CONTEMPORARY SOCIAL THEORY

INVESTIGATION AND APPLICATION

TIM DELANEY, Ph.D.

State University of New York at Oswego

PEARSON

Prentice
Hall

Upper Saddle River, NJ 07458

Library of Congress Cataloging-in-Publication Data

Delaney, Tim.
  Contemporary social theory : investigation and application / Tim Delaney.
    p. cm.
  Includes bibliographical references and index.
  ISBN 0-13-183756-7 (alk paper)
    1. Sociology—Philosophy. I. Title.

HM461.D45 2005
301'.01—dc22   2004044610

AVP/Publisher: Nancy Roberts
Senior Marketing Manager: Marissa Feliberty
Prepress and Manufacturing Buyer: Mary Ann Gloriande
Production Editor: Cheryl Keenan
Copyeditor: Margaret Ritchie
Proofreader: Beatrice Marcks
Editorial Assistant: Lee Peterson
Director, Image Resource Center: Melinda Reo
Manager, Rights and Permissions: Zina Arabia
Manager, Visual Research: Beth Brenzel
Image Permission Coordinator: Joanne Dippel
Photo Researcher: Teri Stratford
Cover Art Director: Jayne Conte
Cover Designer: Jayne Kelly

This book was set in 10/12 Palatino by Laserwords Ltd. and was printed and bound by Phoenix Book Technology. The cover was printed by Phoenix Color Corp.

Excerpts from George Ritzer's *Modern Sociological Theory*, fifth edition are printed with permission of the publisher, McGraw-Hill. Portions of the biographical sketches in this text appear in Tim Delaney's *Classical Social Theory* published by Prentice Hall.

Pearson Education LTD.
Pearson Education Singapore, Pte. Ltd
Pearson Education, Canada, Ltd
Pearson Education–Japan
Pearson Education Australia PTY, Limited
Pearson Education North Asia Ltd
Pearson Educación de Mexico, S.A. de C.V
Pearson Education Malaysia, Pte. Ltd
Pearson Education, Upper Saddle River, New Jersey

10 9 8 7 6 5 4 3 2 1

ISBN 0-13-183756-7

"...The Story Continues"

Contents

6   Social Exchange Theory: George Homans, Peter Blau, and Karen Cook   134

11   Modern and Postmodern Theory   259

Preface

Generally speaking, a social theorist is a person who seeks to understand the social world by means of reason and rational thought. Some social thinkers attempt to understand the world from a philosophical standpoint driven by abstract thinking. Abstract thinking allows for creative and innovative thought processes. Other social thinkers attempt to explain the world from a rational standpoint. These scientifically driven theorists seek validity of their theories through empirical research and data analysis and interpretation. It should be understood that all forms of social inquiry are valuable in the pursuit of knowledge and in presenting credible explanations of the world in which we live .

Classical social theorists (for example, Marx, Simmel, Weber, and Durkheim) were influenced by the ideas of earlier philosophers, such as Kant and Hegel. These early philosophers in turn were influenced by social thinkers that preceded them, such as the ancient Greek philosophers (like Aristotle and Plato). In other words, all social thinkers are influenced by those who came before them. Logic, if nothing else, dictates this reality. Current social thinkers are influenced by the works of those people to whom they were exposed. Students of social theory today are in turn influenced by contemporary social thinkers. We all benefit from the knowledge of others. For example, it is not necessary to reinvent the law of gravity, it has already been established. We move on from the knowledge that can be treated as "givens" in order to make new discoveries. The discoveries of today will be treated as "givens" in the future. This is all a part of the "chain of knowledge." As a result of this "chain of knowledge," contemporary social theorists extend, alter, modify, and/or reject the ideas of those who preceded them.

In classical social theory, the focus is on individual theorists. There are many obvious reasons for this focus. Here are three reasons: First, social thinkers of the classical period were few in number. Second, rights to education had not been extended to the masses, leaving most of them illiterate and unable (or too busy) to read the ideas of others. The lack of educational opportunities also meant that there were very few people who had a chance to go to college where they could develop their own academic skills. Third, the lack of publication opportunities and a near non-existent mass media meant that few social thinkers would have an outlet for their ideas.

As a result, the masses had no access to their works. By the twentieth century this was all changing. More and more people entered college. Publication opportunities increased. Social thinkers with diverse ideas found audiences. Today, there is an abundance of people who claim to be social thinkers. Consequently, it is impossible to review all the social thinkers that some would like included—especially in an already comprehensive contemporary social theory book such as this one.

As a result of the great proliferation of social theorists and the lack of a number of quality "grand theorists" in the modern era, contemporary social theory is divided into "schools of thought." This is easily understood when one realizes that in the social sciences, and sociology in particular, the fields have become very broad, but areas of specialty among individuals have become very narrow. Because of the large number of thinkers in the contemporary era, theorists who share similar interests or perspectives are grouped together into "schools of thought." Consequently, contemporary sociological theory has become dominated by "schools of thought" rather than by single theorists. This is either good or bad depending on one's perspective. Nonetheless, it is the reality of current sociological social theory. Furthermore, there are those who place a great emphasis on paradigm distinctions. Paradigms represent collective schools of thought that can be lumped together. Ever since Thomas Kuhn published his *The Structure of Scientific Revolutions* (1962) the topic of paradigm distinction has remained in popular discourse. Unfortunately, there are nearly as many paradigm classifications schemes offered by individuals, as there are "schools of thought." As a result, the focus of this book is on the major "schools of thought."

Contemporary Social Theory: Investigation and Application begins with an examination of social theory and is followed by a review of the major schools of thought. Chapter One provides an in-depth analysis and examination of social theory and its relevancy to social society in general, and sociology, specifically. In each of the chapters on the major schools of thought (2–11) a review of the basic tenets is provided along with a discussion of some of the major theorists found in each school, their influences, and their concepts and contributions to social theory. Each of these chapters concludes with a relevancy section which serves to review the theory, assess the school of thought, and apply select concepts to the relevancy of contemporary society. Chapters 12 and 13 are dedicated to the works of two of the more brilliant theorists of the contemporary era, George Ritzer and Jonathan Turner, respectfully. Additionally, Chapter 14, *"Applying Social Theory to Future Society,"* was written as an attempt to apply many of the established social trends that have existed for the past five centuries and show their relevancy to future society. In this chapter, the author introduces a number of his own concepts and theories; including: the *Human Species Convergence Theory* and the *Five Horrorists* (an updated version of Malthus's Four Horsemen). Students, and professors alike, should find this chapter of particular interest.

ACKNOWLEDGMENTS

I want to thank a number of people who assisted in one way or another in the publication of this book. Special thanks go to Tim Madigan, who proofread the first draft of this book and offered valued suggestions and ideas.

Three former students of mine contributed a great deal of research assistance by retrieving large numbers of books and journal articles from local libraries. Thanks to Danielle Fraher, Fiora DiGiannantonio, and Raymond Kropczynski. I wish them all great success in graduate school and beyond.

My thanks also go to the following people, who reviewed the text and provided additional insight and guidance: Karen A.

Callaghan, Barry University; Arthur P. Jipson, University of Dayton; and James P. Marshall, University of Northern Colorado. As always, I am very grateful for the great support given to me by Nancy E. Roberts and Lee W. Peterson of Prentice Hall. Their friendship and professionalism are greatly appreciated. Special thanks to Margaret Ritchie and Cheryl Keenan for their assistance in the final editing process and production.

And, of course, many thanks to Christina.

Tim Delaney, Ph.D.

About the Author

Tim Delaney, assistant professor of Sociology at the State University of New York at Oswego, holds a B.S. degree in sociology from the State University of New York at Brockport, an M.A. degree in sociology from California State University–Dominguez Hills, and a Ph.D. in sociology from the University of Nevada at Las Vegas.

Dr. Delaney is the author of *Community, Sport and Leisure,* Second Edition (2001), coeditor of *Values, Society, and Evolution* (2002), coeditor of *Social Diseases: Mafia, Terrorism and Totalitarianism* (2004), and author of both *Classical Social Theory: Investigation and Application* (2004) and *American Street Gangs* to be published in 2005. He has published over fifty book reviews, book chapters, and journal and encyclopedia articles and has served as guest Editor for *Philosophy Now.*

Dr. Delaney has presented thirty-five papers at regional, national, and international conferences, including papers at the Russian Academy of Sciences during international conferences at both St. Petersburg (1999) and Moscow (2001). He has been invited to give guest lectures at Moscow State University in 2004 and 2005. Delaney is the cofounder of the Anthropology Society (of Western New York) and founder of the Social Theory Society, an academic society that promotes "learning through thinking and experience." Delaney maintains membership in ten professional associations. He served his second term as president of the New York State Sociological Association in 2003–2004. He is a charter member of the Wall of Tolerance sponsored by the national campaign for Tolerance, and co-chaired by Rosa Parks and Morris Dees, in recognition of his community activism and scholarship efforts in the fight against social injustice. Dr. Delaney is listed in Marquis *Who's Who in America* for his outstanding achievements.

1

Examining Social Theory

What is social theory? The word *theory* is often misunderstood. It seems to imply speculation or uncertainty because it is viewed *merely* as a theory, not a statement of "truth." Theories are generally contrasted with "facts." It is usually believed that facts are established truths, whereas theories are speculations about what might be true. Mainstream sociology is grounded in the scientific tradition, and that is the general approach embraced by most sociological social thinkers. It is important to note that the scientific approach is not embraced by all social thinkers. Furthermore, any theory that contributes to the "chain of knowledge" has merit and deserves recognition. Nonscientific approaches to the study of human behavior are often open to explanations of human behavior ignored by those grounded in the scientific tradition.

The vast majority of sociologists *do* treat their profession as a science and therefore prefer to see theories grounded in facts and supported by empirical data. "To a scientist, a 'theory' is not mere speculation. In fact, theories may already be established as true. To a scientist, theories possess three characteristics: First, they are *empirically verifiable;* second, they provide an *explanation* or *account*

for; third, *a general class of phenomena*" (Goode, 1997:65–66). *Empirically verifiable* refers to sociology's commitment, as a science, to support theory with systematic observation and data collection, known as research. Scientific research allows researchers to go beyond common sense, faith, and tradition. Research offers a cause-and-effect account of phenomena; it provides an *explanation* of why something occurs. When the explanation is general, it can be applied to some cases (such as, *a general class of phenomena,* Newton's theory of gravitation).

Theory is not used by scientists alone. In reality, people use theories regularly. As Williams and McShane (1994) explained, people seem to "think of theory as something abstract and not really applicable to the 'real world'" (p. 1). Williams and McShane used rain as an example of theory in everyday life. When you see dark clouds forming in the sky and state, "It is going to rain," you have just expressed a simple theory. A more complex theory of rain would be: Under certain circumstances, surface water evaporates and rises into the atmosphere. Certain atmospheric conditions cause the water to condense, first into clouds and ultimately into drops of rain. This second theory of rain is more complex, for it specifies the conditions and processes involved (evaporation and condensation).

A theory is a statement that proposes to explain or relate observed phenomena or a set of concepts. Theory involves a set of interrelated arguments that seek to describe and explain cause-effect relationships. A "good theory" is one that can be tested and supported by empirical research. "Good theory offers new explanations for patterns that have been observed through research, or predicts findings that might be expected based upon the theory's argument. Good research may test a relationship proposed in a theory, or it may identify new patterns or relationships in need of explanation by a theory" (Farley, 1998:3–4). As an example, here is a theory that most students have heard from their teachers: "The more hours a student studies, the higher his or her grade will be." This statement represents an attempt to link two specific variables, the number of hours one studies (the independent variable) and the grade that one will receive for the class (the dependent variable). Students can test this theory for themselves by keeping track of the hours they study for each class and examining the grade they receive. Thus, through the use of research, a theory can be tested for validity. Additional research may reveal that other variables are involved, such as the varying difficulty of courses and the interest in one class over another. But even these new ideas of variables related to one's grade represent theory in action.

Presenting ideas (theories) in the form of statements allows empirical testing. Jonathan Turner agreed with the importance of forming theories in terms of statements. Turner (2003) stated that theory is constructed with the basic elements of concepts, variables, and statements/formats. Concepts (such as power, violence) are developed through the process of definitions. "Those who believe that sociology can be like other sciences prefer concepts that

are translated into variables—that is, into states that vary. We want to know the variable properties—size, degree, intensity, amount, and so forth—of events denoted by a concept" (Turner, 2003:7). Most important, concepts must somehow be linked to one another in the form of a theoretical statement. This is necessary in order to demonstrate the relationship between variables. Statements must specify the interrelatedness. "When these theoretical statements are grouped together, they constitute a *theoretical format*" (Turner, 2003:7).

Adams and Sydie (2001) defined *sociological theory* as "an abstract, symbolic representation of, and explanation of, social reality" (4). In his second edition of *Sociological Theory* (1988), Ritzer defined *sociological theory* as "a wide-ranging system of ideas that deals with the *centrally important* issues of social life" (3). Ritzer amended his definition of sociological theory in *Modern Sociological Theory* (2002) to those theories which "have a *wide range* of application, deal with *centrally important social issues,* and have *stood the test of time*" (4). Goode (1988) explained that theory can also be used in a broader sense as a *paradigm.* Thus, Goode defined a *theory* as "a general approach, a perspective, a paradigm; an explanation for a general class of phenomena, such as Darwin's theory of natural selection" (20). A paradigm, then, serves as a model that links similar theoretical ideas into "schools of thought." Contemporary theory is characterized by this broader perspective of theory, in that "schools of thought" dominate the description of modern sociological theory. Grand theorists, such as those found in the classical era, seem to be as extinct as the dinosaurs.

Generally speaking, sociological theory is grounded in the scientific tradition of belief that social patterns exist and that therefore general abstract "laws" can be created through empirical study. As Turner (2003) stated, "Scientific theories begin with the assumption that the universe, including the social universe created by acting human beings, reveals certain basic and fundamental properties and processes that explain the ebb and flow of events in specific contexts. Because of this concern with discovering fundamental properties and processes, scientific theories are always stated abstractly, resign above specific empirical events and highlight the underlying forces that drive these events" (p. 1). Wallace and Wolf (1999) also stressed the importance of the systematic approach to social theory. They stated that sociological theorists "express their assumptions or hypotheses systematically and discuss in a comprehensive way how far their theories explain social life. Even more important, they provide new insights into behavior and the workings of societies" (3). Most sociologists are grounded in the scientific tradition of explaining social behavior, but social inquiry did not begin with them, or other scientists. Contemplating the social world surrounding us is a trait shared by humans throughout history.

ORIGINS OF SOCIAL THEORY

There is no starting date for when people began to think about, and develop theories of, the world around them. However, ancient social thought is of little importance to understanding contemporary social theory. Furthermore, even though the Greeks had philosophical theories about society, these have had little direct influence on sociological theory, for the Greeks did not engage in scientific-empirical research. These philosophers assumed that intelligent observers could learn about the nature of reality simply by thinking and by talking with other intelligent individuals about it. They created an ideal type of society and called upon it to conform to that ideal. Consequently, it is safe to say that the roots of sociological social theory do not lie with the ancient Greek philosophers.

Garner (2000) traced the beginning of sociology to Niccolò Machiavelli and *The Prince*, published in 1513, at the height of the Italian Renaissance. From 1450 to 1525, Europe experienced dramatic social change. In 1453 the Turks captured Constantinople (now Istanbul) from the Greeks and demonstrated the proficient use of cannons and gunpowder. The eastern Mediterranean became part of the Islamic world, and European rulers, merchants, and adventurers felt pressure to expand westward and southward beyond the Straits of Gibraltar. In 1458 Johann Gutenberg printed the Bible on his movable-type printing press and spearheaded the mass dissemination of the printed word. In 1492 Columbus "discovered" the "New" World, triggering the burst of expansion by European nations into the rest of the world. In that same year, the sovereigns of Christian Spain completed their reconquest of the peninsula from Islamic rule and expelled the remaining Moors and Jews (Garner, 2000:6).

Martin Luther (1497–1546), one of the first advocates of mass education, challenged the Catholic church and its assertion that the only true interpretation of the Bible should come from religious leaders. Luther, in contrast, believed that it was the right, even the duty, of all Christians to interpret the Bible for themselves. For this to happen, everyone had to learn to read, which required mass education (Farley, 1998). In 1517, Luther challenged the Catholic church by nailing his ninety-five theses to the door of the cathedral in Wittenberg, Germany, lighting the fires of the Reformation and Protestantism. Luther's ideas represent a nonscientific theoretical approach to understanding his society. He did not rely on statistical analysis to conclude that members of society would be better off if they were granted certain privileges otherwise reserved for the elites.

But it was Machiavelli's work that sparked sociological theory. *The Prince* was a controversial book for its time, as it provided a realistic view of human actions and challenged the long-held belief of the divine right of kings and others (for example, slave owners) that held "legitimate" power. Until the

Renaissance, most books upheld general notions of normative behavior, were nonempirical, and did not observe, describe, or analyze actual human behavior. Machiavelli included in his book all the violent, fierce, savage, coercive, and sometimes even compassionate acts that the ruler must perform in order to stay in power. *The Prince* was based on reality, observations of real people, and not just moral ideals. It is for this very reason that it shocked its readers and was widely censored and banned. This is the very type of publication that illustrates modern social science: writing about society as it really is, not as the power elite says it is or should be. Note that Garner's opinion that sociological theory began with Machiavelli is not shared by all sociologists. Nonetheless, it marks an important event and time frame for tracing social theory.

After Machiavelli, many social thinkers made contributions to the study of society and human behavior. Three of the more influential early theorists are Thomas Hobbes, John Locke, and Jean-Jacques Rousseau. In the following pages a brief review of their significant contributions are discussed.

Thomas Hobbes (1588–1679)

Hobbes was born in Wiltshire, England, on April 5, 1588. His father, the vicar of the parish, could only read the prayers and the homilies of the church and did not value learning. One of the surviving stories about the senior Hobbes involved his being an irresponsible and unpleasant fellow. After a fight with a fellow clergyman, he was threatened with excommunication. As a result, he soon "disappeared from history" (Martinich, 1999). The young Hobbes lived a sheltered and leisured life. His education was provided for by an uncle, a solid tradesman and alderman of Malmesbury. By the time he reached fifteen, Hobbes had mastered Latin and Greek and was sent to Oxford to continue his education. Hobbes then traveled throughout Europe

and did not begin writing until he was forty years old.

Hobbes's primary contribution to social thought was his belief that the social order was made by human beings and that therefore humans could change it (Adams and Sydie, 2001). Even under authoritarian rule, Hobbes believed that authority is given by the subjects themselves, and that it is only by their consent that the rulers maintain sovereign power.

As a political and social theorist, Hobbes wondered what life and human relations would be like in the absence of government. In 1651, Hobbes published his greatest work, *Leviathan.* In this book he provided a disturbing account of society without government. From his viewpoint, society would be filled with fear and the danger of violent death, and human life would be solitary, poor, nasty, brutish, and short.

In his brief introduction to the *Leviathan,* Hobbes described the state as an organism analogous to a large person. He showed how each part of the state parallels the function of the parts of the human body and noted that the first part of his project was to describe human nature, because humans are the creators of the state. To this end, he advised that we look into ourselves to see the nature of humanity in general. Hobbes argued that, in the absence of social conditioning, every action we perform, no matter how charitable or benevolent, is done for selfish reasons. Even giving to charity is a way of showing one's power to do so. Today, this concept is often referred to as "*psychological egoism.*" Hobbes believed that any description of human action, including morality, must reflect the reality that people are self-serving by nature. Hobbes also noted that there are three natural causes of conflict: competition for limited supplies of material possessions, distrust of one another, and glory insofar as people remain hostile to preserve their powerful reputation. Given the natural causes of conflict, Hobbes concluded that the natural condition of humans is a state of perpetual war of all against all, where no morality exists, and everyone lives in constant fear.

For Hobbes, the state of nature was not a specific period in history, but a way of rationalizing how people would act in their most basic state. Advancing on the individualism put forth by René Descartes ("I think, therefore I am"), Hobbes used the individual as the building block for all of his theories. He formulated his theories by empirical observation, believing that everything in the universe is simply made of atoms in motion, and that geometry and mathematics can be used to explain human behavior.

According to his theories, there are two types of motion in the universe: Vital (involuntary motion such as heart rate) and Voluntary (things that we choose to do). Voluntary motion is further broken down into two subcategories that Hobbes believed were reducible to mathematical equations: Desires and Aversions. Desires are things one is moved to do or that are valued by the individual, while aversions are fears or things to be avoided by the individual. Further, individuals' appetites constantly keep them in motion, and in order to remain in motion, everyone needs a certain degree of power. Thus, the pursuit of power is the natural state of humans. Humans are in a constant struggle for power, and above all else, they wanted to avoid a violent death.

Hobbes was considered a liberal in his day. He emphasized the importance of individuals and made them the center of politics. Government should derive from human beings, and not some divine sense of purpose or a birthright. If Hobbes can be thought of as the first liberal thinker, then it is only fitting to turn our attention now to John Locke, considered by some the father of liberal democratic thought.

John Locke (1632–1704)

John Locke was born in a village in Somerset, on August 29, 1632. Locke was the son of a country attorney and small landowner (John Locke, Sr.) who served as a captain in the parliamentary army when civil war broke out, and of Agnes Keene Locke (Cope, 1999). Not much is known about Locke's mother except that she was nearly 10 years older than Locke's father (Cope, 1999). Both sides of the family came from a Puritan background and Locke, Sr., rose on the social ladder by becoming an attorney. Locke had two siblings, but only his brother Thomas survived past infancy (Cope, 1999). His father had hoped that John would follow in his footsteps and become a lawyer, but Locke decided on medicine instead.

Locke embraced many of Hobbes's ideas on the state of nature and the rise of government and society. He differed from Hobbes, however, in believing that God was the prime factor in politics and that individuals were born with certain natural rights given not by government or society but by God. This right is what gives all people equality. Locke and Hobbes shared their view of the importance and autonomy of the individual in society. The extent to which they agreed varies, but one important belief was constant between the two: People had existed as individuals before societies and governments came into being, each possessing certain rights and having the freedom to do as they pleased—unrestricted, according to Hobbes, and with some restrictions placed on them by God, according to Locke. This freedom of the individual was important, for it was the foundation for modern political democracy.

Besides a general right to self-preservation, Locke believed that all individuals had a natural right to appropriate private property. This natural right carried with it two preconditions of natural law. First, since the earth was given by God to all individuals, people must be sure to leave enough property for all to have, and second, nothing may be allowed to spoil. These conditions being met, individuals were granted exclusive rights to any object that they mixed with their labor.

Locke agreed with Hobbes that, human nature being what it is, people eventually would find a way around the natural law restrictions on property accumulation through the creation of money. People were granted the ability to accumulate unlimited money based upon their industriousness. This meant that some people acted more rationally than others and thus were more deserving of property. Locke so despised the use of money that he argued it led to the disproportionate and unequal possession of land.

Locke's *Two Treatises of Government* (1690) has been viewed as the classic expression of liberal political ideas. It is read as a defense of individualism and of the natural right of individuals to appropriate private property. It served as an intellectual justification for the British Whig revolution of 1689 and stated the fundamental principles of the Whigs (Ashcraft, 1987). It would also serve as a primary source to the American Declaration of Independence. The key elements in Locke's political theory are natural rights, the social contract, government by consent, and the issue of private property. Locke also believed that society had the right to overthrow the government. Since the will of a majority established representations to create it, the majority of people have the power to remove it. This belief introduces the idea that government should be accountable to the people. Clearly Locke was in favor of a limited government, not an authoritarian one like the one Hobbes described.

The constitutional and cultural life of the United States was deeply influenced by Locke's *A Letter Concerning Toleration* (1689), which argued for human rights and the necessity of separating church and state. Locke wrote that the commonwealth seems to be a society of men constituted only for the procuring, preserving, and advancing their own civil interests. Locke referred to civil interests as liberty, health, indolency of body, and the possession of outward things, such as money, lands, houses, and furniture. It is the duty of the civil magistrate, by the impartial execution of equal laws, to secure to all the people in general and to every one of his subjects in particular the just possession of these civil interests.

In *A Letter Concerning Toleration*, Locke detailed at great length the need for the separation of church and state. He stated that whatsoever is lawful in the commonwealth cannot be prohibited by the magistrate in the church. Any law created by ordinary vote for the public good overrides the church, and any conflict with interpretations of God's will must be judged by God alone, not religious zealots. Further, the magistrate ought not to forbid the preaching or professing of any speculative opinions in any church because they have no relation to the civil rights of the subjects.

Whether or not Locke can be labeled a *rationalist* is debatable. Some social thinkers view as rationalists those who use reason to interpret the social world. Philosophers insist on labeling Locke an *empiricist*. Thomson (1993), for one, argued that Locke was an empiricist and described empiricism as beginning "with sense experience and claims that all knowledge must be derived from it. . . . Empiricist principles reject the possibility of a priori knowledge of the world" (p. 210). A long-standing interpretation of empiricism is that it is based on information obtained through our senses; the information must be something that can be seen, heard, felt, tasted, or smelled, and that can likewise be verified independently by others' senses (Goode, 1988). Today, *empiricism* is defined far more specifically: It is a method based on observation and experimentation. Most modern sociologists are empirical because they collect evidence (data) that involves real things (for example, the effects of poverty on gang participation) that happen in the real world—a world that is observable. Modern science demands that claims of empiricism must refer to information carefully gathered in an unbiased manner

(Kornblum, 1991). Systematic data collection and statistical interpretation are requirements of modern empiricism, and therefore in order to be labeled an empiricist, one must collect data and statistically analyze them. Thomson provided no evidence that Locke conducted empirical research; in fact, Locke's pursuit of a medical degree was hampered by this critical limitation. The philosophers may label Locke an empiricist during his era, but as the criteria of empiricism have evolved, there are few modern social scientists who would label him an empiricist.

Jean-Jacques Rousseau (1712–1778)

Rousseau was a fascinating individual whose unorthodox ideas and passionate prose caused a flurry of interest in eighteenth-century France. His republican stance on liberty, equality, and brotherhood helped to lead his country eventually to revolution. He was born on June 28, 1712, in Geneva, Switzerland; his mother died during his birth. His father had him reading romances and classical histories such as Plutarch's before apprenticing him to an engraver. Rousseau left his home at age 16. He studied music and devised a new system of musical notation, which was rejected by the French Academy of Sciences. Throughout his life, Rousseau often earned his living by copying music, and he later became a composer. In Paris in the 1740s (he arrived for the first time in 1742), he entered literary society and wrote both words and music for an opera, *Les Muses galanates.* Rousseau lived for thirty years with an uneducated servant girl who bore him five children, according to his *Confessions;* all of the children were given to an orphanage in infancy.

In 1762 Rousseau published his famous book *The Social Contract.* According to Rousseau, society could only be accounted for, and justified, as a means of enabling men to advance to a higher level of achievement than could be arrived at in its absence.

Society had to be regarded as a necessary means to the development of the moral potentialities of a man's original nature. Man's development from primitive to organized societies would provide the foundation for his conception of the necessary elements of social obligations: Man is born free and everything is in chains.

Rousseau believed that nature ordained all men equal and that the state's conformity to natural law involved the maintenance of public order and the provision of opportunities for the happiness of individuals. Rousseau's idea of a "perfect" society includes the following:

- A society which grows only to the extent that it can be well governed.
- A society in which every person is equal to his occupation, and no one is committed to another's function.
- Society and individuals have the same goals.
- All members of society have an equal voice.
- No single member is above the law, and further, no individual is able to dictate to the state that it must recognize individual superiority of power.
- Society is aware of a dramatic increase in new members and makes sure that these new members do not restructure the state so that they enjoy unequal power.
- Society is free from threat of conquest by other societies and should not attempt to gain control of others.
- As society grows, magistrates will "run" it, but their power will be limited.

It is clear that Rousseau wanted a democratic society, but he was also aware of the potential of individuals to act in their own self-interest. He believed that the only primitive instinct of man is the desire for self-preservation, so he will love what tends to conserve life and abhor what tends to harm it. Man's attempt at social order is the source of all evil. For man in his earliest or natural condition is an isolated being; there are no institutions, political or social, no government, no family, no property, none of the usages of society. Man survives in nature by self-sufficiency. The moment man becomes self-conscious is the beginning of his decline. In contemporary European society, reflection has led him to the fatal knowledge of his superiority to the other animals. With human pride comes the divorce of nature. Man, now apart from nature, sets out to subdue the world, to advance himself in knowledge and power, and to perfect his place in the environment by this awakening reason. Man now must agree to created laws, binding all equally, and ensuring the peace and well-being of everyone. But the very vices that render government necessary have rendered the abuse of power inevitable. Rousseau, therefore, believed that the state should have a limited role in societal matters, its primary function being to protect its members from outside threat as well as internal self-concerned individuals.

The work of social thinkers like Hobbes, Locke, and Rousseau emphasized grand, general, and very abstract systems of ideas that made rational sense. Their work, along with that of many other thinkers, such as Voltaire, Charles Montesquieu, and René Descartes, would spearhead a new movement of social reasoning known collectively as the Age of Enlightenment.

AGE OF ENLIGHTENMENT

The Age of Enlightenment, a phrase that describes the trends and writings in Europe and the American colonies during the eighteenth century, began prior to the French Revolution. The phrase was frequently employed by writers of the period itself, who were convinced that they were emerging from centuries of darkness and ignorance into a new age enlightened by reason, science, and a respect for humanity. The Enlightenment was a period of dramatic intellectual development and change in philosophical thought. A number of long-standing ideas and beliefs were

abandoned and replaced during the Enlightenment (Ritzer, 2000).

The Enlightenment thinkers kept a watchful eye on the arrangements of society. "Their central interest was the attainment of human and social perfectibility in the here and now rather than in some heavenly future. They considered rational education and scientific understanding of self and society the routes to all human and social progress" (Adams and Sydie, 2001:11). Progress could be attained because humans held the capacity for reason. Further, reason should not be constrained by tradition, religion, or sovereign power.

The roots of modern sociology can be found in the work of the philosophers and scientists of the Enlightenment, which had its origins in the scientific discoveries of the seventeenth century. That pivotal century began with Galileo's "heretical" proof that the earth is not the center of the universe, as the church had taught, and ended with the publication of Sir Isaac Newton's *Principia Mathematica* (Kornblum, 1994).

The work of Enlightenment thinkers was not dispassionate inquiry, for they were deeply disturbed by the power of the church and its secular allies in the monarchy. Freedom of inquiry and diversity of thought were not tolerated and freethinkers were often tortured and executed (Garner, 2000).

The Enlightenment is most readily characterized as supporting "liberal individualism." It was a movement that emphasized the individual's possession of critical reason, and it was opposed to traditional authority in society and the primacy of religion in questions of knowledge (Hadden, 1997). According to Seidman (1983), liberalism arose as a reaction against a static hierarchical and absolutist order, which suppressed individual freedom.

Of the basic assumptions and beliefs of the philosophers and intellectuals of this period, perhaps the most important was an abiding faith in the power of human reason.

Their insistence on the ability of people to act rationally was anathema to church and state (Hadden, 1997). Social thinkers were impressed by Newton's discovery of gravitation. If humanity could so unlock the laws of the universe, God's own laws, why could it not also discover the laws underlying all of nature and society? Scientists came to assume that through a rigorous use of reason, an unending progress would be possible—progress in knowledge, in technical achievement, and even in moral values. Following the philosophy of Locke, the eighteenth-century social thinkers believed that knowledge is not innate but comes only from experience and observation guided by reason.

The Enlightenment was more than a set of ideas; it implied an attitude, a method of thought. There was a clear desire to explore new ideas and allow for changing values. It is important that not all of the social writers in the collectivity of enlightened reason were intellectuals. Many popularizers engaged in a self-conscious effort to win converts. They were journalists and propagandists as much as true philosophers, and historians often refer to them by the French word *philosophes.*

For the most part, the homeland of the philosophes was France. Political philosopher Charles de Montesquieu, one of the earliest representatives of the movement, published various satirical works against existing social institutions. Voltaire was another famous French writer of political satire, plays, poems, and essays and aided tremendously in popularizing the works of the philosophes. Voltaire and other philosophes relished the concept of a philosopher-king who would enlighten the people.

The philosophes valued both education and practical knowledge. They believed that the educated would exercise their critical reason for their own happiness and that, consequently, their acts and deeds would benefit society overall. The philosophes also placed a great deal of importance on practical knowledge: how to farm, how to construct

bridges and dams, how to relate to fellow citizens (Adams and Sydie, 2001). Hard work and education were believed to be the foundation of human and social progress. As quoted in Gay (1969:170), Denis Diderot (coauthor of the *Encyclopédie* volumes from 1751 to 1765) believed that "nature has not made us evil; it is bad education, bad models, bad legislation that corrupt us." Thus, reason is learned; it is not innate.

The Enlightenment was also a profoundly cosmopolitan and antinationalistic movement with representatives in many other countries: Immanuel Kant in Prussia; David Hume in England; Cesare Beccaria in Italy; and Benjamin Franklin and Thomas Jefferson in the American colonies. All of them maintained close contacts with the French philosophes but were important contributors to the movement in their own right.

THE CONSERVATIVE REACTION

History will show that whenever a new and radical movement begins to challenge and change the very core beliefs and values of society, a corresponding conservative backlash results. The Enlightenment and the French Revolution created a powerful backlash. The Enlightenment thinkers are generally considered the intellectual forbears of the French Revolution (1789–1794). Intellectuals who represented the interests of the absolute monarchy and the aristocracy wrote against the new ideas of freedom of thought, reason, civil liberties, religious tolerance, and human rights (Garner, 2000). They argued for a return to rigid hierarchies, with fixed status groups, established religion, and misery for the masses. Many of the conservatives questioned the legitimacy of individual freedom and rights, including the right to happiness. They argued that society is not a collection of individuals but a social unit in its own right, and that it must be protected from free thought.

Among the ideas of the conservatives was the idea that society should go back to the medieval-era style of rule. Louis de Bonald (1754–1840), for example, was so disturbed by the revolutionary changes in France that he yearned for a return to the peace and harmony of the Middle Ages. In his view, God was the source of society, and he therefore saw reason, which was so important to the Enlightenment thinkers, as inferior to traditional religious beliefs. Furthermore, de Bonald opposed anything that undermined such traditional institutions as patriarchy, the monogamous family, the monarchy, and the Catholic church (Ritzer, 2000c).

The conservatives had idealized the medieval order, conveniently forgetting, or not caring about, the misery that the vast majority of people were subjected to throughout their short, labor-filled lives. As a challenge to the principles of the philosophes and a critique of the postrevolutionary "disorder," the conservatives advanced a number of propositions about society. Zeitlin (1981) outlined ten major propositions of this conservative reaction, which are abbreviated here:

1. Society is an organic unity with internal laws and development and deep roots in the past. Society is greater than the individuals who comprise it.
2. Society is superior to the individual man, for the man has no existence outside a social group or context, and he becomes human only by participating in society.
3. The individual is an abstraction and not the basic element of a society. Society is composed of relationships and institutions.
4. The parts of a society are interdependent and interrelated. Therefore, changing one part undermines the stability of the whole society.
5. Institutions are positive entities because they provide for the needs of individuals.
6. All the various customs and institutions of a society are positively functional. Nothing is dysfunctional, not even prejudice (which can unify groups).
7. The existence and maintenance of small groups is essential to society. The family, the neighborhood, religious groups, and so on (not individuals) are the basic units of society.
8. The conservatives wanted to preserve the older religious forms—Catholicism, not Protestantism—and sought to restore the religious unity of medieval Europe.
9. The conservatives insisted on the essential importance and positive value of nonrational aspects of human existence. Man needs ritual, ceremony, and worship. The philosophes were merciless in their criticism of those activities, labeling them irrational vestiges of the past.
10. Status and hierarchy were also deemed essential to society. A hierarchy was necessary to ensure that the church would remain on top of the social order.

The propositions brought forth by the conservatives would influence such thinkers as Saint-Simon, Comte, and Durkheim. But what is most important is that both the conservatives and the Enlightenment thinkers contributed substantially to the foundation of sociological thought. The Enlightenment thinkers stressed liberal individualism, with its emphasis on reason, individual freedom, contractual relations, and a reverence for science as the way to examine and explain all spheres of experience, including the social. The conservatives stressed collectivism, which emphasizes the importance of maintaining the social order for the good of society itself. Tradition and church authority are sacred and must be maintained.

REVOLUTIONS

The reactionary beliefs and hopes of the conservatives that society should turn back to a way of life that existed in the Middle Ages were, of course, never realized. Progress can never be stopped, and the rise of reason and science had already transformed the social order. The vehicle of social change was not science itself, since relatively few individuals of any society were practicing scientists.

Instead, social change was a product of the many new social ideas that captured people's imagination during the Enlightenment. A series of revolutions took place in Europe and America that were, at least in part, a result of the social movements unleashed by the triumph of science and reason. The ideas of human rights for all, not just the elites, of democracy versus rule by an absolute monarch, of self-government for colonial peoples, and of applying reason and science to human issues in general are all streams of thought that arose during the Enlightenment (Kornblum, 1994).

Political Revolutions

The Age of Reason allowed the questioning of the traditional order of society. Faith and tradition were slowly challenged by secular thinking. Knowledge replaced sacred tradition and ritual. The concept of individual natural rights for all people influenced the study of law and lawmaking, and debates about justice in society began to replace the idea that kings had a "divine right" to rule. From the Renaissance on, especially in Western societies, social thinkers and political revolutionists would extol the virtues of reason and scientific discovery.

From the standpoint of Europeans, the American Revolution and the Declaration of Independence indicated that, for the first time, some individuals were going beyond the mere discussion of enlightened ideas and were actually putting them into practice. The American Revolution would encourage further attacks on and criticisms of existing European regimes. "Thomas Jefferson's preamble to the Declaration of Independence, a prime example of Enlightenment thinking, assumed that all 'rational' individuals would agree with the 'self-evident truths' that 'all men are created equal' and endowed with 'inalienable rights' of 'life, liberty, and the pursuit of happiness" (Adams and Sydie, 2001:12). By praising the value of democracy and citizens' rights,

Jefferson was striking a blow against tyrannical authority.

The British Empire directly felt the impact of the American Revolution and learned that the convictions and desires of the oppressed would not be tolerated by freethinking citizens armed with the tools to fight back. Indirectly, it was the French who were perhaps influenced the most by the revolution in America. The citizens of France were no longer willing to be subjected to traditional forms of authority. The ideas of democracy had a great impact on the French people and provided a spark to ignite the French Revolution of 1789.

The Age of Enlightenment is usually said to have ended with the French Revolution. As mentioned earlier, some see the social and political ferment of this period as being responsible for the revolution. The French Revolution brought the French people the opportunity to build a new social order based on the principals of reason and justice. The changes were indeed revolutionary, as many nobles were killed and their dominant role in French society was ended forever (Cockerham, 1995). A series of laws enacted between 1789 and 1795 produced a number of other fundamental social changes. Churches were now subordinated to the state and forbidden to interfere in politics and the conduct of civil government. Each social class was given equal rights under the law, and each son in a family (rather than just the eldest son) was entitled to an equal amount of inherited property. The total impact of the French Revolution was far more intense than that of the American Revolution. The Americans were fighting for freedom from the imperial British government, while the French were fighting for the near-complete restructuring of society.

While embodying many of the ideals of the philosophes, the French Revolution in its more violent stages (1792–94) served to discredit these ideals temporarily in the eyes of many European contemporaries. France was forced to fight several wars, against Britain, Russia, and virtually all its neighbors in order to preserve its new social and political order. The French society was at total war and would reach its zenith of power under one of its generals, Napoleon Bonaparte, who became a dictator in 1799. For the next fifteen years Napoleon was the dominant figure in European politics. Brilliantly winning a series of battles, Napoleon conquered most of Europe. He met his final demise of power at Waterloo in 1815.

As France returned to a period of stability under an imposed peace settlement, intense debate erupted among French intellectuals about the many social changes that had occurred. As Giddens (1987) stated, the French Revolution marked the first time in history that an entire social order was dissolved by a movement guided by the purely secular ideas of universal liberty and equality.

The long series of political revolutions ushered in by the French Revolution and continuing far into the nineteenth century was a dramatic factor in the rise of sociological theorizing. The impact of these revolutions on many societies was enormous and resulted in many positive changes. It also attracted the attention of many early theorists who concentrated on the negative effects of such changes. These writers were particularly disturbed by the chaos and disorder that revolution and war brought with them, especially in France. The issue of the social order was one of the major concerns of classical sociological theorists, especially Comte and Durkheim.

The Industrial Revolution

The Industrial Revolution was at least as important as the political revolutions in shaping sociological theory. It began in the late eighteenth century in England and quickly spread through many Western societies, including the United States. The Industrial Revolution was not a single event, but a number of interrelated developments that culminated in the transformation of the Western world from a largely agricultural to an overwhelmingly industrial system.

The Industrial Revolution involved the substitution of machines for the muscles of animals and humans. This substitution resulted in a dramatic increase in productivity, which led to an increased demand for more machines, more raw materials, improved means of transportation, better communication, better-educated workers, and a more specialized division of labor.

Large numbers of people left their farms and a rural way of life in hopes of finding employment in the rapidly developing cities. Industrialized factories created a high demand for labor. More and more people left their agrarian lifestyle, not sure of what to expect in the city. Large sections of many medieval cities were transformed into sprawling, chaotic slums characterized by poor sanitation. Laborers worked long hours for little pay.

The Industrial Revolution changed the face of Western society. No longer did the majority of people live in small rural villages with an extended kinship system and produce for themselves most of what they needed in order to survive. The rise of trade had dissolved the subsistence economy of medieval society and created a system of political power based on financial wealth rather than ownership of land. A wide range of social problems that had never existed before industrialization became the new topic of concern among intellectuals and social thinkers. Issues of social change and the social order were joined by questions of why modernization was not occurring elsewhere in the world. Why weren't Africa, China, India, and other nations experiencing the same social changes as the West? These concerns would soon come into the domain of sociological thinking.

CLAUDE-HENRI SAINT-SIMON (1760–1825)

Born in 1760 into a noble family, Saint-Simon lived in comfort as a member of the aristocracy.

He was the eldest of nine children and was educated by private tutors. Saint-Simon met Rousseau and was taught the leading ideas of the Enlightenment philosophers of France. Every morning his servant would greet him, "Remember you have great things to do." In 1776 Saint-Simon joined the military. Three years later he became a captain, as the common experience of the aristocracy was to enjoy rapid promotion. Saint-Simon served in the American Revolution as a volunteer on the side of the colonists. He fought under the command of George Washington at Yorktown. Fighting with the French in the colonial war in the West Indies, he was captured (1782) by the English and served a prison term of several months. In 1783 Saint-Simon went to Mexico and designed the concept of building a canal across Panama. The following year Saint-Simon returned to France. He took no part in the French Revolution, believing that the old regime was weak enough to ensure the outcome. He did, however, use the opportunity to make a fortune through land speculation.

Saint-Simon spent the first forty years of his life as a soldier and speculator. He said that Charlemagne, the first and greatest Holy Roman Emperor, appeared in a dream and told him to become a "great philosopher." This vision persuaded him to pursue a career in "saving humanity." Saint-Simon's desire for social improvement led him to purchase aristocratic and church property from the government, and a financial partnership he formed to this end met with great success. He lavished his wealth on a salon for scientists but spent his later years in poverty, sustained by the faith that he had a message for humanity. With the support of a former servant, Saint-Simon found full time for study and soon began his scientific studies.

Saint-Simon maintained that Newton had uncovered the structure of the universe (structure being the recurrent patterns observed and studied in astronomy). He thought it was possible to study the structure of society and uncover its laws. In his work, Saint-Simon wrote about the necessity of creating a science of social organization. The very term "*organization*" meant "organic structure" to him. He maintained that a society, like an organism, was born and grew. The major challenge was to understand such growth (social change) and the forces behind social stability (social order). He believed that laws exist to explain these issues of organization and social stability.

In his *Introduction to the Scientific Studies of the 19th Century* (1807), Saint-Simon stated that the observation of patterns over a long period of time was essential. Those observations must then be brought together in a general theory of history capable of explaining the fundamental causes of historical change, not only in the past and the present, but also in the future, for the causes of future events must already be in existence. The implication was if one could forecast the future, one might be able to shape the future as well. This line of thought was influenced by Nicolas de Condorcet's belief that he could document the operation of progress in the past and project the course of history for the future. For Condorcet, the idea of infinite perfectibility was a foregone conclusion (Coser, 1977). Ironically, Condorcet was a victim of the Terror during the French Revolution.

In his 1813 *Essays on the Science of Man*, Saint-Simon suggested that the methodology of a social science:

1. One should study the "course of civilization" and look for regularities, patterns, and processes of change.
2. Observations will disclose patterns or "laws of social organization." The broad historical trends will outline the history of social evolution.
3. Once the laws are discovered, they can be used to reconstruct society on the basis of a plan.

In other words, the study of society should be based on science, including the use of history and observation, in the search of regularities.

Foreseeing the triumph of the industrial order, Saint-Simon called for the reorganization of society by scientists and industrialists on the basis of a scientific division of labor. He had an essentially authoritarian and hierarchical view of society, believing that it was inherently divided into rigid social strata. Social classes would be determined by the new social order being ushered in by positivism. Positivism (the reliance on scientific study, laws, regulations, and reason) was to be directed by the most "competent" members of society. Saint-Simon referred to the competent class as people like bankers, lawyers, industrialists, and intellectuals. Saint-Simonian thought dictated that action taken by this class was to be evaluated and analyzed from a positivistic perspective.

Ideologically, Saint-Simon envisioned a planned society, an international community, and therefore he was in favor of technological growth and industrialization. He believed that all societies would unite, forming a worldwide community. Because "common" people could not grasp the concept of a worldwide community based on science, the elites would be needed to oversee and lead society. Worldwide protests in 2000 against globalization and organizations such as the World Trade Organization and the World Bank would seem to support Saint-Simon's contention that the masses still cannot, or will not, grasp the concept of a world community. Saint-Simon felt that the ideas of science should be introduced to the masses through artists and their work, which would reduce it to a level that common people could understand.

The most lasting and important influence of Saint-Simon lies with one of his former pupils and one-time personal secretary: Auguste Comte. It was Comte who more successfully transformed many of Saint-Simon's ideas and formulated them into a new and highly challenging discipline called *sociology*. The many contributions of the early "greats"—Auguste Comte, Émile Durkheim, Karl Marx, and Max Weber—had a strong influence on later sociological thinkers.

THEORETICAL FORMATS: THE STRUCTURE OF SOCIAL THEORY

Social inquiry is guided by a number of diverse approaches which impact the format or structure of social theory. Contemporary sociological thinkers generally utilize a particular course of action, from the options available while developing social theory. There is a lack of consensus on the best approach as reflected by the diverse opinions on how to best create social theory and how to properly categorize contemporary social thought. As Turner (2003) explained, "In sociological theory there is relatively little consensus about just how to organize theoretical statements; in fact, much of the theoretical controversy in sociology revolves around differences concerning the best way to develop theoretical statements and to group them together into a format. Depending on one's views about what kind of science, if any, sociology can be, the structure of theoretical statements and their organization into formats differ dramatically" (p. 7).

Turner (2003) utilized a number of specific schemes in his structural description of social theory. The first category of schemes is the *metatheoretical schemes*, which are used to emphasize basic issues that a theory must address, rather than explaining specific events. These issues include determining the basic nature of human beings, uncovering the fundamental nature of society, and discovering the bonds that unite people into a community. Brian Fay (1975) argued that "there are four essential features of metatheory: first, drawing on the distinction between discovery and validation, its deductive-nomological account of explanation and concomitant modified Humean interpretation of the notion of 'cause'; second, its belief in a neutral observation language as the proper foundation of knowledge; third, its value-free ideal of scientific knowledge; and fourth, its belief in the methodological unity of sciences" (p. 13).

In fact, theoretical paradigms can be divided into the two distinguishing categories of *consensus* and *conflict* in regard to whether there is a general agreement among people in society on values and norms (consensus) or whether people are coerced into accepting the values and norms of society (conflict). The unfortunate downfall of the metatheoretical approach is that "meta-theorizing often gets bogged down in weighty philosophical matters and immobilizes theory building. The enduring philosophical questions persist because they are not resolvable" (Turner, 2003:9). The primary point of sociological theory is to actually conduct a course of action and study of definite behaviors and events.

Analytical schemes are the second category of schemes described by Turner. Analytical approaches attempt to organize concepts into a classification scheme that designates key properties and shows the interrelatedness of such concepts, as found in the social world. This approach can create concrete theories about relatively simple behaviors and represents an advantage over abstract theories that are not tied directly to social reality and therefore are difficult to test. An example of a concrete simple theory is: A ball thrown at a glass door will cause the glass to break and allow the ball to travel through. On the other hand, it is difficult to test the theory that time moves slower the faster one travels once the speed of light has been passed (an abstract theory). Science has a difficult time testing velocities beyond the speed of light and then relating them to the passing of time. But analytical schemes have the problem of rigidness, and when social theory becomes too complex and specific, it cannot be used to generalize. Thus, a ball thrown toward any type of door other than a glass one will not pass through, nor will it cause the destruction of the door. The advantage of abstract theorizing is that it allows for the creation of "grand theory."

According to Turner, *propositional schemes* vary the most among the theoretical approaches and especially along the lines of two critical issues: the level of abstraction and the way in which propositions are organized into formats. "A proposition is a theoretical statement that specifies the connection between two or more variables. It tells us how variation in one concept is accounted for by variation in another" (Turner, 2003:10). The propositional scheme is further divided into a number of subcategories: axiomatic format (propositions are stated in a hierarchical order), formal propositional formats (used to create abstract principles), and empirical propositional formats (consisting of generalizations from specific events that lead to empirical verification).

Modeling schemes represent the final category of schemes outlined by Turner. A model provides a "diagrammatic representation of social events" (Turner, 2003:16). This approach allows both a comparison of social events based on a model format and for causal connections between various social behaviors and phenomenon. Models are helpful when numerous variables are involved and the theorist wants to demonstrate the interconnectiveness of them. Models can be analytical (abstract) or causal (empirical generalizations).

Wallace and Wolf (1999) relied on distinctions between inductive and deductive approaches in their analysis of the structure of sociological theory. They stated that the "classical definition of a theory is essentially a *deductive* one. It starts with definitions of some general concepts (and, often, a few clearly stated assumptions); lays out rules about how to classify the things we observe in terms of these different categories; and then puts forward a number of general propositions about concepts. Once observers have classified their subject matter, a generalized theory allows them to deduce logically a number of quite specific statements about nature and behavior" (p. 3). Thus, deductive theory proceeds from the general to the particular. For example, an investigator examining gang behavior using the deductive approach would begin the study with a number of specific theories and observe behavior to see whether they were true or not. As Adams and Sydie (2001) explained, "The sociological theorist may start with an idea, or theory, about the nature of society and social behavior and proceed to construct in relatively abstract, symbolic terms some sort of model that can explain social life. That is, the sociologist may theorize deductively" (p. 4).

Social thinkers who use the *inductive* approach begin with observations of the social world. "They feel that to start analysis with a clearly defined hypothesis is too rigid and may lead analysts to ignore important aspects of their subject. It is far better, they suggest, to get to know a subject and situation well and gradually build up, or induce, descriptions and explanations of what is really going on. In an inductive approach, the key concepts emerge in the final analysis of the research process" (Wallace and Wolf, 2001:9). Inductive theory proceeds from the particular to the general. Thus, a researcher studying gang behavior would observe, for some time, the various interactions among the gang members and others in the social environment. After a period of time a number of general theories would be established.

Both the inductive and the deductive approaches have been successful in creating good theory. In both approaches, "the theorist is concerned with clearly defined concepts that can be used to help understand what is going on" (Wallace and Wolf, 2001:9). Adams and Sydie (2001) agreed with this conclusion by stating, "Whether theorizing deductively or inductively, the sociological theorist is attempting to provide a comprehensive yet simple and elegant explanation of society and the causes of social behaviors" (p. 4).

Social inquiry is also influenced by the subject matter at hand. Is the study on small-group relations and behaviors (micro theory) or is it a large scale study (macro theory)?

Sociologists who prefer to study social relations on a small scale and enjoy the face-to-face interactional approach to theory building help to develop microsociological theory. Macro theories look at the "big picture" and hope to explain society on a structural and institutional level. Theories are rarely both micro and macro in their explanation. Micro theories generally include sociopsychological issues, and macro theories generally attempt to create grand theory. There are sociologists who use the middle-range theoretical approach because they view constructing grand macro as too abstract and microtheorizing as too limiting.

The subject matter almost always influences whether the theoretical approach will be qualitative or quantitative. In qualitative theory the focus is on gaining insights and descriptions of social behavior. Quantitative theory is guided by the methodological consideration of data collection, measurement and testing, and statistical analysis.

CONCLUSION

Social inquiry and the general contemplation of the social environment have intrigued people throughout history. Early philosophers attempted to reveal the secrets of life, but they did so with little empirical evidence. Their contributions are significant nonetheless. As science became more prevalent in society, social theorizing was guided by the principles of empiricism. Early classical social thinkers and a number of significant social events paved the way for the development of contemporary sociological thought. Despite the various theoretical formats and schemes, contemporary social theory is, for the most part, dominated by the grouping of "schools of thought" rather than by the specific grand theorists who dominated the "classical" period. The primary focus of *Contemporary Social Theory: Investigation and Application* is to describe, explain, and articulate these specific theoretical formats and the relevant social thinkers equated with each school of thought.

2

Edward Wilson, Sociobiology, and Evolutionary Theory

The most influential social thinker in the field of sociobiology is Edward O. Wilson. A Harvard professor for four decades, Wilson has written twenty books, has won two Pulitzer prizes, has discovered hundreds of new species, and is often called the father of biodiversity. Edward Wilson is known worldwide as a highly reputable scientist. He is primarily a biologist, and much of his work involved an examination of the social structure of ants, but he has also studied and written about biogeography, ecosystem diversity, human nature, evolutionary psychology, and the relation of genes and culture. Wilson founded the field of sociobiology, a science that connects biology to human social behavior. Discussion of sociobiology begins with a review of his personal life and significant contributions to social thought followed by a review of evolutionary theory and concludes with a section on the relevancy of sociobiology.

Edward Wilson, American Sociobiologist, Pulitzer Prize winner, and "The Father of Biodiversity".
Source: Harvard Photo Services

EDWARD OSBORNE WILSON (1929–)

Wilson was born in Birmingham, Alabama, in 1929, to Edward Osborne Wilson, Sr., and Inez Freeman Wilson. Many of his younger years were spent on the shores of Mobile Bay, along the Gulf Coast. He schooled himself in natural history during solitary excursions into the woodlands near his home (Alabama

Communication Hall of Fame, 2002). In *Naturalist* (1994), Wilson provided a narrative of his life and described both his growth as a scientist and the evolution of a science he helped to define. During adolescence, Wilson lost part of his hearing. He also struggled with math and a mild form of dyslexia. Any one of these imperfections might have hindered a scientific career but nothing could stop his curiosity about the natural world. Wilson had decided to focus on the tiny creatures he could pick up and bring close to his remaining good eye. He especially enjoyed the study of insects, and particularly ants (*Natural Connections*, 2002).

In 1949, Wilson earned his bachelor of science degree in biology, and in 1950 he earned his master's degree in biology. Wilson first decided to earn his Ph.D. at the University of Tennessee, in Knoxville, primarily because of Arthur Cole, a professor of entomology who specialized in the classification of ants. Wilson conducted his own studies of insects in the nearby Chilhowee and Great Smoky mountains. While working as Cole's laboratory teaching assistant, Wilson honed his knowledge of the anatomy and classification of insects. Wilson stated that the academic challenge was not great at the University of Tennessee and that he became bored there. Understandably, he was unhappy residing in a state known for its statute forbidding the teaching of evolution. By early 1951 he had decided to move on to Harvard University.

Wilson spoke of Harvard as his "destiny": "The largest collection of ants in the world was there, and the tradition of the study of these insects built around the collection was long and deep" (Wilson, 1994:132). By this time, Wilson was publishing detailed accounts of the comparative behavior of the decatine ants found in the southern states. In 1955 Wilson graduated from Harvard with a Ph.D. in biology. Although he received offers from many other prominent universities, Wilson accepted a nontenured five-year assistant professorship at Harvard. He remained at Harvard because of the opportunity to work with well-known faculty and talented undergraduates. Wilson served as an assistant professor of biology from 1956–1958, an associate professor of zoology from 1958–1964, professor of zoology from 1964–1976, and a curator in entomology at the Museum of Comparative Zoology from 1973–1997, and he currently serves as honorary curator in entomology at the Museum of Comparative Zoology.

Wilson's contention that social behaviors have genetic components has changed the study of human behavior and generated plenty of controversy. His specialty is the social life of ants, but his wider reputation comes from his writings on the human condition. In spite of the controversy created by many of his ideas, Edward O. Wilson has many impressive distinctions. He is the only person to have received both the highest award in science in the United States, the National Medal of Science, and its premier literary award, the Pulitzer Prize in literature, twice. Wilson has also received the Crafoord Prize, awarded by the Royal Swedish Academy of Science, an award designed to cover those areas (general biology, oceanography, mathematics, and astronomy) not covered by the Nobel Prizes. Wilson received this award for his work in ecology. He has also received over sixty other prizes, medals, and awards from around the world, as well as twenty-four honorary degrees. Wilson is the author or coauthor of over twenty-four books (among the most noted are *Sociobiology, Insect Societies, On Human Nature, The Diversity of Life, The Biophilia Hypothesis,* and *The Ants*) and 350 scholarly articles. He was recognized in 1996 by *Time* magazine as among its twenty-five Most Influential Americans and has been identified as one of the 100 most influential scientists of all time (Alabama Academy of Honor, 2002). Wilson and his wife, Renee, have a daughter, Catherine.

Influences on Wilson

Wilson has possessed a lifelong curiosity about the various life forms (plants, animals, and humans) found on earth. He is fascinated by insects and their behavior. Eventually, he attempted to apply his evolutionary-natural theories to human behavior. He was raised in a physical environment that allowed him to explore insects firsthand in their natural environment. He also visited many museums and read a wide variety of books on insects and evolution. Consequently, Wilson was influenced by numerous social thinkers and scientists.

One of the most prominent influences on Wilson's work was Ernst Mayr and his book *Systematics and the Origin of Species*, which Wilson read as a young undergraduate. Wilson (1994) stated that he adopted *Systematics* "as my bible when I was eighteen" (232). Wilson (1994) described *Systematics* as "a cornerstone of the Modern Synthesis of evolutionary theory, one of the books that combined genetics with Darwin's theory of evolution by natural selection. Mayr's writing reinforced in my mind the philosophy implicit in Schrodinger. He showed that variety among plants and animals is created through stages that can be traced by the study of ordinary nature around us. Mayr's text told me that I could conduct scientific research of a high order with the creatures I already knew and loved" (pp. 44–45). Mayr was the curator of birds at the American Museum. He stated that a revolution in systematics and biogeography was spreading worldwide, but especially in England and the United States, the strongholds of Darwinian evolutionary theory. This idea encouraged Wilson to believe that he had an academic future in his chosen field. Wilson was convinced that the only reason Mayr never won a Nobel Prize was that none are given in evolutionary biology.

It is safe to say that Mayr strengthened Wilson's attraction to the study of biology and evolutionary sciences. But Mayr would prove to be much more than an academic influence; he ultimately became a colleague of Wilson's at Harvard. When Wilson was under attack by the media and some of his own colleagues for his sociobiological ideas, which critics linked with "racist eugenics and Nazi policies," Mayr was one of the few people who publicly defended his studies (Wilson, 1994:338).

As an evolutionary biologist, it should be clear that Wilson was influenced by the works of Charles Darwin. Darwin's belief in natural selection as a mechanism of evolution is mirrored in Wilson's use of this same mechanism for the predisposition of the mind to select for certain units of culture, which he called "culturgens." Wilson conducted research in the South Pacific, an area that has served many of the key advances in evolutionary biology. "Darwin conceived of evolution by natural selection from what he learned about birds in the Galápagos Islands, and Wallace had the same idea after studying butterflies and other organisms in the old Malay Archipelago, now modern Malaysia, Brunei, and Indonesia" (Wilson, 1994:166).

Wilson developed an interest in chemical communication in the fall of 1953 when Niko Tinbergen and Konrad Lorenz visited Harvard to lecture on the new science of ethology. Twenty years later they shared the Nobel Prize for physiology or medicine, with Karl von Frisch as a third corecipient. Wilson was highly impressed by Lorenz's lectures and "phrases soon to become famous in the behavioral sciences: imprinting, ritualization, aggressive drive, overflow; and the names of animals: graylag goose, jackdaw, stickleback. He had come to proclaim a new approach to the study of behavior. Instinct has been reinstated, he said; the role of learning was grossly overestimated by B. F. Skinner and other behaviorists; we must now press on in a new direction" (Wilson, 1994:285–286). Wilson admits being influenced by Skinner's ideas about the process of learning. As a behavioral theorist, Skinner worked to find ways to predict behavioral patterns. In his operant reinforcement theory he argued that events following a behavior determine the frequency of that behavior (Seligman, 2001).

In 1954, Wilson met Sir Julian Huxley, a great evolutionary scholar and humanist, during his visit to Harvard. Their common interest was a classic topic of general biology. They had both discovered a "problem" while studying caste ants that seemed to violate the rules of natural selection. "The problem of ant castes had attracted the attention of Charles Darwin, who saw it as a threat to the theory of natural selection. Although Darwin had constructed the idea of relative growth intuitively, Huxley and I knew that the ideas and data of our studies had produced the first full and quantitative evolutionary explanation. In 1968 I refined the idea of adaptive demography and developed several new principles of caste evolution with the aid of models in linear programming" (Wilson, 1994:313–314). Because Wilson used mathematical models in his genetic theories on population biology, he was influenced by biologists and mathematicians who also applied formulas and models to such studies. Lawrence Slobodkin is one such ecologist who had shown a link between ecology and genetics by using mathematical models.

This discussion represents a mere sample of the influences on Wilson. An academic position at Harvard University presented Wilson with plenty of opportunities to meet the leading figures of academia; he read a great deal and possessed a highly trained mind. It is no surprise that Wilson would contribute so significantly to social theory.

SOCIOBIOLOGY

Wilson's greatest contribution to sociological thought is his theories of *sociobiology*. This term was coined by Wilson in his controversial 1975 book, *Sociobiology: The New Synthesis*, to refer to efforts to link genetic factors with the social behavior of animals. John Pfeiffer, in the *New York Times Book Review* (1975), wrote of *Sociobiology* as "an evolutionary event. . . announcing for all who hear that we are on the verge of breakthroughs in

the effort to understand our place in the scheme of things" (Wilson, 1980:inside cover). "In a 1989 poll the officers and fellows of the international Animal Behavior Society rated *Sociobiology* the most important book on animal behavior of all time, edging even Darwin's 1872 classic, *The Expression of the Emotions in Man and Animals*" (Wilson, 1994:330–331). *Sociobiology* provided the framework for a new science: the study of the biological basis for social behavior in every species, from one-cell amoebas to humans (Wilson, 1980). Wilson (1975) defined sociobiology as "the systematic study of the biological basis of all social behavior" (p. 4).

Biological Reductionism

Sociobiology is the study of the biological bases of behavior. "The tendency to explain social phenomena in terms of biological causes such as physiology or genes is known as *biological reductionism*" (Kornblum, 1991:102). From this perspective, it is believed that specific genes cause specific behaviors, such as a gene that causes criminal behavior or a gene that causes someone to drink alcohol in such a way as to be labeled an alcoholic. The roots of biological reductionism can be traced to Darwin's biologically based evolutionary theories. Wilson's sociobiology represents a recent version of biological reductionism. Sociobiologists believe "that the human race is a product of evolution and that vast quantities of information are passed on by our genes. It follows that genes as well as environment play [*sic*] a role in society and that behavior has a biological base" (Wallace and Wolf, 1999:383). Pierre L. van den Berghe (1977) stated that "sociobiology applies natural selection theory to behavior. It asserts that the behavior of an animal, like its anatomy, is the product of a process of biological evolution through natural selection" (p. 121). According to Wilson, "Natural selection is the process whereby certain genes gain representation in the following generations superior to that of other genes located at the same chromosome positions. . . . In the process of natural selection, then, any device that can insert a higher proportion of certain genes into subsequent generations will come to characterize the species. One class of such devices promotes prolonged individual survival. Another promotes superior mating performance and care of the resulting offspring" (Wilson, 1980:3).

Sociobiologists are not simplistic genetic determinists who believe that all human behaviors are rigidly controlled by genes. Instead, they argue that biological factors and genetic influences place limits on the range of possible behaviors (Wallace and Wolf, 1999). "The principal goal of a general theory of sociobiology should be an ability to predict features of social organization from a knowledge of these population parameters combined with information on the behavioral constraints imposed by the genetic constitution of the species" (Wilson, 1980:5). Wilson's studies comparing invertebrate and vertebrate societies to human societies and finding them functionally similar have led to much criticism. The controversy set off by this biological reductionist approach to the study of human behavior will be discussed later in this chapter.

Elementary Concepts of Sociobiology

The fundamental belief of sociobiologists is that genes determine behavior, both in animals and in humans. Genes are the core of any organism. Wilson (1980) stated:

> In a Darwinist sense the organism does not live for itself. Its primary function is not even to reproduce other organisms; it reproduces genes, and it serves as their temporary carrier. Each organism generated by sexual reproduction is a unique, accidental subset of all the genes constituting the species. Natural selection is the process whereby certain genes gain representation in the following generations superior to that of other genes located at the same

> chromosome positions. . . . In the process of natural selection, then, any device that can insert a higher proportion of certain genes into subsequent generations will come to characterize the species. (p. 3)

To specify an organism a researcher requires information about the properties of the cells and their spatial positions. To specify a cell the researcher must first find not only the nucleotide sequences but also the identity and configuration of other kinds of molecules placed in and around the cell.

Every organism consists of cells. A number of organisms involved in joint activity can be viewed as a society. Communal activity defines the roles of various members found within the society. As Maslow (1936) found in his study of rhesus monkeys, dominance relations can be examined only in the whole-group context, not in paired groupings. "The monkeys form coalitions in the struggle for dominance, so that an individual falls in rank if deprived of its allies. A second-ranking male, for example, may owe its position to protection given it by the alpha male or support from one or more close peers. Such coalitions cannot be predicted from the outcome of pairwise encounters, let alone from behavior of an isolated monkey" (Wilson, 1980:7).

Wilson (1975, 1980) provided basic definitions of a number of elementary concepts of sociobiology, summarized as follows (7–9):

1. **Society:** a group of individuals belonging to the same species and organized cooperatively. Reciprocal, cooperative communication, transcending mere sexual activity, is an essential intuitive criterion of a society. Aggregation, sexual behavior, and territoriality are important properties of true societies. Bird flocks, wolf packs, and locust swarms are examples of elementary societies.

2. **Aggregation:** a group of individuals of the same species, comprising more than just a mated pair or a family, gathered in the same place but not internally organized or engaged in cooperative behavior. An example of a human aggregate would be those people

waiting for a train at a train station; they gathered there independently of one another.

3. **Colony:** in strict biological usage, a society of organisms which are highly integrated, either by physical union of the bodies or by division into specialized zooids or castes, or by both. In sociobiology, this word is best restricted to the societies of social insects and "colonial" invertebrates.

4. **Individual:** any physically distinct organism.

5. **Group:** a set of organisms belonging to the same species that remain together for any period of time while interacting with one another to a much greater degree than with organisms of other specifies. Group behavior is especially prevalent in societies in which there exists a hierarchy of levels of organization of nested subsets of individuals belonging to a single large congregation.

6. **Population:** a set of organisms belonging to the same species that occupy a clearly delimited area at the same time. This unit—the most basic but also one of the most loosely employed in evolutionary biology—is defined in terms of genetic continuity. A *species* is a population or set of populations within which the individuals are capable of freely interbreeding under natural conditions. Members of one species do not interbreed with those of other species, regardless of how closely related they may be genetically. A population that differs significantly from other populations belonging to the same species is referred to as a *geographical race* or a *subspecies*.

7. **Communication:** action on the part of one organism (or cell) that alters adaptively the probability pattern of behavior in another organism (or cell).

8. **Coordination:** interaction among units of a group so that the overall effort of the group is divided among the units without leadership being assumed by any one of them (such as the encirclement of prey by a pride of lions).

9. **Hierarchy:** in ordinary sociobiological usage, the dominance of one member of a group over another, as measured by superiority in aggressive encounters and order of access to food, mates, resting sites, and other objects promoting survivorship and reproductive fitness.

Technically, there need be only two individuals to make up a hierarchy, but chains of many individuals in descending order of dominance are more frequent. Advanced societies are dominated by a hierarchical structure.

10. **Regulation:** in biology, the coordination of units to achieve the maintenance of one or more physical or biological variables at a constant level. The result of regulation is termed *homeostasis*. Social insects display marked homeostasis in the regulation of their own colony populations, caste proportions, and nest environment.

These concepts are integral to an understanding of Wilson's sociobiological theories.

The Social Insects

A great deal of *Sociobiology* reflects Wilson's attempt to provide an index of social organisms, to further advance his evolutionary ideas, and to articulate explanations of how sociobiology is relevant to the life history of various species. Wilson had established a highly credible reputation for his research on insects before the publication of *Sociobiology*. In 1971, Wilson published *The Insect Societies*, the first comprehensive study of social insects since the 1930s. In it, he wrote that the study of insects is important because insects

> are among the great achievements of organic evolution. . . . The biologist is invited to consider insect societies because they best exemplify molecule to society. Among the tens of thousands of species of wasps, ants, bees, and termites, we witness the employment of social design to solve ecological problems ordinarily dealt with by single organisms. . . . The second reason for singling out social insects is their ecological dominance on the land. In most parts of the earth ants in particular are among the principal predators of other invertebrates. (p. 1)

In the abridged edition of *Sociobiology* Wilson (1980) stated, "The social insects challenge the mind by the sheer magnitude of their numbers and variety. There are more species of ants in a square kilometer of Brazilian forest than all the species of primates in the world, more workers in a single colony of driver ants than all the lions and elephants in Africa. The biomass and energy consumption of social insects exceed those of vertebrates in most terrestrial habitats" (p. 189). Insects provide the biologist with an array of social organizations for study and comparison. "The full sweep of social evolution is displayed—repeatedly—by such groups as the halictid bees and sphecid and vespid wasps. There are so many species in each evolutionary grade that one can sample them as a statistician, measuring variance and partialing out correlates" (p. 189).

Wilson (1980) described a social insect, or eusocial insect as they are often technically labeled, as

> all of the ants, all of the termites, and the more highly organized bees and wasps. These insects can be distinguished as a group by their common possession of three traits: (1) individuals of the same species cooperate in caring for the young; (2) there is a reproductive division of labor, with more or less sterile individuals working on behalf of fecund nestmates; and (3) there is an overlap of at least two generations in life stages capable of contributing to colony labor, so that offspring assist parents during some period of their life. (pp. 189–190)

Wilson continued his research on social insects. In 1990, he published *The Ants* (1990a), the first comprehensive treatise on these insects since the beginning of the twentieth century. The highly impressive book is over 700 pages long and contains almost a thousand line drawings, photographs, and paintings. *The Ants* contains chapters dealing with classification, altruism, kin recognition, communication, homeostasis, and population regulation, among other topics.

In his article "Insects," Wilson (1990b) stated, "If all mankind were to disappear, the world would regenerate back to the rich state of equilibrium that existed 10,000 years ago. If insects were to vanish, the environment

would collapse into chaos" (p. 6). Insects comprise more species than all other organisms combined—including plants, animals, and microorganisms. There are only a few entomologists who specialize in classifying insects. As one of them, Wilson (1990b) reported that every time he made a field trip he turned up new species, often within hours. In fact, "during the past two centuries biologists have discovered and given formal names to somewhat more than 1.5 million species of plants, animals, and microorganisms, yet various methods of estimation place the number of all species of Earth, known and still unknown, between 3 million and 100 million" (Wilson, 2002:86a). The diversity of life is truly amazing. Wilson (2002a) estimated that there are 1 million trillion insects alive on the planet at any given time, and as many as 10 billion bacteria may reside in a single pinch of soil.

Selfish Genes, Kin Selection, and Altruism

Social scientists certainly will not argue with the biological contributions Wilson has made in the plant and animal worlds, but they do question the validity of explaining human behavior through mostly biological methods. In the preface to *Ecology, Evolution, and Population Biology* (1974), Wilson explained:

> Modern biology consists of essentially two disciplines. One, molecular and cellular biology, which elucidates the machinery of life. Its goal is to explain the ways in which cells, tissues, and organs are constructed out of molecular building blocks and run on chemical reactions. The other discipline, evolutionary biology, is the subject of this present book. Viewing life at the level of whole organisms and populations, it interprets the functions of the machinery used in adapting organisms to the natural environment, and it attempts to trace the history of life from the beginning four billion years ago as giant replicating molecules to the eventual origin of living species. Ecology and evolutionary theory are the major components

of this higher level of biology. Ecology cannot fully explain the relation of organisms to their environment without substantial recourse to evolutionary history and population dynamics. (p. v)

Wilson stressed that the basic unit is the gene. Genes are passed from one generation to the next. If an organism contains genes that tend to promote its survival, then that organism has been "selected for" survival.

Kinship groups that share superior genes demonstrate a type of "genetic fitness." The members of this kinship group may live together or be scattered throughout the population. "The essential condition is that they jointly behave in a way that benefits the group as a whole, while remaining in relatively close contact with the remainder of the population. This enhancement of kin-network welfare in the midst of a population is *kin selection*" (Wilson, 1980:55). Through spatial rearrangement kin selection can merge into interdemic selection. "As the kin network settles into one physical location and becomes physically more isolated from the rest of the species, it approaches the status of a true population. A closed society, or one so nearly closed that it exchanges only a small fraction of its members with other societies each generation, is a true Mendelian population" (Wilson, 1980:55).

The idea of kin selection was articulated by Charles Darwin in *On the Origins of Species*. Darwin had realized that Lamarck's theory of evolution—the inheritance of characteristics acquired by individual organisms—needed to be amended, because it was flawed. Consequently, Darwin introduced the idea of natural selection operating at the level of the family rather than of the single organism. Wilson (1980) explained that Darwin's logic is impeccable: "If some of the individuals of the family are sterile and yet important to the welfare of fertile relatives, as in the case of insect colonies, selection at the family level is inevitable. With the entire family serving as the unit of selection, it is the capacity to generate

sterile but altruistic relatives that becomes subject to genetic evolution" (p. 56). Wallace and Wolf (1999) stated:

> This basic theory of natural selection—in which the mechanisms for Darwin's theory is provided by Mendelian genetics—is essentially one of what has been called 'gene selfishness.' This is not to say that genes are *consciously* selfish. Rather the whole theory of natural selection implies that the race goes, by definition, to those who behave in ways that promote the interests (namely survival) of their genes. This, in turn, means that if a particular gene tends to promote the survival of an organism, it will be reproduced. If it does not, it will not. (p. 385–386)

Thus, it seems logical that a biological basis exists for people's tendency to favor members of their kin rather than those not directly related. Members of families generally watch out for one another and assist in raising and nurturing the next generation. This complex set of relationships is referred to as *reciprocal altruism* (Trivers, 1971). Human behavior abounds with reciprocal altruism, but animal behavior seems to be almost devoid of it. "Perhaps the reason is that in animals relationships are not sufficiently enduring, or memories of personal behavior reliable enough, to permit the highly personal contracts associated with the more human forms of reciprocal altruism" (Wilson, 1980:58). Wilson acknowledged that social insects possess altruistic behavior that has evolved by family-level selection. The primary behaviors associated with altruism are the thwarting of predators, cooperative breeding, and food sharing. Wilson (1980) stated that "no behavior is more clearly altruistic than the sharing of food" (p. 61).

Wilson remained steadfast in the idea that the process of natural selection, through kinship, is responsible for altruistic behavior. When genes causing altruism are shared by two organisms because of common descent, the propensity to altruism spreads through the gene pool and into the next generation.

However, cooperation and altruism extend well beyond the bounds of kinship. It would appear that altruism, is not best explained in biological terms. There are many social explanations for altruism, trust being one of them. Trust is something that is learned and extends to many people one might meet outside the family circle.

Sociobiology and the Human Species

In the final chapter of *Sociobiology*, Wilson attempted to extend his sociobiological theories to humans. He discussed the peculiar nature of *Homo sapiens*. They occupy the widest geographical range and maintain the highest local densities of any of the primates. Modern humans are anatomically unique: Their erect posture and wholly bipedal locomotion are not matched by other primates. Furthermore, the reproductive physiology and behavior of *Homo sapiens* have undergone extraordinary evolution. The task of comparative sociobiology is to trace human qualities back through time and identify behaviors similar to those of other species. It is Wilson's belief that the same principles of population biology and comparative zoology that worked so well in explaining the rigid systems of the social insects can be applied to vertebrate animals.

Wilson acknowledged that the human species is unique in the great amount of "plasticity" of human social parameters. This vastness of parameters is due to humans' great variety of behavior. Therefore, Wilson (1975) proposed that genes promoting this plasticity must be strongly selected for at the individual level. The ability to generate such variety comes from a lack of competition from other species. Unlike all other organisms on this planet, "man has temporarily escaped the constraint of interspecific competition" (Wilson, 1975:549). Thus, humans do not have to compete for any resources that could otherwise limit human population growth. Biologists refer to such a lack of competition from

other species as *ecological release*. It should be noted, however, that cultures do replace one another.

The basic proposal put forth by Wilson in the final chapter of *Sociobiology* is that humans inherit a "propensity" to attain behavioral and social structure. This propensity is shared by the human population and can therefore be called *human nature*. Wilson acknowledged that humans have free will and free choice, but the channels of psychological development are imbedded very deep in human genes. Thus, although there is great variation between cultures, there is also a convergence between certain ideas, referred to as a *common humanity* (Wilson, 1975). In brief, the human brain works with the sensory organs to allow an individual to acquire the most favorable traits for survival in the environment (Wilson, 1975).

Wilson (1975) stated that self-knowledge and social behavior are constrainted by the system that works to shape these concepts, namely, the hypothalamic and limbic systems of the human brain. These organs are under the pressures of genetic selection and development, and therefore, they have evolved by natural selection. Consequently, as the organs that constrain them evolve, concepts such as self-knowledge and social behavior must also be constantly evolving, or at least under the pressures of natural selection. Wilson wrote that an understanding of the evolution of social behavior depends on a full understanding of the population information, including the population growth rate, and the genetic structure of the population (Wilson, 1975).

Wilson did not completely ignore social variables as influences on human behavior. Cultural variation is explained as phenotypic rather than genetic in origin. As Wilson (1980) explained, "This view has gained support from the ease with which certain aspects of culture can be altered in the space of a single generation, too quickly to be evolutionary in nature. The drastic alteration in Irish society in the first two years of the potato blight (1846–1848) is a case in point. Another is the shift in the Japanese authority structure during the American occupation following World War II" (p. 274). Another social development is that of world languages. Language elevates humans over other animals in their ability to communicate with each other. Words are given arbitrary definitions and possess a fully symbolic quality. Language allows humans to transcend time and space barriers and represents a quantum jump in evolution.

In the opening sentence of the final chapter of the abridged edition of *Sociobiology*, "Man: From Sociobiology to Sociology," Wilson (1980) stated, "Let us now consider man in the free spirit of natural history, as though we were zoologists from another planet completing a catalog of social species on Earth" (p. 271). Critic Antony Flew (1994) stated that "Wilson did not, either then or later, go on to do it. Instead, he proceeded, by his subsequent off-the-cuff remarks about human nature, to provoke explosions of fury from various individuals and collectives committed to the defense of social democratic or socialist orthodoxies" (p. 323). Flew argued that zoologists should examine the peculiarities of humans, including the extensive period between birth and maturity, the incomparable capacity for learning, the importance of previous experience, and the importance of learned (as opposed to instinctual) behavior. Flew stated that Wilson was far too good a biologist not to have noticed the tremendous differences between humans and other species.

The Controversy with Sociobiology

Antony Flew's criticisms of Edward Wilson and sociobiology are merely the beginning of the controversy that surrounds this field. "When applied to human societies, sociobiology has drawn severe criticism from both social scientists and biologists" (Kornblum,

1991:102). In his 1978 article, "Introduction: What Is Sociobiology?" Wilson admitted that he was

> surprised—even astonished—by the initial reaction to *Sociobiology: The New Synthesis*. When the book was published in 1975, I expected a favorable reaction from other biologists. After all, my colleagues and I had merely been extending neo-Darwinism into the study of social behavior and animal societies, and the underlying biological principles we employed were largely conventional. . . . From social scientists, I expected not much reaction. I took it for granted that the human species is subject to sociobiological analysis no less than to genetic or endocrinological analysis. (p. 1)

In *Naturalist* (1994), Wilson wrote that the liberal dovecotes of Harvard University became reactionary in their attitude toward his *Sociobiology* (1975), and the faculty offered little support. "I know now after many private conversations that the majority of my fellow natural scientists on the Harvard faculty were sympathetic to my biological approach to human behavior but were confused by the motives and political aims of the Science for the People study group. They may also have thought that where there is smoke, there is fire. So they stuck to their work and kept a safe distance" (Wilson, 1994:338). Wilson speculated that perhaps he should have ended *Sociobiology* at his chapter on chimpanzees. "Many biologists wish I had. Even several of the critics said that *Sociobiology* would have been a great book if I had not added the final chapter, the one on human beings. Claude Levi-Strauss, I was later reminded by his friend the historian Emanuel Ladurie, judged the book to be 90 percent correct, which I took to mean true through the chimpanzees but not a line further" (Wilson, 1994:328). Although some of his contemporary biologists questioned his sociobiological theories as applied to the human species, the greatest criticism of Wilson came from social scientists. Wilson acknowledged in the preface to the abridged edition of *Sociobiology* (1980) that he had ventured into many disciplines in which he had no direct experience. Social scientists wished that he had not bothered to venture into "their" domain. "Marshall Sahlins, a cultural anthropologist, made a strong attempt to exempt human behavior from the tenets of sociobiology in his 1976 book, *The Use and Abuse of Biology*. In November of that year the members of the American Anthropological Association, gathering in Washington for their annual meeting, considered a motion to censure sociobiology formally and to ban two symposia on the subject scheduled earlier" (Wilson, 1994:331).

The Marxists attacked sociobiology as well. "I did not even think about the Marxists. When the attacks on sociobiology came from the Science for the People, the leading radical left group within American science, I was unprepared for a largely ideological argument. It was now clear to me that I was tampering with something fundamental: mythology" (Wilson, 1978:1). Wilson believed that social scientists misunderstood the context of sociobiology. In his updated definition, Wilson (1978) called sociobiology "the systematic study of the biological basis of all forms of social behavior, including sexual and parental behavior, in all kinds of organisms including humans" (p. 1). He stated that sociobiology is not something new to the biological sciences. In fact, Wilson explained that the term *sociobiology* had been used by John P. Scott in 1946 and by Charles F. Hockett in 1948, but the word had never caught on.

Sociologists especially disagree with sociobiology. Many sociologists view sociobiology as an attempt "to legitimate aspects of human societies that people wish to reform and to set limits on how far you can change (or perfect) people. Opponents see the human being as *essentially* a creature of cultural norms, in whom biological universals extend no further than such basic activities as eating, excreting, and sleeping. . . . The other major criticism of sociobiology is that cultures are so diverse that biology, which deals with the universal, really cannot be much use in explaining things" (Wallace and Wolf, 1999:383–384). Sociologists recognize that genes determine certain characteristics (such as skin color and eye color) but argue that behavior is not determined by genes. Furthermore, "the hypothesis that genetic programming establishes complex forms of normative behavior is not supported by direct evidence—there is as yet no proof that such genes or sets of genes actually exist" (Kornblum, 1991:103). Not surprisingly, Wilson considered sociobiology the "antidiscipline" of the social sciences, especially sociology and anthropology. Sociologists grounded in the scientific tradition have trouble accepting the legitimacy of sociobiology; social thinkers not grounded in the scientific tradition, understandably, have an even greater difficulty accepting this field.

ADDITIONAL CONTRIBUTIONS BY WILSON

Beyond sociobiology, Edward O. Wilson has made a number of other significant contributions to sociological thought. His theories on biophilia, biodiversity, and consilience are worthy of review.

Biophilia and Biodiversity

In *Naturalist* (1994), Wilson explained that he had coined the term *biophilia* for use in a *New York Times* article on conservation. Later, in 1984, Wilson had used the term as the title and pivotal idea of his book *Biophilia*. It was in this publication that Wilson had defined *biophilia* as "the inborn affinity human beings have for other forms of life, an affiliation evoked, according to circumstances, by pleasure, or a sense of security, or awe, or even fascination blended with revulsion" (Wilson, 1994:360). Among the most basic desires of humans is a preference for certain natural environments as places for habitation; the most obvious choice is living near some body of water. This is certainly understandable because humans need water to survive. Consequently, the question remains: Is this desire to live near water a true example of the validity of biophilia or simply a reflection of fulfilling a basic human need for survival?

In 1993, Wilson and Stephen R. Kellert coedited *The Biophilia Hypothesis*. In their chapter "Biophilia and the Conservation Ethic" Kellert and Wilson (1993) described biophilia as "the innately emotional affiliation of human beings to other living organisms" (31). The attachment that humans have to other forms of life is innate but also mediated by rules of prepared and counterprepared learning. Biophilia is not a single instinct but a complexity of emotional feelings that include attraction and aversion, awe and indifference, and peacefulness and fear-driven anxiety.

> The biophilia hypothesis goes on to hold that the multiple strands of emotional response are woven into symbols composing a large part of culture. It suggests that when human beings remove themselves from the natural environment, the biophilic learning rules are not replaced by modern versions equally adapted to artifacts. Instead, they persist from generation to generation, atrophied and fitfully manifested in the artificial new environments into which technology has catapulted humanity. For the indefinite future more children and adults will continue, as they do now, to visit zoos than attend all major professional sports combined (at least this is so in the United States and Canada), the wealthy will continue to seek dwellings on prominence above water admist parkland, and urban dwellers will go on dreaming of snakes for reasons they cannot explain. (Kellert and Wilson, 1993:31–32).

Although Wilson failed to provide any statistical data to support his hypothesis, he explained, "Were there no evidence of biophilia at all, the hypothesis of its existence would still be compelled by pure evolutionary logic" (Kellert and Wilson, 1993:32). Humanity began millions of years ago with the origin of the genus *Homo*. For nearly 99 percent of human history people have lived in hunter-gatherer types of societies and were intimately involved with other organisms. Biophilia has evolved through bicultural evolution, a process in which culture is elaborated under the influence of hereditary learning propensities while the genes prescribing the propensities are spread by natural selection in a cultural context (Kellert and Wilson, 1993). Lumsden and Wilson (1981) described bicultural evolution as a type of gene-culture co-evolution, which traces a spiral trajectory through time whereby a certain genotype makes a behavioral response more likely, and the response enhances survival and reproductive fitness. This genotype spreads through the population, and the behavioral response grows more frequent. Thus, gene-culture coevolution is viewed as a plausible explanation of the origin of biophilia.

Wilson (1994) admitted that the evidence for biophilia remains thin, and most of the underlying theory of its genetic origin is highly speculative. He remained steadfast in the idea that the most important implication of an innate biophilia is the foundation it holds for an enduring conservation ethic. Wilson (1994) stated, "Biophilia is the most recent of my syntheses, joining the ideas that have been most consistently attractive to me for most of my life. My truths, three in number, are the following: first, humanity is ultimately the product of biological evolution; second, the diversity of life is the cradle and greatest natural heritage of the human species; and third, philosophy and religion make little sense without taking into account these first two conceptions" (p. 363).

Whereas biophilia remains as much a theory as an explanation of human behavior, *biodiversity* is an undisputed reality. There are more than 10 million species alive today, with an even more astronomical number of possible genetic recombinants, which create the field on which evolution continues to play. "The most wonderful mystery of life may well be the means by which it created so much diversity from so little physical matter" (Wilson, 1992:35). The great diversity of life is created through a process referred to as *speciation*. Wilson (1975) defined *speciation* as the processes of the genetic diversification of populations and the multiplication of species. The closer to the equator, the greater the number of species. The increase of species is determined by three factors: energy, stability, and area (or ESA). "The more energy that is available to the evolving community of species, the more species there are. That maximizes as you go towards the equator. The more stable a region, as in a constant-climate area, the more species accumulate because they have more time to adapt and fit together. The larger the area, the larger the population and the more diverse it is. For example, South America has more species than the West Indies" (Wilson, 2002c:3). Speciation slows down after the initial burst of diversification.

Life has divided into millions of species, each unit serving a unique role in relation to the greater whole. And yet, the biosphere and all organisms combined make up only about one part in 10 billion squares kilometers of surface. "Despite the fact that living organisms compose a mere ten-billionth part of the mass of earth, biodiversity is the most information-rich part of the known universe. More organization and complexity exist in a handful of soil than on the surfaces of all the other planets combined" (Wilson, 1993:39). Since Wilson has not conducted research on the surfaces of other planets, this part of his theory remains just that: a theory.

Wilson's participation as an environmental activist was triggered in 1980 when the editors of *Harvard Magazine* asked seven Harvard professors to identify what they considered the most important problem facing the world in the coming years. Four cited

poverty (especially that due to overpopulation), one was concerned about excessive governmental control (focusing on the United States), and another chose the threat of global nuclear war. Only Wilson mentioned the environment. He wrote of his concern over the peril of the biosphere and the depletion of ancient storehouses of biological diversity. As terrible as economic collapse, energy depletion, conquest by a totalitarian government, and limited nuclear war would be, they could be repaired within a few generations, but the loss of genetic and species diversity through the destruction of natural habitats will take millions of years to correct (Wilson, 1994).

Population size is critical to survival. Generally speaking, when populations go below approximately 100 individuals, inbreeding depression occurs. If there are deleterious or lethal genes in the populations (for example, cystic fibrosis in humans), there is a higher incidence of genetic malfunction, which can lead to death or sterility in species members. In larger populations, chances of a lethal gene's being passed on are lower (Wilson, 2002c). With possible extinction happening globally, it is Wilson's belief that the focus of conservation efforts should begin with such hot spots as the tropical forests. "Hot spots are the habitats that are most endangered and have the largest number of species found nowhere else but in them. These include the forests of Hawaii and Madagascar and the rich scrub lands of southwestern Australia and southern Africa. Tropical wilderness, such as the Amazon and the Congo, have the last of the great frontier forests able to support a mega fauna, i.e., large mammals and birds. The preservation of these places is critical" (Wilson, 2002c:5).

Wilson's concern about the preservation of biodiversity has led to a crusade of conservation and the embracing of every kind of living creature. Wilson also pointed out that because he edited the volume *Biodiversity* in 1988, it is widely believed that he coined the term. He has stated that he deserves no credit at all, and that the expression was put into play by Walter Rosen, the administrative officer of the National Academy of Sciences, who organized the 1986 Washington forum on biodiversity.

Consilience

The overwhelming criticism of Wilson is directed at his reductionist attitude when explaining human behavior. In *Consilience: The Unity of Knowledge* (1998), Wilson managed to upset social scientists once again. He argued that everything in the world is organized by a small number of fundamental natural laws that underscore the principles of all forms of learning and behavior. Wilson would like to see a linkage and a consolidation between the natural and social sciences:

> The greatest enterprise of the mind has always been and always will be the attempted linkage of the sciences and humanities. The ongoing fragmentation of knowledge and resulting chaos in philosophy are not reflections of the real word but artifacts of scholarship. The propositions of the original Enlightenment are increasingly favored by objective evidence, especially from the natural sciences. Consilience is the key to unification. I prefer this word over "coherence" because its rarity has preserved its precision, whereas coherence has several possible meanings, only one of which is consilience. (Wilson, 1998:8)

Wilson did not coin this term: rather, he acknowledged William Whewell in his 1840 synthesis, *The Philosophy of the Inductive Sciences*, as the first to speak of *consilience*, which literally means a "jumping together" of knowledge by the linking of facts and fact-based theory across disciplines to create a common groundwork of explanation.

The combining, or consilience, of sciences means that the social scientists are to abandon their approach to the study of human behavior and embrace the idea used by natural scientists: that specific genes cause certain behaviors. It is Wilson's belief that the natural sciences and the humanities (particularly the creative arts) will be the two great branches of learning in the twenty-first century. "The social sciences will continue to split within each of its disciplines, a process already rancorously begun, with one part folding into or becoming continuous with biology, the other fusing with the humanities" (Wilson, 1998:12). Furthermore, Wilson stated that the social sciences are progressing more slowly than the "natural" sciences (medical science being an example), because medical science works by building on the foundation of cellular and molecular biology, as well as chemistry. Meanwhile, the social scientists do not build on their bases. Wilson has recognized that the social sciences are far more complex than the hard sciences, but he added, that the social scientists attempt to oversimplify their theories by basing them on common sense, and by ignoring the findings of psychology and biology that could be useful in providing evidence for such theories (Wilson, 1998). Wilson wrote that the social scientists have "paid little attention to the foundations of human nature, and they have almost no interest in its deep origins" (Wilson, 1998:184). Social scientists certainly do not rest their theories on common sense; in fact, they warn against such an activity. Nor do they ignore the origins of human nature.

Wilson (1998) argued that "the natural sciences have constructed a webworm of causal explanation that runs all the way from quantum physics to the brain sciences and evolutionary biology" (p. 125), and yet there are gaps in the knowledge of culture and its role in human behavior. The understanding of culture represents "the boundary between the natural sciences and the humanities (Wilson, 1998)." In *Sociobiology* (1975), Wilson stated that culture is under the pressures of natural selection and also evolution. To establish the link between culture and genetics, Lumsden and Wilson, in *Genes, Mind, and*

Culture (1981), developed the concept of *gene-culture coevolution* (the coupled evolution of genes and culture). *Gene-cultured coevolution* is defined as "any change in gene frequencies that alters culturgen frequencies in such a way that the culturgen changes alter the gene frequencies as well" (Lumsden and Wilson, 1981:372). It is Lumsden and Wilson's belief that the transmission of culture occurs through genes, and that this process occurs in any species with aspects of advanced culture. Wilson stated that previously, his sociobiology had failed to appreciate the complexity and development of the mind and the diversity of culture; therefore, he proposed mechanisms by which individual mental development is connected to culture, and culture to genetic evolution. In order to do this, sociobiology needs to draw from the fields of population genetics, cultural anthropology, and mathematical physics (Lumsden and Wilson, 1981).

Lumsden and Wilson (1981) proposed the existence of epigenetic rules. These rules are actually procedures that are genetically determined and that in turn direct the assembly of the mind. Mechanisms for this include sensory filters that screen external stimuli, cellular organization processes, and the more profound processes of cognition. Culture occurs when these epigenetic rules are translated into mental activity and behavior. Wilson and Lumsden also introduced the concept of *culturgens*, which are an assortment of transmissible behaviors, mental abilities, and artifacts. A *culturgen* is a basic unit of culture and can be mapped into node-link structures in the individual's long-term memory. Humans can choose from the array of gene-culture fitnesses of all the combinations of genotypes and culturgens that are assembled by a population, known as the *gene-culture adaptive landscape*. A shift from one culturgen to another, because of a change in the epigenetic rules, becomes the equivalent of "pure genetic evolution" (Lumsden and Wilson, 1981:10). Lumsden and Wilson (1981:16–17) identified four classes of evidence for gene-culture coevolution:

1. Nonuniform epigenetic rules exist and can be analyzed.
2. Genetic variance in the epigenetic rules exists in human populations.
3. There is a link between cultural practice and genetic fitness within human populations.
4. There exist cellular and molecular mechanisms that connect genes to cognitive development.

The first point of evidence, that rules can be analyzed, is illustrated by the example of blind children. Sight is an important sensory screen through which stimuli pass, and optic centers in the brain become fully developed in children at about five months of age. Within weeks of this time, there is observable deviant social behavior in blind children (Lumsden and Wilson, 1981). The second point of evidence, that genetic variation exists, has been confirmed in longitudinal studies involving fraternal and identical twins. The third point, a link between cultural practice and genetic fitness, is apparent in such cultural practices as circumcision, diet, marital practice, and economic organization. Specifically, societies that practice circumcision decrease the likelihood of infection; thus, members of that society have a greater chance of surviving and reproducing and a greater genetic fitness. The last point, the existence of cellular and molecular mechanisms, can be illustrated by genetic alterations that would affect the level of the neurotransmitter serotonin, which can act to greatly influence mood and behavior. This view reflects the genetic determinism that dominates the thoughts of Wilson in particular and the natural sciences in general.

Wilson has maintained a strong belief in consilience. His belief is that if sociology allows for the impact of genes on behavior, a more valid scientific theory can be created. Such a theory requires four bridges to be spanned: cognitive neuroscience, human behavioral genetics, evolutionary biology, and environmental sciences (Wilson, 1998). Wilson (1998) praised the natural and social sciences for the respect of both for fine analysis and factual information that is attained by trained intellects.

Understandably, there is a great deal of criticism of Wilson's ideas on consilience, as he basically dismissed the social sciences and argued that human behavior can be explained by biological means. The very idea that all forms of human expression—from philosophy and religion to art—can be explained in genetic terms has been criticized by those outside the social sciences as well. As sociologists have found, social phenomena are generally more than the sum of their individual parts (Begley, 1998). As Allan Mazur explained, social phenomena have their own properties and do not simply arise out of an individual's neurons or genes (Begley, 1998). It is very difficult to predict how a crowd will behave, or how a society will change, even if one knows precisely the thoughts, beliefs, and histories of its individual members.

Stephen Pope (2001) argued that Wilson failed to properly explain the role of genetics in social morality. The term *morality* refers to a community's commonly held beliefs and assumptions regarding issues of right and wrong, ethical and unethical. In *Consilience* (1998), Wilson proposed that moral sentiments need to be defined in terms of the underlying neural and endocrine responses of individuals. Pope (2001) stated, "The speculative nature of Wilson's enterprise has also been its weakness: he typically provides *programmatic* proposals, studded with intriguing hints regarding practices like incest taboos and hypergamy, rather than developing a carefully documented and comprehensive substantive descriptive anthropology" (p. 235). Pope also took issue with Wilson's (1978) claim that emotions are based on intuition, a claim offered without any evidence.

EVOLUTIONARY THEORY

Sociobiology falls within the framework of evolutionary theoretical thought. Over many years, through the process of evolution, genes create a greater probability of survival for the species are passed from one generation to the next. Classical theorists, such as Auguste Comte and Herbert Spencer, made connections between biology and sociology as long ago as the nineteenth century (for example, Spencer's use of the term *survival of the fittest*, which preceded Darwin's use of *natural selection*). However, Spencer's evolutionary framework was primarily culture-based and not genetic in emphasis. Émile Durkheim rejected biological explanations of social behavior. He believed that more advanced societies evolved from *mechanical solidarity* to *organic solidarity*. In the 1980s, Amos Hawley developed an ecological theory suggestive of Spencer and Durkheim. As Jonathan Turner (2003) explained, Hawley's theory of ecological processes begins with three basic assumptions:

1. Adaptation to environment proceeds through the formation of a system of interdependencies among the members of a population.

2. System development continues, other things being equal, to the maximum complexity afforded by the existing facilities for transportation and communication.

3. System development is resumed with the introduction of new information that increases the capacity for movement of materials, people, and messages and continues until that capacity is fully used. (pp. 84–85).

Thus, the three processes of adaptiveness, growth, and evolution are integrated by a system of mutual interdependencies. The social system is also tied to the physical environment, as humans depend on the resources that are made available by the natural ecosystem (Hawley, 1986). Hawley argued that new knowledge (for example, energy information) stimulates change and evolutionary growth in human society.

Contemporary sociobiological evolutionary theories maintain a focus on genes. Everyday behaviors related to religion and morality are all said to stem from our genes. Genes that have assisted humans in survival are maintained, through natural selection, and passed on to succeeding generations. As a popularized example, evolutionary psychologists claim that men are promiscuous because their hunter-gatherer ancestors found it necessary to mate with as many females as possible to guarantee the survival of the human species. If such a trait truly exists (as a specific gene that causes behavior), modern men would be programmed by a promiscuity gene. Sharon Begley (1998) criticized evolutionary psychologists for taking an existing trait and spinning a story to explain how it got there:

> Many traits may not be the result of natural selection; instead, they may be neutral byproducts. For instance, chins don't make us fitter or more evolutionary successful; rather, chins are the unavoidable consequence of the shape of the human jaw, which does help us survive. Similarly, evolution might not have selected for altruism, religiosity, a drive to create art, or any of the other behaviors Wilson identifies. All of these may simply be byproducts of what selection did shape—the large, complex human brain. With a smart brain, people figured out that they were mortal, and so invented religion to ease the pain caused by that knowledge. There need not be any 'religion gene'—or incest-taboo gene, art gene or dance gene. 'What is selected for is flexibility and the ability to think', argues evolutionary biologist Niles Eldredge of the American Museum of Natural History. (p. 62)

The ability to think and to act intelligently is what allows the evolution of the human species. As evolutionary biologist Francisco J. Ayala indicated, morality does not depend on our biological makeup; morality evolved not because it was adaptive, but because of an evolution of eminent intellectual abilities, such as foresight, evaluation, and choice (Pope, 2001).

However, there is a growing amount of research and interest in the area of sociobiology, an area once called *instinct*. Some of this research will be discussed in the final section of this chapter, after a brief review of a few contemporary sociobiological evolutionary theorists and their ideas.

Pierre van den Berghe

Pierre van den Berghe remains a strong proponent of the validity of a biological perspective on human behavior. He argues the very reason humans are "social" is that we find sociability advantageous in reproducing and guaranteeing the survival of our species. Communal forms of bonding allow humans to protect themselves from predators and to more easily dominate and exploit the natural resources necessary for survival (for example, water and food supplies). *Kin selection* (the inclination to favor kin) is the oldest and most basic mechanism necessary for sociality. This mechanism, like all processes that affect human behavior, is explained by sociobiological arguments operating at the genetic level. The gene itself becomes the ultimate unit of natural selection. However, van den Berghe (1977–1978) did acknowledge that the gene's reproduction can be affected by cultural forces. Thus, culture (presumably through the socialization process) is responsible for variations in the degree of altruism and nepotism in kin selection. But the ultimate reason for such things as nepotism, van den Berghe insisted, remains genetics.

Altruistic behaviors, such as providing assistance to those with whom a bond has been formed, are influenced by the process of reciprocity. Organisms help one another increase the likelihood of the survival of their species; such exchanges are described by sociobiologists as *reciprocal altruism* (Turner, 2003:101). In human societies, reciprocity is influenced by a culture's norms and expectations of proper behavior. The role of power is demonstrated through *coercion*, which van den Berghe referred to as the ability to increase fitness and survival at a cost to others. Pure strength and intellectual superiority, developed genetically, allow certain members of the species to dominate others. Laws created by society usually neutralize the role of physical strength (for example, one cannot become the CEO of a corporation by physically beating up the current CEO and claiming his or her job). However, at the macro level, a society can develop a superior army and use coercion, through military threats or action, to establish a power position and thus increase the probability of survival.

Richard Machalek

As Turner (2003) explained, "Machalek has applied modern evolutionary theory to traditional sociological problems. Machalek would like to see a truly comparative sociology or one that crosses species lines. His approach is to search for the foundations and development of 'sociality' wherever it is found, in both human and nonhuman species" (p. 105). Generating research and information on various species results in a comparative sociology. Animal species and human species are obviously quite distinctive, but Machalek (1992) maintained that all species confront the same basic problems of organizational structure and regulation needed to guarantee survival, and that the reason there are so few macro societies (only insects and humans have successfully created them) is that the evolution of any species is limited by a number of constraints (organismic, ecological, cost-benefit, and sociological). Overcoming sociological constraints is the most difficult and important challenge. In order for humans to evolve a macro society, they had to engage in cooperation, adopt a division of labor, and learn how to integrate and coordinate this division of labor (Machalek, 1992).

Kinship bonds helps to explain how humans first learned to cooperate, argued

Machalek. The general principle of kinship evolved to include the cooperation of larger groups of humans. The ability to integrate the behaviors of "anonymous others" enables social insects and humans to form large, complex societies (Machalek, 1992). Insects use chemical communication, whereas humans employ "cognitive culture" and a socially constructed division of labor. It is this capacity that allows complete strangers to work cooperatively within the macro structure. This impersonality allows individuals to distance themselves from anonymous others and maintain an allegiance to kin.

Gerhard Lenski

Lenski has taken a conflict approach to his work in seeking to answer the age-old question of social stratification: Who gets what and why? Lenski equated social stratification with the distributive process in human societies and concentrated on the causes of social stratification rather than the consequences. He examined the mechanisms by which power, prestige, and material wealth are dispersed among the members of the population. Turner (2003) explained that Lenski's theory is evolutionary in that "Lenski's emphasis [was] on distribution of power and privilege in distinct societal types that were seen as stages in humans' long-term evolutionary history: (1) hunting and gathering societies, (2) simple horticultural societies, (3) advanced horticultural societies, (4) agrarian societies, and (5) industrial societies" (p. 109).

Lenski's evolutionary and historical approach to the study of social stratification comes from the perspective of Hegel's dialectic. "Applying the Hegelian dialectic to the past, one easily discovers a meaningful pattern in the otherwise confusing history of stratification theory. . . . The dialectical view of stratification theory is more than a useful device for summarizing the work of the past. It also sensitizes one to current trends and developments, and provides a basis for anticipating future ones" (Lenski, 1966:viii). In *Power and Privilege* (1966) Lenski stated, "The starting point in every sociological discussion of the nature of man is the deceptively simple assertion that *man is a social being obliged by nature to live with others as a member of society*" (p. 25). The human race could not survive without the social bonds created by its culture. Culture and social life are social products essential for the survival of the species and the satisfaction of human needs and desires. It is through cooperative activity that humans can satisfy their many needs and desires. Self-sacrifice and altruistic behavior are still more likely to be directed toward like-minded people and kin. As Lenski (1966) explained, sacrificial action is not disinterested, and such behavior is seldom taken on behalf of strangers, nor do strangers expect it. In order to differentiate patterns of such behavior, Lenski (1966) used the term *partisan self-sacrifice* (p. 28).

In more recent publications, Lenski, along with his wife, Jean Lenski, and their collaborator, Patrick Nolan, have moved away from just stratification processes to a more macrolevel theory of social organization in general (Turner, 2003). Lenski, Nolan, and Lenski (1995) were concerned about random variation and the selection of those traits that promote adaptation to the environment. The authors argued that human society is influenced by biological evolution, where genetic information is transmitted through the reproduction of new organisms. This biological evolution allows speciation to occur over a long period of time and eventually leads to new patterns of differentiation and diversification. With biological evolution, both simple and complex types of species can coexist. However, with social evolution, because new traits can be created, learned, and implemented in a relatively short period of time, simpler societal types tend to dissolve and disappear.

Lenski (1994) wrote that advances in technology are functionally equivalent to adaptive changes in a population's gene pool, and that new energy sources and new materials enable humans to do things that they could not do before. The level of sophistication that one society already possesses affects its ability to absorb new information and technology. Furthermore, the larger the population, the greater the likelihood that its members will create new technology (Lenski, Nolan, and Lenski, 1995). Eventually, new technology is diffused and borrowed by other societies. Consequently, previously powerful societies have the ability to attain new information and technology even when they fail to create it. They may acquire information and technology through force or coercion, or by offering other valued resources.

J. Richard Udry

Udry is a strong proponent of incorporating biology into sociology. It is his belief that most sociologists have accepted the idea that human bodies and brains have evolved through natural selection, and yet they still view the understanding of human behavior as outside the realm of evolutionary forces (Udry, 1995). Udry's theories are primarily centered on issues of gender, and whereas most sociologists (especially feminists) argue that gender roles are culturally determined and a product of gender role expectations associated with a specific sexual category, Udry has sought biological explanations. Udry (1994:562) used the term *sexual dimorphism* to explain characteristics that distinguish males and females. The hormones that control dimorphism are found in all mammals with "sex-dimorphic body structures" and "sex-dimorphic reproductive behaviors."

Through his research (which is a work in progress), Udry has proposed that males and females differ from one another in their average biological propensity to enact the same behaviors: in short, gender differences have biological roots: Women are better suited to certain behaviors than are males, and vice versa. Udry's approach encourages future research in the area of gender theory that incorporates biological explanations and not just sociological approaches when explaining gender differences. As Turner (2003:120) outlined, Udry would like to see the following questions answered:

1. Why do male and female behaviors vary so dramatically in some instances and not in others?
2. Why do these variations in behaviors show such cross-cultural commonalities, despite major societal and cultural differences?
3. Why do some males act much more masculine than other males?
4. Why do some females act much more feminine that other females?

Udry is committed to integrating biological variables into the social sciences and especially into the study of gender.

RELEVANCY

Edward O. Wilson has spent his entire life studying the various species found on our planet. He is recognized as a leading figure in the study of biodiversity, and he created a school of theoretical thought known as *sociobiology*. His attempts to apply his biology-based theories to humans and their behavior have met a great deal of resistance from most social scientists. It is Wilson's insistence that human behavior is, for the most part, dictated by specific genes that remains the most controversial for sociologists. A number of contemporary sociobiologists and evolutionary theorists are convinced of the validity of genetics-based explanations of human behavior. This debate is best illustrated by the nature-nurture continuum. In other words, the question is whether human behavior is a result of genetics (nature), the social environment and the social learning process (nurture), or some combination of both?

Sociologists lean heavily toward the validity of nurture as the best way to explain human behavior. Sociologists believe that

humans have free will and therefore are capable of choosing their courses of action, and that behavior is not dictated by genetic determinism. A number of relevant examples are presented later.

Sociobiologists believe that natural selection, through kinship, creates altruistic behavior and that specific genes are responsible for altruism. This theory is questionable at best. The term *altruism* was first used by Auguste Comte (Heckert, 2000; Hunt, 1990) and can be defined as "behavior that benefits another at some cost to the benefactor, and it is done selflessly without the anticipation of rewards from some outside source" (Hunt, 1990:21). True altruism is unique behavior (Heckert, 2000), as doers of charitable acts generally receive some type of reward for their behavior. This idea is called *generalized exchange*: "In generalized exchange, an individual donates something to another individual in what seems to be an act of pure charity, but the donor eventually is rewarded, just not from the person to whom the donation was made" (Takahashi, 2000:1107). For example, millions of Americans gave blood to blood banks immediately after the September 11, 2001, attacks. This behavior could be viewed as selfless, but in reality the donors felt a sense of patriotism and felt as if they were "doing something" to help those in need. In fact, many acts of charity are fueled by the idea that it is the "right" or "moral" thing to do (especially from a religious standpoint). Is such an act selflessness, or is it dictated by a belief that it is commanded by a higher power and therefore will be rewarded in the afterlife (for example, by a heavenly reward of positive karma)? It is true that some people simply help others without any overt rewards, but their feeling of self-righteousness may itself be a reward.

In *Sociobiology*, Wilson stated that play serves an important role in the socialization of mammals, and furthermore, that the more intelligent and social the species, the more elaborate the play. Play, it seems, actually does contain elements of innate behavior. Steve Craig clearly documented in *Sports and Games of the Ancients* (2002) that certain activities, such as running, archery, and wrestling, were indigenous to all remote ancient cultures, and he described them as innate. It is his belief that the study of the socializational aspects of sports and play in cultures of the past offers insights that help us to understand our own culture. Wilson (1975) struggled to define play biologically. The experts in this area are clearly the sport sociologists. Sport sociology, as a field, was created in 1973 by Harry Edwards. Even before Edward's landmark book, *Sociology of Sport* (1973), theorists such as George Herbert Mead and Jean Piaget had created elaborate theories of socialization through their analysis of play. Jay Coakley (2001), among the most prominent contemporary sport sociologists, defined play as involving "expressive activity done for its own sake; it may be spontaneous or guided by informal norms. An example of play is three four-year-olds who, during recess period at school, spontaneously run around a playground, yelling joyfully while throwing playground balls in whatever directions they feel like throwing them" (21). Sports, on the other hand, represent a concerted effort to organize play into something far more regimented. As Wilson (1980) explained, "Human beings are in fact so devoted to play that they professionalize it, permitting the lionized few who turn it into serious business to grow rich" (85). Play may be viewed as innate, but sport is a cultural, human-made creation. Around the globe, consumers of sports are willing to pay large amounts of money to view games—at a price far greater than most would spend to visit a zoo.

There is a debate in academia over whether intelligence is a matter of socialization (nurture) or genetics (nature). As Pulitzer Prize–winner Jared Diamond (1999) explained, "An enormous effort by cognitive psychologists has gone into the search for differences in IQ between peoples of different geographic origins now living in the same country. In particular, numerous white American psychologists have been trying for decades to demonstrate that black Americans of African origins are innately less intelligent than white Americans of European origins" (p. 20). The problem with measuring IQ based on intelligence tests is the reality that such tests are generally culturally biased. "Our cognitive abilities as adults are heavily influenced by the social environment that we experienced during childhood, making it hard to discern any influence of preexisting genetic difference [and] tests of cognitive ability (like IQ tests) tend to measure cultural learning and not pure innate intelligence, whatever that is" (Diamond, 1999:20). People adapt culturally to their physical environment. Consequently, differences between people of different geographic areas are not due to innate differences in the people themselves, but to differences in their environments. Attempts to measure pure intelligence must take into account cultural differences among humans.

Another controversial area involving the nature-nurture continuum debate is the idea of alcoholism as a disease. If it is a disease, a gene is responsible for someone being labeled an alcoholic. The 1989 Merriam-Webster dictionary defines *alcoholism* as continued excessive and usually uncontrollable use of alcoholic drinks; an alcoholic is someone affected with alcoholism. This definition does not mention genetics as a reason for alcoholism; it implies that it is self-induced behavior. That is, anyone who quits drinking no longer has a drinking problem.

A disease concept, on the other hand, implies an involuntary disability. In fact, there are numerous nondisease explanations for alcoholism. Goode (1997) gave four slightly outdated definitions or criteria for alcoholism: (1) the *quantity* and *frequency* of alcohol consumed (DeLindt and Schmidt, 1971); in order to be labeled an alcoholic, one must drink large amounts of alcohol; (2) *psychological dependence* (see essays in Blane and Leonard, 1987); one must "need" alcohol to function properly; (3) one must suffer from *withdrawal symptoms* upon the discontinuation of drinking (Mendelson and Mello, 1985); and (4) the *life problems* definition, where one must incur serious life problems—divorce, firing from a job, accidents, and so on—because of drinking, and still refuses to stop; this person is an alcoholic. There are additional explanations of why alcoholism is not a matter of genetics. Someone's developing an alcohol problem when there is no family history of alcoholism strongly suggests that alcoholism is not simply a matter of genetics. A freshman in college may never have had a drink before, come from a family without a history of drinking problems, still become a victim of peer pressure to drink in order to fit in, and develop a serious drinking problem in this environment. Studies have shown that environmental factors such as peer pressure, onset of drinking at an earlier age, and acceptance and availability of alcohol may actually drive a person to drink more (National Institute on Alcohol and Alcoholism, 1992). It is in the social environment that individuals learn to drink, and how drinking is reinforced will dictate whether the drinking behavior continues or not. Furthermore, an increasing number of experts are now defining alcoholism as a "use disorder" (Clements, 1999).

Still, a number of people, especially in the United States, insist that alcoholism is a disease caused by a yet unidentified gene. In 1975, Forrest (1975) viewed alcoholism as a chronic disorder involving physiological and psychological variables which render certain individuals incapable of refraining from frequent alcohol ingestion. Two decades later, Forrest amended his view of alcoholism by stating, "that all human beings are biologically addictive. Virtually all people manifest the biological capacity to develop a wide range of drug dependencies." (Forrest, 1995: 63)

Alcoholism is viewed as a disease because it impairs a person's physiological functioning. Alcoholics develop physiological problems such as cirrhosis of the liver and brain damage (Dorgan, 2002). Enoch and Goldman (2002) stated that a genetic predisposition underlies alcoholism that renders certain persons vulnerable to it, regardless of free will. Those who support the idea that alcoholism is a disease caused by genetics have failed to identify the specific gene that causes it; instead, they generally conclude that there is not enough evidence to prove without a shadow a doubt that alcoholism is based on genetics. This theory cannot be ruled out (Denzin, 1987).

Alcoholism as a genetics-based disease has somehow gained favor among some in the academic arena. The theory that specific genes are responsible for specific behaviors remains unvalidated. Sociobiologists and genetic evolutionary theorists would have us believe that all behaviors are predetermined. Does anyone, other than Wilson and sociobiologists, seriously believe that racism, sexism, ageism, and so on are caused by genes and not learned in the social environment? Is a preference for a sports team or a college innate? Is religion innate? Clearly the religion that one chooses to believe in is simply a matter of socialization and culture. Norms, values, language, attitudes, and culture are all learned phenomena. Studies on twins continue to disprove genetic-based reasoning. One thing is true, genetic research and testing is growing by leaps and bounds. If there is any validity to gene-based explanations to human social behavior, we will learn of it during the Third Millennium.

Perhaps the most important contribution of Edward Wilson to social theory and, more important, to human society is his concern about future humanity. Much of Wilson's contemporary work involves his concern for the physical environment and biodiversity. In his books *Biophilia*, *The Future of Life*, and *The Diversity of Life*, Wilson wrote that humans should respect the environment and the diverse species within it. He believes that the next great period of extinction is pending, and this time it will be due to not some environmental catastrophe, but to the actions of human beings (Wilson, 1992). Wilson (1992) wrote that the preservation of diversity is important not only for ecological integrity, but also for human society, as preserved species could be the sources of new medicines, crops, fibers, petroleum substitutes, or pharmaceuticals. In *The Future of Life* (2002a) Wilson stated that humanity has "appropriated the planet's natural resources, we choose to annuitize them with short-term maturity reached by progressively increasing payouts. . . . But there is a problem. . . . Earth's arable land, ground water, forests, marine fisheries, and petroleum, are ultimately finite, and subject to proportionate capital growth. Moreover, they are being decapitalized by overharvesting and environmental destruction" (149).

In addition to the purely environmental cause, Wilson's aforementioned concepts and theories can provide the basis for understanding the effects of another major event affecting the diversity of cultures on this planet: globalization. Wilson's theories about the formation of culture could be important to decisions on how to preserve threatened cultures, as they, too, may have undiscovered value.

3

Functionalism

During the 1950s and 1960s functionalism reigned as the dominant theoretical perspective in sociology. Its primary tenets remain among the cornerstone ideas of social theory. Students of sociology must be exposed to, and clearly understand, the core concepts of functionalism. Functionalism is often referred to as *structural functionalism* because of its dual focus on the structural forces that shape human behavior and the attention given to systems needs. "According to this view social systems tend to perform certain tasks that are necessary for their survival, and sociological analysis, therefore, involves a search for the social structures that perform these tasks or meet the needs of the social system" (Wallace and Wolf, 1999:17). Proponents of functionalism are often called *structural functionalists.* The two leading structural functionalists were Talcott Parsons (grand theory) and Robert Merton (middle-range theory).

THE INTELLECTUAL ROOTS OF FUNCTIONALISM

The most significant intellectual forerunners of functionalism were Auguste Comte, Herbert Spencer, Émile Durkheim, and Max Weber.

Auguste Comte (1789–1857)

In the fourth volume of the *System of Positive Polity* (1854), Comte proposed the word *sociology* for his new positivist science. He proposed that science relies upon empirical knowledge to gain an understanding of human behavior and thus advocated applying the scientific method to the study of society. Through his notions of *social statics* (social processes that hold society together) and *social dynamics* (mechanisms of change), Comte established a direction for social research. He believed that just as biology finds it useful to separate anatomy from physiology, one should also make a distinction in sociology between statics and dynamics. In his description of social statics (today's term is *social structure*), Comte anticipated many of the ideas of later functionalists. Through the use of social statics, Comte maintained that units or levels of investigation were the individual, the family, the society, and the species. Social dynamics (today's term is *social change*) deals with the laws of social movement, or progress. Society is always changing, but change is ordered and subject to social laws; it is an evolutionary process. Thus, to understand how humans are affected by society, the social scientist should examine the social structure and uncover the laws that exist to maintain it, while uncovering the laws that change it. Borrowing from biology, Comte was at the early stages of comparing society to an organism (the *organic analogy*). In his *System of Positive Polity* (1851), Comte anatomically described the social structure as consisting of *elements* (families), *tissues* (classes or castes), and *organs* (cities and communes). As Turner (2003) explained, "In Comte's hands, the organismic analogy was rough and crude. . . . It was left to the British sociologist, Herbert Spencer, to develop more fully the implications of the organismic analogy" (p. 24).

Herbert Spencer (1820–1903)

Spencer reluctantly gave credit to Comte for reintroducing the organic analogy into contemporary thought. Spencer stressed that Plato and Hobbes had made similar analogies and that much of his own organismic thinking had been influenced by Von Baer. Spencer acknowledged the role of environmental variables in social organization and agreed that the superorganism (society) and the organism (body) had a number of similarities (for example, society and individuals grow; as size increases so does complexity; parts of the whole are interdependent) and differences such as the organism is a single, indivisible unit, but in a society, individuals can come and go freely). Spencer believed that the organic and superorganic bodies reveal certain universal requisites that must be fulfilled for these bodies to adapt to the environment. He termed this process *requisite functionalism* (Turner, 2003:25).

Spencer's concept of *differentiation* is of significant importance in the development of functionalism. He believed that increases in the size of both organic and social aggregates are invariably accompanied by an increase in the complexity of their structure. According to Spencer, the process of growth,

by definition, is a process of integration. Furthermore, integration in its turn must be accompanied by a progressive differentiation of structures and functions if the organism or the societal unit is to remain capable of survival. Social aggregates, like organic ones, grow from relatively undifferentiated states, in which the parts resemble one another, into differentiated states in which the parts have become dissimilar. As the level of complexity increases, so, too, does the level of interdependence of the parts of the organism and the social unit.

Spencer (1898) argued that societies change from "a state of relatively indefinite, incoherent, homogeneity to a state of relatively definite, coherent, heterogeneity" (p. 371). By this, Spencer meant that what distinguishes premodern societies from modern societies is differentiation, that is, the development of increasing societal complexity through the creation of specialized social roles and institutions. Premodern societies are characterized by relatively few roles and institutional distinctions, so people must have a wide range of skills that allow them to act independently of one another. In modern societies, however, people master a limited number of skills within a large number of highly specialized institutional roles, so there is a great deal of interdependence. In short, the fundamental processes of growth, differentiation, integration, and adaptive upgrading are, to some extent, conditioned by *external factors* (such as the availability of natural resources), *internal factors* (such as the nature of the interior units), and *derived factors* (such as relations with other societies).

Most functionalist theories share the assumption that as societies develop they become more complex and interdependent. Within sociology, this assumption can be traced to Spencer (1860), who argued that societies change from incoherent undifferentiated homogeneity to coherent differentiated heterogeneity. Much of Spencer's discussion of social institutions and their changes is expressed in functional terms. He analyzed social institutions in relation to the general matrix in which they are variously embedded. Spencer made great efforts to show that social institutions are not the result of the deliberate intentions and motivations of the actors but arise from structural requirements.

Émile Durkheim (1858–1917)

Parsons valued broad comparative studies and found that the two most important programs of research in the last generation had been conducted by Émile Durkheim in his study of suicide rates and Max Weber in his comparative study of religion (Parsons, 1954). Parsons described Durkheim's study on suicide as "intermediate between the broad comparative method and what might be called the 'meticulous' ideal of operational procedure" (Parsons, 1954:16). He criticized Durkheim's crude attempt at statistical method but marveled at his ingenuity in working out a variety of significant combinations of data. Durkheim's study revealed differences in suicide rates based on one's religion that held up internationally; differences between rates in armed forces and in the civil population of the same nations; and variations of rates as they related to the business cycle. Durkheim demonstrated that theory supported by empirical data provides a sense of legitimacy in sociology's claim to be a science.

Durkheim is well known for his study of Aboriginal Australian society (found in *The Elementary Forms of the Religious Life*, (1912), where he emphasized and documented the "pan-religionism" of most primitive societies. Primitive societies are permeated with religious sentiments and activities ruled by the prominence of religiomagical belief systems and the prevalence of ritual activities. Parsons (1966) noticed from Durkheim's study that *sacred* items, like kinship, were not only prominent but also elaborately structured. Parsons came to see the whole sociocultural system as linked to the kinship

system. Furthermore, he interpreted the sacred significance of totems as being linked to the organization of clans as kinship units. "The totemic references are so formed as to symbolize the integration of the social unit within the total order of the human condition" (Parsons, 1966:38). The social system needs to integrate its parts to maintain social equilibrium. Integration involves incorporating individuals into the social order. From Durkheim, then, Parsons came to see the validity of a structural, functioning system linked together through need (kinship) and working toward the greater good of the whole society.

Durkheim's sociology maintained a focus on structural analysis, rather than individual action and motivation. He believed society and social structures are realities at a level above the individual human organism. He shared Comte's functionalist, evolutionary, and positive premises. The functionalist perspective views society as a sum total (the whole) of a large number of persons, groups, organizations, and social institutions (the parts). Social thinkers that utilize this approach examine the role of society as it attempts to execute the functions needed to maintain, for example, national defense, internal social order, consumer production and distribution, and food, clothing, and shelter demands by its citizens. Consequently, the social structure is a complex system, whose parts are said to be well integrated and in a state of equilibrium when functioning properly. During periods of rapid social change, or with the introduction of a new and dramatic force, whether social (such as entrance into an "unwanted" war) or natural (for example, a deadly drought), the social structure may be thrown out of equilibrium. As a result, the various structures of society can become poorly integrated, and what were formerly useful functions can become "dysfunctional."

Functionalism, for Durkheim, was the idea that society is a system, and its parts (institutions) contribute to its stability and continued existence. His functionalist outlook did not include a value judgment, nor did he imply that some societies are "better" than others. Rather, the parts of the system are interconnected and attempt to meet the demands of each particular society. When this occurs over a period of time and stability is met, the system is said to be functioning properly. Durkheim's functionalist approach was evolutionary in that he was interested in how societies change over time. He recognized that societies, as social systems, are not static and are therefore subject to change at any time. Durkheim's view on functionalism is summarized in this quote from *The Dualism of Human Nature and Its Social Conditions* (1914/1973): "A great number of our mental states, including some of the most important ones, are of social origin. In this case then, it is the whole that, in a large measure, produces the part; consequently, it is impossible to attempt to explain the whole without explaining the part—without explaining, at least, the part as a result of the whole" (p. 149).

Durkheim argued that crime and deviance serve a functional role in society because they help to unite its members. When violators are punished, the laws of society are reaffirmed by the rest of society's members. Laws and norms represents a shared sense of morality within a society (the *collective conscience*). In some cases, crime promotes social change. When a violation is not greeted with public opposition, a reevaluation of such behavior may be stimulated. Therefore, an activity that was once considered deviant may be reconsidered and may become part of the norm.

Max Weber (1864–1920)

Weber's influence on functionalism is particularly evident in the works of Talcott Parsons. Max Weber captured Parsons's interest by his spiritual orientation, an outlook that resonated with Parsons's own Calvinist background. "Initially, it was this spiritual and cultural side of Weber that drew Parsons's attention. This was evident in his Heidelberg dissertation and in his early publications. However, in the process of writing *The Structure of Social Action* [1937/1949], Parsons came to be more attuned to Weber's methodology" (Trevino, 2001:31). Parsons's dissertation, "Concept and Capitalism," was based primarily on Weber's *The Protestant Ethic and the Spirit of Capitalism* (1904–1905/1958). Parsons was exposed to Weber's works while he studied in Europe, and he translated Weber (the first four chapters of *Wirtschaft und Gesellschaft*) into English for American sociologists. Parsons felt that Karl Marx's reductionist approach to explaining social structure and social action as being tied nearly exclusively to the economic realm was overly simplistic and not realistic. He favored Weber's unwillingness to simplify explanations of the complexity of the social system. "Weber essentially established certain broad differentiations of patterns of value-orientations, as we would now term them. . . . He showed how these . . . patterns 'correspond' to the broad lines of differentiation of the social structures of the societies in which they had become institutionalized" (Parsons, 1954:15). Weber stated that the Protestant ethic was responsible for creating the rise of the spirit of capitalism. Protestantism succeeded in turning the pursuit of profit into a moral crusade. Ideas such as "time is money," "be frugal," and "be punctual" are all in the *spirit of capitalism.* This spirit allows capitalists to ruthlessly pursue economic riches; in fact, it is their duty. Societies that embraced industrialization were transformed both politically and economically. The impact on social life was dramatic. Parsons felt that Weber's analysis marked the first major development in the systematic discrimination of major types of value systems and their link to social structures, since Ferdinand Tönnies's famous distinction between *Gemeinschaft* and *Gesellschaft.*

Parsons learned of Weber's "problems of meaning" and of the "ideas" behind the cultural symbolic interpretation of "representations" (for example, concepts of gods, totems, and the supernatural), which form ultimate realties but are not themselves such realities. Thus, behavior is influenced by the social system. Parsons (1966), agreeing with Weber, concluded that, since the social system is made up of the interaction of human individuals, interactions are affected by the social environment. Interactions are a part of the greater action system and need to be incorporated into any grand theory. Like Weber before him, Parsons wanted to describe convincingly logical types of social relations applicable to all groups, small and large. Parsons would create a system (grand theory) of social action to include all its aspects. His first attempt at this systematic scheme appears in *The Structure of Social Action* (1937/1949).

Linguistics and the Anthropological Tradition

Among the diverse fields to impact functionalism are linguistics and anthropology. The works of Swiss linguist Ferdinand de Saussure (1857–1913) rank among the more significant in the development of functionalism. Saussure's distinction between langue and parole is especially important. *Langue* is the formal, grammatical system of language, consisting of a system of phonic elements whose relationships are governed by determinate laws. It is structured by a system of signs which have gained meaning among members over a period of interacting time. The meaning of words can therefore be altered (such as the word *gay* once meant "happy": now it also means "homosexual"). Understanding the structure and meaning of language reveals a great deal about a society and the arrangement of its parts. According to Saussure, *parole* is actual speech made possible by langue. The field of *semiotics* is broader than the study of langue in that it examines all other sign and symbol systems, such as facial expressions, body language, and literary texts (Ritzer, 2000).

Among the anthropologists who influenced functionalism are Claude Lévi-Strauss,

A. R. Radcliffe-Brown, and Bronislaw Malinowski (one of the founders of anthropological functionalism). Ritzer (2000) explained that "Levi-Strauss also applied structuralism more broadly to all forms of communication. His major innovation was to reconceptualize a wide array of social phenomena (for instance, kinship systems) as systems of communication, thereby making them amendable to structural analyses. . . . Levi-Strauss even used a system of binary oppositions in his anthropology (for example, the raw and the cooked) much like those employed by Saussure in linguistics" (456).

Radcliffe-Brown argued that organismic analogizing presents certain teleological implications and attempted to eliminate some of the problems associated with this approach. For example, Radcliffe-Brown promoted using the term *necessary condition of existence* in place of the term *system needs* in order to avoid postulating a universal human or societal need. "Furthermore, in recognizing the diversity of conditions necessary for the survival of different systems, analysis would avoid asserting that every item of a culture must have a function and that items in different cultures must have the same function" (Turner, 2003:29).

Parsons's functionalism is closer to the functionalism of A. R. Radcliffe-Brown than it is to Malinowski's. "Both these anthropologists were committed to a scientific methodology and were reluctant to build theory about matters for which little hard evidence exists, for example, the historical development of preliterate societies. Both chose to focus their attention on existing societies that could be observed by the ethnographer, and both chose to conceive of those societies as consisting of customs and practices that helped sustain them as ongoing, integrated wholes" (B. Johnson, 1975:17). Parsons learned from both Radcliffe-Brown and Malinowski to identify the various conventional patterns of behavior that contribute to the maintenance of society.

Defining Functionalism

Functionalism is a macrosociological theory that examines the characteristics of social patterns, structures, systems, and institutions. It views society as having interrelated parts which contribute to the functioning of the whole system. Functionalism has two basic assumptions. The first is the idea of interdependent parts, where all of society's social institutions (for example, religion, politics, military, economics, education, sports, and leisure) are all linked together. As Levin (1991) explained, "Functionalism begins with the idea that any stable system (such as the human body) consists of a number of different, but interrelated, parts that operate together to create an overall order" (p. 76). Any change in one institution inevitably leads to changes in other institutions. In order to function properly, the system seeks equilibrium, or stability. Equilibrium allows a smoothly running system. Second, members of society must have a general consensus on values. A general agreement on issues of right and wrong, basic values, and morality issues allows the system to function properly. If people lose faith in their society (the system), they will seek change. Rapid change within the system is something the functionalist approach is not geared to handle.

It would be incorrect to assume that the functionalist approach ignores social change. It explains social change as a result of such variables as population growth (due to migration and increased childbirth rates) and increased technology (such as computers). Functionalists are so aware of social change that they often wonder how society maintains itself at all. Society's social institutions are running most efficiently when the system is in a homeostatic mode. Consequently, the social system is designed to minimize conflict. This is true at any level (societal, institutional, and family).

TALCOTT PARSONS (1902–1979)

Talcott Parsons, the youngest of five children, was born in Colorado Springs in 1902. He

Talcott Parsons, structural functionalist and grand theorist.
Source: Harvard University News Office

came from a religious family that valued education. His father was a Congregational minister and a professor at Colorado College. His mother was a progressive and a suffragist (Camic, 1991). During his undergraduate studies at Amherst College, Parsons took courses in biology and later in the social sciences. His early exposure to biology, with its focus on the importance of the interdependence of an organism's parts, greatly influenced his outlook on social behavior. He graduated from Amherst in 1924 and a year later entered the London School of Economics. In London, he studied with Malinowski, L. T. Hobhouse, and Morris Ginsberg. Parsons accepted Malinowski's view of societies as systems of interconnected parts.

In 1926 Parsons received a scholarship from the University of Heidelberg, where he first learned of the works of Max Weber. Although Weber had died five years before Parsons's arrival, his widow held meetings at her home on the works of her husband, and Parsons regularly attended. Upon the completion of his dissertation, Parsons was appointed as a nonfaculty instructor of economics at Harvard University. Parsons eventually became an inaugural member of the sociology faculty at Harvard. In 1945 Parsons established the Department of Social Relations, an interdisciplinary collaboration in the behavioral sciences. He served as chair of the department for its first ten years and remained active in the department until its dissolution in 1972. A year later, Parsons retired as emeritus professor. He continued teaching as a visiting professor at such universities as Pennsylvania, Rutgers, and the University of California at Berkeley. Parsons died in May 1979.

Parsons was one of the most prominent theorists of his time. He attempted to generate a grand theory of society that explains all social behavior, everywhere and throughout history, with a single model: structural functionalism or, more simply, functionalism. By design, his theory is often very abstract: it is nonetheless quite elaborate. His theory once dominated sociological discourse and had nearly as many detractors as supporters. Parsons's analysis of social systems and social action remains relevant as a premiere sociological theory.

Functionalism

The structural-functional approach of Parsons was a life-long development and reflected the era in which he lived. The post–World War II era was highlighted by a great prosperity among many Americans. The 1950s were a decade of a relative societal calm and an increasing economic boom. "Structural-functional sociology mirrored these real-life developments. It emphasized societal stability and the match between institutions like the economy, the family, the political system, and the value system" (Garner, 2000:312). Parsons believed social systems strive for stability.

"Parsons argued that the overall system and subsystems of which it is composed work together to form a balanced, stable whole and that the system naturally tends toward stability rather than toward disorder" (Levin, 1991:77). The basic premise of Parsons's functionalism of stability or equilibrium is a sound one, for it stands to reason that for any society to last a great length of time, there must be some sense of social order and interdependence among the various institutions. With its commitment to stable social institutions, the decade of the 1950s provided the perfect years for Parsons's structural-functional theory to dominate sociological thought. The conservative nature of this theoretical approach reflected American society itself.

Parsons believed that sociological theory must utilize a limited number of important concepts that "adequately grasp" aspects of the objective external world. These concepts thus correspond to concrete phenomena. As Turner (1978/1982) explained Parsons's theoretical approach, "Theory must, first of all, involve the development of concepts that abstract from empirical reality, in all its diversity and confusion, common analytical elements. In this way, concepts will isolate phenomena from their imbeddedness in the complex relations that go to make up social reality" (p. 40). Thus, Parsons's theoretical framework is grounded in empirical research on concepts created by the ideas and actions of those under study. In "The Role of Ideas in Social Action" Parsons (1954) explained that his theory of action is an analytical one ("analytical realism") and that any analysis of ideas must be conducted on an empirical, scientific basis. "Parsons did not advocate the immediate incorporation of these concepts into theoretical statements but rather, advocated their use to develop a 'generalized system of concepts. This use of abstract concepts would involve their ordering into a coherent whole that would reflect the important features of the 'real world' " (Turner, 2003:39). Parsons used his analytical concepts throughout his writings, which were first presented in his brilliant book *The Structure of Social Action* (1937/1949).

Social Action Theory

In the preface to *The Structure of Social Action* (1937/1949), Parsons made clear his commitment to empirical research as the guiding force behind his theory: "This body of theory, the 'theory of social action,' is not simply a group of concepts with their logical interrelations. It is a theory of empirical science the concepts of which refer to something beyond themselves. . . . True scientific theory is not the product of idle 'speculation,' or spinning out the logical implications of assumptions, but of observation, reasoning and verification, starting with the facts and continually returning to the facts" (p.v). Parsons acknowledged the subjective nature of human activity and therefore wished to make clear the distinction between the concepts of *action* and *behavior*. For Parsons, behavior seems to have implied a mechanical response to stimuli, whereas action implied an active, inventive process (Ritzer, 2000). "The common feature of all these modes of analysis of action is its conception as a process of attaining specific and definite ends by the selection of the 'most efficient' means available in the situation of the actor. This, in turn, implies a standard according to which the selection among the many possible alternative means is made" (Parsons, 1954:22). Action options depend upon the actor's knowledge of her or his situation, which includes knowledge of the probable effects of the available choices. Parsons (1937/1949) insisted that in order to qualify as an action theory, the subjective aspect of human activity cannot be ignored.

Parsons's social action theory begins with a biological-sociological conceptualization of the basic unit of study as the "unit act." "Just as the units of a mechanical system in the classical sense, particles, can be defined only in terms of their properties,

such as, mass, velocity, location in space, direction of motion, etc., so the units of action systems also have certain basic properties without which it is not possible to conceive of the unit as 'existing' " (Parsons, 1949:43). Parsons then elaborated his meaning of the concept of an act. He stated that an *act* involves the following criteria:

1. It implies an isolated unit, an agent, an "actor."
2. For purposes of definition the act must have an "end," a future state of affairs toward which the process of action is oriented. This fulfills the "rational norm of efficiency."
3. It must be initiated in a "situation" of which the trends of development differ in one or more important respects from the state of affairs to which the action is oriented, the end. The actor is guided by the scientific knowledge of the circumstances of her/his situation.
4. There exists alternative means to the end (randomness), in so far as the situation allows alternatives. In cases where there are no alternative choices (e.g, a prison inmate has few choices of action), a "normative orientation" of action will exist. (Parsons, 1949:44)

Parsons (1937/1949) explained that an act is always a process in time, and that the concept *end* always implies a future reference to a state (or situation) that does not yet exist. Actions consist of the structures and processes by which human beings form meaningful intentions and more or less successfully implement them in concrete situations (Parsons, 1966).

Parsons's theory of social action involves four steps. First, Parsons believed that actors are *motivated* to action, especially toward a desired goal (for example, a college degree). Parsons referred to a *goal* as the time of the termination of the actor's action in which the desired end has been reached (for example, receiving the college diploma on graduation day). Second, the actor must find the *means* to reach the desired goal (for example, a college fund created by the student's parents, student loans, a personal computer). Next, the actor must deal with *conditions* that hinder reaching the goal (obstacles to a student's reaching a college degree might include the lack of a proper intellect or of time to study, or a personal crisis). And finally, the actor must work within the *social system* (such as administrative rules and procedures, test taking, and all the required courses). Working within the social system is often quite challenging.

Social System

In *The Social System* (1951), Parsons attempted to further articulate his social action theory by integrating the role of structure and processes of social systems in their effect on the actor. A social system involves the interaction of a plurality of individual actors oriented to a situation, where the system includes commonly understood cultural symbols. Parsons (1951) stated:

> Reduced to the simplest possible terms, then, a social system consists in a plurality of individual actors interacting with each other in a situation which has at least a physical or environmental aspect, actors who are motivated in terms of a tendency to the "optimization of gratification" and whose relation to their situations, including each other, is defined and mediated in terms of a system of culturally structured and shared symbols. Thus conceived, a social system is only one of three aspects of the structuring of a completely concrete system of social action. The other two are the personality systems of the individual actors and the cultural system which is built into their action. Each of the three must be considered to be an independent focus of the organization of the elements of the action system in the sense that no one of them is theoretically reducible to terms of one or a combination of the other two. Each is indispensable to the other two in the sense that without personalities and culture there would be no social system and so on around the roster of logical possibilities. (pp. 5–6)

This process of reciprocal interrelationism has two other implications. First, a social system

cannot be so structured as to be radically incompatible with individual personalities. Second, the social system depends on the requisite minimum of "support" from each of the systems.

Culture itself is a system of generalized symbols and their meanings. Through the internalization of a culture's norms and values, the individual's personality becomes integrated as a part of the social system. "The principal mechanism by which this is accomplished appears to be through the building up of attachments to other persons—that is, by emotional communication with others so that the individual is sensitized to the *attitudes* of the others, not merely to their specific acts with their intrinsic gratification-deprivation significance" (Parsons, 1965:29). As Parsons's general theory continued to develop, the cultural element occupied a more central place.

Systems have parts, or subsystems. The social system is an arrangement between parts or elements that exist over time, even while some elements change. For example, as members of a college sports team graduate, they are replaced by members of succeeding classes. This succession reflects the reality of the organizational nature of social systems. Organizations, like social systems, are designed to function even as people leave; thus, people are replaceable, and the social system is capable of maintaining itself. Parsons (1965) described an organization as a broad type of collectivity which has assumed a particularly important place in modern industrial societies. Like any social system, an organization possesses a describable structure. The study of organizations represents just one part of the study of the social structure.

Not all social systems are designed equally; some are much more complex than others. Still, a number of general assumptions about the social system can be made:

1. Systems are made of order and the interdependence of parts.

2. The system and all of the subsystems strive for equilibrium (normal activity, a self-maintaining order).

3. Systems are generally static or move in a progressively deliberate matter.

4. A disruption in the "normal flow" of one subsystem can cause a disturbance throughout the whole system.

5. Systems have boundaries, which may involve actual physical space, or time and distance.

In Parsons's late years, he took an interest in the field of *sociobiology*, where he analyzed the differences between a biological system and a social system. He identified four such distinctions, which can be briefly summarized:

1. **Growth:** Biologically, individuals grow to a certain point and then growth stops. A social system may be static for some time and then grow, or it may continue to grow for an extended period of time.

2. **Space:** Biological systems are clearly bounded (for example, one's internal organs are bounded within the physical body), while social system boundaries are not so fixed or limited (for example, the territory of the United States extends beyond the mainland borders).

3. **Time:** A biological unit has a limit: mortality. A social unit can survive for centuries (for examples, nation-states, organized religions).

4. **Parts/Subsystems:** A biological system is often very specialized and dependent on the proper functioning of the whole for its very survival. A major breakdown in one area can lead to the destruction of the unit (for example, heart failure will lead to the death of the biological unit). Within social systems, parts are easily replaceable and the system moves on (for example, sport franchises dissolve, but the league can survive).

With these general descriptions of social systems, Parsons placed social actors in the mix. For Parsons (1951), a social system is a mode of organization of action elements relative to the persistence or ordered processes of change of the interactive patterns of a plurality of individual actors. The role of the actor allowed Parsons (1951) to create three distinct units within the social system. First, he reiterated that the most elementary unit of a social system is the "act." The act becomes a unit in a social system insofar as it is part of a process of interaction between its author and other actors.

Second, Parsons stated that for the purpose of a more macroscopic analysis of social systems, it is convenient to make use of a higher-order unit than an act, namely, the *status role*. (*Status* refers to a structural position within the social system, while a *role* is what the actor does in such a position.) Since a social system is a system of processes of interaction between the actors, it is the structure of the relations between the actors (as involved in the interactive process) which is essentially the structure of the social system. The social system is a network of such interactive relationships. Each individual actor is involved in a plurality of such interactive relationships with one or more members of the social system. Therefore, it is the participation of an actor in patterned interactive relationships that plays the most significant role in the social system. This participation is influenced by one's *location* in the relationship, which is referred to as one's *status* (such as a private in the armed forces has far less status than a general). Parsons (1951) pointed out that the statuses and roles, or the status-role bundle, are not, in general, attributes of the actor but are units of the social system, though possessing a given status may often be treated as an attribute.

The third unit of the social system is the actor. After all, it is the actor who holds a status or performs a role and therefore is always a significant unit. The actors themselves are a composite bundle of statuses and roles.

Pattern Variables

In an attempt to make his abstract theory of action more explicit, Parsons formulated *pattern variables*, which categorize expectations and the structure of relationships. These pattern variables are a set of concepts denoting some of the variable properties of social systems. Parsons had three primary thoughts in mind when developing these variables: They should be general enough to permit the comparison of relationships in different cultures; they should show relevance to action frames or reference; and they should be relevant to all social systems. The following five pattern variables simultaneously allow for "the categorization of the modes of orientation in personality systems, the value patterns of culture, and the normative requirements in social systems. The variables are phrased as polar dichotomies, that, depending on the system under analysis, allow a rough categorization of decisions by actors, the value orientations of culture, or the normative demands on status roles" (Turner, 2003:42). The five pattern variables are

1. **Affectivity–Affective Neutrality:** The concern here is whether the actor can expect an emotional component in the relationship or interaction situation. A newlywed couple should expect a great deal of affection in their relationship, whereas the sales clerk–customer relationship is neutral.

2. **Diffuseness–Specificity:** This part of terms refers to a range of demands and obligations that may be expected in the relationship. If the relationship is a close one, there exists a potential for a wide range of demands and expectations (diffusion), but if the relationship is limited, there are far fewer expectations (specific needs are met).

3. **Universalism–Particularism:** The issue here is how actors are evaluated. Is the actor treated on the basis of a general norm (universalism), or does someone's particular relationship with the other cause particular action?

4. **Achievement–Ascription:** These pattern variables deal with the assessment of an actor. Is performance evaluated on achieved statuses (for example, an earned college degree, setting a state record in the 100-meter dash) or on an ascribed status (such as race, gender, age)?

If someone is judged simply on ascribed characteristics, the quality of the performance evaluation has been compromised.

5. **Collectivity–Self-orientation:** The concern here is with the motivation of the actor. Is the behavior directed toward a particular person, or is the action directed toward the collectivity? Self-interest often overrides a commitment to the group or to specific others.

These five dichotomies represented, for Parsons, the universal dilemmas of action. "Some of these concepts, such as self-–collectivity, were later dropped from the action scheme, but others, such as universalism–particularism, assumed greater importance. The intent of the pattern variables remained the same, however: to categorize dichotomies of decisions, normative demands, and value orientations" (Turner, 2003:43). Parsons believed that these pattern variables provided a set of categories for describing the value components of action at the level of personality, the social system, and the culture (B. Johnson, 1975).

Adaptation, Goal Attainment, Integration, and Latency: Functional Imperatives for All Action Systems

Soon after *The Social System* (1951) was published Parsons developed another schema that was to prove far superior to the pattern variables. He referred to this new schema by a number of different names, including *system problems*, the *functional imperatives of any system of action,* and the *four-function paradigm* (B. Johnson, 1975). The term *functional imperatives* is the one that endured, and students of social theory generally call them *AGIL* (adaptation, goal attainment, integration, and latency) for short.

In 1953, Parsons collaborated with Robert Bales and Edward Shils to publish *Working Papers in the Theory of Action.* It was in this book that the conception of functional imperatives arose and came to dominate the general theory of action. Three years later, Parsons, along with Neil Smelser, published *Economy and Society* (1956) to further outline these imperatives. The experiments of Parsons and Bales (on leadership in small groups) were the source of the data used to develop their classification scheme. Wallace and Wolf (1999) indicated that the subjects used in these studies consisted of mostly white upper-middle or upper-class Protestant males and therefore suggested that the data lack generalization credibility.

The functional imperatives are a set of conditions that Parsons believed must be met if systems of action are to be stable and effective, that is, "the conditions can be thought of as processes that constitute the imperative functions of any system, from a simple two-person interaction to the most complex modern society" (B. Johnson, 1975:29). The functional imperatives are based on Parsons's hypothesis that processes in any social system are subject to four independent functional imperatives, or "problems," which must be met adequately if equilibrium and/or continuing existence of the system is to be maintained (Parsons, 1956a). Thus, these are tasks that must be performed if the system, or subsystem, is to survive:

1. **Adaptation:** Social systems must secure sufficient resources (for example, raw materials, technology) from the environment and distribute them throughout the system. Thus, the system must show that it can adapt to changes in the system and/or environment. Adaptation may involve the manipulation of the environment (for example, building dams to control flooding) in order to secure the resources which are deemed necessary to reach the goal(s) of the social system. The responsibility of this function imperative rests with the economic institutions of a society.

2. **Goal Attainment:** The social system must first clearly establish its goals. This need may seem obvious, but goals vary from one social system to the next. Nonprofit agencies hope to collect resources so that they may be properly distributed to the needy, whereas corporations hope to maximize profits, especially for the stockholders. In order to reach the stated goals, the social system must mobilize resources and energies, while establishing and maintaining priorities. The primary responsibility for this function in a nation-state is the political system (government).

3. **Integration:** This functional imperative involves the regulation and coordination of actors and subsystems within the greater social system in order to keep it functioning properly. The system must coordinate, adjust, and regulate relationships among the various subgroups. This is accomplished by the legal system, or the prevailing court of laws. In its attempt to reach goals, the system must often fight to maintain equilibrium and stability; consequently, it is important to keep deviance to a minimum.

4. **Latency:** Latency consists of two related problems: tension maintenance (internal tensions and strains of actors) and pattern maintenance (displaying "appropriate" behavior). The system must define and maintain a set of common values that guide and legitimate action within the system. Actors must be socialized and sufficiently motivated to play their roles (maintaining a commitment to society), and society must provide mechanisms and safety valves for actors so that they can release pent-up frustrations and other strains that they feel. This function is accomplished through such social institutions as the family, religion, education, and sports and leisure.

Collaborating with Gerald Platt on *The American University* (1973), Parsons infused his AGIL concepts with his general action systems theory (see Table 3.1). The biological organism must learn to adapt behaviorally (*behavioral organization system*) in order to survive in the environment. The *personality system* motivates individuals toward desired

TABLE 3.1 Structure of the General Action System

L	Cultural system	Social system	I
A	Behavioral organization	Personality system	G

goals, while society presents opportunities to achieve these goals. The *social system* is designed to integrate the diverse members of society. The *cultural system* provides the norms, values, and expectations of society that individuals must learn to incorporate into their daily lives.

In their book *Economy and Society* (1956), Parsons and Smelser utilized their functional imperatives on a variety of subjects. One of them is presented as "The Differentiated Subsystems of Society" (p. 53). Starting with the macrosocial system of society, Parsons and Smelser (as described above) projected the adaptation problem onto the economy; the goal attainment problem onto the polity; the integration problem onto an integrative subsystem that includes the legal system; and the latency issue onto such subsystems as religion and education. However, in another figure, "Functional Differentiation of the Economy as a System" (p. 44), Parsons and Smelser projected the functional imperatives onto a subsystem of the society: the economy. Here, the adaptation problem was delegated to the capitalization and investment sector; the goal attainment problem to the production subsystem, including distribution and sales; the integration issue to the organization subsystem of entrepreneurism; and latency to the economic commitments found in physical, cultural, and motivational resources. The point is that functional imperatives can be used on a whole system (society) or on a subsystem (organizations and groups).

Concept of Society

As Parsons (1966) stated, "Treating societies as wholes by no means exhausts the possibilities for empirical application of the concept of social system. Many social systems such as local communities, schools, business firms, and kinship units are not societies, but rather sub-systems of a society. Also, in a sufficiently pluralistic world, many social systems, which are 'partial' systems in terms of the concept of society, may be parts of more than one society" (p. 1). This is especially true of global corporations that conduct business in more than one nation. Parsons's study of societies was guided by both an evolutionary and a comparative perspective. The evolutionary framework implies that humans are integral to the organic world and the life process. Basic concepts of organic evolution such as variation, selection, adaptation, differentiation, and integration are the center of concern. "Socio-cultural evolution, like organic evolution, has proceeded by variation and differentiation from simple to progressively more complex forms" (Parsons, 1966:2).

Parsons provided a number of definitions for *society*. In *Societies* (1966) he stated, "In defining a society, we may use a criterion which goes back at least to Aristotle. A society is a type of social system, in any universe of social systems, which attains the highest level of self-sufficiency as a system in relation to its environment" (p. 9). In *The System of Modern Societies* (1971) Parsons defined a society as "the type of social system characterized by the highest level of self-sufficiency relative to its environments, including other social systems" (p. 8). All societies depend for their continuation on the inputs they receive through interchanges with the surrounding systems. The system has to be coordinated in such a way that sufficient resources may be found in the environment. "The core of a society, as a system, is the patterned normative order through which the life of a population is collectively organized. As an order, it contains values and differentiated and particularized norms and rules, all of which require cultural references in order to be meaningful and legitimate. As a collectivity, it displays a patterned conception of membership which distinguishes between those individuals who do and do not belong" (Parsons, 1969:11). The study of societies is important not only because society represents the most critical social system, but also because of a society's tremendous impact on individuals.

ROBERT MERTON (1910–2003)

Robert King Merton was born in 1910 of Jewish immigrant parents from eastern Europe and was raised in a South Philadelphia slum. The family lived in an apartment above his father's modest grocery store until the building burned down. His father then worked as a carpenter and truck driver. Merton's passion for learning began at an early age and was summed up in an autobiographical statement titled "A Life of Learning" (Merton, 1994/1996). Growing up in a slum did not stifle cultural opportunities for Merton. He spent a great deal of time at the nearby Carnegie library and attended concerts performed by the Philadelphia Orchestra. Interestingly, Merton was not the family name, as he was born Meyer R. Schkolnick. As an admirer of the magician Harry Houdini, who had changed his name from Ehrich Weiss, Meyer Schkolnick decided he wanted to change his name. "And so Meyer Schkolnick became Robert Merlin, after King Arthur's famous magician, and—after being reminded that this was a bit hackneyed—Robert Merton. Five years later Meyer Schkolnick's name was legally changed to Robert King Merton" (Adams and Sydie, 2001:359). As a teenager, Merton often performed magic tricks at birthday parties.

Merton won a scholarship to attend Temple University and became interested in sociology while taking an introductory sociology course taught by George E. Simpson, the translator of Durkheim. Simpson not only instilled an interest in sociology in Merton but also saw to it that Merton attended an annual meeting of the American Sociological Society, where he met Pitirim Sorokin of Harvard. After earning his B.A. at Temple, Merton, with the help of a fellowship, attended and received his doctorate from Harvard University. Merton was far more impressed by the young,

Robert Merton, empiricist, and structural functionalist who emphasized theories of the middle range.
Source: Courtesy of Robert Merton

then-unknown sociologist Talcott Parsons than he was by Sorokin. After earning his Ph.D. in 1936, Merton taught for two years at Tulane, before joining the faculty at Columbia University in New York City. At Tulane, Merton began a working friendship with Paul Lazarsfeld, a mathematically minded methodologist. The two became colleagues in 1941 at the Bureau of Applied Social Research at Columbia and continued to collaborate until Lazarsfeld's death in 1976 (Adams and Sydie, 2001:360).

Merton had always stressed the importance of empirical research, and his approach to functionalism reflected this commitment. Merton's functionalistic approach contrasted with the grand theorizing of Parsons. "Merton's goal was to keep functional assumptions to a minimum, whereas Parsons' intent was to build a functional analytical scheme that could explain all reality. . . . Merton believed that grand theoretical schemes are premature because the theoretical and empirical ground-work necessary for their completion has not been performed" (Turner, 2003:33). Merton formulated empirical hypotheses and often tested them in the real world by gathering data himself and analyzing the data—true empiricism. Merton's functionalist theories are of the "middle-range" variety. He questioned the assumption that all systems have needs and requisites that must be met and that certain structures are indispensable in meeting these needs (Turner, 2003). Despite their differences, Parsons and Merton together would become known as the leaders of the structural functionalism school of thought.

On February 23, 2003, Merton died: he had been residing in New York City. He will be remembered as one of the most influential sociologists of the twentieth century. His cumulative work contributed to his becoming the first sociologist to win a National Medal of Science in 1994 (Kaufman, 2003).

Theories of the Middle Range

One of Merton's greatest contributions to sociology was his emphasis on what he termed "theories of the middle range." He felt that grand theories were too abstract, and he deemed microanalysis pedantic inquiries. What he preferred were studies that led to further inquiry. In *Social Theory and Social Structure* (1949/1968) Merton described sociological theory as logically interconnected sets of propositions from which empirical uniformities can be derived. The focus of his theories is on the middle range. Merton (1949/1968) defined *theories of the middle range* as

> theories that lie between the minor but necessary working hypotheses that evolve in abundance during day-to-day research and the all-inclusive systematic efforts to develop a unified theory that will explain all the observed uniformities of social behavior, social organization and social change. Middle-range theory is principally

used in sociology to guide empirical inquiry. It is intermediate to general theories of social systems which are too remote from particular classes of social behavior, organization and change to account for what is observed and to those detailed orderly descriptions of particulars that are not generalized at all. Middle range theory involves abstractions, of course, but they are close enough to observed data to be incorporated in propositions that permit empirical testing. Middle-range theories deal with delimited aspects of social phenomena, as is indicated by their labels. One speaks of a theory of reference groups, of social mobility, or role-conflict and of the formation of social norms just as one speaks of a theory of prices, a germ theory of disease, or a kinetic theory of gases. (p. 39).

Merton's middle-range theories are functionalist theories that consist of limited sets of assumptions, from which specific hypotheses can be derived and tested empirically. Merton viewed Durkheim's *Suicide* and Weber's *The Protestant Ethic and the Spirit of Capitalism* as examples of middle-range theories.

An important element of middle-range theory is the concept of *role sets*. Merton (1949/1968) stated, "The theory of role-sets begins with an image of how social status is organized in the social structure. . . . Despite the very diverse meanings attached to the concept of *social status,* one sociological tradition consistently uses it to refer to a position in a social system, with its distinctive array of designated rights and obligations. In this tradition, as exemplified by Ralph Linton, the related concept of *social role* refers to the behavior of others (who accord the rights and exact the obligations)" (p. 41). Role sets are multiple role expectations that are parts of the same position or status that any one person holds. For example, a student's role set might include family obligations, study obligations, work demands, significant-other demands, demands from a coach if that student is an athlete, and demands from other friends. This student must somehow find a way to meet all the demands on him or her within this role set.

Merton's theories are functionalist in perspective. For Merton, the term *function* referred to the extent to which a particular part or process of a social system contributes to the maintenance of the system or subsystem. *Function* does not mean the same thing as *purpose* or *motivation* (subjective dispositions); it refers to observable objective consequences. Merton (1949/1968) promoted a process referred to as *codification.* Codification involves orderly, disciplined reflection; it entails the discovery of what has in fact been the strategic experience of scientific investigators, rather than the invention of new strategies of research. One of Merton's most famous middle-range theories involves his analysis of deviance.

Anomie Theory

As initially developed by Durkheim, the concept of *anomie* referred to a condition of relative normlessness in a society or group. Indicators of anomie include the perception that community leaders are indifferent to one's needs; the perception that little can be accomplished in a society which is seen as basically unpredictable and lacking social order; the perception that life goals are receding rather than being realized; a sense of futility; and the conviction that one cannot count on personal associates for social and psychological support. The success goal in American culture leads many to feelings of anomie. According to Merton (1949/1968), it is the conflict between cultural goals and the availability of using institutional means—whatever the character of the goals—which produces a strain toward anomie.

Merton's *Anomie Theory* (first published as "Social Structure and Anomie" in 1938) is a theory on the study of social deviance. Merton notes that at one time it was popular in "psychological and sociological theory to attribute the faulty operation of social structures

to failures of social control over man's imperious biological drives . . . With the more recent advancement of social science, this set of conceptions has undergone basic modifications. For one thing, it no longer appears so obvious that man is set against society in an unceasing war between biological impulse and social restraint . . . Sociological perspectives have increasingly entered into the analysis of behavior deviating from prescribed patterns of conduct" (1949/1968: 185). In his article "On the Evolving Synthesis of Differential Association and Anomie Theory: A Perspective from the Sociology of Science" (1997), Merton stated "that some two-thirds of a century ago I became persuaded that theoretical sociology was too sharply focussed on social patterns of conforming behavior and so I turned to the task of trying to develop a sociological theory of deviant behavior' (p. 517).

In brief, Merton believed that society encourages all persons to attain culturally desirable goals (such as economic success), but the opportunities to reach these goals are not equal among the members of society. Structural barriers such as racism, sexism, and ageism may hamper one's opportunity to reach culturally determined goals. Persons feeling such social pressures, without the means to attain these goals legitimately, may adapt a number of deviant behaviors in order to avoid feelings of anomie. Such terms as *cultural goals* and *institutionalized norms* are examples of explanatory factors consistent with functional analysis. Merton's primary aim "lies in discovering how some social structures *exert a definite pressure* upon certain persons in the society to engage in nonconformist rather than conformist conduct" (Merton, 1957:672). Among the several elements of social and cultural structures that exert pressure on individuals, two are of immediate importance. The first is culturally defined goals, purposes and interests, held out as legitimate objectives for all members of society. The second element is the institutionalized means that the structure defines, regulates, and controls, that is, the acceptable modes of reaching out for these goals. "Every social group invariably couples its cultural objectives with regulations, rooted in the mores or institutions, of allowable procedures for moving toward these objectives" (Merton, 1968: 187; Orig. 1949). The social system must find an effective equilibrium between these two elements. Thus, individuals must have ample opportunities to reach desired goals, but not to the extent that the social structure is threatened.

Merton (1968:194; Orig. 1949) described five types of individual adaptations for pursuing the coveted goals. These adaptations are schematically set out in Table 3.2, where plus (+) signifies "acceptance," minus (−) signifies "rejection," and plus/minus (+/−) signifies "rejection of prevailing values and substitution of new values."

A brief description of each of these modes of adaptation reveals how the social structure operates to exert pressure upon individuals.

Merton stated that to the extent that a society is stable, adaptation Type 1—*conformity* to both cultural goals and institutionalized means—is the most common and widely diffused mode. If this were not the case, the stability and continuity of society would be compromised. This adaptation is not a deviant one, for it implies that a person has attained monetary success by socially acceptable means (by working hard and getting an education). *Innovations* such as bank robbery and racketeering will help the individual attain economic success, but they represent deviant adaptations. Merton wrote of the alarming increase in white-collar crime; he would be alarmed at the rate at which it occurs today. *Ritualistic* types of adaptation involve the "abandoning or scaling down of the lofty cultural goals of great pecuniary success and rapid social mobility to the point where one's aspirations can be satisfied" (Merton, 1968:203; Orig. 1949). This type of person rejects the cultural obligation to attempt "to get ahead in the world" but continues to abide almost compulsively by institutional norms. This type of behavior is labeled deviant. *Retreatism* (for example, in drug addicts, social hermits, and pariahs) represents the rejection of both the cultural goals and the institutional means of attaining them, and it is therefore deviant behavior. *Rebellion* is a type of deviant adaptation that leads individuals to go outside the social structure. It involves a genuine transvaluation, where the direct or vicarious experience of frustration leads to a full denunciation of previously prized values. Rebellion represents the rejection of both societal goals and acceptable means and leads to behavior that attempts to drastically modify or overthrow the existing social structure. In extreme cases, riots or coup attempts may occur.

Robert Dubin and Richard Cloward addressed different aspects of Merton's *Anomie Theory* of socially deviant behavior.

Dubin methodically combines additional elements of social behavior to arrive at subtypes of deviant adaptations that were not distinguished in an earlier classification.

TABLE 3.2   A Typology of Modes of Individual Adaptation

Modes of Adaptation	Cultural Goals	Institutionalized Means
1. Conformity	+	+
2. Innovation	+	−
3. Ritualism	−	+
4. Retreatism	−	−
5. Rebellion	+/−	+/−

Cloward introduces strategic new variables for the analysis of the social and cultural contexts that, by hypothesis, give rise to varying rates of deviant behavior. Otherwise put, Dubin proposes a more exacting analysis of distinct forms of deviant adaptation; Cloward proposes a more exacting analysis of kinds of opportunity-structures that help account for differentials in rates and kinds of deviant behavior occurring in various social groups and social strata. (Merton, 1959:177)

Merton believed that both Dubin and Cloward had helped to contribute toward a more adequate sociological theory of deviance. In a society such as the United States, where the success goal is so predominant, Merton predicted that there would be a great deal of deviant behavior.

Manifest and Latent Functions

Merton argued that the functional approach to sociology is caught up in terminological confusion. All too often, a single term has been used to symbolize different concepts, just as the same concept has been symbolized by different terms. This confusion extends to the very word *function.* "The word 'function' has been pre-empted by popular speech with the not unexpected result that its connotation often becomes obscure in sociology proper" (Merton, 1949/1968:74). By such a word as *function* many theorists mean one thing; specifically, if a behavior is functional, it serves some manifest trait. Merton believed that, too often, functionalists looked only at the manifest (intended) functions of behavior. Durkheim's study of elementary forms of religious life is a classic example of this, according to Merton. In his study of the Hopi Indian raindance Merton expanded upon Durkheim's acknowledgment that the Arunta practiced totemism, and that the symbols on the totem were in fact significant, in that they possessed a functional purpose. But as Merton (1949/1968) noticed, the Hopi raindance served a manifest

function as a means of attaining the needed rain and also the latent function (unintended) of the dance behavior itself, aiding in the maintenance of group solidarity. Thus, Merton came to distinguish two primary usages for the word *function. Manifest functions* are those consequences that are expected, or intended; they are conscious motivations for social behavior. *Latent functions* are consequences that are neither recognized nor intended. The manifest function of the Hopi raindance was rain, whereas the latent function of the dance included bringing the community together for a common cause. As another example, education has the manifest function of providing knowledge to students, but a latent function is providing social interaction opportunities (such as parties, and finding one's future spouse).

As Cuzzort and King (1995) explained, "The manifest-latent distinction is a valuable one; it makes clear the nature of sociological investigation as perhaps few other distinctions do. Manifest functions are essentially 'official' explanations of a given action. Latent functions are the unrecognized or 'hidden' functions of an action. Socially patterned motives and purposes are essentially concepts for understanding the interaction between social structures and individual behavior" (p. 251). When a manifest function fails (if it does not rain after a raindance) but the latent function remains important (communal gathering), there is a tendency to rationalize social action (the lack of rain was not the result of the ceremony itself, but the fault of one, or more, of the participants). With regard to the Hopi raindance, the functionalist explains the persistence of superstitions as functional features of the social order. "Merton, aware of this disturbing feature of structural and functional thought, has tried to get around it by introducing yet another idea—the idea of dysfunctions" (Cuzzort and King, 1995:252).

Dysfunctions

As a functionalist, Merton examined the social structure and patterns of activity within organizations. He noticed that just setting up a system and put it in place does not guarantee that it will work at peak performance or that it will be *functional.* It may in fact have very negative or *dysfunctional* consequences for the organization or the persons who must deal with it. "Merton termed such system-disrupting consequences dysfunctions" (Levin, 1991:78). Furthermore, aspects of the system may be functional for some but dysfunctional for others. For example, a convenience store that remains open while all other grocery stores are closed during some holiday may turn out to be quite functional for the customers who need last-minute purchases; however, the clerk who is stuck working the holiday hours may find the store's remaining open dysfunctional. Merton examined bureaucracy, which he described as a system set up for specific procedural strategies that foster objectivity and the smooth operation of the organization. However, a bureaucracy, by its very design, is conservative (ritualistic) and inflexible (formalistic), and therefore unable to cope with changes or flaws within the system (Merton, 1949/1968). For example, if a courthouse is totally dependent on persons using computers to conduct daily business, it is rendered useless, or *dysfunctional,* during an electrical power outage. Dysfunctional events, then, lessen the effective equilibrium of a social system. "Dysfunctional aspects of a society imply strain or stress or tension. A society tries to constrain dysfunctional elements somewhat as an organism might constrain a bacterial or viral infection. If the dysfunctional forces are too great, the social order is overwhelmed, disorganized, and possibly destroyed" (Cuzzort and King, 1995:252). Wallace and Wolf (1999) stated, "Merton's concept of dysfunctions is also central to his argument that functionalism is *not* intrinsically conservative. It appears to be only when functionalists imply that everything is generally functional in its consequences" (p. 52). A lasting issue is the concern over for whom the social structure is functional and for whom it is dysfunctional. Many institutions and subsystems possess these bipolar effects on different individuals, groups, and even entire societies.

Empirical Research

While working with Paul Lazarsfeld, Merton (with Patricia Kendall) wrote a piece on the focused interview. "Although he was never totally oriented to methods, some of Merton's most insightful pieces concerned the relation between research and theory, and the issue of problem-solving in sociology" (Adams and Sydie, 2001:363). Merton acknowledged that different research methods are necessary for different empirical problems, that research may lead to empirical generalizations, and that empirical research is useful for much more than testing hypotheses drawn from a general theory. Merton consistently drew links between theory and research. In an article written decades ago, Merton (1949/1968) stated, "Like all interpretative schemes, functional analysis depends upon a triple alliance between theory, method and data. Of the three allies, method is by all odds the weakest. Many of the major practitioners of functional analysis have been devoted to theoretic formulations and to the clearing up of concepts; some have steeped themselves in data directly relevant to a functional frame of reference; but few have broken the prevailing silence regarding how one goes about the business of functional analysis" (p. 73). More recently, Merton promoted the techniques employed in focus-group research that were derived from work some forty years prior (Merton, 1987). In his article "The Focused Interview and Focus Groups" (1987), Merton argued for "a set of procedures for the collection and analysis of qualitative data that may help us gain an enlarged sociological and psychological understanding in whatsoever sphere of human experience" (p. 565). Thus, for Merton, theorizing was always important, but it required methodology, research, and data analysis.

NEOFUNCTIONALISM AND POSTFUNCTIONALISM

In the years following the primary contributions by Parsons and Merton, many other functionalists emerged, some in the tradition of the two theorists and others who rejected them. As Turner (2003) stated, "The grand architecture of the Parsonian functional scheme, as it evolved over a forty-year period at the midcentury, inspired a great amount of criticism, both inside and outside the functionalist camp" (p. 54). As a result, a new theoretical set of ideas appeared in the United States and Germany, collectively known as *neofunctionalism*. Among the most eminent neofunctionalists have been Niklas Luhmann, who wrote about social systems and maintained a commitment to producing abstract frameworks for analyzing social reality; Anthony Giddens, who rejected the Parsonian functional scheme and wrote about the process of structuration; Jeffrey C. Alexander, who is recognized as the leading proponent of neofunctionalism in the United States and published a volume titled *Neofunctionalism and After*; and Neil J. Smelser, who coauthored *Economy and Society* with Parsons. The works of these theorists and others are briefly discussed here.

Niklas Luhmann (1927–1998)

Niklas Luhmann was born in 1927 in Luneburg, Germany. In 1949, he completed a law degree at the University of Freiburg/Breisgau. He practiced law for a few years but became disillusioned with the repetitive nature of the legal profession and subsequently joined the civil service. During his free time he read the classic works of Descartes and Kant, as well as the functionalist theories of

Malinowski and Radcliffe-Brown. His own theoretical development took place as a result of his own reading and of his civil service work related to the German reparations post–World War II (Adams and Sydie, 2001:370). Luhmann spent a year in the early 1960s at Harvard studying under Parsons and introduced German social thinkers to his works. Luhmann was highly impressed by Parsons but felt that he had failed to incorporate such critical concepts as self-reference and complexity. Having witnessed firsthand his country's defeat in a world war and German occupation by foreign troops, Luhmann was led to conclude that modern society was not a better place to live. Thus, like any social thinker, he was influenced by the climate of his times, and his pessimistic outlook on life directly contrasted with the outlook most American theorists (especially Parsons) of this era. Luhmann even argued that the modern world is too complex for such things as shared norms and values (the second core assumption of functionalism: shared values that assist in the maintenance of the social system).

Luhmann's own works were an attempt to formulate a universal or grand theory of social systems that includes his ideas described above. The resulting theory is far more complicated than the works of Max Weber. "Niklas Luhmann not only saw the modern world as complicated—more so than during Weber's time—but mirrored it in his writing. The words are complex, the thoughts are complex, and his works are almost prohibitively so. He used a flexible and abstract set of concepts and propositions that could be combined in many different ways" (Adams and Sydie, 2001:370). The difficulty that Americans have in reading Luhmann involves the translation from German, the fact that his ideas are very abstract, and the fact that his sentences include new or little-known words. Luhmann found no reason to make theory noncomplicated, because social life itself is complicated. "The encompassing system is too large and complex to be immediately understandable. Its unity is not accessible, neither by experience nor by action" (Luhmann, 1984:59). His primary works, such as *Social Systems* (1984), have no natural starting point and lack a logical sequence of chapter ordering. Luhmann (1983) stressed the importance of grand theory: "Without universalistic theories or general frameworks, sociology will never be fully accepted" (p. 987). Luhmann (1983) described theory as not "something you invent or produce yourself; it is something already available which only needs interpretation and refinement" (p. 987). He remained steadfast in the idea that grand theory can, and should, be the primary goal of sociological theory. Luhmann (1984) stated, "Despite all skepticism and all the complaints about ideological bias which seem to be a recurrent affair" about hundred years (besides Nietzsche, see von Wiese, 1933, and Tenbruck, 1981) the chances for general theory are exceptionally good today. However, they require interdisciplinary orientations which are overlooked if we continue to focus on the classics" (p. 60).

Luhmann's primary contribution to social theory rests in his work on *systems theory*. "Luhmann employs a *general systems* approach to emphasize that human action becomes organized and structured into systems. When the actions of several people become interrelated, a social system can be said to exist. . . . All social systems exist in multidimensional environments, posing potentially endless complexity with which a system must deal" (Turner, 2003:55). In order for any system to survive, it must learn to adapt to its environment. The complex nature of social environments makes systems integration a major concern. Luhmann (1984) stated:

> Consequently, modern society has to describe itself a highly differentiated system. . . . All systems are based on a difference between system and environment. Therefore, system differentiation means the repetition of this difference within systems. The differentiated systems become decomposed into subsystem and (internal) environment, for instance as the political system and its societal environment. Subsystem and internal environment add up again to the total system, and this may be repeated several times, according to the number of subsystems. In this sense, system differentiation is equivalent to multiplication of the system by different internal perspectives. It means increasing complexity, depending on the ways in which the difference of systems and environments is realized. (p. 63)

The student of social theory should be able to easily recognize that the core premise of interdependent parts is a key element of Luhmann's theory. As Luhmann (1984) explained, "Social systems are self-referential systems. They are composed of elements (actions) which they produce by an arrangement of their elements" (p. 65).

This general framework distinguishes several forms of building subsystems in relation to their internal environment. "Segmentation means that subsystems presuppose their environment in terms of a rank order of systems. Functional differentiation means that subsystems specialize themselves on specific functions and presuppose that their environment cares for the rest. These distinctions coincide roughly with the historical types of primitive societies, culturally developed societies, and modern society" (Luhmann, 1984:63–64). Interestingly, Luhmann did not view modern society as really integrated at all. As Fuchs (2001) interpreted Luhmann, society is instead "characterized by massive parallel processing: think of all the encounters and conversations going on at the same time, with no mega-encounter coordinating or planning how this happens, or with what results. Modern society does not 'go' anywhere but 'drifts,' without anyone at the helm" (p. 130).

Luhmann described *general systems theory* as possessing two important elements. The first (as described above) is the distinction of the whole and its parts as modified by his *distinction of system and environment*. Second is the concept of *self-referential systems,* a condition necessary for the efficient functioning of systems. What this means is that the system is able to observe itself, can reflect on itself and what it is doing, and can make decisions as a result of this reflection. Luhmann (1983) stated:

> The system continually refers to itself by distinguishing itself from the environment. This is done by drawing and maintaining boundaries which can be crossed occasionally. The self-referential system is a self-reproducing or "autopoietic" unit, itself producing the elements which compose the system, and this requires the capacity to distinguish elements which belong to the system from elements which belong to the environment of the system. The distinction between system and environment is, therefore, constitutive for whatever functions as an element in a system. It is not the actor who produces the action. The meaning of the action and therefore the action itself is due to the difference between systems and environment. (pp. 992–993).

Thus, Luhmann's focus remained on the system, and not on individual actors. Individuals were merely a part of the environment.

According to Luhmann, social systems consist primarily of communication networks. The socialization of individuals into the social system is accomplished through communication. Socialization is necessary to align the individual's modes of conduct with society's general shared meanings. Shared meanings are always a result of communication. Luhmann created a *communication theory* that stresses human communication as reflexive. Communication and, presumably, a shared language allow the more effective transmission of the ideas and concepts central to a society (or social

system). Communicative language allows individuals to share the meaning of the key elements found in the environment. Reflexivity allows individuals to understand the meaning behind various forms of communication and therefore assists in the integration process. "However, his departure from Parsons began when he argued that, although there are systems in the modern world, there is not a single overarching and integrated system striving for equilibrium" (Adams and Sydie, 2001:373).

Many of Luhmann's ideas are related to those of British theorist Anthony Giddens.

Anthony Giddens (1938–)

Few theorists have been as productive as Anthony Giddens. He has produced thirty-one books (published in twenty-two languages) and more than 200 articles and reviews. As a result, he is well known throughout the academic world. Giddens was born in North London in 1938 and was the first member of his family to attend college, graduating from Hull University in 1959. He completed his M.A. at the London School of Economics in 1961 and taught at Leicester until the late 1960s. He then went to Simon Fraser in Canada, and then to the University of California at Los Angeles (UCLA). After UCLA, Giddens went to Cambridge, where he served as a sociology lecturer and then a professor from 1970 to 1997. He is now the director of the London School of Economics and Political Science and has been an advisor to Tony Blair and Bill Clinton.

Taking a postmodernist point of view, Giddens believes that contemporary sociology relies too much on the theories and concepts of nineteenth-century European social theory in the application to modern social problems. He believes that the classical ideas must be radically overhauled today, and virtually all of his work is an attempt to develop a change in social theory. Evidence can be found in *Capitalism and Modern Social Theory*

(1971), which Giddens (1976) described as "an exegetical preparation to an extended critique of nineteenth-century social thought" (p. 1), in *New Rules of Sociological Method* (1976); and in some sections of *Studies in Social and Political Theory* (1977), where he undertook critiques of two broad programmatic approaches to social theory: hermeneutics of the forms of "interpretative sociology" and functionalism. Giddens's primary objective is to develop a theoretical position which attempts to draw upon the ideas of structuralism, hermeneutics, and interpretive social theory. He referred to his approach as the *theory of structuration*. Knoke (1990) described Giddens's approach as strongly influenced by Continental hermeneutics and linguistics, and as an attempt to formulate a theory of agency without lapsing into purely subjectivist phenomenology.

According to Giddens (1979), "The theory of structuration begins from an absence: the lack of a theory of action in the social sciences" (p. 2). He continued:

> The theory of structuration substitutes the central notion of the *duality of structure.* By the duality of structure, I mean the essential recursiveness of social life, as constituted in social practices: structure is both medium and outcome of the reproduction of practices. Structure enters simultaneously into the constitution of the agent and social practices, and "exists" on the generating moments of this constitution. As a leading theorem of the theory of structuration, I advance the following: *every social actor knows a great deal about the conditions of reproduction of the society of which he or she is a member.* Failure to acknowledge this is a basic insufficiency of functionalism and structuralism alike; and it is as true of Parsons's "action frame of reference" as it is of other varieties of functionalist thought. The proposition that all social agents are knowledgeable about the social systems which they constitute and reproduce in their action is a logically necessary feature of the conception of the duality of structure. (p. 5)

Giddens (1979) went so far as to state that the theory of structuration could be read as a *nonfunctional manifesto* (p. 7). According to his theory, social systems have no purposes, reasons, or needs whatsoever; only human individuals have. It is clear that Giddens takes exception to the concept of *systems needs* because a system cannot "need" anything; it is an entity that exists because individuals within a system exist, and they are the only ones who could possibly "need" something from the environment. In functionalist theory the guiding model of a "system" is usually that of an organism; therefore, it is viewed as a living, breathing being that has needs (as a biological organism has needs).

In contrast, Giddens (1979) views *social systems* as "regularized relations of interdependence between individuals and groups, that typically can be best analyzed as *recurrent social practices.* Social systems are systems of social interaction; as such they involve the situated activities of human subjects, and exist syntagmatically in the flow of time. Systems, in this terminology, have structures, or more accurately, have structural properties; they are not structures in themselves" (p. 66). As Knoke (1990) observed, "In Giddens' unique terminology, social systems, as continuous flows of conduct in time and space, are distinguished from social structures, which are defined as rules and roles existing as memory traces that are revealed in actions" (p. 16). Social structures become necessary components of social systems. "Giddens believes structure can be conceptualized as *rules* and *resources* that actors use in 'interaction contexts' that extend across 'space' and over 'time'" (Turner, 2003:477). Rules are notions that actors come to understand and generally accept. "All social rules have both constitutive and regulative (sanctioning) aspects to them" (Giddens, 1979:66). A common example of a rule is "not to take the goods of another." Resources are those items that give actors power and allow those who possess resources the ability to "get things done." Giddens emphasizes the inherent "transformative" potential of rules and resources (Turner, 2003). Structural principles operate in cooperation with one another, but they also contravene each other (Giddens, 1984). In addition, structure itself is "both enabling and constraining, and it is one of the specific tasks of social theory to study the conditions in the organization of the social system that govern the interconnections between the two. According to this conception, the same structural characteristics participate in the subject (the actor) as in the object (society). Structure forms 'personality' and 'society' simultaneously—but in neither case exhaustively" (Giddens, 1979:69–70).

A quick summation of Giddens's theory of structuration reveals his structuralist perspective, which is revealed in Knoke's (1990) analysis of the four basic modes of structuration that occur:

1. Rules for signification of meaning.
2. Rules for normative legitimation of social conduct.
3. Authorized resources to command persons (political power).
4. Allocation of resources to command objects (economic property).

Giddens's theory of structuration (1979) links these structural modes to recurrent interactions through a duality of structure and agency. Thus, society, though consisting of social actors who interact with one another, is still a complex matrix of social systems that are interdependent.

For years now, Giddens has been working in the area of globalization, especially in regard to its impact on human behavior, the global marketplace, and international finances. The global marketplace has grown so much that more than a trillion dollars is turned over each day on global currency markets (Giddens, 2000:28a). Among his most recent books are *The Consequences of Modernity* (1989), *Modernity and Self-Identity*

(1991), *Beyond Left and Right* (1994), *In Defence of Sociology* (1996), *The Third Way and Its Critics* (2000), and *Runaway World* (2000). In *Runaway World*, Giddens described how globalization is restructuring the ways in which we live. Globalization is led from the West and bears the strong imprint of American political and economic power. Giddens pointed out that globalization affects the United States as well as the rest of the world. According to Giddens (2000a):

> Globalisation also influences everyday life as much as it does events happening on a world scale. . . . In most parts of the world, women are staking claim to greater autonomy than in the past and are entering the labour force in large numbers. Such aspects of globalization are at least as important as those happening in the global market-place. They contribute to the stresses and strains affecting traditional ways of life and cultures in most regions of the world. The traditional family is under threat, is changing, and will change much further. Other traditions, such as those connected with religion, are also experiencing major transformation. Fundamentalism originates from a world of crumbling traditions. The battleground of the twenty-first century will pit fundamentalism against cosmopolitan tolerance. In a globalizing world, where information and images are routinely transmitted across the globe, we are all regularly transmitted across the globe. . . . Cosmopolitans welcome and embrace this cultural complexity. Fundamentalists find it disturbing and dangerous. (p. 22)

Giddens views globalization as a positive influence on humanity because it is liberating women, spreading democracy, and creating new wealth. The importance that Giddens places on democracy leads him to conclude that it is worth fighting for, and that it can be achieved. It can be achieved through more government. "Our runaway world doesn't need less, but more government" (Giddens, 2000:100).

In 1998, Giddens wrote *The Third Way*, a reference to the growing attraction to a third way of politics. The third way provides a political alternative to leftists and rightists. "Third way politics, I try to show, isn't an ephemeral set of ideas. It will continue to have its dissenters and critics. But it will be at the core of political dialogues in the years to come, much as neo-liberalism was until recently and old-style social democracy was before that. Third way politics will be the point of view with which others will have to engage" (Giddens, 2000b:). In *The Third Way and Its Critics* (2000b), Giddens expanded upon some of the ideas and themes outlined in his 1998 publication. Giddens (2000b) stated, "The idea of finding a third way in politics has become a focus of controversy across the world. The term 'third way,' of course, is far from new, having been employed by groups of diverse political persuasions in the past, including some from the extreme right. Social democrats, however, have made the use of it most often." (p. 1) American Democrats describe the third way as a "new progressivism" (Giddens, 2000b:2). "Partly borrowing from the New Democrats, and partly following its own line of political evolution, the Labour Party in Britain converged on similar ideas. Under Tony Blair's leadership, the party broke with its own 'old progressivism'—Clause 4 of the Labour Party constitution. Blair started to refer to New Labour as developing a third way, eventually putting his name to a pamphlet of the same title" (Giddens, 2000b:3). Giddens described the third way as involving radical politics and "argues that the three key areas of power—government, the economy, and the communities of civil society—all need to be constrained in the interests of social solidarity and social justice. A democratic order, as well as an effective market economy, depends upon a flourishing civil society. Civil society, in turn, needs to be limited by the other two" (Giddens, 2000b:51).

It is Giddens's hope that the third way will provide a fresh approach to issues such as family life, crime, and the decay of many communities. Perhaps his faith in globalization will be realized as the third way of dealing with worldwide inequality.

Jeffrey C. Alexander and Neil Smelser

Alexander's *Neofunctionalism and After* (1985) is an attempt to finalize the bridge between traditional functionalism and reconstructed functionalism. He has succeeded in establishing the legitimacy of some of Parsons's central themes and concepts while articulating newer, more contemporary issues related to functionalist theory. However, Alexander does admit that, despite neofunctionalism's established position in contemporary society, it must continue to produce new and creative sociological studies. Alexander (1985) gave credit to the "emergence of new politically generated theories such as feminism, multiculturalism, civil society, and postcolonialism" (p. 17). Alexander's theorizing has shifted from the Parsonian strict focus on macro issues to a strong focus on microsociological concerns, which include elements of symbolic interactionism.

Alexander is credited with coining the term *neofunctionalism*. *Neofunctionalism and After* (1998) is a volume filled with Alexander's writings on neofunctionalism. Here he described neofunctionalism as

> a movement of ideas that marked a shift in the predicted slope of knowledge/power, to mix a concept from trigonometry with a term of Foucault's (see Chapter 11). Faced with the emergence of a neofunctionalism in the 1980s, theorists whose formation occurred in the 1960s—when a radical sociology was supposed to have broken definitely with Parsons—spoke of a "surprisingly successful comeback" and of neofunctionalism as a refutation of the linear assumptions about scientific development that the preceding generation had continued to hold. (p. 3)

Alexander acknowledged the considerable contributions of Parsons to sociological theory but stated that they are not as revered today as in the past. Alexander (1998) added:

> I have succeeded in helping to (re)establish the legitimacy of some of Parsons' central concerns, I regard this project as completed. It is this very completion that has allowed me increasingly to separate my own understanding of social theory from Parsons' own, to look beyond Parsons, to think about what comes "after Parsons," to build not only upon "Parsons," but upon strands of classical and contemporary work, to create a different kind of social theory. Still, whatever comes after neofunctionalism will be deeply indebted to it. (p. 5)

Alexander views neofunctionalism as part of the evolutionary growth of postwar sociological theory. Parsons dominated the first phase (the 1940s through the mid-1960s). Theories presented in the 1970s by such social thinkers as Giddens, Habermas, and Collins that attempted to integrate different lines of thought represent the second phase of theoretical development. And finally, in a phase that Alexander (1998) described as postclassical, neofunctionalism "was an effort to relate Parsons to different forms of classical and contemporary work" (p. 8). Furthermore, "neofunctionalism has succeeded in helping to establish Parsons as a classical figure" (p. 12).

Neil Smelser coauthored *Economy and Society* (1956) with Talcott Parsons while he was just a graduate student. Smelser is considered a top-level theorist in neofunctionalism. Smelser (1998) believes that people seek to avoid the experience of ambivalence because it is "such a *powerful, persistent, unresolvable, volatile, generalizable,* and *anxiety-producing* feature of the human condition" (p. 6). Smelser (1998) stated that ambivalence refers to such phenomena as death and separation, retirement, and moving away from a community (traditional definitions of ambivalence—simultaneous attraction toward and repulsion from a person—might confuse the reader here with Smelser's usage of the term). When such

moves are "forced" upon the individual, the negative feelings are heightened. For example, if someone loses a job and is forced to move away from a loved community, that person will experience a wide variety of negative emotions, or ambivalence. Additionally, more coercive organizations, or those closed institutions described by Erving Goffman as "total institutions," are especially conducive to ambivalence and its negative consequences. In less extreme cases, people may feel locked to a job, or a career, that they cannot escape without great cost. In such cases, coworkers must learn to cooperate and get along with one another. Unfortunately, all too often those in power abuse their authority because of a personal agenda, and the victim feels great ambivalence (among other feelings).

RELEVANCY

Functionalism dominated sociological theory in the 1950s and 1960s. In 1959, at the height of functionalism, Kingsley Davis (1959) suggested that every sociologist is a functionalist because sociology *is* functionalism. Sociology assumes societies are real and therefore consist of integrated parts. The functionalist perspective was spearheaded by the works of Talcott Parsons, who revolutionized a way of thinking by formulating a grand theory. His functionalistic approach was centered on his social action theory and his analysis of social systems. Parsons's one-time, dominate theoretical perspective came under attack on many fronts by the 1970s. One criticism of functionalism is that it fails to explain social change, that it stresses structure over process. It is argued that structural functionalism is better suited to dealing with static structures than to dealing with processes of change. If the parts of the system are designed to maintain a functional flow, how do they allow for change? Parsons believed that he had addressed this concern about social change in his theory of evolution. However, his explanation was always in the context of strain on the system and the corresponding attempt to reach equilibrium. The emphasis of the social system is on the need for integration of the parts of society and the various actors. Consequently, a more legitimate criticism of Parsons's functionalist theory is its conservative nature.

The conservative nature of functionalism is indeed often criticized. The narrow focus of functionalism prevents it from addressing a number of important issues in the social world. Functionalism's focus on systems equilibrium leads it to support the status quo, so it is highly conservative. The assumption that the parts of the system work in cooperation with one another generally leads functionalists to ignore conflict. Functionalists have a hard time dealing effectively with conflict—another important criticism of functionalism.

Functionalism stresses the importance of shared societal values but ignores the *interests* of people. According to Wallace and Wolf (1999), although functionalism does show "the independent importance of ideas and the links between power and social consent, it neglects the coercive aspects of power and the significance of people's conflicting objectives" (p. 65). Because of the conservatism of his theories, Parsons often ignored issues of conflict and power. The social system needs to maintain equilibrium, and therefore, it must often exercise social control and seek to avoid conflict. Conflict is a cause of strain that must be stabilized so that the system can move along smoothly.

Parsons was aware of conflict but failed to address it in any significant way in his theories. The primary reason he failed to explain conflict is that he did not elaborate on the role of power and how power positions often dictate behavior. The reason most people perform their roles and act as they do is not that their behavior is functional to them, but that they find themselves on the short end of a power relationship. Parsons (1951) did acknowledge that one's participation in the social system is influenced by one's "location" in the relationship. In his article "A Sociological Approach to the Theory of Organization II" (1956b), Parsons discussed what can be achieved with power but did not articulate what constitutes power, nor did he discuss power relationships. Parsons seemed to treat conflict and power as "givens" of normal life that do not need further examination. Even toward the end of his life, when he was surely aware of the criticisms of his theoretical shortcomings, Parsons failed to examine more closely these vitally important variables of human action. In order to be a complete theory, functionalism needs to integrate the role of power and the effects and types of social conflict.

Functionalism is also attacked for its overly macro perspective on social life. It pays little attention to daily interactions among individuals. Functionalism fails to explain adequately its most important terms: *structure, function,* and *social system.* It assumes that there is a general consensus on shared values but fails to demonstrate how these values come about or how they are modified. Parsons was criticized for failing to collect empirical data, even though he admired Weber and Durkheim for using empirical data to support their theories. Parsons did not worry about such complaints as he indicated that there must be specialists in every field: Some are specialists in research, and he considered himself a specialist in theory. His commitment to the development of sociological concepts in order to study human action reveals his dedication to social theory.

There is little doubt of the staying power of many key ideas and concepts of functionalism. Many social thinkers, in the tradition of Parsons and Merton, have continued to focus on structural issues. Other neofunctionalists have contributed to the development of postmodern theory. Despite the criticism of this grand theory, many elements of functionalism remain relevant today.

Society and social systems *do* comprise interdependent parts, and a major failure or breakdown in one part can cause harm to the entire system. This premise can be demonstrated in a number of ways. First, the concept of *role set* reveals itself on a daily basis. Few people are self-sufficient to the point where they do not depend upon a multitude of others. Any role we play (for example, teacher) comes with a role set of rules and norms of behavior, typically specifying how the actor is to behave; it also shows what one person's role is in relation to other people's roles. A teacher does not have time to "hunt and gather" food; the teacher shops at a store, where other people who have performed their roles have made the food available. The same person is dependent upon others for a variety of services, including home heating, car fueling, auto service, and trash removal. In short, every individual depends on others; we all need one another to survive.

The validity of the interdependence of parts is revealed in a second way. For the sake of self-containment, the system will always seek equilibrium. It must show its adaptive capacity. When a dominant corporation fails (such as Enron, at one time seventh largest U.S. company), it sends a ripple effect throughout all the related subsystems. People lose jobs, so they cannot pay their bills, and they may default on mortgages. All the companies and services (outside contractors, such as pest controllers) that did business with the failed organization also suffer. Charities dependent on the organization's contributions may be forced to close social programs. And so on. All of the people hurt by one event, such as a plant closing, understand the value of maintaining equilibrium. The value of the macro, "big-picture" perspective of functionalism demonstrates that despite the harm done to those affected by one system's collapse, the greater system generally absorbs the role left abandoned. For example, even though Enron collapsed and thousands of individuals lost their jobs

and life savings, the financial system of the United States did not fall apart, as other companies moved in after Enron's failure to assume its functions. In other words, the greater social system (the society) reacted to Enron's collapse by maintaining "systems needs." A microsociological approach would concentrate on the social effects of those who lost jobs because of a plant closing (as well as those who benefit when another plant eventually opens elsewhere to meet the needs of the greater system), whereas the macrosociologist is more concerned about the fact that the system and society as a whole survived.

A global perspective, the ultimate in macro analysis, provides evidence of the growing reality of globalization. Beyond global industry (for example, multinational corporations), a number of social institutions are linked internationally. As Thompson (1979) stated, "Concrete efforts at international cooperation in higher education, international agriculture, and the work of the larger private foundations with international programs lends some credence to the functional approach" (p. 103). The global reality of the social world was mild in Thompson's day compared to now.

Thus, at a multitude of levels, systems consist of parts that depend on one another. The global reality of social systems creates a great deal of pressure on political structures. Lane (1994) suggested that "structural-functionalism might again prove useful as a stimulus to coordinated research in comparative politics" (p. 461).

The international sports industry is another social system that works at the global level and creates systems rules that all participants are expected to abide by. Among the more notable sports organizations are the Olympics. When the world protested apartheid in South Africa, international sports authorities, like the International Olympic Committee, banned South Africa from formal competition. Before the United States–led coalition forces waged war against Iraq in

2003, there was a similar movement under way to ban Iraq from Olympic and other international sports, primarily in response to human rights abuse charges (especially against Iraq's own athletes). It is possible to speculate that this attempted ban had more to do with the United States and its threat of war against Iraq. After all, China was awarded the 2008 Summer Olympics in spite of numerous human rights violations accusations.

Functionalism has two guiding principles; first is the idea of interdependent parts and second is the principle of a general consensus on values. It is this second principal that upsets so many critics of functionalism, for they feel it reflects an intolerance of differing viewpoints and is therefore conservative and supports the status quo. The truth remains, however, that in order for any social system (society, organization, family, or personal relationship with others) to remain in tact and to run smoothly, there *must* be some commitment to general values, issues of morality, and goals of the relationship. To deny this reality is naive at the very least. Couples "drift" apart when they no longer share a commitment to the relationship; employees leave an organization when they realize that their attitudes and goals differ from those of the employer; and society risks dissolution when disturbances (for example, internal conflicts, riots, protests, and civil war) cause such strain that the system itself is threatened.

Changes necessary to the value system are often compromised by vested interests. For example, when laws are passed to protect homosexuals from discrimination in the workplace, employers who disapprove of gays cannot deny them equal opportunity for employment. Certain interest groups, usually religions-based, may disagree with such lifestyle choices and fight against such legislation because of moral and value issues. In short, there will *never* be a complete agreement of values in any social system (at either micro or macro levels), but if the system is to

survive, overriding values must be adhered to and followed. This is demonstrated by the fact that society's members do agree on most fundamental norms and issues of right and wrong (such as stealing someone's property is wrong, hard work should be rewarded, and murder is wrong).

Robert Merton's middle-range version of functionalism introduced many key concepts into sociological theory. The distinctions between manifest and latent functions are numerous. Many people attend sporting events to cheer for their favorite team (manifest function), but the communal gathering (especially demonstrated with "tailgating" before football games—America's number one sport) before, during, and after the game also serves a latent function. The manifest function of cellular phones is to help people in a time of crisis, such as when their cars break down, but cell phones also keep people in touch with one another concerning more mundane matters (latent function).

Interestingly, cell phones also help to introduce another key concept of Merton, namely, the dysfunctional aspects of certain behaviors and organizations. Cell phones have proved to be a major source of nuisance to others, as disrespectful cell phone users routinely use this device in inappropriate places (for example, leaving their phones on in the classroom, at movies, and in restaurants or talking loudly in trains and planes or while standing in line in public places). The worst violation of cell phone users is talking on the phone while driving a vehicle. It has been statistically proved that more accidents are caused by people driving and talking than by drunk drivers.

Many Americans have purchased over-priced sport utility vehicles (SUVs) that bring them comfort on the one hand (functional) but that increase the U.S. dependence on foreign oil (dysfunctional) because of their very poor gas mileage performance. A micro analysis of the SUV phenomenon is also quite enlightening. Individuals who are wealthy enough to own such cars enjoy flaunting their privileged status (micro analysis) even though they demonstrate their lack of concern about the negative impacts of environmental damage and foreign oil dependence (macro analysis).

Functionalism is a theory originally designed by Talcott Parsons that now lives on through the ideas of others. Stephen Turner (1993) stated, "Parsons underwent a much promoted posthumous 'revival,' and the historical and interpretive literature on Parsons, both of the hagiographic and critical sort, has expanded ever since. Parsons has been fortunate in attracting scholarly interest—of better quality, in some respects, in death and with nonstudents than in life with his students' (pp. 228–229). The contributions of neofunctionalists and poststructuralists like Niklas Luhmann, Anthony Giddens, Neil Smelser, and Jeffrey C. Alexander demonstrate the staying power of the functionalist tradition. As Levin (1991) stated, "Functionalism is one of the major perspectives in sociology" (p. 82) It is safe to state that the functional approach will remain in sociological discourse for as long as there is sociology. It remains one of the Big Three approaches to social theory.

4

Conflict Theory

The cornerstone of functional theory is the idea that there is a general *consensus* in values and norms of society and that the social institutions are integrated as a functioning whole. In contrast, *conflict theories* emphasize the role of *power* and the inequality found systematically throughout society. Conflict theory claims that there is no true consensus and that, instead, society's norms and values are those of the dominant group. The privileged group imposes its will on the subordinate group in order to maintain its power position. Conflict theory rose to prominence during the 1970s because of growing disenchantment with structural functionalism.

DEFINING CONFLICT THEORY

Conflict theory arose as the primary alternative to functionalism as a macrosociological theoretical perspective that explains the general structure of societies. As Turner (1975) explained, "The growing disenchantment with structural-functional theory has been marked by the rise of alternative theoretical perspectives over the last two decades. One of the most conspicuous of these alternatives has been 'conflict theory' which has presumably rediscovered for the discipline such phenomena as power, force, coercion, constraint, and change in social systems" (p. 443).

The conflict perspective views society as a system of social structures and relationships that are shaped mainly by economic forces. Those who are economically wealthy control the means of production and thus dominate society because of their advantageous power position. Conflict theorists assume that social life revolves around the economic interests of the wealthy and that these people use their economic power to coerce and manipulate others to accept their view of the society—and the world. Social classes are based on economics and one's relative position in regard to the means of production. Furthermore, because there is a clear power differential among individuals and social classes, resentment and hostility are constant elements of society. The obvious implication of this social reality is that conflict is inevitable.

The conflict perspective acknowledges that there are special *interest groups* that fight over the scarce resources of society. These groups have their own best interests at heart and not those of the greater society. Interest groups work to gain a power advantage over others. "Instead of interpreting social life as normally cooperative and harmonious, conflict theorists view society as an arena in which different individuals and groups struggle with each other in order to obtain scarce and valued resources, especially property, prestige, and power" (Lindsey and Beach, 2004:20). The competition between these groups throws off the equilibrium of society until a dominant group gains control and reinstitutes stability by means of power. Conflict theorists believe that *power* is the core of all social relationships. It is the most precious of the scarce social resources. Therefore, conflict theory views society as composed of competing elements (interest groups) that fight over scarce resources (for example, wealth, power, and prestige); power differentials ultimately determine the allocation and distribution of these scarce resources.

HISTORICAL ROOTS OF CONFLICT THEORY

Sociological conflict theory has its roots in the ideas of Karl Marx (1818–1883), Max Weber (1864–1920), and Georg Simmel (1858–1918). All three of these classical theorists contributed to the formation of contemporary social conflict theory. (For biographical backgrounds and a more thorough analysis of these social thinkers, see, for example, *Classical Social Theory: Investigation and Application*, Delaney, 2004).

Karl Marx (1818–1883)

When teaching conflict theory to students I tell them to think of two things when they hear the term *conflict theory*: power and Marx. The role of power in society is a common thread among all conflict theorists, and it is the ideas of Karl Marx that are most evident in the conflict perspective. Marx did not "create" conflict theory; rather, it was his ideas on such subjects as human potential, the historical method, class conflict, class consciousness, and communism that influenced future

social thinkers when they created conflict theory.

As a humanist, Marx wanted all individuals to reach their full *human potential*. He believed that capitalism was an economic system designed to keep power in the hands of the few—the owners of the means of production—while the masses were forced to abide by a social system created by the privileged. Even before capitalism, society had always been distinguished by persons who owned property or controlled the means of production and those who did not. In fact, Marx believed that all of history is characterized by an economic struggle between the haves and the have-nots. This materialistic conception was spelled out in Karl Marx and Friedrick Engels's *The German Ideology*. Marx articulated a dialectical theory which he first called *naturalism* or *Humanism* and later specified as *historical materialism* (Giddens, 1971). In Marx's dialectical approach, mind and matter, spirit and nature, constitute the unified structure of reality. Thus, Marx was attempting to combine material and ideal factors or structural and cultural factors, and to illustrate their reciprocal relationship.

The importance that Marx placed on using the *historical method* reflects his evolutionary ideas about human society. His focus on social change led Marx to believe that humans make their own history. He explained how humans separated themselves from animals once they consciously realized that they could *produce* their own means of subsistence, rather than depending on what nature provided. Some people learned to produce more than they needed to survive. They came to enjoy a power position because they could provide subsistence to others. Controlling material production represented a threshold point in the historical development of humans. It also led to a division of labor in society, and to the formation of economic social classes. Class struggle became the next inevitable step in the historical process of human development. Marx stated that class distinctions are heavily influenced by the possession of personal property.

Reactions to class differences may range from open hostility and revolt against the existing social system to simple acceptance of how things are in society. The latter response is what Marx referred to as *false consciousness*. Marx defined false consciousness as the inability to clearly see where one's own best interests lie. Marx believed that once the exploited became conscious of their plight and misery, they would unite in revolution. The new society would be characterized by *communism* which was to be the economic and philosophical force that would eliminate class struggle. It would also represent the next step in the historical process. Marx's primary ideas of communism are described in *The Communist Manifesto* (1848), cowritten by Marx and Engels. In brief, Marx and Engels believed the world would be a better place under communism. They believed that class inequality would end with the collective control of property and with the growth in size and power of the working class. The governmental abuse of workers would end with the dismantling of government (Pampel, 2000).

The basic elements of conflict theory are clearly found in this brief review of Marx's ideas.

Max Weber (1864–1920)

Weber agreed with Marx that economics was an important variable in determining power differentials among individuals in society. However, he believed that social divisions were based on two other factors as well: social prestige or status and political influence. Weber believed that someone who possesses a great deal of social prestige and yet is economically poor (for example, Mother Teresa, Gandhi) can still hold power in society. A local politician who earns a modest salary may still hold a great deal of power in the community. Additionally, Weber argued that "social groups would identify themselves not merely according to wealth, but more

deeply by ethnic and cultural backgrounds, and by shared 'styles of life'" (Farganis, 2000:263). However, whereas Marx saw society as evolving toward a communist utopia, Weber warned that individual freedoms were likely to be compromised because of the increasing role of modern bureaucracies (Cockerham, 1995).

Conflict theory maintains that the social order existing in society is a result of coercion by the people in the power positions of the social structure. Conflict theorists particularly emphasize the role of power in maintaining order within society. Weber believed that conflict underlies all social relations and determines power (Dronberger, 1971). The possession of power is a critical element in conflict theory, and power is a central aspect in Weber's works on the *types of authority*.

Weber defined *power* as the ability to impose one's will on another, even when the other objects. *Authority* is legitimate power (and a legitimate form of domination); it is power that is exercised with the consent of the ruled. According to Weber, the distribution of power and authority is the basis of social conflict. He stated that whereas power is essentially tied to the personality of individuals, authority is always associated with social positions. Weber also insisted that while power is merely a factual relation, authority is a legitimate relation of domination and subjection. In this sense, authority can be described as legitimate power. Authority is a universal element of social structure; it both realizes and symbolizes the functional integration of social systems.

In every association, the interests of the ruling group (the maintenance of the status quo) are the values that constitute the ideology of the legitimacy of its rule, whereas the interests of the subjected group constitute a threat to the prevailing ideology and the social relations it covers. If the subordinates believe in the legitimacy of the authority figures, conflict may be avoided; if, however, they do not recognize the legitimacy of authority, conflict may occur. Reactions by subordinates to claims of legitimacy by authority figures determine the course of action of those in the power positions. "According to the kind of legitimacy which is claimed, the type of obedience, the kind of administrative staff developed to guarantee it, all the mode of exercising authority, will all differ fundamentally" (Weber, 1978:213). Those with power (who dominate) seek to maintain their dominance (the status quo), and those without power (who are subordinate) seek some level of power and control (social change).

Social class identifies conflict groups that are generated by the differential distribution of authority in society. The *power elites* are always smaller in number, but more organized. The masses are larger in number, but far less organized. Social classes, understood as conflict groups arising from the authority structure, are in conflict primarily over the issue of power. Weber used an *ideal type* as an analytical tool in his discussion of authority relations. Weber proposed that there are three *types of authority*: rational-legal, traditional, and charismatic.

Rational-legal authority is set on rational grounds and anchored in impersonal rules that have been legally enacted or contractually established. This type of authority is common in modern societies like the United States and is characterized by *bureaucracies*. This kind of authority exists in the position that one holds, not in the individual. *Traditional authority* is the dominant type of authority in premodern societies. It is based on the ideal of tradition, where power is handed down from generation to generation (such as royalty). The design of the social system has made it legitimate. *Charismatic authority* resides in the appeal of leaders who claim legitimacy because of the will of the people. In this regard, power is with the individual, not the political system. Weber's analysis of power and authority is critical to conflict theory.

Georg Simmel (1858–1918)

Simmel was interested in identifying universal patterns in human behavior and was committed to developing theoretical statements that reflect these basic social processes. "Simmel (1908, 1950) was concerned primarily with abstracting the 'forms' of social reality from ongoing social processes, whereas Marx (1848, 1867) was committed to changing social structures by altering the course of social processes" (Turner, 1975:619). Simmel insisted that sociologists conduct a systematic analysis of *social forms*. "Whereas Marx and Weber wanted to understand what made a particular society operate, Simmel concentrated on developing what is almost a mathematics of society: a collection of statements about human relationships and social behavior that apply irrespective of the historical setting" (Wallace and Wolf, 1999:76). Simmel pointed out that similar forms of socialization occur with quite dissimiliar content, and similar social interests are found in quite dissimilar forms of socialization. Furthermore, there are similar forms of relationships between individuals in groups which are completely dissimilar in purpose and goal. Superiority and subordination, competition, imitation, division of labor, personal bias, and countless other forms of relationships are found in all types of groups. Therefore, Simmel disagreed with Marx that social classes are formed horizontally (based on economics). People are not divided neatly into self-contained groups that have common interests, and that are different from other self-contained and antagonistic groups (Wallace and Wolf, 1999:77). An individual may agree on some matters related to a particular economic class but disagree on other matters. One thing remains true: A sociologist can easily predict that the larger the group size, the greater the differences in opinions and power.

Simmel's sociological study was guided by the *dialectical approach*. A dialectical approach is multicausal and multidirectional;

integrates fact and value; rejects the idea that there are concrete dividing lines between social phenomena; focuses on social relations; and is deeply concerned with conflicts and contradictions. Simmel believed that "the world can best be understood in terms of conflicts and contrasts between opposed categories" (Levine, 1971:xxxv). The forms of social life constantly influence individual decisions and behavior. According to Simmel, the most important form of relationship in the whole social world is the one between the leader and the followers, between the superior and the subordinates. It is a form of socialization critical to social life and is the main factor in sustaining the unity of groups. Superiority and subordination constitute the sociological expression of psychological difference in human beings (Spykman, 1965).

The *superordinate* and the *subordinate* have a reciprocal relationship. The superordinate (for example, boss, master, leader) expects the subordinate (for example, employee, slave, follower) to follow the rules. Because of the reciprocal nature between the two; domination does not lie in the unilateral imposition of the superordinate's will upon the subordinate. After all, even in the most oppressive social environments, subordinates have at least some degree of personal freedom—although the choices may be limited between submission and punishment. Thus, even submission is not purely passive but has an active aspect as well. Simmel insisted that social action always involves harmony *and* conflict, love *and* hatred. If this is the case, then conflict is always present and varies only in degree.

A final note on Simmel's contribution to conflict theory: Simmel wrote about *secrecy* and how it represents one of the greatest human achievements (that is, the ability to keep a secret and to reveal it when it places the holder of the secret in a position of power). Having secret information about someone puts the concealer of the secret in an advantageous position, especially if the

information may be damaging to the other's authoritarian position. The secret contains a tension that dissolves at the moment of its revelation. The secret is surrounded by the possibility and temptation of betrayal, and an external danger of being discovered is interwoven with the internal danger of giving oneself away. Some groups are formed around secrets and are known as *secret societies*. The secret society depends on the reciprocal confidence of its members. Secret societies are generally in conflict with the greater society.

The works of Marx, Weber, and Simmel had a tremendous impact on the development of conflict theory, and yet their influence was delayed for decades. As Turner (2003) explained, "Despite the genius of these early masters, conflict theory remained recessive during the first half of the twentieth century. . . . The ideas of Marx, Weber, and Simmel on conflict began to resurface in America and assume a central place in sociological theory during the 1950s in the works of two German-born sociologists, Ralf Dahrendorf and Lewis Coser" (p. 131).

Coser and Dahrendorf are two of the four specific conflict theorists to be discussed in this chapter. The other two are C. Wright Mills and Randall Collins.

LEWIS COSER (1913–2003)

Lewis Coser was born in Berlin, Germany, in 1913, to a Jewish family of bankers. He lived in Berlin through high school, where his involvement with the socialist student movement was not met with tolerance during the emergence of Adolf Hitler and his Nazi regime (Coser, 1993). Coser left Germany in 1933 and moved to Paris, explaining (1993), "My parents were not allowed to support me financially outside Germany, and the French government did not allow foreign exiles to take regular jobs in the tough job market of the depression years. I worked as a traveling salesperson for several wholesalers, and somewhat later was privileged to work as a personal secretary to a Swiss author and journalist" (p. 2).

Luckily for Coser, enrollment at the Sorbonne (University of Paris) was free, and so began his academic career. He was unsure of which subjects to take and at first flirted with modern history. Then he decided on comparative literature, mainly because of his command of French and English in addition to his native German. Coser's dissertation was a study comparing nineteenth-century French, English, and German novels in terms of their different social structures. One of his professors told him, "'Social structure, my friend, is not a subject of study in comparative literature— that is something to be studied in sociology'" (Coser, 1993:2). So Coser switched to sociology.

Under the advice of Professor Jean Marie Carré, Coser began to study social structure. At the Sorbonne, the study of social theory was limited mostly to the works of Émile Durkheim. Coser (1993) referred to this situation as the "Durkheimian magic circle," where the only theorist studied outside Durkheim was Karl Marx. Coser (1993) credited Henry Jacoby, a refugee from Hitler's prisons, with freeing him from Marxist orthodoxy, which threatened, for a while, to rigidify his thoughts. When Coser later reached America, he described himself as an "unorthodox Marxist with strong admixtures of Durkheimian thought" (1993:3).

With the outbreak of World War II, Coser was interned as an enemy alien. He was able to escape France with the aid of a local socialist mayor, who managed to get a visa for Coser as a political antifascist refugee (Wallace and Wolf, 1999). Coser arrived in New York via Spain and Portugal and was assigned an agent, Rose Laub, for his case with the International Relief Association. Not only did Coser remain in the United States, but he and Laub also fell in love and were soon married. Rose and Lewis remained happily married, and Coser (1993) claimed that Rose was one of the major influences on his life "I

find it almost impossible to sort out the ideas of hers that later cropped up as mine" (p. 3).

Coser found work with various U.S. government agencies, including, the Office of War Information and the Department of Defense. He also edited a left-wing magazine, *Modern Review*. Meanwhile, Laub had enrolled at Columbia University to study sociology and met Robert Merton. Coser followed in her footsteps, and in 1948, he too enrolled at Columbia as a graduate student. Laub introduced Coser to Merton, who later became one of Coser's greatest academic influences. Coser left Columbia to teach courses on the theories of Weber, Durkheim, and Margaret Mead at the University of Chicago. After two years, however, he left Chicago and returned to Columbia to finish his graduate studies. Coser wrote his dissertation under Merton's guidance. The influence of

Lewis Coser, German-born social thinker, activist, and significant conflict theorist.

Source: Courtesy of the Coser Family and Dept. of Sociology, Stony Brook University

Simmel's ideas is reflected in Coser's work. In 1954, Coser received his Ph.D. from Columbia.

After teaching for a number of years at Brandeis University, Coser taught at the State University of New York (SUNY) at Stony Brook from 1968 to 1988. Since his retirement in 1988, Coser has been professor emeritus of sociology at Stony Brook and adjunct professor of sociology at Boston College. Coser has served as president of the Eastern Sociological Society, president of the American Sociological Association, and president of the Society for the Study of Social Problems. In 1954, he cofounded, with Irving Howe, the magazine *Dissent*, during the height of the Joseph McCarthy "red scare." *Dissent* was created to wake people up—especially intellectual spokespersons—from the irrational behavior and intolerance generated by McCarthyism. Coser contributed to such other "nontraditional" academic publications as the *Partisan Review* and *Commentary*.

Coser's academic writings include his first book *Functions of Social Conflict* (1956), *Men of Ideas: A Sociologist's View* (1965b), *The Continuities in the Study of Social Conflict* (1968), *Greedy Institutions: Patterns of Undivided Commitment* (1974), his brilliant review of social theory found in *Masters of Sociological Thought* (1977), and a large number of journal articles. Coser's work reflects the conflict perspective and his life-long concern with protecting human freedoms from oppressive power groups. His work also centers on the analysis of *greedy institutions* that demand total involvement from their members. Coser was concerned with the threat of human freedom inherent in total involvement. He wrote (1974), "I consider it essential that an open society be preserved above all" (p. 17). After a long and productive life, Lewis Coser died on July 8, 2003, in Cambridge, Massachusetts.

Influences on Coser

It should be clear to the reader that Coser's life experiences played a significant role in his outlook on social life. Born and raised as a Jew in Germany, he was forced to escape from his homeland by the oppression of the Nazi regime. He learned firsthand about direct social conflict and the negative effects that a dominant group can have on a subordinate group—a lesson that, once learned, is seldom erased in future attitudes or action. Among the academic influences on Coser are Émile Durkheim, Georg Simmel, Karl Marx, Robert Merton, Talcott Parsons, and Coser's wife, Rose Laub Coser.

Because Durkheim was the central theorist taught at the Sorbonne, it is obvious that Durkheim's work would have an influence on Coser. Durkheim is generally considered one of the founders of functionalist thought, and Coser enjoyed Durkheim's detailed analysis of the structural aspects of society. Coser learned from Durkheim that the social world can be viewed as a system of variously interrelated parts; that all social systems reveal imbalances, tensions, and conflicts of the interests of the various parts; that processes within and between the system's interlocking parts operate under different conditions; and that many processes, such as violence, dissent, deviance, and conflict, can serve as a device of integration (Turner, 1974).

Georg Simmel also had a great influence on Coser. It was his work on conflict that turned Coser's focus to "the conflictual rather than the harmonious aspects of social phenomenon" (Coser, 1993:7). Simmel was interested in the "web of conflict," or the cross-cutting allegiances that can both bind a society together and create antagonism and confrontations. Coser's major work on conflict theory, *The Functions of Social Conflict* (1956), is an exposition of sixteen separate propositions that attempt to develop Simmel's rather fragmented insights (Wallace and Wolf, 1999). Coser (1956) argued that although conflict always exists in society, society also consists of degrees of consensus.

Combining Simmel and Marx's ideas, Coser came to view the causes of conflict as

1. The greater the deprived groups' questioning of the legitimacy of the existing distribution of scarce resources, the more likely they are to initiate conflict.
2. The more a group's deprivations are transformed from absolute to relative, the more likely the group is to initiate conflict. (Turner, 1974)

Coser (1956) also discussed the intensity, duration, and functions of conflict.

Among his contemporaries, Robert Merton, Talcott Parsons, and Rose Laub Coser provided the greatest influence on Coser. Coser worked with Merton on his dissertation, and many of Merton's ideas and concepts are demonstrated in the works of Coser. On his acknowledgments page in the second edition of *Masters of Sociological Thought* (1977), Coser described Merton as his former teacher and long-term friend, who not only suggested the idea of *Masters* and assisted in its inception but also gave crucial support in the completion of both the first and second editions: "Without his sustained attention, searching discussion, and painstaking comment on each chapter, *Masters of Sociological Thought* would never have become what it is" (Coser, 1977:xi). In turn, Merton, wrote the foreword and described Coser's "skill for epitomizing complex ideas without trivializing them enables him to cut deep below the surface to their assumptions" (Coser, 1977:vii). Merton further stated, "With the publication of *Masters of Sociological Thought*, Second Edition, Lewis Coser takes an even more commanding place than before as sociologist and historian of sociological theory" (Coser, 1977:ix).

Coser had great respect for Talcott Parsons, even though at times he disagreed with Parsons's work. Coser was Parsons's opposition, yet there was common ground between the two. Coser (1993) stated, "Even though my first academic publication in American was a critical review of Parsons' *Essays*, I have never changed my opinion that Parsons and Merton are the two towering figures in the twentieth-century American sociology" (p. 8). Coser's greatest admiration was toward his wife, Rose, whom he described (1977) as "my critical superego, sternly insisting on logical and semantic clarity in the formulation of my thoughts and mode of expression" (p. xi).

Lewis Coser made many contributions to sociological social theory. The following sections present a brief review of some of Coser's more significant concepts and contributions.

Conflict Theory

By the late 1950s, many social thinkers in the United States had revitalized Marxist thought into conflict theory. "The revolutionary and activist Marxism first developed by Marx and Engels in the late 1840s found an echo among 20th century intellectuals. . . . Social existence determined social consciousness. The receptivity to variant Marxist doctrine was largely conditioned by the values and attitudes of the men and women whose concrete social and historical existence was mirrored in their world view, whether as producers or as consumers of ideas" (Coser, 1972a:200).

In *The Functions of Social Conflict* (1956), Coser defined and related conflict to the social world, explored the nature of hostility, discussed how conflict can lead to social change, and paid close attention to the role of people's emotions in conflict. Coser (1956) defined conflict as "a struggle over values and claims to scarce status, power and resources in which the aims of the opponents are to neutralize, injure or eliminate their rivals" (p. 8). Coser believed that conflict may take place between individuals, between collectives, or between individuals and collectives. Intergroup and intragroup conflicts are a constant feature of social life (Hilgart, 1997). Coser (1956) defined power as "the chance to influence the behavior of others in accord with one's own wishes"

(p. 134). Determining the level of power that any one group holds depends on its relation to other groups.

Coser agreed with Simmel that there are aggressive or hostile impulses in people, and that in all close and intimate relationships, both love and hate are present. Love and hate are conjoined because contact is constant in close relationships; the closer the contact, the more intense the conflict. Conflict in a relationship often creates instability (Coser, 1956). Because of close proximity, people have many opportunities to develop resentment; consequently, conflict and arguments are integral parts of people's relationships and need not be signs of instability and breakup.

On the other hand, the nature of hostility and conflict varies for sociological reasons, including social structural factors that include financial stability, clearly defined societal rules, love and nurture from the family, and practical and emotional support from outside the nuclear family. Coser's work is an attempt to explain how structural factors interact with people's underlying emotions (Wallace and Wolf, 1999).

Coser came to realize that conflict serves many functions. Conflict often leads to social change, it can stimulate innovation, and during times of external (war) or internal (civil unrest) threat, it leads to an increase in the centralization of power. (Note: This idea was also articulated by Herbert Spencer.) Thus, as the title of his book implies, it was the *functions* of conflict that Coser explored. He presented a number of arguments in the form of sixteen separate propositions. A selected number of these propositions are reviewed next:

Proposition 1: Group-Binding Functions of Conflict

Conflict serves as an important agent in establishing full ego identity, autonomy, and differentiation of personality from the outside world. Conflict with other groups increases a group's consciousness and awareness of separateness and establishes boundaries between groups. A group is bound together by the individual members' similarities and the reinforcing of group awareness of such similarities. The realization of differences from other groups establishes and strengthens the group's identity. Conflict helps to create and maintain group cohesion. With a high level of conflict comes a high level of group cohesion. Each group relies on conflict for its identity and for the maintenance of the boundaries that divide it from the rest of the social world. Conflict, then, is essential to a society (Coser, 1956).

Proposition 4: Conflict and Hostile Influences

Social conflict cannot be accounted for by drives, impulses, and isolated instances of behavior; rather, it is explained by a pattern of interaction. Aggressive behavior is related to a group's structure of interactive relations. The structural variable linked to direct aggression is the degree of group cohesion. Coser (1956) defined *direct aggression* as "aggression expressed toward members of the group" (p. 57). In unorganized groups, there are many instances of aggression. Therefore, high group cohesion leads to high amounts of aggression (Coser, 1956).

Proposition 5: Hostility in Close Social Relationships

Love and hate are intricately linked. "One frequently hates the person one loves; hence it is often invalid to separate the two elements in concrete reality (Coser, 1956:60). (Note: There is a popular song lyric that expresses this idea: "It's a thin line between love and hate.") This idea is most accurately applied to close, intimate relationships rather than all social relationships. The closer the relationship, the greater the investment, which leads to a likelihood of suppressed, rather than expressed, hostile feelings. This suppression is due to a fear of putting the relationship in danger. As hostility continues to be suppressed, these emotions accumulate and intensify. This intensity creates feelings of hatred, which may eventually be expressed in direct aggression. Therefore, the love-hate phenomenon found in intimate relationships helps to support Coser's contention that the high instances of direct aggression are found in highly cohesive groups. Studies of domestic violence could benefit from Coser's analysis of conflict in loving, close relationships.

Proposition 7: Impact of Conflict on Group Structures

As previously noted, close relationships may exhibit tendencies toward the suppression of conflict. If conflict should occur despite suppression, it tends to be disruptive to the relationship because of the intensity expressed. This intensity is attributed to the total involvement of the personality and the accumulation of hostility. Therefore, it is accurate for the participants to fear conflict because of the effects it may have on the relationship (Coser, 1956).

Proposition 10: Conflict with Another Group that Defines Group Structure

When conflict occurs between groups, the members of each group become more cohesive. They depend on each other's loyalty and dedication in order for the group to come out of the conflict victorious. Groups in conflict expect their individual members to be entirely involved. For example, bickering family members unite when a threat from the outside challenges the very survival of the family. A group engaged in continued struggle with other groups tends to be intolerant of individual deviations within the group. A member of a threatened group may be allowed only limited departures from group unity. Those who choose to deviate must either volunteer or be forced to withdraw from the group. This proposition helped Coser form his future ideas on *greedy institutions* and their demand for total involvement. Coser and his wife described in *Dissent* how the People's Temple cult and the Jonestown tragedy were an example of a greedy institution that expected such a degree of commitment from the group that the members moved away from their homes and loved ones and eventually committed group suicide (Coser and Coser, 1979).

Concluding and Connecting the Functions of Social Conflict

Social conflict creates boundaries between different groups, which, in turn, creates a strong unity between the individual members of a group. Not only does social conflict promote cohesion in individual groups, but it also promotes coalitions and associations with outside groups. Several groups may be threatened by one single other group, so they may unite to fight the single threatening group. Therefore, social conflict creates an increase in cohesion inside a group and among several groups which, if not in conflict, would not normally unite.

Social Change

In a variation of the organic analogy, Coser (1967) explained that a society does not die the way biological organisms do, nor is there a precise point of birth. Furthermore, a society may change or form a new system rather than die. In *Continuities in the Study of Social Conflict* (1967), Coser discussed his theory of *social change*. *Continuities* was designed to update and supplement *The Function of Social Change* (1967). Coser explained that social life always involves change and that societies are not born and do not die as a living organism would. Societies change and evolve over time and have no set pattern. He refered to Talcott Parsons's distinction between change *within* a system and change *of* a system, to demonstrate the two different types of social change that can occur.

Change *within* a system is very slow and marginal. It involves an adjustment of some type within the system itself (Coser, 1967). Such changes are caused by individual members of a society who have deviated from its traditional ways. The second type of change, change *of* a system, involves a more radical change, such as the creation of new institutions within the system (for example, a new economic or political system). Social change of the system involves the entire society's parting from old traditions and embracing new, acceptable norms and expectations of universal behavior. In this regard, the system is actually altered and changed. New things can be added, or old things can be eliminated, and this process may continue indefinitely. In short, social change may result because of external forces, or it may result because of changes within the system (Coser, 1967).

Violence

Violence and conflict are often linked, and therefore, violence itself can lead to social change. Coser believed that violence serves three specific social functions. The first is violence as achievement. Causing violence is an achievement for some people, and the more violence they cause, the more they achieve in their own minds. As Merton articulated in his anomie theory on social deviance, society does not provide equal opportunity for all members to achieve the success goal. Consequently, some people deviate from the normal expectations of behavior and commit acts of deviance, including violence, as a means of achieving success (Coser, 1967).

The second function of violence is as a danger signal. Violence often alerts society and its members to underlying problems that need to be corrected. It acts as a warning signal (or a social barometer) that some course of action must be taken, for clearly a number of people are frustrated by the social system if they feel it necessary to turn to violence to gain attention.

The third function of violence in society is as a catalyst. This catalyst function can start the process of "correction" in solving a social problem, or it can cause an increased level of violence. "Whether given forms of conflict will lead to changes in the social system or to breakdown and to formation of a new system will depend on the rigidity and resistance to change, or inversely on the elasticity of the control mechanisms of the system" (Coser, 1967:29). Violence arouses the public and informs it that something needs to be done about specific social issues. When the society unites to solve the problem, the catalyst has

completed its job. However, violence can act as a catalyst to cause more problems and attract others to join in the violence. Coser (1967) believed that violence has both positive and negative functions in society and viewed it as a necessary aspect of society.

Intellectuals

Coser worked within the tradition of Richard Hofstader in his work on *intellectuals*. According to Coser, Hofstader made distinctions between intelligence and intellect by stating, "Intellect is the critical, creative, and contemplative side of mind. Whereas intelligence seeks to grasp, manipulate, re-order, adjust, intellect examines, ponders, wonders, theorizes, criticizes, imagines" (Coser, 1965b:viii).

Coser (1965) listed five types of intellectuals:

1. **Unattached:** Intellectuals "independent" of structural constraints. They may include, but are not limited to, professional authors. Coser (1965b) stated that this type of intellectual was few in number in contemporary America.
2. **Academic:** Those persons who are tied to an educational institution and devote their lives to research and teaching. Most of these people hold Ph.D.'s, but not all professors with Ph.D.'s are intellectuals. Academic intellectuals are often characterized by their nonacceptance of intellectual status; they tend to be modest. Coser (1982) wrote an article in honor of Al Gouldner as such an intellectual: "What characterizes Al's work, in addition to the generous combativeness, and the combination of sociological imagination, radical stance, and commitment to the role of the intellectual, was the catholicity of his concerns" (p. 886).
3. **Scientific:** Also called *creative intellectuals*. According to Coser (1965b), all scientists considered intellectuals have made major contributions to science.
4. **Washington:** Coser (1965b) identified two different types of intellectuals in Washington: those who had become government officials as a career and those "transitional" intellectuals

who had joined the administration during periods of national emergency or political change. Career officials tended to identify their careers with service in the federal bureaucracy and highly depended on it. These career officials "perform staff functions in helping to formulate or implement policies within a public bureaucracy" (Coser, 1965b:315). Transitional Washington intellectuals, or ad hoc bureaucrats, did not anticipate a permanent governmental career. Thus, they were "less likely to be constrained by bureaucratic pressures, for they do not affiliate permanently with public administration and have ready alternatives in private life or academic positions" (Coser, 1965b:315). When describing this type of intellectual, Coser may have reflected on his own life as a transitional intellectual immediately following his arrival in the United States.

5. **Mass-culture industries:** Intellectuals involved in productions such as movies and magazines. In mass-culture industries, there is a highly developed division of labor, in which no one person has control over the outcome of a particular product. Instead, production is looked at as a group effort, and the product emerges from the workers' coordinated efforts (Coser, 1965b). An example comes from the motion picture industry, where the final product—the film—is the result of the efforts of actors, extras, directors, producers, sound effects engineers, and many other creative people.

Coser concluded that having intellect is not the same as having intelligence. "Intellectuals live for, rather than, off ideas" (Coser, 1965:viii). Intellectuals are found in all spheres of society and contribute to social change through their visionary ideas. Coser (1965b) feared that American society had become too bureaucratic, and that it needed to find a way to inspire others intellectually, in order to end its multitude of social problems.

Social Theory and Methodology

Coser's contributions to social theory were not limited to his works and ideas centered on the conflict perspective. His *Masters of*

Sociological Thought (1977) was once a classic textbook in graduate and undergraduate social theory courses. In this text, Coser provided a detailed description of a number of social theorists. The chapters are divided into five sections: the work, the theorist, the intellectual context, the social context, and a summary of each theorist. Coser provided a wealth of information and offered often brilliant insights into the work of each theorist. Unfortunately, students often found the book difficult to read. It lacks a full bibliographical listing, and the order of the contents within each chapter often make the reading even more difficult. Regardless of these minor criticisms, Coser illustrated the importance of detailing the biography of each social thinker, for one's personal life most assuredly affects one's outlook on the social world. The influences on each theorist reveal the fact that each bit of current knowledge is a mere extension or reinterpretation of past thoughts and ideas. The need to describe the contributions of each theorist is self-evident.

Coser (1976) always emphasized the need for a balanced assessment of theoretical trends. He maintained that each theoretical perspective must be given time to flourish and grow: "Just like young trees that have only begun to bear fruit, their ultimate worth will have to be judged by a generation that is able to evaluate the quality of their products. Some of them, no doubt, will turn out to have been barren, while others will have produced an abundant harvest" (p. 158).

In support of the conflict perspective, Coser (1964) warned that "sociological theory tends too frequently to focus attention exclusively on the dominant norms and patterns of behavior and to disregard the tensions and dysfunctions that full adherence to those norms might entail" (p. 884). In addition, in pursuit of the sociology of knowledge and sound social theory, Coser (1988) recommended utilizing a number of methodological techniques. "The traditional view in the philosophy of science has assumed that there existed a close link between the logic of scientific procedure and the substantive results of empirical inquiry. This view has now been sharply challenged by post-positivist scholars who have demonstrated that the relations between methodology and substantive findings are much looser than had previously been assumed" (p. 85). Furthermore, in his 1975 presidential address delivered at the annual meeting of the American Sociological Association, Coser stated, "I am perturbed about present developments in American sociology which seem to foster the growth of both narrow, routine activities, and of sect-like, esoteric ruminations" (p. 691).

Lewis Coser made a number of significant and lasting contributions to sociological thought. His work as a conflict theorist who attempted to incorporate some of the basic constructs of functionalism is a wonderful addition to social theory. Many of his ideas will remain relevant well into the third millennium. In all societies, conflict is inevitable. Conflict serves to bind members of a group together, and it determines the boundaries of power.

C. WRIGHT MILLS (1916–1962)

C. Wright Mills was born in Waco, Texas, on August 28, 1916, into a middle-class Catholic household. His father was an insurance broker and his mother was a homemaker. By 1939 he had earned both his bachelor's and master's degrees from the University of Texas. He left Texas, for the first time in his life, to work on his doctoral studies at the University of Wisconsin (he had won a research fellowship there). At Wisconsin, Mills studied under Hans Gerth, a German émigré. "Far from the usual student-professor relationship, they soon engaged in a series of collaborative works focusing on social psychology and introducing the work of the German sociologist Max Weber to an English-speaking audience" (Kivisto, 1998:36). While working on his doctorate, Mills taught for a while at the

University of Maryland. The proximity to Washington, D.C., provided Mills his first taste for political life and an exposure to true power.

After earning his Ph.D., Mills moved to New York City and accepted a position at Columbia University in 1945. Mills wrote for many left-wing journals, including the *New Leader*, the *New Republic*, the *Partisan Review*, and the union journal *Labor and Nation* (Scimecca, 1977). He remained at Columbia until his untimely death in 1962 from his fourth heart attack. He was just forty-five when he died, but as we shall see, he contributed a great deal to sociological theory. Among the books that he authored are *The New Men of Power* (1948), *White Collar* (1951), *The Power Elite* (1956), *The Causes of World War Three* (1958a), *The Sociological Imagination* (1959), and *The Marxists* (1962). Mills coauthored other books and published numerous journal articles as well.

The Social Context

C. Wright Mills was a colorful person who seemed to be surrounded by controversy. Ritzer (2000a:67) described Mills's private life as combative and tumultuous, characterized by many affairs and three marriages (there was a child from each marriage). He fought with professors while he was a graduate student and with his colleagues at Columbia. Horowitz (1983) described how Mills published a vaguely disguised critique of the ex-chair at Wisconsin and referred to the senior theorist at Wisconsin, Howard Becker, as a "real fool." Mills even turned on his friend and coauthor Hans Gerth. Gerth retaliated by calling Mills a "cowboy"—as in "a la ride and shoot" (Horowitz, 1983:72). (Note: The term *cowboy* was certainly not meant as a compliment.) According to Kivisto (1998), "Mills had an uncanny ability to irritate people who had befriended him. His life comprised a series of fallings-out with such people, beginning with Gerth and continuing through to include Bell, Macdonald and other luminaries in the New York intellectual scene, and his sociology colleagues at Columbia" (p. 37).

Mills had also established an academic reputation for himself upon his arrival at Columbia, having been published in sociology's major journals (Ritzer, 2000). And yet, his reputation as a rebel and a cowboy, combined with the conservative climate of the times, led to continued complications in Mills's life. As Garner (2000) explained, "Of Texan origin, which contributed to his image as a maverick and radical from the heartland, he was a professor of sociology at Columbia University during the most intense period of the Cold War. The 1950s was a period of political timidity and enforced conformity when many intellectuals avoided expressing ideas and opinions for which they could have been labeled as reds or subversives. Mills courageously opposed this political timidity in his writing and teaching" (p. 322). Despite his growing marginality, Mills did not soften his positions. If anything, he became more vitriolic with the passage of time (Kivisto, 1998).

Mills was critical both of the trends of contemporary sociology and of society. He more than challenged the status quo. He questioned "grand theorizing" and the unbreakable commitment to positivism (at a time when few American sociologists had). He challenged Talcott Parsons, the dominant theorist of his day, and Paul Lazarsfeld, the dominant methodologist and Mills's colleague at Columbia. His disdain toward empirical research was the result of his belief that fragmented data collected from questionnaire responses were no substitute for a broad historical and political understanding of society (Garner, 2000). A commitment to the historical method was just one of Marx's influences on Mills. The criticism that Mills directed toward American society earned him a visit to the Soviet Union, where he was

honored as a major critic of American society. However, true to his confrontational nature, Mills "took the occasion to attack the censorship in the Soviet Union with a toast to an early Soviet leader who had been purged and murdered by the Stalinists: 'To the day when the complete works of Leon Trotsky are published in the Soviet Union'" (Ritzer, 2000:67; the toast quoted from Tilman, 1884:8).

Conflict Theory

Like other conflict theorists, Mills was deeply influenced by the ideas of Karl Marx and Marxist thought. Mills helped to introduce American sociologists to Marxism through his edited anthology, *The Marxists* (1962). Mills did not describe himself as a Marxist, however, as he found clear differences between his ideas and those of Marx.

C. Wright Mills, controversial, brilliant American social thinker and conflict theorist.
Source: Courtesy of Kathryn Mills

Mills did not see all inequality as emerging from the mode of production; like Weber, he identified several distinct dimensions of inequality and treated power as a variable that can be independent from economic class. The concept of power elite, rather than ruling class, signals this difference between Mills and Marxists. He did not insist on the bourgeoisie and the proletariat as the antagonistic classes of a polarized structure, nor did he share Marxist ideas about the unfolding of a historical process. In many ways, his version of conflict theory was much closer to Weber than to Marx, and his concerns about the direction of society overlapped and updated Weber's critique of bureaucracy and formal rationality. Mills also differed from many Marxists in his commitment to North American traditions of social criticism and radical democracy. His solution to the economic inequalities and power differences in corporate America was not a vanguard party and a proletarian revolution, but a reopening of political debate, public discussion, and citizen participation in politics. (Garner, 2000:323)

Political power and class differences were the focus of Mills's publications. *The New Men of Power* (1948) is a study of the American labor movement. In this book, Mills wrote that the working class is not a revolutionary class capable of overthrowing capitalism. He did not believe that the rank-and-file workers were a militant force, and that they were more concerned with basic daily issues than with seeking loftier goals. Furthermore, Mills concluded that labor leaders did not work in the best interests of their workers and were instead coopted by business and government (Kivisto, 1998:37). He believed that most union leaders resembled the character of their organizations, and that few union leaders possessed any real power. Mills (1948) wrote, "It is the task of the labor leaders to allow and to initiate a union of the power and the intellect. They are the only ones who can do it; that is why they are now the strategic elite in American society. Never has so much depended upon

men who are so ill-prepared and so little inclined to assume the responsibility" (p. 291). Because of this lack of leadership, the working class could never become a revolutionary force.

Power

Power is the critical element of analysis for all conflict theorists. This is especially true of C. Wright Mills. "His work remained centered on power—the nature of power, the distribution of power, the uses and abuses of power, the person of power, the power of organizations, the myths of power, the evolution of power, the irrationality of power, and the means of observing and comprehending power in the vastness of modern society" (Cuzzort and King, 1995:178–79). Mills wrote in "The Promise" (1959) that people feel that their lives are a series of traps.

> "They sense that within their everyday worlds, they cannot overcome their troubles, and in this feeling, they are often quite correct: What ordinary men are directly aware of and what they try to do are bounded by the private orbits in which they live; their visions and their powers are limited to the close-up scenes of job, family, neighborhood; in other milieu, they move vicariously and remain spectators. And the more aware they become, however vaguely, of ambitions and of threats which transcend their immediate locales, the more trapped they seem to feel. (Mills, 2002:1–2)

In "The Structure of Power in American Society" (1958b), Mills wrote that "power has to do with whatever decisions men make about the arrangements under which they live, and about the events which make up the history of their times. Events that are beyond human decision do happen; social arrangements do change without the benefit of explicit decision. But in so far as such decisions are made, the problem of who is involved in making them is the basic problem of power" (p.29). Mills (1958) questioned whether American society was truly a society were citizens were ruled by consent and instead suggested that those in power managed to manipulate the consent.

Mills (1958b) described three types of power:

1. **Authority:** Power that is justified by the beliefs of the voluntarily obedient.
2. **Manipulation:** Power that is wielded unbeknownst to the powerless.
3. **Coercion:** The "final" form of power, where the powerless are forced to obey the powerful.

Mills acknowledged that in the modern era, power is more likely to be authoritarian. And yet, the reality remains that most people will always be relatively powerless. Marx wrote in *The 18th Brumaire of Louis Bonaporte* (1852) that "all men are free to make their own history" (p. 31), but Mills (1958b) said that "some men are indeed much freer than others." The reason is that freedom requires access to the means of decision and power.

Major decisions regarding the course of history are made by political, military, and economic institutions, which, according to Mills, make up the power elite. Mills stated that this "triangle of power" is a structural fact and the key to understanding American society.

The Power Elite

Mills was convinced that the American military, industry, and politics were integrated. This connection concerned Mills because "it can lead to a disengagement of leadership from the problems of the people that leadership is supposed to represent" (Cuzzort and King, 1995:179). In *The Power Elite* (1956), Mills wrote:

> The power elite is composed of men whose positions enable them to transcend the ordinary environments of ordinary men and women; they are in positions to make decisions having major consequences. Whether they do or do not make such decisions is less important than the fact that they do occupy such pivotal positions: their failure

to act, their failure to make decisions, is itself an act that is often of greater consequence than the decisions they do make. For they are in command of the major hierarchies and organizations of modern society. They rule the big corporations. They run the machinery of the state and claim its prerogatives. They direct the military establishment. They occupy the strategic command posts of the social structure, in which are now centered the effective means of the power and the wealth and the celebrity which they enjoy. (pp. 3–4)

Mills was concerned that this "triangle of power" or "tripartite elite" was an increasing threat to American democracy.

Mills (1958b) explained the unity of the power elite in psychological and economic terms. The members of the power elite generally share a similar origin, education, and style of life, and because of their similar social type, they easily intermingle. Additionally, since they are the "elites" of society, they share economic goals.

The social context of the mid-1950s was clearly an influence on Mills's writings regarding the power elite. American military technology was superior, the economy was strong but becoming increasingly dependent on foreign markets, and a repressive political climate existed because of the Cold War; all contributed to Mills's "conspiracy" theory of the power elite.

Mills acknowledged that the power elites were not solitary rulers. They were assisted by the advisers and consultants, the spokespeople and opinion makers, and the captains of industry. Immediately below the elite were the professional politicians, as well as those of the new and old upper classes. Thus, the power elites are those who possess scarce resources. As Mills (1956) explained, "The higher circles in and around these command posts are often thought of in terms of what their members possess: they have a greater share than other people of the things and experiences that are most highly valued. From this point of view, the elite are simply those who have the most of what there is to have, which is generally held to include money, power, and prestige—as well as all the ways of life to which these lead" (p. 9). However, simply possessing more scarce resources than others does not automatically bring wealthy people power; such people must be in a position to command situations. Mills (1956) stated, "By powerful we mean, of course, those who are able to realize their will, even if others resist it. No one, accordingly, can be truly powerful unless he has access to the command of major institutions, for it is over these institutional means of power that the truly powerful are, in the first instance, powerful. Higher politicians and key officials of government command such institutional power; so do admirals and generals, and so do the major owners and executives of the larger corporations" (p. 9).

From a Marxist perspective, Mills felt that the American people were subjected to "the will of the bourgeoisie." It is always in the best interests of the powerful to maintain the status quo. Therefore, they promote a conservative society, where challenges to authority are discouraged. History has shown that when extreme conservatism is met with a dramatically changing society, conflict is inevitable. "The challenges to the elite that burst onto the cultural and political landscape in the 1960s—the civil rights movements, the antiwar movement, and the counterculture—called into question Mills's pessimistic assessments" (Kivisto, 1998:40). Mills did not live to see these radical forces of social change, as he died in 1962.

White-Collar Worker

Among the more significant socioeconomic transformations to occur during Mills's lifetime was the development of a new middle class, which was composed mostly of a huge sales force, technicians, administrators, clerical workers, civil servants, and low-level managers and supervisors. In contrast to their blue-collar counterparts, who were paid for manual labor, white-collar workers were employed for their mental labor. In his 1946 article "The Middle Classes in Middle-sized Cities," Mills stated that "theories of the rise to power of white-collar people are generally inferred from the facts of their numerical growth and their indispensability in the bureaucratic and distributive operations of mass society. But only if one assumes a pure and automatic democracy of numbers does the mere growth of a stratum mean increased power for it. And only if one assumes a magic leap from occupational function does technical indispensability mean power for a stratum" (p. 529).

The rising number of white-collar workers did not equate with a new challenge in power. For at the top of the white-collar world remained the old captains of industries who handed over tasks to the managers of the corporations, who in turn gave orders to the workers (Mills, 1951). Mills recognized the importance of studying the growing white-collar world:

> By examining white-collar life, it is possible to learn something about what is becoming more typically "American" than the frontier character probably ever was. What must be grasped is the picture of society as a great salesroom, an enormous file, an incorporated brain, a new universe of management and manipulation. By understanding these diverse white-collar worlds, one can also understand better the shape and meaning of modern society as a whole, as well as the simple hopes and complex anxieties that grip all the people who are sweating it out in the middle of the twentieth century. (p. xv)

Mills's exploration of the white-collar world was groundbreaking work at the time of its publication, and his style of critique was evident throughout *White Collar* (1951). As Kivisto (1998) explained:

> In chapters with such provocative titles as "The Managerial Demiurge," "Brains, Inc.," "The Great Salesroom," and "The Enormous File," Mills (1951), in a style reminiscent of

Veblen, examined the social psychology, the cultural orientations, and the political proclivities of the new middle class. Although conceding that it was premature to draw many conclusions about the character of the new middle class, Mills nonetheless suspected that their location in the middle of the class structure inclined them to be moderate, careful, and conformist in matters cultural and political. The dramatic growth of this class encouraged the homogenizing tendencies of mass society. (p. 38)

Thus, the white-collar world served to maintain the advantageous position of the power elite. On the other hand, white-collar workers enjoyed a certain amount of prestige based on their advantageous position over blue-collar workers and the poor. "White-collar people's claims to prestige are expressed, as their label implies, by their style of appearance. Their occupations enable and require them to wear street clothes at work. Although they may be expected to dress somewhat somberly, still, their working attire is not a uniform" (Mills, 1951:241). Approximately fifty years later corporate America would allow "casual Friday" as another clothing concession to the power of the white-collar worker. The conservative hold that the power elite exhibit over the white-collar worker is still quite evident at the beginning of the third millennium.

Social Motivation

Mills's interest in the sociological motivation of actors dated back to his days at the University of Wisconsin and his published article "Situated Actions and Vocabularies of Motive" (1940). Mills (1940) acknowledged that human actors vocalize and impute motives to themselves and to others. Motives are influenced by many variables and are primarily acted on because of an interpretation of the conduct of other social actors. Thus, individual action is motivated by the social conduct of others. The task of the researcher is to locate "particular types of

action within typal frames of normative actions and socially situated clusters of motive" (Mills, 1940:913).

In *Character and Social Structure* (1953) Mills and coauthor Hans Gerth expanded on the idea of *social motivation* in a chapter entitled "The Sociology of Motivation." "In terms of the *person* we might assume that conduct is motivated by the *expectations* of others, which are internalized from the roles which persons enact, and that important aspects of such motivation are the vocabularies of motive which are learned and used by persons in various roles. Motivation thus has to do with the balance of self-image with appraisals of others" (Gerth and Mills, 1953:112).

With the development of the white-collar professions came increased specialization and a clear division of labor. As a result, individuals became more concerned with their own needs than with those of a collectivity. From a Marxist standpoint, there was no motivation to revolt against the capitalists. Consequently, white-collar workers lack a *class consciousness*. "It is said that people in the United States are not aware of themselves as members of classes, do not identify themselves with their appropriate economic level, do not often organize in terms of these brackets or vote along the lines they provide. America, in this reasoning, is a sandheap of 'middle-class individuals'" (Mills, 1951:294).

The Sociological Imagination

Perhaps the single concept that Mills is most known for is the *sociological imagination*. The sociological imagination reveals how our private lives are influenced by the social environment and the existing social forces. The sociologist can gain insights into human behavior by utilizing the sociological imagination. According to Mills (1959):

The sociological imagination enables its possessor to understand the larger historical scene in terms of its meanings for the inner life and the external career of a variety of individuals. It enables him to take into account how individuals, in the welter of their daily experience, often become falsely conscious of their social positions. Within that welter, the framework of modern society is sought, and within that framework the psychologies of a variety of men and women are formulated. By such means the personal uneasiness of individuals is focused upon explicit troubles and the indifference of publics is transformed into involvement with public issues. (p. 5)

The sociological imagination emphasizes the importance of the historical social context in which an individual is found. Combining personal biography with current behavior allows the sociologist to better understand the individual.

To highlight the importance of this point, Mills made distinctions between "the personal troubles of milieu" and "the public issues of social structure." According to Mills (1959) "this distinction is an essential tool of the sociological imagination and a feature of all classic work in social science" (p. 8):

1. *Troubles* occur within the character of the individual and within the range of her or his immediate relations with others. They have to do with the self and with those limited areas of social life of which the person is directly and personally aware.

2. *Issues* transcend these local environments of the individual and the range of her or his inner life. They have to do with the organization of many milieux into the institutions of a historical society as a whole and form the larger structure of social and historical life.

With this reasoning, the sociologist acknowledges that social forces, often out of the control of the individual, affect the individual's life for both the good and the bad. For example, if a company goes bankrupt and lays off all its workers, the individual employees need not view themselves negatively, because they could not control the causes of their dismissal.

RALF DAHRENDORF (1929–)

Ralf Dahrendorf was born in Hamburg, Germany, in 1929. This time was a turbulent period in Germany. His father was a Social Democratic politician, a member of the Hamburg Diet at the time of Ralf's birth, and then later a member of the German Parliament (the Reichstag). The Social Democrats had political differences with both the Nazis and the Communists. The senior Dahrendorf would lose his job when the Nazis came into power in 1933. Unemployed, he moved his family to Berlin. Ralf's father was arrested twice. The second time he was sentenced to seven years in prison—and was released by the Russians at the end of the war.

Ralf Dahrendorf was also involved in opposition to the Nazi regime. In late November 1944, Dahrendorf was arrested by the Gestapo for letters that he and his friend had written to each other. Dahrendorf was sent to a concentration camp east of the Oder River, in what is now Poland. Dahrendorf escaped on January 29, 1945, while the German guards battled with the Russian army. Throughout his life, Dahrendorf has actively participated in political groups that fight injustice.

In 1952, Dahrendorf earned his first doctorate in philosophy, with classics as the subsidiary subject, from the University of Hamburg. He then moved to London and to the London School of Economics, where he later earned his doctorate in sociology. Dahrendorf is a widely respected social scientist in both Europe and North America. He has held academic positions in Germany, Great Britain, and the United States, including the position of director of the London School of Economics from 1974 to 1984. Lord Dahrendorf is a life peer and consequently a member of the British House of Lords (the upper house of Parliament) (Wallace and Wolf, 1999).

Conflict Theory

At the beginning of this chapter it was explained that functional theorists believe that society is held together informally by norms, values, and a general consensus on issues of morality. Additionally, functionalists believe that society is in a state of moving equilibrium—a slow, evolutionary growth that leads to orderly social change. Conflict theorists, especially Ralf Dahrendorf, believe that social order is maintained through coercion by those at the top or, as Mills put it the power elites. Consequently, tension is a constant in society, and radical social change is likely at any point, in any given society. "For Dahrendorf, the social world is composed of 'imperatively coordinated associations' . . . which represent, in terms of criteria not specified, a distinguishable organization of roles. This organization is characterized by power relationships with some clusters of roles having power over others" (Turner, 1973:236).

Dahrendorf (1959) believed that sociological theories should be divided into two parts: those that concentrate on issues of consensus and those that concentrate on issues of conflict. Dahrendorf believed that conflict and consensus are both evident in any society. In fact, there cannot be conflict unless some degree of consensus has already been established. In other words, one cannot be in conflict with another until there is a lack of consensus on a matter. When a consensus has been reached, conflict disappears, temporarily.

As to whether or not conflict and consensus theories can be linked, Dahrendorf (1959) stated:

> Inevitably, the question will be raised, also, whether a unified theory of society that includes the tenets of both the integration and the coercion models of society is not at least conceivable—for as to its desirability there can be little doubt. Is there, or can there be, a general point of view that synthesizes the unsolved dialectics of integration and coercion? So far as I can see, there is no such general model; as to its possibility, I have to reserve judgment. It seems at least conceivable that unification of theory is not feasible

at a point which has puzzled thinkers ever since the beginning of Western philosophy. (p. 164)

Dahrendorf (1959:162) referred to his conflict theory as the "coercion theory of society," which can be reduced to a small number of basic tenets:

1. Every society is at every point subject to processes of change; social change is ubiquitous.
2. Every society displays at every point dissensus and conflict; social conflict is ubiquitous.
3. Every element in a society renders a contribution to its disintegration and change.
4. Every society is based on the coercion of some of its members by others.

Dahrendorf disagreed with Marx that economic forces are the sole determinant of conflict in society. He believed that the unequal distribution of political power was also a major contributor to conflict. According to Dahrendorf (1959), the structural organization of society and groups is designed so that "some positions are entrusted with a right to exercise control over other positions in order to ensure effective coercion; it means, in other words, that there is a differential distribution of power and authority" (p. 165). Thus, the bases of conflict, and of Dahrendorf's conflict theory, are the concepts of power and authority.

Power and Authority

In the tradition of all conflict theorists, Dahrendorf believed that power and authority are scarce resources, and that those who have them hope to maintain the status quo, while those who lack power and authority hope to attain some portion of them. Dahrendorf (1959) assumed that the differential distribution of power and authority becomes the basis of conflict. "Identification of variously equipped authority roles is the first task of conflict analysis; conceptually and empirically all further steps of analysis follow from the investigation of distributions of power and authority" (Dahrendorf, 1959:-165–166). Dahrendorf believed that power implies the coercion of some by others but recognized that in organizations and associations, the power held by certain persons is legitimate authority (Turner, 1973). In making a distinction from Marx, however, Dahrendorf suggested that authority is not bound by property rights and therefore believed that "class conflict is best seen as arising out of a dispute over the distribution of authority in a given authority structure" (Lopreato, 1967:281).

Dahrendorf used the same definitions of power and authority as Weber (discussed earlier in this chapter). Dahrendorf stated that the important difference between power and authority is that power is essentially tied to the personality of individuals, whereas authority is always associated with social positions or roles. Dahrendorf (1959:166–167) was most interested in the study of authority and came to the following conclusions:

1. Authority relations are always of superordination—and subordination.
2. Where there are authority relations, the superordinate element is socially expected to control, by orders and commands, warnings and prohibitions, the behavior of the subordinate element.
3. Such expectations attach to relatively permanent social positions rather than to the character of individuals; they are in this sense legitimate.
4. Therefore, they always involve a specification of the persons subject to control and of the spheres within which control is permissible. Authority, as distinct from power, is never generalized control over others.
5. Authority being legitimate, noncompliance with authoritative commands can be sanctioned; it is indeed one of the functions of the legal system (and of course of quasi-legal customs and norms) to support the effective exercise of legitimate authority.

In his studies of authority, Dahrendorf also utilized the terms *domination* and *subjection* synonymously.

Two other issues related to authority are also noteworthy. Since authority lies in the position that one holds, it does not extend to other social arenas, and persons who lose their authority also lose their position. For example, nearly everyone has a "boss" who holds legitimate authority. But one person's boss does not have authority over someone outside that setting. Thus, someone can occupy a position of authority in one setting and a subordinate position in another. Additionally, a boss who is fired, resigns, or retires no longer has authority over his or her subordinates. With these ideas in mind, Dahrendorf argued that society is composed of *imperatively coordinated associations* (Max Weber used the term *Herrschaftsverband*). Since imperative coordination, or authority, is a type of social relation present in every conceivable social organization, it is sufficient to describe such organizations simply as associations. These associations are coordinated as organized aggregates of roles by domination and subjection because, in all associations, authority exists. "Authority relations exist wherever there are people whose actions are subject to legitimate and sanctioned prescriptions that originate outside them but within social structure. This formulation, by leaving open who exercises what kind of authority leaves little doubt as to the omnipresence of some kind of authority somehow exercised. For it is evident that there are many forms and types of authority in historical societies" (Dahrendorf, 1959:168). More important, Dahrendorf argued that domination and subjection are a common feature of all possible types of authority.

Class Theory

Dahrendorf explained that the concept of class has invariably displayed a peculiar explosiveness. "If the sociologist uses the concept of class he not only must carefully explain in which of its many meanings he wants it to be understood, but also must expect objections that are dictated less by scientific insight than by political prejudice. . . . Evaluative shifts of meaning have accompanied the concept of class throughout its history" (Dahrendorf, 1959:3). The Romans introduced the word *classis* to divide the population into tax groups, but with this economic distinction came an evaluative one as well. This is true of the American term *income bracket*, which, along with its statistical category, touches on the vulnerable point of social inequality.

Using the historical method in his analysis of class theory, Dahrendorf highlighted the significance of industrialization (as have all historically conscious sociologists). "With the industrial revolution, the history of the concept of class as a tool of social analysis began" (Dahrendorf, 1959:4). Dahrendorf (1959) examined Marx's class theory and pointed out that "Marx regarded the theory of class as so important that he postponed its systematic exposition time and again in favor of refinements by empirical analysis" (p. 8). Marx came to the conclusion that society is a two-class system, the proletariat falling far short of reaching their full human potential because of their limited access to society's scarce resources. His solution to this problem was the promotion of a classless society (under communism), where there is no private property and the people share equally in the resources.

As any student of social theory and Marxist thought is aware, it is commonplace today to point out the many flaws in Marx's general class theory because of his failure to predict the significant changes that occurred in the capitalist system (for example, the rise of the middle class, profit sharing, and stock options). Dahrendorf commented, however, that to ignore Marx completely would be "naive and irresponsible." Marx believed that the theory of class involved a systematic analysis of the causes of the endogenous

structural change in societies. At the root of all social change is social conflict. For Dahrendorf (1959) class theory can be defined as

> the systematic explanation of that particular form of structure-changing conflict which is carried on by aggregates or groups growing out of the authority structure of social organizations. The general theory of class precedes the empirical analysis of given societies in terms of class in that it states the underlying regularities of class conflict in a form that in principle allows application to all societies. But the following formulation of the theory of class does not claim universal applicability, for such applicability is always subject to the test of empirical research; it is confined, instead, to that type of society which we have described as industrial society. (p. 152)

Clearly, Dahrendorf believed that the sociologist can uncover key elements of society, through empirical methods, to the point where a class theory can be applied. He was quick to note that generalizing class theory from one society to another is problematic in that each society is unique.

According to Dahrendorf (1959:153–154), to create a general theory of class, two analytically separable elements must be addressed: the *theory of class formation* and the *theory of class action*, or class conflict.

1. **The Theory of Class Formation:** Concerned with the question of analyzing the "genesis" of social classes. The theory must establish relations which connect the specific "real phenomenon" class by way of the "theoretical phenomenon" class with patterns of social structure, and in this sense derive social classes from social structure.

2. **The Theory of Class Action:** Based on the theory of class formation. Its subject matter consists of the general analytical elements of the interrelations between classes conceived of as structural phenomena. It is concerned in particular with patterns of class conflict and the regulation of class conflict.

Dahrendorf wrote in far greater detail about both the theory of class formation and the theory of class action in *Class and Class Conflict in Industrial Society* (1959).

As for the specific classes found in society, it is not surprising that Dahrendorf found the continual existence of two opposed classes: the "elites" and the "ruling classes" and the "masses" and "suppressed classes." These two groups are forever in conflict, as their collective goals are in direct opposition. Social classes, then, can be understood as conflict groups arising out of the authority structure of imperatively coordinated associations that are in conflict. "In the affluent society, it remains a stubborn and remarkable fact that men are unequally placed" (Dahrendorf, 1968:151). Social stratification is a very real element of everyday life, and every person is aware of her or his "place" within the social structure.

Industrial Conflict

Industrial society witnessed the formation of a new type of conflict. "The intensity of conflict in capitalist society was increased by the superimposition of authority and other factors of social status, especially income. Domination meant, for the capitalists, a high income, while subjection involved for labor extreme material hardship. There was a clear correlation between the distribution of authority and social stratification" (Dahrendorf, 1959:242). Industrial authority does not involve the subordination of total persons under all persons with authority: it is restricted to persons as incumbents in given, limited roles. Thus, my "boss" is boss to me, but everyone else's boss is not boss to me; the authority of any one person is limited to the specific industrial environment.

However, the industrial enterprise does possess an authority structure and is therefore an imperatively coordinated association. Therefore, "we are entitled to assume that the incumbents of positions of domination and subjection within it are united in two

conflicting quasi-groups with certain latent interests. This inference follows from the model of class formation" (Dahrendorf, 1959:251). The interest of workers is generally in conflict with the interest of management; although they both depend on the overall success of the association. Consequently, there exists the establishment of "industrial democracy," consisting of a number of structural arrangements to help minimize conflict:

1. The organization of conflicting interest groups itself.
2. The establishment of "parliamentary" negotiating bodies in which these groups meet.
3. The institutions of mediation and arbitration.
4. Formal representations of labor within the individual enterprise.
5. Tendencies toward an institutionalization of workers' participation in industrial management.

Few people would deny, however, that there are still conflicts in industry, such as wage claims, benefits packages, strikes, and lockouts. Inevitably, then, conflict is resolved in the same manner as it nearly always is, by those with power.

Homo Sociologicus

Essays in the Theory of Society (1968) is a collection of ten essays written by Ralf Dahrendorf. The longest essay, "*Homo Sociologicus*: On the History, Significance, and Limits of the Category of Social Role," published first in book form in Germany in 1959, has gone through six printings and has given rise to great controversy.

Before introducing the *Homo sociologicus*, Dahrendorf (1968) discussed the much-debated *Homo oeconomicus* of modern economics as "the consumer who carefully weighs utility and cost before every purchase and compares hundreds of prices before he makes his decision; the entrepreneur who has the latest information from all markets and stock exchanges and bases his every decision on this information; the perfectly informed, thoroughly rational man" (pp. 20–21). In brief, the *Homo oeconomicus* appears to be a highly rational and organized but perhaps "anal" person. Dahrendorf believed that sociologists can, and should, be as rational in their approach to the study of society as the *Homo oeconomicus* is to the field of economics. "Mere random probability can hardly explain our behavior toward others and toward ourselves. We obey laws, go to the polls, marry, attend schools and universities, have an occupation, and are members of a church" (Dahrendorf, 1968:22). The key issue for sociologists is to find the laws of society.

RANDALL COLLINS (1941–)

Randall Collins was born in Knoxville, Tennessee, on July 29, 1941. His father was a professor of German literature at Maryville College, and during World War II he joined Army Intelligence, later becoming a career diplomat. Because of his father's military career, Collins traveled with his parents to such places as Germany, Uruguay, Russia, and Spain.

Collins received his bachelor's degree from Harvard University in 1963, his master's degree from Stanford in 1964, and his Ph.D. from the University of California at Berkeley in 1969. He has taught at several universities, including Chicago, Harvard, Virginia, Wisconsin, and the University of California at Los Angeles, at San Diego, and at Riverside, where he once served as chairperson of the sociology department. Collins is currently teaching at the University of Pennsylvania. He has been a visiting professor at the Institute for Advanced Study at Princeton, the Institute for Advanced Study in Vienna, the Swedish Collegium for Advanced Study in Social Sciences, and the École Normale Supérieure in Paris. Collins has been the recipient of a number of prestigious awards, including the American Socio-

logical Association (ASA) Theory Prize, the ASA Sociology of Religion Prize, and the ASA Distinguished Contribution to Scholarship Prize in 1999 for his book *The Sociology of Philosophies*. He has been elected a fellow of the American Association for the Advancement of Science and has been the president of the Pacific Sociological Association.

Collins has published a large number of works and was one of the most prolific writers among sociological theorists in the 1970s, 1980s, and 1990s (Farley, 1998). His early work centered on the conflict perspective and is highlighted by the publication of *Conflict Sociology* (1974). In *Conflict Sociology*, Collins incorporated all the major elements of conflict theory: an emphasis on people's interests, a view of society as made up of competing groups whose relative resources give their members more or less power over each other, and an interest in ideas as a

Randall Collins, one of the most significant sociologists and social thinkers of the contemporary era.
Source: Courtesy of Randall Collins

weapon of social conflict and domination (Wallace and Wolf, 1999). As Farley (1998) explained, Collins articulated ways in which the propositions arising from conflict theory can be scientifically tested and applied the conflict perspective to gender inequality (1971a), education (1971b), religion (1974), and marriage (1985).

Other publications include *The Credential Society* (1979), *Weberian Sociological Theory* (1986c), and *Macro-History: Essays in Sociology of the Long Run* (1999). Recently, Collins has sought to combine microsociological aspects within the conflict perspective. His works have been translated into Arabic, Chinese, Dutch, German, Japanese, Korean, Romanian, Russian, Spanish, and Swedish.

Influences

Randall Collins was influenced by some of the greatest minds of sociological and philosophical thought, among them Niccolò Machiavelli, Thomas Hobbes, Émile Durkheim, Karl Marx, Max Weber, George Herbert Mead, and Erving Goffman.

Machiavelli and Hobbes were political theorists in the sixteenth century. Hobbes was one of the first Western thinkers to provide secular justification for the political state. He applied certain principles to explain human motivation and social organization. Machiavelli, author of *The Prince* (1513), spoke out against the unfair political regime of his time. He openly criticized the existing social order and realized that major political change can occur only through open conflict between the ruling class and the ruled. As Collins (1975) explained, "Machiavelli and Hobbes initiated the basic stance of cynical realism about human society. Individuals' behavior is explained in terms of their self interests in a material world of threat and violence (conflict). Social order is seen as founded on organized coercion!" (p. 56).

Collins does not think very highly of functionalism, but he believes that Durkheim

explained a great deal about the role of emotional bonds and how loyalties are created and maintained (Wallace and Wolf, 1999). Collins (2000) explained that in Durkheimian theory, the collective performance of rituals generates feelings of solidarity and that the recognition and use of symbols reinforce membership in the group. His interaction ritual chain theory was undoubtedly influenced by Durkheim.

The interactionist perspective is evident in Collins's interaction ritual chain theory. As Farley (1998) explained, "This theory holds that interaction rituals, like those described by Goffman's dramaturgical perspective, are influenced by the level of resources each participant brings to the interaction. But at the same time, the process of the interaction may increase or decrease each participant's resources. Thus, both the level of resources (as conflict theorists would emphasize) and the interaction ritual (as interactionist theorists would emphasize) influence the outcome of the process of interaction" (p. 58). Mead's idea of verbal thinking, or internalized conversation, explained how our thought processes are carried out through words and expressions that have acquired significance in the group, especially during interaction rituals.

Karl Marx played a significant role in the formation of Collins's work. Collins (1975b) described Marx as "the great originator of modern conflict theory" (p. 428). He does not agree with all Marxian thought, but he does agree with Marx's analysis of the material world and the formation of the division of labor. Marx traced the origin of the division of labor to the primitive family structure, where the man, generally larger in size and physically stronger, left the home to hunt for food for the survival of the family, and the woman stayed home to raise the children. (Thus, biological and social factors lead to the creation of the division of labor.) Marx preached that the capitalist system, by its very structure, separated people into classes, relative to the control of the means of production. When the subordinate group (the workers) become aware of their exploitation by the owners, conflict ensues. Those in power do what they can to maintain their favorable position, while those without power revolt in an attempt to gain some control over their lives.

Among all the theorists that Collins admired the most, Max Weber ranks number one. Collins adopted Weber's pluralistic model using an analytic framework, comparative historical approach, and nonutopian outlook (Wallace and Wolf, 1999, p. 138). Collins used Weber's definition of the state as the monopolization of legitimate force (Collins, 1999). It is most likely that Weber, more than anyone else, influenced Collins's undertaking of geopolitics. Collins prefers Weber's notion of social stratification—that it includes aspects of political power and social prestige—to Marx's economic deterministic perspective.

Sociology as a Science

Some debate whether sociology is a true science. Perhaps the answer lies with how one interprets what a science really is. By definition, sociology is, of course, a science. Definitions of the term *science* usually include such criteria as an area of knowledge and knowledge obtained and tested through the scientific method. The scientific method itself is defined as the pursuit of knowledge involving the stating of a problem, the collection of facts through observation and experiment, and the testing of ideas to determine whether they are right or wrong. Traditional sociology prides itself on its commitment to the scientific method. Other sociologists, especially postmodernists, choose not to use the scientific method and therefore question sociology's commitment to positivism and empiricism. At times, the different theoretical branches found in sociology are downright hostile toward one another's views

and interpretation of what makes "good" sociological theory.

In *Conflict Sociology*, Collins (1975b) explained that sociology is a science, but with goals such as generalized explanation, practicality, ideological evaluation, and aesthetic interpretation, which are very different from those of the natural sciences of physics, chemistry, and biology. It also reflects the general impression of the "natural" sciences as authoritarian and elitist.

> In the postmodernist atmosphere of the late 20th century, it has become unfashionable to ask about the scientific prospects of sociology and the other social disciplines. The natural sciences are regarded by many intellectuals as authoritarian and destructive; hence in the social disciplines we should not try to become a science even if we could. On the other side, science was once considered a liberalizing and enlightening movement in Western culture, and some persons continue to work at exploring the social realm in the same spirit. . . . I stress the social organization of intellectual fields in order to avoid the ideological and philosophical terms in which debates over the scientific character of the social "sciences" have often been carried out. (Collins, 1994:156)

Collins (1994) speculated that the social sciences, except in isolated pockets, will not develop the streams of research technologies of the natural sciences, nor will the social sciences ever acquire the rapid-discovery mode.

Collins insisted that for sociology to make progress as a discipline, it must find some spirit of generosity and cooperation, instead of the factional antagonism that exists within its ranks.

> This is not the same as a policy of "go your own way," tolerating each other but having nothing to do with one another intellectually. Building sociological knowledge is a collective enterprise, and in more ways than one. . . . To come together as scientists, we

need to concentrate on the coherence of theoretical conceptions across different pieces of research. The personal aspect of that intellectual structure is generosity and good will, a positive feeling towards each other's best contributions as we grope our way forward together. (Collins, 1989:137)

Collins (1998) reminded us that "sociology, like everything else, is a product of particular historical conditions" (p. 2). The roots of sociology are firmly embedded in empiricism. For many decades now, there have been some sociologists who feel it is better to abandon scientism. The beginning of the third millennium has marked a historical era anticipated with great interest. Will sociology be proscience? Or will it be antiscience? In rationale-based societies it seems clear that science will always be highly cherished and valued.

Conflict Theory

Conflict theory generally emphasizes the role of power that one group, or person, holds over another group, or person. Kemper and Collins (1990) contended "that power and status are fundamental relational dimensions at the micro level of social interaction and perhaps at the macro level as well. Whatever else may be going on in social life, and however else one may wish to conceptualize it, human actors are deeply involved in relational issues of control and dominance (power) and of acceptance and positive association (status), and social theorists of all persuasions have necessarily dealt with these in one form or another" (p. 32). Inherent in any social system, group structure, or interpersonal relationship is an imbalance of power. Collins (1975) assumed that there are certain "goods"—namely, wealth, power, and prestige—that people in all societies will pursue. Furthermore, all people dislike being ordered around and will therefore do what they can to avoid the subordinate role. Thus, conflict is inevitable, for everyone is in pursuit of scarce resources and the roles related to these desired resources. Collins (1975b)

concluded that coercion and the ability to "force" others to behave a certain way are the primary basis of conflict.

Karl Marx attempted to lead the proletariat, through class consciousness, into a revolution against the established social order spearheaded by the capitalists. Collins believed that Marx's analysis of stratification was too limited. "Marx was primarily interested in the determinants of political power, and only indirectly in what may be called a 'theory of stratification'" (Collins, 1975:57). Collins's conflict approach to stratification has more in common with phenomenological and ethnomethodological theories than with Marxist or Weberian theory (Ritzer, 2000). Though he was clearly influenced by Marx and Weber, Collins did not completely follow in their footsteps. According to Ritzer (2000c:130), Collins's conflict approach to stratification can be reduced to three basic principles:

1. People live in self-constructed subjective worlds.
2. Other people may have the power to affect, or even control, an individual's subjective experience.
3. People frequently try to control the actions of others, who oppose such attempts of control; result is often interpersonal conflict.

From these three principles, Collins developed five principles of conflict analysis (Ritzer, 2000c:130):

1. Conflict theory must focus on real life rather than abstract formulations.
2. Material arrangements affect interaction.
3. In social situations of inequality between persons, those who possess the power position generally attempt to exploit those who lack resources.
4. The role of cultural phenomena, such as beliefs, values, and norms, must be examined in terms of their relationship to interests, resources, and power.
5. There must be a firm commitment to the scientific study of stratification and every other aspect of the social world.

In his conflict theory, it is clear that Collins attempted to bridge the micro-macro division that exists within the sociological perspective. From the macro perspective, Collins incorporated the ideas of Marx and Weber and their analysis of the effect of the economic and political institutions on individuals' behaviors. His focus on individuals and their inner struggles reveals a micro orientation. Collins (1975b) believed that conflict theory should incorporate the social construction of subjective realities and the dramaturgical qualities of historically conditioned material interests, and he provided a typology of the resources people bring with them to social interaction:

1. Material and technical resources, which include not only property, tools, and such skills as literacy, but also—very importantly— weapons.
2. Physical strength and attractiveness and the role they play in personal relationships.
3. Number of contacts people have will directly influence the potential for negotiating material goods and status.
4. The possession of personal resources and qualities deemed desirable by others which will lead to opportunities for emotional bonding among people because of shared interests.

In brief, Collins stressed the idea that individual actions shape the social structure, and that the social structure shapes individual actions.

Collins believed that sociological research should be aimed at solving concrete problems in the world. Applied sociology involves making practical contributions, such as in planning and evaluation. He described the basis of scientific sociology as empirical research, unifying theory, and a sociology with a solid explanatory foundation—causal explanation. For Collins, the path forward to a general explanatory theory is to build on Weber's nominalist conflict approach to stratification and to organizations, and to treat any larger historical pattern as a historicist combination of these elements. Durkheim is to be borrowed from selectively in order to round out the theory at the point of a fundamental understanding of the emotional and cognitive dynamics of interpersonal interaction (Collins, 1975b).

Stratification and Social Change

From a conflict perspective, the basic outlines of stratification theory were set forth by Marx and Engels. "Revolutions were class conflicts: a privileged class faced increasing pressure from a discontented rising class. The revolutionary transfer of power eventually broke through the block, setting off a new period of social change. This process was synchronized with a succession of ideological hegemonies. The ruling ideas were those of the ruling elite; as class challengers emerged, their change in consciousness acted as a barometer as well as a mobilizer for the coming revolution" (Collins, 1993b:117).

In his theory of stratification, Collins (1975) indicated that the crucial dividing lines in the social structure are dominance relations and the number of resources that one possesses. In keeping with his general program of linking structural and interactional levels of analysis, Collins attempted to cast all structural variable in terms of actual differences in the experience of face-to-face encounters. For example, in the world of employment, power relations and situations of giving and taking orders seem to be the most important variables in shaping behaviors. Collins concluded that the basic premise of the conflict perspective is that all pursue their own best line of advantage according to the resources available to them, and that social structures—whether formal organizations or informal acquaintances—are empirically nothing more than continuous negotiating power situations in any encounter.

Collins examined stratification by education as part of his interest in the role of educational qualification (credentials) and their use as a resource in the struggle for power, wealth, and prestige (Wallace and Wolf, 1999). The educational elite use credentials to screen undesired persons from employment. (Note: It is hard to argue against the necessity of "qualified" people in most professional jobs, especially in the medical, scientific, and educational fields. What might be a better example is the law profession, which keeps raising the required LSAT score needed for admission to law school. The score is raised because too many people are already in the law profession.) Thus, the educational system serves as a "gatekeeper," which allows those who have attained a high level of education to climb in the ranks of the social hierarchy. Collins (1979) explained the reemergence of such schools as commercial trade schools and business institutes as a response to this credential requirement. (Note: It is important that professionals such as plumbers, electricians, and exterminators must also be "certified" and have licenses to perform their trades.) Collins (1979) went so far as to suggest that there is a credentials crisis, and he sought to abolish compulsory school requirements.

Beyond the field of education, Collins applied his theoretical analysis of stratification and social change to economics. He has written articles on such topics as the market system and the effects of capitalism on social structures. Collins (1997:843) noted how, historically, capitalism has gone through three key phases:

1. A small leading sector within agrarian-coercive societies set the innovative dynamic in motion.
2. The spread of capitalist market structures made agricultural production dynamic.
3. The Industrial Revolution of production by machines harnessed to inanimate energy sources set off the expansion of nonagricultural production.

Like Weber, Collins examined the role of religion as an explanation of why some world regions evolved with industrialization and others did not.

In his article "Market Dynamics as the Engine of Historical Change" (1990a), Collins concluded that "if past history is any precedent, the capitalism that is dominant today has plenty of upheavals in store in its future" (p. 134).

Interaction Ritual Chain Theory

One of Collins's most interesting and significant contributions to sociological theory is his interaction ritual chain theory. Through the interaction ritual, Collins explained why people behave differently among different groups of people. He believes that all social encounters can be ranked by their degree of ritual intensity. Those who have a highly vested interest in the group will carry out ritualistic behavior more intensely than those who are less committed to the group (or couple). Those who have an emotional attachment to the group, share in its social identity, and participate in the group activities will experience emotional energy (Collins, 2000). Individuals carry symbols of this commitment to indicate membership and to recharge their emotional energy. There are numerous examples of this commitment to membership: married couples wear wedding rings to show their commitment to one another, sports fans wear clothing with symbols of their favorite team, religious persons wear some token of their faith, and gang members wear tattoos to show their allegiance to the gang. In all cases, all members of the group feel accepted and welcomed because of their attachment to the group and the ritualistic behavior. As Delaney's (2001) research indicated, the same ritualistic behavior of bonding and emotional commitment is shared by members of sports booster groups. Cheering for the team and wearing team associated clothing (hats, T-shirts, and so on) contribute to the interaction ritual.

Collins expanded on his ritual theory with ideas on intellectual networks. These networks start with intellectuals, who produce decontextualized ideas and regard them with the same kind of seriousness and respect that Durkheim said believers give to the sacred items of religion (Collins, 2000). Intellectuals make their careers by entering the network of previous participants and building new arguments on past feelings. The new intellectuals try to imitate not the ideas of prior theorists, but the emotional energy (Collins, 2000). The new intellectuals hope to attract attention with their new work, but these opportunities are limited because only a limited number of positions attract proper scholarly recognition.

On certain college campuses scholarly academic pursuits are not rewarded (compared to sports accomplishments, for example), and in some cases, those in power positions who are threatened by the new intellectuals use the resources at their disposal to hinder the careers of the aspiring intellectuals. Many of those in academia must decide whether to forge ahead in an attempt to make a lasting contribution to the field or be content with going "through the motions" so as not to challenge the existing administrative power structure.

Geopolitics

Another important concept articulated by Collins is *geopolitics*. Geopolitics represents a momentous contribution not only to sociology, but to international politics as well. Collins's work on geopolitics paid particular attention to the importance of military technology and organization (Collins was perhaps influenced by his childhood military family lifestyle). It is noteworthy that in 1980, through his geopolitical analysis, Collins predicted the collapse of the Soviet Union.

Other theorists have certainly presented a world-systems view of international politics and economics, but Collins's presentation of geopolitics is original enough to stand out. Collins argued that geopolitics began at the turn of the twentieth century. Powerful nations began to realize that the possession of strategic heartlands on the globe gave the

state dominance over others. Since Collins did not originate the geopolitics concept, his contribution comes in the form of his geopolitical theory. Collins's (1999) geopolitical theory consists of five conditions, or principles, for the expansion and contraction of the territorial power of states. The five principles of geopolitical theory are as follows:

1. Size and resource advantage favor territorial expansion. The bigger, more populous, and more resource-rich states expand militarily at the expense of smaller, less populous, and resource-poor states.
2. Geopositional or "marchland" advantages favor territorial expansion. Those states with enemies on fewer fronts expand at the expense of states with enemies on more borders.
3. A high level of internal conflict hinders efforts to expand, whereas internal harmony, or control, allows a concentration of military efforts externally.
4. Cumulative processes bring periodic long-term simplification, with massive arms races and showdown wars between a few contenders. Bigger states swallow up smaller ones or force them into alliances. Before long there exist just a couple of "superpower" states.
5. Overextension brings resource strain and state disintegration. The costs of expansion have become overwhelming, to the point where the internal state risks dissolution.

It was the review of these five principles that first led Collins to conclude that the Soviet Union had passed its peak of power and would decline.

The State of Sociology

As for the state of sociology, Collins (1986c) did not believe that the rising number of sociologists and the expansion of the field had reached an alarming number. He believed that the social nature of any science creates a community that is engaged in discourse. Therefore, the structure allows a number of rival positions to arise; it also allows new areas of research to begin, and these eventually lead to further explanation and knowledge of the social world. In this case, conflict can lead to advancements in science. On the other hand, the fierce competition among those who label themselves the "new intellectuals" in pursuit of the limited resources (accolades, praise, publication, funding, and so on) will most likely perpetuate the same inequality and elitist discrimination in the field of academia as it does in all other work environments.

Randall Collins: A Summary

Collins provided an excellent version of conflict theory that attempts to incorporate the fundamental micro principles of symbolic interactionism with the traditional macro orientation. He provided concrete propositions that relate the unequal power structures found in the macro social institutions to the unequal distribution and allocation of resources to members of the social system. His commitment to the micro-macro bridge is admirable, and as Collins (1981) stated, "A micro-translation strategy reveals the empirical realities of social structures as patterns of repetitive micro-interactions" (p. 985). As for his methodological approach, Collins believes that sociology has the greatest chance of being an empirical science if it is grounded in micro behaviors. "Sociological concepts can be made fully empirical only by grounding them in a sample of the typical micro-events that make them up" (Collins, 1981:988).

Collins's defense of the field of sociology itself is to be warmly embraced, as he responded to the critics from the "natural" sciences that (still) question the validity of sociology's claim to be a science. As his primary response, Collins (1989) argued that sociology can be concerned with empirical descriptions, including both contemporary social conditions and historical sequences. Sociology can discuss moral issues, propose policy, and compare existing conditions against ideals. But what provides sociology with its intellectual justification is the formulation of generalized explanatory principles, organized into models of the underlying processes that generate the social world.

Collins's work on the interaction ritual is both insightful and fascinating. All personal relationships can easily be examined by means of this theory. The expansion of this ritual theory to intellectual networks provided excellent insights into interpersonal relationships within a structural framework. Randall Collins is certainly a first-rate scholar in the field of sociology, in particular, and a brilliant social thinker in general. Sociological theory has certainly benefited from this gifted social thinker.

RELEVANCY

Conflict theory views society as composed of competing elements, characterized by power differentials, with conflict among groups and individuals as the inevitable outcome. Conflict theorists believe that society is coordinated as a result of power struggles and power differentials. In brief, the conflict perspective proposes that inherent in any social system are interest groups that continually struggle for superiority and power. Those who have power want to keep it. The power elites are those who control the resources needed for the production and distribution of the goods and services deemed desirable and necessary by a society. Because they control the economic strata, the power elites have the money to help maintain their advantageous position. Those without power seek social change. Because of this reality, conflict theorists view society as a setting where groups and individuals are in constant struggle with one another in order to obtain scarce and valued resources, especially money, property, prestige, and, in short, power. Furthermore, the conflict perspective maintains that what social order does exist is the result of the power elites' coercion of the masses.

Karl Marx provided the foundation for modern conflict theory. He viewed power relationships as unnatural and alienating. In his era, society was basically a two-class system: the bourgeoisie (owners of the means of production) and the proletariat (workers). Marx believed that the owners of the means of production used their power position over the workers to maximize their profits. Marx argued that economics was the ingredient that had shaped human society throughout history. Contemporary conflict theorists do not limit their power analysis to the economic-class structural realm. They look at such issues as gender (feminist theory) and race, ethnicity, and sexual preference.

There are three primary criticisms of conflict theory. First, because of its focus on power differentials that are reinforced by coercion, conflict theory tends to ignore the many areas in which most people arrive at an uncoerced consensus about important values of life. The powerful and the powerless alike respect honest, hard-working people who stick by their principles and cherish family, honor, and dignity. Mundane daily behaviors, such as walking and driving on the right (in the United States, anyway), holding the door open for the person behind you, and a slew of basic manners and courtesies, are valued by people of all socioeconomic levels. Therefore, conflict might be an enduring aspect of society, but so are harmony and cooperation among diverse individuals and groups of people.

The second criticism of conflict theory is its seemingly active commitment to side with the people who lack substantial social power (Fay, 1987). The problem with this, is not that the powerless are in need of being helped, but, as critics claim, activism that provides just one group violates the principle of scientific objectivity. Conflict theorists, of course, do not see this as a criticism and would charge that those who see an injustice and do nothing about it are guilty of being "moral bystanders."

A third criticism of the conflict perspective is of its focus on economic factors as the sole criteria for all conflict in society. This criticism is accurate of the Marxist approach, but not of all versions of conflict theory. Most conflict theorists today do not ignore the importance of gender, race, ethnicity, age, sexual orientation, and other factors that lead to conflict.

The following paragraphs cover a few of the elements of conflict theory relevant to contemporary society.

Among the general principles of conflict theory that are most relevant to contemporary and future society is the idea that power differentials exist in nearly all forms of interaction: interpersonal, intergroup, and social class. Among primitive and isolated societies, power is first exercised physically. The stronger person is the more powerful person: Might *does* make right. Primitive man dominated the primitive female because of superior strength. The leader of the clan was the physically stronger. Eventually, empires were made because of physical strength. In many ways, physical power is still a standard of ultimate power. This is especially true in gang behavior and among inmates in prisons. In civilized societies physical strength has been neutralized as a factor in decision making. For example, a professor up for tenure does not physically challenge the department chair to a fistfight to determine tenure status; a physically stronger person cannot legally take a "weaker" person's home or other possessions away by means of might. Physical power has given way to "legal" and "economic" power. A person who legally owns property has claims to it. Those who control the means of production provide jobs that are necessary to the well-being of workers. Thus, being the owner of the means of production is equated with power.

In contemporary society, most societies are characterized by a legitimate means of power: authority. As Weber defined authority, it is power that is exercised with the consent of the ruled. This leads to roles such as superordinate-subordinate and domination-subjection. Since these aspects are prevalent in society, the study of these relationships will remain relevant in the future. Coser documented an interesting aspect of the domination-subjection phenomenon. "To illustrate the sociological point that whenever rulers are greedy for power, whenever they wish to maximize their autonomy in the face of feudal, bureaucratic, or other impediments, they tend to avail themselves of the services of alien groups rootless in the country they rule. The alien, I have argued, is easily bent to the ruler's purposes and an ideal servant of power" (Coser, 1972b:580). The economically powerful often employ servants and other persons to do their housework, and they are, indeed, generally aliens.

The conflict perspective has already demonstrated, because of power differentials between groups, that conflict *is* an inevitable aspect of social relations. Even though consensus and agreement can be found in many areas of society, it remains true that conflict exists in society as well. Conflict has always existed, and it always will. The study of conflict will always be important. At many colleges and universities, conflict resolution courses are taught in an effort to combat this inevitability of social life.

The conflict theorists are also accurate in their assessment that interest groups operate in society. Individuals nearly always act in a manner that is in their best interest. Even altruistic behaviors such as helping others usually result in some benefit to the person performing such acts. The argument over whether any behavior is truly altruistic is generally debated by social psychologists, but for now, it should be clear that most people, most of the time, act in their own best interest. This principle is even easier to accept at the group and class levels. In an effort to maintain a power position, or in an effort to attain a power position, interest groups use political methods such as hiring lobbyists. Lobbyists are hired to work the political system in such a way as to get laws passed that are favorable to their clients. For example, the tobacco industry is among the most powerful interest groups in the world. It uses the political and economic systems to its advantage to maintain its own power position. The proof of its power is obvious: What other single product (tobacco) is responsible for 420,000 deaths per year? If there was a food product, automobile, child's toy, and so on that killed a fraction of this number, it would be banned from the market, and yet tobacco remains a legal product.

It is also very evident that there is a power elite in society. C. Wright Mills described the power elite as political, military, and economic institutions. These three elements are integrated and form what Mills called the *triangle of power*. At the turn of the century, U.S. president George W. Bush attempted to integrate these three powers in his effort to fight terrorism and in his crusade to start a war with Iraq. The power elite are people who transcend the ordinary environments of ordinary persons and make decisions that have major consequences. They are at the top of hierarchies of major organizations and, in short, are in charge of the "machinery" that runs society.

Among the specific contributions by the conflict theorists discussed in this chapter is Lewis Coser's functional conflict theory. Functional conflict theory illustrates the beauty of combining two major theories. "Conflict theorists do not deny that certain types of social arrangements are functional for particular individuals or for groups, but they insist that we must always ask *for whom* they are functional. They view with great skepticism the functional assumption that many existing social arrangements can be interpreted as generally positive for an entire social system" (Lindsey and Beach, 2004:20). For example, when a president announces a "tax cut" and declares that it will benefit all of society, the conflict theorist quickly analyzes this claim and generally discovers that the tax cut is designed to help the rich. A great example of this fallacy is former president Ronald Reagan's claim that his "trickle-down" economics would benefit all of society.

Coser also claimed that external conflict can create unity within a group. This is often true, as group members generally work together to secure the group's future. After the brutal September 11, 2001, attacks on the United States, American citizens were moved to great heights of patriotism. A little more than a year later, the country was radically divided about whether invading Iraq was justified or not. The large number of antiwar protests demonstrate that the external threat of conflict must be clearly visible in order to be an effective means of mobilizing a hugely diverse nation such as the United States. The September 11 attacks also demonstrated Coser's belief that violence is a form of achievement for those who use it as a weapon. American history has been changed because of these brutal terrorist attacks.

C. Wright Mills is best known to college students today because of his sociological imagination concept. The sociological imagination is taught in all introductory sociology courses and is a standard of their textbooks. Mills wrote on the difference between individual troubles and public issues. This analysis is social-psychological. For example, a person who has recently been divorced or has broken up with a significant other has negative self-feelings and may think there is something wrong with him or her. The reality of this individual trouble is that it is a part of a greater public issue. There is a growing divorce rate, and people break up with each other regularly. As another example, people who lose their jobs because of corporate downsizing are not "losers"; instead, they are simply a product of the greater economic reality of a dramatically changing socioeconomic system. Consequently, the negative feelings one may have regarding oneself are simply a reflection of a greater societal occurrence. The bottom line is that, when looking at things sociologically, we see the "big picture," and not a simple snapshot view of the world. The problems that most people have (lack of economic security) are not found in individual pathologies (although there certainly are times when they are), but in mismanagement of the greater society.

Mills was also one of the first sociological theorists to examine the growing phenomenon of the white-collar professions. The number of professional and other white-collar-related jobs has continued to increase since the time of Mills's analysis. The white-collar environment is often very impersonal and sterile, workers being assigned to small, separate workspaces known as *cubicles*. Many workers feel like enclosed laboratory rats who work in a maze of bureaucracy, performing tasks for the reward of a paycheck. In the tradition of Weber, I refer to the workers of the contemporary white-collar work world as trapped in an "iron cubicle." The new white-collar workplace is illustrated daily by cartoonist Scott Adams in his syndicated cartoon *Dilbert*. Dilbert is a fictitious engineer who works in the "iron cubicle" world surrounded by incompetency and petty bureaucrats who attempt to survive one mundane, and often meaningless, day after another.

Ralf Dahrendorf articulated the ideas of domination and subjection and the role of authority. Of particular interest is his insight that a person who holds a position of authority in one setting does not hold a position of authority in other social arenas. Future studies in this area should prove to be very beneficial, especially in the industrial setting.

Randall Collins has contributed a great deal to sociological theory and will continue to do so for some time. His work on geopolitics has already proved useful in the understanding of the global community. Collins's defense of sociology as a science is warmly embraced by the largest percentage of sociologists. Of specific interest are his theories on the role of persons in power positions when they mingle with subordinates in social settings and his interaction ritual chain theory. First, his analysis of power persons in social settings is relevant on numerous occasions. Generally, the "boss" or the person with greater power expects to be shown a certain level of respect and deference, even in social settings. Many bosses expect that when playing a game, like golf, the subordinates will allow them to win. They expect to be allowed to "cut" into the food line rather than waiting their turn at a buffet, and they expect that their jokes will be laughed at. In short, those who hold power generally expect special treatment outside the work environment and exploit their subordinates even in social settings. Collins's interaction ritual chain theory is a revealing look at human behavior and provides an area of study that could benefit from additional research. Collins

has revealed the conditions under which people continue to engage in, or disengage from, relationships with others. This theory is especially insightful on small-group behaviors.

Last, Collins, in an attempt to defend empiricism and scientism in sociology, stated that creating "laws" and making predictions of human behavior would be a more likely scenario at the micro level. George Homans (see Chapter 6), through his use of five basic propositions, has attempted such an endeavor. Homans claimed to be able to predict all micro individual behaviors with five psychological propositions. Much more research should be conducted in this area, as the relevancy of being able to accurately predict behavior should be self-evident.

In short, conflict theory is one of the "big three" theories of sociology. It is taught at all levels of sociology, from introduction courses to advanced graduate courses. There is good reason. Power differentials and conflict are inevitable in human behavior and society. Consequently, the study of social conflict will always be relevant.

5

Symbolic Interactionism

ymbolic interactionism is a term coined by Herbert Blumer and a theoretical perspective most generally associated with George Herbert Mead. Blumer had been asked by Emerson P. Schmidt to contribute an article on social psychology to his book *Man and Society* (1937). Blumer used "the term *symbolic interactionism* in an attempt to clarify how social psychology was largely interested in the social development of the individual and that its central task was to study how the individual develops socially as a result of participating in group life" (Wallace and Wolf, 1999:190). Norman Denzin (1969) stated, "The development of a theoretical perspective appropriate for the joint analysis of social psychological and sociological problems has long concerned the sociologist" (p. 922). As essentially a social-psychological perspective, symbolic interactionism focuses primarily on the issue of self and in small group interactions. Joel Charon (1989) believes that "symbolic interactionism is a perspective in social psychology that is especially relevant to the concerns of sociology" (p. 22). The relevancy of symbolic interactionism will be examined later in this chapter, but attention is first given to the historical roots and development of symbolic interactionism. The major contributions of the significant theorists in this field are then reviewed.

THE ROOTS AND DEVELOPMENT OF SYMBOLIC INTERACTIONISM

The intellectual sources that influenced the development of symbolic interactionism are both numerous and diverse. This highly American social theory includes the European precursors of evolutionism, the Scottish moralists, and German idealism, along with the American intellectual influences of pragmatism, behaviorism, and the works of William James and Charles Cooley. A brief analysis of these influences follows.

Evolution

Charles Darwin's model of an organism in an environment to which it must adapt in order to survive provides the means of understanding and discovering all behaviors, those of humans included. Mead was particularly impressed by Darwin's *Expression of the Emotions in Man and Animals*. In this book Darwin extended his theory of evolution into the field of "conscious experience" (Mead, 1934). He showed that there are a number of acts that express emotions. The part of the organism that most vividly expresses emotions is the face. Mead did not agree with Darwin's theory of consciousness. For example, Mead believed that consciousness is an emergent form of behavior, whereas Darwin viewed consciousness as a psychological state. As Reynolds (1990) explained, "The nineteenth-century Darwinian doctrine of evolution was a major source of ideas for the American pragmatists in general and for George Herbert Mead in particular. It was, however, only to selected aspects of Darwin's theory that the founders of interactionism were to direct their attention. Mead, for example, was critical of Darwin's argument concerning emotions and their expression by animals" (p. 6).

Mead's attraction to Darwin rests on his emphasis on process (evolutionary process), specifically, the idea that process gives rise to different forms (Stone and Farberman, 1970). Mead's interpretation of Darwin's ideas led him to believe that behavior is not accidental or random but formed through individuals' interactions with one another in a social environment. This adaptation to the environment is an ongoing process sustained by social interaction. "As this interaction unfolds, the person's behavior is performed in adaptation to the environment, and person and environment come mutually to influence each other" (Reynolds, 1990:7). Behavioral adaptation during social interaction often leads to emergent behavior that meets the needs of the changing environment. Thus, "the evolutionary conceptions of the processual, emergent character of life, the adaptive function of behavior, and the mutually determinative relationship between organisms and environments were to be a part of the intellectual heritage of symbolic interactions" (Reynolds, 1990:8–9).

The Scottish Moralists

Evolutionism influenced the founders of symbolic interactionism to believe that the "mind" and the "self" possessed emergence characteristics. The Scottish moralists believed that the "mind" and the "self" were social products shaped by individuals' interactions with others. Among the principal spokesmen of the Scottish moralist tradition were Adam Ferguson, Henry Homes, David Hume, Francis Hutcheson, and Adam Smith.

> The principal significance of the Scottish Moralists for the symbolic interactionists is that the former anticipated many of the key or pivotal social-psychological concepts of the latter . . . . The Scottish Moralists' concepts of "sympathy" and of the "impartial spectator" clearly foreshadow the interactionists' working concepts of "roletaking" and the "generalized other," and in the writings of Adam Smith are to be found views anticipating the interactionist conceptions of a spontaneous, or "I," component of self, as well as the self's "me," or internalized view of others, component. (Reynolds, 1990:9).

Smith's ideas not only foreshadowed Mead's concepts of the "I" and the "me," but also Cooley's theory of the self.

German Idealism

The principal spokesmen of the variety of German idealism who influenced Mead and symbolic interactionism were Gottlieb Fichte, Friedrich Von Schelling, and G. W. F. Hegel, whom Mead called the *the Romantic Philosophers*. These philosophers argued that humans construct their own worlds and their realities. "It was Fichte's concept of the 'ethical self' and Schelling's discussion of artistic creativity that led each to conclude that the world in which we live was, at least in part, created by ourselves" (Reynolds, 1990:11). The romantic idealists utilized the self–not-self process in experience and identified this process with the subject-object process. This subject-object process was similar to William James's analysis. Mead learned from the German tradition that there is no consciousness which is not conscious of something;

therefore, the subject and the object are inevitably interrelated. There cannot be a subject without the object's being aware of it, just as there cannot be an object without its being a subject. Mead also believed that the development of self involves the process of reflexivity, which is the ability of an individual to be an object to themselves. This idea would greatly influence Mead's concept of the generalized other.

Mead came to view the German idealists as preoccupied with the relations of the self to its objects. He felt that Fichte was too concerned with about experiences and that Schelling and Hegel focused too much attention on the aesthetic experience and on experience of thought, respectively (Coser, 1977). Above all, Mead found fault with Hegel for not having formulated adequate concepts of the individual and of the future. Hegel's philosophy is thus incapable of grasping individuality in its concreteness (Joas, 1985).

Having studied in Germany, Mead was most directly influenced by Wilhelm Wundt, especially Wundt's theories of language and the gesture. Wundt was the heir apparent of the German idealistic tradition. He was able to relate German idealism to the social sciences through his psychological parallelism (Martindale, 1988). In the introduction to Mead's *Mind, Self, and Society* (1934), Charles Morris clarified the distinction between Darwin and Wundt's conception of the gesture by explaining that Wundt had helped to separate the gesture from its internal emotional implication and to regard it in a social context. In the tradition of Wundt, Mead viewed the gesture as the transitional link to language from human action. The gesture precedes language and mediates the development of language as the basic mechanism that allows the "sense of self" to arise during the course of ongoing social interaction. Thus, Mead came to argue that the gesture can be explained *only* in a social context. Years later, a more mature Mead (1934) would come to describe a gesture as those phases of the act which bring about the adjustment of the response of the other.

From Hegel, Mead took the idea that consciousness and society are dialectically emergent phenomena (Adams and Sydie, 2001). Mead replaced Hegel's "spirit" with a concept of a "unified world" that emerges through the realization of universal human potential. Mead (1938) believed that social development depends on individuals' becoming aware of their "opposition to one another" and working through such oppositions. "From the larger camp of German idealism, then, symbolic interactionism was to draw upon the doctrine that dictated that what Mead termed 'the World that is there' was, in fact, a self-created world. People were to be seen as responding to their own working conceptions and definitions of that self-created world and not to the world per se. And from Wundt would be taken the conception of the gesture as the initial phase of the social act" (Reynolds, 1990:12–13).

Pragmatism

A brief discussion of the American influences on symbolic interactionism follows. A critical influence on symbolic interactionism in general, and on Mead specifically, was pragmatism. In fact, Reynolds (1990) stated, "If forced to single out the one philosophical school of thought that most influenced symbolic interactionism, one would be on safe ground in concluding that pragmatism provides its primary intellectual underpinnings" (p. 13). Pragmatists believe that true reality does not exist "out there" in the real world; it is actively created as we act toward the world (Shalin, 1986).

Although Mead would become one of the key figures in the development of pragmatism, he was initially introduced to pragmatic philosophy by John Dewey, William James, and James Baldwin. Mead (1938) viewed pragmatism as a "natural American outgrowth." It reflected the triumph of science in U.S. society and a belief in the superiority of scientific data and analysis over philosophical dogma and other forms of inferior beliefs. Pragmatists reject the idea of absolute truths and regard all ideas as provisional and subject to change in light of future research (Ritzer, 2000a). Truth is determined by humans' adaptations to their environments, and therefore the transitive character of both truth and consciousness is revealed. Reality, then, is always relative to individuals. Pragmatism helped to develop the idea that people base knowledge on what is most useful to them. Therefore, a construction worker is knowledgeable about tools and how to operate them properly, while an auto mechanic is knowledgeable about the parts and operation of automobiles.

Pragmatists believe that human beings reflect on the meaning of a stimulus before reacting. The meaning placed on various acts depends on the purpose of the act, the context in which it is performed, and the reactions of others to the act (Adams and Sydie, 2001). Mead's notion of the act as social was directly influenced by Dewey and Cooley. Dewey and Mead were colleagues for a short period of time at the University of Michigan. More important, Dewey, while at the University of Chicago, was instrumental in getting Mead an appointment there. As the primary exponent of pragmatism, "Dewey stressed the process of human adjustment to the world, in which humans constantly seek to master the conditions of their environment. Thus, the unique characteristics of humans arise from the *process* of adjusting to their life conditions" (Turner, 2003:345). Dewey believed that reflexive action(s) leads to the construction of such ideas as morality. Thus, Mead came to view even ideas such as ethics and morality as socially constructed and not fixed. Different cultures are easily explained by the realization that people with different life experiences come to different interpretations of events and impose different meanings on acts.

The collaboration of Dewey and Mead was mutually beneficial. On the one hand,

close examination of Mead's social psychology reveals many influences from Dewey. On the other hand, as Charles Morris stated in the introduction to *Mind, Self, and Society* (Mead, 1934) in regard to both Dewey and Mead, "Neither stands to the other in the exclusive relation of teacher to student; both . . . were of equal though different intellectual stature; both shared in a mutual give-and-take according to their own particular genius. If Dewey gave range and vision, Mead gave analytical depth and scientific precision" (p. xi).

Behaviorism

Mead considered himself a behaviorist but not in the radical tradition of behaviorism that focuses on the stimuli that elicit responses, or behaviors (stimulus-response mechanisms). Mead (1934) defined behaviorism as simply an approach to the study of the experience of individuals from the point of view of their conduct (behavior). His version of behaviorism was not consistent with how the term was used by his contemporaries, especially John B. Watson. The behaviorism of Mead's time was borrowed from animal psychology and was applied to humans (Ritzer, 2000a). Watson represented the attempt to account for sociopsychological phenomena in purely behavioristic terms (Martindale, 1988). Because Mead recognized the importance of both observable behavior and the covert aspects of behavior, something that the radical behaviorists ignored, he criticized Watson for ignoring the inner experiences of consciousness and mental imagery. Thus, for Mead, the acts of individuals possess both covert and overt meanings.

Mead believed that the inner experiences of individuals who act can be studied by behaviorists, as long as a social-behavioristic approach is utilized. This social-behavioristic approach led to the development of symbolic interactionism. Instead of studying the mind introspectively, Mead focused on the act (the social act). Acts are behaviors that respond to stimuli. In a variation of the stimulus-response relationship described by behaviorists and exchange theorists, Mead described a stimulus-act relationship. The difference is that the inner consciousness responds to the stimulus before the individual responds, thus creating an act that takes into account the existence of the mind and freewill.

William James

The properties of Mead's social psychology and symbolic interactionism can be traced, at least in part, to William James. "The Harvard psychologist William James (1842–1910) was perhaps the first social scientist to develop a clear concept of self. James recognized that humans have the capacity to view themselves as objects and to develop self-feelings and attitudes toward themselves" (Turner, 2003:344). In his *Principles of Psychology* (1948), James called for a reexamination of the relations between the individual and society (Martindale, 1988). Although James was a product of his time and accepted the instinct theory that was so prevalent then, he began to believe that other aspects beyond biology tended to modify behavior. His works on habit were of special importance, as James recognized that habit reduces the need for conscious attention. If individuals are capable of forming new habits, they are also capable of modifying their behavior. James (1948) believed that the individual acquires a new nature through habit.

A second critical aspect of James's psychology was his rethinking of the role of "consciousness." He noted that consciousness always involves some degree of awareness of the person's self. The person appears in thought in two ways, "partly known and partly knower, partly object and partly subject. . . . For shortness we may call one the *Me* and the other the *I*. . . . I shall therefore treat successively of (A) the self as known, or the *Me*, the 'empirical ego' as it is sometimes called; and of (B) the self as knower, or the *I*, the 'pure ego' of certain authors" (James, 1948:176).

The empirical self, or me, is the sum total of all the person can claim as one's own: their feelings, emotions, actions of self-seeking and self-preservation. People possess as many social selves as there are individuals who have images of them in mind. The self as knower, the I, or pure ego, is a much more complicated subject (James, 1948). The I is what the person is at any given specific moment in time. James developed a typology of selves, but this typology was never adopted by subsequent interactionists. However, his notion of the social self became a part of all interactionists' formulations (Turner, 2003). Mead was clearly influenced by James in his works on the development of the self. Mead even used the same terminology of the "I" and the "me" in explaining the structure of the self.

Charles Horton Cooley

Cooley was a student of John Dewey and was well acquainted with the writings of both William James and James Mark Baldwin. Cooley and James both identified the influence of the environment on behavior. The self is viewed as a process in motion, in which individuals see themselves as objects, are aware of other objects in the environment, and modify their behaviors as the situation dictates. Individuals learn to act as society (others) wants them to act, not as they themselves might want to act (thus, individuals do not react solely on a stimulus-response mechanism). For example, two youths cannot play catch with a football during church services just because they want to; the negative reactions of others will be enough to stop the inappropriate behavior of those properly socialized. Society itself is an interweaving and interworking of mental selves. Through socialization, society is internalized in the individual psyche; it becomes a part of the individual self through the interaction of many individuals, which links and fuses them into an organic whole. Consequently, Cooley realized that the self emerges from communication and interaction with others. Through interaction and the evaluation and interpretation of acts by others, the self is developed as both an object and a subject.

Cooley argued that a person's self develops through contact and interaction with others. By identifying a sense of self, individuals are able to view themselves the same way they do any other social object. Cooley (1964) stated that there can be no isolated selves: "There is no sense of 'I' . . . without its correlative sense of you, or he, or they" (p. 182). Individuals gain a sense of self when they receive consistent messages from others. Actors are most interested in, and value most, the reactions of significant others, especially primary-group members. Cooley is perhaps best known for introducing sociologists to the concepts *primary groups* and the *looking-glass self.*

What Is Symbolic Interactionism?

Symbolic interactionism is based on the idea that social reality is constructed in each human interaction through the use of symbols (Levin, 1991). Symbols include such things as words and gestures. The ability to communicate by the use of language becomes the primary method of symbolic interaction. Language allows individuals to discuss and understand ideas and events that transcend the immediate environment. "Symbolic interactionism takes as a fundamental concern the relationship between individual conduct and forms of social organization. This perspective asks how selves emerge out of social structure and social situations. . . . The interactionist assumes that human beings are capable of making their own thoughts and activities objects of analysis, that is, they can routinely, and even

habitually, manipulate symbols and orient their own actions towards other objects" (Denzin, 1969:922–923). Symbolic interactionism is a micro approach in sociological theory. The focus is primarily on individuals and their interactions with others. What is of utmost concern are the meanings that actors place on social acts committed by themselves and by others. Because objects found in human environments carry no intrinsic meaning, humans are capable of constructing objects' meanings. In addition, because actors are objects themselves, their sense of self is open to meaning and thus amendable.

Symbolic interactionists believe that studying social interaction is the key to understanding human behavior. "Instead of focusing on the individual and his or her personality characteristics, or on how the social structure or social situation causes individual behavior, symbolic interactionism focuses on the *nature of interaction*, the dynamic social activities taking place between persons. In focusing on the interaction itself as the unit of study, the symbolic interactionist creates a more active image of the human being and rejects the image of the passive, determined organism" (Charon, 1989:22).

The interactionist perspective maintains a belief in the ability of actors to modify their behaviors to meet the needs of the present and the immediate environment. Interactionists are steadfast in the idea that reality exists in a present. As Mead (1959) stated, "The present of course implies a past and a future, and to these both we deny existence. . . . Existence involves non-existence; it does take place. The world is a world of events" (p. 1).

Additionally, during interaction, social acts and events come to be defined in some matter by participating interactants. "Because human interaction involves behavior of both the covert and overt variety, and because the meanings attached to objects often change during an encounter, and the interactionist endeavors to relate covert symbolic behavior with other patterns of interaction. This additionally demands a concern for the unfolding meaning objects assume during an interactional sequence" (Denzin, 1969:925). The basic concepts and theoretical constructs of symbolic interactionism are elaborated in the following pages as the focus of this chapter shifts to the discussion of the major contributors to the field.

GEORGE HERBERT MEAD (1863–1931)

George Herbert Mead was born on February 27, 1863, in South Hadley, Massachusetts. When he was seven, the family moved to Oberlin, Ohio. Mead entered Oberlin College at age sixteen and was described as a serious, cautious, quiet, mild-mannered, and kind-hearted person (Miller, 1973). After graduating from Oberlin, Mead was admitted to the graduate program in philosophy at Harvard University. At Harvard, Mead's philosophical interests lay in the romantic philosophers and Hegelian idealism, as taught by Josiah Royce (Baldwin, 1986). Mead studied under William James, whom he worked for; he also tutored James's children (Miller, 1973). Both Royce and James left a permanent mark on Mead's life and outlook (Coser, 1977). Although he found James's philosophy courses stimulating, Mead also felt that they were too abstract and isolated from the real world (Pampel, 2000). Unhappy with the abstract nature of philosophy, Mead decided to change his course of study to physiological psychology. He accepted a scholarship to study in Germany, the location of the world's most renowned specialists in physiological psychology (Pampel, 2000). Mead first went to Leipzig to study with Wilhelm Wundt, whose conception of the *gesture* would greatly influence Mead's later works. In 1899, Mead went to Berlin to study both psychology and philosophy taught in the tradition of Simmel. Mead never earned his doctorate. In 1891 he accepted a lecturer's teaching position at the University of Michigan, teaching

philosophy and psychology (Scheffler, 1974). Mead's colleagues at Michigan included Charles Cooley, James Tufts, and John Dewey. Mead and Dewey quickly recognized their similar interests and became life-long friends. In 1893, Dewey received an offer to become the chair of the department of philosophy at the University of Chicago. Dewey insisted that Mead be allowed to join the department as well. Mead remained at the University of Chicago for the rest of his life. Mead is generally considered the most influential of the social thinkers in the field of symbolic interactionism. His primary contributions are discussed in the following pages.

Symbolic Interactionism

Mead, the most important thinker associated with the Chicago School and symbolic interactionism, was not a sociologist but a philosopher. It must be made clear that there was no

George Herbert Mead, Pragmatist, philosopher, social scientist, and principle founder of symbolic interactionism.
Source: Courtesy of National Library of Medicine

such field as symbolic interactionism when Mead first started teaching social psychology at Chicago. It was Herbert Blumer, following in the tradition of Mead and Cooley, who coined the term in 1937. Mead's students, who put together their notes on his courses and published *Mind, Self, and Society* (1934) posthumously under his name, had a primary influence on Blumer and the development of symbolic interactionism. Mead had published several articles by the time Blumer completed his doctoral dissertation on "Method in Social Psychology." A number of Mead's works were made available to Blumer before his assertion that he "was compelled to develop a symbolic interaction methodology to deal '. . . explicitly with many crucial matters that were only implicit in the thought of Mead.' It is not clear by what criteria Blumer made his judgement that Mead's methodological perspective was 'implicit' in his written work. Our comparison of their respective epistemologies will establish that Mead's position is far more detailed and explicit than Blumer suggests. It is also quite different from the position Blumer felt compelled to develop" (McPhail and Rexroat, 1979:450).

Mead believed that human beings have the capacity to think and decide on their own how they should act in given situations, and that they react on the basis of their perceptions and definitions of the situations in which they find themselves (Cockerham, 1995). Mead did not ignore legitimate social forces that strongly influence or limit alternate plans, such as being born into an economically lower-class family, or losing one's job because of downsizing. But the symbolic interaction approach suggests that people cope with the reality of their circumstances according to their comprehension of the situation (Cockerham, 1995).

Mind, Self, and Society

Mead's *Mind, Self, and Society* (1934) represents his attempt to understand individual social experiences in relation to society. He argued that there can be no self, no consciousness of self, and no communication, apart from society. Mead felt that social experience is the sum of the total dynamic realities observable by the individual, who is a part of the ongoing societal process (Kallen, 1956). Society must be understood as a structure that emerges through an ongoing process of communicative social acts and through interactions between persons who are oriented toward each other (Coser, 1977).

Mead viewed the mind as a process and not a thing, as an inner conversation with oneself, which arises and develops within the social process and is an integral part of that process. The mind reflects the human capacity to conceive what the organism perceives, define situations, evaluate phenomena, convert gestures into symbols, and exhibit pragmatic and goal-directed behavior. Mead was concerned with intelligence on the human level and with

> the adjustment to one another of the acts of different human individuals within the human social process; an adjustment which takes place through communication: by gestures on the lower planes of human evolution, and by significant symbols (gestures which possess meanings and are hence more than mere substitute stimuli) on the higher planes of human evolution. The central factor in such adjustment is "meaning." Meaning arises and lies within the field of the relation between the gesture of a given human organism and the subsequent behavior of this organism as indicated to another human organism by the gesture. If that gesture does so indicate to another organism the subsequent (or resultant) behavior of the given organism, then it has meaning. (Mead, 1934:75–76)

The mind, or mentality, resides in the ability of the organism to respond to the environment, which in turn responds, so that the individual can control responses to stimuli from the environment. The mind emerges when the organism demonstrates its capacity to point out meanings to others and to itself (Strauss, 1956). Mead felt that the human animal has the unique capacity of controlling its responses to environmental stimuli and isolating those responses during the very act itself. This ability is the product of language (Miller, 1973). Language becomes the mechanism of control during the reflection process of interaction between the organism and the environment.

The concept of *self* is critical in Mead's works. The self involves the process whereby actors reflect on themselves as objects. Thus, the self has the rare ability to be both object and subject. Mead (1934) stated, "The self has a character which is different from that of the physiological organism proper. The self is something which has a development; it is not initially there, at birth, but arises in the process of social experience and activity, that is develops in the given individual as a result of his relations to that process as a whole and to other individuals within that process. The intelligence of the lower forms of animal life, like a great deal of human intelligence, does not involve a self" (p. 135). The developmental process of the self is not a biological one; rather, it emerges from social forces and social experiences. Even the human body is not representative of the self until the mind has developed and recognizes it as such. The body can simply be there as an existent structure in the real world, but the self has the characteristic that it is an object to itself, and that characteristic can then distinguish itself from other objects and from the body (Pfuetze, 1961).

Language represents the developmental process, from interpreting gestures to the capability of utilizing symbolic communication and interaction. Sharing a language allows people to put themselves in the role of the other and to understand why the other acts as it does. It is this reflexivity that allows for the development of the self because persons are able to consciously adjust and modify their own behavior (Mead, 1934).

In regard to society, Mead (1934) stated, "Human society as we know it could not exist without minds and selves, since all its most characteristic features presuppose the possession of minds and selves by its individual members; but its individual members would not possess minds and selves if these had not arisen within or emerged out of human social process in its lower stages of development" (p. 227). Mead believed that the behavior of all humans has a basic social aspect. The experience and behavior of the individual are always a component of a larger social whole or process. The organization of human experience and behavior is society. Because humans have the ability to manipulate their environment, a wide variety of human societies may exist.

The "I" and the "Me"

Mead is the earliest of the social thinkers to examine the socialization process from the interactionist perspective. He believed that human behavior is almost totally a product of interaction with others. The self, which can be an object to itself, is essentially a social structure that arises from social experience. A baby is born with a "blank slate," without a predisposition to develop any particular type of personality. The personality that develops is a product of that person's interactions with others. According to Mead, the self is composed of two parts: the "I" (the unsocialized self) and the "me" (the socialized self). Both aspects of the self are part of an individual's self-concept (Cockerham, 1995). The self is a product of the dialogue between the "I" and the "me." The "I" is the spontaneous, unsocialized, unpredictable, and impulsive aspect of the self. It is the subject of one's actions. The "me" is the part of the self that is formed as the object of others' actions and views, including one's own reflections on oneself (Garner, 2000). An individual who fails to conform to the norms and expectations of society is under the influence of the "I."

The "me" is the judgmental and controlling side of the self that reflects the attitudes of other members of society, while the "I" is the creative and imaginative side of the self (Pampel, 2000). The "me," then, represents the organized set of attitudes which one introjects on one's private self, and the "I" represents the organism's response to others' acts, behaviors, and attitudes (Pfuetze, 1961). The "me" has a self-control aspect, in that it acts to stabilize the self, while the "I" is associated with change and the reconstruction of the self. The combining of the "I" and the "me" leads to the creation of individual personality and the full development of self (Pfuetze, 1961).

Mead believed that we are never totally aware of the "I" aspect of ourselves, and that is why we periodically surprise even ourselves by our own behavior. We see and know the "I" only after the act has been carried out. Consequently, we know the "I" only in our memories (Ritzer, 2000a). The self appearing as the "I" is the memory image of the self who acted toward itself and also acts toward other selves. Additionally, the process that goes into making up the "me," whom the "I" addresses, is the experience which is induced by the action of the "I" (Reck, 1964). The "I" of introspection is the self which enters into social relations with other selves. It is not the "I" that is implied in the fact that one presents herself or himself as a "me." And the "me" of introspection is the same "me" that is the object of the social conduct of others (Reck, 1964).

Development of Self

The development of the self is critical for the creation of consciousness and the ability of the child to take the role of the other and to visualize her or his own performances from the point of view of others. To understand the formation of the self, Mead studied the activities and socialization of children. Mead (1934) noted that newborn babies do not have a sense of themselves as objects; instead, they respond automatically and selfishly to hunger, discomfort, and the various stimuli around them. Very young babies do not have the ability to use significant symbols, and therefore, when they play, their behaviors are little different from those of puppies or kittens, which also learn from imitating their parents. Through play and as children grow, they begin to learn to take the role of others: "A child plays at being a mother, at being a teacher, at being a policeman; that is, in taking different roles" (Mead, 1934:150).

In his theory of the development of the self, Mead traced patterns of interaction that contribute to the emergence of the social self during childhood (Pampel, 2000). To learn the role of others, the child must come to understand the meanings of symbols and language. Much of this learning takes place through various forms of play. The development of the self takes place through a number of stages, and although many reviewers of Mead's stages of development concentrate on just two stages (the play and game stages), it is more useful to identify a third (the imitation stage). The first stage of development is the imitation stage. At this stage the child is capable of understanding gestures (for example, the parent coaxes the child to roll the ball by rolling the ball herself) and imitating behavior. This is an elementary stage of learning, but it represents learning nonetheless, as even imitation implies learning, and babies learn that some behaviors are positively rewarded and other behaviors bring punishment (Pampel, 2000).

The play stage is the second stage of development. At this point of development the child has learned the use of language and the meanings of certain symbols. Through language the child can adopt the role or attitude of other persons. Children's imagination allows them to "act out" the roles of others. By role playing, the child learns to become both subject and object, an important step in the development of the self.

The game stage represents the final stage of development. As Mead (1934) stated, "The fundamental difference between the game and play stage is that in the latter the child must have the attitude of all the others involved in the game. The attitudes of the other players which the participant assumes organize into a sort of unit, and it is that organization which controls the response of the individual" (pp. 154–155). Mead used the game of baseball to illustrate his point. All the players must know the role of the others in order to efficiently maintain team play. Understanding the roles of others is just one critical aspect of the game stage. Knowing the rules of the game indicates the transition from simple role taking to participation in roles of a special, standardized order (Miller, 1973). Abiding by the rules implies the ability to exercise self-control, especially when one is frustrated by others or the rules of the game (or society). The ability of individuals to adopt the attitude of the generalized other is what allows diverse and unique persons to share a sense of community. The generalized other is a kind of corporate individual or a plural noun; it represents the attitudes of the whole community. Thus, the development of the self depends on interactions with others within the community, and these interactions help to shape the individual's personality. Embracing the standards of the community is accomplished by recognizing the generalized other.

The Act

Mead's analysis of the act reveals his social-behaviorist approach to the stimulus-response process. "All perception involves an immediate sensuous stimulation and an attitude toward this stimulation, which is that of the reaction of the individual to the stimulation" (Mead, 1938:3). The response to a stimulus is not automatic because the individual has a choice of the behaviors with which to react. Mead (1982) stated, "We conceive of the stim-

ulus as an occasion or opportunity for the act, not as a compulsion or a mandate" (p. 28). In *The Philosophy of the Act* (1972; Orig. 1938) Mead identified four basic and interrelated stages in the act:

1. **Impulse:** The impulse involves the "gut" reactions or immediate responses to certain stimuli. It refers to the "need" to do something. If individuals are hungry, an impulse will tell them to eat. Reactions to this impulse still involve a level of contemplation and decision making. If the immediate environment does not offer something to eat (nothing at home), then the individual must now decide whether or not to leave the environment (go to the store) to find food, put off the decision to eat until later (wait for a roommate or spouse to come home with groceries), or order take-out delivery. The environment may provide a source of food (vending machine) but still put up obstacles to obtaining it (the machine is out of order). The impulse, like all other elements of Mead's theory, involves both the actor and the environment (Ritzer, 2000a).

2. **Perception:** The second stage of the act is perception. The individual must know how to react to the impulse. "Perception is a relation between a highly developed physiological organism and an object, or an environment in which selection emphasizes certain elements. This relation involves duration and a process. The process is that of action through media which affect the sense organs of the biologic individual" (Mead, 1938:8). Individuals use their senses as well as mental images in an attempt to satisfy impulses. Because people are bombarded by potential limitless stimuli, they must choose among sets of stimuli that have the characteristics most beneficial to them and ignore those which do not.

3. **Manipulation:** Once the impulse has been manifested and the object has been perceived, the individual must take some conscious action with regard to it. The individual conforms to the environment or perhaps conforms the environment itself in order to satisfy the impulse. Thus, if one is tired of waiting for an overdue roommate and still feels hungry, she

or he may decide to go to the store and purchase food.

4. **Consummation:** At this, the final stage, the individual has followed through on a course of action and can consummate the act by satisfying the impulse (eating food). Mead (1938) stated:

> The full completion of the act which the distance stimulus initiates is found in some such consummation as that of eating. It is not the consummation of the act, however, which is the perceptual thing that the distance stimulus sets going. One eats things. In other words, there is an experience of contact with the object which constitutes its perceptual reality and which comes in between the beginning of the act and its consummation. To this experience is referred both the visual experience and consummatory act. They both become characters or adjectives of the thing. . . . We approach the distant stimulus with the manipulatory processes already excited. We are ready to grasp the hammer before we reach it, and the attitude of manipulatory response directs this approach. (pp. 23–24)

Mead viewed the four stages of the act as interrelated. He also viewed the act as involving one person, while the social act involves two or more persons.

The Social Act and Gestures

A *social act* may be defined as one in which the stimulus (or occasion) sets free an impulse (found in the very character or nature of its being) that then triggers possible reactions by those in the environment (Reck, 1964). Mead restricted the social act to the class of acts which involve the cooperation of more than one individual, and whose object, as defined by the act, is a social object (Reck, 1964). The basic mechanism of the social act is the gesture.

According to Thayer (1968), the importance that Mead placed on gestures was influenced by Darwin's *Expression of Emotions in Man and Animals,* in which Darwin described physical attitudes and physiological changes as expressive of emotions (the dog baring teeth for attack). This suggested an evolutionary biological origin of the gesture of language, which Mead found appealing (Thayer, 1968). However, he objected to Darwin's subjectivistic psychological theory that emotions are inner states and gestures are the outward expressions of these ideas and meanings (Thayer, 1968). Mead emphasized the importance of the vocal gesture because the individual who sends a vocal gesture can perceive that vocal signal in much the same way as the listener. That shared perception does not guarantee that the listener will respond in the manner that the sender anticipated (Baldwin, 1986). Verbal gestures represent signs, which, being heard by the maker as well as other parties in the social act, can serve as a common sign to all parties in the social act. The mutually understood gesture becomes a significant symbol (Martindale, 1988). Common gestures allow the development of language, which consists of a number of significant symbols. Only humans have developed to the point of being able to use language and create significant symbols. Symbols allow people to communicate more easily. Consequently, a shared language greatly assists the whole society to function more efficiently. The development of symbolic communication leads to inner conversation with the mind, and to reflective intelligence (Baldwin, 1986). The "same" responses to a significant symbol lead to organized attitudes, which we arouse in ourselves when we talk to others (Reck, 1964).

Communication through vocal gestures has a special quality, in that we cannot see our own facial gestures, but we can hear our own vocal gestures, and therefore, they potentially carry the same meaning to both the listener and the speaker. The speaker can also formulate the answer he or she hopes the listener will (Pampel, 2000). Thinking about responses appropriate in social settings is what Mead called the *generalized other.*

HERBERT BLUMER (1900–1987)

Blumer taught sociology at the University of Chicago from 1927 to 1952, having completed his doctoral dissertation in 1928 under the guidance of Ellsworth Faris, a disciple of George Herbert Mead. Although Mead was a philosopher, his courses on social psychology routinely drew a large number of sociology students. Blumer took courses from Mead, and during Mead's illness in his last quarter of instruction at Chicago, he asked Blumer to take over his major course, "Advanced Social Psychology." As Wallace and Wolf (1999) stated:

> Blumer carried on Mead's tradition for twenty-five years at the University of Chicago and for another twenty-five years at the University of California at Berkeley, where he taught until his retirement. During his Chicago era Blumer was involved in such diverse activities as playing professional football, serving as a mediator in labor disputes, and interviewing underworld figures from the Al Capone gang. Blumer's stature in the profession and the profound respect he commands are indicated by his editorship of the *American Journal of Sociology* from 1941 to 1952, his presidency of the American Sociological Association in 1956, the festschrift in his honor, and several memorial sessions at professional meetings after his death on April 15, 1987. (p. 206)

Blumer was one of sociology's most prominent and esteemed practitioners, and for an entire generation he was the leading spokesperson for the Chicago style of symbolic interactionism. His writings "attempt to capture the fluidity of social action, the reflexivity of the self, and the negotiated character of much of everyday life" (Farganis, 2000:349). Blumer believed that humans construct their own actions and are free of internal drives. Instead, actions are a consequence of reflexive and deliberate processes determined by the individual in response to the environment. Furthermore, humans act on the basis of meaning. Meanings arise during the interactive process, which itself is mediated by language. Language allows individuals to take the role and perspective of the other in order to better understand the true meaning of one's own and others' behavior.

Symbolic Interactionism

Herbert Blumer coined the term *symbolic interactionism* in 1937. According to Blumer (1969):

> Symbolic interactionism rests in the last analysis on three simple premises. The first premise is that human beings act toward things on the basis of the meanings that the things have for them. Such things would include everything that the human being may note in his world—physical objects, such as trees or chairs; other human beings, such as a mother or a store clerk; categories of human beings, such as friends or enemies; institutions, as a school or a government; guiding ideals, such as individual independence or honesty; activities of others, such as their commands or requests; and such situations as an individual encounters in his daily life. The second premise is that the meaning of such things is derived from, or arises out of, the social interaction that one has with one's fellows. The third premise is that these meanings are handled in, and modified through, an interpretative process used by the person in dealing with the things he encounters. (p. 2)

Blumer insisted that the first premise—that "humans act toward things on the basis of meanings"—is merely common sense and cannot be argued against. And yet, many social scientists ignore or downplay the importance of this reality. Blumer stated, "Meaning is either taken for granted and thus pushed aside as unimportant or it is regarded as a mere neutral link between the factors responsible for human behavior and this behavior as the product of such factors" (p. 2).

"Blumer views symbolic interactionism as a uniquely human process in that it requires the definition and interpretation of language and gestures and the determination of the meaning of the actions of others as well" (Farganis, 2000:350). For humans to interact, they must be able to communicate; to communicate effectively, they must share a language. The simple realization that humans interpret each other's actions is the foundation of symbolic interactionism. The process of interpretation has two distinct steps:

> First, the actor indicates to himself the things that have meaning. The making of such indication is an internalized social process in that the actor is interacting with himself. . . . Second, by virtue of this process of communicating with himself, interpretation becomes a matter of handling meanings. The actor selects, checks, suspends, regroups, and transforms the meanings in the light of the situation in which he is placed and the direction of his action. Accordingly, interpretation should not be regarded as a mere automatic application of established meanings but as a formative process in which meanings are used and revised as instruments for the guidance and formation of action. It is necessary to see that meanings play their part in action through a process of self-interaction. (Blumer, 1969:5)

The importance that Blumer placed on interpretation is an elaboration of Mead's argument against Watsonian behaviorism or any mechanical stimulus-response approach. Blumer and Mead insisted that both covert (subjective meanings, the thinking process) and overt (actual, observable) behaviors be analyzed when scientific explanations of human interaction are offered (Wallace and Wolf, 1999). Furthermore, gestures are a key element in the interpretation process: They help to shape an awareness context. This awareness context is illustrated in Glaser and Strauss's (1965) study of dying patients, in which the patients learned to interpret the gestures of their nurses.

Having established his three basic premises of symbolic interactionism, Blumer (1969:50)

elaborated on the methodological implications of symbolic interactionists' view of human group life and social action. These implications led to four central conceptions in symbolic interactionism:

1. People, individually and collectively, are prepared to act on the basis of the meanings of the objects that comprise their world.
2. The association of people is necessarily in the form of a process in which they indicate to one another and interpret each other's indications.
3. Social acts, whether individually or collective, are constructed by actors' noting, interpreting, and assessing the situations confronting them.
4. The complex interlinkings of acts that comprise organization, institutions, division of labor, and networks of interdependency are moving and not static.

The fact that people act on the basis of the meanings that objects have for them presents profound methodological implications. It signifies that if researchers hope to truly understand social action, they must see the objects in the same way as do the subjects of their study.

Methodology

Throughout his academic life, Blumer attempted to articulate his methodology. As Wallace and Wolf (1999) explained, "One of Herbert Blumer's chief contributions to symbolic interactionism has been his elaboration on the methodology of this perspective. In 1983 Blumer received the American Sociological Association Award for a Career of Distinguished Scholarship. The citation stated that Blumer's discussion of methodological issues deeply affected 'the adoption and diffusion of field methods, ethnography, and qualitative sociology. As early as 1937 Blumer discussed the techniques researchers used in analyzing the 'inner career of action'" (p. 217). Despite his lifelong attempts to clarify the methodological needs and guidelines that are essential to the interactionist approach, McPhail and Rexroat (1979), in their article "Mead vs. Blumer: The Divergent Methodological Perspectives of Social Behaviorism and Symbolic Interactionism," drastically misinterpreted Blumer's works. In his article "Mead and Blumer: The Convergent Methodological Perspectives of Social Behaviorism and Symbolic Interactionism," Blumer (1980) blasted the assertions of McPhail and Rexroat. He referred to their article as "flawed by serious misrepresentations" (p. 409) and as "completely wrong" (p. 412).

Blumer (1980) clarified his methodology on a number of key points. First, his approach to the study of human conduct was "naturalistic: By 'naturalistic' study I mean the study of conduct and group life as these occur naturally in the everyday existence of people—in the interaction of people as they associate in their daily lives, as they engage in the variety of activities needed to meet the situations that confront them in their day-to-day existence. This natural makeup of human conduct and group life covers what is done by individuals, organizations, institutions, communities, and collectivities as they carry on their lives" (p. 412). Second, Blumer stressed the need for exploratory studies for two reasons: (1) A great deal of human group life is obscured or is hidden from immediate notice, and (2) social scientists generally do not initially have firsthand intimate familiarity with the group life that they propose to study. For these two reasons, Blumer (1969, 1980) advocated and stressed the need for exploratory study. Exploratory studies are, by definition, flexible, enabling researchers to move in new directions as their study progresses, and they allow scholars an opportunity to form a close and comprehensive acquaintance with a sphere of life that is unfamiliar and hence unknown to them.

The symbolic interactionist approach to methodology is inductive, committed to the understanding of human behavior. The researcher is to gain in-depth knowledge of a group with whom she or he becomes thoroughly familiar. This approach is the opposite of the deductive functionalist approach, which begins with a set of hypotheses. The primary modes of inquiry include exploration (as described previously); inspection, by using "sensitizing concepts," that is, clear definitions of the attributes of the persons and objects under study; and qualitative analysis, or in-depth knowledge gained by interviews and observations of the group under study. The use of concepts is critical in scientific research. Blumer warned against vagueness in defining concepts. "The vagueness of the concept means that one cannot indicate in any clear way the features of the thing to which the concept refers; hence, the testing of the concept by empirical observation as well as the revising of the concept as a result of such observation are both made difficult" (Blumer, 1940:707). Blumer suggested that students are often repelled by the vagueness of certain concepts and theories and therefore turn their attention to the more solid character of the natural sciences. Agreeing with Blumer, I feel it is necessary to show the relevance of abstract theory to concrete events and contemporary people.

Blumer vehemently denied that symbolic interactionism treats the act of scientific inquiry as beginning with a "blank mind." Blumer (1973) stated:

> Neither Mead nor I ever advanced such an absurd position.... Both Mead and I see the act of scientific inquiry as beginning with a problem. Any reasonable consideration of what is involved in the experience of the investigator when he perceives, poses and addresses a scientific problem should show how ridiculous it is to characterize this experience as starting with a "blank mind." Confronted with a problem, the investigator must note given empirical happenings that give rise to the problem; he must pay attention to the prevailing generalizations or beliefs being challenged by the noted empirical happenings; he must give shape

to the problem as it emerges before him; he must identify an area of inquiry implied by the problem; he must form some idea of the kinds of empirical data relevant to clarifying and possibly resolving the problem; and he must sketch out lines of empirical inquiry. (p. 797)

Social Theory

Blumer's focus on social theory was limited to theories grounded in empirical science. Blumer (1954) stated, "The aim of theory in empirical science is to develop analytical schemes of the empirical world with which the given science is concerned. This is done by conceiving the world abstractly, that is in terms of classes of objects and of relations between such classes" (p. 3). Although Blumer's theory is generally micro in its orientation, his conception of society provides a structural framework. Blumer (1969) freely acknowledged the role of structure in human society: "There are such matters as social roles, status positions, rank orders, bureaucratic organizations, relations between institutions, differential authority arrangements, social codes, norms, values and the like" (p. 75). However, Blumer (1969) made it clear that "social interaction is obviously an interaction between *people* and not between roles, the needs of the participants are to interpret and handle what confronts them—such as a topic of conversation or a problem—and not to give expression to their roles." Theoretical schemes are essentially proposals as to the nature of relations between persons and their social environments. "Theory, inquiry and empirical fact are interwoven in a texture of operation with theory guiding inquiry, inquiry seeking and isolating facts, and facts affecting theory. The fruitfulness of their interplay is the means by which an empirical science develops" (Blumer, 1954:3). Blumer wrote *Industrialization as an Agent of Social Change* in the early 1960s, but because he was never happy with this book, it was not published. Maines and Morrione, however, had

it published posthumously in 1990. Maines and Morrione suggest that this book reveals Blumer's macro and objectivist side. Blumer wrote this book in an attempt to explain the role of industrialization as a cause of social change.

ERVING GOFFMAN (1922–1982)

Another important figure in the field of symbolic interactionism is Erving Goffman. Goffman was born in Manville, Alberta, Canada, on June 11, 1922. He graduated from the University of Toronto in 1945 and, for his graduate studies went to the University of Chicago, where he studied with Herbert Blumer. He obtained his master's degree in 1949. His master's thesis was an attempt to use statistics to understand an audience's response to a then-popular American radio soap opera called *Big Sister* (Manning, 1992). His academic focus would shift dramatically from the quantitative approach in his thesis. One of his publications before his dissertation, "On Cooling the Mark Out" (1953), foreshadowed this dramatic departure. "'Cooling out' refers to the efforts of the con artist to control the anger of the 'mark' (the person who has been 'taken') in order to defuse the risk of police intervention or other forms of retaliation on the part of the person who has been wronged" (Adams and Sydie, 2001:505). Goffman received his Ph.D. in 1953. His dissertation was based on fieldwork on a remote Shetland Island. Goffman was fascinated by the various ways that islanders spoke with one another and with strangers and visitors:

> The island was a small, barren place, with only 300 families as permanent residents. Everyone lived in almost constant sight of one another. This provided Goffman with an ideal social microcosm in which to study face-to-face interactions. His Ph.D. study of social interactions and self-presentation, titled "Communication Conduct in an Island

Community" (1953), was published in 1959 as *The Presentation of Self in Everyday Life.* (Adams and Sydie, 2001:506)

In 1954, Goffman served as a visiting scientist at the National Institute of Mental Health in Bethesda, Maryland. Posing as a ward orderly at the hospital, Goffman was able to conduct participant observation research on the interactions among patients, doctors, and administrators. This work would appear later in his publication *Asylums* (1961) and deals with issues related to performance alterations found within total institutions. In 1957 he joined the department of sociology at Berkeley, where he became a colleague of Herbert Blumer. Goffman stayed at Berkeley until 1969, when he accepted a position as professor of anthropology and sociology at the University of Pennsylvania, where he taught until his death in 1982.

Goffman's works reveal a great deal of influence of the symbolic interactionist tradition (participant observation supplemented by data from case histories, autobiographies, letters, and so on), especially the influence of Everett Hughes, who is best known for his studies of occupations, and George Herbert Mead's concept of the self. The influence of Durkheim's analysis of ritual in *The Elementary Forms of the Religious Life* (1912/1965) can be found in Goffman's discussion of ceremonial practices in a total institution *(Asylums)* and in *Interaction Ritual* (1967). Goffman was also influenced by social anthropology, especially the works of W. Lloyd Warner (Collins, 1986c). "Goffman's graduate work was in social anthropology as well as in sociology, and he was Warner's research assistant at Chicago when Warner was working on his analysis of social stratification" (Adams and Sydie, 2001:506). The combination of Warner's work and the Chicago empirical tradition shaped Goffman's studies of the rituals of everyday life. Goffman believed that an individual becomes attached to society through ritual. Georg Simmel's concept of *sociation* established the importance of the study of interaction as

basic to sociological analysis and influenced Goffman's commitment to the study of face-to-face interaction.

In short, Goffman's works were influenced by a wide variety of sources. His theoretical contributions to the field of symbolic interactionism are enormous, but as Manning (1992) revealed, Goffman felt that calling himself a symbolic interactionist was too vague and narrow. He created the field of dramaturgy; he helped to shape the sociology of everyday life, ethnomethodology, and conversation analysis. As Ritzer (2000c) stated, "In fact, a number of important ethnomethodologists (Sacks, Schegloff) studied with Goffman at Berkeley and not with the founder of ethnomethodology, Harold Garfinkel" (p. 228). Late in his life Goffman was elected president of the American Sociological Association. He died in 1982, at the peak of his fame, before being able to give his presidential speech.

Presentation of Self

Perhaps Goffman's most famous work, and his first major publication, is *Presentation of Self in Everyday Life* (1959). *Presentation of Self* is very much in the tradition of symbolic interactionism because of its focus on the individual as an active and reflective self capable of making a vast number of choices in determining how the self should be presented in the varied social situations in which it must perform. In the preface Goffman stated that the perspective used in this book "is that of the theatrical performance; the principles derived are dramaturgical ones. I shall consider the way in which the individual in ordinary work situations presents himself and his activity to others, the ways in which he guides and controls the impression they form of him, and the kinds of things he may and may not do while sustaining his performance before them" (p. xi). The dramaturgical perspective compares all human interaction to a theatrical or dramatic performance. Society is viewed as a stage where humans are actors giving performances for audiences. While *acting*, individuals attempt to *present* themselves according to their identity constructs. The "self label" is an identity that one presents to others in an attempt to manage their impression of him or her. Individuals deliberately give off signs to provide others with information about how to "see" them.

> Information about the individual helps to define the situation, enabling others to know in advance what he will expect of them and what they may expect of him. Informed in these ways, the others will know how best to act in order to call forth a desired response from him. For those present, many sources of information become accessible and many carriers (or "sign-vehicles") become available for conveying this information. If unacquainted with the individual, observers can glean clues from his conduct and appearance which allow them to apply their previous experience with individuals roughly similar to the one before them or, more important, to apply untested stereotypes to him. They can also assume from past experience that only individuals of a particular kind are likely to be found in a given social setting. (Goffman, 1959:1)

A few important points can be made from this analysis. Individuals who are with unacquainted persons can present themselves as they want others to see them, and they may be successful in this presentation because the audience has no past knowledge of them and they therefore cannot be discredited. However, audience members will attempt to fill in the pieces of missing information and may or may not be accurate in their assessment of the actor. Actors with an audience of acquainted persons can successfully present themselves if their behavior is consistent with the audience's knowledge of them. Thus, a respected professor can gain the approval of students because they already know about that professor from other students and their own previous experience. On the other hand, a professor who has already been discredited as incompetent cannot present

himself or herself as a respected educator. In another example, a significant other with a history of cheating (discredited) will not be able to present herself or himself effectively by saying, "Trust me; you know I would never cheat on you." On the other hand, when one is dating someone and has little knowledge of that person's past, and he or she states, "Trust me; I would never cheat on you," he or she will be judged on the basis of past experiences that one has had in previous relationships as much as he or she is likely to be judged on his or her own merits (presentation of self). Persons who present themselves may or may not be sincere in their performance. The audience members must always guard against the likelihood that the performers are hiding their true attitudes, beliefs, emotions, and even factual accounts of events. This is especially important because most people interact with others using certain presuppositions. "A *presupposition* (or assumption, or implication, or background expectation) can be defined very broadly as a state of affairs we take for granted in pursuing a course of action" (Goffman, 1983a:1).

The person performing implicitly requests that the observers take seriously the impression that is fostered before them. They are asked to believe that the character they see actually possesses the attributes presented. Performers may sometimes believe in the sincerity of their own performance, and at other times they may doubt the effectiveness of their own performance. For example, when interviewing for a job, the actor may believe that her or his presentation was effective and showed a strong candidacy for the job, or the actor may leave the interview believing she or he failed in the interview. Utilizing the correct props helps the actor in a presentation. When interviewing for a professional job, it is advisable to dress appropriately (for example, in a business suit). Gregory Stone (1962) conducted a study of appearance and dress in this context and concluded that dress is important in telling others who we are, or in announcing our identities. Proper dress is important in many settings, and how one dresses often influences the way one is perceived. If one goes to court one should have a dignified manner and dress properly. How one dresses when giving a student presentation to the class, attending a business function or a ballgame, and going on a date indicates the presentation of the self and reveals how one is perceived by the self and by others.

Dramaturgy

Dramaturgy in sociology was developed by Goffman as a method of examing social interaction as a series of small plays, or dramas (Levin, 1991). This is an easy concept to grasp, as many individuals already recognize that their lives are filled with drama and constant turmoil—leading to such contemporary phrases as "She acts like a drama queen." As Deegan (1989) explained, "Dramaturgy is a powerful tool for analyzing social life. Invoking the dramatic world of the theater, it allows us to analyze the profane world of everyday life and the sacred world of extraordinary life" (p. 6). Goffman's analysis of the presentation of the self is guided by the dramaturgical perspective; that is, he attempted to explain human interaction by comparing life to a staged drama. Interacting persons are viewed as *actors*, who give *performances* for *audiences* in *settings*, by using *props* and allowing their true selves to be known in the *backstage* region; but they perform for others through their *appearance* and *manner* on the *front stage*. Goffman explained the use of the dramaturgical perspective in *Presentation of Self in Everyday Life* (1959):

> In developing the conceptual framework employed by this report, some language of the stage was used. I spoke of performers and audiences; of routines and parts; of performances coming off or falling flat; of cues, stage settings and backstage; of dramaturgical needs, dramaturgical skills, and

dramaturgical strategies. Now it should be admitted that this attempt to press a mere analogy so far was in part rhetoric and a maneuver. The claim that all the world's a stage is sufficiently commonplace for readers to be familiar with its limitations and tolerant of its presentation, knowing that at any time they will easily be able to demonstrate to themselves that it is not to be taken too seriously. An action staged in a theater is a relatively contrived illusion and an admitted one; unlike ordinary life. (p. 254)

During social performances it is common for actors to manipulate others and engage in *impression management* in order to give and sustain a particular definition of the situation. Impression management affects the *self,* which Goffman referred to as the *product* of a particular scene that is being played out. To protect oneself in the presentation of the self, impression management is used to guard against unexpected actions, such as unintended gestures, inopportune intrusions, and other unforeseen events that may influence one's performance. Performing social actors attempt to construct a particular definition of the situation and must therefore pay close attention to details (for example, props, the setting) if they are to have any chance of success in convincing others of their role. Many times, social actors do not perform alone; they perform with others. Goffman used the term *performance team* or simply *team* to refer to any set of individuals who cooperate in staging a single routine (1959:79). "A team is not identical to a group. In fact, members of the team may not know each other; certainly, they do not have to like or care particularly about each other" (Curra, 2003:51). For example, professionals such as hairdressers and dentists who help with one's appearance would be considered team members. Coworkers may be viewed as team members as well. In a restaurant, hostesses, waiters and waitresses, buspersons, cooks, bartenders, and management personnel are all team members who attempt to make the dining experience of customers a positive one.

Two critical distinctions in settings affect the presentation of performance: the *front stage* and the *backstage*. Front stage behaviors are designed to give intentional performances through the use of specific props to illustrate the role that one is playing. A surgeon needs a sterile operating room, a cab driver needs a taxi, and the waitress needs a restaurant to serve patrons. Goffman (1959) described the front stage as "that part of the individual's performance which regularly functions in a general and fixed fashion to define the situation for those who observe the performance. Front, then, is the expressive equipment of a standard kind intentionally or unwittingly employed by the individual during his performance" (p. 22). The front stage is where the individuals perform a role as they wish to be perceived, whether that is their "true" identity or not. Most people who work do not see their coworker's entire identity (for example, a clerk has an identity and life beyond the work label); instead, workers perform certain roles in given situations (the clerk may also be a parent who needs to take care of a child or a member of a band that must perform at a club).

In the *backstage* actors act as they really are and let their guard down (for example, a police officer off duty and relaxing at home may wish to watch a ballgame and have a few drinks). "Here the performer can relax; he can drop his front, forgo speaking his lines, and step out of character" (Blumer, 1959:112). The backstage is a region closed and hidden from the audience, where the techniques of impression management are relaxed and the actors can be themselves. Thus, a waitress, hoping to earn big tips, will be polite and courteous and act as if she is genuinely concerned about the well-being of her customers (front stage behavior), but in the kitchen, she may be making fun of the patrons with the cooks and busboys (backstage

behavior). "By drawing our attention to the backstage region, Goffman helps us to understand all of the hidden work involved in accomplishing successful presentation of self in public. He shows us how, in the drama of everyday life, individuals manage to look good when they present themselves to others, at home, school, work, neighborhood, and in other microinteractive settings" (Wallace and Wolf, 1999:231). "Maintaining the separation of front and back stage is important for impression management. This separation is found in all areas of social life" (Adams and Sydie, 2001:512).

Mary Jo Deegan (1989) interpreted Goffman's view of teamwork as "negative unity," that is, unity in opposition to others. In other words, team members are often "forced" to cooperate with one another in their front stage performance (for example, the waitress may not like the chef, and the bartender may not like the manager) and act friendly toward one another in the presence of each other and of the patrons. However, in their backstage behavior their true feelings are revealed, and as Goffman concluded, social actors are more likely to unite with one another over the degradation of others than in their praise of others. "Secret derogation seems to be much more common than secret praise, perhaps because such derogation serves to maintain the solidarity of the team, demonstrating mutual regard at the expense of those absent and compensating, perhaps, for the loss of self-respect that may occur when the audience must be accorded accomodative face-to-face treatment" (Goffman, 1959:171). Thus, people who think their colleagues are talking about them behind closed doors should assume they are being "bad-mouthed" and not praised. Furthermore, praise is offered in face-to-face interaction, and degradation (negative gossip) is done in private.

The degree to which individuals separate themselves from a given role (front-stage–backstage separation) is described in

Goffman's concept of *role distance*. As Goffman wrote in *Encounters* (1961), if the role being performed by an actor negatively impacts his self-image, he will want to quickly distance himself from that role-performance. "It is important to note that in performing a role the individual must see to it that the impressions of him that are conveyed in the situation are compatible with the role-appropriate personal qualities effectively imputed to him: These personal qualities, effectively imputed and effectively claimed, combine with a position's title, when there is one, to provide a basis of *self-image* for the incumbent and a basis for the image of his role that others will have of him" (p. 87).

A judge is supposed to be deliberate and Sober; a pilot, in a cockpit, to be calm; a bookkeeper to be accurate and neat in work.

Stigma

Stigma is a term that describes a mark of disgrace or dishonor. Persons who are stigmatized are lacking in full social acceptance, and their self-identity is negatively affected by this label. In one of his most fascinating works, *Stigma: Notes on the Management of Spoiled Identity* (1963), Goffman presented an analysis of persons who are unable to conform to the standards which society has established as "normal." Tracing the origins of the word *stigma* and its meaning, Goffman (1963) stated:

> The Greeks, who were apparently strong on visual aids, originated the term *stigma* to refer to bodily signs designed to expose something unusual and bad about the moral status of the signifier. The signs were cut or burnt into the body and advertised that the bearer was a slave, a criminal, or a traitor—a blemished person ritually polluted, to be avoided, especially in public places. Later, in Christian times, two layers of metaphor were added to the term: the first referred to bodily signs of holy grace that took the form of eruptive blossoms on the skin; the second, a medical allusion to this religious allusion,

> referred to bodily signs of physical disorder. Today the term is widely used in something like the original literal sense, but is applied more to the disgrace itself than to the bodily evidence of it . . . . Society established the means of categorizing persons and the complement of attributes felt to be ordinary and natural for members of each of these categories. (pp. 1–2)

Stigmas are not simply physical markings (such as scars, moles, the lack of a nose, or obesity); they may be seen as "blemishes of individual character" in people who are perceived as weak, those labeled as dishonest, distrustful, afraid, cowardly, traitor, and so on. A stigma can be applied at the macro level as well; there are tribal stigmas of race, nation, and religion, which can be transmitted through lineages and equally contaminate all members of a family. In the years immediately following the terrorist attacks of September 11, 2001, Arabs and Muslims were stigmatized in the United States. The same can be said of Americans in many nations of "The East."

Persons considered "normal" often discriminate against those who are stigmatized. Goffman said we believe that the person with a stigma is not quite human. "We construct a stigma-theory, an ideology to explain his inferiority and account for the danger he represents, sometimes rationalizing an animosity based on other differences, such as those of social class. We use specific stigma terms such as cripple, bastard, moron in our daily discourse as a source of metaphor and imagery, typically without giving thought to the original meaning" (Goffman, 1963b:5). Cuzzort and King (1995) concluded that "stigmata fall into three broad classes: gross physical defects, defects in character, and membership in a social class or group that is not acceptable. A stigma may be acquired at birth or at any time during the life of the individual. Although there are variations caused by the kind of stigma or the time of its acquisition, most stigmatized persons share a number of common problems and common strategies for meeting these problems" (p. 337). A stigma does not dictate all the social performances of the person having it, but it precludes social acceptability in certain settings. Goffman's sociological analysis of stigma also involves the techniques used by "different" persons in dealing with the refusal of others to accept them. The stigmatized individual uses techniques that do not fit the general categorization of that specific category of stigmas. Goffman's examples include the Jew "passing" in a predominantly Christian community and persons who lie about their past but must constantly be on guard that the audience does not learn of the deception—this is referred to as a *discreditable stigma* (Ritzer, 2000c).

Stigma, then, is viewed as a type of deviance from the normal. In an early publication, "Embarrassment and Social Organization" (1956), Goffman stated that "it is only natural to be at ease during interaction, embarrassment being a regrettable deviation from the normal state . . . . He who frequently becomes embarrassed in the presence of others is regarded as suffering from a foolish unjustified sense of inferiority and in need of therapy" (p. 264). Those who face public speaking may become flustered and feel discomfort, and being unable to cope with these feelings they become rattled. "An individual may recognize extreme embarrassment in others and even in himself by the objective signs of emotional disturbance: blushing, fumbling, stuttering, an unusually low- or high-pitched voice, quavering speech or breaking of the voice, sweating, blanching, blinking, tremor of the hand, hesitating or vacillating movement, absent-mindedness, and malapropisms" (Goffman, 1956:264). People who fail in public speaking not only feel embarrassed but are also stigmatized. Given their desire to conceal then embarrassment, they may attempt to control their performance by maintaining poise or "hiding" behind the podium. Since individuals dislike feeling or appearing embarrassed, tactful persons will avoid placing themselves in such a situation.

ARLIE RUSSELL HOCHSCHILD (1940–)

Arlie Hochschild is considered the founder of a new subfield of sociology: the sociology of emotions (Wallace and Wolf, 1999). She received her B.A. from Swarthmore and her M.A. and Ph.D. (1962) from the University of California at Berkeley. She taught at the University of California at Santa Cruz for two years and then returned to Berkeley, where she is currently a sociology professor. Unlike the advantages that women have today in entering the college job market, Hochschild (1994) faced many obstacles in attempting to combine graduate study, an academic job, and child care during the late 1960s and early 1970s. Hochschild indicates that her focus on emotions was inspired by the "collective consciousness" of the women's movement and by Goffman's work. She did not take classes from Goffman while he was at Berkeley, but she had met him and wrote to him on several occasions. His positive response to her academic writings further encouraged her to continue her sociological work on emotions (Adams and Sydie, 2001).

Hochschild's work on emotions has extended Goffman's work in two ways: "First, she expanded on his studies of embarrassment and shame to incorporate a whole range of emotional responses. Second, she examines the outward signs of emotional response and work as Goffman did, but unlike Goffman, she also examines the inner emotional life of the self" (Adams and Sydie, 2001:518). However, Hochschild (1983) was critical of Goffman, arguing that he ignored the emotive self that exists separate from "outer watchers":

> To develop the idea of deep acting, we need a prior notion of a self with a developed inner life. This, in Goffman's actors, is generally missing. From no other author do we get such an appreciation of the imperialism

of rules and such a hazy glimpse of an internally developed self. Goffman himself describes his work as a study of "moments and their men, not men and their moments" (1967). This theoretical choice has its virtues, but also its limitations . . . . Where is the self as subject of emotive experience? What are the relations of *act* to *self*? Goffman speaks as if his actors can induce, or prevent, or suppress feeling—as if they had a capacity to shape emotion. But what is the relation between this *capacity to act* and the self? Whatever other problems they posed, William James and Sigmund Freud proposed a self that could feel and manage feeling. Goffman does not. (pp. 216–217).

Hochschild (1983) described emotion as a biologically given sense; like the other senses—like hearing, touch, and smell—it is a means by which we know about our relation to the world, and it is therefore critical for the survival of human beings in group life (p. 219). She believes that emotion is a unique sense because it is related to cognition: "Broadly interpreted, cognition is involved in the process by which emotions 'signal' messages to the individual" (p. 220). Emotional states such as happiness, sadness, and jealousy are viewed as senders of signals about our way of approaching the inner and outer environment.

Emotion Work

Hochschild's theory of emotion is an expansion of symbolic interactionist ideas but is designed to expand on the limitations of the work on emotions. Her theory encompasses a wide range of emotions and focuses on how actors attempt to manage (work at) their feelings. Hochschild (1979) stated:

> By "emotion work" I refer to the act of trying to change in degree or quality an emotion or feeling. To "work on" an emotion or feeling is, for our purposes, the same as "to manage" an emotion or to do "deep acting." Note that "emotion work" refers to the effort—the act of trying—and not to the

outcome, which may or may not be successful. Failed acts of management still indicate what ideal formulations guide the effort, and on that account are no less interesting than emotion management that works. . . . Emotion work differs from emotion "control" or "suppression." The latter two terms suggest an effort merely to stifle or prevent feeling. "Emotion work" refers more broadly to the act of evoking or shaping, as well as suppressing, feeling in oneself. (p. 561)

Hochschild explained that there are two broad types of emotion work: *evocation*, in which the actor's cognitive focus is on a desired feeling that is initially absent, and *suppression*, in which the actor's cognitive focus is on an undesired feeling which is initially present. Often, emotion work is aided by creating emotion work systems. An example used by Hochschild involves a person telling

Arlie Russell Hochschild, founder of the sociology of emotions.
Source: Estrada Studio

friends of all the worst faults of the person one wants to "break up" with and then going to those friends for reinforcement of this view of the ex-beloved. Hochschild stated that "emotion work can be done by the self upon the self, by the self upon others, and by others upon oneself" (p. 562).

Using a content analysis study of 261 protocols given by university students, Hochschild (1979:562) identified other techniques of emotion work:

1. **Cognitive:** The attempt to change images, ideas, or thoughts in the service of changing the feelings associated with them.
2. **Bodily:** The attempt to change somatic or other physical symptoms of emotion (such as trying to breathe slower, trying not to shake).
3. **Expressive:** Trying to change expressive gestures in the service of changing inner feeling (for example, trying to smile or to cry). This differs from simple display in that it is directed toward a change in feeling.

Emotion work becomes most necessary when the actors' feelings do not fit the situation they find themselves in. For example, a person who has recently received some very good news (like, a new job, the birth of a child) but finds himself or herself in an environment that dictates displaying emotions of sorrow (for example, attending a funeral) needs to suspend the feelings of happiness until he or she leaves the environment demanding displays of emotional sorrow. All of this is necessary because social guidelines direct how we are to feel in given social situations. Thus, persons who display signs of sorrow overtly may actually be quite happy covertly. In other words, outward behaviors can be, and often need to be, controlled, depending on social protocols whereas feelings can be masked and kept "hidden" from the audience members. Hochschild (1979) explained, "Feeling rules differ curiously from other types of rules in that they do not apply to action but to what is often taken as a precursor to action. Therefore they tend to be latent and resistant to formal codification" (p. 566). In short, individuals try to manage what they feel in accordance with rules.

Emotion Culture

The emotion culture consists of a series of ideas about how and what people are supposed to experience in given situations. This culture is filled with emotional ideologies about the behaviors, attitudes, and feelings that members should share (these are similar to subcultural expectations placed on members within their circle of associates). Hochschild stresses that individuals are often put in situations where a great deal of emotion work must be performed; consequently, a number of Hochschild's publications deal with various work and nonwork environments that expect certain levels of conformity.

In *The Unexpected Community* (1973) Hochschild provided a descriptive account of the interactions among forty-three retired people who lived in a small apartment building near the shore in San Francisco (the Bay Merrill Court Senior Citizen Housing Project). She described the social isolation that many senior citizens experience as the norm. In preindustrial society a large proportion of old people owned or controlled the modes of production and consequently maintained a positive sense of self. Postindustrialization has led to the decline of small-business owners and has caused a corresponding lowering of self-esteem among the elderly because they find themselves relatively powerless. A large number of elderly people find themselves living in retirement homes as their last years disappear. They are an example of de facto segregation, living separate from the greater society and their immediate families. Hochschild (1973) explained, "There is a well-known theory in gerontology called the theory of disengagement. According to it, as people grow older, they reduce ties to the outside world and invest less emotion in the ties they retain. In doing so they gradually "die" socially before they die biologically. This process, according to the theory, is "natural" and is linked to the nearness to death" (p. 32). Within the retirement home it is common to form a new sense of community that develops new norms and expectations of behavior. There is a structure of "parallel leadership." The members assist in the planning of activities, purchasing flowers for those who die, helping out the disabled among them, and so on. But there are always those who refuse to join in group activities beyond having their meals together—they become deviants within the community. Ingroups and outgroups are formed, rivalries are created, and some members are judged while others do the judging.

In *The Managed Heart* (1983), Hochschild presented data that demonstrate certain consequences for many airline attendants and bill collectors. "She suggests that while laborers doing manual work may become alienated from what they produce, laborers doing emotional work may become estranged from their own emotional expressions and what they actually feel" (Reynolds, 1990:195). The growing service industry has created a large number of disenchanted workers who are required to do a great deal of emotional labor. From her studies on flight attendants, Hochschild (1983:187–188) believes there are three categories of workers:

1. Workers who identify too wholeheartedly with the job and therefore risk burnout. They have little or no awareness of a "false self." They are likely to offer warm, personal service, but they are also warm *on behalf of* the company.

2. Workers who clearly distinguish themselves from the job are less likely to suffer burnout. They have a truer sense of self.

3. Workers who distinguish themselves from their actions, do not blame themselves for doing so, and see the job as positively requiring the capacity to act; for these workers there is some risk of estrangement from acting altogether and some cynicism about it.

In *The Time Bind: When Work Becomes Home and Home Becomes Work* (1997), Hochschild provided an accurate portrayal of the growing reality for many workers: working at home. Working at home creates images of "freedom" from corporate and management demands. But if the home worker has children at home, the job becomes far more complicated. The home is being invaded by the time pressures and efficiencies of work (for example, fax machines, home computers); while for some workers the workplace is becoming a type of "surrogate home." These workers find their primary "self" identified with their work/occupation; they tend to lack an emotionally stable home environment, or they simply have no life outside the office. Hochschild spent three years at a Fortune 500 company and interviewed workers from factory hands to top executives in a variety of environments ranging from corporate meetings to the home and at the golf course. She stated that, "as the social worlds of work and home reverse, working parents' experience of time in each sphere changes as well" (p. 45). The implication is that a trend in modern life may be that few people feel totally secure either at work or at home.

RELEVANCY

In this chapter, the micro-oriented sociological theory of symbolic interactionism was analyzed, beginning with the its roots in evolutionism, idealism, behaviorism, and pragmatism. The diverse influences from both European and American sources have led to the development of a very intriguing school of thought. The core ideas presented by George Herbert Mead, Herbert Blumer, and Erving Goffman center on the presentation of the self and the fact that human communication and interaction often involve attempts to manage one's image and environment. Recent developments in the interactionist tradition are more diverse and have expanded its original focus. "The work of Hochschild and others on emotion extends the focus of interaction in important ways. . . . The social psychological focus of interactionism takes seriously the premise that people are active, creative interpreters of their social worlds" (Adams and Sydie, 2001:523).

Undoubtedly, the strongest influence on symbolic interactionism remains George Herbert Mead. Through the works of Charles Darwin, Mead came to believe that behavior is not accidental or random but is instead formed through interactions among individuals in the social environment. Behavioral adaptation during social interaction often leads to the creation of new behavior. From the pragmatic perspective, Mead learned that humans not only interpret, shape, and adapt their behaviors but can also do so because they can place meanings on various acts. Reflective meaning and interpretation allow humans to create an image of the self, and that is why symbolic interactionists believe that studying social interaction is the key to understanding human behavior.

George Ritzer (2000a:243–244) provided an excellent summary of the basic principles of symbolic interactionism, summarized here:

1. Human beings, unlike lower animals, are endowed with a capacity for thought.
2. The capacity for thought is shaped by social interaction.
3. In social interaction, people learn the meanings and the symbols that allow them to exercise their distinctively human capacity for thought.
4. Meanings and symbols allow people to carry on distinctively human action and interaction.
5. People can alter the meanings and symbols that they use in action and interaction on the basis of their interpretation of the situation.
6. People can make these alterations because, in part, of their ability to interact with themselves, so that they can examine the possible courses of action, assess the relative advantages and disadvantages, and then choose a course of action.
7. The intertwined patterns of action and interaction make up groups and societies.

Despite the seemingly obvious merit of the symbolic interactionist approach and its contributions to sociological theory there are critical attacks from all sides. Psychologists interested in some of the same topics as symbolic interactionists tend to regard both the ideas and the methods of symbolic interactionists as lacking in rigor and replicable procedures (Stryker, 1987). Mainstream sociology is also critical of symbolic interactionism's seeming departure from the canons of scientific methodology and the quest for objectively verifiable generalizations, which are the cornerstone of traditional sociology. "Symbolic interactionism places great emphasis on a methodology which focuses on subjective meanings, symbols, and interpretation in the determination of how actors arrive at their courses of action. Because the processes are mental and internal, some interactionists rely on subjective and introspective insights rather than readily observable and objective data" (Farganis, 2000:350). This unscientific approach is hence "little more than tenured journalism" (Fine, 1993:65). Bear in mind, of course, that not all social thinkers believe it is necessary to ground theory scientifically.

Ethnomethodologists are critical of the symbolic interactionism derived from Blumer, "regarding the description of social processes produced in that vein as a total gloss of human social interaction, demanding in its place the minute description of behavior, in particular language behavior, without reference to the 'mind,' or 'self' or 'society' that were the conceptual mainstays deriving from Mead that organized accounts of social life in the manner of Blumer" (Stryker, 1987:84). The strongest criticism of symbolic interactionism seems to rest on its commitment to, and over emphasis on, everyday life and the social formation of the self while virtually ignoring social structure. "There are times when symbolic interactionists write as if the poor, the homeless, and the victims of economic dislocations were not a part of everyday life. Class relations and the constraints they place on the lines of action open to individual actors are ignored or overlooked in favor of a more optimistic view of an open society in which negotiated joint action is the relevant characteristic of human action" (Farganis, 2000:350). Fine (1993) added, "Critics might accept symbolic interactionist dominance over the study of face-to-face interaction and microrelations but reject its relevance elsewhere" (p. 65). Of all the criticisms of symbolic interactionism, this (its lack of focus on structure) is the fairest and is of greatest concern. However, it should be noted that the symbolic interactionist perspective *is* a micro approach and the focus *is* on individual social interaction.

Over the past few decades, symbolic interactionism has become more accepted by mainstream sociology, many of its core concepts having been accepted. "Symbolic interactionism has experienced resurgence since the founding of the journal *Symbolic Interaction*. In addition, leading sociological journals now typically include symbolic interactionists on their editorial boards and, as a result, these journals are publishing more research articles informed by tradition" (Wallace and Wolf, 1999:251). Fine (1993) stated, "Symbolic interactionism has changed over the past two decades, both in the issues that practitioners examine and in its position within the discipline. Once considered adherents of a marginal oppositional perspective, confronting the dominant positivist, quantitative approach of mainstream sociology, symbolic interactionists find now that many of their core concepts have been accepted" (p. 61). The symbolic interactionists have done such a good job within their domain that "the process of interaction is

probably the best-understood dimension of the social universe" (Turner, 2003:364).

The relevancy of symbolic interaction is demonstrated primarily by the fact that so much is known about the interaction process. There have been studies conducted on seemingly every possible variable that affects humans. For example, researchers at the University of California at San Diego looked at twenty-seven years' worth of California death certificates (5 million in total) in order to determine whether sets of initials can be "good" or "bad." It seems that names really will hurt you! According to psychologist Nicholas Christenfeld (year 5) people with initials such as JOY or HUG (good initials) had a better chance of living longer—and were less likely to commit suicide or die in an accident—than those with neutral or "bad" initials such as APE, BUM, HOG, or RAT. "The findings do seem to support the idea that liking your name and liking yourself may be linked, and that parents should be sensitive when naming children, said Penelope Wasson Dralle, a professor in LSU Medical Center's psychiatry department" (McConnaughey, 1998:A10). Despite the abundance of research conducted on a wide variety of subjects and behaviors, it should be noted, as all of us have experienced, there are times when our own behaviors baffle us. Consequently, additional research is always needed, particularly in the area of the self.

The study of the self and especially of self-esteem has exploded since the mid-1980s not only in psychology, social psychology, and sociology but also in education. "The California legislature funded a task force whose purpose was to study self-esteem as a potential means of solving such pressing problems as addiction and delinquency" (Hewitt, 1998:xi). In fact, great emphasis is placed on the value and importance of self-esteem "promulgated in advice books directed at managers, nurses, teachers, bankers, and other professions, as well as the general public" (Hewitt, 1998:xi). Parents, teachers, and sports coaches are taught to socialize with young people in such a way as not to compromise their self-concept. Positive self-esteem is assumed to be a good thing. But is it? John Hewitt, professor of sociology at the University of Massachusetts at Amherst, and author of *Self and Society: A Symbolic Interactionist Social Psychology* (1998) and coauthor of "Disclaimers" and "Aligning Actions", stated in *The Myth of Self-Esteem* (1998) that the contemporary emphasis on self-esteem can be irritating and sometimes appalling. Poor self-esteem is now used as an explanation for every imaginable personal problem. "Moreover, the word seems to confirm our worst fears about the decline of ethics and morality, for people increasingly seem to use low self-esteem as an excuse for their every sin and shortcoming. Where even the vilest act can be explained away as an unfortunate but inevitable result of a poor self-image, our capacity to distinguish between good and evil seems to be in jeopardy" (p. xii). John Rosemond (2000), family psychologist and nationally syndicated columnist, prefers people with low self-esteem. "Once upon a not-so-long-ago time, low self-esteem was known as humility and modesty. I believe in those old fashioned virtues if for no reason other than that there's nothing so charming as a humble, modest individual, whether child or adult" (p. A10). Rosemond agrees with Hewitt in proclaiming that, for more than a generation now, members of the health professions have urged parents and teachers to promote high self-esteem in children. Even when a child failed at something (losing a ball game), adults were supposed to pretend he or she won, and if a child misbehaved, adults were to look the other way, ensuring that the child would not feel bad about what he or she had done. The result of such a philosophy is a disdain for authority, cravings for instant gratification, and a dramatic rise in child and teen violence. "In 1996, researchers at Case Western Reserve University of Virginia found that high self-esteem is characteristic of violent criminals, spouse abusers, rapists, gang members, and people with borderline (sociopathic) personalities. In other words, from toddlerhood on, high self-esteem and antisocial behavior go hand-in-hand" (Rosemond, 2000:A10).. Clearly, the debate on the merits of promoting self-esteem will continue for sometime, and self-esteem is just one of many issues related to the self.

The study of gestures has led to a great deal of research on nonverbal communication, which has shown how people in different cultures use different nonverbal signs and align themselves spatially in different ways during their interactions. Recognizing these differences in attitudes is important in interpersonal relations. Additionally, because of the great global diversity in cultures, this understanding and acceptance of cultural differences are critical if peace and harmony are to have any chance. The inevitable force of globalization has made it clear that world leaders and business people need to understand that cultural diversity is revealed in gestures and nonverbal behaviors. Proper interpretation of the cues provided will aid in cooperative and successful interactions.

Symbolic interactionism applies a number of sound methodological procedures to the study of human behavior. The first is the "naturalistic" approach where the researcher observes firsthand the conduct of group life in the natural environment of the interactants. The second is exploratory studies, where the researcher does not bring any preconceived notions regarding the subjects. The third, a qualitative inductive method, allows greater flexibility in conducting research. These techniques of study remain valuable for many forms of study of the social world.

Among the most interesting contributions of symbolic interactionism is Erving Goffman's dramaturgy. Everyone, at some point, interacts with others in the manner described by Goffman's as the front stage and backstage personas. When a young man meets the parents of his new girlfriend, it is best to behave politely and respectfully (front stage), making such comments as "I respect your daughter very much," "When would you like me to have her home?" and "You have a lovely home," rather than saying what he might be thinking (backstage): "I can't wait to make out with your daughter," or "I have no idea when, or if, I will get your daughter home tonight." Job interviewing demands that interviewees put forth their front stage persona by highlighting their job skills and relevant experience. This behavior is opposed to what might be one's true character (backstage) and is revealed by mentioning being fired for stealing and/or embezzlement. Examples of the relevancy to the dramaturgical approach are nearly limitless. Goffman's work on stigma and embarrassment are similar to the relevancy of Garfinkel's (Chapter 4)

work on degradation ceremonies. People are always at risk of being stigmatized by society, and many people already bear this burden. There are few people who have never experienced public (or at least private) embarrassment.

Symbolic interactionism is of great value to sociology, and it is a tremendous complement to more traditional, macrosociological theories. "The focus on the micro relations of social life, and the inductive and qualitative nature of the methodology generally employed, provides a rich source of data and raises important, usually overlooked, issues that can put the proverbial 'meat' on the bones of abstract theoretical constructions" (Adams and Sydie, 2001:523). In short, symbolic interactionism is one of the "big three" of sociological theories, and its relevance to sociological theory will remain indefinitely.

6

Social Exchange Theory: George Homans, Peter Blau, and Karen Cook

xchange theory emphasizes people's abilities to act rationally in their social interactions. For that reason, some scholars refer to exchange theory as a rational choice theory. George Homans described the first three propositions of his explanation of human behavior in terms of "rational choice." However, this categorization often leads one to fail to acknowledge the many dynamics of this truly brilliant theory and its significant contributions to social thought. The rational choice distinction also implies that exchange theory ignores the role of emotions, which is untrue.

INTELLECTUAL ROOTS

The intellectual influences on exchange theory include cultural anthropology, B. F. Skinner and psychological behaviorism, and utilitarian economics. The creator of social exchange theory is George Caspar Homans; direct influences on his creation of exchange theory will be discussed later in this chapter.

CULTURAL ANTHROPOLOGY

At one time, cultural anthropology was a dominant academic discipline. Cultural anthropologists, such as Clyde Kluckhohn, insisted that every culture is unique, especially in terms of social rituals. George Homans disagreed and instead insisted that human nature is generally the same the world over. He believed that, in terms of basic behavioral modes, even remote Aboriginal societies engage in typical interactional patterns. While anthropologists generally wrote about the unique beliefs of Aboriginal societies, Homans took note of their similar behavioral patterns. Consequently, he concluded that societies are not unique and that people around the world are stimulated to act by common goals and aspirations. In other words, all people have common aspirations and similar purposes for their interactions with others. The goal of social science should be to unveil these ordinary behavioral patterns.

British anthropologist Bronislaw Malinowski acknowledged social exchange considerations in his studies. Malinowski believed that exchange plays an important role in social life. He spent many years among the Trobriand Islanders of the Melanesian Islands, where he concluded that exchange is the basis of social cohesion. Malinowski (1926) found that Trobriand society is guided by the principle of legal status, which involves well-balanced chains of reciprocal services. The whole division of totemic clans is characterized by a game of give-and-take, by reciprocity. The concept of reciprocity became a critical element in Homans's exchange theory. The concept of exchange itself was influenced by Malinowski's discussion of the gift. Anthropologists and exchange theorists argue that a crucial aspect of gift exchange binds society together through mutual obligations and increases social cohesion (Wallace and Wolf, 1999).

B. F. SKINNER AND PSYCHOLOGICAL BEHAVIORISM

Burrhus Frederic Skinner, a highly esteemed Harvard professor of psychological behaviorism, was another important influence on the creation of social exchange theory. Skinner was famous for his pigeon studies and the Skinner box (an instrument used to trace changes in animal behavior). Skinner viewed social theories such as structural functionalism, conflict, symbolic interactionism, ethnomethodology, and phenomenology as "mystical enterprises." He saw these theories as constructing mystical entities that distract sociologists from the only concrete entities of study: behavior and the consequences that make behavior more or less likely to occur. Culture itself is nothing more than a collection of human behaviors. Concepts such as ideas and values are useless. What needs to be understood are things such as costs and rewards.

B. F. Skinner was a pioneer in the study of operant behavior and was fascinated by the prospects of the control of behavior of animals and human beings (Martindale, 1988). (Homans would use the word *activity* instead of *operant*). At the core of his psychology was the notion of the stimulus-response arc: When the subject is presented with a stimulus, a response is automatically triggered (for example, when a golfer yells,

"Fore," at a golf course, nearby golfers respond by "ducking" and protecting themselves). In his studies of pigeons, Skinner proved that by reinforcing a desired behavior, he could train his birds to perform bizarre stunts. For example, he was able to get his pigeons to perform a parody of table tennis by rewarding them with corn (Martindale, 1988). Both imitation and willingness to follow instruction are the basis of reinforcement effectiveness. Skinner explained that language, the most significant human skill, arises on the basis of differential reinforcement, through the building of a basic repertoire of words and expressions. The biologically functional child is capable of learning language and does so by imitating the sounds of the parents. Through reinforcement, the child is encouraged and rewarded for furthering her or his vocabulary skills. Even creativity is explained by the principles of reinforcement, by the positive response that originality elicits from most humans.

GEORGE CASPER HOMANS

Homans treated the social exchange between Skinner and his pigeons as the paradigm of all social exchange. Thus, in formulating his version of exchange theory, Homans turned to the behavioral school of experimental psychology founded by his friend Skinner (Wallace and Wolf, 1999). Homans's sociology is an attempt to build a theory about social life from the basic behavioristic propositions of Skinner's psychology of operant conditioning. Homans (1967) believed that all behavior can be reduced to psychological organismic behavior and that those people who dislike a theory based on pigeons simply suffer from "sentimental" problems.

Exchange theory is deterministic. There are two types of determinism: strong ontological (nature of being) and weak epistemological (nature of knowing). Homans falls into the category of strong ontological determinism, which denies conscious beings. Homans felt that consciousness is metaphysical—a left-over of religion. There is no soul; the mind replaces it. For Skinner, the mind is a "black box" and people simply react to stimuli. Consequently, the researcher does not have to understand what is going on in an individual's consciousness (as phenomenology stresses); instead, the researcher merely needs to observe actual behavior. In regard to methodology, Homans's exchange theory advocates experiments. Experiments are used within an axiomatic theoretical format in which a few highly abstract statements lead to hypotheses that can then be tested.

UTILITARIAN ECONOMICS

Basic economic theory, developed by such great thinkers as Adam Smith, David Ricardo, and Carl Menger rests on certain premises about individual psychology and their implications for people's behavior in the marketplace (Wallace and Wolf, 1999). Rational choice theorists have adopted four basic economic propositions. These propositions, as outlined by Wallace and Wolf (1999:299), are

1. Individuals are rational profit maximizers, making decisions on the basis of their tastes and preferences.

2. The more of something an individual has, the less interested he or she will be in yet more of it.

3. The prices at which goods and services are sold in a free market are determined directly by the tastes of the prospective buyers and sellers. The greater the demand for a good, the more "valuable" it will be and the higher will be its price.

4. Goods are generally more expensive if they are supplied by a monopolist than if they are supplied by a number of firms in competition with each other.

The first two propositions are clearly based on the psychological interests of persons. Individuals always seek a profit in any given interaction, and their course of action is nearly always driven by specific preferences such as one's choice of whom to date or have as friends. The second proposition may need a little clarification. It is hard to imagine that anyone who has a lot of money, property, wealth, or fame would not want even more of it. A fan of music wants as many compact disks as possible but generally has little interest in having multiple copies of the same cd. The last two propositions highlight the willingness of persons to pay market prices, especially if they must give up other goods and services. There are a few commodities that most people cannot live without and therefore are willing to pay any "reasonable" price for (for example, water, gasoline, heating oil, and cigarettes). However, if they have options (because of competition), many will seek the best deal in order to maximize their profits. For example, gasoline prices are generally the same from one retailer to the next, and those dependent on automobiles for transportation will pay what the market demands. On the other hand, those who smoke cigarettes and can no longer afford the increasing price of the leading brands often resort to maintaining their habit by purchasing "generic" brands of tobacco.

Homans adapted and applied these basic economic premises to human behavior. He argued that the parties involved in a social exchange approach it with a variety of interests or values, such as material rewards (certain tangible goods and products) and nonmaterial rewards (enjoyment, power, self-esteem). The tobacco industry is obviously not concerned about the health of the customers; it merely wants to increase profits. Cigarette smokers either wish to take care of the addictive need of smoking or simply wish to enjoy the "pleasurable" experience of smoking. When all of the parties involved in the exchange are happy, group equilibrium, or balance, has occurred. Homans called fair exchange *distributive justice.*

Homans's exchange theory has its roots in utilitarianism. The utilitarian approach describes people as self-interested in the sense of maximizing pleasure and avoiding pain (this approach is similar to hedonism, which emphasizes maximizing pleasure and minimizing pain.). Utilitarians argue that behavior is more or less a moral activity according to the amount of utility it bestowes on individuals. Utilitarianism is a theory that the greatest good for the greatest number should be the main consideration in making a choice of actions. For example, during a war, the death of soldiers (and some civilians) is justified in the name of serving the "greater good."

DEFINING SOCIAL EXCHANGE THEORY

Social exchange theory illustrates an effort to fuse the principles of behaviorism and economics with other ideas and apply them to the concerns of sociologists. Exchange theory originated during the 1950s, primarily through George Homans. Most of Homans's exchange theory can be viewed as a reaction against Talcott Parsons, Émile Durkheim, and structural functionalism in general. Exchange theory is positivistic in that it assumes that human behavior can be explained by natural "laws." Because there is an exchange in behavior, this theory is concerned with the interactions between people and focuses on what people seem to be getting out of their interactions and what they in turn are contributing to the relationship. Exchange theorists believe that in every interaction something is being exchanged. These exchanges are not limited to the economic realm (money or commodities), for incentives to behave socially (to take action) also come in the form of approval, esteem, love, affection, allegiance, and other nonmaterialistic or symbolic expressions. "When two actors at least occasionally satisfy each other's interests somewhat, and do so as an exchange, we say that together they form an exchange relation. An exchange network is a set of exchange relations in which every exchange relation shares an actor with at least one other exchange relation" (Whitmeyer, 2001:141). The larger the number of the interacting members, the more complex these exchanges become. Furthermore, "location in a network of exchange will affect the outcomes an actor experiences when actions in one relationship affect the course of negotiations in other relationships involving that actor. Negotiations comprise a sequence of actions by which agreement is (or is not) reached" (Skvoretz, Willer, and Fararo, 1993:97). Those with power are always in a better negotiation position.

Because Homans was the creator of social exchange theory and most of the guiding principles, it is time to shift focus to this brilliant social thinker.

GEORGE CASPAR HOMANS (1919–1989)

It was Homans's belief that all human behaviors could be explained by behavioral psychology. To that end, he implemented a number of propositions, all psychological in origin, to comprise a theory of rational behavior centered on the assumption that individuals act to increase their rewards and decrease their costs. For all those theorists who disagree with his basic assumption, Homans argued that the burden of proof rests on their shoulders (Martindale, 1988).

A Brief Biographical Sketch

George Caspar Homans was born in Boston to a wealthy Brahmin-style family on August 11, 1910. In his autobiography Homans (1984) described the Brahmins as gentlemen and ladies who were conscious of their class standing. The Homans lineage consisted of three consecutive generations of successful surgeons, all residing in Boston. George was the eldest of four children. He would always value academics, and he took advantage of the outstanding library in his family home—something that can only happen in a financially privileged household. "Much of what I learned from books I learned not at school but at home, from our excellent library" (Homans, 1984:46). He also benefited from the top private schools in Boston until he eventually entered Harvard, following in the footsteps of previous generations of Homanses. In September 1928, Homans entered the freshman class. As an English literature major, he learned from Bernard DeVoto, who was his English instructor and tutor. Homans credited DeVoto with being the biggest single influence on his intellectual life. Homans was particularly indebted to DeVoto for introducing him to Lawrence Joseph Henderson. DeVoto and Henderson were friends, and it was Henderson who had introduced DeVoto to sociology. In turn, it was DeVoto who introduced Homans to sociology.

George Homans, founder of Social Exchange Theory.
Source: Courtesy of the Harvard University Archives

Homans earned his bachelor's degree from Harvard in 1932, with an in English literature major. Homans's sociological background came from those with whom he associated at Harvard, but his real interest in the field came as a result of reading the works of Vilfredo Pareto. His exposure to the works of Pareto would forever alter his academic and professional pursuits. In 1934, Homans coauthored (with Charles Curtis) *An Introduction to Pareto.* "The publication of this book made Homans a sociologist even though Pareto's work was virtually the only sociology he had read up to that point" (Ritzer, 2000d:55). Pareto especially influenced Homans's detailing of the basic laws of psychology that guide human behavior, his application of general concepts associated with economics, and his desire to establish full deductive theories or explanations (Wallace and Wolf, 1999).

The publication of *An Introduction to Pareto* led directly to Homans's appointment as a junior fellow in sociology at Harvard in 1934. The Society of Fellows had been created to explore the possibility of graduate training that was more adequate than that for the Ph.D. (Martindale, 1988; Ritzer, 2000). Even though Homans himself never earned a Ph.D., he became one of the major sociological figures of his day (Ritzer, 2000d). Homans was a junior fellow at Harvard from 1934 to 1939, and during this time he immersed himself in the field of sociology. In 1939, Homans became an instructor of sociology, remaining so until 1941, when he left to serve in the U.S. Navy in World War II. After four and half years in the navy, Homans returned to Harvard and was given the position of associate professor of sociology in the Department of Social Relations founded and chaired by Talcott Parsons. Homans did respect Parsons but would come to be highly critical of his style of theorizing. In fact, a long-running public feud would develop between the two colleagues that often manifested itself in books and journals. Homans believed that social theory should be centered on empirical observation and deductive reasoning. He felt that Parsons created theoretical constructs and then found examples to fit these preconceived categories.

During the 1950s, Homans was very productive as he became a full professor in sociology in 1953, earned an M.A. in English in 1955, and had significant empirical studies published. His major publications are *The Human Group* (1950), in which he analyzed the structures and processes of human groups in various settings ranging from a factory setting to that of an aboriginal tribe found in the Pacific; *Social Behavior: Its Elementary Forms* (1961), where he wrote that all human behaviors can be explained by basic psychological principles; *Sentiments and Activities* (1962), which centers on his criticism of Parsons and other functionalists, along with an elaboration of his own methodological principles; and *The Nature of Social Science* (1967), which continued the themes found in *Sentiments and Activities.*

Homans served as the president of the American Sociological Association (ASA) and in his 1964 address followed the tradition of making controversial statements about the state of sociology. Homans verbally attacked functionalists because of their rejection of the validity of using psychological propositions, by stating that functionalism was unable to generate any adequate explanations of human behavior. Homans spent his entire academic career at Harvard, and in 1988, while serving as professor emeritus, he was awarded the ASA's Distinguished Scholarship Award.

Influences on Homans

Because of his micro orientation, the most significant influences on Homans's work came from a variety of sources that attempt to explain small-group analysis. These influences include such disciplines as biochemistry, behavioral psychology, functional anthropology, utilitarianism, and basic economics and such social theorists as Lawrence Henderson, Elton Mayo, B. F. Skinner, and Georg Simmel.

When Homans was an undergraduate, he became a close friend of a junior faculty member named Bernard DeVoto ("Benny"). DeVoto assigned many books (beyond Pareto's *Sociologie generale*) that interested Homans. However, as Homans (1984) stated, "The greatest service Benny did me was to introduce me to Professor Lawrence Joseph Henderson" (p. 89). Henderson (a biochemist) was conducting research on industrial work with his colleague Elton Mayo (a psychologist). Mayo was the director of the famous studies conducted at the Hawthorne Plant of the Western Electric Company in Chicago. (*Note:* Homans dedicated *Sentiments and Activities* to the memory of Elton Mayo.) Homans conducted his own follow-up studies of the Bank Wiring Room at Hawthorne years later and concluded that workers share a body of sentiments. In his 1951 article "The Western Electric Researches," Homans described how workers know better than to turn out too much work. Any worker that did so was considered a "rate-buster." "The theory was that if an excessive amount of work was turned out, the management would lower the piecework rate so that the employees would be in the position of doing work for approximately the same pay. On the other hand, a person should not turn out too little work. If he did he was a 'chiseler;' that is, he was getting paid for work he did not do" (Homans, 1951:235). In other words, workers expected new employees to work at the same rate of production as the established norm. This "expected" pace produced enough to keep management happy but controlled an impression that other workers were not working hard enough. Newcomers to the workforce were quickly indoctrinated into these shared sentiments in the workplace culture.

Homans's *The Human Group* (1950) was partially rooted in the functionalist tradition of Durkheim and of the British anthropologists

Bronislaw Malinowski and A. R. Radcliffe-Brown. His subsequent work abandoned this functional viewpoint in favor of an exchange perspective. Homans eventually broke away from these influences after he met B. F. Skinner. Homans came to view Skinner's operant conditioning research as applicable to research on humans. Homans was not implying that animals and humans are similar in behavior, however. "We begin at what may seem a long distance from human social behavior—at the behavior of individual animals. And a long distance it is: not for one moment do we imply that the behavior of men and the behavior of animals is the same. But if they are not the same they may yet be similar, and similar in just those ways that will most interest us" (Homans, 1961:17). Homans believed that the explanations of animal behavior are more firmly established than those of human behavior; therefore, it was logical to borrow from other sciences the knowledge that they had already tested (especially because investigators can more easily experiment with animals under controlled conditions than with humans). Skinner's psychological propositions became the foundation of Homans's social exchange theory. These ideas were fused with basic economic premises to yield a cost-benefits analysis of behavior.

Georg Simmel had an impact on Homans as well. Simmel was one of the first early major social theorists who attempted to identify universal characteristics of human behavior. He was especially interested in why people are moved to make contact with others. Like modern exchange theorists, he came to believe that their motive is to satisfy needs and pursue individual goals. Simmel suggested that even though people do not always receive equal returns, their interactions are always based on some expectation of reciprocity and therefore should be viewed as kinds of exchanges (Wallace and Wolf, 1999). Simmel, then, sought to capture the fundamental nature of human life as an interactive process involving reciprocal relations, or exchange, within social associations (Farganis, 2000).

In 1958, Homans wrote an article ("Social Behavior as Exchange") for a special issue of the *American Journal of Sociology* in honor of Simmel. Homans suggested that Simmel was the ancestor of postwar small-group research, which Homans had taken to the edge of a growing scientific sociology. Homans urged small-group researchers to integrate laboratory experiments with quantified fieldwork, and to limit the propositions to psychological explanations. He proudly stated in *Sentiments and Activities* (1962), "I hold myself to be an 'ultimate psychological reductionist'" (p. 279). Furthermore, Homans (1962) stated that the special virtue of exchange theory is that it brings sociology closer to economics, the oldest and most practical of the sciences of humanity.

Social Exchange Theory

Homans's basic view was that the study of sociology should concern itself with explaining individual behavior and interaction. He showed little interest in consciousness or in the various types of large-scale structures and institutions that were of primary concern to most sociologists. His interest centered on reinforcement patterns and the history of rewards and costs that lead individuals to do what they do (Ritzer, 2000c). The most basic premise of exchange theory is that people continue to engage in behaviors they find rewarding and that they cease to engage in behaviors where costs have proven too high. Homans believed that self-interest is the motive that makes the world go around and that individuals, just like Skinner's pigeons, modify their behavior according to the positive or negative reinforcement provided by their environment (Coser, 1977). The human social world consists of interacting persons exchanging rewards and punishments, and people continue to engage in relationships that they find rewarding.

However, when people become aware that they are being exploited or treated unfairly, they leave the relationship or quit the group (Homans, 1961). In Homans's industrial observations he concluded that if workers feel that they are not being paid enough for their work, they may form a union, bargain collectively with the employer, or even go on strike. But in taking such action, workers must weigh the potential benefits against the potential costs: losses in pay and in friendship and perhaps even their jobs. Such choices are never easy, nor are the motivations always obvious. When multiple values are involved, the rational calculation of benefits and costs becomes very difficult.

In short, Homans's exchange theory is based on both behavioral psychology and elementary economics. It is a theory that "envisages social behavior as an exchange or activity, tangible, or intangible, and more or less rewarding or costly, between at least two persons" (Homans, 1961:13). Homans outlined five clear-cut propositions that he felt explain all human behavior. Although he admitted that his "set of general propositions gets no high marks for originality" (Homans, 1961:13), they do form the foundation of his social exchange theory.

The Five Propositions of All Human Behavior

Homans made it clear that his five basic propositions used to explain all human behaviors are psychological. They are psychological in two ways. First, they are usually stated and empirically tested by persons who consider themselves psychologists. Second, they are propositions about individual behavior, rather than propositions about groups or societies. Although a particular kind of reward may be valuable to members of one group and a different kind of reward may be of value to another, and since the pursuit of different rewards may require different action, the same proposition is used. The proposition "The more valuable the reward,

the more frequent or probable the action that gets the reward" holds true for both. Even if people differ genetically and biologically, they still pursue the action that is most likely to be rewarded (Homans, 1967).

Homans (1984) believed that all human behaviors can be explained by five general propositions. He stated:

> The general propositions relate four main classes of variables to one another: frequency with which a person performs an action (in B. F. Skinner's language an operant); the frequency with which an action is followed by a reward, a punishment, or nothing at all (in Skinner's language, the frequency with which an action is *reinforced*, positively or negatively); the degree of reward or punishment experienced by the actor (in my language, not Skinner's, the *value* of the reinforcement); and finally the environmental conditions, *stimuli*, that attend a person's action. Note that a person need not get a reward *because* he performed a certain action. The reward may be the result of wholly different causes. To serve as a reinforcer, it is enough that it follows the action, which leaves an opening for superstition behavior. (p. 334)

Of his five propositions, four of them were from Skinner, while the "frustration-aggression" proposition was stated in 1940 by Dollard in his book *Frustration and Aggression*. The propositions are as follows (Delaney, 2004: 269–271).

1. **The Success Proposition:** The principle of reward. If in the past an activity was rewarded, then the individual is more likely to repeat the activity in the present. The shorter the interval of time between the behavior and the reward, the more likely the person is to repeat it. Furthermore, the more often a particular action of a person is rewarded, the more likely the person is to perform that same action. This is referred to as the *success proposition* because the individual is rewarded for certain courses of action and activity. In *The Human Group* (1950), Homans attempted to make a distinction between action and activity in stating

that an activity is "an *element* of social behavior. . . . It might be called *action*, if *action* had not been given a more general meaning, or *work*, if *work* did not have a special meaning" (pp. 34–35).

Homans explained that in the pursuit of rewards certain costs are incurred. "For an activity to incur cost, an alternative and rewarding activity must be there to be foregone" (Homans, 1961:59). A *cost* is a value foregone, and it is a negative *value.* "The *cost,* then, of a unit of a given activity is the value of the reward obtainable through a unit of an alternative activity, foregone in emitting the given one" (Homans, 1961:60). A *profit* is measured in terms of successful rewards minus all costs. Homans (1961) stated, "We define psychic *profit* as reward less cost, and we argue that no exchange continues unless both parties are making a profit. Even the pigeon, when it finds its rewards and costs nicely balanced, may try to get out of the situation or indulge in emotional behavior rather than continue its exchange with the psychologist. But our argument is more familiar in the field of human buying and selling" (p. 61). For example, an individual will not continue to purchase a regular product (something consumed often, such as coffee or soda) at a high price at one store if it can be purchased cheaper at a second store. Furthermore, the seller at the first store will not be able to reduce the price if she or he does not receive a reduction in the wholesale cost. Homans regularly used economic examples to demonstrate the validity of his propositions. Homans (1961) believed that the "principles of elementary economics are perfectly reconcilable with those of elementary social behavior, once the special conditions in which each applies are taken into account. Both deal with the exchange of rewarding goods" (p. 68).

2. **The Stimulus Proposition:** The principle of experience. If a similar stimulus, or set of stimuli, presents itself and resembles an originally rewarded activity, the individual is likely to repeat that course of action. The more often, in a given period of time, an individual's activities reward the activity of another, the more often the other will emit the

activity. This proposition reflects the concepts of *value* and *quantity*. In quantity, frequency is measured by some sort of counting over a period of time, such as the quantity of desired activities during exchange. According to Homans (1961), "Frequency is a measure of the quantity of activity; it is the number of units of the activity that the organism in question emits within a given period of time: the frequency of pecking is the number of pecks per minute or per hour. Frequency is measured by some kind of counting and presupposes units of activity that can be counted" (p. 36). Value may be measured in terms of the "degree of reinforcement" an individual receives per exchange. Value is a matter of degree varying from one person to another, and it is equated with rewards. The connection between the stimuli and the action is subject to both generalization and discrimination. The individual works within the bounds of how similar a stimuli must be to past rewarding stimuli in order to be considered as valuable as the original. For example, a grandchild tells her grandfather that she loves playing video games. The grandfather, not thinking about what type of video games his granddaughter likes to play, assumes she will like a video game for a gift because she love to play games (generalization) and purchases a video game for a gift. But the grandchild does not like the game her grandfather purchased, preferring (discrimination) instead some other game.

3. **The Value Proposition:** Reward and punishment, the principle of value of outcome. The more valuable to an individual a unit of the activity another gives him or her, the more often he or she will emit the activity rewarded by the activity of the other. Thus, if one person highly values the company of the other, she or he is far more likely to engage in behavior that the other finds desirable. For example, she or he tolerates watching football on television because the friend likes football. However, Homans was quick to notice that this proposition needed to be altered, for if one person highly values the company of another but the other is always accompanying the original, a feeling of satiation may occur.

Rewards, then, vary by degree of value. The value in question is always that of a given unit of the reward, no matter how that unit is defined. The variable, value, may take either a positive or a negative form. The results of an individual's behavior that have positive values are called *rewards,* while the results that have negative ones are called *punishments.* Action that has the result of allowing an individual to avoid punishment is rewarded by that result, and that behavior is more likely to be performed in the future. Consequently, there are two classes of reward: intrinsic reward and the avoidance of punishment. In addition, there are two classes of punishment: intrinsic punishment and the withholding of a reward. Punishment, or its threat, becomes a potentially powerful motivator of action.

Homans combined these first three propositions to form the rationality proposition, or rational choice. These first three propositions assign value to our actions as individuals seek to collect favorable outcomes (rewards). As Homans explained, in choosing between alternative actions, a person chooses the one for which, as perceived by him or her at the time, the value, V, of the result, multiplied by the probability, p, of getting the result, is the greater. Thus, Action A equals p times V ($A = pV$). If a person faces a choice between two courses of actions, with the first, if successful, bringing a result, let us say, of three units of value to him, but he or she estimates the chance that the action will be successful as only one out of four, he or she may choose to pursue a different course of action. The second course of action will bring a result worth only two units, but its chance of success is estimated as one out of two. Thus, since $3 \times 1/4$ is less than $2 \times 1/2$, the rationality proposition predicts that the individual will take the second course of action (Homans, 1961). Although this proposition may sound complicated, humans use this system daily. Decisions such as choosing what type of camcorder, automobile, or television to purchase are all determined by a rational calculation of the costs versus the rewards. One camcorder may cost more than another, but if the additional extras justify

the additional money, it may still be more valuable to purchase. On the other hand, if someone is working on a tight budget, it may be more rewarding to purchase the cheaper model without a lot of extras.

4. **The Deprivation-Satiation Proposition:** The principle of diminishing returns. Homans (1961) stated that "deprivation and satiation are not, of course, separate variables but low and high values, respectively, of the same variable, and we have not stated two different propositions but a single proposition" (p. 19). In Skinner's studies, deprivation was explained in terms of the pigeon's going a long period of time without food. Hunger increased the desired activity of pecking at the lever to receive a food pellet. Homans believed that this principle could also be applied to human needs beyond (and including) food. A person who goes a long period of time (deprivation) without a desired reward (for example, contact with a loved one) becomes far more willing to engage in behavior that will lead to the desired reward. When people miss one another so much that they "ache" without the other, they will alter their behavior so that they can be with the desired one. This idea is somewhat similar to the adage that absence makes the heart grow fonder. However, an individual who is forced to go a long period of time without the desired reward will lose interest and move on, seeking other rewards from other sources. Homans referred to this as changes in kind of activity. Since human activities are not standardized exchanges incapable of change, people will change their activities to increase profits and rewards. Thus, when engaging in the dating ritual of "playing hard to get" one must be prepared for the other's simply giving up and moving on.

When someone has more than enough of the desired reward satiation takes place and the motivation to act a certain way is missing. In Skinner's studies, when a pigeon had had an abundance of food, its need to participate in the desired behavior (pecking at the target) disappeared. This proposition can be applied to humans in a wide variety of activities. For example, when two people spend a great deal of time together, they may grow tired of the relationship. In some cases "familiarity breeds contempt" (as is generally the case when two bitter rivals are placed in close proximity).

Homans further elaborated that the deprivation-satiation proposition is not very precise and is subject to the value of the reward in question in relation to the time it was last presented. Food and sex satiate a person quickly, but they soon recover their value, whereas most persons are not so easily satiated by money, power, or status.

5. **The Aggression-Approval Proposition:** The principle of distributive justice. Homans (1961) noted that "when a behavior does not receive the expected reward, or is punished unexpectedly, the response is anger or aggression. Interestingly, the aggressor will find such aggression rewarding" (p. 37). Additionally, when a person's action receives a greater reward than expected, or he or she does not receive a punishment when expected, he or she will be pleased and is more likely to perform approving behavior.

The principle of distributive justice is applied here. In Skinner's pigeon's study, "when a pigeon pecks but gets no grain, although the stimulus-conditions resemble those under which it was previously rewarded for pecking, the pigeon displays what looks to a human observer for all the world like anger and frustration: it turns away from the target, flapping its wings and cooing hurriedly" (Homans, 1961:72–73). This principle certainly applies to humans. When individuals do not receive the same rewards as others, frustration occurs. For example, if two students both receive the same numerical grade, they expect the same letter grade. If one receives a grade lower than the other, frustration and anger will occur. As Homans (1961) explained, humans "express anger, mild or severe, when they do not get what their past history has taught them to expect. The more often in the past an activity emitted under particular stimulus-conditions has been rewarded, the more anger they will display at present when the same activity, emitted under similar conditions, goes without its rewards: precedents are always turning into rights" (p. 73). This anger and frustration are especially directed at the person responsible for the distribution of the reward. Additionally, the more unfairly one is treated, the more frustrated and angry one becomes.

The Group System

Homans was quite clear about the elements that comprise the group system (Martindale, 1981). These elements are activity, interaction, sentiment, and norms. *Activity* refers to what the members of the group do as members. *Interaction* involves the relation of the activity of one member of the group to that of another. The *sentiment* of the group is the sum of the feelings of group members with respect to the group. The *norms* of the group are a code of behavior adopted consciously or unconsciously by the group. Homans's group system is in the tradition of Pareto, who viewed a group as "external in contrast to the internal system" (Martindale, 1988). The group is external in that it responds to the needs of the outside environment. These environmental needs can be physical, technical, and/or social. The group is an internal system because the elements of behavior are mutually dependent.

In *The Human Group,* (1950), Homans defined a group as "a number of persons who communicate with one another often over a span of time, and who are few enough so that each person is able to communicate with all the others not at secondhand, through other people, but face to face" (p. 1). Homans analyzed a series of previously conducted studies of groups found in a variety of environments, including families, school cliques, and coworkers.

Power and Authority

Homans (1961) felt that a person who influences other members has authority. An individual earns authority by acquiring esteem and acquires esteem by rewarding others. Similarly, power can be defined as the ability to provide valuable rewards. Those with power and authority are small in number, and the smallness of the number is the seed for future conflict. The leader, when directing others, inevitably causes the members to incur costs. The leader's also incurring costs will help to prevent conflict. For example, workers are less upset when the boss tells them they have to work late if the boss also stays to work late. When the rewards that are distributed seem fair (distributive justice), the individual is satisfied, especially if the reward is received within a given period of time. Humans act as if they find it valuable to realize fair exchange, and they will express emotion toward this end (the pursuit of distributive justice).

George Homans's greatest contribution to sociological theory is his development of social exchange theory. His focus was primarily on the individual and social groups, but his ideas helped to influence such exchange theorists as Peter Blau, Karen Cook, and Richard Emerson. These theorists helped to transform exchange theory from its micro-oriented roots to addressing issues at the macro level.

PETER BLAU (1918–)

Peter Blau expanded Homans's exchange theory by extending his analysis to more complex issues such as social structures, organizations, and bureaucracy. He explored "the development of social structures and the reciprocal relationship between these larger structures and social interaction on the individual level" (Farganis, 2000:295). Blau's exchange theory is closer to mainstream sociology (Wallace and Wolf, 1999).

A Brief Biographical Sketch

Peter Blau was born in Vienna, Austria, on February 7, 1918. He emigrated to the United States in 1939, and after serving in the military during World War II (earning a Bronze Star), he became an American citizen in 1943. Blau received his undergraduate sociology degree from Elmhurst College (Illinois) in 1942 and his Ph.D. from Columbia University in 1952. He taught at Wayne State University, Cornell University, the University of Chicago (from 1953 to 1970), Columbia University (becoming a professor of sociology), and then at the University of North Carolina at Chapel Hill. Blau has received many honors during his career, including serving as president of the American Sociological Association in 1964 and winning the Sorokin Award from the ASA in 1968 for a book he coauthored with Otis Dudly, entitled *The American Occupational Structure* (1967). He has written many articles and books. Among his more significant publications are *The Dynamics of Bureaucracy* (1955); *Bureaucracy in Modern Society* (1956); *Formal Organizations* (1962), coauthored with W. Richard Scott;

Peter Blau expanded Social Exchange Theory beyond its original micro roots.
Source: Courtesy of Judith R. Blau

Exchange and Power in Social Life (1964); *The Structure of Organizations* (1971), coauthored with Richard A. Schoenherr; *The Organization of Academic Work* (1973); *Continuities in Structural Inquiry* (1981), coauthored with Robert Merton; *Structural Contexts of Opportunities* (1994); and the second edition of *Crosscutting Social Circles* (1997), coauthored with Joseph E. Schwartz.

Blau has made significant contributions to two distinct theoretical approaches: exchange theory and functionalism. "Blau's interest in social structure is common to both his theories of social exchange and his later work, in which he is no longer directly concerned with exchange per se. . . . Whereas Homans believes that such properties are ultimately explained by psychological factors, Blau argues that distinctively social factors are involved as well" (Wallace and Wolf, 1999:328). Blau maintains a belief that the social exchange process is crucial to the understanding of both small-group dynamics and complex social structures. It was, however, his *Exchange and Power in Social Life* (1964) that propelled Blau's status as a major theorist and is of greatest relevancy to exchange theory and, consequently, this chapter.

Blau's Exchange Theory

In *The Organization of Academic Work* (1973), Blau discussed the role of theory. "A formal theory from which empirical predictions can be logically deduced plays the dominant role in research that is designed to test the predictions and thereby indirectly the theory" (p. 45). Thus, a theory needs to be presented in such a way that it allows itself to be tested empirically. Exchange theory is such a theory.

Exchange and Power in Social Life (1964) represents Blau's major contribution to exchange theory. "Its analysis of the origins and principles governing exchange behavior is close to Homans's. However, Homans is essentially concerned with setting out a deductive theory of behavior in general. By contrast, Blau sees exchange as one particular aspect of

most social behavior. . . . His analyses suggest how an exchange perspective can provide explanation rather than offering strict deduction and exposition" (Wallace and Wolf, 1999:328).

In *Exchange and Power in Social Life,* Blau acknowledged his devotion to Simmel's idea of exchange. Blau described social exchange as a central principle in social life, which is derived from primitive terms, and from which complex social forces are derived. Blau stated that social exchange theory can explain behavior in groups as well as in individuals. In short, he believed that social exchange may reflect any behavior oriented to socially mediated goals. In Chapter 1 of *Exchange and Power,* Blau discussed the structure of social associations. He analyzed Durkheim's conception of suicide as a social fact by suggesting that a social fact emerges only when it has been transformed by association. Association itself is an active factor in producing social behavior. It creates social life, and it assists social integration. "Blau argues that exchanges increase social integration by creating trust, encouraging differentiation, enforcing conformity with group norms, and developing collective values" (Wallace and Wolf, 1999:329). Thus, social exchange creates bonds of friendship and establishes social positions of subordination and domination.

Processes of social association can be conceptualized, if one follows Homans's lead, as an exchange of social activity, tangible or intangible, rewarding and costing, between at least two persons (Blau, 1964). Exchanges of gifts in simpler societies served latent functions of establishing bonds of friendship and establishing superiority over others. The basic foundation of any social exchange is one person's offering another person a reward at a certain cost. The relationship continues as long as both persons find the exchange beneficial or necessary. A variety of conditions affect social exchange: the stage in development and the character of the relationship between the exchange partners; the nature of the benefits in the transactions; the costs of providing them; and the social context in which the exchanges take place.

According to Blau, the social exchange process also creates opportunities for impression management. People want to be seen in a certain way to maximize their potential profits. Impressions often come at a cost to the actor, as he or she must perform the role that brings the most rewards. For example, someone who is in the early stages of dating generally behaves in a manner that ultimately brings the greatest rewards (for example, additional dates, sex). Blau acknowledged, as Homans did, that in any relationship, one person almost always has more power than the other. Blau (1964) referred to Willard Waller's principle of least interest, whereby the partner who is less committed to the relationship has an advantage over the person who is more involved in the relationship.

Blau's conception of *reciprocity* in exchange implies the existence of balancing forces that create a strain toward equilibrium. The simultaneous operations of diverse balancing forces produce imbalances in social life, and the resulting dialectic between reciprocity and imbalance gives social structures their distinctive nature and dynamics (Blau, 1964). Humans choose between potential associates or courses of action by evaluating the experience or expected experiences with each in terms of preference ranking, and then they select the best alternative. Blau believed that the main force that draws people together is social attraction (Farganis, 2000). *Attraction* is defined in terms of potential rewards for participating in the social exchange. When there are inadequate rewards, the social ties between individuals and groups is (more) likely to deteriorate. In other words, individuals continue to associate with others as long as they are getting something (rewards) out of the relationship. Irrational as well as rational behaviors are governed by these considerations. Of particular

importance is the realization that not all individuals (or groups) value the same alternatives equally. Thus, one person may be willing to do just about anything to maintain the company of another, while those outside the relationship may wonder why the first person would even want to associate with the other (as in "What does he see in her?"). Blau also makes distinctions between intrinsically rewarding exchanges (love relationships) and associations primarily concerned with extrinsic benefits (getting paid to tutor a student).

Unlike Homans, Blau never listed specific propositions designed to explain all human behaviors. Jonathan Turner (2003:295), however, extracted basic principles from Blau's theories and established what he called "Blau's Implicit Exchange Principles." They are listed here:

1. **Rationality Principle:** The more profit people expect from one another in participating in a particular activity, the more likely they are to engage in that activity.

2. **Reciprocity Principles:**
   A. The more people have exchanged rewards with one another, the more the reciprocal obligations that emerge and guide subsequent exchanges among these people.
   B. The more the reciprocal obligations of an exchange relationship are violated, the more disposed deprived parties are to sanction negatively those violating the norm of reciprocity.

3. **Justice Principles:**
   A. The more exchange relations have been established, the more likely they are to be governed by norms of fair exchange.
   B. The less norms of fairness are realized in an exchange, the more disposed deprived parties are to sanction negatively those violating the norms.

4. **Marginal Utility Principle:** The more expected rewards have been forthcoming from a particular activity, the less valuable the activity is and the less likely its performance is.

5. **Imbalance Principle:** The more stabilized and balanced one set of exchange relations is among social units, the more likely are other exchange relations to become imbalanced and unstable.

This impressive review by Turner provides a valuable summation of Blau's exchange theory.

Group Formation

Social exchange must be directed toward other persons; consequently, social interaction begins with social groups. Individuals choose what groups to interact with based on the rewards they can receive. Groups that offer the greatest number of rewards are the ones sought out, whereas "closed" groups, or groups that offer few rewards, will be ignored. Groups that offer rewards are attractive, and because a group is attractive, individuals want to be accepted.

> To be accepted, they must offer group members rewards. This involves impressing the group members by showing the members that associating with the new people will be rewarding. The relationship with the group members will be solidified when the newcomers have impressed the group—when members have received the rewards they expected. Newcomers' efforts to impress group members generally lead to group cohesion, but competition and, ultimately, social differentiation can occur when too many people actively seek to impress each other with their abilities to reward. (Ritzer, 2000a:283)

A good example would be pledges to a fraternity or sorority. A fraternity that has a good reputation and therefore is capable of offering many rewards (for example, job connections, good house parties) will be sought out by many who want to be pledges, and who will attempt to impress the organization with their own ability to provide rewards (for example, athletic ability, being from a politically powerful family).

The formation of a group involves the development of integrative bonds that unite individuals in a cohesive unit. Some of the integrative bonds discussed by Blau (1964) are

1. **Impressing others:** Expectation of rewards makes association attractive. Strategies that appear impressive include taking risks, performing role distance, and being able to exhibit both strain and ease, depending on the social occasion.

2. **Social Approval:** Humans are anxious to receive social approval for their decisions and actions, opinions, and suggestions. The approving agreement of others helps to confirm their judgments, to justify their conduct, and to validate their beliefs. Preoccupation with impressing others impedes both expressive involvement and instrumental endeavors. Restraints imposed by social approval are confined to circles of significant others.

3. **Attractiveness:** opinions that are met with approval, and one's approval of another's opinion, increase one's level of attractiveness. We all like to associate with people who agree with our opinions. On the other hand, serious and persistent conflicts of opinions lead to personal rejection (unattractiveness). The role of first impressions is involved in perceived attractiveness, for impressions may be self-fulfilling as well as self-defeating. One must be cautious of first impressions, for their reflection may be distorted. Bluffing is a mechanism utilized by some people in hopes of creating a positive early impression. However, the cost of having a bluff called may be too high. For example, claiming to be economically wealthier than one really is can be embarrassing when the person of one's desire agrees to a date at an expensive restaurant where one cannot afford to dine (bluff was called).

4. **Love:** Love is the extreme case of intrinsic attraction. Love appears to make human beings unselfish, since they themselves enjoy giving pleasure to those they love, but this selfless devotion generally rests on an interest in maintaining the other's love. The exchange process is most evident in love attachments, but the dynamics are different

because the specified rewards are not as clear as in social exchanges. In love relationships, there quite often is one person who is "more in love" than the other (the principle of least interest). The person less in love has the power advantage and may manipulate this advantage to gain more rewards. Although expressions of affection stimulate another's love, freely giving rewards depreciates their value, which is the dilemma of love.

Group Cohesion and Power

Group cohesion promotes the development of consensus on normative standards and the effective enforcement of these shared norms because integrative ties of fellowship enhance the significance of the informal sanctions of the group (such as disapproval and ostracism) to its individual members. Whereas social control strengthens the group as a whole, social support strengthens its members individually, particularly in relation to outsiders (Blau, 1964). Blau (1955) stated, "Common expectations and orientations arise or crystallize in the course of interaction and subsequently influence it" (p. 144).

Simmel's discussion of the dyad and the triad influenced Blau's conception of power. The simple addition of a third person to a two-person group radically changes the structure of the group. The power of an individual over another depends entirely on the social alternatives, or the lack of alternatives, of the subjected individual. Unilateral exchange generates differentiation of power. The exercise of power, as judged by norms of fairness, evokes social approval or disapproval, which may lead to legitimate organization and to social opposition, respectively. Collective approval of power legitimizes that power; collective disapproval of power engenders opposition. Furthermore, equilibrium forces on one level are disequilibrating forces on another (Blau, 1964).

Turner (2003:297) summarized Blau's conditions for the differentiation of power in social exchange:

1. The fewer services people must exchange for the receipt of particularly valued services, the more compliance those providing these particularly valued services can extract.
2. The fewer the alternative sources of rewards, the more compliance those providing valuable services can extract.
3. The less those receiving services from particular individuals can employ physical force and cohesion, the more compliance those providing the services can extract.
4. The less those receiving the valuable services can do without them, the more compliance those providing the services can extract.

Blau has successfully demonstrated the role of power at the dyad level, the group level, and the social structural level. Power differential inevitably leads to the potential for conflict. The group system, at all levels, must find a way to successfully integrate differences in power and authority among group members if it is to succeed in maintaining its structure.

Bureaucracy and Social Organization

Blau attempted to bridge the micro-macro gap of social theory. Do to this, he realized that sociological analysis must be of bureaucracy and social organizations; it cannot rely on an examination of individual social exchanges. In his *Bureaucracy in Modern Society* (1956), Blau described how frustrating it can be to deal with bureaucracies and red tape. Imagine how he would react today, especially in light of the growing number of automated phone processes and prerecorded menus that individuals must deal with before they can speak to a "live" person. It is as if organizations want nothing to do with their customers. Even bank tellers prefer customers to make deposits at and small withdrawals from an automatic teller machine (ATM), presumably freeing them for more important transactions.

Blau (1956) defined a *bureaucracy* as a "type of organization designed to accomplish large-scale administrative tasks by systematically coordinating the work of many individuals" (p. 14). He added, "This concept, then, applies to organizing principles that are intended to improve administrative efficiency and that generally do so, although bureaucratization occasionally has the opposite effect of producing inefficiency. Since complex administrative problems confront most large organizations, bureaucracy is not confined to the military and civilian branches of the government but is also found in business, unions, churches, universities, and even in baseball" (p. 14). Bureaucracy is the result of the increasing rationalization of society. The consequences of rationalization have often been deplored, although there is no conclusive proof that such things as alienation actually occur because of it (Blau, 1956). Nearly fifty years ago Blau wrote that learning to understand bureaucracies is more important than it ever had been, and that the study of bureaucratic organization makes a particular contribution to the advancement of sociological knowledge.

Blau's study of bureaucracy began with *The Dynamics of Bureaucracy* (1955), in which he presented systematic investigations of the bureaucratic structure and function, utilizing the case study method. Blau used the comparative approach in *Formal Organizations* (1962) to explore the role of modern humans in the organizational society. He stated, "Our ability to organize thousands and even millions of men in order to accomplish large-scale tasks—be they economic, political, or military—is one of our greatest strengths" (p. ix). In *The American Occupational Structure* (1967), coauthored with Otis Dudley Duncan, Blau provides a systematic analysis of the American occupational structure. "By analyzing the patterns of these occupational movements, the conditions that affect them, and some of their consequences, we attempt to explain part of the dynamics of the stratification system in the United States" (Blau and Duncan, 1967:1) (p. 1). In *The Organization of*

Academic Work (1973) Blau used quantitative empirical data on 115 American universities and colleges to present a systematic study of the relationship between bureaucracy and scholarship, particularly the influences of the administrative structure on academic work. Blau examined how the administrative structure establishes itself in order to organize the many students and faculty members in a university or college. In *On the Nature of Organizations* (1974), Blau presented an overview of his work on organizations and organizational power over twenty years.

Throughout his analysis of organizations Blau has examined the role of organizational substructures, and has found that the system still depends on costs and rewards. If the organization does not make a profit, or a large enough profit, it fails. When it can no longer provide rewards, it has failed. As Turner (2003) stated, "Organizations in a society must typically derive rewards from one another, thus creating a situation in which they are both attracted to, and in competition with, one another" (p. 303). Thus, the principles of exchange theory apply even at the organizational macro level.

KAREN COOK (1946–)

Among the most notable contributions that Karen Cook has made to social thought is her attempt to bridge the micro-macro gap inherent with all social theories. Following in the tradition of Peter Blau and Richard Emerson, Cook has articulated her own version of social exchange theory.

A Brief Biographical Sketch

Karen Schweers Cook was born on July 25, 1946, in Austin, Texas, where she was raised. Karen and her twin brother, Ken, attended college together as undergraduates at Stanford University. She received her bachelor's degree in sociology with distinction and honors in 1968. She remained at Stanford and earned her master's degree in 1970. Cook then served as acting instructor in the Sociology Honors Program and research associate for the Laboratory of Social Research at Stanford. Cook received her Ph.D. with distinction in sociology from Stanford in 1973.

In the fall of 1973, Cook began her academic career as an assistant professor of sociology at the University of Washington. She was promoted to associate professor in 1979 and full professor in 1985. From 1995 to 1998, Cook served as the James B. Duke Professor of Sociology at Duke University. At Duke, she was the director of the Sociology Laboratory for Research. Cook left Duke in 1998 and took her current position at Stanford University as the Ray Lyman Wilbur Professor of Sociology.

In the area of publishing, Cook both edits and authors a large number of works. Cook has published extensively in the area of social exchange theory, social justice, power and trust in social relationships, and social psychology. She is currently coauthoring, with Toshio Yamigishi, *The Structure of Social Exchange* and *Social Structure and Trust*.

Influences on Cook

Cook is primarily an exchange theorist who is attempting to establish empirical links between specific behaviors and traditional exchange theory. A great deal of her work has been conducted with the help of such contemporaries as Karen Hegtvedt, Mary Gillmore, and Toshio Yamagishi. As an exchange theorist, Cook has been influenced by many of the traditional sociologists associated with the field, especially George Homans, Peter Blau, and Richard Emerson.

Among Homans's concepts, Cook was interested in his idea of distributive justice. In an article titled "Distributive Justice, Equity, and Equality" (1983), Cook and Hegtvedt provided a general review of the research conducted since the mid-1980s on individuals' ideas of equity and distributive justice

and their reactions to inequality. Cook and Hegtvedt concluded that microlevel concepts of distributive justice have certain limitations, and they suggested that macrolevel concepts should be used to integrate equity and distributive justice theories with the grand sociological theories of power, conflict, and collective action. If this integration could be achieved, it would bring notions of justice to the forefront in the analysis of social change.

Cook was employed by Peter Blau. Blau had extended the ideas of Homans, especially agreeing with his analysis of individual behavioral processes. However, Blau and Cook were interested in the general characteristics of social structure, rather than just an analysis of small or informal groups, and established social institutions and organizations. Thus, where Homans's focus is on elementary forms of behavior, Blau and Cook's primary focus was the analysis of complex structures. Blau (1964) hoped to establish "an understanding of social structure on the basis of an analysis of the social processes that govern the relations between individuals and groups" (p. 2).

Blau was interested in the process of exchange. He envisioned a four-stage process that represents the transformation from interpersonal exchange to social change, as described by Ritzer (2000c:118):

> Step 1: Personal exchange transactions between people give rise to . . .
>
> Step 2: Differentiation of status and power, which leads to . . .
>
> Step 3: Legitimization and organization, which sow the seeds of . . .
>
> Step 4: Opposition and change (Ritzer, 2000c:418).

This four-step sequence will become a critical element in the attempt to link micro with macro exchange theory. Blau's attempt to link micro and macro considerations of social exchange theory was an important influence on Cook as she has attempted to do the same thing.

In 1972, Richard Emerson published two essays on power dependence relations. So important were these essays that they "marked the beginning of a new stage in the development of social exchange theory" (Molm and Cook, 1995:215). Power is critical in exchange theory, and Emerson articulated this very fact.

Like Blau, Emerson has attempted to create a link between the micro and macro aspects of social theory. Emerson's exchange theory has been expanded by his study of "exchange social structures" (Cook, 1987). The actors in Emerson's macrolevel exchange theory can be individuals as well as collectivities (such as groups, societies). Cook (1987) indicated that the idea of exchange network structures is critical to the micro-macro link.

Exchange Theory

Like Emerson, Cook began with the basic, microlevel premises of exchange theory. In general, exchange theory is based on the idea that in any social relationship, people calculate the benefits and costs associated with their interaction. People seek to minimize the costs and maximize the rewards, and when a situation is identified as rewarding, attempts to ensure the continuation of the relationship manifest themselves. Cook has examined the costs and reward structures found in social interactions.

For example, Cook examined the relationship between general exchange and social dilemmas. A social dilemma is "a situation involving a particular type of incentive structure, such that, 1) if all group members cooperate, all gain, whereas, 2) for each individual it is more beneficial not to cooperate" (Yamagishi and Cook, 1993:236). Yamagishi and Cook (1993) explained that "in generalized exchange, the rewards that an actor receives usually are not directly contingent on the resources provided by that actor; therefore, free riding can occur" (p. 235). The

center of this problem relates to the fact that, if everyone "free-rides"—that is, takes the benefits while contributing nothing—society will eventually suffer. To illustrate this point, Yamagishi and Cook used the example of the stranded motorist. If the car is disabled, eventually someone will come to the rescue. Those coming to the motorist's aid do not expect any immediate reward from the motorist; however, they expect that someone will help them out similarly in the future. If most, or all, people refuse to stop and help others, the exchange system will eventually collapse and everyone may suffer—including society itself. Blau had also addressed the issue of free riders. He believed that the norm of reciprocity is what keeps everyone from being free riders (takers). However, the irony is that without "takers," there cannot be "givers."

Exchange Networks

Research on social exchange networks began with Emerson's (1972a) work on powerdependence and his attempt to go beyond small-group analysis. By incorporating networks into exchange theory, Emerson, Cook, and others have extended exchange theory beyond the dyad and have attempted to integrate network-structural principles and power-dependence theory in order to explain the dynamics of power in exchange networks (Bienenstock and Bonacich, 1993:117). An exchange network consists of the following elements (Cook et al., 1983:277):

1. There is a set of either individual or collective actors.

2. Valued resources are distributed among the actors.

3. There is a set of opportunities for exchange among all actors in the network.

4. Exchange relations, or exchange opportunities, exist among the actors.

5. Exchange relations are connected to one another in a single network structure.

In short, "An exchange network is a specific social structure formed by two or more connected exchange relations between actors" (Cook et al., 1983:277). Once this exchange network has been established, the connection between dyadic (two-person) exchange and macrolevel structural phenomena is revealed (Yamagishi, Gillmore, and Cook, 1988). Every exchange relation is embedded in a larger exchange network consisting of two or more such networks.

In their study of exchange networks and social dilemmas, Yamagishi and Cook (1993) distinguished between two different types of generalized exchange structures: group-generalized exchange and network-generalized exchange. Group-generalized exchange occurs when all members of the group pool their resources and then eventually share in the rewards generated by pooling (Yamagishi and Cook, 1993). Structures of this type are subject to collapse because everyone involved receives an equal part of what is being shared, but each person within the group may not have contributed resources to the group (free riders). This situation can be illustrated by the classroom group project assignment. Inevitably, not all members of the group participate at an equal rate, and yet the slackers will receive the same rewards as those who worked harder on the project. In other words, within almost any group, there are free riders who take advantage of those who work hard for the benefit of the collectivity. Able-bodied persons who abuse the welfare system are examples of free riders.

Network-generalized exchange is a structure in which each person provides benefits for one other person in the group, rather than benefiting from the group as a whole. Thus, the rewards that one person receives are directly related to the resources given by another specific person (Yamagishi and Cook, 1993).

The research conducted (several four-person groups with multiple variations in testing) by Yamagishi and Cook (1993) revealed that both structures have the benefit of cooperation and the enticement of reaping the rewards but not contributing resources. However, they differ greatly in structure. "Group-generalized exchange involves no internal group structure, whereas the network-generalized exchange takes place in a network of unidirectional relations" (p. 239). Yamagishi and Cook also found that it is easier not to cooperate in group-generalized exchange structures than in network-generalized exchanges. The reason is that it may be more difficult for the rest of the group to notice when someone is failing to participate. Conversely, it is more difficult for someone to free-ride in network-generalized exchange because the group can create and impose sanctions, making it mandatory to participate.

Trust is an extremely important factor in both exchange structures. Because of its strong effect on cooperation in relationships, trust is a necessary component of a functioning exchange structure. Yamagishi and Cook's results showed that people who are more trusting are more likely to contribute their resources to the group than those who are less trusting of others. Interestingly, Yamagishi and Cook also found that within social groups, exchange structures may actually develop trust among group members. Network-generalized exchange groups promote higher levels of trust among their participants, because everyone is directly responsible for benefiting specific members of the group. In group-generalized networks it is easier for people to become free riders because they are not directly responsible to any one person. Yamagishi and Cook (1993) stated that network-generalized exchange networks are more likely to survive and flourish than group-generalized exchange networks. However, this survival depends on the other members of the group being aware of the actions of others and imposing sanctions to ensure their cooperation. If these sanctions are not implemented, one noncooperative person in the group can cause a domino effect that leads to the degradation and failure of the system.

In sum, network-generalized exchange networks are more likely than group-generalized networks to produce higher levels of profit, to promote greater trust, and to flourish in regard to group implementation (Yamagishi and Cook, 1993).

Power and Equity

A key element of social exchange theory is the role of power in any given relationship. In Blau's (1964) examination of his large-scale social structures, within an exchange perspective, analysis centered on the development of legitimate institutional power. He argued that the major determinant of legitimacy is found in the exchange aspect of power, specifically, whether subordinates feel that power is exercised fairly and generously. Legitimacy transforms power into authority because legitimacy makes it right and mandatory to obey. The legitimacy of authority develops through group norms that help to enforce members' adherence to the laws (norms).

Emerson (1972b) defined *power* as "the level of potential *cost* which one actor can induce another to 'accept' " and *dependence* as "the level of potential cost an actor will accept within a relation" (p. 64). These concepts became the cornerstone in the development of Emerson's power-dependence theory. Cook and her colleagues summarized Emerson's power-dependence theory this way: "The power of one party over another in an exchange relation is an inverse function of his or her dependence on the other party" (Yamagishi et al., 1988:837).

Karen Cook has examined the role of power and equity in social relationships in a number of articles. In Cook and Emerson's article "Power, Equity, and Commitment in Exchange Networks" (1978), the issue of power, in both the traditional dyadic setting and the macro setting, is explored. They

emphasized the importance of social exchange theory in the discussion of power and equity issues.

Cook coauthored with Karen Hegtvedt an article entitled "Distributive Justice, Equity, and Equality" (1983), where they explored how society conceptualizes justice and equity. The sociological approach to justice is to examine how individuals behave when confronted with the distribution of resources in a social setting. They believe that justice is related to individuals' perceptions of fairness.

In their article "Power and Equity: What Counts in Attributions for Exchange Outcomes?" Hegtvedt, Thompson, and Cook (1993) attempted to combine the theoretical perspectives of social exchange and attribution. They proposed a theoretical model that depicts the influence of two fundamental social factors—structural power and outcome equity—on causal attributions for exchange outcomes. Hegtvedt et al. attempted to show how the social factors of structural power and the equity of exchange outcomes affect individuals' causal attributions about these outcomes. The authors made several assumptions in order to complete their study; one assumption is that individuals have the ability to assess the equity of social exchanges, and another is that a balance of power exists when each actor in a social relationship is equally dependent on the others' resources (Hegtvedt et al., 1993). In addition, the authors defined the parameters of attribution in exchange situations (where an individual draws conclusions about another actor's behavior) as the individual's own self, the other individual in the situation, the situation itself, and the interaction between the individuals.

By conducting extensive research on a number of dyadic groups, Cook and her associates attempted to empirically support a number of hypotheses. They found when individuals believe they have greater power, they are more likely to attribute it to their own actions and are thus less likely to attribute their power to the actions of the other members, the situation, or the interaction between the individuals. However, there were some inconsistencies among the dyadic groups: "In same-sex dyads, the direct effect between structural power and situation attributions is in the direction predicted for perceived power. In opposite-sex dyads, it appears that attributions to self mediate the relationship between perceived power and situation attributions" (Hegtvedt et al., 1993:114).

Other hypotheses tested by the authors relate to the idea that an individual's perceived treatment, fair or unfair (in the tradition of Blau), affects the object of the individual's attribution of exchange outcomes, and that the strength of these attributions affects her or his reaction to the situation. The data supported the hypotheses. Cook and associates also found that the results of their study were consistent with the idea that females are more relationship-oriented and tend to see other females as status equals. While there were several limitations to this study, the authors demonstrated the need and value of future research linking exchange relationships with attribution theory.

Social Psychology

Like any theorist who attempts to bridge the micro-macro gap in social theory, Cook has a strong interest in social psychology. Social psychology is a wonderful attempt to inject micro aspects into sociological theory, while reminding psychologists of the major flaw in their discipline: the nearly complete neglect of the effect of macrostructural factors on human behavior. Cook has published a number of articles in this area, among them "Recent Theoretical Advances in Social Psychology: Progress and Promises," coauthored with Judith Howard (1992). Cook and Howard believe that the focus of social psychology should be primarily on the relations between individual actors or collectivities and various social factors or forces.

They cited Blau (1964) in his work on exchange and power as an example of a theorist who focuses on the dialectic between micro-macro phenomena.

In 1959, Thibaut and Kelley published *The Social Psychology of Groups*. The majority of the book is devoted to dyadic relationships. The concepts of costs and rewards are central to their analysis:

> The reward-cost positions the members of a dyad may achieve in the relationship will be better (1) the more rewarding to the other is the behavior each can produce and (2) the lower the costs at which such behavior can be produced. If both persons are able to produce their maximum rewards for the other at minimum cost to themselves, the relationship will not only provide each with excellent reward-cost positions but will have the additional advantage that both persons will be able to achieve their best reward-cost positions at the same time. (p. 31)

Molm and Cook (1995) proposed that Thibaut and Kelley's book offers three important contributions to the development of exchange theory:

1. Their interest in power and dependence would later become critical to Emerson and his followers. Unfortunately, Thibaut and Kelley concentrated primarily on dyads, where structural relationships are clearly different from those in triads and larger groups. As Simmel had discovered, in a dyad, each participant is dependent on the other, and therefore each has a degree of power over the other.

2. Thibaut and Kelley discussed the ideas of comparison level and comparison level for alternatives. Both are important in the evaluation of outcomes of relationships. This will become important for future theorists, such as Emerson, who will develop ideas on social networks.

3. The notion of the *outcome matrix* is a way of visually depicting all the possible events that may occur when two persons interact. This matrix provides the individual with options of courses of actions in order to maximize rewards and minimize costs.

The primary task of social psychology is to find the link between micro and macro issues related to social interaction. Consequently, social psychological elements are inherent in a theory that attempts to sufficiently address the micro and macro variables.

Network Analysis

Contemporary exchange theorists strive to link the microdynamics of human behavior with the influence of macrostructural and organizational influences. Simmel discussed the "web of group affiliations," throughout his works but contemporary sociologists generally use the term *network*. As discussed previously in this section, Cook, Emerson, and a number of other social theorists have established a field of study referred to as *exchange networks*. Network analysis involves the discovery of patterns of behavior in order to determine how such ramifications "influence the behavior of the people involved in the network" (Mitchell, 1974).

Cook and associates have published a great deal of work in the area of network analysis. In an article titled "Two Approaches to Social Structure: Exchange Theory and Network Analysis" (1992), Cook and Whitmeyer described social structure as "a configuration of social relations among actors where the relations involve the exchange of valued items" (p. 110). Cook explained that the term *network analysis* refers to the patterns of interactions between many actors. These interactions and patterns can be seen as networks. To better understand the concept of social structure, Cook and Whitmeyer used a historical approach by examining the ideas of three exchange theorists: Homans, Blau, and Emerson. Homans studied individuals in the work environment and examined the employee-employer relationship between actors who come into direct contact with each other. Blau has examined social exchange principles in terms of group formation, cohesion, social integration, opposition, conflict, and dissolution. Emerson has attempted

to link social structures with exchange principles. Cook and Whitmeyer (1992) concluded that all three theorists had successfully combined exchange theory and social structural parameters. In their network analysis, Cook and Whitmeyer made note that rewards (of some type) always exist, despite the great variety of social actions taken by individuals in a wide disparity of social groups, organizations, and structures.

RELEVANCY

Social exchange theory was founded by George Homans. He argued that self-interest is the universal motive for behavior and that people shape their behaviors in terms of the positive or negative reinforcement provided by their environment (Coser, 1977). Homans believed that humans interact with one another by exchanging rewards and punishments. The individual is viewed as a rational being capable of calculating pleasures (rewards) and pains (costs) and is always motivated to maximize profits. Homans's exchange theory is micro-oriented. He believed that all social behaviors could be explained by five psychological principles.

Peter Blau has attempted to extend exchange theory from its micro roots to the macrolevel, especially by emphasizing the importance of norms (Ritzer, 2000c). Clearly influenced by Homans, Blau has attempted to remedy some of the deficiencies he perceived in Homans's conceptualizations and to reconcile them within the structural perspective (Coser, 1977). Blau felt that there were three basic reasons why one should look beyond microlevel interaction patterns. First, humans rarely pursue one goal, forgetting about all others. Second, humans are inconsistent in their performance. Third, humans never have complete information regarding the alternative behaviors that might be available. Turner (2003) stated that "even Blau himself increasingly believed that the isomorphism between micro-level and macro-level exchange processes was forced" (p. 306).

Where Blau has left off, contemporary theorists Richard Emerson and Karen Cook (among others) have continued to transform the microsociological perspective of exchange theory to the macrolevel (Ritzer, 2000c). Contemporary exchange theorists emphasize network analysis and conflict theory's dependence on power differentials as a determinant of behavior. Emerson emphasized the concepts of power and dependence and the alternatives available. Cook and Emerson have conducted a number of laboratory studies of exchange relationships in order to determine what costs people are willing to endure in their pursuit of rewards (Wallace and Wolf, 1999). Cook is a significant contemporary social theorist. She has provided invaluable information on the field of sociology in general, and on exchange theory in particular. Along with a number of associates, Cook has conducted a great deal of empirical research. Her micro-analysis of small-group behavior is inspiring. Her attempt to transform exchange theory so that it may properly address macrostructural issues, relabeled *network analysis,* is to be applauded. Network analysis can be applied to any number of large social systems, such as television networks. Each major television network is a conglomerate of businesses consisting of local affiliations that serve, and interlink with, the central office. Home offices of chain retail stores use a form of network analysis to keep tabs on individual franchises.

Exchange theory and the rational choice perspective have enjoyed considerable attention recently. "Some argue that they must be given pride of place as the basis of sociological theory in the next century; others criticize them as based on a flawed or incomplete view of human nature, unable to explain many of the major concerns of sociology, and essentially tautological in their propensity to first assume in advance that actions must be rational, and then explain them as such" (Wallace and Wolf, 1999:363).

George Homans has been labeled a reductionist by several of his critics, who have attempted to show that his deductive schemes tend to be either tautological or ad hoc (Coser, 1977). The criticism of reductionism does bring up the question: Should exchange theory incorporate the ideas of symbolic interactionism in order to address the issue of the symbolic meanings of behaviors? Mead's discussion of value has definite exchange implications. Exchange theory has benefited by emphasizing some of the core concepts of conflict theory, and there are those who feel that exchange theory would benefit by integrating elements of symbolic interactionism, especially Mead's categories of mind, self, and society. Peter Singleman (1972) made such an attempt. He believes that exchange theory is one of the most stimulating sociological theories because it provides a general rationale for generating distinctive propositions for predicting concrete behaviors. He correctly pointed out that Homans's behaviorist approach ignores aspects of subjectively meaningful behavior. Singleman added Mead's concepts of mind (the actor perceives something as a reward), self (which is generally treated as a given by exchange theorists), and society (which is constructed and reconstructed through a series of interaction patterns, or exchange processes). Exchange theory in general has been criticized for its inattention to the mental processes of actors. Such critics believe that exchange theorists fail to take into account the ability of human actors to reflect on their own behavior, and to evaluate it in terms of decision making with the many options of behavior available to them. Homans's exchange theory has been criticized for ignoring large-scale structures. Network analysis is an attempt to answer this criticism.

Social exchange theory has a great deal of relevancy to contemporary and future society. Beginning with Homans's five propositions that explain behavior, it is clear how applicable exchange theory is to sociology and the understanding of human behavior. The bigger challenge is to find a behavior, *any* behavior that cannot be explained by Homans's five propositions. The success proposition, for example, assumes that individuals will seek out, and maintain, interactions where the rewards outweigh the costs, so that there is a profit. Measuring costs against rewards is not limited to economics; all personal relationships can be measured this way. A person will maintain a relationship with another for as long as it is profitable (the rewards outnumber the costs).

The stimulus proposition illustrates the processes of generalization and discrimination, concepts utilized on a regular basis during social interactions. For example, waitresses will find that good service almost always generates good tips, while poor service generally leads to a much smaller tip (generalization). A consumer who prefers "dark" beer will not like "lite" beers (discrimination). The fact is that demonstrating the relevancy of Homans's five propositions would, in itself, fill an entire book. Furthermore, the challenge is offered again to identify *any* behavior that cannot be explained by these propositions.

Homans, Blau, and Cook have all described the importance of understanding group behavior. They have identified elements that lead to its development and maintenance. Nearly everyone is involved in some type of group behavior. It might be a sports team, a study group, a card game gathering, a street gang, or any number of other options. In the analysis of group dynamics, inevitably there must be some discussion of power and authority. Much of the research conducted on power in the exchange tradition is similar to that in conflict theory. In fact, conflict theory and exchange theory are in agreement that power affects the dynamics of the group structure and corresponding interactions. The study of groups and

power relationships will always be relevant to sociological theory.

Analysis of bureaucracy and organizations is at least as important as the examination of groups. Blau's work in this area provides a wealth of information relevant to the study of such structures today. Not only do people interact with others in a variety of group settings, but they also often do so within an organizational environment. Cook's network analysis demonstrates how the core premises of micro exchange theory can be applied at the macrolevel. Entire societies deal with one another in a manner similar to that of individuals. In 2003, because of American president George Bush's desire to go to war with Iraq as an extension of his war against terrorism, the United States and the coalition forces did indeed go to war with Iraq. All the countries of the world (especially those in the immediate geographic area) had to decide whether to side with the United States or not. They had to weigh the costs (for example, internal dissension, a possible religious war) against the rewards (such as allying themselves with the world's most powerful country). In short, even at the global level, the basic element of profit comes into play. Countries decide what course of action to take based on the perceived acquisition of rewards.

Blau and Cook (along with other theorists like Emerson) have attempted to bridge the micro-macro divide. All social theories seem to take one approach or the other to their study of human behavior. Symbolic interactionism, ethnomethodology, and phenomenology, are micro theories, while functionalism and conflict theory tend to be macro. Conflict theory and feminism both possess concepts that are concerned with macro and micro issues, but no theory other than social exchange theory has so actively attempted to construct this bridge. Only when a theory has successfully addressed issues of both micro and macro elements will sociology have a true "grand" theory. This grand theory will demonstrate sociology's relevance to the other academic disciplines, and consequently, this grand theory will be responsible for sociology's one day reaching the elite status that it so deserves. Social exchange theory is the theory closest to this ultimate goal. This contention underscores the idea that social exchange theory is the most underrated theory in sociology. It is one of the most relevant theories in the explanation of human behavior and therefore deserves much greater recognition from within the discipline as well as outside it.

Current and future social theorists must come to grips with the reality that social exchange theory offers valuable insights into social behavior and structural phenomenons.

7

Ethnomethodology and Harold Garfinkel

Everyday conversation among the masses of society seldom revolves around a discussion of ethnomethodology or Harold Garfinkel. This is somewhat ironic in that it is Harold Garfinkel and the field of ethnomethodology that study everyday people and their social worlds, interactions, and conversations. Garfinkel is interested in mundane and commonsense knowledge, and in the range of procedures and considerations by means of which the ordinary members of society make sense of, find their way about, and act on the circumstances in which they find themselves. In this chapter, the focus is on the life and contributions of Harold Garfinkel, the field of ethnomethodology that he created, contributions by other theorists in this area, and the relevancy of ethnomethodology to contemporary society.

HAROLD GARFINKEL (1917–)

Harold Garfinkel was born in Newark, New Jersey, on October 29, 1917. His father was a businessman who hoped that Harold would learn a trade, but he wanted to attend college. He initially learned to compromise by both working in his father's business and taking

business courses at the then-unaccredited University of Newark. His academic career began in 1935 when he became a student of economics. The courses were taught mostly by graduate students from Columbia University, and because of their lack of practical research experience, their approach to teaching was generally theoretical. Ritzer (2000a) explained that Garfinkel was comfortable at Newark because of the other Jewish students who were taking courses there. Many were sociology majors who later became social scientists.

Garfinkel graduated from Newark in 1939 and spent the summer in a Quaker work camp in rural Georgia. "There he learned that the University of North Carolina had a sociology program that was also oriented to the furtherance of public works projects like the one in which he was involved" (Ritzer, 2000a:246). He was accepted into the program with a fellowship and chose Guy Johnson as his thesis adviser. Garfinkel received an M.A. from the University of North Carolina in 1942, some of his work on interracial homicide being published in an award-winning short story. After serving in the military in World War II, Garfinkel attended Harvard University to study with Talcott Parsons. While still a doctoral student, Garfinkel taught for two years at Princeton. After obtaining his Ph.D. in 1952, he taught for two years at Ohio State University. Garfinkel "then joined a project researching juries in Wichita, Kansas. In preparing for a talk on the project at the 1954 American Sociological Association meetings, Garfinkel came up with the term 'ethnomethodology' to describe what fascinated him about the jury deliberations and social life more generally" (Ritzer, 2000a:247). In the fall of 1954 Garfinkel accepted a position as an assistant professor at the University of California at Los Angeles (UCLA), where he continued to develop and conduct research in the field of ethnomethodology. His career at UCLA has remained a distinguished one, and he is now a professor emeritus. In 1995 he received the Cooley-Mead Award for lifetime contributions to the intellectual and scientific advancement of sociology and social psychology.

As a university instructor, Garfinkel was well respected but known for being quite a character and a "hard" grader, and for giving out perplexing assignments. One of his former students, Jill Marie Stein (1997), wrote:

> When I decided to enroll in his grad course on Ethnomethodology, I did so knowing that there was as much chance of getting an "F" as an "A" (he had been known to fail otherwise excellent students) and that I was willing to risk that just for the experience of working with him. The entire class was like an experiment in EM [ethnomethodology]. I had the sensation the whole time that I was chasing a mirage. . . . Just as I started to come upon something that I could grasp, my previous understanding would disappear as I took another step forward. It was absolutely exhilarating. Harold often created his own vocabulary for referring to things (I suppose he found the given language too constraining), and once you got the meaning of words, he would make up new ones. He would give us vexing assignments (i.e.: go home and watch the phone ringing), which

he would rarely explain or discuss even after we completed them. He patently disavowed not only others' interpretations of his work (and their own EM studies), but the value of almost anything he had ever done up until what he was currently working on (scientific discovery). . . . His final assignment for the course was for us to write a "Dear Harold" letter telling him what we got out of it [the course]. I called him to ask whether I could turn the paper in late and he hung up on me. I took that as a "no" and made the deadline. I won't say here what grade I got, it wasn't the point. What I can say is that studying with him was one of the great highlights of my career as a sociologist, and perhaps beyond.

Influences

Garfinkel has relied on many theorists, in various fields, to help stimulate his ideas on ethnomethodology, along with his related works. Ethnomethodolgy (EM) is influenced by phenomenology, linguistics, anthropology, symbolic interactionism, and other mainstream concepts found in sociology. In *Studies in Ethnomethodology* (1967), Garfinkel wrote that his work had been particularly influenced by Talcott Parsons, Alfred Schutz, Aron Gurwitsch, and Edmund Husserl. "For twenty years their writings have provided me with inexhaustible directives into the world of everyday activities. Parsons' work, particularly, remains awesome for the penetrating depth and unfailing precision of its practical sociological reasoning on the constituent tasks of the problem of social order and its solutions" (p. ix). Garfinkel, as stated earlier, had studied under Parsons at Harvard, and while it is true that Garfinkel gave high recognition to Parsons, they certainly had not agreed on many matters. As Ritzer (2000c) stated, "While Parsons stressed the importance of abstract categories and generalizations, Garfinkel was interested in detailed description. When Garfinkel achieved prominence within the discipline, this became a focal debate within sociology" (p. 247).

As Heritage (1984) explained, one of Parsons's central claims in *The Structure of Social Action* (1949) is that all the various social sciences essentially deal with systems of social action. The basic units of such systems, Parsons argued, are "unit acts," which are composed of the following irreducible elements:

1. **An actor:** The agent of the act.
2. **An end:** A future state of affairs which the actor seeks to bring about by the act.
3. **Action:** A current situation within which the actor acts and which he or she seeks to transform by his or her behavior.
4. **Means:** A mode of orientation.

According to Parsons, successful social action begins with the internalization of norms and continues when actors engage in behavior with complementary role expectations. Parsons insisted on an objective, scientific study of human behavior in order to understand human behavior. Garfinkel denied that the social scientific formulation of objectively rational courses of action under given conditions could be useful, or even feasible, in the study of human action. Similarly, he denied that such formulations could be useful "yardsticks" (measuring devices) with which to evaluate the rationality of actors' action. Garfinkel took great exception to Parsons's view that mundane social action can be treated as irrelevant. It is the Parsonian disregard for the entire common sense world which constitutes the departure of Garfinkel's treatment of the theory of action (Heritage, 1984). "Garfinkel wanted to construct a perspective that would fill in one aspect of Parsons' theory of action, the motivated actor" (Wallace and Wolf, 1999:259). Nonetheless, Garfinkel (1988) himself attested to Parsons's influence, stating that ethnomethodology's earliest initiatives were taken from Parsons's four-volume *The Structure of Social Action*. "Inspired by *The Structure of Social Action* ethnomethodology undertook the task of respecifying the production and accountability of immortal, ordinary society" (Garfinkel, 1988:104).

The influence of Parsons on Garfinkel was extended by the fact that he had introduced Garfinkel to the theories of Alfred Schutz and Edmund Husserl. Garfinkel visited and studied with Schutz at the New School for Social Research. From Husserl, Garfinkel adopted "indexical expressions" and cited the philosopher's solution to the problem of relativity in sociology. However, even though Husserl was the leading philosopher to found phenomenology, Schutz had a greater influence on Garfinkel (Rogers, 1983). *"Studies in Ethnomethodology* [Garfinkel, 1967] is replete with references to Schutz, and Garfinkel says that his own work is heavily indebted to him" (Wallace and Wolf, 1999:259). Schutz's phenomenological ideas (especially those involving attitude and the commonsense world), methodology, and concepts were crucial in the development of ethnomethodology. Schutz concluded that each individual carries with him or her a "stock of knowledge at hand" consisting of constructs and categories that are common sense and of social origin when interacting with others in the social world. Schutz viewed phenomenology as the process by which we typify the basic stream of meaningless sense-experience into "stocks of knowledge" which are shared; together all stocks of knowledge constitute the "life-world" (our reality and our knowledge of it are one and the same). Schutz argued that these constructs are utilized dynamically, presuppositionally, and in a taken-for-granted fashion; they are revisable and directed by a collage of "recipe knowledge" possessing an intersubjective understanding between interacting individuals (Borgatta and Borgatta, 1992).

Brief mention should also be made of a number of other theorists who had an influence on Garfinkel in general, and on ethnomethodology specifically. Ethnomethodology is close to the Weberian emphasis on the empirical study of ideas in history and also resembles Durkheim's original analysis of anomie.

Branching out from ethnomethodology, Garfinkel became famous for his "breaching experiments." "Garfinkel argued, one must 'breach' constitutive expectancies in radical ways, since the natural attitude guarantees that people assimilate 'strange' into 'familiar' without dismantling the presuppositions underlying a shared world" (Rogers, 1983:80).

ETHNOMETHODOLOGY

Ethnomethodology is an approach to understanding social interaction and is "based on the assumption that social reality is the result of our agreement to agree with one another. That is, we negotiate reality by exchanging accounts of what is going on between us, with the unstated assumption that we will reach an agreement eventually" (Levin, 1991). "The beginnings of ethnomethodology can be traced to Harold Garfinkel's analysis of tapes of jury deliberations, which he conducted in 1945" (Wallace and Wolf, 1999:260). He became interested in why jurists came to view what they were doing as indeed the work of jurists. He wondered what knowledge, especially that rooted in the taken-for-granted worlds, the jurists drew upon during their deliberations and decision-making processes. In fact, he was studying the methods of how people come to see the social world. "The term itself was coined when, working with the Yale cross-cultural files, Garfinkel came to a section entitled 'ethnobotany, ethnophysiology, ethnophysics.' It occurred to him that on the jury deliberation project he was 'faced with jurors who were doing methodology,' and he decided that the label seemed adequate to convey the notion was *ethnomethodology*" (Wallace and Wolf, 1999:260). The term *ethnomethodology*, given its Greek roots, literally means the methods of ordinary people that are used on a daily basis to accomplish their everyday needs.

There are many definitions and interpretations of the term. "*Ethno*—refers to 'people.' *Method*—refers to 'method.' And *-ology* refers to 'study.' Ethnomethodology, then, is an examination of the methods people commonly use to sustain some kind of consensus about the world and to solve problems characterized by highly irrational features" (Cuzzort and King, 1995:357). Ritzer (2003) stated that "the definition of ethnomethodology is the study of ordinary members of society in the everyday situations in which they find themselves and the ways in which they use commonsense knowledge, procedures, and considerations to gain an understanding of, navigate in, and act on those situations" (p. 154). Wallace and Wolf (1999) stated, "If we translate the 'ethno' part of the term as 'members' (of a group) or 'folk' or 'people,' then ethnomethodology can be defined as members' (or people's) methods of making sense of their social world. Ethnomethodology's interest is in how people make sense of everyday activities" (p. 260). In *Studies in Ethnomethodology* (1967), Garfinkel used the term "to refer to the investigation of the rational properties of indexical expressions and other practical actions as contingent ongoing accomplishments of organized artful practices of everyday life" (p. 11). More recently, Garfinkel (1996) stated that "ethnomethodology gets reintroduced to me in a recurrent episode at the annual meetings of the American Sociological Association. . . . The question is asked: 'Hey, Hal, what IS ethnomethodology?' The elevator doors close. We're on our way to the ninth floor. I'm only able to say, 'Ethnomethodology is working out some very preposterous problems'" (p. 5). Garfinkel was not being cute in using the term *preposterous*. What he meant was that the first order of business for ethnomethodology is to pursue and examine a preposterous problem. Garfinkel (2002) explained how preposterous events present the greatest opportunity to analyze the orderliness of things:

Preposterous is what practitioners, making use of formal analysis, bear witness for each other about Ethnomethodology. Preposterous is what practitioners with their use of formal analysis can find and demonstrate to be the case in Ethnomethodology's fundamental phenomenon and central claim—namely, that there is endless orderliness in the plenum; that this orderliness is found in the curious *things* that *methods* could possibly be; let alone what *details* could be; let alone the *coherence of things* could be if the unavoidable way to provide for that *made* coherence of things and the only way is that it is the workings of immortal, ordinary society, and it is done without remedy or alternatives as the *things* the territory consists of. That immortal society isn't anything other than—*not* the achieved coherence of *activities*—but the *familiar* coherence of ordinary *things.* (p. 139)

Garfinkel believed that life consists of many ordered things and activities. Most people take comfort in the familiar. Garfinkel (1996) refined his definition of *ethnomethodology* as follows: "Ethnomethodology's fundamental phenomenon and its standing technical preoccupation in its studies is to find, collect, specify, and make instrutably observable the local endogenous production and natural accountability of immortal familiar society's most ordinary organizational things in the world, *and to provide for them both and simultaneously as objects and procedurally, as alternate methodologies*. The identity of objects and methodologies is key" (p. 6). The study of ordinary society reveals how individuals work hard to maintain consistency, order, and meaning in their lives (Garfinkel, 2002).

Accounts

Garfinkel's ethnomethodology seeks to understand the methods people employ to make sense of their world. "He placed considerable emphasis on language as the vehicle by which this reality construction is done. Indeed, for Garfinkel, interacting individuals' efforts to account for their actions—that

is, to represent them verbally to others—are the terms, *to do* interaction is *to tell* interaction, or in other words, the primary folk technique used by actors is verbal description. In this way, people use their accounts to construct a sense of reality" (Turner, 2003:421). The accounts of people reflect how social order is possible. "For Garfinkel (1967) the answer merges a Durkheimian concern for large collective representations with an interactionist conception of the rules, norms, and meanings that members of any social order daily take for granted" (Denzin, 1969:926–927). In this regard, Garfinkel's social facts are different from Durkheim's social facts. "For Durkheim, social facts are external to and coercive of individuals. . . . In contrast, ethnomethodology treats the objectivity of social facts as the accomplishments of members—as a product of members' methodological activities. In other words, ethnomethodology is concerned with the organization of everyday, ordinary life" (Ritzer, 2003:154).

Ethnomethodology attempts to reveal the subjective nature of human interaction. It has a microfocus on daily life and on the thoughts and actions of human behavior. "One of Garfinkel's key points about ethnomethods is that they are reflexively accountable. *Accounts* are the ways in which actors explain (describe, criticize, and idealize) specific situations" (Ritzer, 2003:155). Agreeing with Ritzer, Turner (2003) stated, "Garfinkel placed enormous emphasis on indexicality—that is, members' accounts are tied to particular contexts and situations" (p. 421). Garfinkel uses the term *indexical expressions* not merely to capture the traditional philosophical problem of points of reference but also to note that ordinary descriptive terms are powerfully influenced by the context in which they are uttered.

Garfinkel's ethnomethodological studies regard the subject they are studying as the result of accountability production. Accounts are social creations and constructs built from past interactions. "*Accounting* is the process by which people offer accounts in order to make sense of the world. Ethnomethodologists devote a lot of attention to analyzing people's accounts, as well as to the ways in which accounts are offered and accepted (or rejected) by others" (Ritzer, 2003:155). The principle aim of ethnomethodology is to investigate the procedural accounts that individuals bring with them during interaction with others. Behaviors that are present in the everyday world are especially interesting to Garfinkel's ethnomethodological studies. As Garfinkel explained in *Studies in Ethnomethodology* (1967):

> In accounting for the stable features of everyday activities sociologists commonly select familiar settings such as familial households or work places and ask for the variables that contribute to their stable features. Just as commonly, one set of considerations are unexamined: the socially standardized and standardizing, "seen but unnoticed," expected, background features of everyday scenes. The member of the society uses background expectancies as a scheme of interpretation. With their use actual appearances are for him recognizable and intelligible as the appearances-of-familiar-events. Demonstrably he is responsive to this background, while at the same time he is at a loss to tell us specifically of what the experiences consist. When we ask him about them he has little or nothing to say. For these background expectancies to come into view one must either be a stranger to the "life as usual" character of everyday scenes, or become estranged from them. As Alfred Schutz pointed out, a "special motive" is required to make them problematic. (pp. 36–37)

Garfinkel believes that the goal of the sociologist is to reveal the unknown background features of everyday activities and "to treat as problematic what is taken for granted in order to understand the commonsense everyday world" (Wallace and Wolf, 1999:260).

The Commonsense World

From the theoretical writings of Schutz, Garfinkel created a number of "determinants" to define an event as an occurrence in the commonsense world (Rogers, 1983). In brief, some of the determinants that assume the label of commonsense include viewing specific events as objective facts; viewing the meanings of events as products of a socially standardized process of naming, reification, and idealization of the user's stream of experience (that is, as the products of language); applying past determinants of events to similar present and future events; and viewing alterations of descriptions of events as remaining in the control of the participating actors. Interacting members of society are not the only ones to utilize a commonsense approach to interaction. Garfinkel acknowledges that researchers often rely on a taken-for-granted, commonsensical approach to the study of human behavior.

Garfinkel (1967) stated that "sociologists distinguish the 'product' from the 'process' meanings of a common understanding. As 'product,' a common understanding is thought to consist of a shared agreement on substantive matters; as 'process,' it consists of various methods whereby something that a person says or does is recognized to accord with a rule. With his concepts of *begreifen* and *verstehen*, each with its distinct character as method and knowledge, Weber provided sociologists an authority for this distinction" (pp. 24–25). Furthermore, Garfinkel (1967) stated, "Much of 'core sociology' consists of 'reasonable findings.' Many, if not most, situations of sociological inquiry are common sense situations of choice. Nevertheless, textbook and journal discussions of sociological methods rarely give recognition to the fact that sociological inquiries are carried out under common sense auspices *at the points where decisions about the correspondence between observed appearances and intended events are being made*" (p. 100). Nonetheless, Garfinkel remains steadfast in the idea that *scientific* sociology is a fact, and not merely based on common sense. It can be a science if it follows certain policies of scientific procedure.

Policies of Scientific Ethnomethodological Study

No doubt, students of sociology have already learned of the complex nature of examining human behavior scientifically because of the problematic and dynamic nature of the subject of study: human behavior. Garfinkel (1967:32–34) proposed that five policies be implemented in ethnomethodological studies:

1. An indefinitely large domain of appropriate settings is available for study. If researchers use a search policy that *any occasion whatsoever* has an opportunity to be chosen, objectivity is more likely. Such a policy provides for inquiries of every imaginable kind. No inquiries can be excluded no matter where or when they occur, no matter how vast or trivial their scope.

2. Scientific sociology is continually engaged in counting, graphing, interviewing, sampling, recording, reporting, planning, decision making, and so on. In other words, to achieve objectivity in the name of science, traditional sociology relies on empirical data collection and analysis. Garfinkel argues that sociology must go beyond this approach, and he therefore insists that ethnomethodology examine the mundane and taken-for-granted phenomena that engulf the social setting. Researchers must describe all the actual behaviors involved in the setting to provide a subjective reality of interaction.

3. Methodological approaches must reveal the subjective nature of human behavior and therefore should not rely on a standard approach, or a preconceived rule of research procedure, obtained from outside the actual setting under study. All aspects of behavior are to be examined. Garfinkel (1967) wrote, "All logical and methodological properties of action, every feature of an activity's sense, facticity, objectivity, accountability, communality

is to be treated as a contingent accomplishment of socially organized common practices" (p. 33).

4. Every social setting is to be viewed as self-organizing with respect to the intelligible character of its own appearances as either representations of or evidence of a social order. Garfinkel (1967) wrote, "Any setting organizes its activities to make its properties as an organized environment of practical activities detectable, countable, recordable, reportable, tell-a-story-aboutable, analyzable—in short, *accountable*. Organized social arrangements consist of various methods for accomplishing the accountability of a setting's organizational ways as a concerted undertaking. . . . In exactly the ways that a setting is organized, it *consists* of members' methods for making evident that setting's ways as clear, coherent, planful, consistent, chosen, knowable, uniform, reproducible connections—i.e., rational connections" (p. 33). Thus, all settings are a result of accountable methods used by the participating members.

5. Garfinkel (1967) wrote, "Every kind of inquiry without exception consists of organized artful practices whereby the rational properties of proverbs, partially formulated advice, partial description, elliptical expressions, passing remarks, fables, cautionary tales, and the like are made evident, are demonstrated. The demonstrably rational properties of indexical expressions and indexical actions is [*sic*] an ongoing achievement of the organized activities of everyday life" (p. 34).

Utilizing these guidelines, or policies, will assist the ethnomethodologist while doing ethnomethodology.

APPLYING ETHNOMETHODOLOGY

A basic interest of the ethnomethodologist is to disturb the normal situations of interaction in order to uncover taken-for-granted rules (Denzin, 1969). "A methodological key used by ethnomethodologists is intentional disruption of the process of reality negotiation or meaning construction. When a researcher upsets the process by which the meaning of a situation is negotiated, the normally hidden methods of the negotiation can be starkly highlighted" (Levin, 1991:62). Early ethnomethodological studies conducted by Garfinkel and his associates generally took place in casual, noninstitutionalized settings like the home. More recently, there has been a movement toward studies of institutional settings such as courtrooms, medical facilities, and police departments, and with formal analytic technology. The various methods used by ethnomethodologists to collect data generally include open-ended or in-depth interviews, participant observation, videotaping, the documentary method of interpretation, and ethnomethodological experiments, often called *breaching experiments* (Wallace and Wolf, 1999). Breaching experiments involve violating the everyday rules as a technique for discovering social order through its disruption. "The format was introduced in the early 1960s by Harold Garfinkel (1963) under the title "breaching demonstrations" as a way to make tacit understandings clearer and to show the power of the taken-for-granted world. The concept and procedure immediately became a popular way to conduct research into everyday life and, in particular, to train students to see and experience the complex web of rules in which we live" (Deegan, 1989:33). Discussion of the application of ethnomethodology begins with breaching experiments.

Breaching Experiments

In an attempt to validate their assumptions about what is real, Garfinkel and his associates conducted several empirical studies. "One line of empirical inquiry became known as the *breaching experiment*, in which normal course of interaction was deliberately interrupted" (Turner, 2003:421). As Ritzer (2000a) explained, "In breaching experiments, social reality is violated in order to shed light on the methods by which people construct social reality. The assumption behind this research is

not only that the methodical production of social life occurs all the time but also that the participants are unaware that they are engaging in such actions. The objective of the breaching experiment is to disrupt normal procedures so that the process by which the everyday world is constructed or reconstructed can be observed and studied" (p. 251). Garfinkel believes that one must "breach" constitutive expectancies in radical ways, since the natural attitude guarantees that people assimilate "strange" into "familiar" without altering the presuppositions underlying a shared world (Rogers, 1983). These breaching experiments demonstrate the fundamental EM principles. They are not formal and are not based on things that can be empirically observed.

Garfinkel's quasi-experimental field studies are designed to modify the familiar, known-in-common environment by rendering the background expectancies inoperative. Garfinkel (1967) stated:

> Specifically, this modification would consist of subjecting a person to a breach of the background expectancies of everyday life while (a) making it difficult for the person to interpret his situation as a game, and experiment, a deception, a play, *i.e.*, as something other than the one known according to the attitude of everyday life as a matter of enforceable morality and action, (b) making it necessary that he reconstruct the "natural facts" but giving him insufficient time to manage the reconstruction with respect to required mastery of practical circumstances for which he must call upon his knowledge of the "natural facts," and (c) requiring that he manage the reconstruction of the natural facts by himself and without consensual validation. (p. 54)

Individuals have no alternative except to try to normalize the resultant incongruities in their social world. Seeking balance and normality in one's life is viewed as a natural need of humans. We like to think that we are capable of putting meaning on our world, to the point where it can be taken for granted. It makes us feel better, or "normal." Thus, breaching experiments become an effective means of observation of how humans bring order and stability to their lives. Studies have been conducted in conversation analysis, walking, face-to-face communication, and interactions in various settings. These studies examine how people construct and reconstruct social reality. The researcher enters a social setting, violates or breaches the rules that govern it, and studies how the interactants deal with the breach.

Many of the breaching experiments that Garfinkel utilized were undertaken by his students in casual settings. One example involves the breaching of the basic rules of the game tic-tac-toe. The rules of tic-tac-toe are very simple: Each of the two participants takes a turn placing a mark within one of the cells. In the breaching experiment, the "operative" places a mark between two cells, thus creating confusion about which cell the mark actually belongs in. The game cannot continue "normally" as the taken-for-granted rules have been violated. Ethnomethodologists would examine the reaction of the participant who was being duped.

In another study, Garfinkel had his students act as if they were boarders in their homes. They were instructed to conduct themselves in a circumspect and polite way. "They were to avoid getting personal, to use formal address, to speak only when spoke to" (Garfinkel, 1967:47). Five of his students refused to participate, and four were "unsuccessful." In the other cases, "reports were filled with accounts of astonishment, bewilderment, shock, anxiety, embarrassment, and anger, and with charges by various family members that the student was mean, inconsiderate, selfish, nasty, or impolite" (Garfinkel, 1967:47). Family members demanded to know why the student was behaving in such a way. This attempt to put meaning to the breaching behavior reflects their attempt to readjust the social situation to normality. In addition, many students also reported having difficulty with the assignment because of the drastic way it altered their own taken-for-granted world.

One other example of a breaching experiment conducted by Garfinkel and his students involves the counseling study. "Ten undergraduates were solicited by telling them that research was being done in the Department of Psychiatry to explore alternative means to psychotherapy 'as a way of giving persons advice about their personal problems'" (Garfinkel, 1967:79). Each subject was paired with a person who was portrayed as a trainee counselor. The subject was escorted to a room and told to formulate a series of yes/no questions about a personal problem he or she had. The subject then asked the "counselor" the questions and received either a yes or a no response. After each response, the subject was instructed to comment privately into a tape recorder about what she or he had learned. The catch was that the answers provided by the "counselor" were completely random and had nothing at all to do with the questions being asked. Some answers were confusing and contradictory. For example, a subject might be told yes in response to a question about whether someone would make a suitable mate. But a short time later, when the subject asked whether to continue dating this person, the answer would be no. Many of the subjects expressed tremendous frustration and anger, but they kept trying to find a pattern of meaning in the replies. Some subjects thought the counselor had learned something new about them between the two contradictory replies or had discovered some sort of deeper meaning. The subjects were always able to come up with a "sensible" explanation for the confusing responses they had received. If the counselor advised against continuing to date a desirable mate, the subject might conclude that the counselor was telling him or her to "test" his or her love for the other person (Garfinkel, 1967).

By showing how people can give meaning to an intrinsically meaningless situation, Garfinkel provided insight into the creation and maintenance of reality in everyday life. One of the taken-for-granted assumptions we make in social interactions is that events are relatively orderly and predictable. Thus, even confusing developments "make sense" to us on further examination (Garfinkel, 1967). From these experiments, Garfinkel came to believe that experiences provide the meaning of language and facilitate communication. He does not believe that language holds a shared, or a consistent, meaning for everyone. Garfinkel contends that the words of language are not the basis of communication; but that previous and present interactions are the cornerstone of communication.

Conversation Analysis

Garfinkel interprets an individual's use of words as a means of clarifying or repairing social problems created by human communication. He believes that a large part of human communication is not what *is* said, but what *is not* said. What people leave out of conversation is often far more important than the actual words spoken. The nonverbal communication between the speaker and the spoken-to is of extreme importance. Furthermore, everyone uses anticipatory knowledge gained from previous interactions during verbal discourse: If we did not utilize past knowledge, each conversation would have to begin with a lengthy history lesson of past interaction. Thus, insinuation and alluding to previous events provide an undertone in effective communication. However, until the undertones of discourse are fully exposed, through verbal language, honest communication cannot exist. Garfinkel believes that communication is made possible by a communal agreement, or the appearance of consensus in the spoken word. Previously acknowledged acceptance of events sets patterns of understanding in communication.

These patterns are carried into encounters by each participant and assist in effective interaction. Garfinkel and other ethnomethodologists see language as a tool that is used to interpret and clarify social interactions. Breaching the taken-for-granted rules of conversation provides valuable insight into the behaviors of interactants.

One of the major forms of research within ethnomethodology is conversation analysis. The goal of conversation analysis is to examine how conversation is organized. A great deal of research has been conducted in this area. Emmanuel A. Schegloff (1979) examined telephone conversations in an effort to understand the orderly nature of such interactions, especially in regard to how interactants come to identify and recognize cues given by the other in an attempt to maintain a sense of systematic normality. Research has been conducted to ascertain how individuals know when it is appropriate to laugh during the course of conversation (Jefferson, 1979, 1984). Heritage and Greatbatch (1986) studied devices by which speakers generate applause from their audiences; Clayman (1993) studied booing as an expression of disapproval in the context of public speaking; and Goodwin (1984) examined the integration of talk and nonvocal activities (Ritzer, 2000a). These are just a few examples of research conducted by ethnomethodologists in the area conversation analysis inspired by the Garfinkel's examination of communication.

Phenomena of Order

Breaching experiments and communication analysis reinforce the idea that individuals continually attempt to bring balance and order into their lives. We seem to crave orderliness over chaos, and clearly rational thinking reinforces the need for social order. In his later writings, Garfinkel (1988) began to stress the importance of ethnomethodologists' conducting more studies on the social order (a number of such studies are identified later in this chapter). Such studies should "specify the production and accountability of immortal, ordinary society—that miracle of familiar organizational things—as the local production and natural, reflexive accountability of the phenomena of order" (p. 103). For Durkheim, the objective reality of social facts is sociology's fundamental principle. Garfinkel (1988) argued that "for ethnomethodology the objective reality of social facts, in that and just how it is every society's locally, endogenously produced, naturally organized, reflexively accountable, ongoing, practical achievement, being everywhere, always, only, exactly and entirely, members' work, with no time out, and with no possibility of evasion, hiding out, passing, postponement, or buy-outs, is *thereby* sociology's fundamental phenomenon" (p. 103). From this viewpoint, social order is as an ongoing process subject to constant change and even misinterpretation by the members of the society. But always, members of the society "concert their activities to produce and exhibit the coherence, cogency, analysis, consistency, order, meaning, reason, methods" (Garfinkel, 1967:108) which bring order to their lives. For the researcher, distinctive emphases should be placed on the production and accountability of order, and especially on the methods that individuals utilize to maintain order and normality.

Experience teaches us that not everything in social life or natural life fits a nice orderly pattern. Sexual identity is one such example.

Intersexuality: The Case of Agnes

In the orderly world, biology dictates two sexual categories: male and female. In the social world, this distinction is not always so simple. Garfinkel (1967) stated, "Every society exerts close controls over the transfers of persons from one status to another. Where transfers of sexual statuses are concerned, these controls are particularly restrictive and rigorously enforced" (p. 116). For those people

who consider themselves sexually "normal," the environment has a sexually normal component. The taken-for-granted world consists of a reality that an individual is either a male or a female. The lives of persons are made easier by this "reality." "This obstinacy points to the omnirelevance of sexual statuses to affairs of daily life as an invariant but unnoticed background in the texture of relevances that comprise the changing actual scenes of everyday life" (Garfinkel, 1967:118). The perception that one's sex fits neatly into one of two categories—male or female—is altered by the reality that "for a variety of reasons, one out of every 2,000 births is characterized by a distinguishable degree of *intersexuality;* that is . . . they are difficult to classify as male or female because they possess both male *and* female sexual characteristics. . . . Persons of intersexual status may be born with male and female attributes; that is, the category of intersexual may be thrust upon them" (Goode, 2001:322). In this regard, some people "accomplish gender." Garfinkel's study of Agnes remains a classic in the field of intersexuality, or accomplishing gender.

In this study, Garfinkel gave a genuine methodological description of the uninterrupted nature of social gender production. Specifically, the focus was on Agnes and her ability to accomplish the assignment of passing as a "normal" woman. *Passing* is defined as *"the work of achieving and making secure her rights to live as a normal, natural female while having continually to provided for the possibility of detection and ruin carried on within socially structured conditions"* (Garfinkel, 1967:137). Passing as a female was critical to Agnes's self-identity. Garfinkel (1967) described a number of "passing devices" used by Agnes in order to secure her appearance as a woman.

Garfinkel first met Agnes at the department of psychiatry at UCLA in October 1958. At the time, Agnes was a single, white nineteen-year-old girl who was at the time self-supporting and working as a typist for a local insurance company. Garfinkel (1967) described Agnes' appearance as convincingly female.

> She was tall, slim, with a very female shape. Her measurements were 38-25-38. She had long, fine dark-blonde hair, a young face with pretty features, a peaches-and-cream complexion, no facial hair, subtly plucked eyebrows, and no makeup except for lipstick. . . . She appeared as a person with feminine body contours. . . . She had large, well-developed breasts coexisting with the normal external genitalia of a male. An abdominal laparotomy and pelvic and adrenal exploration, performed two years before she was first seen at UCLA, revealed no uterus or ovaries, no evidence of any vestigial female apparatus nor any abnormal tissue mass in the abdomen, retroperitoneal area, or pelvis. Bilateral testicular biopsy showed some atrophy of the testes. . . . Agnes was born a boy with normal-appearing male genitals. A birth certificate was issued for a male and she was appropriately named. Until age seventeen she was recognized by everyone to be a boy. (pp. 119–120)

Garfinkel's study involves the analysis of how Agnes achieved her right to live the gender identity of a female. His concept of *passing* refers to how she accomplished this feat (Michener, DeLamater, and Schwartz, 1986).

At age sixteen, Agnes ran away from home and began dressing like a woman. She realized that dressing like a woman was not enough; she would have to learn to "pass" as a woman if she was going to be accepted as one. Learning the expected behaviors and mannerisms of a woman, Agnes came to define herself as a woman and was defined by others as a one. Years later, Agnes revealed that she had lied about her gender identity. From the age of twelve she had been taking estrogen—hormone pills that she stole from her mother—which had induced female secondary sex characteristics (Goode, 2001). However, Garfinkel was always primarily concerned about the passing techniques that Agnes had used to function as a woman in society. As Ritzer (2000c) explained, "The more general point here is that we are not simply born men or women; we also learn and routinely use the commonplace practices that allow us to pass as men or women. It is only in learning these practices that we come to be, in a sociological sense, a man or a woman" (p. 253). Furthermore, nonintersexed persons use passing techniques as well in order to help secure their respective identities as a man or a woman. Some people are far less secure than others and engage in a number of activities to maintain positive sexual identities.

The Degradation Ceremony

One's identity is affected by many factors, including both internal reflection (such as sexual identity) and external projection (for example, a sports coach who states that a player is a discipline problem). Degradation ceremonies are public attempts to inflict identity alteration. They are acts of embarrassment done purposely rather than accidentally. "With the exception of planned embarrassment, most embarrassing incidents emerge unpredictably; neither their definers nor their actors anticipate their occurrence. These incidents are haphazardly, rather awkwardly accepted instances of status-forcing. The problematic individual is forced to accept an otherwise unacceptable definition of self. Degradation ceremonies describe planned and anticipated instances of status-forcing in which derelict individuals know in advance that they will lose self-credibility" (Lindersmith, Strauss, and Denzin, 1991:256). Examples of accidental embarrassing moments that cause harm to one's stature are numerous, such as a politician who mistakenly uses an ethnically offensive term while making a speech. If the slur is harmful enough, it may cost the politician an election. Among more mundane embarrassing moments that cost someone a degradation of status are a student's falling asleep in the classroom. This student has forever lost status with the professor and will never again be considered a serious student.

Identity degradation involves destroying the offender's current identity and transforming it into a "lower" social type. In 1956, Garfinkel's article "Conditions of Successful Degradation Ceremonies" was published in the *American Journal of Sociology*. In this famous article, Garfinkel described a degradation ceremony as an attempt to transform "an individual's total identity into an identity lower in the group's scheme of social types" (p. 420). Furthermore, "any communicative work between persons, whereby the public identity of an actor is transformed into something looked on as lower in the local scheme of social types, will be called a 'status degradation ceremony'" (p. 420). Garfinkel described the conditions and parameters that give rise to successful degradation ceremonies. Ultimately, individuals who are being degraded must be placed outside the everyday moral order and defined as a threat to that order (Lindersmith et al., 1991). Additionally, since degradation poses a threat to the status of the subject, the ceremony is generally forcibly imposed. The degradation ceremonies discussed by Garfinkel were restricted to those concerned with the alteration of total identities. "The identities referred to must be 'total' identities. That is, these identities must refer to persons as 'motivational' types rather than as 'behavioral' types, not to what a person may be expected to have done or to do (in Parsons' term to his 'performance') but to what the group holds to be the ultimate 'grounds' or 'reasons' for his performance" (Garfinkel, 1956:420).

Garfinkel proposed that all moral societies have degradation ceremonies and only those with total anomie do not. In fact, it is highly unlikely that any society does not feature conditions and organization sufficient for inducing shame. Simply put, "There is no society whose social structure does not provide, in its routine features, the conditions of identity degradation. Just as the structural conditions of shame are universal to all societies by the very fact of their being organized, so the structural conditions of status degradation are universal to all societies" (Garfinkel, 1956:420). Garfinkel argued that only the communicative tactics used for the degradation ceremony vary by society.

Degradation ceremonies used at the societal level fall within the scope of moral indignation. They are designed to bring shame and guilt to the violator of the moral code. Moral indignation is equated with public denunciation. In this regard, the accuser is attempting to rally the entire group into believing that the accused is guilty of some wrongdoing. The actions of the violator (accused) are "cast in moral terms which threaten the existence of the social group, and their accuser must be defined as a person who is morally superior. The accuser will evoke higher moral values which witnesses accept, and he will be defined as a legitimate upholder of those values. If the accuser is successful in his attempts, the accused must accept their new status. Degradation ceremonies force them to yield to the wishes of others. They give up control over their own moral career, finding that their fate now lies in the hands of others" (Lindersmith et al., 1991:257). Moral indignation causes the destruction of status of the person denounced, and through ritualistic ceremonies it generally reinforces group solidarity. However, in some cases, the degradation of status inflicted on the accused by one social group may actually lead to rewards by another group. For example, Rosa Parks was a victim of degradation by many southern whites because she refused to give up her bus seat to a white man, but she became a hero and champion of civil rights to the greater American society.

The successful degradation ceremony results in the recasting of the objective character and status of the condemned (accused) person. The person "becomes in the eyes of his condemners literally a different and *new* person. It is not that the new attributes are added to the old 'nucleus.' He is not changed, he is reconstituted. The former identity, at best, receives the accent of mere appearance. . . . The new identity is the 'basic reality' " (Garfinkel, 1956:421–422). Garfinkel (1956:422–423) identified eight conditions for a successful denunciation:

1. Both event and perpetrator must be removed from the realm of their everyday character and be made to stand as "out of the ordinary."

2. Both event and perpetrator must be placed within a scheme that shows that no preferences were given. If the accused has a personal agenda against the accused, objectivity is lost. Witnesses must not be swayed by such biases.

3. The denouncer must so identify himself to all the witnesses that during denunciation they regard him not as a privately but as a publicly known person (an attempt to demonstrate objectivity without bias). The denouncer must be presenting facts to the witnesses.

4. The denouncer must make the dignity of the suprapersonal values of the tribe salient and accessible to view, and the denunciation must be delivered in their name. This reinforces the values of the group in the name of the greater society.

5. The denouncer must arrange to be invested with the right to speak in the name of these ultimate values—the denouncer represents society.

6. The denouncer must be recognized as this representation of society and its moral code.

7. The denouncer must maintain proper social distance from the accused and the witnesses.

8. Finally, the denounced person must be ritually separated from a place in the legitimate order. She or he must be placed "outside" and made to feel "strange."

Garfinkel (1956) concluded by stating, "These conditions must be fulfilled for a successful denunciation. If they are absent, the denunciation will fail. Regardless of the situation when the denouncer enters, if he is to succeed in degrading the other man, it is necessary to introduce these features" (p. 423). Unfortunately, for many falsely accused persons, the denouncer is often successful in denouncing an accused in spite of biases and personal agendas.

STUDIES BY OTHER ETHNOMETHODOLOGISTS

A number of ethnomethodologists other than Harold Garfinkel have continued in his tradition. Garfinkel (1988:106–107) briefly acknowledged the work of several studies by ethnomethodologists:

- Medicines among the Kpelle of Liberia (Bellman, 1975).

- Proving the schedule of thirty-seven theorems and their proof accounts that make up, as instructions, Godel's proof by mathematicians (Livingston, 1986).

- Designing and administering a medical school curriculum in pediatrics, and evaluating the competence with that curriculum of medical students, interns, and residents (Robillard and Pack, 1976–1982).

- Teaching English as a second language to preschool children from immigrant families (Meyer, 1985, 1988).

- Coordinating work site practices of 911 dispatchers in "working" a call (Zimmerman and Whalen, 1987).

- Learning to play improvised jazz piano (Sudnow, 1978).

- Talking the convict code in an inmate halfway house (Wieder, 1974).

- Designing a Xerox copier to ensure complaint-free operation by office personnel (Suchman, 1985).

These are only a few studies recognized by Garfinkel. He feels that these studies are examples of good ethnomethodology and its attempt to explain everyday behavior and individuals' pursuit of order.

Aaron V. Cicourel

Cicourel (1964) is a critic of the notion that using quantitative methods guarantees a more objective research study and reduces bias. Although he questions Garfinkel's assertion that interaction and verbal accounts are the same process, he believes that humans see, sense, and feel much that they cannot communicate in words. "Humans use 'multiple modalities' for communicating in situations. Verbal accounts represent crude and incomplete translations of what is actually communicated in interaction. This recognition has led Cicourel to rename his brand of ethnomethodology: *cognitive sociology*" (Turner, 2003:423). In his research, Cicourel attempts to uncover the universal "interpretive procedures" that humans use to give meaning to social situations. Through these interpretive procedures humans can put order in their lives and engage in interaction successfully. These techniques include searching for a normal form (including methods of maintaining or creating one), doing a reciprocity of perspectives (especially through the use of gestures that attempt to assure others that a reciprocity of perspectives does actually exist), and using the et cetera principle (what is left unsaid, as in the *Seinfeld* television show, where the interactant fills in the blanks with "yada, yada, yada").

Dierdre Boden

Boden (1990b) attempted to integrate ethnomethodology with the more sociological traditional approach to incorporate the role of social structure into human behavior. Boden (1990a) also attempted to incorporate ideas of symbolic interactionism. Her approach to ethnomethodology lies in conversation analysis, with a specific focus on talk. All forms of talk are relevant: work talk, home talk, and every form of mundane talk. Boden has attempted to redefine conversation analysis with her term *interactional analysis*. As Ritzer (2000a) explained, "By using the term *interactional analysis*

to describe the interest in both verbal and nonverbal phenomena, Boden clearly aligns conversation analysis with symbolic interactionism" (pp. 268–269). From this standpoint, Boden attempts to highlight the importance of the thought process involved in conversation. People not only react to talk, but must also interpret the meaning of it; that is, they must think about it.

Harvey Sacks

Sacks attempts to expand "Garfinkel's concern with verbal accounts, while eliminating some of the problems posed by indexicality" (Turner, 2003:424). He believes that researchers, through the use of words to describe phenomena, alter the meaning set forth by interactants. The words chosen by researchers are not neutral and may represent a biased opinion, or at least they may create an untrue analysis of conversation. Consequently, Sacks generally records entire conversations verbatim. "Such a tactic resolved the problem of indexicality because Sacks simply ignored the substance and contexts of conversation and focused on its form. For example, 'sequences of talk' among actors might occupy his attention" (Turner, 2003:424). Sacks and various collaborators have come to realize that interactants involved in conversation expect each other to take turns ("turn talking"). When conversation occurs face-to-face they look for cues from one another to know when it is their "turn" to talk. Interruptions in the normal flow of conversation are often viewed as breaches. Sacks's research has involved the attempt to discover universal forms of interactions that apply to all conversations. He hopes to find laws of reality construction common to all interacting individuals.

Donald Zimmerman, Melvin Pollner, and Lawrence Wieder

Donald Zimmerman and Melvin Pollner (1970) argued that sociology fails to pay attention to the most important aspect of human behavior. Conventional sociologists use the everyday social world as a *topic* rather than treating the everyday world in its own right, as a *resource*. Traditional sociologists examine communication looking for evidence of values, norms, and prevailing attitudes; the ethnomethodologist examines communication as evidence of how social life is actually carried on. Furthermore, the sociologist attempts to provide causal explanations of observations in terms of patterns and repetitive actions. The ethnomethodologist is concerned with how "members of society go about the task of *seeing, describing,* and *explaining* order in the world in which they live" (Zimmerman and Wieder, 1970:289). Zimmerman, Wieder, and Pollner have all drawn inspiration from Garfinkel, and they have sought to identify universal procedures that people use to maintain a sense of order or normality.

RELEVANCY

Ethnomethodology is a theoretical perspective that seeks to understand human behavior by examining the methods that people employ to make sense of the world. Created by Harold Garfinkel, ethnomethodology is the study of the everyday practices of people and their attempts to deal with day-to-day life. Clues are provided by individuals through their verbal accounts of social action. People attempt to maintain a sense of normality and prefer to live in a commonsense world built by a stream of past experiences and interpretations of events.

Ethnomethodology falls outside the parameters of mainstream sociology. Ethnomethodologists are generally critical of traditional sociologists because they impose their sense of social reality on interactants rather than use the descriptions of those persons under study. In an attempt to be objective and rational, traditional sociologists use some working interpretation of rationality.

"Commonly, sociological researchers decide a definition of rationality by selecting one or more features from among the properties of scientific activity as it is ideally described and understood. The definition is then used methodologically to aid the researcher in deciding the realistic, pathological, prejudiced, delusional, mythical, magical, ritual, and similar features of everyday conduct, thinking, and beliefs" (Garfinkel, 1967:262). Ethnomethodologists remain steadfast in the idea that the everyday world must be treated as a resource rather than as a topic. The primary goal of ethnomethodologists is to specify general rules and procedures that people utilize to maintain a sense of order, a taken-for-granted reality.

Despite much research, ethnomethodology has failed to produce such "laws" of general behavior. Many contemporary sociologists value the contributions of ethnomethodology but feel that its scope of analysis is far too narrow. Macrostructural factors are almost completely ignored, although Garfinkel's study of degradation ceremonies makes cross-cultural reference to the fact that all societies throughout the world utilize such status-reducing rituals.

The relevancy of ethnomethodology will continue long into the twenty-first century. Experiments are generally conducted by natural scientists and considered the domain of natural science (partly because of the complex nature of controlling the numerous variables found in the human social environment). However, experiments are seldom conducted in mainstream sociology. Ethnomethodologists remind us all that very important human research can indeed be collected through its methodological approach. If ethnomethodologists and social psychologists find value in the experimental-design approach to data collection, perhaps traditional sociologists should consider this approach more often than they generally do.

Breaching experiments reveal the taken-for-granted world that humans live in. Disruptions in the typical flow of activity result in attempts to bring things back to normal. It is this reality that illustrates the phenomenon of order: the coherent attempt to bring things back into balance. To test this premise, I had my social psychology students conduct a number of simple breaching experiments on campus: walking backward, walking on the wrong side of the stairwell, standing facing the back of the elevator, a male student's wearing a dress to class, suddenly barking like a dog during class, placing a "wet paint" sign on a wall that has not been freshly painted, and so on. In one case, a student invited friends over to his apartment for a keg party. He actually purchased nonalcoholic beer but did not tell any of the guests. By the time the keg was nearly finished, most of the guests were acting *as if* they were drunk (which would be the normal order of things if one were actually drinking alcohol). It was not until the next day that the student informed his guests they had been drinking nonalcoholic beer—much to their dismay and anger! Breaching experiments reveal many of the taken-for-granted realities that interactants construct in order to proceed smoothly with their daily life. These experiments are useful tools for examining human interaction.

The greatest contribution of ethnomethodology is conversation analysis. The description and explication of everyday talk reveal the many "rules" participants use and rely on while interacting with others. General rules such as taking turns while talking and watching for nonverbal cues indicate to conversation analysts that participants look for order. Conversation analysts generally use audiotapes and videotapes to collect accurate data on naturally occurring dialogues. Garfinkel first used this approach in his research on jury deliberations. This ethnomethodological approach has influenced the labeling school and social psychology, (another branch of sociology). The

success of many professions is tied directly to effective conversation analysis. Callers to emergency services (for example, police, fire fighters, 911) benefit if the receiver is trained to properly understand what message is being communicated, especially in creating a relaxed conversational tone in order to clearly identify the emergency and the proper method of response. Effective communication skills help to save the lives of those in need and time for those attempting to aid others. Conversation analysis has also been effective in the medical fields. Properly trained doctors and consultants can reduce unnecessary prescribing, overprescribing, and errors in surgery (for example, amputating the wrong leg). Conflict mediators, marriage counselors, and even politicians can benefit from learning skills in effective public speaking. All persons benefit from effective communication. In short, conversation analysis can assist nearly everyone positively.

Garfinkel's Agnes study illustrates the fact that gender identities are socially produced, not biologically produced. For most people sexual identity is quite simple, perhaps the simplest thing they will ever have to come to grips with. However, many other people feel confused by their sexual identity, reporting that they feel like "a man trapped in a woman's body" (or vice versa). This confusion brings with it doubts and uncertainty, and often remorse. Being able to discuss this issue with a trained professional helps to reassure people of their place in their own bodies and, consequently, in the social world. In contemporary society there is greater acceptance of intersexed persons and same-sex partners preference than ever before. However, it is also true that many people are not as tolerant of alternative viewpoints, which challenge their taken-for-granted worlds. The U.S. military generally applies the "don't ask, don't tell" policy to sexual preference. In other words, the military will not ask whether or not someone is gay and also expects not to be told. Interestingly, since the September 11, 2001, attacks, the U.S. military has been in great need of service personnel who speak Arabic. In November 2002, two potential translators were dismissed when it was revealed that they were gay. Seemingly, the gay lifestyle was considered more of a threat to national security than terrorism. Esera Tuaolo, a former player in the National Football League (NFL), recently said that he was gay. In an article written in *ESPN the Magazine* (2002), Tuaolo stated, "The NFL is a super-macho culture. It's a place for gladiators. And gladiators aren't supposed to be gay. . . . for nine years I made my living as a gladiator in the NFL . . . and I am a gay man" (p. 74). Tuaolo hid this fact while he played football because he feared retribution and lack of acceptance by his teammates, other professional football players, the media, and the fans. Considering the reaction of current players and fans, he was right to hide his true sexual identity.

Research in the area of degradation ceremonies remains very relevant. Garfinkel was correct in his assertion that all societies use such techniques to control behavior. It is also true that nearly all social groups and organizations have such disciplinary reviews in place to punish those who stray from the expected norm. Degradation ceremonies alter the identity of the subject, who is given a label that is of lesser status than previously held. This new label brings with it a new identity that compromises full acceptance within the group or society. Among the many examples is the military court martial, where the convicted person is stripped of former rank and privileges. The disgrace is often too much to bear. Government workers may also be subjected to degradation ceremonies.

Perhaps no label has a more extreme stigma than "traitor to the country." Robert Hanssen has the label of "the most damaging FBI agent in U.S. history." In a book review of *The Spy Next Door,* Delaney (2002c) wrote,

"Robert Hanssen, an unassuming man . . . pretending to be a religious family man who hated communism, used his top-secret clearance to gain information on the activities of FBI agents and double agents in Moscow—secrets he leaked to the Soviets over the years for a total of $470,000. His betrayal is linked to the execution of at least three U.S. spies" (p. 162). Hanssen's degradation ceremony scarred his reputation forever and links with the likes of Benedict Arnold and Samuel Mudd (Mudd was the doctor who set the leg of John Wilkes Booth, the man who assassinated President Lincoln, and despite a full pardon from President Andrew Johnson, Mudd remains stigmatized). The authors of *The Spy Next Door* relied on ethnomethodological data collection in the form of more than 150 interviews with Hanssen's friends, neighbors, colleagues, lawyers, professors, classmates, roommates, psychiatrists, and priests.

Other degradation ceremonies include mental health officials' labeling someone insane and the criminal courts' labeling someone a sex offender. The status of sex offender is especially compromised as those so labeled must register with local officials and inform neighbors whenever they move into a new neighborhood.

Although ethnomethodology does not receive complete respect from traditional sociology, it has certainly contributed a great deal to the general accumulation of knowledge. It is difficult to discount a field that studies everyday life, but it is hard to defend when it ignores macrostructural factors in microbehavioral interactions. Ethnomethodology continues to develop new research, especially on work and the workplace. It has developed the study of human-machine relations in the business setting by helping organizations develop computer hardware and software systems that fit workers, rather than demanding that workers fit systems. In fact, ethnomethodology seems to be keeping up with current advancements, as many recent articles have a very technological and computer flavor to them. Garfinkel's 1996 article "Ethnomethodology's Program" relates formal analytic (FA) technology within the ethnomethodology tradition: "The premier achievement of FA studies of work is the generality of work and occupations, not in occupations' aesthetics but as labor described in their generically represented details of structure: e.g., in their details of generality and comparability, staffed by interchangeable and surveyable populations, the descriptions being responsive across occupations, disciplines, and literatures to inductive inference without incoherence, etc." (p. 13). Clearly, Garfinkel is taking greater notice of structural issues in the workplace and adapting it to the micro needs of participants. It is difficult to determine the future of ethnomethodology, but if research continues to examine macro issues, criticism of it will not be so loud. Above all Harold Garfinkel will be given full credit for its roots.

8

Phenomenology: Edmund Husserl, Alfred Schutz, and Peter Berger

The term *phenomenological sociology* refers to the work of a number of sociologists who share certain sympathies regarding phenomenological philosophy. Phenomenological analysis has as its subject matter the world of conscious experience. The world consists of the numerous and shifting inputs of perception. Since most perception is quickly and effortlessly organized into certain customary patterns, the world appears as a familiar one. It is common for the familiarity of the world to become so compelling that the work that goes into achieving this familiarity is overlooked. The major goal of phenomenology is to reverse this process by exploring and analyzing the formative core of consciousness (Douglas, 1980). Phenomenology can be defined as a philosophical sociology that begins with the individual and his or her own conscious experience as the focus of study and attempts to avoid prior assumptions, prejudices, and other dogmatic forms of thinking while investigating social behavior. A phenomenologist would like people not to take for granted the social world and, instead, to question its formation and maintenance.

SOCIOLOGIES OF EVERYDAY LIFE

Phenomenology studies common sense, conscious experience, and routine daily life. In this regard, phenomenology may be placed in the category of sociologies of everyday life. In the preface of *Introduction to the Sociologies of Everyday Life*, Jack Douglas (1980) argued that the sociologists of everyday life have for many years been rebuilding the foundation for understanding all human life and thus rebuilding the foundation of all theory and method in the social sciences. These concentrated efforts have led to five major bodies of theoretical ideas called the sociology of everyday life:

1. Symbolic interactionism
2. Dramaturgical analysis
3. Labeling theory
4. Phenomenology and ethnomethodology
5. Existentialism

The sociology of everyday life is a sociological orientation concerned with experiencing, observing, understanding, describing, analyzing, and communicating about people interacting in concrete situations. The sociologist of everyday life studies face-to-face social interactions by observing and experiencing them in natural situations, that is, in situations that have not been scientifically manipulated. The sociologist begins with an analysis of the members' meanings of their behaviors.

179

The Role of Consciousness

There are many differences between phenomenology and sociology. Phenomenologists rely on a reflexive experience as it takes form in consciousness. Their research proceeds on the certain ground of intentional consciousness. Through the techniques of reduction and the capacity for imaginative variation, the phenomenologist is able to find the rudimentary structures and processes of experience. Sociologists, on the other hand, often rely on taking the perspective of the other and imposing a sense of order on the environment so that they may collect data. Phenomenologists are much more concerned with the way individuals construct in their own consciousness the meanings of things. They see the social world as ultimately made up of many more individual constructions than do other sociologists. "Phenomenological sociology is characterized as a subjective or creative sociology because it seeks to understand the world from the point of view of the acting subject and not from the perspective of the scientific observer. Initially then, the relevant world of study for the sociologist is the world that is inhabited by ordinary people and defined as their commonsense reality" (Farganis, 2000:311). People interact with one another on the basis of a socially created world, where meanings come about through constant negotiation in their everyday lives. Generally, they come to see the world as a natural order, rather than as the socially created one that it is. Phenomenologists question the legitimacy of an "objective" world and therefore prefer to examine the subjective natural of social reality. Edmund Husserl and Alfred Schutz, in particular, concentrate on the reciprocity of perceptions. Their analysis is a result of reflection, attention, and awareness.

The Phenomenological Approach

It was Edmund Husserl who first developed the phenomenological approach. For him, the term *phenomenology* designates two things: a new kind of descriptive method which made a breakthrough in philosophy at the turn of the nineteenth century and a science which is intended to supply the basic instrument (*Organon*) for a rigorously scientific philosophy and, in its consequent application, to make possible a methodological reform of all the sciences (McCormick and Elliston, 1981). The roots of phenomenology are firmly entrenched in the German tradition, some of the most important intellectual debates taking place between the world wars. The complex ideas that come under the phenomenology umbrella were generated in an atmosphere of heightened social conflict and anxiety about the future. Husserl's phenomenological approach was to examine the phenomena of consciousness and bracket them in order to test their truth.

Husserl was influenced by such social thinkers as Descartes, Hume, and Kant. It was in reading Descartes's *Mediations* that Husserl first conceived of the possibility of seeking a universally rational "science of being" by turning his theoretical focus on an objective world to a reflective one. Descartes argued that the social world exists only in the context of presentations of experiences of people. Descartes promoted the idea of *transcendental subjectivity*, a philosophy founded through a psychology of inner experience. In the introduction to *Phenomenology and the Crisis of Philosophy* (1965), Quentin Lauer stated, "Unlike Descartes, however, Husserl will not look upon this knowledge of the subject as a first indubitable principle from which all other knowledge can be derived. Instead, taking the *cogitatum* as the objective correlate of the *cogito*, he will see in subjectivity the one and only (transcendental) source of all absolute, objectivity valid knowledge, because in the subjectivity of consciousness and only here is the being of objectivity absolute" (p. 20).

Husserl was convinced that Hume had effectively put an end to the possibility of any causal metaphysics or theory of knowledge. "Hume had refused to see in appearance anything more than appearances—they reveal only themselves and not something which appears. In this Husserl agrees, but the conclusion he draws is diametrically opposed to that of Hume. The latter had never advanced beyond a 'phenomenism,' according to which appearances yield no necessary knowledge at all. Husserl, on the contrary, will find in phenomena all the knowledge he wants, and it will be an absolute knowledge" (Lauer, 1965:20–21). From Kant, Husserl was convinced that objectivity could never be the measure of subjectivity. Husserl came to find "reality" in the phenomena themselves, with the contents of the consciousness as a priori forms. There is no need to discuss "things," as "things" are revealed in consciousness. William Dilthey and the neo-Kantians had already made a distinction between the realm of nature (*Naturwissenschaften*) and the realm of culture (*Geisteswissenschaften*). This development helped to spark the growth of sociology in Germany, as did the influence of Max Weber. Schutz's adaptation of phenomenology included Weber's concept of *verstehen* (subjective meaning). "For Schutz, the meaning that the individual imparts to situations in everyday life is of prime importance; he puts the spotlight on the individual's own definition of the situation" (Wallace and Wolf, 1999:255).

Edmund Husserl delivered five lectures from April 26 to May 2, 1907, in Göttingen. They introduced the main ideas and concepts of his phenomenology (Husserl, 1965). Discussion of the most significant social thinkers in phenomenology rightfully begins with Edmund Husserl.

EDMUND HUSSERL (1859–1938)

Edmund Husserl is known as the father of phenomenology. His ideas are often very complex and confusing; also, the translation of his German works into English often complicates the clarifications of his theories. As George Nakhnikian explained in the introduction to *The Idea of Phenomenology* (1964), "To the student reared in the English-speaking tradition in philosophy, Husserl's phenomenology may seem bizarre" (p. ix). Lauer (1965) described the "forbidding style" of Husserl, adding that the early translation of Husserl's works by Boyce-Gibson was lacking in accuracy, and that Dorion Cairns's translation reveals the difficulty of presenting a readable English version of Husserl's German.

Husserl was born April 8, 1859, into a Jewish family in the town of Prossnitz in Moravia, then a part of the Austrian Empire. His father was a merchant of sufficient means to send Edmund to the finest schools. Prossnitz was a leading center of textile and clothing manufacturing and a leading religious center for a number of famous rabbis during

Edmund Husserl, philosopher and social thinker who helped form phenomenology.
Source: Corbis/Bettmann

the two centuries before Husserl's birth. The minority Jewish community enjoyed a middle-class existence and had established a technical school in 1843 for all the town's children. The number of Jewish families was controlled in Austria as dictated by the Bohemian *Familianten Gesetz* in 1787. The Jewish population was therefore controlled through marriage licenses. Prossnitz was allowed 328 Jewish families, and that is exactly how many it had just prior to Husserl's birth. This population control policy was stopped in 1849 but the requirement that Jews obtain special marriage licenses remained in effect until late 1859.

Edmund's father had decided to send Husserl away to school in Vienna at age ten to begin his German classical education at a *Realgymnasium*. One year later he transferred to the *Staatsgymnasium* in Olmutz and graduated in 1876. He then went to Leipzig University and studied mathematics, physics, and philosophy. After two years he went to Berlin for further studies in mathematics. Husserl finished his doctoral work at Vienna, completing his dissertation on the theory of the calculus of variations. Husserl married Malvine Charlotte Steinschneider, a Jewish woman from Prossnitz. They had three children. From 1886 to 1901 Husserl held the position of *Privatdozent* at Halle University. In 1901 Husserl joined the faculty at Göttingen, where he taught for sixteen years. He accepted a professorship at Freiburg im Breisgau in 1916 and stayed there until he retired in 1928. At Freiburg, Husserl succeeded Heinrich Rickert, a leading figure in the neo-Kantian school of Baden in southern Germany.

Calvin O. Schrag wrote in the introduction to *The Phenomenology of Internal Time-Consciousness* (1966), "It was during his career at Freiburg, as well as during the period following his retirement, that he assimilated his later and mature reflections with his earlier insights. It was this whole course of development that gave to the world the seminal ideas of phenomenological philosophy.

Some of the main themes and ideas that emerged throughout this development were: a critique of psychologism, the intentionality of consciousness, the phenomenological and eidetic reduction, the phenomenological ego, transcendental intersubjectivity, time-consciousness, and the life-world" (p. 11).

In *The Foundation of Phenomenology* (1943), Marvin Farber reviewed Husserl's development:

> Husserl's own special preparation included mathematics and psychology. His doctor's degree was taken in mathematics, his studies under Weierstrass giving him a firm basis for later logical work. In psychology he was interested primarily in the pure descriptive type of investigation, "empirical" in Bretano's sense. The fusion of these two apparently diverse streams of scholarship determined the setting for his career. The important changes in his development are to be explained to a larger extent by difficulties encountered in integrating these elements. (p.15)

Among the most significant publications of Husserl are *On the Concept of Number* (1887), *Philosophy of Arithmetic* (1891), *Logical Investigations* (and 1901), and *Ideas* (1913). Many of Husserl's publications originated from his lectures. His last major philosophical work, *Die Krisis der Europaischen Wissenschaften und die Transzendental Phanomenologie*, appeared as Parts I and II in *Philosophia* (1936). "It was Husserl's intention to publish Part III in the same review, but the manuscript was never sent to the publisher. The entire work, in which for the first time the author dealt explicitly with the relation between history and philosophy, grew out of a lecture he had delivered on May 7, 1935, at the University of Prague" (Lauer, 1965:6).

Phenomenology

Husserl's philosophy begins with the assumption that every certainty is questionable. In *Ideem I* (1950) Husserl described phenomenology as a "doctrine of essences" and a doctrine concerned with what things are, not with whether they are. Husserl was not looking to establish absolute presuppositions on which to build a whole system of knowledge. Consequently, he was not interested in being a system builder. "He abhorred system-building as much as did [Søren] Kierkegaard and [Friedrich] Nietzsche. He was always a beginner, reexamining the foundations of his investigations, resisting all fixed formulations and final conclusions. Philosophy for Husserl was a never-ending pursuit of serious and open-ended questions, which lead to further questions that may require a resetting of the original questions. This at the same time accounts for the fertility of his investigations and for the philosophical freedom which his whole philosophy illustrates" (Schrag, Husserl, 1966:11).

Nakhnikian (Husserl, 1964) described "Husserl's phenomenology as an outgrowth of his attack on psychologism. Psychologism is a species of the view that philosophy is reducible to a factual science, in this case to psychology. Husserl is just as strongly against `biologism' and `anthropologism' as he is against psychologism" (p. x). Psychologism is an attempt to reduce the fundamental laws of logic and mathematics to psychological generalizations about the way people think; it is a type of scientific generalization. "The significance of Husserl's critique of psychologism is basically understandable only in terms of the final goal of the *Logical Investigations*, and that goal in fact lies beyond the two published volumes. The *Investigations* as we have them consist of epistemological clarifications of principles and essential concepts, in the service of laying the theoretical groundwork of a new discipline, pure logic—what Husserl would later call the `logic of the absolute science'" (Sheehan, 1981:143). In his article "A Reply to a Critic of My Refutation of Logical Psychologism," Husserl (1972) stated that "logic reflects on the reflected consciousness, and endeavors to raise our knowing processes to a higher power by

investigating the laws of our reflected consciousness. Psychology, on the other hand, will try to carry reflection raised to a higher power by logic over into the investigation of unreflected consciousness" (p. 13).

Additionally, phenomenology is not interested in the metaphysical world. Husserl's focus on individual consciousness led his phenomenology to be metaphysically neutral. He believed that only through consciousness could a researcher find the true meaning behind behavior. For Husserl (1965), "Consciousness was the `absolute' being with which philosophy is concerned—his is not a theory of being, as the metaphysician understands it, but only a theory of philosophical (scientific) being" (p. 67). As Husserl saw it, personal reflection was not a psychological activity of consciousness, but the ideal act of consciousness, which is inescapably linked to an objective structure. The objective world consists of the *Unwelt* (the environing world) and the *Lebenswelt* (the everyday world). "The *Unwelt* or *Lebenswelt*, then, is the objective counterpart of pre-philosophical consciousness: it is a world in consciousness that has not been rendered `thematic,' which is simply taken for granted—it is the familiar world in which men perforce live. . . . Phenomenology is what it is because it neither seeks nor accepts evidence other than that offered by consciousness itself" (Husserl, 1965:67–68). In short, phenomenology is not a science of facts, but a science of essential being, an eidetic science (meaning an insubstantial empirical science); it is a science that aims at establishing the "knowledge" of essences (Husserl, 1931).

Husserl distinguished between facts and essences. He described sciences of experience as sciences of "fact." Such "facts" are determined by acts of cognition which underline human experiences. Something is real and thus a fact because it possesses a spatiotemporal existence, having a particular duration of its own and a "real" content

(Husserl, 1931). An essence is that which an individual discloses as a "what is," an empirical possibility—a possibility which is itself to be understood not as empirical, but as an essential possibility (Husserl, 1931). Husserl noted that whatever belongs to the essence of one individual can also belong to another individual. This reality allows for the formation of categories of essences.

Natural Thinking and the Scientific Method

Empirical verification of theories and ideas is the goal of any science. In order to claim empirical authenticity, a science must demonstrate that it employs objective methods when collecting data. For the phenomenologist, objectivity is found in the world of individual consciousness that can be verified by others when objects attain temporal matter (for example, sound). Husserl questioned whether any discipline, especially philosophy, can be a science. Husserl (1965) stated that "from its earliest beginnings philosophy has claimed to be rigorous science. What is more, it has claimed to be the science that satisfies the loftiest theoretical needs and renders possible from an ethico-religious point of view a life regulated by pure rational norms. . . . During no period of its development has philosophy been capable of living up to this claim of being a rigorous science" (p. 71). Husserl indicated that philosophy had long placed itself among the loftiest and most rigorous of all the sciences in its attempt to acquire pure and absolute knowledge. His criticism of philosophy was not that it is an imperfect science, but that "it is not a science at all" (Husserl, 1965:73). Husserl added that all sciences are incomplete, even the "exact" (natural) sciences, because of the many defects in their doctrines.

Husserl, then, questioned the very thinking, or cognitive, approach of science in its study of human behavior. "*Natural thinking* in science and everyday life is untroubled by the difficulties concerning the possibility of cognition. *Philosophical thinking* is circumscribed by one's position toward the problems concerning the possibility of cognition. . . . What do things in themselves care about our ways of thinking and the logical rules governing them? These are laws of how we think" (Husserl, 1964:1). Husserl was indicating that the scientific method is not nearly as important as understanding the meaning of behavior based on one's consciousness. The critique of naturalism and the cognitive approach to the study of humans are the methods of phenomenologists, who question all cognition. In "Philosophy and the Crisis of European Man," (Lauer, 1965) Husserl questioned whether a "natural science" is possible because such a science is still vulnerable to spiritual activities. "Blinded by naturalism (no matter how much they themselves may verbally oppose it), the practitioners of humanistic science have completely neglected even to pose the problem of a universal and pure science of the spirit and to seek a theory of the essence of spirit as spirit, a theory that pursues what is unconditionally universal in the spiritual order with its own elements and its own laws. Yet this last should be done with a view to gaining theory scientific explanations in an absolutely conclusive sense" (Lauer, 1965:154–155).

Husserl viewed phenomenology as a type of science but, above all, as a method and an attitude of mind. It is a philosophical attitude of mind that incorporates a philosophical method. The research focus of phenomenology is the understanding of the pure transcendental consciousness and involves suspending the "givens" of the "natural" world (as perceived by the researcher). Martin Heidegger (1889–1976), a brilliant student of Husserl, developed a type of phenomenology in *Being and Time* (1996), sometimes called *hermeneutic phenomenology.* This designation is more than a subdivision within the field, as Heidegger "explicitly refers to his method as 'a hermeneutic' (Palmer, 1969:127). In this regard, Heidegger emphasized the study of what is "open" to study, or what has become manifest.

Perception

Objectivity is a goal of science, but objectivity is always influenced by perception. Perception itself is influenced by many factors, but especially by retention and memory. Husserl hoped to explain the origin of such notions (perceptions):

> As far as *memory* is concerned it is not anything simple, and from the start it presents different forms of objects and, interconnected with these, different forms of Givenness. Thus one could refer to the so-called *primary memory*, the *retention* which is necessarily bound up with every perception. The mental process which we are now undergoing becomes objective to us in immediate reflection, and thenceforth it displays in reflection the same objectivity: the self-same tone which has just existed as an actual "now" remains henceforth the same tone, but moving back into the past and there continually constituting the same objective point in time. (Husserl, 1964:52)

In other words, what one "sees" is a product of past memories and immediate reflection and interpretation of events. An individual refers back to some particular intuition (of past behavior) and applies some sort of meaning from it to the present situation, doing so whether the objects truly relate to one another or not. For example, a woman who has been cheated on by a man in the past may now suspect her current boyfriend of cheating despite his denial. Her perception of current events is tied to past events (via retention of past memories) through her current intuitions.

From this phenomenological approach, Husserl viewed humans acting in accordance with both past behaviors (memories) and current situations (that need to be interpreted for possible courses of action). Husserl (1931) stated:

> Every perception of a thing has such a zone of *background intuitions* (or background awareness, if "intuiting" already includes the state of being turned towards), and this also is a *"conscious experience,"* or more briefly a "consciousness of" all indeed that in point of fact lies in the co-perceived objective "background." . . . What we say applies exclusively to that zone of consciousness which belongs to the model essence of a perception as "being turned towards an object," and further to that which belongs to the proper essence of this zone itself. But it is here implied that certain modifications of the original experience are possible, which we refer to as a free turning of the "look"—not precisely nor merely of the physical but of the *"mental look"*—from the paper at first *described* to objects which had already appeared before, or which we had been "implicitly" aware, and whereof *subsequent* to the directing of one's look thither we are explicitly aware, perceiving them "attentively," or "noticing them near by." (p. 117)

Humans, then, are aware of things not only in perception, but also consciously in recollections and in representations similar to recollections. Reflexivity provides the individual an opportunity for an inner *mental glance* toward itself.

Recollections make it possible for individuals to perceive acts in certain ways.

> Recollection can make its appearance in different forms of accomplishment. We accomplish it either by simply laying hold of what is recollected, as when, for example, a recollection "emerges" and we look at what is remembered with a glancing ray [*Blickstrahl*] wherein what is remembered is indeterminate, perhaps a favored momentary phase intuitively brought forth, but not a recapitulative memory. Or we accomplish it in a real, re-productive, recapitulative memory in which the temporal object is again completely built up in a continuum of presentifications, so that we seem to perceive it again, but only seemingly, as-if. The whole process is a presentificational modification

of the process of perception with all its phases and levels, including retentions. However, everything has the index of reproductive modification. (Husserl, 1966:59)

The retention of memories is an important factor in perception, and consequently in one's consciousness. "Retention is a characteristic modification of perceptual consciousness, which is primal impression in the primordial, temporally constitutive consciousness, and, with reference to temporal objects, whether or not it is consciousness of the immanent—as an enduring sound in the tonal field or a color-datum in the visual field—perceptual consciousness is immanent (adequate) perception" (Husserl, 1966:159). By definition, memories are in the realm of the past, a time that has gone by, and yet, we remain conscious of them, and they shape our perception of current events.

Time Consciousness

Husserl (1977) explained that "the totality of one's consciousness at any given time is a unity within which every element is bound up with every other element. However, in the *manner* of the unification of these elements, as well as in the degree of its fixity and in its immediacy or mediacy, significant differences are to be found" (p. 297). Husserl believed strongly in the link between time and consciousness. The events and content of the past do in fact influence one's present consciousness; they are simultaneously linked. Husserl (1931) stated, "All the essential characteristics of experience and consciousness which we have reached are for us necessary steps towards the attainment of the end which is unceasingly drawing us on, the discovery, namely, of the essence of that `pure' *consciousness* which is to fix the limits of the phenomenological field. Our inquiries were eidetic; but the individual instances of the essences we have referred to as experience, stream of experience, `consciousness' in all its senses, belonged as real events to the natural

world" (pp. 125–126). This intentional unity, which we are conscious of, is a continuous flow of perceptual patterns which pass off onto one another. "These patterns themselves have always their *definite descriptive nature (Bestand)*, which is *essentially* correlated with that unity. To every phase of perception there necessarily belongs, for instance, a definite content in the way of perspective variations of colour, shape, and so forth. They are counted among the '*sensory data*,' data of a particular region with determinate divisions, which within every such division gather together into concrete unities of experience *sui generis (sensory 'fields')*" (Husserl, 1931:131–132).

Husserl (1966) described the analysis of time consciousness as an age-old crux of descriptive psychology and the theory of knowledge. Time consciousness involves putting objective time and subjective time consciousness into the right relation in order to ascertain how temporal objectivity relates to past subjective realities. The analysis of time consciousness, of the temporal character of objects of perception, memory, and expectation, assumes an objective "flow of time" and a true knowledge of time. In *The Phenomenology of Internal Time-Consciousness* (1966), Husserl stated, "With reference to the problem of time, this implies that we are interested in *lived experiences* of time. That these lived experiences themselves are temporally determined in an Objective sense, *that they belong in the world of things and psychical subjects* and have their place therein, their *efficacy,* their empirical origin and their being" (p. 28). Husserl concluded that there are self-evident laws associated with time consciousness:

1. That the fixed temporal order is of an infinite, two-dimensional series.
2. That two different times can never be conjoint.
3. That their relation is a nonsimultaneous one.
4. That there is transitivity, that to every time belongs an earlier and a later.

Husserl also indicated that although present behaviors are influenced by past memories and recollections, all present acts are subject to modification on behalf of the actor. Modification often entails the alteration of perceived events (for example, when new information becomes available, one can alter her or his view about someone or something). Furthermore, one modification can lead to a series of modifications. Husserl did not write much about the future except to indicate "what is determined is only that after all something will come" (1966:140).

Edmund Husserl, philosopher and social thinker, influenced many students and other theorists who would continue in his tradition, and who formed the theory of phenomenology.

ALFRED SCHUTZ (1899–1959)

Alfred Schutz was responsible for developing phenomenology as a sociological science. Schutz studied law and social science under Hans Kelsen (philosopher of law) and Ludwig von Mises (economist) at the University of Vienna. His *Phenomenology of the Social World* (1967; Orig. 1932) combined Weber's sociology with Husserl's phenomenological method. Schutz worked with Husserl briefly at Freiburg.

Schutz was born in Vienna, Austria, in 1899. Along with Kelsen and von Mises, Schutz studied under sociologist Othmar Spann and was very interested in the work of the greatest of German sociologists, Max Weber, especially in his methodological approach to the social sciences. As George Walsh stated in the introduction to *The Phenomenology of the Social World* (1967):

> Weber's approach was dependent on his central concept of meaning (*Sinn*), which was supposed to be distinctive of human action as opposed to mere reactive behavior and which was also supposed to be open to interpretive understanding (*verstehen*) by the sociologist. Schutz found this notion, and all its dependent ideas, ambivalent. Seeking for a consistent theory of meaning,

he found it in Husserl. By applying Husserl's concept of meaning to action he was able to recast the foundations of interpretive sociology, in other words, to give the latter a phenomenological grounding (p. xvii).

Schutz's primary academic goal was to establish a rigorous philosophical foundation grounded in phenomenological methodology.

After twelve years of research, Schutz published his main work *Der Sinnhafte Aufbau der Sozialen Welt: Eine Einleitung in die Verstehende Soziologie* (translated as *Meaningful Construction of the Social World*) in 1932. When he completed the work, Schutz dedicated a copy of the book and sent it to Husserl, who replied by inviting Schutz to meet with him at Freiburg. Schutz joined Husserl and a group of phenomenologists in intellectual debates regarding phenomenology. Husserl asked Schutz to become his assistant, but Schutz turned down the offer for personal

Alfred Schutz developed phenomenology as a sociological science.

Source: Courtesy of Evelyn S. Lang. Photograph of Alfred Schutz taken by Ilse Schutz in the mid 1920s from the Schutz Family Collection.

reasons. The two continued to visit one another and corresponded with one another until Husserl's death.

With the coming occupation by Nazi Germany, Schutz was forced to leave Austria. He lived in Paris for one year before emigrating to the United States, arriving here in July 1939. Shortly after, he accepted a position on the graduate faculty of the New School for Social Research in New York City. Through the initiative of Marvin Farber, Schutz was asked to join in the establishment of the International Phenomenological Research. The academic atmosphere was rich in opportunity for Schutz, who now found himself with colleagues and friends who had also studied with Husserl, especially Dorion Cairns and Aron Gurwitsch. He became familiar with the work of George Herbert Mead and admired American society, philosophy, and sociology. He was admired by students and colleagues alike. His warm and delightful personality made him an object of admiration and affection to his students and colleagues. Schutz died in the spring of 1959 in the midst of preparations for a book (*The Structures of the Life-World*) he had worked on for many years. His primary publications are *Collected Papers* (1962); *The Phenomenology of the Social World* (1967); and with Thomas Luckmann, *The Structures of the Life-World* (1973).

The Phenomenology of the Social World

Schutz spent many years working on *The Phenomenology of the Social World* (1967), and his study is centered on an intensive concern with Weber's subjective approach to the study of human behavior. He concluded that "only a philosophically founded theory of method can exorcise the pseudo-problems which today hinder research in the social sciences, and especially in sociology" (p. xxxi). Schutz believed that only the works of Henri Bergson and especially Husserl's transcendental phenomenology have a sufficiently deep foundation in the proper methodological approach.

When studying the social world, Schutz (1967) argued that we must accept "the existence of the social world as it is always accepted in the attitude of the natural standpoint, whether in everyday life or in the sociological observation" (p. 97). We must accept our own existence and the existence of others. When observing his or her own lived experiences, the individual must perform a reflective act of attention. When observing others, it is not necessary to live their experiences, but rather simply to "look" at (observe) their experiences. Schutz (1967) explained:

> This means that, whereas I can observe my own lived experiences only after they are over and done with, I can observe yours as they actually take place. This in turn implies that you and I are in a specific sense "simultaneous," that we "coexist," that our respective streams of consciousness intersect. . . . In trying to understand this sychronism we can hardly ignore the fact that when you and I are in the natural attitude we perceive ourselves and each other as psychological unities. . . . I see, then, my own stream of consciousness and yours in a single intentional act which embraces them both. (pp. 102–103)

Thus, one's stream of consciousness is in simultaneous relation to others' streams of consciousness (for examples, as in the expression "growing old together"). Individual's acts are influenced by other people's acts. However, the simultaneity of two streams of consciousness does not mean that the same experiences are shared. For example, a couple may attend a concert; one enjoys it very much, while the other finds the experience unenjoyable. Therefore, even when sharing an experience with someone, one may not share the same stream of consciousness.

In Chapter 4, "The Structure of the Social World," in *The Phenomenology of the Social World* (1967), Schutz explained that once the existence of individuals and the social world is assumed, we have already entered the realm of intersubjectivity. "The world is now experienced by the individual as shared by his fellow creatures, in short, as a *social world*. . . . This social world is by no means homogenous but exhibits a multiform structure. Each of its spheres or regions is both a way of perceiving and a way of understanding the subjective experiences of others" (p. 139). In his study of the multiform structure of society, Schutz (1967) attempted to answer three primary questions:

1. How is such an inner differentiation possible?
2. What grounds are there for supposing that the social world has both unity and inner differentiation?
3. Which of these differentiations may usefully serve as a basis for an analysis of understanding the other self?

Schutz (1967) stated that in a certain sense one becomes a social scientist in everyday life whenever one reflects upon his or her fellow humans and their behavior instead of merely experiencing them. The starting point of social science, then, is this *everyday life*. Schutz quickly pointed out that there is a difference between the naive person studying human behavior and the social researcher, who studies behavior scientifically.

Interdifferentiation is evident to all. We are aware of others and can reflect upon their different characteristics; we are consciously aware of this reality. This awareness extends beyond the spatial (the physical space our bodies take within the natural environment); it is a conscious awareness that the world is both united, through streams of consciousness, and divided, based on individual experience and interpretation of events. We not only attend to our own stream of consciousness but can also attend to others, and therefore, we become aware of what is going on in the minds of others. Understanding others is possible because we share the same world and many of the subjective meanings attached to experiences. In this manner, someone else's subjective experiences are "accessible" to me

because we share the same world. However, what one interprets as the other's stream of consciousness may not be accurate, because of misinterpretation, as illustrated by the expression, "I don't know what you mean by that" (just as many students may wonder, "What does the author mean by this?"). Assessing someone else's stream of consciousness is affected by what Schutz called *degrees of interpretability*. Through observation it is generally clear whether certain people are engaged in social relationships (for example, a couple walking hand and hand or store employees talking to one another are sure to know one another). However, certain presumptions are often not true; we may misinterpret the interactions among the people we are observing.

So, how do we come to understand social action objectively? Schutz altered Weber's definition of *social action* ("Action is social insofar as, by virtue of the subjective meaning attached to it by the acting individual (or individuals), it takes account of the behavior of others, and is thereby oriented in its course"—to "intentional conscious experiences directed toward the other self" (Schutz, 1967:144). Schutz (1967) expanded on this idea:

> Conscious experiences intentionally related to another self which emerge in the form of spontaneous activity we shall speak of as *social behavior*. If such experiences have the character of being previously projected, we shall speak of them as *social action*. Social behavior so defined will embrace all specific Ego-Acts (*Ich-Akte*) which are intentionally directed upon a Thou as upon another self having consciousness and duration. Here we include experiences such as feelings of sympathy and antipathy, erotic attitudes, and feeling-activities of all kinds. (p. 144)

Individuals have many choices in social action. Action represents options of conduct. Action may be covert (the intention of the act is kept private) or it may be overt (the intention of the act is made obvious). In short,

"Action may take place—purposively or not—by commission or omission" (Schutz, 1962:67). Acts of omission occur when the individual decides not to act in a given situation (for example, choosing not to help up off the floor someone who has just fallen).

When two people become reciprocally oriented, we have what Weber called a *social relationship*. In this regard, the behavior (social action) of a plurality of actors is oriented toward each other. Once people are in a social relationship there are two ways in which a person can become aware of whether her or his intentional acts of consciousness, directed toward another person, are reciprocated. She or he can either live in the mutually related conscious experience (accepting at face value that the relationship is mutual), or she or he can "step out" of the social relationship for a period of time to contemplate whether she or he is the object of attention of the other person (Schutz, 1967). A significant other, in any given social relationship, can be described as a person within reach of direct experience and with whom one shares a community of space and a community of time. In other words, a person who spends a great deal of time and space with someone has a social relationship with that person.

Persons who are in reach of each other's direct experience are involved in "face-to-face" situations. "The face-to-face situation presupposes, then, an actual simultaneity with each other of two separate streams of consciousness. . . . Spatial and temporal immediacy is essential to the face-to-face situation. All acts of other-orientation and of affecting-the-other, and therefore all orientations and relationships within the face-to-face situation, derive their own specific flavor and style from this immediacy" (Schutz, 1967:163). Face-to-face relationships grow into "we-relationships," where the streams of consciousness are so intertwined that it becomes common for one person to think of the other as a "natural" extension of expression. Schutz also made a distinction between reciprocal and one-sided relationships. In the reciprocal relationship each partner is benefiting by the experience. As a one-sided relationship would imply, one person is enjoying far more benefits than the other. Friendships are examples of reciprocal relationships, especially in light of the question of why anyone would maintain a friendship that was one-sided. (Work relationships are generally one-sided.) Schutz (1967) described friendship as a series of face-to-face relationships, where behavior is oriented to the "expected and, external obstacles aside, the friends can always get together again and again.

Schutz (1967) concluded that social action is a lived experience; that is guided by a plan or project arising from the subject's spontaneous activity; and that it is distinguished from all other lived experiences by a peculiar act of intention.

Method of Study

Phenomenology stresses that the social scientist should act as a disinterested observer of the social world. By adopting this role "the social scientist detaches himself from his biographical situation within the social world. What is taken for granted in the biographical situation of daily life may become questionable for the scientist, and vice versa; what seems to be of highest relevance on one level may become entirely irrelevant on the other" (Farganis, 2000:333). Schutz (1967:174–175) explained that observers who seek to interpret the subjects' motives will have to be satisfied with three indirect approaches:

1. They can search their memory for similar actions of their own and, finding such, can draw from them a general principle concerning the relation of their in-order-to and because motives. The observers can then assume that this principle holds true for the other person's actions by putting themselves in his or her place. This reading of one's own hypothetical motives into another's behavior can

take place either at once, on the spot, or through a later consideration of what could have made the person act as he or she did.

2. Lacking such a guideline, they can resort to their own knowledge of the customary behavior of the person observed and, from this, deduce the latter's in-order-to and because motives (knowing what role someone holds allows for the deduction of related behaviors).

3. But it may be that the observers lack significant information about the person they are observing. The last resort will be to try to infer the in-order-to motive from the act by asking whether such and such a motive could be furthered by the act in question. They must, while observing the ongoing action, interpret it in terms of the effect which it actually has and assume that the effect is what was intended.

It should be obvious that some of these methodological procedures are not always reliable. As Schutz (1967) admitted, "The further away from the concrete We-relationship (and, therefore, the more abstract) the interpretation is, the less chance it has of hitting its mark" (p. 175). Furthermore, it is more difficult to examine social relationship behaviors than individual behavior. But still, observers must fall back upon their experience of social relationships in general in order to understand certain observed relationships (this includes resorting to "filling in the blank spaces" of the unknown issues of study). Once again however, the presuppositions of the observer may interfere with the true analysis of the group under study.

Stock of Knowledge

As stated above, researchers must often draw upon their own experiences in order to fill in the blanks of the social situation under examination. They are drawing upon their stock of knowledge. Individuals must also draw upon their stock of knowledge while interacting with one another in the social environment. "For Schutz, the definition of the situation includes the assumption that individuals draw

on a common *stock of knowledge*, that is, social recipes of conceptions of appropriate behavior that enable them to think of the world as made up of 'types' of things like books, cars, houses, clothing, and so on. Schutz's idea of the stock of knowledge is similar to Mead's *generalized other*. Schutz thus views individuals as constructing a world by using typifications (or ideal types) passed onto them by their social group" (Wallace and Wolf, 1999:255).

The stock of knowledge that people possess is determined by their life experiences and education. A diverse awareness of events will dramatically increase one's stock of knowledge. Schutz (1973) categorized a number of types of stocks of knowledge, some of which seem to overlap. *Routine knowledge* refers to the ability to differentiate between common situations (routine) and unique ones. *Useful knowledge* refers to the awareness of everyday events and being able to accomplish acts that represent a "means to an end." These types of knowledge allow the individual to solve problems. *Knowledge of recipes* is a standardized means of dealing with specific situations that possess a "self-evident" quality or implication. Schutz used as examples a hunter reading tracks, a sailor or mountain climber orienting herself or himself to changes in the weather, and an interpreter who "automatically" translates phrases. *Habitual knowledge* presents "definitive" solutions to problems, which are organized in the flow of lived experiences, and require little attention (for example, being able to dress and talk on the phone at the same time, or whistling a song while thinking about a mathematical problem). Schutz stated that a certain amount of habitual knowledge belongs to everyone's stock of knowledge. "The 'content' of this knowledge is indeed variable, but not in the same sense that the partial contents of the stock of knowledge are variable from one society to the next and within a society" (Schutz, 1973:109). Everyone has a certain degree of knowledge; experience is what dictates differences between the stock of knowledge of individuals. As Schutz and Luckman (1973) explained:

> The acquisition of knowledge is the sedimentation of current experiences in meaning-structures, according to relevance and typicality. These in turn have a role in the determination of current situation and the explication of current experiences. That means, among other things, that no element of knowledge can be traced to any sort of "primordial experience." In analyzing the processes of sedimentation which lead to the development of the stock of knowledge, we always encounter prior experiences in which we already determined, albeit minimal, stock of knowledge must be conjoined. (p. 119)

The acquisition of knowledge is a life-long process, and it continually reshapes our perception of the world.

Common Sense

Stocks of knowledge, especially the habitual, come to be so taken for granted, that the individual may come to view certain situations as being dictated by rules of common sense. Labeling situations and events as being dictated by common sense presents many potential dangers (for both the researcher and the interactants). Schutz (1962) stated that "even the thing perceived in everyday life is more than a simple sense presentation. It is a thought object, a construct of a highly complicated nature. . . . in other words, the so-called concrete facts of common-sense perception are not as concrete as it seems. They already involve abstractions of a highly complicated nature, and we have to take account of this situation lest we commit the fallacy of misplaced concreteness" (pp. 3–4). All of our knowledge of the world, including common sense and science, involves constructs (for examples, generalizations, formalizations, idealizations). This does not mean that we are incapable of understanding the reality of the world; it just means that we merely grasp only certain aspects of it.

"Common-sense constructs are formed from a 'Here' within the world which determines the presupposed reciprocity of perspectives. They take a stock of socially derived and socially approved knowledge for granted. The social distribution of knowledge determines the particular structure of the typifying construct, for instance, the assumed degree of anonymity of personal roles, the standardization of course-of-action patterns, and the supposed constancy of motives" (Schutz, 1962:38). These taken-for-granted and commonsense patterns are relevant only to those with shared life experiences. Thus, the behaviors of one person may seem to violate the common sense of another person, but the person who has no awareness context of the expected and "proper" course of action has not violated common sense. Add to this the reality that many people regularly violate so-called common sense.

The Structure of the Life-World

The Structure of the Life-World (1973) represents the final focus of twenty-seven years of Schutz's labor, encompassing his work between 1932 and his death in 1959. It represents his attempt to achieve a comprehensive grasp of the nature of social reality, and "it presents an integration of his theory of relevance within his analysis of social structures" (quote from Zaner and Engelhardt, translators of *The Structure of the Life-World*, 1973:xxvii).

It is the everyday-life world that remains the cornerstone of interest to phenomenologists. Schutz and Luckmann (1973) stated that "the everyday life-world is the region of reality in which man can engage himself and which he can change while he operates in it by means of his animate organism. . . . Only in this realm can one be understood by his fellow-men, and only in it can he work together with them. Only in the world of everyday life can a common, communicative, surrounding world be constituted. The world of everyday life is consequently man's fundamental and paramount reality" (p. 3). Thus, the life world is found in the everyday world. The everyday reality of the life world includes both natural elements found in the environment and the social elements created by culture.

Schutz argued that Husserl's concept of the life world was unacceptable and unworthy of the phenomenological method. It failed because it cannot solve the problem of intersubjectivity. "Schutz asserted a mundane constitution of intersubjectivity as the foundation of the life-world; he solved the difficult problem of life-worldly transcendences in terms of his rethinking of the concept of the symbol, be deriving 'the structure of the life-world from the lived experience of transcendence'" (Grafholf, 1989:215). Schutz believed that the life world is intersubjective and presents itself as a subjective meaning context. That is, it appears meaningful in one's consciousness. In the life world, individuals come to find others who are "like me." Action is therefore imbedded for them in meaning contexts and is subjectively motivated and articulated purposefully according to their particular interests and according to what is feasible for them (Schutz and Luckmann, 1973:15). The everyday-life world is the primary reality for individuals because it encompasses most of their daily activities.

Alfred Schutz was a major influence in the development of phenomenological sociology in the English-speaking world and has received recognition as one of the foremost philosophers of social science. Among the more significant contemporary phenomenologists is Peter Berger.

PETER BERGER (1929–)

Peter Berger is a renowned sociologist and social critic, theologian, and novelist. In his work, Berger attempts to understand reality in modern society.

Berger was born in Vienna, Austria, in 1929. He emigrated to the United States in his late teens. He earned his B.A. at Wagner College in 1949 and his M.A. and Ph.D. in 1950 and 1954 from the New School for Social Research in New York City. While at the New School, Berger studied under Alfred Schutz. After serving two years in the U.S. Army, he taught at the University of Georgia and the University of North Carolina. From there, Berger became an assistant professor in social ethics at the Hartford Seminary Foundation and then moved to Rutgers University and Boston College. He most recently taught at Boston University.

Among his many publications, Berger's most significant contribution to sociology is *The Social Construction of Reality* (1966), which he coauthored with Thomas Luckmann. His other books include *A Rumor of Angels* (1969); *Movement and Revolution* (1970), coauthored with Richard Neuhaus; *The Homeless Mind* (1973), coauthored with Brigitte Berger and Hansfried Kellner; *Pyramids of Sacrifice* (1974); *Protocol of a Damnation* (1975); *Facing Up to Modernity* (1977); *The Heretical Imperative* (1979); *The War over the Family* (1983), coauthored with his wife, Brigitte Berger; and *The Capitalist* (1986). As many of these book titles imply, Berger wrote a great deal on the sociology of religion. He consistently discusses the importance of religion in society and maintains a belief in the existence of the supernatural that is, a reality that transcends the reality of the natural world of everyday life. Much of his work on religion is tied to aspects of modern society (for example, globalism, capitalism, the division of labor) and the sociological analysis of the social forces that have led to the creation of organized religions and the effect of religion on the social world. Berger's interest in religion was partly influenced by his studies at Lutheran Theological Seminary in Philadelphia and at Yale Divinity School. He is also a past president of the Society for Scientific Study of Religion. His later work on the family, which he cowrote with his wife, examines many of the controversial issues of contemporary society: sexual norms, abortion, women's and children's rights, and gender roles.

The Social Construction of Reality

The Social Construction of Reality (Berger and Luckmann, 1966) was intended as a systematic, theoretical treatise in the sociology of knowledge. Berger and Luckmann argued that reality is socially constructed and that the sociology of knowledge must analyze the processes in which this occurs. "The key terms in these contentions are 'reality' and 'knowledge,' terms that are not only current in everyday speech, but that have behind them a long history of philosophical inquiry. . . . for our purposes, [we] define 'reality' as a quality appertaining to phenomena that we recognize as having a being independent of our own volition (we cannot 'wish them away'), and to define 'knowledge' as the certainty that phenomena are real and that they possess specific characteristics" (p. 1). It is difficult to argue with the premise that sociology has a strong interest in regard to "reality" and "knowledge" if for no other reason than their social relativity. Sociology involves the scientific study of society. To study society scientifically (or philosophically) it must consist of a "social reality," and the means about which we examine society is representative in our knowledge of it. However, social reality is greatly influenced by culture, and therefore, one person's (such as a Tibetan monk's) sense of reality may be drastically different from another's (such as an American businessman's). It is the contention of Berger and Luckmann (1980) that

> the sociology of knowledge must concern itself with whatever passes for "knowledge" in a society, regardless of the ultimate validity or invalidity (by whatever criteria) of such "knowledge." And insofar as all human "knowledge" is developed, transmitted and maintained in social situations, the sociology of knowledge must seek to understand the processes by which this is done In such a

way that a taken-for-granted "reality" congeals for the man in the street. In other words, we contend that *the sociology of knowledge is concerned with the analysis of the social construction of reality.* (p. 3)

The term *sociology of knowledge* (*Wissenssoziologie*) was coined by German philosopher Max Scheler in the 1920s. This is an important note when one is considering the genesis and development of this new discipline. It is from Marx's *Economic and Philosophical Manuscripts of 1844* that the sociology of knowledge derived its root proposition; that human consciousness is determined by his social being. "The sociology of knowledge inherited from Marx not only the sharpest formulation of its central problem but also some of its key concepts, among which should be mentioned particularly the concepts of 'ideology' (ideas serving as weapons for social interests) and 'false consciousness' (thought that is alienated from the real social being of the thinker). The sociology of knowledge has been particularly fascinated by Marx's twin concepts of 'substructure/superstructure'" (Berger and Luckmann, 1966:5). According to Berger and Luckmann, other significant social thinkers linked to the origins of the sociology of knowledge include Durkheim, Weber, Pareto, Mannheim, and Parsons.

The foundation of reality is found in everyday life, more precisely, the knowledge that guides conduct in everyday life. Berger and Luckmann (1966) explained:

> Everyday life presents itself as a reality interpreted by men and subjectively meaningful to them as a coherent world. As sociologists we take this reality as the object of our analyses. Within the frame of reference of sociology as an empirical science it is possible to take this reality as given, to take as data particular phenomena arising within it, without further inquiring about the foundations of this reality, which is a philosophical task. . . . The world of everyday life is not only taken for granted as reality by the ordinary members of society in the subjectively meaningful

conduct of their lives. It is a world that originates in their thoughts and actions, and is maintained as real by these. (p. 19)

With the foundation established, the continued construction of social reality is contingent on a number of processes. One such process is externalization, "wherein individuals, by their own human activity, create their social worlds. They view the social order as an ongoing human production" (Wallace and Wolf, 1999:278). From this standpoint, the social construction of reality is accomplished by individuals as a result of their past behaviors and can be continually modified and re-created with current activities. On the other hand, the process of objectivation influences the individual to view the everyday-life world as an ordered reality with phenomena prearranged in patterns that seem to be independent of the actor. It is this level of consciousness that causes the actor to see the world in a taken-for-granted fashion. The common objectivations of everyday life are maintained primarily by language. The reason for immigrants reluctance to change their language is not only that it implies giving up their past heritage but that it also results in dramatic changes in their everyday-life world—their very construction of social reality. The same reasoning holds for those who are reluctant to embrace policies that encourage a bilingual society: Their life worlds will be altered. A third process, internalization, is a process in which society attempts to link individual members in a community through the socialization process. When people share the same norms, values, and behavioral expectations, they share a similar social world.

Marriage and the Construction of Reality

Berger had been contemplating ideas on the social construction of reality since the summer of 1962. In an article that he coauthored with Hansfried Kellner, "Marriage and the Construction of Reality" (1964), a specific social institution (marriage) is examined in the context of social construction. "The process that interests us here is the one that constructs, maintains and modifies a consistent reality that can be meaningfully experienced by individuals" (Berger and Kellner, 1964:2). The authors indicated that every society has its own specific way of defining and perceiving reality, and this is true of the institution of marriage. Many rules have been constructed over the years that apply to marriage (for example, the incest taboo, age restrictions, gender parameters) in any given culture. Society's rules impact the everyday experience and conduct of individuals. The monogamous character of marriage has a profound influence on Americans.

Society's expectations of proper social relationships illustrate the merging point between individual desires and socially acceptable behaviors. As Berger and Kellner (1964) explained:

> Every social relationship requires objectivation, that is, requires a process by which subjectively experienced meanings become objective to the individual and, in interaction with others, become common property and thereby massively objective. The degree of objectivation will depend on the number and the intensity of the social relationships that are its carriers. A relationship that consists of only two individuals called upon to sustain, by their own efforts, an ongoing social world will have to make up in intensity for the numerical poverty of the arrangement. This, in turn, accentuates the drama and the precariousness. The later addition of children will add to the, as it were, density of objectivation taking place within the nuclear family, thus rendering the latter a good deal less precarious. It remains true that the establishment and maintenance of such a social world makes extremely high demands on the principal participants. (pp. 9–10)

Two people who decide to marry realize that each partner's actions must be projected in conjunction with those of the other. Lifestyle changes are implied when one gets married; in other words, the old social reality is abandoned, or at best reconstructed, and a new social reality is constructed. Each partner has new modes of meaningful experience of the world in general, of other people, and of himself or herself. In short, with marriage comes a reconstruction of the everyday-life world. These changes come voluntarily and internally, as few people are literally "forced" to get married.

In *The War over the Family* (1983), coauthored by Brigitte Berger and Peter Berger, the social construction aspect of marriage is expanded to include the changing role of the family in contemporary society. The ideas in this book also demonstrate that changes in the everyday-life world can be caused by external forces, over which actors have little control. The Bergers presented three basic contemporary views of the family: the leftist and feminist critique calling for radical change, the new and largely reactionary "profamily" movement, and the value-free analysis of social scientists. They traced the historical development of the family, giving special notice to the effects of modernization and its pressures. According to the Bergers (1983), "There is the view that the family and its values are in a steep decline. The decline is variously interpreted in terms of its causes—broad social trends or specific ideological movements or changes in religion and morality—but most of those holding this view agree that the alleged decline of the family is harmful both to the individual and to society" (p. 85). Thus, social forces (for example, an economic down spiral) which are external to the actor may dictate a change in her or his everyday-life world.

Reification and Consciousness

How is it that external processes come to influence so strongly the individual construction of reality? Berger and Luckmann (1966) believe that the reification process is related to internalization. Treating external products, created by human activity, *as if* they are something other than human products implies that humans are capable of forgetting their own authorship of the social world. Reification leads to alienation and a false sense of consciousness. Berger and Pullberg (1965) defined *alienation* as the process by which the unity of producing and product is broken, where the product now appears to the producer as an alien facticity. Alienation is the process by which people forget that the world they live in has been produced by them. "By reification we mean the moment in the process of alienation in which the characteristic of thing-hood becomes the standard of objective reality. That is, nothing can be conceived as real that does not have the character of a thing. . . . Reification is objectification in an alienated mode" (Berger and Pullberg, 1965:200). In producing such an alienating world, the human is devalued. "This consciousness is reifying consciousness and its objects are reifications" (Berger and Pullberg, 1965:204).

Examining the role of reification and its effect on consciousness more closely, Berger and Pullberg (1965) distinguished between three levels of consciousness:

> First, there is direct and pre-reflective presence to the world. Secondly, founded on the latter, there is reflective awareness of the world and one's presence to it. Thirdly, out of this second level of consciousness there may in turn arise various theoretical formulations of the situation. We may, then, distinguish between the pre-reflective, the reflective, and the theoretical level of consciousness. Reification may occur on the last two levels. . . . But even in an alienated and reified world man continues to reflect and often to formulate theoretically the results of his reflection. (p. 204)

Berger and Pullberg added, "Reification, on all levels of consciousness, converts the concrete into the abstract, then in turn concretizes the abstract. Also, reification converts quality into quantity" (p. 208).

Modernity, and especially technological production, further complicates the reification process and consequently individual consciousness. The level of technological knowledge that one possesses, or fails to possess, affects the individual's everyday life (for example, reliance on the Internet and e-mail to keep in communication with others). Berger et al. in *The Homeless Mind* (1973) explained that a sociology of knowledge that attempts to understand consciousness must also examine the role of technology. "In the language of phenomenology, the knowledge is deeply sedimented in his consciousness even though it cannot be thematized. Put more simply, the worker's specific knowledge derives its location and significance from this larger body of knowledge, although the latter is not available to the worker in his immediate situation" (Berger et al., 1973:25). The inference here is that individuals are aware of their spatial location by such means as their knowledge of technology.

Social Control and Political Authority

The reality of the social world does not present itself all at once. It must be constructed and reconstructed over and over again. The social world is affected by such external factors as society's norms and values (which are learned through socialization). At other times, society exerts its power position in an attempt to coerce individuals into behaving in specific ways. Individuals have freewill and individual consciousness, but they are under constant surveillance by a great number of social control agents. Cuzzort and King (1995) stated: "A person is simply born into society and then controlled by it. We are, as Berger nicely puts it, prisoners of society. Society forms the walls of our imprisonment in history. Furthermore, we are guarded closely; even seemingly harmless acts, such as growing a beard or mispronouncing a word, are apt to bring ridicule or some other forms of social constraint. Society is an external force, as coercive and constraining as the physical and biological environments with which we must cope" (p. 299).

In order to achieve a reasonable certainty that people will behave as they are told, a number of devices are put into place. First, people are threatened by imprisonment if they violate laws; second, society tells them what they are to believe (for example, President Bush explaining to Americans—in late 2002—that we need to go to war with our enemies because they have threatened our collective life world); third, the threat of ridicule often controls behavior; fourth, fraud, lies, and deceit are used to control people; fifth, the threat of ostracism controls people; sixth, there is occupational control; seventh, there is a device Berger called *sphere of intimates,* where individuals are motivated to behave in a manner that benefits their significant others (as opposed to some political agenda on the part of the government); and eighth, social control is maintained through systems of mutual obligation.

In *Movement and Revolution* (1970), Berger and Neuhaus explained that social control is accomplished primarily by political authority. "Politics is the process by which power is acquired and exercised in human affairs. There can be no society, or indeed no human group of even moderate size and continuity, without this process. Thus there will always be individuals who act in society as men of politics, be it professionally or as amateurs" (Berger and Neuhaus, 1970:13).

Globalism

Berger had little to say about the macrostructure and globalization, but he did recognize the role of politics at the international level. Generally, political power is exercised to maintain law and order within the boundaries of a national sovereignty. History has shown us that there have always been political entities that hoped to extend their power beyond their boundaries. Economic power is the primary motivator for aggressive political maneuvers. Berger stated in *Pyramids of Sacrifice* (1974), "There can be no doubt that American political and military power relates to

American economic power, and in some places it may well do so in the manner depicted in the theory of imperialism" (p. 206). Berger wrote, nearly three decades ago, on his experiences traveling abroad and facing anti-American sentiments. At the beginning of the third millennium, many parts of the world have expressed anti-Americanism. All world powers have experienced this hostility throughout time, whether it be the Romans, the English, or some other politically and economically superior power.

The Role of Religion in Society

Berger published a great deal in the area of the sociology of religion. In *The Precarious Vision* (1961) Berger discussed the role of individuals in society and the affect of society on individuals. "For most of us, as we grow up and learn to live in society, its forms take on the appearance of structures as self-evident and as solid as those of the natural cosmos. Very likely society could not exist otherwise. Nor is it likely that socialization could take place if this were not the case" (p. 10). Berger described how religion is an integral part of the American social order and how it is a part of the taken-for-granted life world of most members of society. It is a part of our consciousness. Berger questioned how one can take religion for granted as it is such a precarious social creation. How can a rationally based society coexist with a social system based solely on conjecture and belief? People who attempt to balance a religious belief and yet function in a rational world experience what Berger called *alternation*. "It is an experience that leads to a very specific form of consciousness, particularly a certain consciousness of existence in society. Perhaps the most characteristic feature of this consciousness is an overwhelming sense of the precariousness of social existence" (Berger, 1961:10). As religious people interact in society, they bring with them this precarious vision of the social world. This precarious

vision enters decisively into certain moral choices that individuals act upon.

In 1967, Berger published *The Sacred Canopy—Elements of a Sociological Theory of Religion,* where he attempted to summarize specific elements of a sociological perspective on religion. He tried to apply this perspective to an analysis of the contemporary religious situation. Berger maintains that he has always attempted to be "value-free" (in the tradition of Weber) with his sociological analysis of religion. Responding to the climate of the 1960s and the philosophical question that generated a great religious and social debate—"Is God dead?"—Berger published *A Rumor of Angels* (1969), a reference to Berger's belief that angels are God's messengers or "signals." Berger emphatically stated that God is not dead, and that religion is still of great importance to society. Berger insisted that only through a belief in the existence of the supernatural—that is, a reality that transcends the reality of the natural world of everyday life—can humans grasp the true proportions of their experience. He argued that any discussion of the demise of the supernatural says more about modern humans than it does about the supernatural. Here, Berger's values do interfere with his analysis, for he ignores the possibility that it may be that modern humans has become too intelligent to believe in supernatural forces and organized religious beliefs. This is clearly not the case for most people, however. (Note: It may be the case that Berger followed Weber's belief that value neutrality applies to the classroom and not to research publications, where opinions are supported by facts.) Berger suggested that modern theologians should examine the natural conditions of human life, and in this way they might discover those "signals of transcendence" that might be linked to the supernatural. Berger concluded in *A Rumor of Angels* that humans have come a long way from their one-time belief in gods and angels. He stated, "The breaches of this-worldly reality which these mighty figures embodied have increasingly vanished from our consciousness as serious possibilities. They linger on as fairy tales, nostalgias, perhaps as vague symbols of some sort" (p. 120). However, unable to escape his own grip on a religion-based reality, Berger (1969) added, "A rediscovery of the supernatural will be, above all, a regaining of openness in our perception of reality" (p. 120).

Berger's *Pyramids of Sacrifice* (1974) examines the role of capitalism and socialism in contemporary times. He suggested that the economic structures of capitalism and socialism are representations of "pyramids of sacrifice," with the workers giving of their labor (the sacrifice) to the planners and intellectuals (the new priests and their altars). Religion and modern politics are the primary themes in Berger's *Facing Up to Modernity* (1977). *The Heretical Imperative* (1979) continues Berger's primary focus throughout the 1970s: the role of religion in modern society. He worried that reducing religion to a secular experience, a reductionist option, negates religion and religious experience. Berger proposed turning from external authority to individual experience (the inductive option). In 1975, Berger wrote a novel on religion, *Protocol of a Damnation,* a book about the demonic and the sacred, of the holy and the corrupt. It is a unique way of expressing a sociological view of religion in an "entertaining" format.

Peter Berger has made significant contributions to the field of sociology in general, and to phenomenology specifically. His and Luckmann's book *The Social Construction of Reality* (1966) remains a classic for all social thinkers.

RELEVANCY

Phenomenology is a micro-oriented sociological theory which has as its subject matter the conscious experience of individuals. People's view of the world is shaped by varying perceptions that influence their consciousness. Framing our perceptions of the world allows us to envision some sort of social structure, or social order. Most perceptions are quickly organized into customary patterns, which reinforce previous outlooks on things. Phenomenologists attempt to break down these preconceived notions of social reality in order to explore and analyze the formative core of individual consciousness. Phenomenologists attempt to break down the taken-for-granted world of the actors and instead question its formation and maintenance.

Phenomenology is one of the theories of the sociology of everyday life, which involves studies of face-to-face interactions by observation. It examines routine life, conscious experience, and common sense. A basic premise is that people interact with one another on the basis of a socially created, reified world, where meanings come about through constant negotiation in everyday life. Phenomenology was created by Edmund Husserl, who was heavily influenced by the German tradition. Husserl's primary goal was to examine the phenomena of consciousness and bracket them in order to test their truth.

The critics of phenomenology are generally those who prefer a more scientific or grounded approach to social theory. The concepts used by phenomenologists are very vague and subject to interpretation. This abstract nature clouds the contribution of phenomenology to sociology. But even those who prefer alternatives to scientific social theory question whether the conclusions reached by phenomenologists can be supported by concrete evidence. Scientifically driven social theorists need to acknowledge this diverse approach to the study of human behavior.

The relevancy of phenomenology is, in many respects, similar to the relevance of most micro-oriented approaches. It provides us with great insights into the everyday, taken-for-granted approach that people utilize in their life worlds. The importance that phenomenologists place on perception is understandable. Perception regularly affects the daily lives of all of us. People *do* "judge a book by its cover," just as they initially judge others based on first perceptions. The qualitative aspects of individuals are determined later through interaction. In some cases, people avoid contact with others solely because of first impressions. The way we see strangers and friends alike is determined by our perception of others. Do we perceive a group of young males hanging around a convenience store as a street gang and therefore a potential threat? Or do we see this group as a sports team that just finished their practice?

If I describe a group of young males who have a group name, identify one another with specific clothing, use secret hand signals, and commit deviant acts, does that make you think of a street gang? This description is actually of a college fraternity. Phenomenologists point out that our perceptions are influenced by memories, conscious experience, and recollections. All of these factors influence the way we perceive social situations and others. We draw upon our stock of knowledge in order to put order to a given social situation. For example, perhaps the group of young males you have just encountered is a gang, and they now see you as a target. What will you do? Do you know how to react in this situation? The answer lies with your stock of knowledge (Have you had past experience with these types of encounters?) and your common sense. A regular citizen will react to this situation differently from a police officer. The police officer will perceive the situation differently and will react according to her or his role and stock of knowledge.

The very point of studies of the everyday life *is* their relevancy. All individuals can examine for themselves how perception enters all interactions. Did that cute clerk just "hit" on me? Or was the clerk merely trying to make a sale? Reading the cues of others is a common occurrence in everyday life. Past experiences allow people to bracket possible courses of action in the everyday-life world. An increased stock of knowledge increases the probability of properly interpreting the situation.

One's stock of knowledge includes the items found within the realm of common sense. People generally act on what they consider obvious, or what is often referred to as common sense. The problem with "commonsense" attitudes and outlooks on life is highlighted by the reality that people violate common sense regularly. Going through life with a commonsense approach is sure to include many misunderstandings and misinterpretations in the taken-for-granted world. The violation of common sense is so regular and so profound in the life world that I plan on writing an entire book on this subject.

Phenomenologists acknowledge the role of social structure. In *The Social Construction of Social Reality* (1966), Berger and Luckmann acknowledged that social reality is constructed by the everyday interactions of individuals, and also by social institutions. These social institutions are greatly influenced by culture. Thus, perception is influenced by culture and social expectations. In the mid-1990s a white buffalo was born on a southern Wisconsin farm. News of its birth, an extremely rare occurrence, spread among American Indians, inspiring pilgrimages by many tribes who believe that a white buffalo is a sacred, apocalyptic animal. The white buffalo is especially sacred to the Cheyenne, Sioux, and other nomadic tribes of the Northern Plains that once reified the buffalo for subsistence. The white buffalo's spiritual significance stems from its rarity. Legend has it that the birth of a white buffalo will bring peace among all people, unifying the nations of the four colors—the black, red, yellow, and white. Clearly the perception of these tribes is clouded by pagan cultural beliefs. Peace and harmony did not occur, nor will it ever be tied to the birth of a rare animal. But the perceptions of the tribes' people were directly influenced by their stock of knowledge, which was built on the historical significance of the buffalo.

Interestingly, the birth of another animal has inspired people to another type of pilgrimage. The *Washington Post* reported in 2002 that the birth of a goat with a birthmark resembling the number 3 has led to a large number of fans of racing star Dale Earnhardt to visit a farm about fifty miles south of Jacksonville, Florida. The goat, nine months old (in December 2002), was born with a white 3—Earnhardt's car number—on her right side. People have flocked to the farm to have their pictures taken with the goat; presumably it is a reincarnation issue! However, as nearly any motorist in the past year will tell you, racing fans have adorned Earnhardt's Number 3 on their cars in honor of their deceased hero. The fact is, people often see what they want to, and such visions are heavily influenced by culture, especially religion. Many people have claimed to have seen visions of various religious leaders (for example, Jesus, Mary, Allah) in such odd places as grocery store freezer doors, various clothing articles, and even food. Like-minded people will reinforce these perceptions in an attempt to incorporate them into their life worlds.

As Berger wrote, the impact of religion on society remains very strong. Even in a country that claims the existence of the separation of church and state, the United States, the role of religion as a social structure exerting power over individuals continues. Elements of the Christian religion can be found in many aspects of American culture (for example, currency, the pledge of Allegiance). President George W. Bush, a religious man, continues to cross the line between the separation of church and state and employs religious ideals in his spiritual attempt to unite Americans in impending wars. Berger's analysis of the social institution of marriage is another example of how social structures exert an influence over individuals. There are laws governing marriage; there are social expectations to get married (and have children), although these expectations are not as rigid as in the past; and the reality is that an individual's everyday-life world certainly changes from living life as a single person to living life as a married one.

Phenomenology offers some very interesting insights into human behavior. However, as Wallace and Wolf (1999) stated, "Phenomenology is far from being conventional or traditional sociology. It is distrusted by many mainstream sociologists, particularly those who favor quantitative research" (p. 291). It is important for advanced students of social theory to familiarize themselves with phenomenology. Other than that, phenomenology is clearly a marginal theory in sociology.

9

Feminist Theory

In this chapter, feminist thought is examined, beginning with definitions and a brief history of the development of feminism, continuing with a review of the many variations of feminist theory, and ending with analysis of some of the leading feminist theorists.

FEMINISM AND ITS ROOTS

Feminist theory is an outgrowth of the general movement to empower women worldwide. It is a broad-based theoretical perspective that attempts to demonstrate the importance of women, to reveal the historical reality that women have been subordinate to men (beginning with the sexual division of labor), and to bring about gender equity. Feminism is a women-centered approach to the study of human behavior. It serves as an advocate for oppressed women. Through analysis of gender roles and gender appropriateness, feminist theory demonstrates how women have historically been subjected to a double standard in both their treatment and in the evaluation of their worth. With these ideas in mind *feminism* can be defined as "a recognition and critique of male supremacy combined with efforts to change it" (Hartmann, 1998:41).

Feminism is a social movement and an ideology in support of the idea that a larger share of scarce resources (for example, wealth, power, income, and status) should be distributed to women. Feminists hope to show that gender differences are a result of historically created social conditions and not the result of natural, biological differences. In short, feminists fight for the equality of women and argue that women should share equally in society's opportunities and scarce resources.

The Early History of Feminism

Early feminists have been fighting the ideas of the likes of Jean-Jacques Rousseau, who believed that the development of rationality was the most important educational goal for boys, but not for girls, and that, rational man is the perfect complement for the "emotional woman" and vice versa. Throughout the eighteenth, nineteenth and twentieth centuries feminists have been fighting for the equality of women with men (Tong, 1989). There have been political activists working on behalf of the rights of women for centuries. These activists have come from diverse economic, religious, and racial backgrounds. The underling goal of these activists was always to improve women's social position in society.

Early feminists in the United States strove to gain equal rights for women and especially in education. The origins of feminism are also found in the abolitionist movement of the 1830s. Seneca Falls, New York, has the distinction of being the birthplace of American feminism. A group of women led by Elizabeth Cady Stanton and Quaker preacher Lucretia Mott spearheaded the first Women's Rights Convention, in Seneca Falls, in 1848. The convention brought to light the many social institutions that were designed to keep women subordinate to men. The existing sociopolitical structure worked against women. For example, "Once a woman married, she forfeited her legal existence. She couldn't sign a contract, make a will, or sue in court of law. If she received property from her father or some other source, her husband could sell it and keep the money for himself" (Gurko, 1974:8).

More than 300 people attended the first convention of women's rights in the Wesleyan Methodist Chapel. The convention was gathered to discuss the social, civil, and religious condition of women. It also led to the Declaration of Sentiments. Elizabeth Cady Stanton wrote the first draft of the Declaration of Sentiments out of a strong desire to fight social injustice. The Declaration of Sentiments was modeled on the Declaration of Independence. Paragraph 2 states, "We hold these truths to be self-evident; that all men and women are created equal; that they are endowed by their Creator with certain inalienable rights; that among these are life, liberty, and the pursuit of happiness; that to secure these rights governments are instituted, deriving their just powers from the consent of the governed" (Source: Declaration of Sentiments).

The Declaration of Sentiments also addressed concrete issues that concerned the early feminists. Stating that men have "framed the laws of divorce, as to what shall be the proper causes of divorce; in case of separation, to whom the guardianship of the children shall be given, as to be wholly regardless of the happiness of women—the law, in all cases, going upon the false supposition of the supremacy of man, and giving all power into his hands. . . . He has monopolized nearly all the profitable employments, and from those she is permitted to follow, she receives but a scanty remuneration. . . . He has denied her the facilities for obtaining a thorough education— all colleges being closed against her" (Source: Declaration of Sentiments).

This convention also marked the beginning of a seventy-two year battle to gain women the right to vote in the United States. In 1920, the United States became the seventeenth country in the world to give women the right to vote. New Zealand was the first country to do so, in 1893.

Meanwhile, in early-twentieth-century Germany, feminist thought was being led by such social thinkers as Marianne Weber and grew out of a reaction to the oppressive social system. Germany had been unified in 1871 under the authoritarian and militaristic regime of the monarchy of Prussia led by Otto von Bismarck. The feminist movement in Germany was an active attempt to reach economic and political equality between men and women. Around 1905, another German feminist group emerged whose primary concern was sexual autonomy, which led to what is known as the *erotic movement.* Helene Stocker became the leader of the erotic movement in 1906, and under her leadership the issues of sexual politics and matrimonial law became the focus. These feminists fought for the right of women to engage in sexual relations regardless of marital and legal considerations (Mommsen and Ostehammel, 1987:486).

Max Weber criticized these women, believing that they were promoting rights of "free love" and "illegitimate" children. He viewed the erotic movement as unethical and hedonistic. Weber's wife, Marianne Weber, agreed and wrote in her own book, *Ehefrau und Mutter in der Rechtsentwicklung* (1907), that the focus of the women's movement should be the equality of women and not sexual and moral emancipation. Marianne Weber believed that marriage should be a lasting relationship between man and woman, with mutual obligations. From this standpoint, Weber made two critical points. First, women should be treated equally in the social institution of marriage, along with all the other social institutions. And second, she made it clear that marriage was strictly a union between a man and a woman, which alienated many other feminists (especially lesbian feminists).

Weber was a feminist. She promoted a woman's right to sexual pleasure and she believed that women should have rights equal to those of men in all social institutions. Her fight for equality was in direct contrast to the patriarchal society of Germany. Patriarchal societies are designed so that males can reach a fulfillment of their essential needs, while women are expected to be subordinate to the male and help him reach his full potential. Marianne Weber wanted this type of system to change so that women might also reach their full potential. Weber emphasized that women should have the right to financial independence, including the idea that women should be paid for their domestic chores. This idea continued with the second wave of feminism in the 1960s.

The Contemporary Feminist Movement

The second, and most effective, wave of feminism began in the 1960s. This decade was witness to many changes in the social systems of societies throughout the world. Social protests, Vietnam War protests, and civil rights movements all coexisted with the women's rights movement. The issues addressed by previous feminists gained ground-level support from many members of society, men included. The "free love" attitude of the 1960s helped women to slowly escape the clutches of the sexual double standard—where young men who had sex with multiple partners were merely sowing wild oats and women who had sex with many partners were labeled whores and sluts. Divorce became so easy to obtain that it is now commonplace. The idea that women were to be happy housewives basking in the glory of their husbands' triumphs was no longer acceptable to many women. The doors to higher-level employment were being knocked down, and women were finding fulfillment outside the home.

A commitment to core feminist beliefs continued during this period. Examining the race-class-gender linkage originated with African American feminists in the 1960s. Concepts such as the feminization of poverty arose because of this research. Women are far more likely than men to be poor. Furthermore, poor women are more likely to be single women, women of color, and elderly women living alone. Thus, mainstream white feminists were often negligent of the reality that women of color living in poverty might be more concerned about their economic status than about the disadvantages associated with gender (Lindsey and Beach, 2003). Contemporary feminism is consumed with the idea that women should have equal rights and is reaching this end through legal reform and legislating antidiscriminatory policies. The women's movement does not end with legal reform. It seeks a radical transformation of basic social institutions. Sociological feminist thought was at the forefront of the academic pursuit of equality between the sexes. In fact, more than 700 gender-related articles in sociology journals alone appeared between 1974 and 1983 (Turner, 2003:250).

Today, feminists are concerned about civil rights, gay and lesbian issues, homelessness, AIDS activism, environmental concerns, and human rights. The growth of women's studies programs on college campuses has further assisted the feminist agenda. There are over 600 universities and colleges that teach feminist ideas in their women's studies programs. The world of music has also contributed to feminism. "Women's agency and feminist themes are celebrated in rap, rock, and alternative forms of music. In 1997, Lilith Fair, a musical extravaganza featuring female artists and feminist activists, played to sell-out crowds across the U.S. and Canada. Female rappers with feminist sensibilities adorn the cover of popular magazines and are demanding more artistic freedom within the industry" (Hartmann, 1998:44).

The course of humanity has changed radically in the past two centuries, women having gained greatly in every field and social institution. Much of this improvement is directly attributed to feminism.

VARIATIONS OF FEMINIST THEORY

Feminism is one of the largest subject areas in sociological discourse. There is so much work being conducted in feminism that it takes many diverse forms. "The feminist movement is not completely unified in part because it *is* inclusive, and that very inclusiveness makes it difficult for agreement on some issues. As a result, the movement has several different branches that are divided according to general philosophical differences" (Lindsey and Beach, 2003:266). The variations of feminist theory are discussed briefly in the following pages.

Liberal Feminism

Liberal (sometimes called *egalitarian*) feminism is the most mainstream perspective. It is based on the idea that all people are created equal and should not be denied equality of opportunity because of their gender. Men who support gender equality are most likely to take the liberal approach to feminism. Liberal feminism is best exemplified by the National Organization for Women (NOW), formed in 1966. It works within the established socioeconomic and political systems to advocate for social changes on behalf of women (Anderson, 1997).

In the mid-1970s, liberal feminism was dismissed as a bourgeois white women's movement. But the gains inspired by liberal feminism in recent years have made significant changes in women's lives. On issues ranging from equity in employment to reproductive rights, liberal reforms have resulted in increased opportunities for women and increased public consciousness of women's rights. Working within existing social institutions has most likely contributed to its broad-based support (Anderson, 1997). Believing that all humans have equal rights and should have equal opportunities to secure self-actualization, liberal feminists focus their efforts on social change through the construction of legislation and the regulation of employment practices. They feel that obstacles to equality lie in the traditional laws and behaviors that deny the same rights to women that men enjoy.

The primary obstacle to equality is sexism. Liberal feminists believe that sexist attitudes about appropriate gender role expectations for men and women continue to lead to discrimination and prejudice against women. When women are encouraged to play the role of housewife, it makes them dependent on a male. When men have access to the economic institutions and women do not, females are in a disadvantageous position, a position that leads to an imbalance of power between the sexes. Liberal feminists argue that inequality, then, stems from the denial of equal rights. It is further hampered by women who are reluctant to exercise their rights. Liberal feminism strives for equality and civil rights for all individuals. Equality can best be accomplished through programs that prohibit discrimination and education programs that teach children that society's roles are not gender-specific (for example, males are doctors, while females are nurses). Education programs can be effective because gender roles are learned and not innate. Consequently, by stressing egalitarian gender roles, the once dominating patriarchal structure of gender roles found in society's social system will diminish.

Liberal feminism is based on the premise that individuals are autonomous beings; that all individuals are equal; and that women are independent of men. In stressing that women should be treated equally to men, liberal feminism fails to answer "equal to *which* men?" Not all men are treated equally. Class and race also play a role in how people are treated. Thus, liberal feminism is criticized for failing to explain institutionalized social classes and racial oppression (Anderson, 1997). Additionally, liberal feminists have been criticized by nonliberal feminists on a number of grounds, particularly their tendency to overemphasize the importance of individual freedom over the common good and their tendency to valorize a gender-neutral humanism over a gender-specific feminism. Liberal feminists also have a tendency to overestimate the number of women who want to be like men, who want to abandon roles such as "wife" and "mother" for roles such as "citizen" and "worker" (Tong, 1989). As a result, liberal feminism leaves much unanswered. It does not explain the emergence of gender inequality, nor can it account for the effects of class and race. The liberal approach believes that social change can occur through gradual reform and legislation via the existing social institutions. Many other feminists disagree with this approach.

Marxist Feminism

At its most fundamental level, feminism is very similar to the thoughts of Karl Marx and conflict theory. Marx and Engels had shown, starting with the family, how the division of labor was related to gender role expectations. (Delaney, 2004) The female, because of her ability to give birth, was generally left to be the homemaker and primary caregiver to children. The male was left to provide for the family, initially as a hunter, and then as the "breadwinner." Marx utilized a theoretical perspective which is often called *historical materialism*. It has as a central thesis that materialism and material conditions caused by capitalism shape people's lives, their behaviors, and their beliefs. Where Marx stated that the means of production were controlled by the bourgeoisie, feminists substitute men. The workers, or proletariat, who are the ones being exploited by the existing social system, are the women, according to the feminist perspective. Marx stressed that through productive work, humans can reach their full potential. If women are discriminated against in the economic and political sectors, they will never be able to reach their full human potential.

Marxist feminists stress that only a revolutionary restructuring of property relations can change a social system where women are more likely to be exploited than men. They note that working-class women are hired and paid a cheaper wage than their male counterparts. They produce the necessary work to sustain the capitalistic system, and yet, they do not benefit in the same manner as men (Farganis, 2000). Marx believed that systems of production that distort human potential must be transformed by changing social relations and through revolution (Anderson, 1997).

Karl Marx's theories maintained a focus on how economic systems give rise to social classes; therefore, sexism is a secondary concern, yet something that could be eliminated through a restructuring of society. Marx believed that social classes emerge as society produces a surplus. The accumulation of a surplus can be appropriated by one group and places this group in an exploitive position over the workers. Women, because they were left out of the productive system, were always exploited. Consequently, the social system needs to be changed to the point where women have equal access to the control of the means of production. Entering the paid labor force was the first step in equality. Advancing to management positions was the second step. Women owning the means of production is the ultimate goal of Marxist feminists.

Marxist feminists acknowledge class differences, noting that bourgeois women do not experience the same kind of oppression that proletariat women do (Tong, 1989). However, Marxist feminists believe that bourgeois women are also exploited. "Bourgeois women are not propertied but are kept by propertied men as possessions to perform services that perpetuate the class interests of the bourgeoisie. They produce the heirs to property and provide the emotional support, the nurturing family, and the sexual gratification for the men of property" (Farganis, 2000:370). Thus, Marxist feminism invites all women, whether proletariat or bourgeois to understand that women's oppression is the product of the political, social, and economic structures associated with capitalism (Tong, 1989).

Radical Feminism

Radical feminism views patriarchy as a sexual system of power in which the male possesses superior power and economic privilege. Sexism is the ultimate tool, used by men, to keep women oppressed. It emphasizes that male power and privilege is the basis of social relations. As Tong (1989) explained, radical feminists generally agree on the following:

1. That women were, historically, the first oppressed group.
2. That women's oppression is the most widespread (it exists in all societies).
3. That women's oppression is the deepest (it can not be removed as potentially social classes can be removed from society).
4. That it causes the most suffering (for example, false consciousness).
5. That women's oppression provides a conceptual model for understanding all other forms of oppression.

Radical feminists view patriarchy as having emerged from men's attempt to control, females sexuality. Through patriarchal gender socialization, men attempt to control the bodies of women through the creation of norms of acceptable sexual behavior (MacKinnon, 1982). In MacKinnon's radical feminist perspective, sexuality is the primary sphere of men's power. Men exercise their sexual power over women in many violent forms, including rape, incest, sexual harassment, and battery. Violence against women is not always physical. It can be hidden in more subtle ways, such as encouraging a certain style of dress, beauty standards, motherhood for women, and unpaid housework (Rich, 1976; Wolf, 1991). Heterosexuality is the institution through which men's power is expressed and is consequently viewed as a tool in institutionalizing male dominance (MacKinnon, 1982). Thus, radical feminists have proposed several ways to free women from the cage of feminity. These proposals have ranged from working toward an androgynous culture, in which male and female differences are minimized, to replacing male culture with female culture. To escape from the sexual domination of men, women can resort to celibacy, autoeroticism, or lesbianism. Radical feminists believe that refusing to reproduce is the most effective way for women to escape the snares of patriarchy (Tong, 1989).

Radical feminists speak out against all existing social structures because they are believed to be created by men. For example, organized religion generally teaches that God is a "He," and that He is so remote and aloof that He dwells in a place, heaven, that is beyond earth, reminding us that ultimate power over also implies absolute separation from (Tong, 1989). MacKinnon (1983) argued that the law views and treats women the same way as men do, and that the state is coercive and ensures men's control over women's sexuality. Although the state professes to be objective, in practice women are "raped" by the state just as they are raped by men (MacKinnon, 1983:643). The implication here is that the state is "male" and acts like a male on behalf of the needs of males. Thus, even though many feminists have demanded state intervention in areas such as sexual abuse, discrimination, and family policy, radical feminism suggests that women cannot entrust their liberation to the state.

Socialist Feminism

Whereas radical feminism sees the oppression of women as the result of men's control of female sexuality and the patriarchal institutions that structure sex and gender systems, socialist feminism views women's oppression as stemming from their work in the family and the economy. Socialist feminists believe that the inferior position of women in the social system is the result of class-based capitalism (similar to Marxist feminism). Unpaid housework is used as the primary example of the equal treatment of men and women.

Socialist feminists argue that women's oppression cannot be reduced to capitalism alone, although capitalism remains a significant factor. The creation of socialist feminism stemmed largely from feminists' dissatisfaction with classical Marxist perspectives on women and the family. Socialist feminists (like Alison Jaggar, Iris Young, and Nancy Fraser) seek to draw components of the radical, Marxist, and psychoanalytic insights under one conceptual umbrella. This feminist perspective attempts to adapt socialist principles to both the workplace and the home in order to increase gender equity (Lindsey and Beach, 2003). Socialist feminism believes that gender relations may be as important as economic class relations in determining women's status. Eradicating social class inequality will not necessarily eliminate sexism (Anderson, 1997). Social change will occur through increased consciousness and knowledge of how society's social structures are designed and operate to oppress women.

The link between the workplace and the home can be illustrated by the concepts of *private sphere* and *public sphere*. Men have typically been associated with the public sphere (the workplace) and women with the private sphere (the home). The private sphere has traditionally been an "invisible" economic factor in terms of production. The goal of feminists is to make the activities of women in the private sphere more visible. Socialist feminists criticize traditional theory because it assumes that the only place where history can be made is in the public sphere. This renders the private sphere (and women) inferior to the public sphere (and men). Women's relegation to the private sphere excludes them from public life and from equal access to sociopolitical and economic resources. Therefore, in order to improve the status and value of women, socialist feminists argue for two things:

1. An increased emphasis on the private sphere and the role of women in the household.
2. Equal opportunities for women in the public sphere.

Socialist feminists argue that change in women's social status will occur only through a transformation of the economic system, along with a change in the way household work is evaluated. It shares with Marxist feminism the position that oppression of women is an economic fact, but it is supplemented by demands for ideological transformation in how women are treated in the private sphere.

Postmodern Feminism

Postmodern feminists attempt to criticize the dominant order, particularly its patriarchal aspects, and to valorize the feminine woman (Tong, 1989). As the name of this perspective implies, postmodern feminism utilizes postmodern theory and its assumption that we no longer live under conditions of modernity, but of postmodernity. The postmodern world is a global economic world highlighted by technology that controls and promotes consumerism. Postmodernists believe that concepts and outlooks used to examine the world in the past no longer apply to the analysis of the world today. Thus, basic forms of knowledge are in question. Postmodernists question definitions from the past that attempt to establish what can be referred to as knowledge in a postmodern world. "Postmodern theorists take the position that all theory is socially constructed and reject the claim of modernists that only rational, abstract thought and scientific methodology can lead to valid knowledge (Baber and Murray, 2001:23).

Kristine Baber and Colleen Murray (2001) explained that a "postmodern approach stresses the importance of historical context, variations among people and the expectation of change over time. Postmodernism provides a sophisticated and persuasive critique of essentialism—rejecting the reductionistism and naive dualism that result in dichotomous, either-or thinking and embracing ambivalence, paradox, and heterogeneity" (pp. 23–24). Baber and Murray (2001) used a postmodern feminist approach to teaching human sexuality courses. They argued that "such an approach encourages a careful consideration of taken-for-granted information; helps students understand their experiences, even if they are contradictory or incoherent; and is committed to providing information that will be personally and professionally useful to students" (p. 23). Baber and Murray concluded that teaching human sexuality courses from a postmodern feminist perspective offers great opportunities and also considerable challenges. When information is provided as subjective experience, rather than through empirical means, students question its legitimacy.

Paula Moya, in her article "Chicana Feminism and Postmodernist Theory" (2001), cautioned feminists who believe that postmodern feminist thought is the most productive theoretical framework for feminist discourse. Just as most social thinkers have been hesitant to jump on the postmodern bandwagon, many feminists (such as Barbara Christian, Linda Singer, and Maria Lugones) have acknowledged postmodernism's theoretical limitations. When studying Chicanas and other women of color, feminists are drawn to postmodernism's focus on subjectivity and identity construction. On the other hand, some Chicana feminists demonstrate an ambivalent relationship to postmodernist theory even though they accept many of its presuppositions and claims (Moya, 2001:443).

Attention now shifts to the contributions to contemporary feminist theory of specific feminist social thinkers.

DOROTHY E. SMITH (1926–)

Dorothy E. Smith was born in 1926 in Great Britain. She earned her B.A. degree in sociology from the London School of Economics in 1955. Smith met her husband while attending college in London. They moved to Berkeley, California, where Smith earned her Ph.D. in sociology from the University of California at Berkeley in 1963. Erving Goffman supervised her Ph.D. studies. By the time she earned her doctor's degree, she had children and her husband had left her. She found work in the academic world as a lecturer in sociology at Berkeley (Smith, 1979). Smith's personal experiences led her to realize that she occupied two distinct realms of personal identity: in academia, as a member of the public sphere, and in the private sphere as a mother of two small children (Smith, 1987). After teaching at Berkeley (1964–1966), Smith moved back to England, where she taught at the University of Essex from 1966 to 1968; she then taught at the University of British Columbia (1968–1976) and then the Ontario Institute for Studies in Education in Toronto, where she is currently a professor emeritus. Smith's feminist thinking and sociological approach were deeply influenced by her years at

Berkeley, where nearly all the professors were males, and of course, by her experiences as a single mother.

Construction of Knowledge and Bifurcation

Smith's ideas are linked by her concept of *bifurcation*. Bifurcation is a "conceptual distinction between the world as we experience it and the world as we come to know it through the conceptual frameworks that science invents. In formulating the problem in these terms, Smith is adopting the phenomenological perspective articulated by Alfred Schutz in his distinction between the scientific and the commonsense ways of knowing the world" (Farganis, 2000:371). Smith attempts to expose the gender-biased assumptions within the social sciences. She believes that the male-power-based gender construction of roles has legitimized gender inequality in

Dorothy Smith, English-born feminist and women's rights advocate.
Source: Courtesy of Dorothy Smith

society. Smith proposes a sociology that utilizes a woman's standpoint and a woman's *construction of knowledge.* Smith believes that mainstream sociological theory has not accessed women's experiences. However, in *The Conceptual Practices of Power: A Feminist Sociology of Knowledge* (1990), Smith questioned whether a feminist sociology can describe the realities of women in terms of the sociological discipline merely by extending the field of interest to include the work on gender roles, the women's movement, women in the labor force, sexuality, and so on. Smith does not believe that it is enough to supplement established sociology by addressing gender issues because the established objective knowledge in sociology is biased on a male perspective. It is the challenge of feminism to create a new objective knowledge from a female perspective based on female experiences. Smith, then, is attempting to develop a sociology *for,* rather than *about,* women (unfortunately this creates a new set of biases). Smith (1990) did not propose a radical transformation of the sociological discipline, nor did she promote eliminating all of its methodological procedures. She did suggest that sociology needs a reorganization. Smith especially emphasized the subjective nature of methodology, assuming that the only way researchers can understand subjects under study is from within the subjects themselves. Understanding of this type leads to a bifurcated consciousness. A bifurcated consciousness is an actual representation of the self in the world in which we participate during our daily work life.

Methods

A sociology for women is concerned with how women construct their social realities. Smith believes that the best way to understand human behavior is not through the empirical scientific method but through a subjective approach. This type of methodological approach involves observation,

interviewing, recollection of work experience, use of archives, and other such related
methods (Smith, 1990). Smith insists that the
only way to know human behavior is through
a subjective reality.

Smith (1993) recommended that the feminist approach involve the examination of
human behavior through the actual recollections of experiences of those under study.
The subject of study should be the everyday
world in which humans reside.

Family

Smith (1993) described the standard North
American family as that of a legally married
couple sharing a household. The adult male
is in paid employment, his earnings providing the primary economic basis of the family
and household. The adult female may also
earn an income, but her primary responsibility is the care of the family and the household.
The ideals of family life are produced and reinforced by corporate entities such as Martha
Stewart and magazines like *Ideal Home* and
Home and Gardens, which produce an image
of a stress-free environment. The responsibility for creating such a home falls to the wife
and mother. The reality of today's family
presents many variations on this standard
family. "For example, women may have children with more than one father, all of whom
maintain their relationship to their children;
kin terms are extended to those connected in
networks of reciprocal support and exchange;
and 'daddies' and 'mommas' may be identified by the care they have provided a child
and not by legal status" (Smith, 1993:53).

During the course of her research on
schooling and families, Smith (1993) maintained
her feminist approach to data collection—
remaining subjective and neutral. However,
Smith came to realize that during the course of
her research she had fallen victim to the moth-
ering discourse. Smith (1993) stated:

> Mothering discourse in North America de-
> veloped historically during the first two

decades of the 20th century. It was and is actively fed by research and thinking produced by psychologists and specialists in
child development and is popularly dis-
seminated in women's magazines, television programs, and other popular media.
An important aspect of it is directed toward
"managing" women's relation to their children's schooling, enlisting their work and
thought in support of the public educational system. Women, particularly middle-
class women, were much more involved in
the early development of this discourse.
(pp. 54–55)

As housewives and mothers, many of the
women in Smith's study were caught up in
the role that society expected of them. Consequently, when interviewing these women,
Smith reflected this perspective. She warns
researchers not be caught in the methodological traps that feminists oppose.

Schooling

In "Schooling for Inequality" (2000), Smith argued that "the topic of schooling as an institution productive of inequalities—of gender, as
well as race and class—has never been, as I
believe it should be, a major issue for feminism" (p. 1147). She wrote that for more than
twenty years she had worked with various
women's groups and helped to build women's
organizations, and yet, when talking to activists in other areas, she found profound lack
of interest in, and a turning away from, issues
concerning girls and women in the school system. Smith (2000) stated, "Although feminism
has grown and developed among educators,
the inequalities produced by the school system have never become a central topic for
feminist thought and debate" (p. 1147). Smith
acknowledged that at the university and college levels feminists are very organized, have
successfully marketed their agenda in the curriculum, and have successfully convinced administrators to develop women's studies
programs. But the same cannot be said about
the public school system.

Smith would like to see more classes on gender equity, more textbooks that are sensitive to women's (and girls') needs, and attention to the women's movement. Smith believes that, otherwise, schools will continue to reproduce the social organization of inequality. "Research on gender and schooling shows a persistent replication of gender relations that develop over time as exclusive gender groupings marked by the privileging of male voices and male activity in the classroom, playground, sportsfield, and hallway" (Smith, 2000:1149). Smith would like to see the school system changed to allow girls a larger say in school dynamics.

SANDRA HARDING (1935–)

Sandra Harding is a professor of education and women's studies at the University of California at Los Angeles, where she also

Sandra Harding, feminist philosopher who was critical of traditional sociological theories.
Source: Courtesy of Sandra Harding

directs the Center for the Study of Women. She is a leading feminist and philosopher who taught for two decades at the University of Delaware before joining UCLA in 1996. She is the author or editor of ten books and special journal issues, including *The Science Question in Feminism* (1986) and *Is Science Multicultural? Postcolonialisms, Feminisms and Epistemologies* (1998). Harding has given over 200 lectures at various universities and conferences internationally and has served as a consultant to several United Nations organizations. Harding has written in such areas as feminist theory, sociology of knowledge, and methodological issues related to objectivity and neutrality.

Feminist Theory

In her article "The Instability of the Analytical Categories of Feminist Theory" (1986), Harding criticized all sociological theories. She believes that theories such as functionalism, critical theory, and hermeneutics somehow fail to apply to women and gender relations. She claims that sociological theories of the past and present are gender-biased (although she fails to offer any support for this claim). Harding also criticizes feminist theory from the perspective of the social experience of Western, bourgeois, heterosexual, white women because it is not applicable to other women. Harding (1986) stated:

> The patriarchal theories we try to extend and reinterpret were created to explain not men's experience but only the experience of those men who are Western, bourgeois, white, and heterosexual. Feminist theorists also come from these categories—not through conspiracy but through the historically common pattern that it is people in these categories who have had the time and resources to theorize, and who—among women—can be heard at all. In trying to develop theories that provide the one, true (feminist) story of human experience, feminism risks replicating in theory and public policy the tendency in the patriarchal theories

to police thought by assuming that only the problems of *some* women are human problems and that solutions for them are the only reasonable ones. (pp. 646–647)

Harding clearly does not believe in the idea of a universal theory that applies to all humans and their behaviors. She promotes the idea that specific theories should be designed for specific categories of people. Furthermore, Harding (1986) seems to question the validity of theory itself: "Theorizing itself is suspiciously patriarchal, for it assumes separations between the knower and the known, subject and object, and the possibility of some powerful transcendental, Archimedean standpoint from which nature and social life fall into what we think is their proper perspective" (p. 647).

If a social scientist cannot separate the subject from the object and cannot stand outside the realm of study, how is *any* theory or knowledge possible? Harding answers this question in two ways. Harding (1986) stated:

> On the one hand, we can use the liberal powers of reason and the will, shaped by the insights gained through engaging in continuing political struggles, to piece what we see before our eyes in contemporary social life and history into a clear and coherent conceptual form, borrowing from one androcentric discourse here, another one there, patching in between in innovative and often illuminating ways, and revising our theoretical frameworks week by week as we continue to detect yet further androcentrisms in the concepts and categories we are using. . . . On the other hand, we can learn how to embrace the instability of the analytical categories; to find in the instability itself the desired theoretical reflection of certain aspects of the political reality in which we live and think; to use these instabilities as a resource for our thinking and practices. No "normal" science; for us! (p. 648)

Thus, Harding does believe that theory is possible, so long as "normal" science is not used. The implication that males cannot do

this and have failed to do this in the past is difficult to accept.

Returning to the idea that no theory can be universal or present itself as a "scientific worldview," not even feminism, Harding (1986) stated, "The subject matters of feminist theories are not containable within any single disciplinary framework or any set of them" (p. 649). She added, "Instead of fidelity to the assumption that coherent theory is a desirable end in itself and the only reliable guide to action, we can take as our standard fidelity to *parameters* of dissonance within and between assumptions of patriarchal discourses. This approach to theorizing captures what some take to be a distinctively women's emphasis on contextual thinking and decision making and on the processes necessary for gaining understanding in a world not of our own making" (p. 649).

Harding promotes the use of "good science" instead of science that has been created by a masculine bias—"science as usual." Harding argues that science created without women researchers is biased, and that subject areas chosen without input from women is also biased. The very idea of empirical research is biased. Harding (1986) stated that since "the very concepts of nature, of dispassionate, value-free, objective inquiry, and of transcendental knowledge are androcentric, white, bourgeois, and Western, then no amount of more rigorous adherence to scientific method will eliminate such bias, for the methods themselves reproduce the perspectives generated by these hierarchies and thus distort our understandings" (p. 653). Not surprisingly, Harding ignores empirical data (for example, the poor, war veterans, and the homeless) and believes that all males and all whites benefit from their ascribed status. "Objectively, no individual men can succeed in renouncing sexist privilege any more than individual whites can succeed in renouncing racist privilege—the benefits of gender and race accrue regardless of the wishes of the individuals who bear them" (Harding, 1986:658).

In short, Harding believes that social theory must be created by women and must include issues that are central to women.

Sociology of Knowledge

The feminist viewpoint regarding the sociology of knowledge rests primarily on the idea that knowledge was created from the standpoint of men, which implies that it is biased. During the second wave of the women's movement (beginning in the 1960s):

> Feminist research has attempted to add understandings of women and their social activities to what we all thought we knew about nature and social life. . . . Within the theories, concepts, methods and goals of inquiry we inherited from the dominant discourses we have generated an impressive collection of "facts" about women and their lives, cross-culturally and historically—and we can produce many, many more. . . . We cannot understand women and their lives by adding facts about them to bodies of knowledge which take men, their lives, and their beliefs as the human norm. Furthermore, it is now evident that if women's lives cannot be understood within the inherited inquiry frameworks, than neither can men's lives. The attempts to add understandings of women to our knowledge of nature and social life have led to the realization that there is precious little reliable knowledge to which to add them. (Harding and Hintikka, 1983:ix)

Harding and Hintikka (1983) argued that sexist distortions and perversions in epistemology, metaphysics, methodology and the philosophy of science must be rooted out if an accurate sociology of knowledge is to exist.

In her article "Women as Creators of Knowledge" (1989b), Harding acknowledged that some women are making important advances within the social structures of the sciences, and that feminist critiques of the sciences have opened the doors to new research. She described the long battle women have had in their attempts to gain access to

the opportunities in sciences that have been available to many men. Harding emphasized that the term *history* should be replaced by *herstory*, which would focus on the achievements of great women (for example, Maria Mitchell, Dorothy Wrinch, and Rosalind Franklin) who have been otherwise ignored or trivialized, and of less famous women who have also made contributions to science and technology. Harding's description of the lack of women in most academic scientific departments of the past does not apply today, and that is a sure sign of the growing power of women in such areas as the sociology of knowledge. "In conclusion, I, for one, feel lucky to be living at this exciting, if problematic, moment in the history of women and the history of science. . . . A science that is to be 'for humanity' will have to be for women as well as for men; it will have to be a science directed by feminists—males as well as females. . . . It will have to be directed by a global feminism, not by a movement that seeks merely to add women to the group of men in the West who are overadvantaged. The scientific environment and the environment for women today conjoin to create auspicious projects for women as creators of knowledge" (Harding, 1989b:706–707).

Neutrality and Objectivity in Science

Feminists routinely criticize science as being male-dominated, biased, and lacking in objectivity. "The ideal of objectivity as neutrality is widely regarded to have failed not only in history and the social sciences, but also in philosophy and related fields such as jurisprudence" (Harding, 1992:569–570). Harding believes that the sciences are confronted with the demise of objectivism and the threat of relativism. Harding (1992) stated:

> The epistemological relativism that makes unnecessary trouble in the postneutrality discussions is sometimes conflated with sociological relativism. The latter simply describes the obvious fact that different people or cultures have different standards

for determining what counts as knowledge; there is no one standard to which they all agree. Sociological relativism simply states a fact that is uncontested by either the epistemological absolutists or relativists, who go on to further, conflicting, judgments about how to respond to this fact. The absolutists, such as objectivists, say that there is one and only one defensible standard for sorting belief to which—alas—some peoples and societies haven't caught on. (p. 575)

Clearly, an absolutist perspective is no place from which to conduct research. Issues of relativism have confronted scientists, both natural and social, since the beginning of scientific inquiry. Objectivist methods are encouraged in order to eliminate the social and political values and interests of researchers (although it is tough to extend this goal of objectivity to those who finance research).

Harding notes that objectivity is difficult in most spheres of life. In academia, issues related to funding requests, hiring, promotion, and tenure are all subject to the whims and wishes of those with their own agendas. Thus, in these matters, as well as in science, subjectivity continues to interfere with those attempting to conduct "good science." Neutrality is a requirement of objectivity. Those with a bias, or agenda, are not neutral and therefore are not objective. A person in a position of authority who "has it in" for someone is lacking objectivity. According to Harding (1992:580), objectivity in research can be accomplished if the following strategies are used:

1. Enter research in the context of discovery.
2. Use the values and interests of "legitimate" collective others.
3. Structure the institutions and conceptual schemes of disciplines. These systematic procedures would be capable of . . .
4. Distinguish between those values and interests that block the production of less partial and distorted accounts of nature and social relations ("less false" ones).

Utilizing these techniques should help with the goal of objectivity and neutrality in science.

In her article, "How the women's movement benefits Science: Two Views" (1989), Harding described the differences among feminists in their use of science. She encouraged women to stop disagreeing among themselves and encourage more feminists to enter science. Harding's primary motivation for encouraging women into science was to blow the whistle on scientists who failed to adhere to their often-expressed principles of impartiality, disinterest and value-neutrality. Harding also recognized that most of the status and authority positions of academia resided in the scientific field. Harding (1982) also stated that the women's movement needed feminists outside science, as well as within it, in order to present a critical examination of those conducting science.

The Third Millennium

In the year 2000, Harding wrote an interesting article entitled "After the Common Era." Reflecting on the new millennium, as have many professional social thinkers and laypersons, Harding described how she was not so overwhelmed by the whole "new" millennium "thing." She mentioned that she is not a religious person, so the new millennium held no spiritual significance—no one knows for sure, anyway, what date Jesus was born. She feels no loyalty to Western civilization's claims to ancient Greek and early Christian origins. In addition, Harding finds no positive connection between millennial history and the history of women. She hopes to commemorate a new millennium of history in which women and feminism are celebrated. Harding (2000) concluded that the new millennium could mark the beginning of the emergence of an envisioned "democratic time" for women's rights (p. 1044).

PATRICIA HILL COLLINS (1948–)

Patricia Hill Collins was born in Philadelphia in 1948. She earned her B.A. from Brandeis in 1969, her M.A. from Harvard in 1970, and her Ph.D. from Brandeis in 1984. She is currently teaching at the University of Cincinnati, serving as an associate professor of sociology and African American studies. Her general sociological concerns mirror her experiences as an African American woman who broke many barriers and who often felt marginalized. Her 1990 book, *Black Feminist Thought: Knowledge, Consciousness, and the Politics of Empowerment,* represents her attempt to explain her personal and professional experiences as an African American female. These experiences are expressed in her concept of the *outsider within.* The outsider within is similar to Simmel's idea of the *stranger,* where one is a part of the group but feels distanced from the group (in Collins's case because of her race and gender). Collins (1990:xi) recalled how she was often "the first," or "one of the few," or the "only" African American and/or woman in certain schools, communities, and work settings.

Feminist Theory and Methodology

Collins does not ground her analysis in any single theoretical approach. Collins (1990) indicated that her theoretical work was influenced by diverse sources, including Afrocentric philosophy, feminist theory, Marxist theory, the sociology of knowledge, critical theory, and postmodernism. She believes that the focus of sociological theory should be the "outsider" groups, especially those that usually lack a "voice" in the scientific framework. True to the feminist methodological tradition, Collins promotes using subjective analysis of the concrete experiences and definitions of those under study. To get to the heart of a group of people (under scientific study), Collins advocates the use of a wide variety of "voices." These people could be street musicians, poets, activists, and scholars.

Collins agrees with Harding that white male interests have pervaded traditional scholarship. She discards the use of empirical data and statistical analysis in favor of a

reliance on the documentation of voices of black women from all social settings. Collins (1989a) described positivism as "Eurocentric masculinist." She does not think that researchers should distance themselves from the subjects under study. Collins believes that emotional components, such as feelings are important in the accumulation of knowledge. Consequently, Collins values the symbolic interactionist approach, and it is evident in her work that she is concerned with black women's self-definitions (for example, their self-esteem). Collins uses the ethnomethodological approach as well, including autobiographies and other written and oral forms of communication. Observing black church services provides a wonderful opportunity to examine the use of dialogue among group members.

Collins's views on whether analysis should be conducted at the individual level or the group level are revealed in her discussion of feminist standpoint theory. In her article "Comment on Hekman's `Truth and Method; Feminist Standpoint Theory Revisited': Where's the Power?" (1997), Collins stated:

> First, the notion of a standpoint refers to historically shared, *group*-based experiences. Groups have a degree of permanence over time such that group realities transcend individual experiences. For example, African Americans as a stigmatized racial group existed long before I was born and will probably continue long after I die. While my individual experiences with institutionalized racism will be unique, the types of opportunities and constraints that I encounter on a daily basis will resemble those confronting African Americans as a group. Arguing that Blacks as a group come into being or disappear on the basis of my participation seems narcissistic, egocentric, and archetypally postmodern. In contrast, standpoint theory places less emphasis on individual experiences within socially constructed groups than on the social conditions that construct such groups. I stress this

difference between the individual and the group as units of analysis because using these two constructs as if they were interchangeable clouds understanding of a host of topics. (p. 375)

Individuals have their own reality constructs, but these are linked to the groups in which the individuals belong. In the absence of constraints, individuals are free to join many groups, and to move from one association to another. To understand individual behavior, the researcher must know the individual and must know the individual in a group context.

Black Feminism

Collins utilizes her "outsider within" approach to sociological theory throughout her presentations on Black feminism. In her article "Learning from the Outsider Within: The Sociological Significance of Black Feminist Thought" (1986), Collins described how many black women have been privy to some of the most intimate secrets of powerful white families while they have served as domestic servants. "These women have seen white elites, both actual and aspiring, from perspectives largely obscured from their Black spouses and from these groups themselves" (Collins, 1986:514). Their role as servants places them "inside" the house and family structure, but the dual reality that these black women experienced made them realize that they could never join their white families. This "outsider within" status provides Afro-American women with a special standpoint on self, family, and society.

"Black feminist thought consists of ideas produced by Black women that clarify a standpoint of and for Black women. . . . While Black feminist thought may be recorded by others, it is produced by Black women" (Collins, 1986:516). According to Collins (1986) there are three key themes in black feminist thought:

1. **The Meaning of Self-Definition and Self-Valuation:** "Self-definition involves challenging the political knowledge-validation process that has resulted in externally-defined, stereotypical images of Afro-American womanhood. In contrast, self-valuation stresses the content of Black women's self-definitions—namely, replacing externally-derived images with authentic Black female images" (pp. 516–517). Black feminist thought insists on a black self-definition framework when one is studying the social reality of African American women. Self-valuation involves taking this self-image one step further, to the point where black women learn to value themselves and empower themselves within the societal structure.

2. **The Interlocking Nature of Oppression:** For Collins, gender, race, and class are variables that are interconnected. "The Black feminist attention to the interlocking nature of oppression is significant for two reasons. First, this viewpoint shifts the entire focus of investigation from one aimed at explicating elements of race or gender or class oppression to one whose goal is to determine what the links are among the systems. . . . Second, Black feminist attention to the interlocking nature of oppression is significant in that, implicit in this view, is an alternative humanist vision of societal organization" (pp. 520–521). In *Black Feminist Thought* (1990) Collins argued that society has attempted to teach black women that racism, sexism, and poverty are inevitable aspects of everyday life for them. Such images are designed to keep black women oppressed. Awareness of this interlocking nature will help make black women more powerful and united in their fight against oppression and discrimination. Patricia Hill Collins further reiterated her position on the interlocking nature of the variables of race, gender, and class in her article "A Comparison of Two Works on Black Family Life" (1989a) when she stated, "The analysis presented in this essay suggests that removing any one piece of the triad of race, gender, or class from the analysis seriously jeopardizes a full understanding of the experiences of any group of people" (p. 884).

3. **The Importance of African-American Women's Culture:** "A third key theme characterizing Black feminist thought involves efforts to redefine and explain the importance

of Black women's culture. In doing so, Black feminists have not only uncovered previously unexplored areas of the Black female experience, but they have also identified concrete areas of social relations where Afro-American women create and pass on self-definitions and self-valuations essential to coping with the simultaneity of oppression they experience" (1986:521). Collins believes that an examination of family life is important in the black women's culture, especially the relationship between black women and their biological children. "In reassessing Afro-American motherhood, Black feminist researchers have emphasized the connection between (1) choices available to Black mothers resulting from their placement in historically-specific political economies, (2) Black mothers' perceptions of their children's choices as compared to what the mother thought those choices should be, and (3) actual strategies employed by Black mothers both in raising their children and in dealing with institutions that affected their children's lives" (1986:522).

When considering these three key themes in black feminist thought, Collins (1986) wrote that the sociological significance lies in two areas: "First, the content of Black women's ideas has been influenced by and contributes to on-going dialogues in a variety of sociological specialties. While this area merits attention, it is not my primary concern. Instead, I investigate a second area of sociological significance: the process by which these specific ideas were produced by this specific group of individuals" (p. 525).

Collins's importance placed on using the black women's experiences of everyday life in relation to oppression is furthered examined in her 1989 article "The Social Construction of Black Feminist Thought" (1989b):

> Black women's everyday acts of resistance challenge two prevailing approaches to studying the consciousness of oppressed groups. One approach claims that subordinate groups identify with the powerful and have no valid independent interpretation of their own oppression. The second approach assumes that the oppressed are less human

than their rulers and, therefore, are less capable of articulating their own standpoint. Both approaches see any independent consciousness expressed by an oppressed group as being not of the group's own making and/or inferior to the perspective of the dominant group. More important, both interpretations suggest that oppressed groups lack motivation for political activism because of their flawed consciousness of their own subordination. Yet African-American women have been neither passive victims of nor willing accomplices to their own domination. (pp. 746–747)

Collins's description of the oppressed certainly is nothing new to sociological thought, as this same argument has been used to describe many other groups that were not willing participants in their oppression by more powerful groups (such as the English over the Irish for centuries), but it does remind us that black women were obviously not willing participants in the discriminatory practices and behaviors that they have been subjected to. The political and economic status of black women directly affects their self-definition and self-valuation.

In her 1996 article "What's in a Name? Womanism, Black Feminism, and Beyond," Collins stated that African American women are a part of a new history, and the recurring theme of giving women a voice resurfaces. "Black women appear to have a voice, and with this new-found voice comes a new series of concerns. For example, we must be attentive to the seductive absorption of black women's voices in classrooms of higher education where black women's texts are still much more welcomed than black women ourselves. . . . At this point, whether African American women can fashion a singular `voice' about the black *woman's* position remains less an issue than how black women's voices collectively construct, affirm, and maintain a dynamic black *women's* self-defined standpoint" (p. 9). Collins believes that such solidarity is essential to ensuring group unity while still recognizing the tremendous heterogeneity that operates among black women. "Current debates about whether black women's standpoint should be named `womanism' or `black feminism' reflect this basic challenge of accommodating diversity among black women" (Collins, 1996:9–10).

CAROL GILLIGAN (1936–)

Carol Gilligan is a distinguished psychologist and feminist social thinker with a commitment to providing a forum for female voices. Her most noted theory is the stage theory of moral development for women. Gilligan's works are influenced primarily by Sigmund Freud, Jean Piaget, and Lawrence Kohlberg.

Gilligan received an A.B. (with highest honors in English literature) from Swarthmore College in 1958, an A.M. (with distinction in clinical psychology) from Radcliffe College in 1961, and her Ph.D. from Harvard University in 1964. Her commitment to giving a voice to women began during her graduate studies when she spoke with people in Cleveland at their kitchen tables about voter registration and the need to have a voice in democratic society. She was also involved in the antiwar movement during the 1960s, protesting the University of Chicago's use of grades to determine who would be drafted to serve in Vietnam (Gilligan, 1998). Lower grades increased the likelihood of being drafted. Gilligan began her teaching career as a lecturer at the University of Chicago (1965–1966); moved to Harvard as a lecturer (1967–1969), as an assistant professor from 1971 to 1979, and as an associate professor from 1979 to 1986; and currently serves as a professor in the Harvard Graduate School of Education. She has published over seventy articles and seven books, *In A Different Voice* (1982) being her most notable.

Developmental Theory

Gilligan's analysis of the developmental theoretical works of Freud and Piaget led her to believe that a masculine bias is prevalent. Freud's theory of psychosexual development centers on the male child and his Oedipus complex. Freud believed that a girl's attachments to her mother constituted a developmental failure where the superego was less independent of emotions than male's, concluding that women are more influenced in their judgments by feelings and emotions.

Gilligan's idea that human moral development comes in stages is directly influenced by Piaget. Piaget's theory involves four stages of Cognitive Development:

1. **The Sensorimotor stage (birth to 2 years):** At this stage the child is dominated by an overwhelming interest in making physical contact with the surrounding environment and his or her own body. When objects are removed, the infant forgets about them (out of sight, out of mind).

2. **The Preoperational stage (2 to 7):** By this stage in development the child has learned of object permanence (for example, when a favorite blanket is removed for washing, it still exists). The child is very egocentric and can only take the view of the self, not others.

3. **The Concrete operational stage (7 to 12):** Intellectual development grows quickly within the child, but he or she still lacks the skills to solve abstract or hypothetical problems.

4. **The Formal operation stage (12 years and older):** Adolescents begin to think abstractly and to perceive analogies and can use complex language forms such as metaphors and sarcasm.

Gilligan was influenced by Piaget's examination of the rules of the game. In his observations Piaget noted the fascination that boys have with the legal elaboration of rules and fair procedure to solve conflicts. He found that girls do not develop such interests and that they are more tolerant of rule exceptions. Piaget concluded that the legal sense, which is essential to moral development, is less developed in girls (Gilligan, 1982).

Lawrence Kohlberg, a friend and colleague of Gilligan, also influenced Gilligan's moral developmental theory. In 1970, Gilligan began to teach with Kohlberg, and she noticed that the males in Kohlberg's class were reluctant to speak about their feelings in regard to the draft. She concluded that men were uncomfortable talking about their feelings and assessed such discussions as morally undeveloped. Kohlberg had also created a moral developmental theory, consisting of various stages that are similar to Piaget's.

Gilligan's concern about development lies in moral dilemmas. Gilligan believes that men and women *do* have differences in moral reasoning. Her theory represents an attempt to explain these differences. Among the more significant differences in men and women is their commitment to either a justice or a care orientation. In *Mapping the Moral Domain: A Contribution of Women's Thinking to Psychological Theory and Education* (1988), Gilligan (Ward and Taylor) made a distinction between a justice and a care orientation: "A justice perspective draws attention to problems of inequality and oppression and holds up an ideal or reciprocity and equal respect. A care perspective draws attention to problems of detachment or abandonment and holds up an ideal of attention and response to need. Two moral injunctions—not to treat others unfairly and not to turn away from someone in need—capture these different concerns" (p. 73). In her studies, Gilligan found that both men and women have concerns about justice and care, but that the care orientation is most often present in women and a justice orientation is most often predominant among men (Gilligan, 1988).

Gilligan's stages of moral development for women emphasizes the development of self, rather than changes in cognitive development as one passes from one stage to the next. She also refuses to assign ages to the stages as Piaget and Kohlberg had.

Gilligan's Stages of Moral Development for Women

1. **Orientation to Individual Survival (Preconventional Morality):** The primary goal is individual survival (selfishness). A transition occurs when one changes from a selfish focus to a responsibility to others. This is an egocentric level of development where a woman has no feeling of *should* (as in "I should be more tolerant of others"). Gilligan points out that prospective motherhood often brings about a change in self-concept. Nature has made it difficult for a pregnant woman to feel detached from her fetus, the father, or other mothers. An internal dialogue sparks moral responsibility (Griffin, 1991).

2. **Goodness as Self-Sacrifice (Conventional Morality):** Women define their sense of self-worth by their ability to care for others. They search for solutions in which no one gets hurt. Self-sacrifice is goodness, and goodness is measured by caring for others. The woman must seek a balance between helping others and feeling manipulated. A successful transition to the final stage of moral development occurs through a shift from goodness to the truth that she is a person, too.

3. **Responsibility for Consequences of Choice (Postconventional Morality):** The essence of a moral decision is the exercise of choice and the willingness to take responsibility for that choice. The principle of nonviolence is critical at this stage. Unlike conventional goodness, the concept of truth requires that a woman extend nonviolence and care to herself as well as to others. She must seek to eliminate tension between herself and others.

The moral development of women can be summed up as a transition from caring only for oneself (Stage 1) to seeing the virtue in caring for others (Stage 2) to the final realization that a woman must seek moral equality between caring for herself and caring for others (Stage 3).

Giving Voice to Women

In her 1982 book *In a Different Voice* Gilligan pointed out how the developmental theories of Freud and Piaget treat women like men and were built on observations of men's lives. She believes that a different voice needs to be heard in regard to developmental theory and women's lives. "The failure of women to fit existing models of human growth may point to a problem in the representation, a limitation in the conception of the human condition, an omission of certain truths about life. The different voice I describe is characterized not by gender but theme. Its association with women is an empirical observation, and it is primarily through women's voices that I trace its development" (Gilligan, 1982:2). *A Different Voice* represents Gilligan's attempt to show the contrasts between male and female voices and to highlight a distinction between two modes of thought. She points to the interplay of these voices within each sex and suggests that their convergence marks times of crisis and change. "Clearly, these differences arise in a social context where factors of social status and power combine with reproductive biology to shape the experience of males and females and the relations between the sexes. My interest lies in the interaction of experience and thought, in different voices and the dialogues to which they give rise, in the way we listen to ourselves and to others, in the stories we tell about our lives" (Gilligan, 1982:2). Furthermore, Gilligan (1982) argued that "women's place in a man's life cycle is to protect this recognition while the developmental litany intones the celebration of separation, autonomy, individuation, and natural rights. . . . Only when life-cycle theorists divide their attention and begin to live with women as they have lived with men will their vision encompass the experience of both sexes and their theories become correspondingly more fertile" (p. 23).

Between Voice and Silence (1995) represents the further attempts of Gilligan, and her colleagues, Jill McLean Taylor and Amy M. Sulli, to give a forum to the voices of females, especially adolescent girls. The authors reported that when adolescent girls remain silent or censor themselves to maintain relationships, they often become depressed and develop eating disorders or other

psychological problems. In contrast, when adolescent girls are outspoken, it is often difficult for others to stay in relationships with them, and they may be excluded or labeled as troublemakers. The research centered on twenty-six girls who were designated "at risk" of high school dropout and early motherhood and covered what they were feeling and thinking about themselves, their relationships, their lives, their futures, their experiences in school, and their decisions concerning sexuality. Taylor, Gilligan, and Sullivan found that it was the women (especially those who shared the same experiences) in these girls' lives who were most likely to listen, to care, to be interested in knowing about them.

JOAN JACOBS BRUMBERG (1944–)

Joan Jacobs Brumberg is an award-winning author of such publications as *Body Project* (1997a), *Fasting Girls* (1988), and numerous articles on the American woman's experience. She was born and raised in Ithaca, New York, where she continues to live and work as a professor at Cornell University. Brumberg teaches in the areas of history, human development, and women's studies. Her research and publications have received praise from the Guggenheim Foundation, the National Endowment for the Humanities, and the Rockefeller Foundation. She credits much of her writing direction to her husband, David Brumberg, who helps her with her historical judgments. Joan Jacobs Brumberg is a graduate of Harvard.

One of the major influences on Brumberg's life is Margaret Mead's research in Samoa (although much of Mead's research has been discredited, many find continued worth in her observations). Brumberg took interest in Mead's observations that there are cultures where girls do not experience self-consciousness in adolescence or discomfort with their changing bodies. This reality reveals that gender roles and gender expectations are cultural products. Brumberg decided to trace the female plight of self-consciousness in American and European societies, where women have experienced a great deal of concern about their body image and the physical changes that occur during natural development. Brumberg utilized the feminist methodological approach by examining historical sources, unpublished diaries by adolescent goals, and photographs that conjure up images of the past.

Female Bodies and Self-Image

In contemporary Western society there is an obsession with the female body. In *The Body Project* (1997a) Brumberg described in great detail how girls' bodies change (they mature much earlier) and why the experience of physical changes affects girls' emotional state and self-image more now than ever before. The mass media, as an agent of culture, has reinforced an ideal image that girls are to strive for and attain, therefore placing more emphasis on "good looks" than on "good works." Parents themselves are responsible for this cultural ideal and often do great disservice to their daughters when they focus too much on physical appearance and attractiveness. In *The Body Project* Brumberg provided intimate excerpts from girls diaries between the 1830s and the 1990s. This information reveals how girls' attitudes toward their bodies and sexuality have changed and suggests that although young women today enjoy greater freedom and more opportunities than their counterparts of the past, they are under more cultural pressure to look good:

> At the close of the twentieth century, the female body poses an enormous problem for American girls, and it does so because of the culture in which we live. The process of sexual maturation is more difficult for girls today than it was a century ago because of a set of historical changes that have resulted in a peculiar mismatch between girls' biology and today's culture. Although girls now mature sexually earlier than ever before, contemporary American society provides fewer social protections for them, a situation that leaves them unsupported in their development and extremely vulnerable to the excesses of popular culture and to pressure from peer groups. But the current body problem is not just an external issue resulting from a lack of societal vigilance or adult support; it has also become an internal, psychological problem: girls today make the body into an all-consuming project in ways young women of the past did not. A century ago, American women were lacing themselves into corsets and teaching their adolescent daughters to do the same; today's teens shop for thong bikinis on their own, and their middle-class mothers are likely to be uninvolved until the credit card bill arrives in the mail. (pp. xvii–xviii)

Brumberg suggested that adolescent girls have always felt angst about their bodies, but the historical moment defines how they reacts to their changing bodies. The historical moment is a specific environment at a specific point in time. Whether it is the style of the 1920s flapper or the hourglass figure of the 1950s, women have placed great emphasis on their body image as a means of defining themselves. Brumberg believes that nineteenth-century girls were not as concerned about their physical appearance because of society's emphasis on spiritual rather than physical matters. Many issues related to the changes in the female body were not considered polite public discourse. "In fact, girls who were preoccupied with their looks were likely to be accused of vanity or self-indulgence. . . . Character was built on attention to self-control, service to others, and belief in God—not on attention to one's own, highly individualistic body project" (Brumberg, 1997a:xx).

A diary entry of an adolescent girl in 1892 provides a nice summary of this creed: "Resolved, not to talk about myself or feelings. To think before speaking. To work seriously.

To be self restrained in conversation and actions. Not to let my thoughts wander. To be dignified. Interest myself more in others" (Brumberg, 1997a:xxi). As the twentieth century came to an end, the focus of adolescent girls was that their bodies are something to be managed and maintained, usually through expenditures on clothes and personal grooming items. A diary entry from an adolescent girl in 1982 reveals the dramatic differences in girls' self-image from that of a century ago: "I will try to make myself better in any way I possibly can with the help of my budget and baby-sitting money. I will lose weight, get new lenses, already got new haircut, good makeup, new clothes and accessories" (Brumberg, 1997a:xxi). This diary entry captures how many contemporary girls feel about their physical appearance and about defining their self worth. Commercial industries have made huge sums of money by taking advantage of contemporary girls' angst concerning their bodies and self-image.

Gender Differences

In contemporary society, girls begin to menstruate at an earlier age than ever before, so girls have to cope with physical changes and maturation at an earlier age than boys. Generally speaking, until puberty, girls are considered the stronger sex in physical and mental health. They are less likely to injure themselves, are generally bigger, and are more competent in social settings. Brumberg suggests that once a girl begins to menstruate, her advantage over her male counterparts diminishes, partly because girls begin to suffer bouts of clinical depression from the frustrations they experience when their bodies change. Beyond depression and thoughts of suicide, girls are more vulnerable to eating disorders, substance abuse, and dropping out of school. Brumberg's thoughts on the differences between the sexes are derived from the ideas of Carol Gilligan and Mary Pipher. Gilligan's studies of girls between the ages of eleven and sixteen reveal that they

are likely to lose their confidence and become insecure and self-doubting. Pipher's *Reviving Ophelia* described how adolescent girl's self-esteem crumbles. Brumberg concurs with Gilligan and Pipher (among others) that the body is at the heart of the crisis of confidence for adolescent girls. "By age thirteen, 53 percent of American girls are unhappy with their bodies; by age seventeen, 78 percent are dissatisfied. Although there are some differences across race and class lines, talk about the body and learning how to improve it is a central motif in publications and media aimed at adolescent girls" (Brumberg, 1997a:xxiv).

Society's Influence on Women's Image

Women found in their body image a sense of self-definition and a way to announce who they are to the world. "Today, many young girls worry about the contours of their bodies—especially shape, size, and muscle tone—because they believe that the body is the ultimate expression of the self" (Brumberg, 1997a:97). Contemporary adolescent girls learn from their mothers, as well as from the larger culture, that modern femininity requires some degree of exhibitionism. Since the 1920s, it has been fashionable to display certain body parts, such as arms and legs. Currently, part because of the popularity of Britney Spears, it is common for girls to display their navels and to wear the hip-hugger pants that were popular in the 1960s and 1970s. This freedom to display the body is accompanied by a demand for beauty, and dietary regimens (which involve money and self-discipline) must be met if the young woman is to successfully "pull off the look." As Brumberg (1997a) explained, "What American women did not realize at the time was that their stunning new freedom actually implied the need for greater internal control of the body, an imperative that would intensify and become even more powerful by the end of the twentieth century" (p. 98).

Fashion and the film industry are two huge influences on societal expectations that women display their bodies sexually. The sexual revolution liberated women from the Victorian restraints of modesty but also demanded a commitment to diet and beauty. The 1920s represented the first era when teenage girls made systematic efforts to lower their weight by food restriction and exercise. This dieting craze was referred to as *slimming* and was motivated by new cultural ideals of female beauty. The dominant fashions of the 1920s revealed the shift from the voluptuous Victorian hourglass body shape to an interest in a body shape highlighted by exposed slender legs and a relatively flat-chest. After World War II, voluptuous movie stars such as Marilyn Monroe and Jane Russell served as the model for the ideal American woman. The focus became fixated on the size of a woman's breasts, a fascination that continues today, as adolescent boys and men prefer big-breasted women. This cultural reality has led many women to have their breasts enlarged through surgery. In her article "Silicone Valley" (1997b) Brumberg drew attention to the recent phenomenon of plastic surgery. Women not only are changing their breasts, they are changing their noses, and having cellulite sucked from their bodies. The pursuit of self-perfection through surgery is now easier than ever before because of greater affluence, decreasing costs, and more board certified physicians which make plastic surgery an "acceptable" alternative toward attaining the perfect body. Brumberg (1997b) stated that it is one thing for adult women to have surgery, but it is entirely different for adolescent girls to have plastic surgery as it is potentially damaging to young girls both mentally and physically (p. 2).

Breasts provide visual significance and validation for many women. This is nothing new, as "throughout history, different body parts have been eroticized in art, literature, photography, and film. In some eras, the ankle or upper arm was the ultimate statement of female sexuality" (Brumberg, 1997a:108). The preoccupation with female breasts led to the development of brassieres (bras), a French word for an infant's undergarment or harness. In the United States, the first bras were introduced during the "flapper" era of the 1920s and were designed to flatten the chest in order to conform to the ideal slim, boyish figure that was in vogue. When society placed an emphasis on larger busts, the bra was designed to maximize size and make the breasts conform to an ideal round shape. Today, women are faced not only with wearing a bra, but with wearing a fashionable, sexy bra. Western cultures are characterized by industrial marketers who have cashed in on this preoccupation with fashion and bras. Victoria's Secret and Fredericks of Hollywood specialize in exotic and sexy lingerie. These companies and their advertisers reinforce the image of what a desirable female in contemporary American society should look like.

The focus on women's bodies is now "hitting below the belt." Now big breasts are not the fashionable imperative they once were. The real heat is on the lower body, especially the thighs and the behind. This current emphasis comes from the idea that sleek thighs and a sculptured behind symbolize objects both of desire and of success. "As jeans became a national uniform, particularly for adolescents, the upper leg, crotch, and buttocks were all brought into focus. But it was the bikini, and more recently—bathing suits with legs cut upward toward the pelvic bone, that really made the tone and shape of thighs such a pervasive female concern" (Brumberg, 1997a:125). Women work out and exercise in hopes of attaining the perfect body and willingly display it in thong bikinis. At beaches and night clubs girls wearing thongs are a common sight. Advertisers use such marketing gimmicks as "Girls Gone Wild" to further reinforce the ideal image of young, attractive women. Brumberg makes an astute observation regarding the recent trend of piercings and tattoos. Body piercing, once regarded as primitive artistic expression, and getting tattoos, once reserved for the "lower" and "deviant" members of society, have become fashionable for young women. Brumberg believes that this self-mutilation represents a powerful revolution in sexual mores and behavior. It reflects a turn from a preoccupation with beauty to nonsexual exhibitionism.

BARBARA RISMAN (1956–)

Barbara J. Risman was born in 1956 in Lynn, Massachusetts. She was raised in an extended family environment that included grandparents, aunts, uncles, and cousins, often living in the same house. Her grandparents were Jewish immigrants from Russia who spoke only Yiddish. Risman characterizes her family as very traditional. Her father worked for the Army Corps of Engineers, and her mother was a homemaker and nurse. Risman's own family reflects a typical contemporary family as she and her husband are divorced and have one daughter, Leah. Leah KaneRisman has a last name that is a combination of both her parents'. Risman indicates that people constantly misspell Leah's last name, and that this is a sign that the world is not geared to nontraditional names.

Risman attended college at Northwestern University during the height of the feminist movement. She earned her B.A. in sociology in 1976 and her Ph.D. in 1986 from the University of Washington. Risman eventually became a professor of sociology at North Carolina State University and currently holds the administrative position of Director of Graduate Studies at NCSU. Risman has involved herself in many academic projects, including coediting the journal *Contemporary Society* and being author and coeditor of many journal articles and author of *Gender Vertigo: American Families in Transition* (1998), her most famous book.

Risman has conducted a great deal of her own research in the area of single parenthood. She believes that men are capable of being single parents and that parent-child attachment, household organization, and child development can all occur successfully in both single-mother and single-father homes (Risman, 1988). The research she collected over the years culminated in *Gender Vertigo* (1998). Risman has attempted to uncover the processes that influence people to act in certain ways regarding gender, and she admits that this has always been her intellectual preoccupation. Basing her conclusions on her own graduate studies and the research of others, Risman (1998) theorized that gender is merely a social structure. She is a supporter and member of the Alternatives to Marriage Project (AMP), an organization that encourages diversity in family structure. The AMP believes that marriage is just one form of family structure and that other healthy alternatives exist (for example, the single-parent family, same-sex partners). The AMP gives a voice to those raising a family nontraditionally and plays an active role in creating policies and legislation designed to provide same-sex health benefits, family and medical leave, survivor's benefits, and so on.

Doing Gender

Many feminist theorists believe that an individual is labeled at birth as a member of a sex category, either male or female, and from that point on, is held to acting accordingly. The individual succumbs to society's expectations, often through the use of, or the threat of, sanctions and therefore "does gender." Individuals who deviate from these expectations are unable to have normal interactions with other members of society. Feminists believe that such expectations reflect a patriarchal society that devalues what is defined as female or feminine and claims that biological differences between males and females exist to justify male dominance (Risman, 1998).

Thus, gender is not something that one has or something that one is; rather, it is something that one *does*.

The doing-gender perspective was later extended by West and Fenstermaker (1995) to "doing difference," claiming that what we actually create through interaction is inequality. Risman (1998) believes that just as one uses race to guide interactional encounters despite its lack of biologically based differences, one also uses gender to determine where one stands in daily interactions. Perceived differences between two people play a large role in determining behavior, hence the change from doing gender to doing difference. Risman believes that there is a great difference in how people are treated simply because of their gender categorization. "Gender polarization is the assumption that not only are women and men different, but that this difference is super-imposed on so many aspects of the social world that a cultural connection is thereby forged between sex and virtually every other aspect of human experience, including modes of dress and social roles and even ways of expressing emotion and experiencing sexual desire" (Risman, 1998:2–3). Since the mid-1990s, Risman has tried to understand why men and women behave so differently, particularly in their intimate relationships. She feels that the doing-gender perspective is helpful, yet incomplete, and that the extension from doing gender to doing difference is an important direction of focus in gender research.

Gender as Social Structure

Risman does not accept the criteria of nature (biology determines males and females and thus corresponding gender expectations) as a way to distinguish behavior expectations. She is especially upset by the field of sociobiology. By assigning people to one of two categories—male or female—society has created differences between them. According to Risman, this distinction becomes the cornerstone for inequality. Gender differences become entrenched in the social system.

> Although empirically documented sex differences do occur, structuralists like me have argued that men and women behave differently because they fill different positions in institutional settings, work organizations, or families. That is, the previous structural perspectives on gender assume that work and family structures create empirically distinct male and female behavior. Structuralist feminist sociologists have not usually conceptualized gender itself as a structure. Rather, most have argued that empirically documented sex differences are more apparent than real. Within this perspective, men and women in the same structural slots are expected to behave identically. (Risman, 1998:19)

Clearly, many facets of everyday life are organized or categorized according to gender. However, this structure seems so natural and is so widely accepted that, without careful analysis, most people do not ever recognize its influence. Risman feels that gender's strongest influence is found at the interactional level, and therein lies the deepest liability for the continuation of inequality in American family life (Risman, 1998). Men have historically enjoyed certain advantages while women have enjoyed others (for example, child custody is usually awarded to the mother just because she is a female, and alimony is usually awarded to the female because the male is the one "assumed" to be the breadwinner).

Gender Vertigo

Gender vertigo is a term coined by Robert Connell in the final chapter of his book *Masculinities* (1996). Risman asked, and was granted permission, by Connell to use this term for the title of her book. Risman suggests that the best solution to society's gender inequalities is going beyond gender, ignoring gendered rules, and "pushing the envelope until we get dizzy" (Risman, 1998:11).

> Gender vertigo can only help us to destabilize deeply held but incorrect beliefs about the natural differences between women and men. I believe that we will have to be dizzy for a time if we are to hope to deconstruct gender and construct a society based on equality. I argue that as long as behavioral expectations, material advantages, and cultural ideology divide human beings into types based on their ascribed sex (that is, the shape of their genitals), male privilege will continue. (p. 11) (Risman, 1998:11)

Risman admits that it will be difficult to change people's perceptions of gender and gender role expectations but insists that it must be done in order for equality to occur.

Risman chose the term *gender vertigo* because it is indicative of the profound effect the elimination of gender would have on every person's psyche. Doing gender determines how one walks, talks, dresses, eats, and socializes and nearly all other aspects of everyday life. Gender often plays a significant role in the definition of the self. Freeing individuals from gender restraints will be difficult and marked by feelings of vertigo and disorientation. For these reasons, Risman suggested that society first attack the features of gender structure that immediately uphold differentiation. Family roles requiring women to be financially dependent on men, an economic structure that allows male workers to escape family responsibility, and interpersonal sexism are among the issues that Risman finds the most important. In *Gender Vertigo*, (1998), Risman concluded that in order "to move fully toward justice for women and men, we must dare a moment of gender vertigo. My hope is that when the spinning ends we will be in a post-gendered society that is one step closer to a just world" (162).

RELEVANCY

It is truly amazing how poorly women have been treated historically in so many societies. Negative treatment has led to discrimination and oppression at both the interpersonal and the institutional levels. Patriarchal social systems found throughout the world have usually oppressed women in the economic and political domains. In the family structure women have generally been relegated to household caregiver status. Equal rights advocates, most notably feminists, have attempted to change the existing social structures that have stratified individuals based on gender. Feminism can be defined as a social movement and an ideology in support of the idea that a larger share of scarce resources (for example, wealth, power, income, and status) should be allocated to women. Feminists believe that women should enjoy the same rights in society as men and that they should share equally in society's opportunities. Feminists hope to show that gender differences are a result of historical man-made conditions and not natural, biological differences.

Feminist sociological theory arose from the feminist movement in general and maintains as its core mantra expanding the role, power, significance, and status of women. Feminist sociological theory represents an attempt to give a voice to women and the female perspective. It demonstrates how gender roles are learned and not determined by biology. Thus, an individual is doing gender because of the cultural determinants of appropriate behavior based solely on what type of genitals the person has. When boys are taught "big boys don't cry" they are being taught to be strong and emotionally distant. When girls are taught to play quietly with their dolls and to "play house" they are being taught to be subservient. Boys and girls, then, are doing differences in gender expectations. These gender expectations extend throughout all the social institutions (such as economics, politics, military, and family) and are reinforced by the agents of socialization (for example, the media, the church, the workplace). Dorothy Smith's concept of bifurcation—seeing the world through a preconceived framework—reflects this idea.

It is certainly true that men and women share fundamental needs: survival, self-esteem and confidence, intimacy, personal growth, achievement, recreation, and a sense of control over their lives. But it is also true that men and women have differences, especially physical ones. As Joan Jacobs Brumberg indicated, because of earlier menstruation, girls develop and mature earlier than boys. Earlier development in girls makes them aware of their bodies at an earlier age than boys of the same age. Adolescent girls become very self-conscious of their image and presentation of self. Societal influences such as fashion and the media are responsible for adding pressure to the already vulnerable minds of adolescent girls. Contemporary society places a high emphasis on a slender physical look that involves baring certain body parts. Girls who are caught up in the need for "good looks" will diet and sometimes resort to cosmetic surgery to meet this ideal image. Barbara Risman encourages an abandonment of society's social construct of how one is to look based on a biological distinctions. She realizes that such an idea will lead to "gender vertigo" during this transition toward a more gender-neutral society.

Feminist sociological theory is generally critical of the traditional scientific sociological approach that stresses a commitment to neutrality, objectivity, and empirical research. Feminist standpoint theory has become a staple of feminist theory where the development of a sociological method from the "standpoint of women" is the norm (Hekman, 1997; Smith, 1997). Feminists encourage the collection of subjective data, such as life histories, and the content analysis of such materials as diaries and photographs. They strongly encourage a focus on female issues and giving voice to female concerns. Sandra Harding questions the validity of nearly all sociological theories, believing that they are male-biased, and that traditional feminism

has a white middle-class women's bias. Feminists are in basic agreement that in order to gain knowledge of women, one must use a women's perspective.

There are many criticisms of feminists. One is that they leave themselves wide open to attack because they themselves are very biased in their approach. Giving a voice to women is important, but one must question any theory that purposely ignores one-half of the population: men. For example, Carol Gilligan has articulated a unique developmental theory, in which, instead of concentrating on cognitive development, she examined moral development. This is a fascinating idea. And yet, her moral development theory is applied to women only. There is no reason why this theory should ignore men. The fight against injustice should not be limited to female injustice; it should include all those who are harmed by a social system designed to disadvantage one person over another.

Second, although a commitment to empirical research is not a must in designs of social theory; relying on such techniques as oral testimony and the analysis of such content as diaries risk a lack of objectivity and bias. When an individual is asked for his or her story, it is always biased from his or her perspective. It is also highly questionable that anyone will find the "truth" in diary entries, as only one side of the story is given voice. Diary entries do provide valuable insights into personal interpretations of events—assuming that the truth is told in a diary. Feminist scholar Jesse Bernard, in her 1972 best-seller *The Future of Marriage,* was among the first to propose the idea that men benefit emotionally from marriage while women suffer. This idea fueled the belief that the social institution of marriage has oppressed women. This theory has persisted among feminists (and is viewed as common knowledge) despite scientists' subsequent findings that Bernard's studies were flawed, and more recent research contradicts her results. Research involving over 10,000 people conducted by

David De Vaus, a sociologist at La Trobe University in Melbourne, revealed that emotional problems (for example, depression and other mental disorders) are equally common among husbands and wives (Ross, 2002). Empirical verification of theory will always make it more valid and believable.

Third, most feminists claim that all sociological theories are gender-biased but fail to provide any proof of this claim. It is true that Carol Gilligan provided evidence that Freud's psychological developmental theory is male-biased, but this is hardly a new observation, as relatively few academics take any of Freud's theories seriously today. But just how is a macrostructural theory such as functionalism biased in favor of males? It is an odd accusation. Functionalism is generally criticized for ignoring individuals because of its focus on social structures. It is not designed to deal with such issues as differences between males and females. The five basic propositions that are the cornerstone of Homans's exchange theory apply to women and men. For example, if in the past a behavior was rewarded, that behavior is likely to be repeated in the future; this statement is clearly gender-neutral. The challenge to feminist sociological theory is to support its claim that these two, or any other, sociological theories are biased. Furthermore, how can the sciences of mathematics and biology be gender-biased (Harding claims that past science is "bad science")? Is the law of gravity gender-biased? Are basic mathematical formulas gender-biased? Clearly, they are not.

Fourth, gender is just one variable in human interaction. Many feminists believe that interactions are based solely on gender distinction. Other feminists realize that it is not that simple. Sandra Harding has noted that gender, class, and race are interlocking variables and cannot be separated. Barbara Risman attempted to deemphasize the importance of gender as a variable in an attempt to eliminate a gender stratification system. As conflict theory has clearly demonstrated, it is

power and power differentials that determine interactions among people, as well as individual interactions in the greater social system. "Power corrupts" is not a gender distinction. Women in power positions can be as vindictive, ruthless, and unfair as men. People in legitimate authority positions have power over others; their sex has little bearing on this reality.

A fifth criticism of feminism comes from within feminist sociological theory itself. The fact that there is such a great variety of sociological feminist theories (for example, liberal, Marxist, radical, socialist, and postmodern) represents a clear lack of consensus among feminists as to the best means to go about fighting sexism, discrimination, and oppression. If, and when, feminists can provide a united front, they will have developed a legitimate sociological theory. When they can provide a clear answer to questions such as "How are women to be paid for housework?" and "How are single moms and single dads to paid for housework?" they will advance a legitimate sociological theory.

Feminist thought is very relevant to contemporary society. Feminists have brought attention to many past injustices, especially in the workplace. Despite the enlightenment of most males, there are still many who hold onto the old patriarchal belief that a woman's place is in the house. At the 2000 Aspen U.S. Comedy Festival, comedian Jerry Lewis was quoted as saying "A woman doing comedy doesn't offend me, but sets me back a bit. I, as a viewer, have trouble with it. I think of her as a producing machine that brings babies in the world" (*Buffalo News*, 2000). Feminists have drawn our attention to such institutional sexist practices as the glass ceiling, the idea that women are promoted close enough to see the top positions (through the glass) but that a barrier (the ceiling) prevents her from reaching the top. (It should be noted that the glass ceiling applies to men as well, as exemplified by the class action suit by 115 men against the Girl Scouts because qualified men were denied promotion owing to their sex.) Feminists have also fought for equal pay for equal work in the job market. In most industries this is a reality. It is rare to find a case where a male and a female doing the exact same job with the exact same experience are not paid the same. Laws have been passed to enforce this equality. Some people cite statistics such as a woman makes 76 cents for every dollar a man makes as evidence of salary inequity, but this represents the misuse of statistics. The fact is that women are found at lower-paid jobs and therefore when wages for all jobs are averaged, the average male is making more money than the average female. Many jobs that women have are part-time jobs by choice. As women have increased their levels of education (the truest indicator of economic success) their position in the socioeconomic system has also risen.

Sexism and discrimination exist in nearly all social institutions. Religion is a long-time perpetuator of gender inequality. The Catholic church forbids females from being priests. The Southern Baptists, at a convention held in 1998, reaffirmed their gender inequality status by dictating that "a wife is to submit graciously to the servant leadership of her husband" (*Los Angeles Times*, 1998). In addition, the media continue to bombard girls with unrealistic images of beauty. A few supermodels grace the covers of nearly every magazine on the newsstands, and young girls grow up thinking that if they don't look like these models something is wrong.

Every individual can look at his or her own family environment and determine whether he or she was raised with gender-specific ideals of what is appropriate for boys and girls. If a boy has a later curfew than his sister, the sister has been discriminated against. The social institution of sport was a long-time promoter of gender inequality. The passage of Title IX of the Education Amendment in 1972 mandated that any high school or college that receives federal aid, must provide equal funding (what is actually used is equality of playing opportunities, scholarships, and other athletic resources in proportion to male and female enrollment) for male and female sports programs. Although Title IX has come under attack recently because of the large number of men's programs "cut" from school budgets, it is directly responsible for a dramatic increase in the number of female athletes. Before Title IX was enacted in 1972, fewer than 30,000 women participated in intercollegiate sports programs governed by the National Collegiate Athletic Association (NCAA); by 2000, nearly 151,000 women were NCAA athletes. At the high school level, the number of girls in sports increased from 294,000 to nearly 2.8 million during the same time period. The fight for gender equality in sports has been quite successful.

The great discrepancy in the fight for female empowerment is illustrated in such a mundane topic as a beauty contest. In the United States, many feminists view the beauty contest, especially the swimsuit round, as demeaning to women. In October 2002, the first Miss Tibet beauty contest was held. Only five of the original thirty entrants remained after extreme pressure forced the others to quit. The Tibetan Women's Association and the female deputy speaker of the parliament-in-exile, Dolma Gyari, both favored the contest, saying it would help Tibetan women gain confidence. Thus, for Tibetan women, beauty contests are viewed as a way to demonstrate the power of women in a society where women wear mostly ankle-length dresses and long-sleeved blouses, while in the United States, many women's organizations view such pageants as demeaning and a variation of objectification.

Giving a voice to women remains feminist sociological theory's greatest contribution to the field of sociology specifically and society in general.

10

Critical Theory

Critical theory is the school of thought that emerged from the work of German theorists collectively referred to as the Frankfurt School. Centered on the work of Jurgen Habermas, critical theory started in 1923 with the founding of the Institute for Social Research at the Frankfurt School in Germany. Funded by private money, the Institute enjoyed considerable autonomy and developed with minimal external pressure from the more formal University of Frankfurt (Held, 1980). German ex-patriot Hermann Weil, who lived in Argentina, was persuaded by his son Felix, who obtained a doctorate in political science from Frankfurt, to establish the endowment for an independent research institute to study Marxism and anti-Semitism (Adams and Sydie, 2001).

THE ROOTS OF CRITICAL THEORY

The roots of critical theory are directly in the creation of the Institute for Social Research in Frankfurt and a number of social thinkers who promoted the idealism of Karl Marx.

The Institute for Social Research

The institute was the first Marxist-oriented research school in Europe. Its members attempted to revise both Marx's critique of capitalism and the idea that revolution was the best way to change the social and political structures that had evolved since Marx's death (Bronner and Kellner, 1989). As a result, these social thinkers developed a "critical theory" of society. These German scholars initially used the term *kritische Theorie* to designate a specific approach to interpreting Marxist theory, "but the term has taken on new meanings in the interim and can be neither exclusively identified with the Marxist tradition from which it has become increasingly distinct nor reserved exclusively to the Frankfurt School, given extensive new variation outside the original German context" (Morrow, 1994:6–7).

The institute, under Carl Grunberg's leadership (1923–1929), was the starting point of the Austro-Marxist tradition. Marxism was made the inspiration and theoretical basis of the institute's program (Held, 1980). Under the directorship of Grunberg, the institute was characterized by a rather orthodox scientific Marxism, but this approach was abandoned when Max Horkheimer assumed control in 1930. Horkheimer and his inner circle of scholars adopted a more philosophical, less dogmatic Marxism that was open to diverse intellectual currents (Jay, 1973). The most active years of the institute (1930–1944) coincided with the prominence of Nazism and fascism. The dilemma of the first generation of critical theorists was "to reconcile Marx's emancipatory dream with the stark reality of modern society as conceptualized by Max Weber. . . . There seemed little reason to be optimistic about developing a theoretically informed program for freeing people from unnecessary domination. The defeat of the left-wing working-class movements, the rise of fascism in the aftermath of World War I, and the degeneration of the Russian Revolution into Stalinism had, by the 1930s, made it clear that Marx's analysis needed drastic revision" (Turner, 2003:201). Max Horkheimer, Theodor Adorno, and others who tried to study the power of the masses were put under restraints by Hitler's ascent to power. Anti-Semitism was increasingly evident during the 1930s in Germany, and the Jewish members of the institute were forced into exile. "The Institute relocated to Columbia University in 1934 under the directorship of Max Horkheimer. Thus, the 'revolutionary and Marxist' research Institute resettled in the 'center of the capitalist world', New York City" (Adams and Sydie, 2001:396)

Emigration of the prominent German thinkers of the Frankfurt School to the United States would lead to the first usage of the concept *critical theory*:

The term *critical theory* itself was only coined in 1937, after the majority of the Institute's members had already emigrated to the United States following the triumph of Hitler. The concept was initially a type of code which, while differentiating its adherents from prevailing forms of orthodoxy, also tended to veil their radical commitments in an environment that was hostile to

anything remotely associated with Marxism. But the term stuck and soon was used to encompass and define the general theory of contemporary society associated with Max Horkheimer, Herbert Marcuse, T. W. Adorno, Leo Lowenthal, and Frederick Pollock—as well as with Jurgen Habermas and others who later undertook to continue the tradition. (Bronner and Kellner, 1989:1)

Max Horkheimer, Friedrich Pollock, and Theodor Adorno represented the institute during the years of exile and its initial reconstitution in New York. In the 1940s, the three theorists went to Los Angeles and remained there until their return to Frankfurt in 1950. Other institute exiles found positions elsewhere (Adams and Sydie, 2001). By 1953 the institute had been reestablished in Germany. In the atmosphere of postwar reconstruction and the cold war, many key intellectuals from Germany's past were subject to attack in the press and in academia because of their continual support of Marxist doctrines (Held, 1980). Most members of the Frankfurt School believed that the individual is enmeshed in a world where capital is highly concentrated and where the economy and the polity are increasingly interlocked.

A number of specific theorists are associated with the formation of critical theory. Steven Smith believed that Hegel was a central figure, while other reviewers of critical theory generally agree that Gyorgy (Georg) Lukacs, Max Horkheimer, and Theodor Adorno are the most important scholars who directly influenced the intellectual development of critical theory and subsequent work by Herbert Marcuse and Jurgen Habermas.

G. W. F. Hegel (1931–)

Steven Smith (1987) stated that "Hegel is often regarded as a central figure in the development of the school of modern Critical Theory. Yet while his contribution to this school is often acknowledged, his own practice of critique is seldom given the attention it deserves" (p. 99). Hegel never described himself or his work as critical, but in his *The Phenomenology of Mind* (1931), he revealed a conception of critical theorizing that would have at least two important influences on the development of critical theory:

First, whereas Kant meant by *critique* an inquiry into the nature and limits of rationality as such, for Hegel it took the form of an internal or immanent examination of the various sources of deception, illusion, and distortion that the mind undergoes in its journey to Absolute Knowledge. Such an activity is critical, or in Hegel's term "negative," precisely because it entails a conception of liberation from those historical sources of domination and coercion. Like Marx, Nietzsche, and, later, Freud, Hegel sought to free human agents not only from the coercive illusions that inhibit their capacities for free thought and action, but from the forms of social life within which those coercive illusions thrive and find expression. Philosophical critique necessarily spills over into social theory. Second, underlying the Hegelian conception of critique is the belief that human history expresses an immanent telos the aim of which is the liberation of both the individual and the species from a system of constraints that are at least partially imposed by the minds of the agents to whom the theory is addressed. Hegel's argument depends upon the assumption that human agents are driven by a powerful common interest in freedom that persists through the interplay of their passions and actions. (Smith, 1987:99–100)

Questioning what is deemed "absolute knowledge" and realizing that human history is the result of a struggle between interest groups fall within both the Marxist tradition and the critical paradigm.

Antonio (1983) explained that "critical theory is based on the meta-assumptions that derive from Hegel's dialectics, modified by Marx's materialist critique. Hegel's philosophy, which stresses immanent principles of contradiction, change, and movement, constitutes an alternative to the formal and static nature of Kantianism. . . . For Hegel, the nature of being is characterized by the subject continuously creating, negating, and recreating itself and its object world. Through *labor,* the subject not only makes history, but also produces a movement in history away from 'self-estrangement' toward 'freedom'" (pp. 343–344).

Georg (Györgby) Lukacs (1885–1971)

Lukacs was a part of the early Frankfurt School. In his 1923 publication *History and Class Consciousness* (1923), Lukacs argued that subjectivity is "annihilated" by "commodity production." The capitalistic system creates a "phantom objectivity" that undermines class consciousness. "In his view, emancipatory change does not automatically follow material evolution. Material conditions make revolution possible, but its realization depends upon the 'free-action of the proletariat itself.' Lukacs' analyses of alienation, commodity fetishism, subjectivity, consciousness, and spontaneous action constitute the theoretical bridge to critical theory; but on the way over, the Frankfurt school discarded other key elements of his approach" (Antonio, 1983:328). Lukacs had come to emphasize the importance Marx placed on the fetishism of commodities, a condition caused when the worker assumes that the commodity produced has an objective quality of its own, rather than realizing the commodity is a result of the worker's labor. "Lukacs' interpretation of Marxism as a dialectical critique of reification placed the problem of ideology to the forefront of attention" (Bailey, 1994:14). According to Jonathan Turner (2003), Lukacs blended Marx's ideas of fetishism of commodities with Weber's belief that rationality is penetrating more spheres of modern life. Combining Weber's and Marx's ideas, Lukacs came to believe that as traditional societies change "there is less reliance on moral standards and processes of communication to achieve societal integration; instead, there is more use of money, markets, and rational calculations. As a result, relations are coordinated by exchange values and by people's perceptions of one another as 'things'" (Turner, 2003:202).

Lukacs's *History and Class Consciousness* (1923), and Karl Korsch's *Marxism and Philosophy* (1971) were written as

> Contributions to the widespread European debates about the "crisis of Marxism" in the early twenties. In the aftermath of World War I, the European socialist movements entered a period of ferment and critical reflection. The experiences of the preceding decade, which had included the capitulation of the German Social Democratic Party to the war effort, the Bolshevik success in Russia and failed revolutionary attempts in Germany, Austria, Hungary and Italy, all seemed to demand a thorough rethinking of the prevailing forms of theory and practice. Lukacs and Korsch had been active participants in the Communist parties of Hungary and Germany respectively, and both were concerned to draw the essential lessons from those experiences. (Bailey, 1994:7–8)

Both Lukacs and Korsch were singled out for official denunciation at the Fifth World Congress of the Third International, held in Moscow in 1924, because they questioned prevailing communist sentiments within the party. Lukacs had challenged the philosophical and political assumptions of orthodox dialectical materialism held by party members (Hardt, 1986). By the late 1920s, Soviet Marxism had been transformed into dialectical materialism (Marxism-Leninism), which increasingly contained ideological elements contradictory to Marx's original historical materialism (Antonio, 1983:330; Ulmen, 1978). In short, "both Lukacs and Korsch fell victim to the 'Bolshevization' of the European Communist parties in the aftermath of the Russian Revolution" (Bailey, 1994:9). However, "the influence of *History and Class Consciousness* was nonetheless evident in many essays published during the 1930s by Horkheimer,

Marcuse, and Adorno in the Institute's journal, the *Zeitschrift für Sozialforschung*" (Bailey, 1994:22).

Max Horkheimer (1895–1973)

Horkheimer attended the universities of Munich, Freiburg, and then Frankfurt, where he earned his doctorate in 1922 with a thesis on Kant. He became a lecturer in 1925 at the Institute for Social Research, and in 1929 he was appointed to the new chair of social philosophy at the institute. A year later, he became director of the institute (Adams and Sydie, 2001). Under Horkheimer, the institute was oriented to developing social theory on an interdisciplinary basis. He wanted theory to benefit from both the reflective capacity of philosophy and the rigorous procedures of the individual sciences. From his inaugural address onward, he stressed the necessity of forging a new unity between philosophy and science, science and criticism, fact and value. For Horkheimer, society was a totality which is "continuously restructuring itself." (p. 179) As a result, the idea of a social absolute—a complete or perfect state of social phenomena—is criticized. All factors in the total societal process are held to be in "the process of movement," including the relation of "parts to whole" (Held, 1980:181).

In the 1930s Max Horkheimer found himself in an intellectual milieu that was marked by a sharp swing away from previously dominant forms of neo-Kantianism and toward pronounced forms of antirationalism. Horkheimer, in his 1934 discussion of "The Rationalism Debate in Contemporary Philosophy," endorsed the idea that there is no absolute truth of reality but warned against extreme antirationalism represented by *Lebensphilosophie* and existentialism (Hoy and McCarthy, 1995). Horkheimer explained that

> critical theory required more than the simple invocation of concrete-sounding but no less essentialistic, determinations of this sort. It called for a continuation-through-transformation of the critique of reason, a

materialist account of its nature, conditions, and limits. If the subject of knowledge and action could no longer be viewed as solitary, disengaged, and disembodied, and if the structures of reason could no longer be viewed as timeless, necessary, and unconditioned, then the transformation called for carried the critique of reason in the direction of sociohistorical inquiry. (Hoy and McCarthy, 1995:9)

Horkheimer was also concerned about the increasingly influential sociology of knowledge being developed at the time by Karl Mannheim. "The appearance of Karl Mannheim's *Ideology and Utopia* in 1929 presented an important challenge to the Marxian theory of ideology. . . . By linking the ideological distortion of thought to social position, Marxism had raised doubts about the very possibility of its opponents ever attaining an adequate knowledge of social reality" (Bailey, 1994:1). Horkheimer and other members of the Frankfurt School believed that Mannheim's extension of the concept of ideology to encompass all forms of social thought had deprived it of all critical content, by severing it from any definite relation to a concrete historical conception of truth. In short, "Horkheimer judged Mannheim's sociology of knowledge to be practically, no less than theoretically, wrong-headed" (Hoy and McCarthy, 1995:11). Consequently, the Frankfurt School paid close attention to Mannheim's work and subjected it to close scrutiny in order to distinguish it from its own critical theory of society (Bailey, 1994:1–2). Horkheimer's 1937 essay "Traditional and Critical Theory" constitutes the institute's basic manifesto of its theoretical stand and at the same time distinguishes itself from the ideas of Mannheim. In this essay, Horkheimer emphasized a dialectical reinterpretation of Marx's critique of political economy as providing the basic analytical framework for the development of critical theory. During the early 1940s, however, the Frankfurt School's critical theory of society would begin to undergo

important changes in orientation (Bailey, 1994:29).

Horkheimer maintained a commitment to the idea that there are no general criteria for critical theory as a whole, for such criteria always depend on a repetition of events and thus on a self-reproducing totality. Critical theory depends on particular historical conditions. Horkheimer maintained that there is a hiatus between concept and object, and between word and thing. These concepts are interdependent but irreducible aspects of the total societal process. Thus, critical theory aims to assess "the breach between ideas and reality." The method of procedure is immanent criticism (Held, 1980:183).

Theodor Wiesengrund-Adorno (1903–1969)

Theodor Adorno was born in Frankfurt. His father was a successful Jewish merchant, and his mother had had a successful singing career prior to her marriage. The name Adorno was from her side of the family (Adams and Sydie, 2001). Martin Jay (1973) explained that some of the members of the institute felt that there were too many Jewish-sounding names on the roster, so Adorno dropped the Wiesengrund part of his name while he was in the United States. Adorno earned his doctorate at the University of Frankfurt in 1924 after completing his thesis on Husserl's phenomenology. He became associated with the institute in 1931 and a full member in 1938.

Adorno attempted to establish a "critical social consciousness, (p. 213)" especially in terms of how a philosophy expresses the structure of society. Adorno believed that art expresses social contradictions and antinomies in a mediated form, and so, too, philosophy embodies similar objective structures. Just as forms and pieces of art involve critical perspectives, so could particular philosophies. Adorno's goal was to show how the history of mind—which he conceived of as the attempt of the subject to gain distance from the object—continually reveals the "superiority of objectivity. (p. 213)" Adorno argued that objects exist for us through conceptuality (Held, 1980). "Adorno's complex, aphoristic, and fragmented style is consistent with his view that the language within which we must think and work is not a transparent mirror of reality. What the plain speech of easy and efficacious everyday communication reproduces is the illusion of social harmony and intelligibility. Adorno's highly self-conscious constructions are designed to disrupt the disguised interest in smooth social functioning presupposed by most verbal interchange" (Hoy and McCarthy, 1995:132).

In *Negative Dialectics* (1973) Adorno insisted that the dialectic approach is not a middle point between absolutism and relativism. He was also against the idea that critical theory should merely criticize one point of view in favor of another. "This response will not work if the principle and its negation

Theodor Adorno, German critical theorist in the "Frankfurt School" tradition.

Source: A/P Wide World Photos

are the only alternatives, and if a double negation formally entails the affirmative" (Hoy and McCarthy, 1995:132). Furthermore, attacking someone else's position as relative does not prove that one's own position is any less relative. As Turner (2003) explained, "the goal of negative dialectics was to sustain a constant critique of ideas, conceptions, and conditions. This critique could not only by itself change anything, for it operates only on the plane of ideas and concepts. But it can keep ideological dogmatisms from obscuring conditions that might eventually allow emancipatory action" (p. 203).

Adorno and Horkheimer shared many ideas and collaborated on a number of works. Adorno was more philosophical but also more research-oriented than Horkheimer. But Adorno was also pessimistic about the chances of critical theory's making great changes in society. Even so, his essays were designed to expose patterns of recognized and unrecognized domination of individuals by social and psychological forces (Turner, 2003:203).

Defining Critical Theory

There is no clear-cut definition of critical theory. "Even a casual glance at general portrayals (Jay, 1973; Held, 1980) or at collections of essays on the topic (Arato and Gebhardt, 1978), reveals a stunning range of methods, theories, and substantive analyses. Critical theory is immune to brief summary, and even basic familiarity requires effort that few nonspecialists are willing to expend" (Antonio, 1983:326).

The term *critical theory* is itself an unfortunate one for it is confused with literary criticism, and a number of other approaches to social theory could be considered "critical" in some sense. Marxist theory is a critical approach to the study of society, feminist theory is a constant criticism of the perceived male-dominated society, and even positivist researchers make a claim to criticizing the existing understanding of social reality. Thus, to claim to be critical of social conceptions is nothing new or unique. Regardless, a number of social thinkers are drawn to the critical perspective because of a growing dissatisfaction with dominant views of understanding reality.

> Critical theory offers a multidisciplinary approach to society which combines perspectives drawn from political economy, sociology, cultural theory, philosophy, anthropology, and history. It thus overcomes the fragmentation endemic to established academic disciplines in order to address issues of broader interest. . . . Critical theory maintains a nondogmatic perspective which is sustained by an interest in emancipation from all forms of oppression, as well as by a commitment to freedom, happiness, and a rational ordering of society. Eschewing divisions between the humanities and the social sciences, it thus sets forth a normative social theory that seeks a connection with empirical analyses of the contemporary world. (Bronner and Kellner, 1989:1–2)

In this regard, critical theory is always subject to change. And yet, it remains fundamentally inspired by the dialectical tradition of Hegel and Marx.

Held (1980:41–42) argued that there are six Marxian tenets associated with critical theory:

1. We live in a society dominated by the capitalist mode of production, and a society based on exchange principles of value and profit.
2. The commodity character of products is not simply determined by their exchange, but by their being abstractly exchanged (through labor).
3. Capitalist society ensures fetishism and reification.
4. Capitalism is not a harmonious social world. Contradictions between socially generated illusions (ideology) and actuality (performance, effects) lead to potential crisis.
5. The free market is progressively replaced by the oligarchies and monopolistic mass production of standardized goods.
6. The progressive rise in the organic composition of capital—the amount of fixed capital per worker—exacerbates the inherently unstable accumulation process. In order to sustain this process, its protagonists utilize all means available—including imperialist expansion and war.

Members of the institute maintained that a breakdown of capitalism was "objectively necessary" and "exactly calculable." (Held, 1980:42)

Critical theorizing involves a critical assessment of capitalism, disparages the optimism of the Enlightenment, and views the use of science for constructing a better society as naive, illusional, or even harmful. Most critical theorists see "objective" science as an extension of capitalism. "Postmodern" society is also viewed in a negative light (Turner, 2003). The disdain that critical theorists have for science comes from their assumption that dominant political and social interests shape the development of science and technology and their belief that science and technology is not fully neutral with respect to human values because they inevitably mediate social relations. In other words, science and technology possess ideological implications. (Morrow, 1994:63)

HERBERT MARCUSE (1898–1979)

Herbert Marcuse was born in Berlin to a prosperous Jewish family. After serving in the German army in World War I, Marcuse became associated with the Social Democratic Party and the revolutionary Soldiers Council in Berlin. In 1919, he left the Social Democratic Party in protest over what he perceived as the betrayal of the proletariat (Jay, 1973). Marcuse then went on to study philosophy at the universities of Berlin and Freiburg. He earned his doctorate in 1923 with a thesis on literature. After spending six years as a bookseller and publisher in Berlin, Marcuse returned to Freiburg in 1929 to study with the philosophers Edmund Husserl and Martin

Heidegger, whose right-wing views clashed with his own Marxist views. Despite contradictory philosophical views Marcuse became a member of the institute in 1933 on Husserl's recommendation (Adams and Sydie, 2001:398). Furthermore, Marcuse maintained throughout his life that Heidegger was the greatest teacher and thinker whom he had ever encountered (Kellner, 2003).

When the Nazis came into power, and upon Heidegger's advice, Marcuse fled Germany to Geneva, Paris, and finally New York City. Marcuse became a colleague of Horkheimer at the Institute for Social Research—which had emigrated from Germany to New York, at Columbia University—from 1934 to 1940. In December 1942 Marcuse joined the Office of War Information as a senior analyst in the Bureau of Intelligence. In March 1943 he joined the Office of Secret Services (OSS) and identified Nazi and anti-Nazi people and groups and helped to draw up a plan for the "denazifaction" of Germany. After the OSS dissolved in 1951, Marcuse taught at Columbia (1952–1953) and Harvard (1954–1955) and then became a professor of political science at Brandeis (1958–1965). While at Columbia and Harvard, Marcuse began research which led him to the writing of *Soviet Marxism.* In 1967 be began teaching at the University of California. Marcuse gained world status during the 1960s as a philosopher, social theorist, and political activist. Through his writings, travels, and media exposure he became known as the father of the New Left (Kellner, 1984). He tirelessly propagated his critiques of contemporary society and demands for radical social change and attracted a group of devoted followers. "Critiques and commentaries on Herbert Marcuse abound and they abound because his works got hooked up with the global student-youth revolt as have those of no other contemporary Western theorist" (Breines, 1970:1).

Among Marcuse's more significant publications in social theory and political sociology are *Reason and Revolution* (1941), *Eros and Civilization* (1955), *Soviet Marxism* (1958), *One-Dimensional Man* (1964), *A Critique of Pure Tolerance* (1965), *Negations: Essays in Critical Theory* (1968a), *An Essay on Liberation* (1969), *Counterrevolution and Revolt* (1972), *Studies in Critical Philosophy* (1973), and *The Aesthetic Dimension* (1978).

Marcuse shared Adorno's concern about the critique and transcendence of reification and fetishism. In a vein similar to that of Horkheimer, he stressed the unconcluded nature of the dialectic, a potential in humans that is yet to be realized, the centrality of human practice in the constitution and assessment of knowledge, and the importance of interdisciplinary approaches to the comprehension of the social totality. However, despite these overlaps, there are also major differences in their positions (Held, 1980). Marcuse's writings engage more fully than those of Horkheimer and Adorno with the interests of classical Marxism. Politics plays a key, if not central, role in his life and work. His career represents a constant attempt to examine, defend, and reconstruct the Marxist enterprise. He was preoccupied by the fate of revolution, the potentiality for socialism, and the defense of utopian objectives. The goals of his critical approach to society are the emancipation of consciousness, the nurturing of a decentralized political movement, and the reconciliation of humanity and nature (Held, 1980).

Critical Theory

Marcuse did not define explicitly his crucial and critical concepts, nor did he really define *critical theory* itself. Instead, he used abstractions to described critical theory. For example, critical theory is a process of "bringing to consciousness potentialities that have emerged within the maturing historical situation" (Marcuse, 1968a:158). Critical theory is a theory which was "confronted with the presence of social forces . . . in the established society which move . . . toward more rational and freer institutions" (Marcuse, 1964:254). And it is a theory guided by "political practice" (Marcuse, 1969:5). Marcuse believed that "one key task of philosophy is to criticize other philosophy, not only—even if most importantly—in the interests of truth but also because, whether philosophers will it so or not, philosophical ideas are influential in social, moral, and political life" (MacIntyre, 1970a:1).

Marcuse's critical theory was influenced by Hegel and Marx. "For Marcuse, a critical turning point in the history of philosophy is Hegel's transvaluation of the concept 'reason.' He sees Hegel as the thinker who projected reason from the subjective sphere in which he found it to its proper role as 'a critical tribunal' in and of the world" (Bleich, 1977:5–6). Marcuse placed great value on reason. "In summarizing Hegel's objection to Kant, Marcuse argues that if 'things-in-themselves' are beyond the capacity of reason, reason will remain a mere subjective principle without relevance to the objective structure of reality" (Bleich, 1977:9). Furthermore, Marcuse (1989) stated:

Reason is the fundamental category of philosophical thought, the only one by means of which it has bound itself to human destiny. Philosophy wanted to discover the ultimate and most general grounds of Being. Under the name of reason it conceived the idea of an authentic Being in which all significant antitheses (of subject and object, essence and appearance, thought and being) were reconciled. Connected with this idea was the conviction that what exists is not immediately and already rational but must rather be brought to reason. Reason represents the highest potentiality of man and of existence; the two belong together. For when reason is accorded the status of substance, this means that at its highest level, as authentic reality, the world no longer stands opposed to the rational thought of men as mere material objectivity (*Gegenstandlichkeit*). Rather, it is now comprehended by thought and defined as concept (*Begriff*).

That is, the external, antithetical character of material objectivity is overcome in a process through which the identity of subject and object is established as the rational, conceptual structure that is common to both. (p. 58)

Marcuse's study of Hegel contributed to Hegel's renaissance, which was taking place in Europe during the 1930s.

Like all first-generation critical theorists, Marcuse was influenced by the ideas of Karl Marx. Marcuse himself insisted that the primary inspiration and source of critical theory comes from Marx. Interestingly, Marcuse published the first major review (in 1933) of Marx's recently discovered and published *Economic and Philosophical Manuscripts of 1844*. His review of Marx's work revealed Marcuse to be an astute student of Germany philosophy (Kellner, 2003). "Even in works where Marx is never mentioned, such as *Eros and Civilization*, or in those where traditional Marxism is radically questioned, such as *One-Dimensional Man*, Marcuse is using Marxian concepts and methods to expand Marxian theory, to overcome its limitations and to question aspects that he believes should be revised or rejected. On the whole, Marcuse's version of Marxism consists of a series of revisions and renewals of Marxian theory that provides a theoretical project seeking to comprehend and transform contemporary society" (Kellner, 1984:5). As Marcuse (1989) explained:

Critical Theory of society is essentially linked with materialism. . . . The theory of society is an economic, not philosophical, system. There are two basic elements linking materialism to correct social theory: concern with human happiness, and the conviction that it can be attained only through a transformation of the material conditions of existence. The actual course of the transformation and the fundamental measures to be taken in order to arrive at a rational organization of society are prescribed by analysis of economic and political conditions in the given historical situation. (pp. 58–59)

Marcuse praised Marxist materialism because "Marxist materialism both envisaged a contrast between what man happens to be at the moment and what man could become, and also distinguished between how things really are in a capitalist society and the false consciousness that men in such a society possess, it restored the concept of essence to a central place" (MacIntyre, 1970a:8).

Combining the thoughts of Hegel and Marx, Marcuse concluded that history is the arena in which humans seek the freedom to manifest universal rationality (Bleich, 1977). Lipshires (1974) noted that "following Marx, Marcuse argues that the material and ideal coexist with neither having priority over the other. While 'there exists an objective world of nature transcendentally beyond consciousness' (as Hegel would agree), that world cannot be assigned an ontological character as an infrastructure that determines in any way either human nature or human history" (p. 3).

Marx was a critic of society and proposed courses of action to change it. However, Marcuse felt that Marxism had neither absorbed the most advanced currents of contemporary thought nor kept pace with changes in contemporary society (Kellner, 1984). Marcuse's critical theory had roots in Marxism, but his reconstruction of it led to the uniqueness of Marcuse's thinking. In short, "for Marcuse, Marxism is a method of analysis and instrument of critique and social transformation and is not a dogma or system of absolute knowledge" (Kellner, 1984:9).

Technological Rationality

In *One-Dimensional Man* (1964), Marcuse extended Weber's idea of rationalization by employing the concept of *technological rationality*. Weber had pointed out that Western society had come to be dominated by science and the "iron cage" of bureaucracy.

"The rationalization process not only manifested itself in the rational behavior of individuals in bureaucratic settings, but also referred to their method of thinking. Instrumental rationality, a calculating and *means*-oriented mode of thought, had gradually come to replace substantive rationality, or thought dealing with morality, with the validity of the *ends* of action" (Farganis, 2000:384). Marcuse argued that modern industrial society was dominated by a technological rationality, with the working middle class as its vocal supporter and defender.

Among the many shortcomings of Marx's theory was his failure to foresee the development of the middle class. The workers of industrial societies enjoy benefits that were never realized at any other time in history. Technology created affluence, and this freedom from material want led to a relatively happy and materialistically satisfied middle class. When workers are satisfied, their reasons for dissent and protest are eliminated and they become passive members of the dominating system. Marcuse was concerned that the cost of material satisfaction was the loss of individual freedoms and liberties. "The forms of consumption in an affluent society have, according to Marcuse, a twofold effect. They satisfy material needs which might otherwise lead to protest; and they foster identification with the established order. . . . Moreover the conditions of work in an advanced industrial society tend to render the worker passive. The rhythm of production in a semi-automated factory, the nature of skilled work, the increase in the proportion of white-collar workers all destroy any consciousness of being in opposition to the work system" (MacIntyre, 1970b:64–65). Thus, Marcuse was making two claims. First, the workers of industrial society are suffering from false consciousness. Second, the workers should not be happy with material satisfaction but should be striving for some unidentified (by Marcuse) nonmaterial satisfaction. Marcuse ignored the fact that the history of human kind *is* the pursuit of material success.

Marcuse insisted that modern industrial society produces a "surplus repression" by imposing socially unnecessary labor, unnecessary restrictions on sexuality, and a social system organized around profit and exploitation. Marcuse argued for an end of such "repression" and promoted the creation of a new society. Marcuse believed that industrial society creates false needs, which integrate individuals into the existing system of production and consumption (Kellner, 2003). Technology, mass media, popular culture, and leisure systems are all guilty of being modes of thought that reif the existing social structures.

One-Dimensional Man was criticized by a number of theorists with various political and theoretical commitments. But it also drew the attention of many who identified themselves as the New Left.

The New Left

One-Dimensional Man (1964) was followed by a series of books and articles which articulated New Left politics and critiques of capitalist societies (Kellner, 2003). "Repressive Tolerance" (1965) attacked liberalism and those who refused to take a stand during the protests and controversies of the 1960s. Marcuse's *Essay of Liberation* (1969) praised the work of such diverse radical groups as the hippies and Vietcong sympathizers. *Counterrevolution and Revolt* (1972) describes the social system's predictable movement toward normality—the lack of protests and social uncertainty. In fact, Brandeis had refused to renew Marcuse's teaching contract in 1965 because of his radical stand. He would move on to teach at the University of California at La Jolla, where he remained until his retirement.

Marcuse's radical writings were a perfect match for his place in time. The idealistic 1950s had ended, and the turbulent 1960s provided a breeding ground for a new generation of idealistic radicals. "Of course the new radicals had obvious limitations: they possessed no clear program, no viable organization, not even a formidable constituency. And they were innocent of the disastrous potentialities of moral vision insufficiently tempered by political realism" (Clecak, 1973:233). After a decade of hope, vision was modified by experience, and the hopes of a generation of radicals soured. Marcuse was looked upon as the guru of the New Left and enjoyed his greatest influence throughout the 1970s as he gave lectures and advice to the student radicals who remained around the world. Marcuse used the media to spread the word of Marxian theory, revolutionary vision, and libertarian socialism—ideals that he remained committed to until his death.

Revolution

Entrenched in the Marxist tradition is the necessity for revolution. Marxists believe that revolution is necessary to free humans from the negative grip of capitalism. In "Re-examination of the Concept of Revolution" (1968b) Marcuse wrote:

> The concept of revolution in Marxian theory telescopes an entire historical period: the final stage of capitalism, the transitional period of proletarian doctorship, and the initial stage of socialism. It is in a strict sense a historical concept, projecting actual tendencies in the society; and it is a dialectical concept, projecting the counter-tendencies within the respective historical period, in as much as they are inherent in this period. These tendencies and counter-tendencies are manifestations of which Marxian theory and practice themselves are essential elements. Marxian theory itself is a power in the historical struggle, and to the degree to which its concepts, "translated" into practice, become forces of resistance, change and reconstruction; they are subject to the vicissitudes of this struggle, which they reflect and comprehend, but do not dominate. (p. 17)

Marcuse (1968b) argued that the Marxian concept of revolution implies continuity in change: development of the productive forces contained by capitalism, taking over of the technology and of the technical apparatus by the new producers (p. 18). Marcuse proposed a global revolution where capitalism is replaced by socialism. The revolutionists, or the character of the opposition, that would challenge corporate capitalism are concentrated at two opposite poles of society: the ghetto population and the middle-class intelligentsia, especially the students (Marcuse, 1968). But these two groups do not make up the majority of society, and Marcuse recognized that they would face hostility and resentment from organized labor and corporate entities. Marcuse was concerned that such counterforces could strike a fatal blow against revolutionary hopefuls. "The awareness of this possibility should strengthen and solidify the opposition in all its manifestations—it is the only hope" (Marcuse, 1968b:26).

The Sexual Revolution

Marcuse was in favor of the sexual revolution. For one thing, it implied a type of revolution against oppressive social control apparatuses (as represented by Marcuse's concept of *surplus repression*), and for another, sexual freedom allowed individuals to pursue happiness—and perhaps reach their full human potential. Marcuse was against those who tried to impose sexual codes of conduct on others in the name of religion (transcendental ethical systems) or especially those who would invade the realm of individual privacy. "But Marcuse is no less the foe of all who reduce the definition of human liberation to the dimension of pure sexuality, a reduction which leads in the end to the simplistic equation that unhampered sexual intercourse (on- or off-stage, in public or private) is identical with freedom" (Ober, 1970:101–102). Marcuse, then, was against both Puritan taboos and the wanton sexual abandon which emerged in the 1960s.

Eros and Civilization (1966) contains influences from Freud and psychoanalysis. As early as the 1930s Marcuse considered bodily repression, and in particular sexual repression, one of the most important attributes of the exploitive social order. He was more sensitive to the sexual dimension of repression than either his orthodox Marxist forbears or his revisionist contemporaries (Robinson, 1969). For Marcuse, sexual repression was more than just "another" evil of capitalism; it represented the bourgeois concept of love. "Under the capitalist order, Marcuse argued, sexual love was stripped of its playfulness and spontaneity (qualities which were still preserved, if only vicariously, in the physical artistry one encounters in circus and variety shows). Love became a matter of duty and habit, carefully circumscribed by the ideology of monogamic fidelity. Its sole function, beyond perpetuating the species, was the hygienic one of maintaining the physical and mental health necessary to the continued functioning of the economic apparatus" (Robinson, 1969:189). The workers were allowed to have sex only in the brief period of free time allotted from their commitments to provide labor for the bourgeois.

In his chapter "On Hedonism" in *Negations*, Marcuse (1968a) condemned the bourgeois era as an attempt to isolate individuals from their natural drives (a Freudian perspective). "The individual appears as an ego isolated from and against others in its drives, thoughts, and interests. This isolating individuation is overcome and a common world constructed through the reduction of concrete individuality to the subject of mere thought, the rational ego. . . . The gratification of his wants and capacities, his happiness, appears as an arbitrary and subjective element that cannot be brought into consonance with the universal validity of the highest principle of human action" (pp. 159–160). Marcuse's concern about humans' attaining "happiness" is at odds with Hegel, as Marcuse himself recognized, and also with Marx. "It is perhaps because of these differences that Marcuse has found it possible to be in many respects a Freudian as well as a Marxist when most Marxists have been extremely critical of and antagonistic to psychoanalysis" (MacIntyre, 1970a:43). The convergence of Freudian and Marxist ideas could be summed up in the idea that in order for individuals to reach their full human potential, they must be happy.

Throughout the 1960s and 1970s, Marcuse was one of the most influential radical theorists. Since his death in 1979, Marcuse's influence has been steadily declining.

JURGEN HABERMAS (1929–)

Jurgen Habermas was born in Gummers-bach, near Düsseldorf, in 1929. He grew up during the Nazi regime and World War II, two influences that would have a profound effect on his thinking and future writings. His work has reflected his commitment to a social framework that ensures that fascism will not reappear (Adams and Sydie, 2001).

Habermas studied philosophy at Göttin-gen, Zurich, and Bonn, where he earned his doctorate in 1954. He then worked as Adorno's assistant at the Institute for Social Research in Frankfurt. In 1961 he received his second doctorate at Mainz and began teaching at the University of Heidelberg during the same year. In 1964 he became a professor of philosophy at Frankfurt, where he assumed Horkheimer's chair in philosophy and sociology. Habermas then joined the Max Planck Institute for the Study of the Conditions of Life in the Scientific-Technical World, in Stranberg, near Munich, in 1971. In 1982, he returned to the University of Frankfurt as the chair of sociology and philosophy and remained until his retirement. Among Habermas's significant publications are *Communication and the Evolution of Society* (1962), *Knowledge and Human Interests* (1968), *The Theory of Communicative Action* (Volume 1, 1981; Volume 2, 1984), and *The Philosophical Discourse of Modernity* (1987a).

Habermas is perhaps the most well known and prolific of the second generation of critical theorists. He was influenced by the works of Marx, Weber, and the early members of the Frankfurt School. Habermas's writings are steeped in the German tradition (Held, 1980). In particular, Habermas developed

> Marxist ideas of consciousness, critical theory's critique of instrumental reason, and Weber's critique of rationalization. He attempts to rescue rationality from Weber's pessimistic tendency to couple it with formal rationalization. He also transforms Marxist theory by adding increased emphasis on communication and interaction; this new emphasis, based on twentieth century

Jurgen Habermas, German philosopher and critical social thinker.
Source: A/P Wide World Photos

phenomenology, interactionist theory, and modern theories of communication and cognitive development, clarifies the process by which subjective consciousness can be transformed. Habermas also expands Marxist notions of crisis from economic crisis to crises in political, cultural, and intra-personal spheres—crises of legitimation, rationality, and motivation. (Garner, 2000:371)

Habermas seeks a society with the self-emancipation of people from domination. The issue of morality goes hand in hand with this transformation. "In his discussion of the sociocognitive and moral dimensions of the generalized other, Habermas not only underlines the importance of this distinction but also stresses the need to focus on the moral dimension per se" (Strydom, 2001:177). His critical theory is an attempt to further the self-understanding of social groups capable of transforming society.

Critical Theory

In his article "The Tasks of a Critical Theory" (1989) Habermas stated that the work of the Institute for Social Research was basically dominated by six themes until the early 1940s, when the circle of collaborators that had gathered in New York began to break up. These themes were:

1. **The Forms of Integration in Postliberal Societies:** Whether in a democracy or totalitarian regimes.
2. **Family Socialization and Ego Development:** For example, the structural change of the bourgeois nuclear family and the weakening of the authoritarian position of the father.
3. **Mass Media and Mass Culture:** The development of a culture industry for the manipulative control of consciousness.
4. **The Social Psychology behind Cessation of Protest:** Political consciousness of workers and employees.
5. **The Theory of Art:** The arts as the preferred object of an ideology, whether utopian or critical.
6. **The Critique of Positivism and Science:** science as a tool of the bourgeoisie.

This spectrum of themes reflected Horkheimer's conception of an interdisciplinary social science (Habermas, 1989:292). But this foundation was unable to support an empirical research program, something championed by Habermas.

Utilizing his theory of communicative action, Habermas promoted an analysis that begins reconstructively (or unhistorically) and describes structures of action and structures of mutual understanding that are found in the intuitive knowledge of competent members of modern societies. Furthermore, Habermas (1989) stated:

There is no way back from them to a theory of history that does not distinguish between problems of developmental logic and problems of developmental dynamics. In this way I have attempted to free historical materialism from its philosophical ballast. Two abstractions are required for this: (i) abstracting the development of cognitive structures from the historical dynamic of events, and (ii) abstracting the evolution of society from the historical concretion of forms of life. Both help in getting beyond the confusion of basic categories to which the philosophy of history owes its existence. A theory developed in this way can no longer start by examining concrete ideals immanent in traditional forms of life. It must orient itself to the range of learning processes that is opened up at a given time by a historically attained level of learning. It must refrain from critically evaluating and normatively ordering totalities, forms of life and cultures, and life-contexts and epochs *as a whole*. And yet it can take up some of the intentions for which the interdisciplinary research program of earlier critical theory remains instructive. (p. 296)

Habermas's critical theory was inspired by classical Greek and German philosophy, which stressed the inseparability of truth and virtue, of facts and values, and of theory and practice (Held, 1980). The imperative of critical theorists is to reformulate society from its course of history. Habermas maintained that twentieth-century history was primarily shaped by capitalism and Soviet socialism. Agreeing with Horkheimer, Habermas believed that knowledge is historically rooted and interest-bound. The first stage in the redevelopment of society is to provide objectivity in knowledge. Habermas wanted a society where people are free to assemble and communicate openly (politically). In a detailed, historical analysis, Habermas traced the emergence of "public opinion" to the eighteenth century. Forums for public discussion developed rapidly in Europe to mediate the growing division between the state and civil society, a division which developed from the expansion of market economies (Held, 1980).

Communication and the understanding of language are the keys to understanding and comprehending knowledge. "Habermas argued that linguistic communities are predicated upon an understanding that communication should be based upon a free flow of information undistorted by coercion" (Antonio, 1983:335). Habermas described the ideal speech situation as one that is uncoerced, free for all people, and in which all people are treated equally.

Communication Theory

Habermas found the Marxist philosophy of history fragile, especially in regard to its ability to support empirical research. As Horkheimer and Adorno had scaled down Marx's analysis of history in *Dialectic of Enlightenment* (1944), Habermas also retooled Marxian theory. "Like his critical theory predecessors, Habermas is concerned with reformulating Marxian theory in the light of twentieth-century social changes, and most especially in light of the expansion of state power into all spheres of social life. Habermas expands Marx's conception of humanity by adding language (communication) to work (labor) as a distinct feature of species-being" (Adams and Sydie, 2001:413). Antonio (1983) argued that Habermas's ideas about communication

and language are linked to his ideas of social evolution. "His analysis of the role of language in social evolution rejected views that assign knowledge, values, and ideology a pure epiphenomenal status. Thus, Habermas abandoned the base/superstructure relation and its strict concept of material determinism. He suggested that evolutionary, structural differentiation (rationalization) of productive forces interacts with, establishes limits for, and creates possibilities for the development of communicative action, but does not strictly determine this action" (Antonio, 1983:336).

Habermas was especially concerned about Marx's historical-materialist analysis:

> Historical-materialistic assumptions regarding the dialectical relation between productive forces and productive relations had been transformed into pseudonormative propositions concerning an objective teleology in history. This was the motor force behind the realization of a reason that had been given ambiguous expression in bourgeois ideals. Critical theory could secure its normative foundations only in a philosophy of history. But this foundation was not able to support an empirical research program. . . . The theory of communicative action can ascertain for itself the rational content of anthropologically deep-seated structures by means of an analysis that, *to begin with*, proceeds reconstructively, that is, unhistorically. It describes structures of action and structures of mutual understanding that are found in the intuitive knowledge of competent members of modern societies. There is no way back from them to a theory of history that does not distinguish between problems of developmental logic and problems of developmental dynamics. In this way I have attempted to free historical materialism from its philosophical ballast. (Habermas, 1989:296)

To "escape" the philosophical historical materialism of Marxist thought, Habermas proposed that theory cannot be tied to concrete ideals of human life; instead, it must orient itself to the range of learning processes that are opened at any given time. A theory must refrain from critically evaluating and normatively ordering totalities, forms of life and cultures, and life contexts and epochs *as a whole.* Such a theory must feature communicative action (Habermas, 1989:296–297).

As Adams and Sydie (2001) explained, the use of language as a significant aspect of human development led Habermas to concentrate on how undistorted communication might lay the foundation for the emancipation of individuals. Distorted communication is similar to Marx's false consciousness, whereas undistorted communication assists a more rational, egalitarian society. Habermas's use of *undistorted communication* reveals the influence of Freudian psychoanalysis on his communication theory. "As with the psychoanalyst, the role of the critical theorist is to assist the repressed to recognize and understand their collective, social situation and, as a result, formulate emancipatory practices. Habermas regards this endeavor as particularly important today because of the extent to which science and technology distort communication in the interest of technological rationalization and the political reinforcement of repression" (Adams and Sydie, 2001:413).

The Freudian influence is reflected in the following passage from Habermas's *The Theory of Communicative Action,* Volume 2 (1987):

> The theory of communicative action provides a framework within which the structural model of ego, id, and superego can be recast. Instead of an instinct theory that represents the relation of ego to inner nature in terms of a philosophy of consciousness—on the model of relations between subject and object—we have a theory of socialization that connects Freud with Mead, gives structures of intersubjectivity their due, and replaces hypotheses about instinctual vicissitudes with assumptions about identity formation. This approach can (i) appropriate more recent developments in psychoanalytic research, particularly the theory of object relations and ego psychology,

> (ii) take up the theory of defense mechanisms in such a way that the interconnections between intra-psychic communicative barriers and communication disturbances at the interpersonal level become comprehensible, and (iii) use the assumptions about mechanisms of conscious and unconscious mastery to establish connection between orthogenesis and pathogenesis. (pp. 388–389)

With regard to the media and their role in culture, Habermas (1987b) stated:

> With the shift from writing to images and sounds, the electronic media—first film and radio, later television—present themselves as an apparatus that completely permeates and dominates the language of everyday communication. On the one hand, it transforms the authentic content of modern culture into the sterilized and ideologically effective stereotypes of a mass culture that merely replicates what exists; on the other hand, it uses up a culture cleansed of all subversive and transcending elements for an encompassing system of social controls, which is spread over individuals, in part reinforcing their weakened internal behavioral controls, in part replacing them. The mode of functioning of the culture industry is said to be a mirror image of the psychic apparatus, which, as long as the internalization of paternal authority was still functioning, had subjected instinctual nature to the control of the superego in the way that technology had subjected outer nature to its domination. (1987b:389–390)

Habermas argued that individual's life worlds are influenced by constant interaction with others and with society's social structures.

> The structures of the lifeworld lay down the forms of the intersubjectivity of possible understanding. It is to them that participants in communication owe their extramundane positions vis-à-vis the innerworldly items about which they can come to an understanding. The lifeworld is, so to speak, the transcendental site where the speaker and hearer meet, where they can reciprocally

raise claims that their utterances fit the world (objective, social, or subjective) and where they can criticize and confirm those validity claims, settle their disagreements, and arrive at agreements. (Habermas, 1987b:126)

As Jonathan Turner (2003) explained, "In other words, intrinsic to the process of communicative action, where actors implicitly make, challenge, and accept one another's validity claims, is a rationality that can potentially serve as the basis of reconstructing the social order in less oppressive ways" (p. 219). In short, communicative action, via language, provides meaning to actors and shapes their life worlds. Habermas's (1987) communication theory can be summarized as follows:

Under the functional aspect of *mutual understanding*, communicative action serves to transmit and renew cultural knowledge; under the aspect of *coordinating action*, it serves social integration and the establishment of solidarity; finally, under the aspect of *socialization*, communicative action serves the formation of personal identities. The symbolic structures of the lifeworld are reproduced by way of the continuation of valid knowledge, stabilization of group solidarity, and socialization of responsible actors. The process of reproduction connects up new situations with the existing conditions of the lifeworld; it does this in the *semantic* dimension of meanings or contents (of the cultural tradition), as well as in the dimensions of *social space* (of socially integrated groups), and *historical time* (of successive generations). Corresponding to these processes of *cultural reproduction, social integration*, and *socialization* are the structural components of the lifeworld: culture, society, person. (p. 137–138)

Habermas is perhaps best known for his communication theory. He tried "to salvage the rational kernel of modern philosophy through his linguistic turn, he thinks that French philosophers like Derrida and Foucault abandon this kernel. . . . Whereas Habermas takes the linguistic turn to restore and legitimate reason and philosophy, he sees the French poststructuralists' version of the linguistic turn as threatening the preeminence of both reason and philosophy" (Hoy and McCarthy, 1995:153). Habermas (1991) made it clear, however, that he "never had the false ambition of wishing to develop something like a normative political theory from the principle of discourse" (p. 264).

Rationality and Modernity

Habermas was critical of Western industrial democracies for their reduction of the human world to some form of economic efficiency. Habermas believed that *rationality*—the ability to think logically and analytically—is more than a strategic calculation of how to achieve some chosen end; it is a form of communicative action. Rational behavior serves the individual's best interest and is a key ingredient in understanding others during social behavior. "The change in perspective from solitary rational purposiveness to social interaction does not promise to illuminate the very processes of mutual understanding [*Vertandigung*]—and not merely of understanding [*Verstehen*]—that keep present the world as an intersubjectively shared lifeworld background. We can find in language used communicatively the structures that explain how the lifeworld is reproduced even without subjects, so to speak, through the subjects and their activity orientated toward mutual understanding" (Habermas, 1987a:149). Thus, the communicative action of individuals in everyday life is possible only in relation to others.

Max Weber had attempted to explain why the rational economic system of industrialization had not taken place outside Europe. He found the answer in religion. Habermas (1987a) described Weber's explanation:

He described as "rational" the process of disenchantment which led in Europe to a disintegration of religious world views that issued in a secular culture. With the modern empirical sciences, autonomous arts, and theories of morality and law grounded on principles, cultural spheres of value took shape which made possible learning processes in accord with the respective inner logics of theoretical, aesthetic, and moral-practical problems. What Weber depicted was not only the secularization of Western *culture,* but also and especially the development of modern *societies* from the viewpoint of rationalization. The new structures of society were marked by the differentiation of the two functionally intermeshing systems that had taken shape around the organizational cores of the capitalist enterprise and the bureaucratic state apparatus. (p. 1)

Ideas of rationality led Habermas to explain modernity. Through research, Habermas discovered that many scholars had used the term *modernity.* Originally found in Christian lore, the "new world" had meant the still-to-come age of the world of the future, which was to dawn only on the last day (Judgment Day). The secular world eventually used the term *modernity* to apply to chronological eras; this usage implies that the future has already begun (Habermas, 1987c:5).

The term *modernity* is as problematic as the term *postmodernity.* Habermas (1997) traced the usage of the word *modern* to the late fifth century:

> The word 'modern' was first employed in the late fifth century in order to distinguish the present, now officially Christian, from the pagan and Roman past. With a different content in each case, the expression 'modernity' repeatedly articulates the consciousness of an era that refers back to the past of classical antiquity precisely in order to comprehend itself as the result of a transition from the old to the new. This is not merely true for the Renaissance, with which the 'modern age' begins *for us;* people also considered themselves as 'modern' in the age of Charlemagne, in the twelfth century, and in the Enlightenment—in short, whenever the consciousness of a new era developed in Europe through a renewed relationship to classical antiquity. (p. 39)

Thus, the expression *modern age* is applied whenever a new consciousness is developed. Claiming to be modern or postmodern leads to many obvious criticisms, for as time progresses, those who claimed to be modern or postmodern leave themselves open to ridicule by those in the future. Nonetheless, Habermas (1987:6) believed that the modern world is distinguished from the old by the fact that it opens itself to the future, the epochal new beginning is rendered constant with each moment that gives birth to the new. Modernity, then, is characteristic of a historical consciousness, with the present enjoying a prominent position as contemporary history.

The concepts of *rationality* and *modernity* come together in Habermas's (1987) examination of the lifeworld.

> A considerably rationalized lifeworld is one of the initial conditions for modernization processes. It must be possible to anchor money and power in the lifeworld as media, that is, to institutionalize them by means of positive law. If these conditions are met, economic and administrative systems can be differentiated out, systems that have a complementary relation to one another and enter into interchanges with their environments via steering media. At this level of system differentiation modern societies arise, first capitalist societies, and later—setting themselves off from those—bureaucratic-socialist societies. A capitalist path of modernization opens up as soon as the economic system develops its own intrinsic dynamic of growth and, with its endogenously produced problems, takes the lead, that is, the evolutionary primacy, for society as a whole. The path of modernization runs in another direction when, on the basis of state ownership of most of the means of production and an institutionalized one-party rule, the administrative action system gains a like autonomy in relation to the economic system. (p. 384)

Advanced modern societies rely on technology, thus forming a "technocratic consciousness."

At the core of technocratic consciousness is instrumental reason. At the center of institutional domination is the creeping erosion of the institutional framework of society, the realm of symbolic interaction, by systems of purposive-rational action. "The paradoxes of planning rationality can be explained by the fact that rational action orientations come into contradiction with themselves through unintended systemic effects. These crisis tendencies are worked through not only in the subsystem in which they arise, but also in the complementary action system into which they can be shifted" (Habermas, 1987:385).

As the administrative system expands in late capitalism into areas traditionally assigned to the private sphere, there is a progressive demystification of the naturelike process of social fate. "The expression 'late capitalism' implicitly asserts that, even in state-regulated capitalism, social developments are still passing through 'contradictions' or crises" (Habermas, 1973:39). The state's very intervention into the economy, education, and so on draws attention to issues of choice, planning, and control. The "hand of the state" becomes increasingly more visible and intelligible than "the invisible hand" of liberal capitalism (Held, 1980).

Habermas was also critical of *scientism*—identifying knowledge with science—because of its relation to positivism, since positivism provides scientism's most sophisticated defense. Although positivism began as a critique of certain ideologies (such as religious dogma and speculative metaphysics) it became a central element of technocratic consciousness and a key aspect of modern ideology. Since Habermas believed that (critical) theory should be a critique of knowledge, he opposed positivism because it attempted to objectify knowledge. He believed that knowledge must discard the "illusion" of objectivity—a world viewed as a universe of facts and laws. For Habermas, the goal of the critical sciences is to facilitate the process of methodical self-reflection and

to dissolve barriers to the self-conscious development of life (Held, 1980). Habermas prefers a subject-centered philosophy, rather a rational, scientific, objective science. (Rasmussen, 1990)

Democracy

Habermas's ideas on *democracy* emerged out of his experience with the reconstruction of government in postwar Germany and the ideas of Marx and Weber. Habermas believed that Marx did not properly understand democracy and criticized Marx for attempting to reduce social life simply to the realm of work and labor. Habermas did not abandon Marxism, but instead revised and reformulated it (Kivisto, 1998). Habermas also disagreed with Weber's pessimistic conclusion that future society would fall trap to an "iron cage." Habermas believed that open dialogue of social issues and concerns would be far more rational; and thus allow individuals freedom from bureaucracy. "For Habermas, democracy must be seen first and foremost as a process that results when a certain kind of social interaction prevails. More specifically, democracy should be seen as a particular way by which citizens make collective and rational decisions." (Kivisto, 1998:77) Citizens would eventually come to a consensus on decision-making after an open discussion of ideas free from domination (Habermas, 1970). Such a public sphere mandates the existence of independent voluntary associations of citizens and a political structure that permits the unrestricted dissemination of information and ideas (Kivisto, 1998:78).

Habermas envisioned a "deliberate democracy" where a government's laws and institutions would be a reflection of free and open public discussion. He believed that men and women would support this utopian belief, because they were aware of their collective interest in autonomy (self-government) and responsibility and would agree to adhere to each other's rights.

According to Habermas, modern democracies of the West are dominated by political legitimation. Such societies recognize the legitimacy of law. "That is, law requires more than mere acceptance; besides demanding that its addressees give it de facto recognition, the law claims to *deserve* their recognition. Consequently, all the public justifications and constructions meant to redeem this claim to be worthy of recognition belong to the legitimation of a government organized in the form of law" (Habermas, 1998:87). Furthermore, human rights are simultaneously connected to the morality of the law. "*Like* moral norms, they refer to every creature 'that bears a human countenance,' but *as* legal norms they protect individual persons only insofar as the latter belong to a particular legal community—normally the citizens of a nation-state. Thus a peculiar tension arises between the universal meaning of human rights and the local conditions of their realization" (Habermas, 1998:91). In light of globalism, the concept of universal human rights becomes of utmost concern in contemporary society.

Habermas realized that he would have his critics. After all, he is attacking one of the most fundamental "rights" of Western citizens—individualism—protected by the state. But Habermas (1998) insisted that "citizens are autonomous in a political sense only when they give themselves their laws" (p. 98). Habermas agreed with Kant's conception of autonomy. "Kant conceived autonomy as the capacity to bind one's own will by normative insights that result from the public use of reason. This idea of self-legislation also inspires the procedure of democratic will-formation that makes it possible to base political authority on a mode of legitimation that is neutral toward worldviews. As a result, a religious or metaphysical justification of human rights becomes superfluous. To this extent, the secularization of politics is simply the flip-side of the political autonomy of citizens" (Habermas, 1998:98).

This concludes the discussion on Jurgen Habermas. There are a number of contemporary critical theorists producing quality work. However, because of space limitation, the work and ideas of one of the more prominent contemporary critical theorists, Douglas Kellner, are presented in the following pages.

DOUGLAS KELLNER (1943–)

Douglas Kellner was born in 1943 and received his Ph.D. from Columbia University in 1973. Kellner is especially known for his systematic and critical review of television in the United States. He believes that the media—and in particular, television—have long served the interests of the powerful.

Critical Theory

In his book *Karl Korsch: Revolutionary Theory* (1977), Kellner reviewed the work of Karl Korsch. Kellner described Korsch as "being increasingly recognized as one the most interesting, neglected, and relevant political theorists of the century. . . . Korsch was also an early opponent of nazism and developed a theory of fascism and counterrevolution on a world-wide scale to explain the defeats of the working-class movement and their failure to follow the Marxian scenario. . . . Further, Korsch was one of the first Western theorists to call attention to developments in the so-called Third World, which he perceived might be a locale for the sort of social revolution that had failed to materialize in Europe and America" (p. 3). The relevance of this book to Kellner's critical theory lies in the fact that while Kellner reviewed Korsch's concern about such issues as the crisis of Marxism, he remained committed to the core ideas of Marxist thought. In his review of Jean Baudrillard (*Jean Baudrillard: From Marxism to Postmodernism and Beyond*, 1989b), Kellner specifically defended Marx's concepts of *use values* and *commodities.* Kellner (1989b) stated:

> I would suggest that most individuals and societies *do* prioritize needs and the use values of commodities in everyday consumer practices and social policies, although individuals and societies may not always be clear as to what they actually need or what is useful. Here processes of experimentation and inquiry can help determine whether commodities, practices, ideas and so forth are really useful and valuable. Then processes of dialogue or struggle can help build a consensus as to what a given society needs at a certain stage of its development. But, I would see it as more useful to be clear and discriminating about the hierarchy of one's needs and the use values of different products than simply to expel altogether, as Baudrillard does, the concepts of needs and use values as part of the capitalist system of domination which have no relative autonomy or autonomous value for the individual. (p. 38)

Kellner remains committed to Marxist analysis and critical scrutiny of human behavior, especially in regard to commodities and consumption.

Kellner's critical theory is "based on the premise that we have not moved into a postmodern, or postindustrial, age, but rather that capitalism continues to reign supreme, as it did in the heyday of critical theory. Thus, he feels that the basic concepts developed to analyze capitalism (for example, reification, alienation) continue to be relevant in the analysis of techno-capitalism" (Ritzer, 2000c:151). Kellner (1989a:178) described *technocapitalism* as a capitalist society structured so that technical and scientific knowledge, automation, computers, and advanced technology play such a significant role in the process of production that they parallel the role of human labor power in early capitalism. Technocapitalism is a variation of capitalism, but it is, nonetheless, capitalism. "Kellner does not endeavor to develop a full-scale theory of techno-capitalism. His main point is that although it has changed dramatically, capitalism remains predominant

in the contemporary world. Thus, the tools provided by the critical school, and Marxian theory more generally, continue to be relevant in today's world" (Ritzer, 2000c:152).

Kellner's examination of the media—and in particular, television—reveals his technoapproach to the understanding of human behavior, society, and culture.

Media and Culture

Kellner's ideas on the effect of the media on culture are influenced by the work of Baudrillard. As Kellner (1989b) stated, "During the 1980s Jean Baudrillard has been promoted in certain circles as the most advanced theorist of the media and society in the so-called postmodern era. His theory of a new, postmodern society rests on a key assumption that the media, simulations and what he calls 'cyberblitz' constitute a new realm of experience and a new stage of history and type of society. To a large extent Baudrillard's work consists in rethinking radical social theory and politics in the light of developments in the consumer, media, information and technological society" (p. 60). But Kellner (1989b) criticized Baudrillard for ignoring the important terrain of cultural politics, for not addressing alternative media practices, for believing that all media are mere producers of noise and are devoid of meaning, and for believing that the media are merely an example of one-way communication.

Kellner's views of the effect of media on culture are presented in his *Television and the Crisis of Democracy* (1990). In Chapter 1, Kellner provided statistics (which are outdated now but still illustrate his point) that demonstrate how prevalent television is in contemporary society: "In excess of 750 million TV sets in more than 160 countries are watched by 2.5 billion people per day" (p. 1). Nearly every home in the United States has a television set that is turned on for more than seven hours per day. Furthermore, Kellner stated that watching television is the most popular leisure activity of Americans. Frey and Delaney (1996) found that watching television was the most popular leisure activity among prison inmates as well.

In short, television has a tremendous impact on culture, and consequently, many people have analyzed the effects of television on viewers. "Television thus has many critics, commentators, and celebrants—but few theorists. The critiques themselves have largely been determined by the political views of the critics. Conservatives, for example, claim that television is a liberal medium that subverts traditional values. Liberals and radicals, by contrast, often criticize television for its domination by business imperatives and conservative values" (Kellner, 1990:3). Postmodern theorists have conceptualized contemporary capitalist society in terms of the proliferation and dissemination of images, citing the media as the primary culprit in creating "hyperreal" images that replace reality. In contrast to the postmodern theory of the media, and to Horkheimer and Adorno's 1972 study of the media *(Dialectic of Enlightenment)*, Kellner (1990) presented a multidimensional approach:

> My aim, by contrast, is to develop a critical theory that analyzes television in terms of its institutional nexus within contemporary U.S. society. Moreover, rather than seeing contemporary U.S. society as a monolithic structure absolutely controlled by corporate capitalism (as the Frankfurt School sometimes did), I shall present it as a contested terrain traversed by conflictual mass medium in which competing economic, political, social, and cultural forces intersect. . . . I contend that U.S. society is highly conflictual and torn by antagonisms and struggles, and that television is caught up in these conflicts, even when it attempts to deny or cover them over, or simply to "report" them. (pp. 14–15)

Kellner criticized the early critical school because of its narrow view of the media and mass culture as mere instruments of capitalist ideology. Kellner does not see television as a tool of oppression used by corporate entities to subvert the members of society.

However, Kellner is concerned that television is a threat to democracy. The term *democracy* is problematic in its own right, but Kellner (1990) stated, "In its broadest signification, democracy refers to economic, political, and cultural forms of self-management. In an 'economic democracy,' workers would control the work place, just as citizens would control their polity through elections, referenda, parliaments, and other political processes. 'Cultural democracy' would provide everyone access to education, information, and culture, enabling people to fully develop their individual potentials and to become many-sided and more creative" (p. 15). From this standpoint, the United States has a political democracy (citizens have the right to vote), but certainly not an economic democracy (workers do not control the workplace) or a cultural democracy (there is unequal access to education and information). Kellner argued that the United States does not have a fully democratic polity.

Kellner realizes what many first-generation critical theorists failed to notice: the importance of conflicts within the ruling class and challenges to liberal and conservative positions by radical movements and discourses.

> Given the ubiquity and power of television, it is a highly desired prize for ruling groups. Unlike most critical theorists, however, I attempt to specify both the ways in which television serves the interests of dominant economic and political forces, and the ways in which it serves to reproduce conflicts that traverse contemporary capitalist societies. Accordingly, I shall attempt to present a more comprehensive and multidimensional theoretical analysis than the standard Marxist and neo-Marxist accounts, which tend to conceptualize the media and the state simply as instruments of capital. (Kellner, 1990:15)

Kellner believes that television contributes to social integration and implies that democratized media could be the basis for a revitalized public sphere (Antonio, 1983:340). Through his examination of television in the 1980s, Kellner concluded that television has worked increasingly to further conservative hegemony. In so doing, television has helped produce a crisis in democracy. To his credit, Kellner goes beyond mere criticism of television and offers alternative models to the existing structure of commercial broadcasting—ones that may enhance political knowledge and participation.

Many of these "alternative" approaches to broadcasting have been realized, especially with the Federal Communication Commission's (FCC) implementation of deregulation in 1984. Among the alternative television systems promoted by Kellner (1990) is public access television, which he described as "one of the few real forms of alternative television, and it provides the best prospect for using the broadcast media to serve the interests of popular democracy" (p. 207). The advent of cable television in the 1970s was directly responsible for the increase in public access programs, channels for government, and educational programming. The disappearance of the dominance by the big-three networks also decreased the potential manipulation of television by government and capitalist interests.

Much of Kellner's analysis of the media (of the 1980s)—and in particular, of television—has come to be realized, as today, the media are much more than a one-way flow of communication with the audience serving as passive receptors of information. Call-in radio shows, interactive television (for example, viewers can interact with the shows being broadcasted via their computers while watching programming), and the Internet are just a few examples of two-way forms of contemporary media. The advent of cable and satellite television provides such a large array of broadcasting choices that no government in a free society can suppress the abundance of viewpoints available to the public. Many television shows are very critical of political leaders. The shows include both news programming, at one extreme, and comedy satires (for example, *Saturday Night Live* and *Mad TV*) that openly mock political leaders, at the other extreme. It is difficult to imagine how the creation of the so-called reality shows on television (which have dominated broadcasting in the early 2000s) benefits the capitalists or the government—let alone the viewers or culture in general.

Postmodernism

As critical theory evolves, it seems to lean ever closer to postmodern theory. Postmodern thought extends to many disciplines, most notably art, but has also crept into sociological discourse since the mid-1980s. As Ritzer (2000c) explained, "While many sociologists, and some sociological theorists, still consider postmodern social theory to be a fad (and it continues to look to some more like a carnival than a serious scholarly endeavor), the simple fact is that postmodern social theory can no longer be ignored by sociological theorists" (pp. 468–469). It was Kellner who referred to the hoopla that surrounds postmodernism as a carnival: "I refer here to 'the postmodern carnival' because the new phenomena of the postmodern scene give rise to a carnivalesque situation (in Bakhtin's sense) in which dominant norms are transgressed and a fundamentally different situation erupts. Like Bakhtin's 'carnival king'—and this is no doubt a Baudrillardian imaginary—Baudrillard laughs at the pretensions of modernity and its (now obsolete) political economy, philosophy, politics, sexuality, fashion and culture, while mocking its exhibitions and discourses" (Kellner, 1989:93). Kellner noted that the primary methods of postmodernism are deconstruction, reversal, and inversion. This implies that the theorist must question the taken-for-granted world, the rules of the game, and the claims to authority found in a society. Kellner (1989a) viewed postmodernism as a new stage of society, a break with the previous social order (p. 121).

Kellner had a particular interest in post-modern art. He (1989) traced the origins of postmodernism in the arts to France in the late 1970s, and in fashion to 1940s French existential phenomenologists like Jean Paul Sartre and Merleau-Ponty. Kellner (1983) viewed postmodern art as an opportunity to rebel. This was especially true of the ex-pressionists:

> The expressionist rebellions affirmed the primacy of a passionate subjectivity against traditional social norms and artistic forms. While maintaining a posture of artistic and social revolt, the Expressionists attacked the values and institutions of German bour-geois society and culture through provoca-tive artistic attitudes and productions. Yet the Expressionists championed subjectivity, passion, and rebellion. . . . From this per-spective, Expressionism is not only impor-tant as an artistic phenomenon, but also as a social movement and integral part of the emergence of twentieth-century conscious-ness which provides critical insights into an epoch that is not yet over. (p. 3)

Kellner (1983:13) found Marxist ideas in ex-pressionism. Expression itself, Kellner ar-gued, arose in a period in which analyses of the alienation, reification, and dehumaniza-tion of the individual and the fragmentation of the human personality had become wide-spread.

The postmodern attitude is reflected in expressionist art. Kellner (1983) stated, "Ex-pressionist art can be interpreted as a critical source of knowledge, depicting the odysseys of modern subjectivities disintegrating yet trying to reintegrate, dying yet attempting to be reborn" (p. 31).

RELEVANCY

There is no single definition of critical theory, nor is there a single approach to its examina-tion of society. Critical theory is generally about the role of power in social relations. It is also concerned with action and political involvement. It separates itself from conflict theory by avoiding the idea of economic de-terminism, and it disagrees with the posi-tivistic style of functionalist theory and its attempt to explain social life by discovering universal "social laws."

Critical theory has existed since the for-mation of the Institute for Social Research at Frankfurt University in 1923. The institute conducted independent studies of Marxism and anti-Semitism. Critical theory can be di-vided into three eras: the first generation of Frankfurt philosophers who maintained a commitment to Marxist ideology; the sec-ond generation, beginning with Jurgen Habermas, among others, who reconstruct-ed Marxist ideology; and the contemporary generation of critical theorists such as Dou-glas Kellner (and Ben Agger), who have used a more multidimensional approach to their study of modern culture (especially the media). In light of the rise of Nazism, fascism, and socialism, the first generation of critical theorists had a difficult time de-fending Marxist idealism and a single-focused (the economic realm) approach to explaining behavior. Axel van den Berg (1980) went as far as stating, "Perhaps the first generation of Frankfurt philosophers can be accused of a certain cowardice for not directly facing up to the seamier sides of Soviet reality until after World War II" (p. 450).

The second generation of critical thinkers made amends for the short-sightedness of the original Frankfurt scholars. However, "after the dissolution of the Frankfurt School, the meaning of critical theory was more elusive than ever" (Antonio, 1983:337). Habermas maintained the belief that Western society promotes a distorted conception of ration-ality and continues its destructive impulse to dominate. Contemporary critical theo-rists have increasingly turned their attention to the media and other forms of enter-tainment in their examination of modern culture.

In summary, "Critical theory cannot be characterized by a particular set of methodological techniques and theoretical propositions; however, it is still a coherent approach to the social world that is separate from other types of sociology and Marxism. This fact is obscured by the great diversity of studies in critical theory and by the loose application of this term by some sociologists" (Antonio, 1983:343). Critical theory is comfortable with its commitment to a critique of society by attempting to uncover distorting forms of consciousness, or ways of thinking. "To be sure, the results of rational dialogue and critique cannot add up to absolute knowledge; but in the current intellectual and political context, it seems important to stress that they are not entirely trivial either" (Bailey, 1994:121).

Critical theorists may be happy with merely criticizing society and other theoretical approaches, but critics of this school of thought are not. "What makes a theory 'critical'? To be critical must one have a theory? These two questions are provoked by the label 'critical theory,' which seems initially to be an oxymoron. If not a contradiction in terms, the two words are at least in tension, and pull in different directions" (Hoy and McCarthy, 1995:103). By criticizing and drawing upon a variety of seemingly quite different schools of thought, critical theorists break out of the protected positions often given to established members of a theoretical tradition. With their focus on a critique of all existing social theories, the critical school risks alienating all established approaches (Held, 1980). Consequently, there are a number of criticisms of critical theory. The first four criticisms originated with David Held (1980) and the fifth with George Ritzer (2000c).

The first criticism of critical theory is that it reproduces idealist (utopian) positions. For example, Habermas's concepts of ideal speech (uncoerced, free for all), undistorted communication (communication is seldom free from bias, whether purposeful or not),

and political autonomy (self-rule) are philosophical ideals not grounded in everyday reality. The second criticism is related to the first: Critical theory shows undue concern about philosophical and theoretical problems. In this regard, critical theorists are accused of failing to support their ideas with facts, data, and research. The critical approach has a general disdain for positivistic methods. As Antonio (1983) explained, "Though critical theory should neither embrace positivist methods uncritically nor fuse with sociology, it should be open to those techniques that can be harmonized with dialectical method as well as be useful for collecting and analyzing data necessary for the empirical moment of immanent critique" (p. 348). It is important for critical theorists to at least provide adequate empirical grounding for their theories (for example, as Kellner did in his analysis of television broadcasting).

The third criticism of critical theory is its preoccupation with negativity. This should be treated as a given, really. Since the purpose of this theoretical approach is to criticize, it will always be viewed as "negative." Some people value the role of critics (for example, movie critics, sports critics, and food critics) because of their "valued" and "knowledgeable" opinions. However, critics must have some legitimate credential to claim such a role. On the other hand, most members of society do not like to be criticized (even "constructively"), especially if a viable alternative is not provided. For example, if a parent criticizes a child's school science project without providing help toward the desired goal, of what benefit is the criticism? Eliminating this negative slant remains critical theory's biggest challenge.

The fourth criticism of critical theory is the claim that it developed from a purely academic setting and thus was isolated from working-class politics (add to this, the fact that Marx's conception of the working class as a revolutionary force is untrue) and became increasingly embroiled in abstract issues and "second-order" discourse. This criticism is reflected in the lack of empirical research conducted by critical theorists. Contemporary critical theorists are increasingly meeting this concern.

The fifth criticism leveled against critical theory is that it is ahistorical. Critical theorists have examined a variety of events without paying much attention to their historical and comparative contexts (Ritzer, 2000c:147). This is especially true of the first generation of critical theory. "The first generation of critical theorists (most of whom were trained in philosophy, not sociology), though they stressed the importance of history, did not go far enough in incorporating concrete historical and empirical work into their analyses. Their philosophical training and overly broad definition of positivism caused some of their theoretical work to rely upon less than adequate empirical/historical grounding" (Antonio, 1983:348).

Criticisms such as these have led many sociologists to consider critical theory, at best, a marginal field. Tom Bottomore (1984:76), a traditional Marxist, declared the Frankfurt School "dead." Harvey Greisman (1986:273) labeled critical theory "the paradigm that failed." Despite these criticisms, critical theory is relevant and has been applied to such areas as postmodernity, popular culture (for example, music), education, and crime and delinquency. Ruane and Todd (1988) believe that "the application of critical theory to the practical world has been a goal of critical theorists since the foundation of the Frankfurt School. The early critical theorists stressed the practical relevance of their project but their most influential work was highly theoretical and remote from concrete issues and problems" (p. 533).

As society reaches the "postmodern era" Marxism and critical theory seem to be at a crossroads. Will they continue to find supporters, or will they be overwhelmed by postmodernists? Critical theorist Ben Agger (1992) addressed this issue:

> It is commonly said that civilization has entered an era (sometimes called postmodernity) in which political contention can be put behind. . . . In this context, the crisis of Marxism requires a serious reappraisal of traditional left "certainties" such as the inevitability of capitalism's demise. Both *perestroika* and postmodernism seem to call into question venerable Marxist speculation about the direction of history. Everywhere old-guard leftists fall by the wayside, overtaken by all manner of political factions who have little use for the Marxist catechism. Some of these factions claim to be neoconservative, others post-Marxist. In any case, to be a Marxist today is to be unfashionable. (p. 3)

Agger argues that the left has developed its own right wing, composed of both orthodox Marxist and postmodern theorists. Critical, or left, postmodernists like Fredric-Jameson (see Chapter 11) use postmodernism as a way to defend the significance of Marx's world historical eschatology against other postmodernists, like Baudrillard, who celebrate postmodernity's break with modernity (Agger, 1996). Promoting a more enduring, flexible critical theory, Agger encourages interrogating traditional Marxist ideas by means of postmodern thought.

According to Agger (1996), *postmodernity* is a utopian category—something to be achieved. In this regard, postmodernism is viewed as an extension of Marxism. "Postmodernism, conceived within the eschatological or 'critical' framework of Marxist critical theory, does not betray Marxism but extends Marxism into the late 20th century, formulating postmodernity as the latter-day version of Marx's socialism. In particular, postmodern critical theory is the first narrative to pose a possible utopian future not as a determinate outcome of nature-like social laws but rather as one conceivable discursive accomplishment among many" (p. 37).

Agger (1996) views postmodernism as Marxist because Marx foresaw the need to fulfill the "project of modernity," as Habermas termed it. In summary:

> Postmodernity, then, is not to be located off the Marxist map, a time after when leftist eschatological aims no longer apply. Instead, postmodernity is a contemporary formulation of utopia that can only be reached through modernity. It has much the same status as Marx's notion of how socialism would end prehistory. Only with postmodernity will modernity achieve its telos—dialogical democracy. In appearing to claim postmodernism "for" Marxism I am not making a one-sided appropriation. Marxism is transformed by its engagement with postmodernism and feminism, perhaps beyond recognizability. I contend that it is also revivified now that discursive politics and personal politics matter like never before. (Agger, 1996:45)

The key to any theory's relevance to society is in its application. In that regard, critical theory can either be a museum piece or a living medium of political self-expression (Agger, 1976:12). Applying theory to issues of concern in popular culture is one sure way to guarantee its relevance. Many critical theorists have examined the role of the media and other forms of communication. Music has always been important in any culture. "Music like poetry is a *form* of critical theory in that it stimulates and solicits resignation or rebellion" (Agger, 1976:19). Whether it is classical, heavy metal, rock, or country, music *does* something for people. For example, "rock music and drugs are sources of prepolitical ecstasy which in their ecstatic moments free the person from the spacetime of serial bourgeois life" (Agger, 1976:29). The study of music is relevant because music itself is relevant to people's lives. Certain songs remind individuals of past events, and these songs allow the individual to transcend the present place and time. "Critical theory must surpass *itself* in remaining within the dialectic of the real and the possible. New science recovers grounds for positive rebellion in the carnal body, the body politic. 'Critical theory' is not a school but rather the way we choose to oppose inhumanity in different songs of joy" (Agger, 1976:32).

Critical theory is relevant to the field of education. *Critical Theories in Education* by Popkewitz and Fendler (1999) is a book about the changing discourses of critical educational theory that examines claims to "truth" about knowledge that are imposed on students from the dominant class's point of view. In the preface, the editors wrote, "Critical theory addresses the relations among schooling, education, culture, society, economy, and governance. The critical project in education proceeds from the assumption that pedagogical practices are related to social practices, and that it is the task of the critical intellectual to identify and address injustices in these practices. . . . In education, critical theory has been an important impulse for a wide range of educational practices. In short, critical theory is concerned with the workings of power in and through pedagogical discourses" (Popkewitz and Fendler, 1999:xiii). A critical assessment of the educational system remains an important and relevant topic in contemporary society.

Critical theory has also been applied to issues related to crime and delinquency. "In general terms, critical theorists have clarified theoretical and methodological boundaries which have on occasion been blurred by criminologists, and their unified model of empirical and interpretive analysis can help make sense of recent developments in criminological theory. In addition, critical theory draws its orientation from a broad range of disciplines, including linguistics, psychology, sociology, philosophy, and Marxism" (Groves and Sampson, 1986:538). The critical approach to the study of crime and delinquency challenges the status quo, examines power (class) differentials, and investigates the creation of law.

Sociology has its roots strongly entrenched in the birth and rise of industrialization. When new social problems arose, many moral reformers criticized the existing social order and called upon the powers that be to make amends. Many of these early moral reformers were sociologists. It is perhaps in the blood of sociologists to criticize the perceived injustices of society. If this is true, then critical theory surely has its place in sociology. As Adams and Sydie (2001) acknowledged, "Sociology, as a critical theoretical enterprise, still has a place in the twenty-first century. The global crises that threaten the freedom of citizens, the fragility of democratic institutions in the face of global market forces, and the various siren calls for ideological purity in the name of a race, religion, or nation, all need to be critically and publicly analyzed" (pp. 422–423). There will be social thinkers criticizing the injustices of the world until they cease to exist. In other words, there will always be a need for constructive criticism and a place for those who offer alternative approaches in the fight against injustice.

11

Modern and Postmodern Theory

As we learned from the discussion on critical theory (see Chapter 10) many contemporary social theorists have grown tired of the mainstream and traditional sociological theories of functionalism, conflict, and symbolic interactionism. This discontent led to the development of alternative sociological theories and mirrored Western societies' transition from "modernity" to "postmodernity." Modern and postmodern theorists have attempted to develop new concepts and new ways of analyzing society in light of this transitionary period. As Allan and Turner (2000) explained:

> Sociology emerged as a discipline to explain the dramatic transformations associated with modernity, and by the beginning of the twentieth century, sociological theory and research were directed at understanding the rise of industrial capitalism, the spread of rational-legal social forms, the emerging dominance of science and the exponential increase in technologies, the expansion of urban areas, the commodification generated by new market forces, and other events associated with modernity. Over the last two decades of the century, however, a good deal of social theory in general and sociological theory in particular shifted to understanding "postmodernity" (p. 363).

THE ROOTS OF MODERN AND POSTMODERN THEORY

Many disciplines use the terms *modernism* and *postmodernism,* as they are vague concepts and are arbitrarily applied to social phenomena. Stephen Feldman (2000) applied the terms to his study of the legal profession: "To travel from premodernism through modernism and into post-modernism might take several centuries and even millennia" (p. 3). Postmodernism is especially prevalent in the world of art but has found its way into sociological discourse for the past few decades. As described in Chapter 10, scholars have been using the term *modernism* for centuries, usually in connection with technological advancements or new levels of consciousness. Habermas (1997) traced the use of the word *modern* to the late fifth century, when Christians used the term to distinguish the present from the pagan and Roman past. Bill Martin (1992) used a Hegelian explanation of modernity in terms of eras of time: "With Western humanity's emergence into modernity, the conditions, in totality, are finally set for the 'completion' of history. Hegel's philosophy of history is most of all a recognition of these conditions in his own day: the passage of humanity through the four cultural and spiritual levels of development (called by Hegel the 'Oriental,' 'Greek,' 'Roman,' and 'Christian' Worlds), the emergence of the modern nation state and the instantiation of Christian Universality in modern individuality (p. 34). Thus, each era considers itself modern. This implies that all of history leads to any given era. "Hegel does not say that history has reached its point of completion with the achievement of the Christian World; rather the stage is set for this completion" (Martin, 1992:34).

When scholars think beyond the present (modernity), they allow for both a future (postmodernity) and, consequently, postmodern thought. According to Alexander Riley (2002), "The history of postmodern thought . . . begins in the French Third Republic, roughly during the second half of the life of the Republic, from about 1900 to the outbreak of World War II in 1939. In the aftermath of the fall of the second Bonaparte Empire and of the Paris Commune's rise and demise, the late nineteenth century saw the emergence of a great number of political and cultural debates that would touch on the entire French society" (p. 245). The social force that would change French society was secularism. C. Wright Mills (1959:166) simply stated that the modern age was being succeeded by a postmodern period. John Deely (1994), agreeing with the simplicity of the term *postmodernism,* argued that there is "a nearly indisputable consensus that the word 'post' can only exist in opposition, continuity, or complementarity with the universe which it presupposes, that is, the world of modernity" (p. xi). Kellner (1989a) explained that when society breaks from current modes of thinking, it has emerged into a postmodern era. To accomplish this, social thinkers must question the taken-for-granted world, the rules of society, and the claims to authority found in society. The use of such methodological techniques as deconstruction, reversal, and inversion assist the postmodern thinker. Kellner (1983) believed that the postmodern

attitude is reflected in expressionist art because it can be viewed as a critical source of knowledge.

As for American sociological theory, postmodernism followed the dominance of functionalism in the 1950s and the prevalence of neo-Marxist and conflict theory in the 1960s and 1970s. Many social theorists point to Thomas Kuhn's book *The Structure of Scientific Revolutions* (1962) as a significant indicator that a reliance on science and scientific analysis was not a criterion shared by sociologists. Michael Friedman (1993) argued that Kuhn's book had forever changed the perception of the philosophical importance of the history of science: "Reacting against what he perceived as the naively empiricist, formalist, and ahistorical conception of science articulated by the logical positivists, Kuhn presented an alternative conception of science in flux, of science driven not so much by the continuous accumulation of uncontroversial observable facts as by profoundly discontinuous conceptual revolutions in which the very foundations of old frameworks of scientific thought are replaced by radically new ones. When such a revolution occurs, we do not simply replace old 'false' beliefs with new 'true' beliefs; rather, we fundamentally change the system of concepts" (p. 37). Kuhn described these revolutions in thought as *paradigm shifts.* Kuhn had argued that the history of science is not gradual and cumulative but punctuated by a series of more-or-less radical "paradigm shifts." Summarizing Kuhn's ideas of paradigm shifts in simplistic terms, Conant and Haugeland, in their editors' introduction to *The Road since Structure* (2000), wrote "Shifts happen" (p. 1).

Kuhn questioned scientific claims to objectivity, absolute truth, and rationality. "Kuhn's critique called into question many of the central elements of the traditional picture—the concept of absolute truth, the observation/theory distinction, the determinacy of rational choice, and the normative function of philosophy of science—and it provided an alternative model of scientific change that dispensed with these notions altogether. Kuhn's radical views have been the focus of much debate not only by philosophers, historians, and sociologists of science but also by large numbers of practicing scientists" (Horwich, 1993:1). Postmodernists continue in the tradition of Kuhn by challenging claims to objectivity and the neutrality of "facts."

According to Dmitri Shalin (1993), "Postmodernism has been around for decades now, but it was not until the 1980s that social scientists started paying this intellectual current serious attention" (p. 303). Many sociologists in the 1980s and 1990s believed that there was a "decisive shift in the nature of society, from 'modernity' to 'postmodernity'; that, as a result, the distorted nature of many of the concepts and ideas used by modern theorists (including scientists and social scientists) is increasingly apparent; and that a postmodernist vocabulary and discourse should henceforth be adopted instead" (Wallace and Wolf, 1999:402). Charles Lemert (1997) in particular argued that there has been a major shift in the nature of society, and that the description *modern* is no longer characteristic of the present day.

Shalin (1993) believed that the primary reason that postmodernism has received a "half-hearted" reception by social scientists is that postmodernists do not look favorably at the scientific model, especially such ideals as objective reporting and valid generalizations. Symbolic interactionists were among the first in the social science community to join with the concerns of postmodernism (Faberman, 1991; Denzin, 1991; Fontana and Preston, 1990; Shalin, 1991), perhaps because of symbolic interactionism's relatively marginal status in sociology, along with their "maverick" status. "The postmodernist critique of formal logic, positivism, and scientism also strikes a responsive cord with interactionist sociologists, as is the emphasis on the marginal, local,

everyday, heterogeneous, and indeterminate" (Shalin, 1993:303).

DEFINING POSTMODERNISM THEORY

Although most classically trained sociologists consider sociology a science, there has always been an active debate about whether the scientific model is an appropriate one for studying society. The earliest sociologists (beginning with Claude-Henri Saint-Simon and Auguste Comte), in an attempt to gain some credibility for the field of sociology, borrowed the methodologies utilized by the natural sciences in the hope that they to could establish "laws" just as the natural scientists had. Traditionally, most classical social theorists embraced the concept that science could help change society for the better. Postmodernists strongly disagree with this outlook. "The most important component of postmodernism is its rejection of this scientific canon, of the idea that there can be a single coherent rationality or that reality has a unitary nature that can be definitively observed or understood" (Wallace and Wolf, 1999:406). Postmodernists go so far as to proclaim traditional sociological theory dead and say that postmodernism will revitalize social theory. Steven Seidman (1991) encouraged a renunciation of scientism and its "absurd" claim to speak the truth. There are some postmodernists who "concede that the physical world might operate by laws, [but] the very process of discovering these laws creates culture that, in turn, is subject to interests, politics, and forms of domination. For example, law-like knowledge in subatomic physics has reflected political interests in war-making or the laws of genetics can be seen to serve the interests of biotechnology firms. . . . From a postmodernist's view, 'truth' in science, especially social science, is not a correspondence between theoretical statements and the actual social universe, but a cultural production like any other sign system" (Turner, 2003:228–229).

Defining postmodernism is difficult. Many postmodernist theorists disagree with one another about what are the parameters of postmodernism:

> For example, Norman Denzin (1991:vii), a sociologist whose thinking has made the postmodern turn, provided a number of definitions of the term postmodern, one of which was that it is "undefinable." Second, postmodernists all too frequently write and speak in an impenetrable jargon, and as such their ideas sometimes appear to be comprehensible only to those who are initiates into the mysteries attached to such concepts as antifoundationalism, logocentrisism, hyperreality, and simulacra. A third reason, clearly related to the second, has to do with the French intellectual origins of postmodernism, in which there is a tendency to accentuate the novelty of the claims that are being made and the positions that are being staked out—a phenomenon resulting from the peculiar intellectual fashion consciousness in France. (Kivisto, 1998:139)

George Ritzer (2000c) shared Kivisto's view of the difficulty of defining postmodernism:

> For one thing, there is great diversity among the generally highly idiosyncratic postmodern thinkers, so it is difficult to offer generalizations on which the majority would agree. . . . For clarity it is useful to distinguish among the terms "postmodernity," "postmodernism," and "postmodern social theory." *Postmodernity* refers to a historical epoch that is generally seen as following the modern era; *postmodernism* to cultural products; and *postmodern social theory* to a way of thinking that is distinct from modern social theory. Thus, the postmodern encompasses *a new historical epoch, new cultural products,* and *a new type of theorizing about the social world.* All these, of course, share the perspective that something new and different has happened in recent years that can no longer be described by the term "modern," and that those new developments are replacing modern realities. (p. 469)

Carol Nicholson (1989) also agreed that there is a great deal of controversy among scholars about how to interpret and evaluate postmodern theory:

> Given the complexity and diversity of the postmodern movement, it would be foolish to try to capture its significance in a precise definition. . . . Two influential texts that attempt to draw out the pedagogical implications of postmodernism are Jean-Francois Lyotard's *The Postmodern Condition: A Report on Knowledge* and Richard Rorty's "Hermeneutics, General Studies, and Teachin [g]." . . . There is general agreement among interpreters that postmodernism reflects a crisis in the authority and the conceptual systems of Western culture. . . . Postmodernism in philosophy can be construed in a broad sense to include a number of theoretical approaches—e.g., poststructuralism, deconstructionism, postanalytic philosophy, and neopragmatism—whose goal is to move beyond the tradition which began with Descartes and Kant. (pp. 197–198)

With such a lack of consensus on how to define *postmodern,* some working definition must be used. Riley (2002) stated that the most celebrated definition is that of Lyotard (1979), "who talks of the postmodern condition as the collapse of grand narratives, that is, of uniform and orthodox worldviews that can encompass everything and claim widespread adherence based on this purported epistemological inclusivity and certainty. Pluralism is an obvious outcome of this situation, something Lyotard regards as salutary, but others have contended that a certain anxiety equally arises with the death of these comforting grand narratives" (p. 244). Allan and Turner (2000:365) define social postmodernism as "a critical form of theorizing that is concerned with the unique problems that are associated with culture and subjectivity in late capitalist societies" (p. 365).

BASIC PREMISES

To a large degree, postmodern thought has been the product of nonsociologists, such as

Jacques Derrida, Jean-Francois Lyotard, and Fredric Jameson. Recently, a number of sociologists have incorporated the ideas of postmodernism into sociological discourse. "In social theory, postmodernism rejects grand narratives on the nature of the universe, doubts the advantages of technology, reduces science to a language game, criticizes the exigencies of the market and the hyperreality of advertising, and offers no vision of theory beyond many voices in continual play" (Allan and Turner, 2000:364). In general, postmodern thinkers attack the idea of objectivity in social research, an autonomous rational mind, and grand narratives (grand theorizing). In addition, "postmodernism emphasizes the role of unconsciousness, reinterpreting knowledge as socially constructed and historically situated instead of a timeless representation of the world by separate individuals. In the absence of criteria for distinguishing discourse that accurately represents reality from other uses of language, the traditional distinctions between logic and rhetoric, literal language and metaphor, argument and narrative break down" (Nicholson, 1989:198). Wallace and Wolf (1999) stated that two famous names in postmodernism are Jacques Derrida and Michel Foucault, both of whom are French. This in itself is noteworthy, in that the French intellectual tradition is in conflict with the Anglo-Saxon approach of North American, Australian, and British social scientists.

There are a number of significant postmodern theorists who deserve to be mentioned. In the pages that follow, discussion will center on the concepts and contributions of Jacques Derrida, David Riesman, Jean-Francois Lyotard, Jean Baudrillard, Fredric Jameson, and Michel Foucault.

JACQUES DERRIDA (1930–)

Jacques Derrida was born in El-Biar, Algeria, in 1930. Derrida is a French philosopher and essayist, rather than a sociologist. His works utilize a deconstructivist approach (Martin, 1992). Deconstruction is a strategy of analysis that has been applied to such areas as literature, linguistics, philosophy, law, and architecture. Derrida's deconstructive approach is illustrated in his three 1967 books; *Speech and Phenomena, Of Grammatology,* and *Writing and Difference.* Additional publications include *Glas* (1974) and *The Post Card* (1980). Derrida's publications are focused on the deconstructive analysis of language. The concept of *discourse* is derived from his works. In using the term *discourse,* "Derrida and other postmodernists mean to emphasize the primacy of the words we use, the concepts they embody, and the rules that develop within a group about what are appropriate ways of talking about things. They mediate between us and reality" (Wallace and Wolf, 1999:407).

Logocentrism

Derrida was critical of grand narratives and viewed their construction as the product of what he referred to as *logocentrism.* Logocentrisms are modes of thinking that apply truth claims to universal propositions.

> In other words, our knowledge of the social world is grounded in a belief that we can make sense of our ever-changing and highly complex societies by referring to certain unchanging principles or foundations. The postmodernist stance articulated by Derrida (1976, 1978) calls for a repudiation of logocentrism, which entails taking what postmodernists refer to as an antifoundational stance. In its most extreme versions, postmodernism constitutes a profound repudiation of the entire Western philosophical tradition and represents a form of extreme skepticism about our ability to carry on the sociological tradition as it has been conceived since the nineteenth century. (Kivisto, 1998:139–140)

The Hermeneutical Method

Social thinkers that do not employ the methods of science (empiricism, data collection, and data analysis) must find alternative ones. Max Weber (1864–1920) promoted the use of *verstehen* as a method of study. *Verstehen* is the German word for "to understand." Weber's sociological approach was primarily interpretive and based on *verstehen*. He believed that sociologists should look at the actions of individuals and examine the meanings attached to behaviors. Weber's use of the term *verstehen* was common among German historians of his day and was derived from a field of study known as *hermeneutics* (Pressler and Dasilua, 1996). "The German tradition of *hermeneutics* was a special approach to the understanding and interpretation of published writings. The goal was not limited to merely understanding the basic structure of the text, but the thinking of the author as well" (Delaney, 2004:137).

In response to Foucault's *The History of Madness in the Classical Age* (1961), Derrida wrote an article "To Do Justice to Freud: The History of Madness in the Age of Psychoanalysis" (1997). Derrida (1997:60) wanted to study the "role of psychoanalysis in the Foucauldian" tradition of a history of madness. Derrida utilized the hermeneutical method in his analysis of Foucault. Derrida (1997) stated that the hermeneutical method is "valid for the historian of philosophy as well as for the psychoanalyst, namely, the necessity of first ascertaining a surface or manifest meaning, and, thus, of speaking the language of the patient to whom one is listening; the necessity of gaining a good understanding, in a quasi-scholastic way, philologically and grammatically, by taking into account the dominant and stable conventions, of what Descartes *meant* on the already so difficult surface of his text, such as it is interpretable according to classical norms of reading; the necessity of gaining this understanding *before* submitting the first reading to a symptomatic and historical interpretation regulated by other axioms or protocols, *before and in order to* destabilize, wherever this is possible and if

it is necessary, the authority of canonical interpretations" (p. 61). This quote of Derrida reflects his commitment to the hermeneutical approach, but it also reveals how difficult his translated works are to read.

DAVID RIESMAN (1909–2002)

David Riesman was born in Philadelphia in 1909 and was the son of a professor at the University of Pennsylvania Medical School. Riesman graduated from Harvard College in 1931 and earned a degree from Harvard Law School in 1934. He served as a clerk for U.S. Supreme Court Justice Louis Brandeis and later taught at the University of Buffalo Law School. In 1949, he joined the social science faculty of the University of Chicago. "*The Lonely Crowd* was published in 1950, and became a best seller, as well as winning the admiration of his academic peers. He co-authored the book with Nathan Glazer, professor emeritus of education and social structure, and Reuel Denney, but, according to Glazer, Riesman was the real author of the work" (American Sociological Association, 2002:1). Riesman's other publications include *Faces in the Crowd* (1952, in collaboration with Nathan Glazer), *Thorstein Veblen: A Critical Interpretation* (1953), *Individualism Reconsidered* (1955), *Constraint and Variety in American Education* (1956), *The Academic Revolution* (1968, with Christopher Jencks), *On Higher Education* (1980), and many others. Riesman taught at Chicago until 1958 and then moved to Harvard University, where he taught for over thirty years. Riesman attained much recognition throughout his academic life. However, as Orlando Patterson (2002), professor of sociology at Harvard, explained, "David Riesman died discarded and forgotten by his discipline. Even Harvard's department of sociology, which he had served for over 30 years, recently discontinued a lecture series named for him after only two years. I gave the last David Riesman lecture in October 2000. It was, I think, the last public event David attended, and he was very happy about it. As he was my mentor, so was I" (p. 15).

The Lonely Crowd

The Lonely Crowd (1950–2001) can be viewed as a modern to postmodern discourse in that Riesman discussed dramatic social changes that were reshaping American society. According to Todd Gitlin, who wrote the foreword in the 2001 publication of *The Lonely Crowd*, this book represents a study of the changing American character:

> As America was moving from a society governed by the imperative of production to a society governed by the imperative of consumption, the character of its upper middle classes was shifting from "inner-directed" people, who as children internalized goals that were essentially "implanted" by elders, to "other-directed" people, "sensitized to the expectations and preferences of others." In Riesman's wonderful metaphor, the shift was from life guided by an internal gyroscope to life guided by radar. The new American no longer cared much about adult authority but rather was hyperalert to peer groups and gripped by mass media. . . . *The Lonely Crowd* went on to become, according to a 1997 study by Herbert J. Gans, the best-selling book by a sociologist in American history, with 1.4 million copies sold, largely in paperback editions. For years, the book made "inner-direction" and "other-direction" household terms, canapes for cocktail party chat. (p. xii)

The Lonely Crowd was jargon-free, so it was easier for the general public to understand.

In the preface to *Faces in the Crowd* (1952) Riesman spelled out his (and his collaborators') intent for *The Lonely Crowd* as a "wholly tentative effort to lay out a scheme for the understanding of character, politics, and society in America. The book moved on the most general levels (as in its discussion of the possible relations between growth of population and change in character type) and also on the most concrete (as in its use of particular American movies and comic strips as illustrations of some of its theses)" (p. v).

The postmodern approach is illustrated by Riesman's attention to the change in America's social character from the nineteenth century to the mid-twentieth century. Riesman defined social character as that part of "character" which is shared by significant social groups and is the product of the experiences of these groups. "The link between character and society . . . is to be found in the way in which society ensures some degree of conformity from the individuals who make it up. In each society, such a mode of ensuring conformity is built into the child, and then either encouraged or frustrated in later adult experience" (Riesman, 1950/2001:5–6). In other words, the agents of socialization (beginning with the family and extending to the media, employers, religion,

David Riesman, postmodern theorist who incorporated the impact of technology on society and individuals.
Source: Harvard Photo Services

and so on) attempt to make individuals conform to the expectations of specific social groups and of society in general. Riesman used the term *mode of conformity* interchangeably with the term *social character,* although noting that conformity is just one aspect of social character. "However, while societies and individuals may live well enough—if rather boringly—without creativity, it is not likely that they can live without some mode of conformity—even be it one of rebellion" (Riesman, 1950/-2001:6).

Riesman analyzed the anxieties of American life that were associated with the fast-changing post–World War II culture. In other words, society was changing, from a modern one to a postmodern one, and with this change, Americans expressed a great number of concerns. In *The Lonely Crowd,* along with his other works, Riesman

> provided middle-class Americans with a sharply focused view of their major cultural preoccupations. Then as now, Americans were concerned about the threat to personal freedom posed by the conformism and homogeneity inherent in mass-consumption society. They longed for connection in their pursuit of suburban affluence. They struggled with the contradictory tendency of capitalist individualism to undermine other forms of individualism through a ruthless "ethic of callousness" and celebration of greed. And they tried to reconcile their autonomy with genuine compassion. (Patterson, 2002:15)

Riesman used a number of significant terms in *The Lonely Crowd.* Among them are *tradition-direction, inner-direction, outer-direction, the oversteered child, bohemia,* and *self-consciousness.*

In *tradition-directed* societies, social change is at a minimum. Conformity is ensured by incorporating a near-automatic obedience to tradition. Individuals learn

> to understand and appreciate patterns which have endured for centuries, and are modified but slightly as the generations

succeed each other. The important relationships of life may be controlled by careful and rigid etiquette, learned by the young during the years of intensive socialization that end with initiation into full adult membership. Moreover, the culture, in addition to its economic tasks, or as part of them, provides ritual, routine, and religion to occupy and to orient everyone. (Riesman, 1950/2001:11)

Little effort is spent on alternative ways of thinking: as a result, technology seldom finds a welcome in tradition-based societies.

The concept of *inner-direction* is intended to cover a very wide range of social types. Riesman (1950/2001) stated:

> In western history the society that emerged with the Renaissance and Reformation and that is only now vanishing serves to illustrate the type of society in which inner-direction is the principle mode of securing conformity. Such a society is characterized by increased personal mobility, by a rapid accumulation of capital (teamed with devastating technological shifts), and by an almost constant *expansion:* intensive expansion in the production of goods and people, and extensive expansion in exploration, colonization, and imperialism. The greater choices this society gives—and the greater initiatives it demands in order to cope with its novel problems—are handled by character types who can manage to live socially without strict and self-evident tradition-direction. These are the inner-directed types. (p. 14)

Riesman is clearly utilizing the modern-postmodern analysis approach by describing such issues as technology and economic production affecting the very character of individuals, which, in turn, led to a dramatic change in society. "The problem facing the societies in the stage of transitional growth is that of reaching a point at which resources become plentiful enough or are utilized effectively enough to permit a rapid accumulation of capital" (Riesman, 1950/2001:17). To secure rapid development, countries are often dependent on the resources of other countries.

Riesman (1950/2001) applied the term *other-direction* especially to upper-middle-class persons in large cities: "The type of character I shall describe as other-directed seems to be emerging in very recent years in the upper middle class of our larger cities: more prominently in New York than in Boston, in Los Angeles than in Spokane, in Cincinnati than in Chillicothe. Yet in some respects this type is strikingly similar to the American, who Tocqueville and other curious and astonished visitors from Europe, even before the Revolution, thought to be a new kind of man" (p. 19). The other-directed person is shallow, freer with money, friendlier, and more demanding of approval. The other-directed person gains his or her sense of self from the reactions of others. "Of course, it matters very much who these 'others' are: whether they are the individual's immediate circle or a 'higher' circle or the anonymous voices of the mass media; whether the individual fears the hostility of chance acquaintances or only of whose who 'count.'" In other words, the other-directed person cares more about the feelings and reactions of significant others than those of strangers or ancestors. Riesman (1950/2001) acknowledged that people of all eras cared about how others felt about them, but "it is only the modern other-directed types who make this their chief source of direction and chief area of sensitivity" (p. 21).

Individuals who attempt to meet the standards of significant others risk being "oversteered." This is especially true of children. There is a danger for children who are born to and raised by exemplary persons to be *oversteered*, that is, to find themselves set on a course they cannot realistically follow. Although some children can handle the pressure of being born into famous families (for example, the son or daughter of a politician or a professional athlete), the result for many is a dreadful insecurity about whether they

can live up to these exalted models (Riesman, 1950/2001:95).

An aspect of any "modern" society is the fact that some individuals do not wish to conform or blend into the mode dictated by "other-directed" forces. Such people attempt to find autonomy or harmony. Riesman believed that *Bohemia* was such a "place." "Among the groups dependent on inner-direction the deviant individual can escape geographically or spiritually, to Bohemia; and still remain an individual. Today, whole groups are matter-of-factly Bohemian; but individuals who compose them are not necessarily free" (Riesman, 1950/2001:258). On the contrary, they are often zealously tuned in to the signals of a group that finds the meaning of life in a strict adherence to alternative codes of acceptable behavior.

Riesman (1950/2001) believed that *self-consciousness* constitutes the insignia of the autonomous in an era dependent on other-direction:

> For, as the inner-directed man is more self-conscious than his tradition-directed predecessor and as the other-directed man is more self-conscious still, the autonomous man growing up under conditions that encourage self-consciousness can disentangle himself from the adjusted others only by a further move toward even greater self-consciousness. His autonomy depends not upon the ease with which he may deny or disguise his emotions but, on the contrary, upon the success of his effort to recognize and respect his own feelings, his own potentialities, his own limitations. This is not a quantitative matter, but in part an awareness of the problem of self-consciousness itself, an achievement of a higher order of abstraction. (p. 259)

Riesman had a very profound idea regarding self-consciousness. Achieving self-consciousness is undoubtedly difficult, and even those who attain it often fail to mold it into the structure of an autonomous life and succumb to anomie. "Yet perhaps the anomie of such processes is preferable to the less self-conscious, though socially supported, anxiety of the adjusted who refuse to distort or reinterpret their culture and end by distorting themselves" (Riesman, 1950/2001: 259–260).

In *Faces in the Crowd* (1952) Riesman and Glazer continued with the same sorts of issues presented in *The Lonely Crowd*, but with a greater emphasis on individuals. Research came as a result of interviews conducted with a number of people in the continental United States. *Faces in the Crowd* contains the stories of individuals who are grouped roughly in terms of the character types they illustrate (for example, forty interviews were conducted with residents of East Harlem). Riesman and Glazer concluded that most individuals attempt to be both a part of society and alone from it.

> Indeed the moving about between being in the crowd and being in the wilderness, between society and solitude contains much of the American experience and the American tension. We did not invent the elevator so that we could jam together, but the invention helped spur our "need" to do so, to build cities which would loom like mirages over the all too open spaces. . . . By moving in a crowd, we seek to deny the accidental and chancy nature of our national life. But we also, the more autonomous of us for whom accident is more liberating than frightening, win the courage to single out the faces in the crowd that please us and stimulate us. By moving about both in crowds and in the wilderness, we assure ourselves that we still have room "inside" and "outside" us. (pp. 740–741).

Thus, someone may be just as alone and lonely in Los Angeles as in rural Montana. On the other hand, one may find peace and self-consciousness as easily in Los Angeles as in rural Montana.

Individualism

Sociologists are generally concerned about the role of individuals in society. The relationship between society and the individual was very important to Riesman. However, as Cuzzort and King (1995) explained, Riesman's approach was different from others:

> First of all, Riesman is not especially concerned with resolving the problem of the priority of society or the individual. He is not concerned with proving that society dominates the individual. Nor is he interested in proving that society is a collective manifestation of individual instincts—an elaborately spread out form of human nature. Instead, he takes the problem of the relationship between the individual and society as a point of departure for an investigation into national character. All we need to do is to presume that if there is some kind of relationship between society and the individual—and this seems apologetically reasonably—then the historical experiences of our society may have a bearing on what we, as individuals, have become today. (p. 227)

Thus, certain societies produce specific social characters. *Traditional-directed* societies, for example, will develop in their people a social character that is typified by a tendency to follow long-held customs. Furthermore, *tradition-directed* individuals possess a social character uncritical of tradition and resistant to innovation.

In the introduction to *Individualism Reconsidered* (1955), Riesman stated that he was "defending individualism (of a certain sort) and being critical of conformity (of a certain sort). Yet, I am perfectly sure that I would not be attacking 'groupism' in America if I could not rely on its durable achievements—it is just these that make individualism possible" (p. ix). Consequently, individuals may have unique personality traits, but they are products of their environment and subject to "outside" social forces. Society, defined by Riesman (1955) as a system of social organization, "often provides the mechanisms by which the individual can be protected against the group, both by the formal legal procedures as bills of rights, and by the social fact that large-scale organization many permit the social mobility by which individuals can escape from any particular group" (p. 12). In this regard, groups allow people to become the individuals they hope to be. If someone is uncomfortable with her or his self, joining more compatible groups will assist her or him in reaching self-consciousness. For example, someone who is not comfortable with her or his poor social economic status can work hard, go to college, and find a job that will allow her or him the opportunity to get ahead. The corporate drone who is unhappy with the monotony of his or her life can leave the profession and find a more "spiritual" or "fulfilling" environment or occupation, such as helping those less fortunate. Simply doing volunteer work in a group atmosphere can enhance one's level of self. In short, anyone unsatisfied with his or her self can alter his or her consciousness by joining groups that enhance his or her quality of life.

Education

Riesman wrote many publications related to education and the academic world. In 1956, *Constraint and Variety in American Education* was published. In this book, Riesman attempted to place American higher and secondary education in a cultural context. He suggested that some colleges and universities serve as models for one another, while others are so remote from leading centers that they are not influenced at all by what happens at the major institutions. Other characteristics of educational settings that influence the social character are found in such areas as the level of commitment they have to activities such as athletics, the arts, Greek life, or the snobbiness of such institutions as Harvard. The reputations of many colleges and secondary-level schools are centered on the character they portray (whether actively or not). Thus, because of Harvard's level of prestige, graduating from Harvard is highly desirable. Outstanding athletes might prefer

such institutions of higher education as Florida State University or the University of Tennessee.

The category of society also dictates the type of education available. In the tradition-directed society, children are not likely to receive formal education. They learn what they need to survive in society from direct interaction with adults and peers. In the inner-directed society, issues of education become more complicated. "Children must be infused with general goals that they are willing to pursue even though they may exact a cost in terms of indifference and hostility on the part of others. . . . The character of schooling in the inner-directed society can be summed up as follows: The task of the teacher is to train children in matters of decorum and intellectual subjects. The approach is impersonal. . . . Standards are unequivocal—they are immutable" (Cuzzort and King, 1995:231). Schooling in the other-directed society is designed to ready students for their place in society, with a focus on problems of group relations.

In *The Academic Revolution* (1968), coauthored with Christopher Jencks, Riesman described the rise to power of professional scholars and scientists, especially in America's leading universities. "This book attempts a sociological and historical analysis of American higher education. It begins with a general theory about the development of American society and American colleges, then moves on to discuss different species of colleges and their relationships to the various special interest groups that founded them" (Jencks and Riesman, 1968:ix). Riesman discovered decades ago what scholars still describe today, namely, that colleges and universities are highly politicized. Professors who do not fit the social character of the institution are ostracized, or at the least, their lives are made difficult.

Seventeenth-, eighteenth-, and early-nineteenth-century American colleges were conceived and operated as pillars of the locally established church, political order, and social conventions. They were tradition-directed. By the second quarter of the nineteenth century the character of American universities changed with the evolving American society. A strong central government, the disestablishment of state churches, and the movement westward to California made it clear that no single group had the power to shape society as a whole. However, the trend for wealthy benefactors to provide sizable contributions to colleges and universities (in order to have buildings named after them) revealed the continuing political nature of academia. This trend still exists. Jencks and Riesman (1968) described the rise of the university as one of the most profound changes in higher education. The rise of the university had many consequences. "College instructors have become less and less preoccupied with educating young people, more and more preoccupied with educating one another by doing scholarly research which advances their discipline. Undergraduate education has become less and less a terminal enterprise, more and more a preparation for graduate school. The result is that higher education has ceased to be a marginal backward-looking enterprise shunned by the bulk of the citizenry. Today it is a major growth industry" (Jencks and Riesman, 1968:12–13). The trend has also continued, as by the year 2000, one out of four Americans has a four-year degree.

In 1980, Riesman published *On Higher Education*. Riesman noted that a lot had changed since he published *The Academic Revolution*. In this period of time the power of the faculty had seemed to shift to the students. The student protests of the late 1960s were the first signs of this changing character of education. Student "needs" have become the focus of concern at most colleges and universities. Specialized study programs, demands for tuition-assistance, and minority admissions, have become the norm of the college. Riesman also described student "consumerism" as a characteristic of contemporary education.

Social Research, Theory, and Narratives

In his article "Some Observations on Social Science Research" (1951), Riesman stated, "Every work of social science today establishes itself on a scale whose two ends are 'theory' and 'data': that is, the great theoretical structures by which we attempt to understand our age at one end, and the relatively minuscule experiments and data which we collect as practicing social scientists at the other" (p. 259). Sociologists generally accept the scientific method and empiricism as the "standard" for conducting sound research. It is what makes them "scientists." Other people who claim to be sociologists argue against the use of the scientific method— among them, the postmodernists. Patterson (2002) is one such theorist who disagrees with empirical social research in sociology:

> Anxious to achieve the status of economics and other "soft sciences," the gatekeepers of sociology have insisted on a style of research and thinking that focuses on the testing of hypotheses based on data generated by measurements presumed to be valid. This approach works reasonably well for the study of certain subjects like demographics in which there is stability in the variables studied. Business schools, for example, have increasingly turned to organizational sociologists for a more realistic interpretation of the behavior of firms than that provided by economists. Unfortunately, for most areas of social life—especially those areas in which the general public is interested—the methods of natural science are not only inappropriate but distorting. (It is important to note here that the issue is not the use of statistics. Mr. Riesman encouraged their use where appropriate). (p. 15)

Although, Patterson underestimated the American public's desire for scientific validity in social matters, he is correct that Riesman utilized statistical analysis.

For *Faces in the Crowd* (1952), Riesman and Glazer collected data from 180 interviews. "Interviews are simply one of a number of ways of understanding human character in a society that trains people in many analogous kinds of social conversation and encounter" (Riesman and Glazer, 1952:31). They found that working with interviews preserves the "freshness of first impression" while the data allowed them to quantify their results. The importance of interviewing reflects Riesman's postmodern commitment to social research because it avoids the narrative, grand-theorizing approach of traditional sociology.

JEAN-FRANCOIS LYOTARD (1924–1998)

Jean-Francois Lyotard was born in Versailles, France, in 1924. He was one of the world's foremost philosophers and a noted postmodernist. His interdisciplinary discourse covers a wide variety of topics, including the postmodern conditions, modernist and postmodernist art, knowledge and communication, language, metanarratives, and legitimization. Lyotard taught at many universities, including the University of California at Irvine for several years. At the time of his death in 1998, Lyotard was professor emeritus of the University of Paris VIII and professor at Emory University in Atlanta.

Art, Architecture, and Postmodernism

A number of letters written by Lyotard which take up the issue of postmodernity appear in *The Postmodern Explained* (1993). The translator's foreword explains that this book "approaches the postmodern as a way of maintaining the possibility of thought 'happening'—in philosophy, art, literature, and politics; of thought preceding when it has lost faith in its capacity to repair the crimes of the past by guiding the present toward the end of the realization of ideas" (p. ix). Lyotard (1993) argued that we are in an era of relaxation:

> Everywhere we are being urged to give up experimentation, in the arts and elsewhere. I have read an art historian who preaches

realism and agitates for the advent of a new subjectivity. I have read an art critic who broadcasts and sells "transavantgardism" in the marketplace of art. I have read that in the name of postmodernism architects are ridding themselves of the Bauhaus project, throwing out the baby—which is still experimentation—with the bathwater of functionalism. . . . I have read from the pen of an eminent historian that avant-garde writers and thinkers of the 1960s and 1970s introduced a reign of terror into the use of language, and that the imposition of a common mode of speech on intellectuals (that of historians) is necessary to reestablish the conditions for fruitful debate. (pp. 1–2)

These demands, among others, were cited by Lyotard because they were made in the name of postmodernism, whether by those in favor of a postmodernist approach or by those who were against it. These demands were designed to challenge the status quo. The concept of *realism* is itself subject to changing parameters. Realism finds itself between academicism and kitsch (shoddy or cheap literary material). "When authority takes the name of the party, realism and its complement,

Jean-Francois Lyotard, French-born philosopher and postmodernist social thinker.
Source: ULF Andersen Gamma

neoclassicism, triumph over the experimental avant-garde by slandering and censoring it. Even then, 'correct' images, 'correct' narratives—the correct forms that the party solicits, selects, and distributes—must procure a public that will desire them as the appropriate medicine for the depression and anxiety it feels" (Lyotard, 1993:7).

Lyotard (1993:15) believed that the postmodern artist or writer is in the position of a philosopher because the text she or he creates is not governed by preestablished rules and cannot be judged according to the application of given categories to this work. Thus, the postmodern can be defined as that which in the modern invokes the unpresentable in presentation itself, and that which refuses to fit predetermined categorization and inquires into new presentations. Postmodernity is a product, or an effect, of the development of modernity itself (Lyotard and Larochelle, 1992:415). Lyotard (1993:76) explained that the *post* of postmodernism generally implies a simple succession, a diachronic sequence of periods in which each one is clearly identifiable. The *post* indicates something similar to a conversion—a new direction from the previous one. As for architecture, the postmodern

> finds itself condemned to abandon a global reconstruction of the space of human habitation. The perspective then opens onto a vast landscape, in the sense that there is no longer any horizon of universality, universalization, or general emancipation to greet the eye of postmodern man, least of all the eye of the architect. The disappearance of the Idea that rationality and freedom are progression would explain a "tone," style, or mode specific to postmodern architecture. I would say it is a sort of "bricolage": the multiple quotation of elements taken from earlier styles or periods, classical and modern; disregard for the environment; and so on. (Lyotard, 1993:76)

True to the postmodern tradition, Lyotard's criticism of the rational positivist approach to the study of society is prevalent throughout his work.

Postmodernism and Knowledge

In *The Postmodern Condition: A Report on Knowledge* (1999) Lyotard drew attention to the shift in thinking among many social scientists, namely, away from a reliance on and belief in universals (positivism). In this book, Lyotard wrote about the condition of knowledge as a postmodern one and believed that this condition can be used to describe the condition of knowledge in most highly developed societies. In the introduction to *The Postmodern Condition* Lyotard (1999) wrote, "The object of this study is the condition of knowledge in the most highly developed societies. I have decided to use the word *postmodern* to describe that condition. The word is in current use on the American continent among sociologists and critics; it designates the state of our culture following the transformations which, since the end of the nineteenth century, have altered the game rules for science, literature, and the arts" (p. xxiii). Lyotard described positivist science as a "fable" with a methodology that produces legitimization with respect to the rules of its own game.

Lyotard (1999) used as a working hypothesis the idea "that the status of knowledge is altered as societies enter what is known as the postindustrial age and cultures enter what is known as the postmodern age. This transition has been under way since at least the end of the 1950s, which for Europe marks the completion of reconstruction. The pace is faster or slower depending on the country" (p. 3). The pace of development is especially contingent on technological knowledge. Societies that possess computer knowledge are especially at the forefront in the transformation to postmodernity. Thus, advancing technology has a direct effect on knowledge. "It is widely accepted that knowledge has become the principle force of production over the last few decades; this has already had a noticeable effect on the composition of the work force of the most highly developed countries and constitutes the major bottleneck for the developing countries. In the postindustrial and postmodern age, science will maintain and no doubt strengthen its preeminence in the arsenal of productive capacities of the nation-states" (Lyotard, 1999:5). Economically powerful nations have always exerted their will on the less-developed nations. Armed with increased technological knowledge, the dominant societies will continue this bipolar power relationship.

Lyotard (1999) made it clear that there is a distinction between knowledge and science:

> Knowledge [*savoir*] in general cannot be reduced to science, not even to learning [*connaissance*]. Learning is the set of statements which, to the exclusion of all other statements, denote or describe objects and may be declared true or false. Science is a subset of learning. It is also composed of denotative statements, but imposes two supplementary conditions on their acceptability: the objects to which they refer must be available for repeated access, in other words, they must be accessible in explicit conditions of observation; and it must be possible to decide whether or not a given statement pertains to the language judged relevant by the experts. (p. 18)

Knowledge includes notions of "knowing" how to do things, such as knowing how to listen, how to live, how to enjoy life. Science is a type of knowledge.

With the above position in mind, Lyotard proposed a postmodern approach to the study of society and the advancement of knowledge, one that does not involve positivism. "Science does not expand by means of the positivism of efficiency. The opposite is true: working on a proof means searching for and 'inventing' counter examples, in other words, the unintelligible; supporting an argument means looking for a 'paradox' and legitimating it with new rules in the games of reasoning" (Lyotard, 1999:54). Lyotard believed that with every new theory, hypothesis, statement, or observation, the question of legitimacy remains. He explained that legitimation "is the process by

which a 'legislator' dealing with scientific discourse is authorized to prescribe the stated conditions determining whether a statement is to be included in that discourse for consideration by the scientific community. . . . For it appears in its most complete form, that of reversion, revealing that knowledge and power are simply two sides of the same question: who decides what knowledge is, and who knows what needs to be decided?" (1999:8).

In short, Lyotard wanted to abolish the monopoly that certain orthodoxies have enjoyed over claims to "truth" and "knowledge production."

Legitimation, Language, and Narratives

Lyotard's (1999) definition and usage of *postmodernism* are linked to the three concepts of *legitimation, language,* and *narratives:*

> Simplifying to the extreme, I define *postmodern* as incredulity toward metanarratives. This incredulity is undoubtedly a product of progress in the sciences: but that progress in turn presupposes it. To the obsolescence of the metanarrative apparatus of legitimation corresponds, most notably, the crisis of metaphysical philosophy and of the university institution which in the past relied on it. The narrative function is losing its functors, its great hero, its great dangers, its great voyages, its great goal. It is being dispersed in clouds of narrative language elements— narrative, but also denotative, prescriptive, descriptive, and so on. (p. xxiv).

Lyotard firmly believed that the grand narratives of knowledge had lost their credibility in the postmodern society and that proponents of positivism had lost their claims of legitimacy. Lyotard used the term *metanarratives* to mark the progressive emancipation of reason and to draw attention to the postmodern break from tradition dominated by positivistic grand narratives.

According to Lyotard (1999:19–23) narration is a quintessential form of customary knowledge in at least five ways:

1. Popular stories recount the successes and failures of the hero's undertakings. These successes bestow legitimacy upon the hero (which may be an individual or a social institution). Thus, the narratives allow the society in which they are told, on the one hand, to define its criteria of competence and, on the other hand, to evaluate according to those criteria what is performed or can be performed within it.

2. The narrative form, unlike the developed forms of the discourse of knowledge, lends itself to a great variety of language games.

3. The pragmatic rules that constitute the social bond are transmitted through these narratives.

4. Rhythm, time, and metrical beat are emphasized because they make narratives easy to remember.

5. A culture that gives precedence to the narrative form doubtless has no more of a need for special procedures to authorize its narratives than to remember its past. It is even harder to imagine a society handing over the authority for its narratives to some opposing narrator.

Narratives are an integral aspect of culture and directly affect the language of any given society.

Lyotard utilized a methodology he called *language games*. "In *The Postmodern Condition* Lyotard uses the method of language game analysis to contrast the pragmatics of narrative and scientific knowledge. He defines modernism as the attempt to legitimate science by appeal to 'metanarratives,' or philosophical accounts of the progress of history in which the hero of knowledge struggles toward a great goal such as freedom, universal peace, or the creation of wealth" (Nicholson, 1989:198). In describing language games, Lyotard used Wittgenstein's study of language, where he focused on the effects of different modes of discourse or what he called the various categories of utterances. Lyotard (1999) wrote that "each of various categories of utterance can be defined in terms of rules specifying their properties and the uses to which they can be put—in exactly the same way as

the game of chess is defined by a set of rules determining the properties of each of the pieces, in other words, the proper way to move them" (p. 10). Lyotard (1999) continued to articulate on language games by making three observations: "The first is that their rules do not carry within themselves their own legitimation, but are the object of a contract, explicit or not, between players (which is not to say that the players invent the rules). The second is that if there are no rules, there is no game, that even an infinitesimal modification of one rule alters the nature of the game, that a 'move' or utterance that does not satisfy the rules does not belong to the game they define. The third remark is suggested by what has just been said: every utterance should be thought of as a 'move' in a game" (p. 10). Language can be used for the sheer pleasure of "making a move" in the game of life, and it can be used as a weapon, for if knowledge is power, communicating in a tactical and purposeful manner may allow individuals (or societies) to gain an advantage over others.

Language exampled the first efforts of legitimacy. Rulers of past societies utilized language constructs when they formed governments and regimes (*forma regiminis*). Kant referred to this as the legitimation of the normative instance. Rigid designators define the world. Each human who is born into the world comes to a place that has been previously labeled, or constructed. Furthermore, these labels or constructions have been legitimized by past events, and by those in power (Lyotard, 1993:45). Lyotard explained in his 1992 article "Mainnise" that it is up to all infants to emancipate themselves, to become owners of themselves. Language is a tool of emancipation. Language is also a requirement for a society to exist. Therefore, to understand social relations, what is necessary is not only a theory of communication, but also a theory of language games.

JEAN BAUDRILLARD (1929–)

Jean Baudrillard was born in 1929 in the northern French town of Reims. Jean's parents were civil servants, and his grandparents were peasant farmers. He was the first member of his family to attend university. He taught German in a lycée before completing his doctoral thesis in sociology under the guidance of Henri Lefebvre. Baudrillard became an assistant professor in September 1966 at Nanterre University of Paris. Identifying with student protests at Nanterre in 1968, Baudrillard began publishing a number of theoretical articles bashing capitalist affluence and the growth of technology. Over the years, Baudrillard became a notorious French sociologist (Baudrillard, 2003).

Baudrillard is a postmodern theorist and social philosopher and the author of such publications as *System of Objects; Consumer Society, Critique of the Political Economy of the Sign, The Mirror Production, Symbolic Exchange and Death, On Seduction, America, On the Beach,* and *Cool Memories.*

Baudrillard is a radical among postmodernists. "Baudrillard was trained as a sociologist, but his work has long since left the confines of that discipline; indeed, it cannot be contained by any discipline, and Baudrillard would in any case reject the whole idea of disciplinary boundaries" (Ritzer, 2000c:477). Baudrillard's work is quite diversified and ever-changing. In the 1960s he was both a modernist and a Marxist. He was especially critical of the consumer society. As Ritzer (2000c) explained, his works were also influenced by linguistics and semiotics. By the 1980s Baudrillard could be considered both a postmodernist and a critic of Marxism. Douglas Kellner (1989b) wrote in the introduction to *Jean Baudrillard* that Baudrillard "is now sliding toward center stage of the cultural scene in some circles. In a number of 'postmodern' journals and grouplets, Baudrillard is being proclaimed as a fundamental challenge to our orthodoxies and the

conventional wisdom in Marxism, psycho-analysis, philosophy, semiology, political economy, anthropology, sociology and other disciplines" (p. 1). Christopher Norris (1990) added, "Baudrillard is undoubtedly the one who has gone furthest toward renouncing enlightenment reason and all its works, from the Kantian-liberal agenda to Marxism, Frankfurt Critical Theory, the structuralist 'sciences of man,' and even—on his view—the residual theoreticist delusions of a thinker like Foucault" (p. 164).

Postmodernism

Baudrillard was a part of the French tradition challenging traditional sociological thought. In the 1960s and 1970s his ideas included Marxist criticism of capitalism in studies of consumption, fashion, media, sexuality, and the consumer society. "From this perspective, Baudrillard's early work can be interpreted as a response to neo-capitalism, which, in the 1960s, came with a vengeance to France, with contradictory consequences. The Monnet Plan of the 1940s had inaugurated state planning, and by the 1960s modernization, technological development and the growth of both monopoly firms and a technocratic state sector were evident" (Kellner, 1989b:2). France was also experiencing new architecture and many new expressions of the consumer society such as drugstores, advertising, and mass media—especially television. The France of the 1960s was dramatically different from the France of the 1950s. Social theorists attempted to explain this societal transformation. "These socioeconomic developments stirred a remarkable series of attempts to reconstruct radical social theories to account for the changes in social conditions and everyday life, and spawned many new critical discourses" (Kellner, 1989:3). Baudrillard refers to France as a "consumer society."

The critique of society is a postmodernist creed, where ideas of truth, validity, or claims to being "right" are challenged. Baudrillard (1981b) argued that the empirical object is a myth. He believes that there was a time when signs stood for something real; now they refer to little more than themselves. Thus, signs are created for their own sake; they have become self-referential. Distinctions between what is real and what is fabricated are the cornerstone of the postmodern world. "We can no longer tell what is real; the distinction between signs and reality has *imploded.* More generally, the postmodern world (for now Baudrillard is operating squarely within that world) is a world characterized by such implosion as distinguished from the explosions (of productive systems, of commodities, of technologies, and so on) that characterized modern society. Thus, just as the modern world underwent a process of differentiation, the postmodern world can be seen as undergoing *dedifferentiation*" (Ritzer, 2000c:478).

In a world where signs no longer have a "natural" meaning and are instead manufactured, they take on symbolic meaning. In this regard Baudrillard's postmodernist thinking is familiar to symbolic interactionists. For example, in the medieval world, symbols had an unbroken bond with reality—an individual's identity was brutally and unequivocally stamped by the rigid estate system. Everyone *was* exactly as he or she appeared to be (Shalin, 1993). Today, this is not necessarily true. Instead, the postmodern world is characterized by simulation. According to Baudrillard (1983b), we live in the "age of simulation." Simulations dominate society and have produced a new kind of social order. Simulations lead to the creation of simulacra—the reproductions of objects or events:

> For Baudrillard, "simulacra" are reproductions of objects or events, while "orders of simulacra" form various stages or "orders of appearance" in the relationships between simulacra and "the real." . . . Baudrillard claims that modernity broke with the fixed

feudal-medieval hierarchy of signs and social position by introducing an artificial, democratized world of signs which valorized artifice (stucco, theater, fashion, baroque art, political democracy) over natural signs, thereby exploding fixed medieval hierarchies and order. . . . In Baudrillard's terminology, a "natural law of value" dominated this stage of early modernity, in which simulacra (from art to political representation) were held to represent nature or to embody "natural" rights or laws. (Kellner, 1989b:78)

During industrialization, when infinite reproducibility appeared in the world, industrial simulacra dominated. Mass production replaced the "natural" form of production that existed in feudal-medieval times.

Dramatic changes in society cause a ripple effect throughout the social system. The technological world of capitalism requires a technical language (signs, simulacra) to describe the new systems of objects and their relations. Baudrillard's postmodernist perspective led him to believe that the new technical world of objects causes changes in values, modes of behavior, and relations to objects and to other people. The modern individual is portrayed as a "cybernetician" who is induced to order objects in accordance with the imperatives of the technical world (Baudrillard, 1968). The new morality ushered in by technical advancements affects all the structures of society, and life in its totality. (This is similar to structural functionalist thought: A dramatic change in one part of the system causes dramatic changes in the remaining parts.) "In short, the system of objects leads people to adapt to a new, modern world which represents a transition from a traditional, material organization of the environment to a more rationalized and cultural one. Baudrillard provides a multidimensional analysis of this new world, and attempts to elucidate the ways in which objects and individuals are 'liberated' from traditional systems and usages, yet constrained by the technical imperatives of the new environment" (Kellner, 1983:10–11).

According to Baudrillard (1981), we live in a world that is not "real." (Note: He influenced the novel *The Matrix*.) Instead, we live in a *hyperreal* world where signs have acquired a life of their own and serve no other purpose than symbolic exchange. Symbolic exchange involves the continuous cycle of taking and returning, giving and receiving, a cycle of gifts and countergifts (Baudrillard, 1973/1975:83). Furthermore, individuals caught up in this exchange are convinced that the objects they consume have intrinsic use value. However, this use value is really a "sign exchange value" that the technical system maintains only because consumers choose to give it meaning (a classical Marxist perspective). Shalin (1993) argued that Baudrillard took his cue from Thorstein Veblen (for example, Veblen's study of the leisure class) and supplemented it with his own original insights into the age of mass media, mass production, and mass consumption.

In sum, Baudrillard (1983) argued that society in the postmodern era is dominated by simulacra and simulation and falls into the domain of a hyperreal sociality, where "referential reason disappears."

Beyond Marxism

Initially, Baudrillard employed many Marxist ideas in his own works. However, as Kellner (1983) explained:

> Baudrillard's relation to Marxism is extremely complex and volatile. . . . His first two books can be read as a supplement to and development of the Marxian critique of political economy which follow Marxian explorations of production into the mode of consumption and can be utilized to develop a neo-Marxian critical theory of capitalism. For in these books Baudrillard at least occasionally relates consumption to the mode of production, focuses on the commodity and its uses, and engages in class analysis and critical demystifications of dominant ideologies of consumption, leisure and so on.

> But his third book, *For a Critique of the Political Economy of the Sign* [1972/1981], begins to criticize certain Marxian notions more aggressively, and the later books, *The Mirror of Production* [1973/1975] and *L'échange symbolique et la mort* [English edition, 1976] carry out a wholesale rejection of Marxism and thus constitute a break with Marxian theory. (p. 33)

Norris (1990) argued that Baudrillard's split with Marxism developed most fully in *The Mirror of Production* (1973/1975). "Here he sets out to deconstruct the opposition between use-value and exchange-value, the one conceived in terms of 'genuine' needs and productive resources, the other identified with a late-capitalist or consumer economy which invades and distorts every aspect of human existence" (Norris, 1990:166). Baudrillard (1973/1975) felt that Marxist analysis of labor power, production, use value needs, and so on is a leftover product of an era long gone. Theorists who continue to use Marxist terms are merely producing a mirror image of conservative political economy. Baudrillard (1973/1975:39) argued that Marx's approach was infected by the "virus of bourgeois thought." "Specifically, Marx's approach was infused with conservative ideas like 'work' and 'value.' What was needed was a new, more radical orientation" (Ritzer, 2000c:477). Baudrillard believes that Marx's concepts and theory are too conservative to be useful to revolutionary theory because they are too dependent on the analysis of the political economy. "Baudrillard thus rejects Marxism both as a 'mirror,' or reflection, of a 'productivist' capitalism and as a 'classical' mode of representation that purports to mirror 'the real.' He thus participates in the poststructuralist critique of representational thought" (Kellner, 1983:40).

In short, Baudrillard denounces Marxist theory as simply another variant on the old, self-deluding enlightenment theme—the idea that one can criticize existing beliefs from some superior vantage point of truth, reason, or scientific method (Norris, 1990:168). Postmodern society, characterized by Baudrillard as "cybernetic-technocratic," is no longer subject to analysis from a Marxist perspective.

Contemporary Society

Baudrillard pays close attention to contemporary society. In his second book, *La Société de consommation* (1970), Baudrillard continued his systematic theoretical and empirical investigations of objects and activities in the new world of consumption and technique. "Whereas his first book contains rather theoretical studies of the world of objects, his second book presents a sketch of the nature and structures of the new worlds of leisure and consumption for a more popular audience" (Kellner, 1983:12). He believed that society was no longer dominated by production, but by developments of consumerism, the media, entertainment, and information technologies. "It could be said that we have moved from a society dominated by the mode of production to one controlled by the code of production. The objective has shifted from exploitation and profit to domination by the signs and the systems that produce them" (Ritzer, 2000c:478). Postmodern society is dominated by issues of consumption. People find it necessary to have and use a wide range of goods and services, whether they have a real need for them or not.

Baudrillard's focus on culture led him to conclude that society has undergone a "catastrophic" revolution that has led to the demise of "social" society (for example, idealized resonances of human interaction, civility). Baudrillard blamed the proliferation of media communication and mass entertainment as the chief culprits of this demise. The postmodern society is bombarded by too many messages, advertisements, ideological discourses, signs, and meanings, which eventually lead to an oversaturation.

The Mass Media and Entertainment

"Contemporary culture in the advanced industrial societies is often characterized as being saturated by the media, entertainment, and new information systems. The question is what are the implications of this saturation?" (Kivisto, 1998:142). Baudrillard (1983) believed that the mass media are so dominant and powerful that they have created a culture characterized by hyperreality. That is, the media no longer mirror reality: they have become more real than reality itself. Entertainment media present images that are both not real and, yet, more real than real (Baudrillard, 1983b). As Delaney and Wilcox (2002) explained:

> Contemporary society can be characterized as a *mass-mediated culture,* that is, a culture in which the mass media play a role in both shaping and creating cultural perceptions. The media do not simply mirror society, they help to shape it. With a nearly endless array of events occurring constantly around the world, the media require some way to selectively manage a number of items. This is accomplished by the "categorization of news," selecting events to cover that "fit" the given format. Categorization limits the number of stories deemed worthy of coverage, and also helps to shape how the coverage is presented. Consequently, if the media decide not to cover an event, it is not *news*— at least not public news. (pp. 202–203)

Ryan and Wentworth (1999) argued that another important element of the media's presentation of events is their "over-simplification of complex issues." In this regard, events are streamlined by the media and are limited by time and space. The categorization and over-simplification of events by the media are packaged in such a way as to appeal to the largest audience of consumers.

Best and Kellner (1991) used as an example of Baudrillard's hyperreality a television show where the actor Robert Young played the role of Dr. Welby. Young received thousands of letters asking for medical advice because the audience could not separate the "real" Robert Young from the "unreal" Dr. Welby. Young later capitalized on this misinterpretation of his television role by appearing in commercials saying that he was not a doctor, but that if he were, he would recommend this product. Ritzer (2000c:478) described tabloid news shows and "infomercials" as examples of the hyperreal because the falsehoods and distortions they peddle to viewers are not real and often form the spectacle. In fact, even real events seem to take on the character of the hyperreal (such as the trial of the former football star O. J. Simpson for the murders of Nicole Simpson and Ronald Goldman).

According to Baudrillard, the mass media are not the only social institution responsible for hyperreality. He believed that hyperreality extends to all aspects of postmodern culture and comes in the form of entertainment as well. Baudrillard (1983b) was critical of Disneyland and remarked, "Disneyland is presented as imaginary in order to make us believe that the rest is real, when in fact all of Los Angeles, and the America surrounding it are no longer real, but of the order of the hyperreal and of simulation" (p. 25). (Imagine how Baudrillard must have reacted to Euro Disney in Paris!) Such generalized statements certainly leave Baudrillard open to criticism (Kivisto, 1998:143). Citizens of the United States, in general, and of Los Angeles, specifically, may live in a hyperreal world as described by Baudrillard, but their world *is* real, as demonstrated by the daily events and chores that each person must accomplish in order to live. Kivisto (1998) took exception to Baudrillard's rather unflattering portrait of the role of individuals in postmodern society:

> We appear to have been reduced to the roles of mall rats in quest of objects of desire and excitement, couch potatoes playing with the TV remote control, and voyeurs peering into the private lives of the rich of famous. . . . We are . . . thoroughly enmeshed in our social worlds but incapable of controlling them or of operating in a genuinely autonomous way. This view of social actors is far removed from Marx's vision of the potential for beneficial change arising from collective action. (p. 143)

We are, as Baudrillard claims, in an era in which new technologies (for example, the media, cybernetic models, and computers) have replaced industrial production and political economy as the organizing principle of society. The important issue is: What will we, as a society, do about it? Will we find a way to survive with an emphasis on industry? The next "modern" or "postmodern" era will reveal the answers.

FREDRIC JAMESON (1934–)

Fredric Jameson was born April 14, 1934, in Cleveland, Ohio. He received his M.A. from Yale University in 1956 and his Ph.D. from Yale in 1959. He taught at Harvard University from 1959 to 1967; at the University of California at San Diego from 1967 to 1976; at Yale from 1976 to 1983; at the UC at Santa Cruz from 1983 to 1985; and at Duke starting in 1986. Jameson is now serving as Distinguished Professor of Comparative Literature at Duke University, where he directs the Graduate Program in Literature and the Center for Cultural Theory. Among his publications are *Marxism and Form* (1971), *The Political Unconscious* (1981a), and "Postmodernism, or, After the Cultural Logic of Late Capitalism" (1984).

Postmodernism

Jameson equates postmodernism with late capitalism. He believes that distinct phases of the mode of production have distinct "cultural dominants," or forms of culture. "Jameson gives relatively little attention to classes as coherent purposive social actors. Rather, the cultural dominant is a pattern of representation that appears across different media and art forms. It is an indirect reflection of the underlying mode of production and social conditions, not the product of a class-conscious dominant class" (Garner, 2000:536). Late capitalism is characterized by commodity production, "high tech" or electronic technology, multinationalism and globalization, and media penetration into our unconscious, as well as into our consciousness. Late capitalism represents the shift from modern society to postmodern society. According to Jameson (1981b), in late capitalism, culture is dominated by consumerism and mass media. Never, at any other point in history, has society been so saturated with signs and messages (for example, advertising, information, and communication technologies). The impact of consumerism and the mass media is felt in all spheres of life, including socialization, education, and leisure.

Unlike many postmodern theorists, Jameson does not reject Marxian theory. Jameson used a Marxist analyses of six continental writers in his 1971 publication *Marxism and Form.* More important, as Ritzer (2000c) proclaimed, "Jameson is not only rescuing Marxian theory, but endeavoring to show that it offers the best theoretical explanation of postmodernity. . . . Consistent with the work of Marx, and unlike most theorists of postmodernism, Jameson (1984:86) sees both positive and negative characteristics, 'catastrophe and progress all together,' associated with postmodern society" (p. 473). Jonathan Turner (2003) also sees a Marxian perspective in Jameson's analysis of postmodernism.

> Drawing from Marx's philosophy of knowledge, Jameson still attempts to use the method of praxis to critique the social construction of reality in postmodernity. Marx argued that reality did not exist in concepts, ideas, or reflexive thought but in the material world of production. . . . According to Jameson, the creation of consciousness through production was unproblematically

represented by the aesthetic of the machine in earlier phases of capitalism, but in multinational capitalism, electronic machines like movie cameras, videos, tape recorders, and computers do not have the same capacity for signification because they are machines of *reproduction* rather than of production. (p. 234)

Jameson (2000) believes that with late capitalism, aesthetic production has become integrated into commodity production. Aesthetic production has spilled over into architecture as well, with many new buildings described as postmodern. According to Jameson, styles such as those produced by Frank Lloyd Wright illustrate this point, while Las Vegas epitomizes aesthetic populism.

An interesting concept of Jameson's is *hyperspace,* an area where modern conceptions of space are useless in helping us to orient ourselves. Jameson (1984) used as an example the Los Angeles Hotel Bonaventure with its lobby design that leaves visitors unable to get their bearings. The lobby contains rooms surrounded by four absolutely symmetrical towers, which contain the rooms. Visitors to Las Vegas's gambling rooms complain of the same thing: Where is the exit? It is very easy to lose one's bearings in the casinos of Las Vegas. Jameson uses the concept of *hyperspace* to illustrate the point that people develop cognitive maps in order to maneuver in the complexity of society. The use of maps reinforces the reality that people define the world spatially rather than temporally. Interestingly, Jameson (1989) admitted that cognitive mapping is in reality nothing but a code word for "class consciousness."

It is highly questionable whether the concepts of *hyperspace* and *cognitive mapping* are unique to the postmodern era. Throughout history, cultures have designed unique architecture that may have left visitors confused. The pyramids come to mind immediately, and a number of castles have been designed symmetrically. The University of Moscow has an awesomely huge administrative and dorm building designed in a mirror fashion. As a visitor to that wonderful campus, this author was left confused more than once about whether he was facing the front or the back of the building. As a final note, this building is more than 150 years old—clearly not a product of postmodernism.

Modernism and Capitalistic Imperialism

History has shown that imperialism and colonization have existed for thousands of years and therefore are clearly not to be blamed on modernism or postmodernism. Jameson (1990), however, attempted to show a relationship between modernism and imperialism in his article "Modernism and Imperialism" (1990), in which he wrote, "if it is the link between imperialism and modernism that is in question here (and between imperialism and Western modernism at that), then clearly imperialism must here mean the imperialist dynamic of capitalism proper, and not the wars of conquest of the various ancient empires" (p. 46). Thus, Jameson had to admit that imperialism is not a modern construct; however, he relabeled imperialism to fit his argument against capitalism. Jameson believed that most people think of Marx when they think of imperialism, but even Marx's theories of imperialism are subject to a historical qualification.

Jameson (1990) focused on imperialism not as the relationship between metropolis and colony, but as the rivalry of the various imperial and metropolitan nation-states:

> For it is in our time, since World War II, that the problem of imperialism is as it were restructured: in the age of neocolonialism, of decolonization accompanied by the emergence of multinational capitalism and the great transnational corporations, it is less the rivalry of the metropolitan powers among each other that strikes the eye (our occasional problems with Japan, for example, do not project that impending World War-type conflict that nagged at the awareness of the *belle epoque*); rather, contemporary

theorists, from Paul Baran on to the present day, have been concerned with the internal dynamics of the relationship between First and Third World countries, and in particular the way in which this relationship—which is now very precisely what the word "imperialism" means for us—is one of necessary subordination or dependency, and that of an economic type, rather than a primarily military one. (pp. 47–48)

Jameson's belief that imperialism is significantly different from in the past is flawed. Imperialism has always been about expanding markets and spreading culture (including religion). The danger of late-capitalistic imperialism is expanding military modes of destruction. Since the third millennium began, the threat of worldwide war has been ever-present. The terrorist attacks on New York City on September 11, 2001, were a wake-up call to all citizens of the world.

The Political Unconscious

Jameson wrote in *The Political Unconscious* (1981a) that our understanding of the world is influenced by the concepts and categories that we inherit from our culture's interpretive tradition. With this in mind, Jameson (1981a) wondered, "How can readers of the present understand literature of the past when it was written in such a culturally different context?" (p. 281). The answer, according to Jameson, lies in Marxism and Marx's perspective that history is a single collective narrative that links past and present:

> The most influential lesson of Marx—the one which ranges him alongside Freud and Nietzsche as one of the great negative diagnosticians of contemporary culture and social life—has, of course, rightly been taken to be the lesson of false consciousness, of class bias and ideological programming, the lesson of the structural limits of the values and attitudes of particular social classes, or in other words of the constitutive relationship between praxis of such groups and what they conceptualize as value or desire

and project in the form of culture (Jameson, 1981:281–282)

Determining what is "false" and what is "objective" fact continues to dominate modern thought. When it is applied to the political arena, the distinction becomes increasingly cloudy.

Jameson (1981a:296) maintained a commitment to the Marxist approach of understanding literature by promoting a general theoretical framework in which a Marxist negative hermeneutic and a Marxist positive hermeneutic method is used. "It is only at this price—that of the simultaneous recognition of the ideological and Utopian functions of the artistic text—that a Marxist cultural study can hope to play its part in political praxis, which remains, of course, what Marxism is all about" (Jameson, 1981a:299).

MICHEL FOUCAULT (1926–1984)

Foucault led an interesting life that was cut short when he died of AIDS in 1984 at fifty-seven. He was born on October 15, 1926, in Poitiers, France, and was named after his father, Paul-Michel Foucault. In 1940 he enrolled at the Jesuit secondary school Collège St. Stanislas. In 1946 he was admitted to École Normale Supérieure, where he received the *licence de philosophie* (1948), the *licence de psychologie* (1949), and the *agrégation de philosophie* (1952). After teaching at the University of Uppsala in Sweden (1955–1958) and the University of Clermont-Ferrand (1960), Foucault received his doctorate degree in 1961. He then taught at various colleges around the world and first visited the United States in 1970. Foucault continued to travel and teach at a variety of places globally.

Foucault's works are in areas familiar to sociologists: prisons, asylums, medicine, and changing sexual attitudes and practices. Among his more significant publications are *Mental Illness and Psychology, Discipline and Punish, Madness and Civilization,* and *The Birth of the Clinic.* His book trilogy devoted to

sex—*The History of Sexuality* (1976), *The Care of the Self* (1984), and *The Use of Pleasure* (1984)—revealed his life-long obsession with sex. His personal lifestyle included homosexuality and sadomasochism and a deep attraction to San Francisco's flourishing gay community. He was particularly attracted to the impersonal sex that was available in the gay bathhouses at that time (Ritzer, 2000c). Foucault also experimented with the drug LSD in the spring of 1975 and spoke highly of its positive effect in expanding his mind and redirecting his focus on the "truth"—a reference to his homosexuality (Miller, 1993).

Foucault's Theories

There is some debate as to whether Foucault was a postmodernist, a functionalist, or something else. Lemert and Gillan (1982) asked the questions that many social thinkers ponder when examining Foucault's works. Was he a Marxist? A structuralist? A semiotician?

> He uses Marx's terms: class, political economy, commodity, capital, labor power, struggle. Yet, if this is Marxism, its affiliation is unclear. The structuralist interest in the universal forms of culture is there in Foucault's talk of "order in its primary state" and his attempt to "uncover the deepest strata of Western culture." Yet, again and again, he renounces his structuralism. A semiotician's hand is surely at work in his studies of General Grammar in *The Order of Things* [1966a] and of the relation between signs and symptoms in *Birth of the Clinic* [1975]. Yet, Foucault is obviously much more than a semiotician. Marxist, structuralist, semiotician. These labels are those of his readers, not his. (p. 1)

Strictly speaking, Foucault was not a structuralist, although he thought that structuralism was the most advanced position in the human sciences. "Foucault was primarily an historian of psychiatry who saw the connections between his specialty and other institutional spheres" (R. Collins, 1990:462). Additionally,

"Foucault never posited a universal theory of discourse, but rather sought to describe the historical forms taken by discursive practices" (Dreyfus and Raninow, 1982:vii). Ritzer (2000b) described Foucault's theories as possessing a phenomenological influence, a strong element of structuralism without the formal rule-governed model of behavior, and an adoption of Nietzsche's interest in the relationship between power and knowledge, but that link is analyzed much more sociologically. "This multitude of theoretical inputs is one of the reasons that Foucault is thought of as poststructuralist" (Ritzer, 2000c:459).

David Shumway (1989) did not completely agree with Ritzer's conclusion, stating:

> Poststructuralism is really a category of convenience that names at most an intellectual tendency and perhaps merely a historical moment in French thought. It is thus impossible to articulate a set of doctrines that all poststructuralists share. Of all the major figures, however, Foucault fits least comfortably in the category. . . . What distinguishes him from others [is that] Foucault finds new ways to write history. It is, I think, this historical dimension that has enabled Foucault's work to have a much broader impact than that of the other poststructuralists. . . . As most poststructuralist theory suggests, genuinely new thought must be new discourse. Thus Foucault writes in a style and in a vocabulary that is strange to most readers. (preface)

Foucault's work is difficult to understand because of his wide range of historical reference and his use of new concepts, but perhaps most of all because his theories do not fit very well into any of the established disciplines. His early works (*Madness and Civilization*, 1965; *Birth of the Clinic*, 1975) center on the analysis of historically situated systems of institutions and discursive practices. "The discursive practices are distinguished from the speech acts of everyday life. Foucault is interested only in what we will call *serious* speech acts; what experts say when

they are speaking as experts. And he furthermore restricts his analyses to the serious speech acts in those 'dubious' disciplines which have come to be called the human sciences" (Dreyfus and Rabinow, 1982:xx).

Methodology

Foucault presented a further paradox in his use of methodology. He embraced value neutrality, a strong tenet of positivism, and seemed to downplay the method of hermeneutics. In *The Archaeology of Knowledge* (1969) Foucault insisted that human sciences (social sciences) can be treated as autonomous systems of discourse. In methodological approaches to the study of human societies, the researcher must remain neutral as to the truth and meaning of the discursive system studied. He proposed to treat all human sciences as a "discourse-object." Dreyfus and Rabinow (1982) stated that "Foucault is not interested in recovering man's unnoticed everyday self-interpretation. He would agree with Nietzsche and the hermeneutics of suspicion that such an interpretation is surely deluded about what is really going on. But Foucault does not believe that a hidden deep truth is the cause of the misinterpretation embodied in our everyday self-understanding" (p. xix). This statement strongly suggests that Foucault did not value the hermeneutic approach because he did not attempt to uncover any hidden meanings behind written words.

Discipline and Punishment

In his book *Discipline and Punish: The Birth of the Prison* (1977), Foucault described how prisons are examples of coercive social institutions found in all societies and throughout most of human history. Institutions such as prisons and asylums are highlighted by regularized routines designed to control and repress human behavior. Foucault examined the last three centuries of the history of prisons and found that one form of torture had been replaced by another:

> From the point of view of the law, detention may be a mere deprivation of liberty. But the imprisonment that performs this function has always involved a technical project. The transition from the public execution, with its spectacular rituals, its art mingled with the ceremony of pain, to the penalties of prisons buried in architectural masses and guarded by the secrecy of administrations, is not a transition from one art of punishing to another, no less skillful one. It is a technical mutation. From this transition spring a symptom and a symbol: the replacement, in 1837, of the chaingang by the police carriage. (Foucault, 1977:257)

Foucault's structural analysis of total institutions led him to conclude that modern prisons reflect modern views of appropriate forms of discipline, especially as determined by those who possess power. "To Foucault, the prison and the asylum exemplify the modern world. However, while we commonly see the advent of the modern mental hospital and the decline of the death penalty as signs of progress, Foucault sees them as epitomizing a shift in the way power is exercised in a society. They embody discipline, deprive those involved of liberty, and exist to serve the interests of those in power (Wallace and Wolf, 1999:407). Farganis (2000) elaborated on this idea by stating, "Foucault demonstrates how the human sciences have become techniques of power by shaping the views and behaviors of human subjects. Scientific knowledge, in this instance the human sciences, is not a separate sphere of activity engaging the talents and interests of a rarified community of scholars. On the contrary, the knowledge produced in these disciplines has had a profound impact on the lives of ordinary people and has shaped their views of themselves and others around concepts of normality and deviance" (p. 408).

Sexuality

In *The History of Sexuality* (1978), "Foucault challenges the hermeneutic belief in deep meaning by tracing the emergence of sexual confession and relating it to practices of social domination" (Dreyfus and Rabinow, 1982:xxi). Foucault was concerned about such social systems as psychotherapy and medicine. He questioned their power position and their corresponding ability to dictate to others what is "normal" and how one "should" feel. "Foucault saw these changes in the treatment of the mad and the criminal as a central feature of the modern discursive formation, characterized by the dominance of the sciences—biology, psychology, sociology—and by the translation of these disciplines' claims into fields of practice such as medicine, psychotherapy, and social work. All of these fields constitute disciplines of power; that is, they are focused on the imposition of order, regulation of behavior, and social control" (Garner, 2000:433). Technologies of all kind are designed to control the free-thinking behavior of individuals (for example, surveillance cameras in many walks of life). Individuals are taught self-control. In short, the modern world attempts to suppress impulses of all kinds, especially sexual, violent, and unruly ones (Garner, 2000). As Collins (1990b) explained, "In Foucault's effort to theorize, he hit on a more modern sociological theme, the relationship between micro processes and the macro structure of power. Again, bravo; but frankly, it is an amateur's performance" (p. 462).

Power

From the tradition of Nietzsche, Foucault believed that power and knowledge were intertwined. Social institutions that are in power positions generally have the knowledge to manipulate others in an effort to maintain the status quo (especially in regard to norms, values, and expectations). Foucault (1983) argued that one's very identity and sense of self are shaped by one's position in the power struc-ture. Foucault (1983) stated that power "ap-plies itself to immediate everyday life which categorizes the individual, marks him by his own individuality, attaches himself to his identity, imposes a law of truth on him which we must recognize and which others have to recognize in him." (p. 212). Markula (2003) noted that in his later years, Foucault "concen-trated on the relationship of the self to power and truth: how the human being turns him- or herself into a subject through the technologies of the self" (p. 94). Throughout his life, Fou-cault sought to understand the role of the indi-vidual in society, the changing nature of the self as power relations change, and the "effects of power relations and the possibilities of their transformation" (Markula, 2003:97). No doubt, some of his own questions about his sense of self, his sexuality, and his corresponding posi-tion in society reveal themselves in his work.

Wallace and Wolf (1999) argued that since the death of Foucault there have been no major sociological theorists who can be categorized as active and unequivocally postmodern. "At the same time there *are* important continuities between postmodernism and some of the major concerns and emphases in contempo-rary sociology and in social science as a whole" (Wallace and Wolf, 1999:409). David Harvey, for example, writing at the end of the 1980s, de-scribed a number of contemporary concerns of society that fit the postmodern mode. "Post-modernism has come of age in the midst of this climate of voodoo economics, of political image construction and deployment, and of new social class formation. That there is some connection between this postmodernist burst and the image-making of Ronald Reagan, the attempt to deconstruct traditional institutions of working-class power (the trade unions and the political parties of the left), the making of the social effects of the economic politics of privilege, ought to be evident enough" (Har-vey, 1989:336). More current examples of the application of postmodernism are found in the following pages.

RELEVANCY

Modern and postmodern theories are pro-moted as alternatives to the more traditional sociological theories. The terms *modern* and *postmodern* are themselves problematic, in that they are vague and have been applied to a wide variety of phenomena over a period of many centuries. The concepts of *modernism* and *postmodernism* are usually used in con-nection with technological advancements and new modes of thinking (such as prein-dustrial, industrial, and postindustrial). Not surprisingly, every era (since at least the fifth century) has considered itself "mod-ern." When social thinkers and policymak-ers think beyond the current era, they may be thought of as postmodernists. Thus, in order to think as a postmodernist, a social the-orist must break from the taken-for-granted world, the given rules, and the claims to au-thority found in a society. The popular image in American society currently is "thinking out-side the box." In other words, social thinkers must break from current modes of thinking *and* doing. The doing aspect refers to the methodological techniques used by social thinkers. Modern and postmodern theorists have disdain for positivism and the scientif-ic methods of data collection and analysis. They reject the grand theorizing and narra-tives that are common in the more tradition-al sociological theories. With their French origins, modern and postmodern theories became relatively popular in the 1980s fol-lowing the heyday of functionalism in the 1950s and conflict theory in the 1960s and 1970s.

There are those who wonder whether modern and postmodern theories are actually theories at all. Sociological theory has tradi-tionally consisted of grand narratives and "big ideas" (Ritzer, 2000c:479). Consequently, rejecting grand theorizing is similar to reject-ing sociological theory. Sociological analysis is the examination of large social events: so-cieties, organizations, cultures, and so on.

Successful sociological analysis is, for the most part, dependent on a broad and macro approach. With this reality in mind, it is easy to understand why a large number of criticisms are levied against modern and postmodern social thought.

The first criticism directed toward modern and postmodern theories is aimed at their refusal to employ empirical studies with statistical analysis. It is difficult to examine whether their observations and theories are accurate because "there are no systematic tests of these assertions" (Turner, 2003:246). In this regard, modern and postmodern theories offer no more to social theory than do the critical theorists; they question existing sociological interpretations of events but offer little concrete evidence that their perspective is any better. Sociological theory must be, at the very least, falsifiable; otherwise, we are no better than philosophy. It may be that modern and postmodern theorists are indeed onto some new revelation and insight regarding society and social interaction. However, if it remains unsubstantiated with proof, we will never know its validity. The obvious suggestion is not to be afraid to try empirical testing of theories that lead to grand narratives. Insights regarding social life are the goal of sociological theory. Free and unconstrained by the rules of science and the dispassionate rhetoric of the modern scientist, postmodernists have allowed themselves to create broad generalizations without qualification (Ritzer, 2000c:484).

Since every society has considered itself "modern," the term is too vague to apply to a theoretical approach. Within a short period of time (50–100 years) from now, future generations will look back at this era and laugh at claims of modernity and postmodernity just as we do to past generations. Thus, modern and postmodern theory may not really be a theory at all; it may more accurately be viewed as an ideological belief system. Furthermore, postmodern discourse is itself vague and abstract, so it is difficult to connect to the social world (Calhoun, 1993).

Postmodernists work with the vague assumption that society indeed made a decisive shift in the 1980s and 1990s. By some definitions this may be true. Western societies have evolved into what is referred to as the *service economy*, and yet industrialization is as prevalent as ever before. Industry has slowly left the dominant societies and has shifted into Third World nations, but it remains the fuel that runs the global market. Kivisto (1998) concurred with this idea: "By claiming that we have moved from production to consumption, this version of postmodernism shows evidence of a serious blind spot. It is obvious that goods continue to be produced, although in a global economy this might mean that they are being produced in poor countries, where workers (too frequently including children) are paid abysmal wages and are forced to work exploitatively long hours in unsafe and unsanitary factories" (p. 145). The point remains, then, for postmodernists to show proof that such a dramatic change in society has occurred that it warrants the label *postmodernism.*

Ritzer (2000c:484) offered a number of other criticisms of postmodern theory. Postmodern critics of sociological theory reveal the questionable validity with which they work, for they generally lack a normative basis with which to make their judgments. Given their rejection of an interest in the subject and subjectivity, postmodernists often lack a theory of agency. Postmodern social theorists are best at critiquing society, but they lack any vision of what society ought to be. Postmodern social theory is very pessimistic. Postmodern social theorists argue about what they consider major social issues, while ignoring what many consider the key problems of our time.

Many other criticisms could be made of postmodern theory and many specific criticisms of each postmodern theorist described in this chapter. However, it is also important to demonstrate the relevance of each theory, and postmodern social thought can in fact be applied to many areas of contemporary society. Many of the ideas brought forth by the postmodern theorists discussed in this chapter are relevant to a contemporary analysis of society. A few of them are discussed here.

David Riesman articulated a premise that is common among postmodernists, namely, that society has become increasingly oriented toward consumerism. Evidence of this orientation is bountiful. Citizens of Western societies are treated as a collection of consumers eager to purchase products, even if their purchases mean going into debt. We are encouraged to purchase items that we cannot afford by using credit cards and taking out loans. The federal government and many state governments utilize this very principle by operating on a deficit budget that exceeds $100 billion. College students and even high school students are encouraged to use credit cards, even though most of them lack the income to pay off their credit debts. The same phenomenon applies to cell phones. Many students have told me that their monthly bills exceed $100. How can this be? Who do they talk to to run up a bill this high? The ideology of consumerism encourages these irresponsible behaviors. Food and drink are allowed in college libraries now. This was unheard of just a few short years ago. The librarian at my college explained that in keeping up with changing times (postmodernism?) and competition from such bookstore chains as Barnes and Noble, which allow food and drink in their stores, college libraries have decided to cater to the needs of students. Vending machines in libraries are clearly a "postmodern" reflection of consumerism.

Riesman also described the changing nature of colleges and universities and especially the modern trend toward designing specialized courses and majors to meet the needs of students. It is also common now for students to take courses via instructional television and online. Does this represent a postmodern approach to higher education? Some professors worry about the potential harm in changing the traditional format, which consists of students and professors together in the classroom. Would professors become obsolete? After all, if courses can be taught online and on television, the rerun of taped broadcasts could phase professors out of jobs. Lyotard sounded an alarm to educators when he predicted the "death of the professor." "His proposal to replace professors with computers poses more problems than the obvious one in massive unemployment for those of us in the teaching profession" (Nicholson, 1989:199). A truly postmodern thought has occurred to me. Why would professors be phased out when really what can be eliminated is the institution itself? Professors could become accredited, teach from their home computers online, and collect tuition payments directly from students (the plan is a little more complicated than presented here, but this would be the general idea and illustrates "thinking outside the box"). When this happens, we have reached a postmodern form of education.

Jean Baudrillard's ideas on symbolic exchange are especially noteworthy and offer an expansion on the prevalence of consumerism. Gift giving has indeed become a part of a continuous feedback loop of giving and receiving. When one receives a gift from another, there is a social expectation that the "receiver" will return the gesture to the "giver." Although it is true that there cannot be "givers" without "takers," it is a social faux pas to take and take without ever giving something in return. There are also a growing number of occasions where giving gifts (among close friends and relatives) are the expected norm: birthdays, weddings, anniversaries, Valentine's Day, job promotions, book publications, graduations, house warmings, religious holidays, and so on. This expectation of gift exchange often leads to frustration and the realization that one is seemingly always purchasing a gift for someone for some reason. Receiving a "last-minute" holiday card from someone whom you did not send a card to results in a last purchase and mailing of a card on your part. Giving gifts is not unique to the modern world, but the excess emphasis on materialism and consumerism is a characteristic of modern society.

In his book *The Self after Postmodernity* (1997), Calvin Schrag challenged the bleak deconstructionist and postmodernist views of the human self as something ceaselessly changing. Schrag described the self as a being open to understanding through its discourse, its actions, its being with other selves, and its experience of transcendence. When examining the self, the theorist needs to realize that the self is exposed to a wide diversity of external stimuli but can only be truly understood through introspection. Schrag's (1997) postmodern perspective on the self is exemplified in this quote:

> Human bodies exist in space, are open to inspection by external observers, and are subject to the laws of mechanics that govern the movements of physical objects. Human minds, in contrast, are not in space, are known through introspection rather than by observation, and are exempt from models of mechanistic explanation. Human bodies are public, and the events that they exhibit are external; the career of mind is private, and the events that compose its workings are internal. It is thus that the official doctrine delivers a dualism—a dualism of body versus mind, the public versus the private, the external versus the internal, and the mechanistic versus the vitalistic. (p. 11)

Schrag attempted to avoid what he called the modernists' overdetermination of unity and identity and the postmodernists' self-enervating pluralism. "The portrait of the self has been . . . designed to bring the legacy of modernity into confrontation with the sensibilities and deconstructive strategies of postmodernity" (Schrag, 1999:148).

Interestingly, Schrag also addressed the issue of gift giving but came to a different conclusion from Baudrillard. Schrag (1997) stated that "a gift, to be genuinely a gift, is given without any expectation of return. There can be no expectation of a 'countergift,' for such would place the giving within the context of a contractual rather than a gift-giving relation" (p. 139). Schrag acknowledged that there is a phenomenon of gift giving and gift receiving that is a part of the economy of production and consumption, distribution and exchange.

John Caputo has applied a postmodern perspective to the Catholic tradition. According to Caputo (1999), "Postmodernism offers Catholicism an opportunity to counter what it dislikes about modernity without undertaking a full-scale retreat into *pre*modernity or antimodernity. . . . We are relieved of the need to measure up to the requirements of modernity which have come under fire from other quarters, and we are all ears for what these postmodernists are saying. For if modernity means secularism, how can postmodernism fail to be postsecular?" (p. 253). Thus, Caputo criticized modern society because of its increasingly secular nature and assumed that postmodernity would be the opposite. Caputo will be greatly alarmed if postmodernity means the abandonment of organized religion completely. In his 2000 article "Philosophy and Prophetic Postmodernism: Toward a Catholic Postmodernism" Caputo reiterated his displeasure with the modern world, referring to modernity as secularizing and reductionistic, and saying that "rigidly divides faith from reason, fact from value, subject from object, and mind from body, and if all that were not enough, its religion is Protestant not Catholic" (p. 549). He again indicated that modernity is equated with secularism and that postmodernity "must" mean a society marked by spirituality.

Jagtenberg and McKie (1997) envisioned a postmodern society marked by social movements that will help the ecology. They predict "the greening of social movements" and the utilization of "green maps": "Green maps and new paradigms have their origins in this changing world, but they have not come from the reflexive, relativizing social theory of postmodernism or from the reflection of sociologists on globalization, new communications technology, and risk society. The green ideas we are exploring here have come mainly from the cultures of social movements" (pp. 90–91). According to these authors, there is a growing "culture of the environment," one that has been ushered into existence because of a paradigm shift away from a patriarchal, European, human-centered focus. Only time will tell whether a significant enough change occurs in society to bring about a "greening of culture."

Modern and postmodern theorists pay a great deal of attention to the media and other forms of entertainment. There is good reason, as the mass media and their influence are highly evident. Furthermore, the study of entertainment, including sports and leisure, is extremely important because of its vital role in human society. Delaney and Wilcox (2002) examined the role of the media on sports and concluded that the sports media serve a number of functions and have both positive and negative influences on sports. Among the functions of the sports media are that they provide information (scores, highlights, interviews, live coverage); interpretations of sports events; entertainment, in the form of a wide array of sports events; excitement; and escape and diversion from the monotony of daily events. Among the media's positive roles in sport are economics (the media provide great revenue for university and professional sports organizations); social events (people interact with one another, forming a community); exposure to a variety of sports, many of which would go unnoticed without media coverage; and a public

forum where athletes and fans can discuss aspects of the game and the social ramifications of sports-related behavior. For example, when the players on St. Bonaventure's men's basketball team voted not to play the last two games of the 2002–2003 season, the media provided the public forum to discuss this disgraceful behavior and the illegal activities that had led to the players' decision (the university president and head coach had been involved in allowing an ineligible player play on the team, which eventually led to Atlantic 10 Conference and NCAA sanctions). The negative effects of the mass media on sports include economics, (overpriced, overly commercialized sports have led to increased ticket prices); rule changes, which have been labeled as both positive and negative; controlled production (for example, scripted stop in play for commercials); and the loss of heroes because we now know too much about athletes' on- and off-field behavior.

Modern and postmodern theories offer an alternative approach to sociological theory, an alternative that has not been embraced by most sociologists. Riley (2002) warned that "we must be careful to be critical of sociological pronouncements on the futility or ridiculousness of all postmodern theory, as it seems clear that the rise of this perspective offers unique tools and self-reflexive possibility for the sociologists to more fruitfully account for their own activity and engagement in their work" (p. 260). According to Ritzer (2000c:487), at the very least, postmodern social theory represents a challenge to sociological theory, and at the maximum, it stands as a rejection of much, if not all, sociological theory. Postmodern discourse adds to sociological thought, but if it is to stand the test of time, it will need to empirically ground itself substantially and present some sort of coherent and concise social theory.

12

George Ritzer

Georger Ritzer ranks among the leading contemporary social thinkers. He has taught sociology for more than thirty years, has written extensively about sociology, has lectured around the world on the topic of sociology, and yet, none of his degrees are in sociology. Because of this lack of formal training in sociology, Ritzer has dedicated his academic career to the study of sociology in general, and of sociological theory specifically.

Ritzer was born in New York City in 1940 and spent his formative years there. He received his high school diploma from Bronx High School of Science in 1958. Then he attended the City College of New York and earned his B.A. in psychology in June, 1962. In September, 1962 Ritzer entered the University of Michigan and attained his M.B.A. in June, 1964. After earning his master's degree, Ritzer was employed by the Ford Motor Company in personnel administration. Having acquired an interest in the field of labor, Ritzer worked toward his Ph.D. at the New York State School of Industrial and Labor Relations at Cornell University. He majored in organizational behavior and minored in sociology and collective bargaining. He graduated with his doctoral degree in June, 1968 (Ritzer, 1969:ii).

George Ritzer, a leading contemporary social theorist, introduced the concept of McDonaldization.
Source: Courtesy of George Ritzer

Ritzer began teaching immediately after graduating from Cornell, first as an assistant professor at Tulane University (1968–1970), then as an associate professor at the University of Kansas (1970–1974), and then as a professor at the University of Maryland (1974–present). His list of academic accomplishments is extensive. Internationally, Ritzer held the UNESCO chair in social theory at the Russian Academy of Science, earned a Fullbright-Hays fellowship to the Netherlands in 1975, spent a year as fellow-in-residence at the Netherlands Institute for Advance Study in 1980–1981, spent two terms as a visiting professor at Shanghai and Peking Universities (1988), was a fellow-in-residence at the Swedish Collegium for Advanced Study in the Social Science (1992), and was a visiting professor at the University of Tampere, Finland in 1966 (*Off-Line Production,* 1997).

Domestically, Ritzer has served as chair of the American Sociological Association's Selections on Theoretical Sociology (1989–1990) and Organizations and Occupations (1980–1981). He was named a distinguished scholar-teacher at the University of Maryland and has a teaching-excellence award.

Ritzer has taught a wide variety of courses including the history of theory, contemporary theory, postmodern theory, metatheory, sociology of consumption, theories of consumption, economic sociology, occupational sociology, sociology of science, Parsonian theory, Weberian theory, Durkheimian theory, Marxian theory, industrial sociology, race relations, formal organizations, introductory sociology, and political sociology (*Off-Line Production,* 1997). Currently, Ritzer's major areas of interest are sociological theory and the sociology of consumption (Ritzer, 2000d).

Ritzer's publications are numerous. Among them are twenty-five monographs and undergraduate texts; six advanced texts, seven professional volumes of which he was the editor, twenty-nine major papers, more than sixty-five articles, and twenty-five book reviews. His major publications include *Sociology: A Multiple Paradigm Science* (1975, 1980), *Toward an Integrated Sociological Paradigm* (1981), *Sociological Theory* (2000d), *Metatheorizing in Sociology* (1991), *Classical Sociological Theory*

(2000a), *The McDonaldization of Society* (1993), *Expressing America: A Critique of the Global Credit Card Society* (1995), *The Mc-Donaldization Thesis* (1998), and *Enchanting a Disenchanted World: Revolutionizing the Means of Consumption* (1999). Ritzer's work has been translated into a number of European languages, as well as Chinese and Japanese. There are a dozen translations of *The Mc-Donaldization of Society* (Ritzer, 1996), which remains Ritzer's most popular book and has spearheaded his global influence on how the modern capitalist system is examined.

ACADEMIC INFLUENCES ON RITZER

Ritzer's formal academic training in sociology was severely limited, and consequently, he took it upon himself to study both general and theoretical sociology. Ritzer (2000a) referred to himself as a student of all "schools of thought," but the ideas of Max Weber and Karl Marx stand out as having the most significant influence on his work.

Max Weber (1864–1929)

Ritzer (2001b) considered Weber's theory of rationalization the most famous and important theory in the history of sociology. In Weber's view, modern society, especially the Western world, is growing increasingly complex and dominated by rationalization and bureaucratization. Max Weber recognized that bureaucracies are organized rationally and that offices are ranked in a hierarchical order, in which their operations are characterized by impersonal rules. The bureaucratic world prefers rational decision making over personal involvement driven by emotion. Weber was so concerned about the ever-expanding role of rationality in society that he described the future as an "Iron Cage" in which human society would become trapped by its very own creation.

Weber described four types of rationality (Ritzer, 2001b):

1. **Practical rationality:** Found in people's mundane, day-to-day activities and reflecting their worldly interests.
2. **Theoretical rationality:** Theoretical mastery of abstract concepts, logical deduction, the attribution of causality, and the increased use of symbols in society.
3. **Substantive rationality:** The creation of values and value clusters that shape people's daily action.
4. **Formal rationality:** The rational calculation of means to reach desired ends, which are reinforced by rules, regulations, and laws.

Weber's deep concern about rationality influenced Ritzer so much that it became the cornerstone of his sociology.

From Weber, Ritzer learned of the interpretive approach in sociology. This micro orientation to the understanding of human social action attempts to provide casual explanations of human behaviors. These explanations remain grounded in the rationality principle. Additionally, from Weber's concept of the *ideal type,* Ritzer utilized the McDonalds fast-food restaurant chain as a "measuring rod" when describing the problems of the modern, rational, capitalist society.

Karl Marx (1818–1883)

Karl Marx, one of the most brilliant social thinkers of the second millennium, and a noted authority on the economic system during early capitalism, provided the primary influence on Ritzer's work related to the means of production and consumer production. According to Marx, the owners of the means of production, in order to maximize profits, increase the level of production to provide enough commodities for consumers to purchase. Consumers who have enough money (wages) purchase commodities for consumption (Ritzer, 1999). The ideas and concepts used by Marx helped Ritzer create his theory on the modern means of production and consumption.

Many other ideas of Marx can be found in Ritzer's works, among them the concept of *false consciousness*. The owner, the worker, and the consumer are all influenced by the rationalization, or McDonaldization, process, which, in turn, reaffirms its very "need" of existence. Ritzer attempts to demonstrate that the so-called most efficient means of production are not necessarily the best. Marx indicated that the rational-efficient means of production often creates feelings of alienation. The continued growth of efficiency in such areas as automation, robotics, and other technological innovation yet to be utilized will lead to a continuing restructuring (downsizing, American corporations moving overseas, and so on) of the means of production that will surely guarantee high rates of alienation in the future.

CONCEPTS AND CONTRIBUTIONS

George Ritzer has taken the central elements of Karl Marx and Max Weber, expanded and updated them, and provided a critical analysis of the impact of social structural change on human interaction and self-identity. Weber was concerned with the processes associated with a bureaucracy. He described a bureaucracy as a formal organization characterized by a hierarchical authority structure, a well-established division of labor, written rules and regulations, impersonality, and a concern with technical competence. Ritzer has come to view the restaurant chain McDonalds as the case model (ideal type) to examine the increased influence of rationality on society and its ultimate consequences in human behavior. He terms the continuation and even the acceleration of rationality the "McDonaldization" of society (Ritzer, 1983).

The McDonaldization of Society

According to Ritzer (1993:91), *McDonaldization* is "the process by which the principles of the fast-food restaurant are coming to dominate more and more sectors of American society as well as the rest of the world" (p. 91). Ritzer explained that since 1955, McDonalds has grown to over 12,000 outlets (a number that is probably higher currently) worldwide— including one in St. Petersburg, Russia. It's not just the food industry that represents this process; toy stores (such as Toys R Us), bookstores (B. Dalton's), newspapers (*USA Today*), child care (Kinder Care), learning (Sylvan Learning Centers), and a host of other businesses have followed the Mc-Donaldization trend. Ritzer does not intend to discredit McDonalds per se; rather, he offers a social criticism of the manifestations of the rationalization process. This rationality-based process does produce such advantages as efficiency, predictability, calculability, and control, but it also gives rise to the irrationality of rationality.

Ritzer (2001b) outlined five dominant themes within the McDonaldization process. These five key elements are the same as Weber's five dimensions of rationalization:

1. **Efficiency:** Refers to choosing the means to reach a specific end, rapidly, and with the least amount of cost or effort. This approach should benefit the customer because, after all, the less time the customer has to wait for an order at a "fast" food restaurant, the happier she or he will be. Unfortunately, in an effort to speed along the process of delivering food quickly, many restaurants provide the basics of the meal, but the customer must still take the time to go the "fixing bar" in order to add such items as onions, lettuce, ketchup, and napkins and straws. Customers are often expected to throw away their own trash and clean their own table. Consequently, they spend almost as much time waiting on themselves as they spent waiting in line for their food. The "salad bar" is the ultimate example of an effort by the restaurant to make customers do the work by "serving" themselves. There are plenty of other examples of businesses that utilize "efficient" means of service that result in the customers' doing the majority of the work themselves: the drive-up window,

filling one's own cup with the just-purchased beverage, "self-serve" gasoline pumps, automatic teller machines (ATMs), electronic voice mail systems, and buffets. In the name of efficiency, the customer is doing the work that paid employees used to do. As for the employees, they often find themselves in a non-decision-making work environment, characterized by a sharp division of labor, with repetitive, nonstimulating job functions.

2. **Calculability:** McDonaldization involves an emphasis on things that can be calculated, counted, and quantified. "Quantification refers to a tendency to emphasize quantity rather than quality. This leads to a sense that quality is equal to certain, usually (but not always) large quantities of things" (Ritzer, 1994:142). Examples of this element include the "Big Mac," the "Whopper," the "Big Gulp," and Taco Bell's eight-ounce burrito. The large portions mask what is often a lack of quality in such fast-food products. Time is another element related to calculability; fast-food restaurants often microwave foods to quicken the process of food preparation and delivery. Microwaving food obviously detracts from its quality. Ritzer (2001b) described the *USA Today* newspaper as "junk-food journalism" for the lack of substance in its stories. Ritzer believes that this newspaper offers fast, quick bits of information without overwhelming its readers with substance and quality. It should be noted that the *USA Today* does excel in its sports coverage (providing a large number of quantitative charts and statistics, box scores, standings, and point spreads, but limited written analysis of most games) and feature articles.

   According to Ritzer, the calculability element of McDonaldization leaves the employees with little or no chance of any personal meaning, and therefore they are filled with feelings of alienation. The creation of automation and its further implementation in the workplace are responsible for many people's losing their jobs. In short, calculability serves to benefit only the corporations (the owners of the means of production). As Ritzer (1996) stated, the name of the game is "service by numbers."

3. **Predictability:** Rationalization involves an increasing effort to ensure predictability. *Predictability* refers to the attempt to structure our environment so that outside forces do not cause disequilibrium within the system. People like to think that they have some control over their lives, so they like a certain amount of accurate predictability. Weather forecasts, for example, are critical for many people because no one wants to get caught in a storm or flood due to improper planning. Rational people have a need to know what to expect, when to expect it, and what courses of action to take in the event of any given situation. Americans who travel far from their homes seem to find comfort in places like McDonalds because a Big Mac in Syracuse is likely to taste the same as in Los Angeles or Orlando. This idea helps to explain why the movie industry produces so many sequels of originally financially successful films: People find comfort in movies from which they know what to expect. Shopping malls present the same type of "comfort" by providing stores that are nearly the same throughout the country.

   Many people do not like shopping malls for the very reason that they are so similar and lacking in true character and originality. Ritzer (1996) was concerned that the United States, a society that stresses individualism, is suffering terribly from the McDonaldization process. He believes that this process has reduced vital human beings to a uniformed group that dresses the same, talks the same, and acts the same. Even the architecture of McDonalds is similar from one location to the next.

4. **Control and replacement of people with nonhuman technologies:** Uncertainty is problematic for rationalists. Ultimately, the McDonaldization process would like to control the primary sources of uncertainty and unpredictability found in any rational system: people, both the people who work within system and the people served by them. Replacing humans with nonhuman technology allows greater control by those who control the means of production.

   In an effort to maintain control, everything is prepackaged, premeasured, and automatically controlled. The human is not required to think, just follow instructions and push a button periodically. Checkers at supermarkets don't have to think either; they just scan the barcode on the products being purchased. Ritzer comments that soon customers will scan their own food before they make payment; after all, they are already trained to stand in line and wait their turn. In fact, many retail stores now have "self-check" lines. Thus, the customer must find the items, check the items out, and bag them as well. Service is no longer a concern for many retail stores. I suppose that next they will expect customers to unload the delivery trucks and stock the shelves Airplanes are under the control of computers and nearly fly themselves. Pilots merely oversee the process. Airlines now provide self-check-in lines for customers with electronic tickets. The result of these efforts of control and replacing people with nonhuman technology is the diminishing skills and capabilities of the human actor and significantly less service being provided to customers by the owners of the means of production.

5. **Irrationality of rationality:** There are many advantages in the increased level of rationalization in society, but there comes a point where rationality becomes irrational. "Most specifically, irrationality means that rational systems are *unreasonable* systems. By that I mean that they deny the basic humanity, the human reason, of the people who work within or are served by them" (Ritzer, 1994:154). The lines at fast-food restaurants can be very long, and waiting in line at the drive-through can take longer than going inside. These rational systems do not save customers money; furthermore, even when prices are low, the customers do most of the work by serving themselves. Ritzer states that fast food is often less nourishing than home-cooked meals, being loaded with stabilizers and flavor enhancers, fats, salt and sugar, and coloring (for example, to keep lettuce looking "green fresh," a color additive is applied to browning lettuce).

Ritzer's primary question is: How long will it be before these rational systems evolve beyond the control of people and how much of our lives is already subject to their influence and control? Additionally, Ritzer wonders what happens when the people who control the systems succumb to being controlled. Ritzer answers these questions in part by examining the effects of the introduction of Coca-Cola to the French in the 1940s by American capitalists. For one thing, Coca-Cola was met with great opposition by the French wine industry because it feared competition. French society in general feared that new consumer goods and products would upset the French way of life. On a visit to Paris, Ritzer was appalled that the old-style French bakeries had become fast-food shops, taking on the image of the new capitalist system (*Off-Line Production*, 1997). The traditional pubs of Ireland and England, known for selling warm beer, have now nearly all been replaced by the Americanized way of selling beer ice cold. For American tourists, this is a welcome change; for Irish and English patrons the change has met with mixed reactions.

In Moscow, when McDonalds, faced with Russia's ruble crisis in 1999, imposed take-it-or-leave-it part-time work positions on its employees, many decided to set up a trade union. Unions have historically enjoyed little success in Russia, but this effort to form a union seems to be moving forward. According to Andrei Isayev, Labour Commission Vice-President, "Russian trade unions are changing. It's happening very slowly, but at last the idea of workers defending their rights is beginning to sink in" (Francoise, 2001:1). Thus, the McDonaldization effect has indirectly led to valuable social change in Russia.

McJobs

In his article "McJobs: McDonaldization and Its Relationship to the Labor Process" Ritzer (2002c) acknowledged that the spread of McDonaldized systems has led to the creation of a large number of jobs (fast-food restaurants

employ over 40 percent of the approximately 6 million people employed in restaurants of all types), but unfortunately, "the majority of them can be thought of as McDonaldized jobs, or 'McJobs'" (p. 141). As Ritzer (2002c) noted, "For many, the fast-food restaurant is likely to be their first employer. It is estimated that the first job for one of every 15 workers was at McDonald's; one of every eight Americans has worked at McDonald's at some time in his or her life" (p. 141). Most of these employees work part time and earn little more than minimum wage, and the high turnover rate is reflected in the fact that one-half of McDonald's employees remain on the job for a less than one year.

Ritzer (2002c) characterized McJobs as a dimension of McDonaldization and defined McJobs, first, as jobs that

> tend to involve a series of simple tasks in which the emphasis is on performing each as efficiently as possible. Second, the time associated with many of the tasks is carefully calculated and the emphasis on the quantity of time a task should take tends to diminish the quality of the work from the point of view of the worker. That is, tasks are so simplified and streamlined that they provide little or no meaning to the worker. Third, the work is predictable; employees do and say essentially the same things hour after hour, day after day. Fourth, many nonhuman technologies are employed to control workers and reduce them to robot-like actions. Some technologies are in place, and others are in development, that will lead to the eventual replacement of these "human robots" with computerized robots. Finally, the rationalized McJobs lead to a variety of irrationalities, especially the dehumanization of work. (p. 142)

Spokespersons for McDonaldized systems claim that they offer a large number of entry-level positions that help provide employees with the basic skills that they will need to advance upward in the occupational structural system. Ritzer admitted that this claim is often true, especially in management positions, but insisted that "the skills acquired in McJobs are not likely to prepare one for, help one to acquire, or help one to function well in, the far more desirable postindustrial occupations which are highly complex and require high levels of skill and education. Experience in routinized actions and scripted interactions do not help much when occupations require thought and creativity" (Ritzer, 2002c:142).

Ritzer views McJobs as another aspect of the McDonaldization process designed by those who control the means of production to exploit both their employees and their customers. The workers are exploited because they are paid less than the value of their labor in proportion to the profit made by the corporation. Consumers are exploited even more because they "are not only paid less than the value they produce, they are paid *nothing at all.* In this way, customers are exploited to an even greater degree than workers" (Ritzer, 2002c:144). Ritzer concluded that many workers and customers have simply internalized these norms of behavior and have conformed to them of their own accord (false consciousness). One might think that Ritzer has neglected to note that many consumers today *do* have an impact on the McDonalds of the world. Because of consumer demands, many fast-food restaurants, including McDonalds, are offering a variety of "healthy" foods (for example, green salads), leaner beef, and charts that provide nutritional information regarding their food products).

According to Ritzer, the McDonaldization process is just capitalism run amuck. Since no corporation can last an indefinite period of time without change, they must find a way to maintain profits through the process of sneakerization—having a diverse line of products. Consequently, consumers may not be responsible for the "healthier" changes in menus at fast-food restaurants; the changes may simply be the corporate response to the need for diversification of the product line. Ritzer (1996) warned that eventually the McDonaldization process itself will

succumb to the "Iron Cage," which is either an ironic fate or social justice.

Occupational Life

Weber, who worried that humankind would end up "trapped" in its very own creation of professionalism, rationalization, and bureaucracy because of increased rationalization, coined the term *Iron Cage.* The study of occupational life is an important subarea within sociology. The focus in occupational sociology is on the reciprocal effects of organizational structure on occupational life. According to Ritzer (1972): "When a doctor is employed in a hospital, his occupational behavior is affected by the organization and, conversely, his presence in the hospital affects its structure. Further, when the occupational sociologist studies occupations in organizations, he is also concerned with the impact of the various occupations on each other. Thus in the hospital setting he may focus on the conflict and cooperation between doctors, nurses, and administrators" (p. 1). Members of some occupations (for example, the independent merchant, the independent taxi driver, the doctor in the private practice, and the poolroom hustler) have relative autonomy and freedom. Other occupations, such as those of the janitor and the night guard, exist within a formal organization in which workers have very little freedom.

In his *Man and His Work* (1972), Ritzer examined many of the elements found in the occupational setting, including conflict, conflict resolution, alienation, the division of labor, technological advances, bureaucratization, unionization, professionalization, and the role of rationalization. Ritzer utilized the four dominant theoretical perspectives in the analysis of occupation from the sociological perspective. He concluded that conflict and functional theories have the greater utility in explaining issues at the macrolevel, while exchange theory and symbolic interactionism offer us the most help in understanding the micro relationships and issues found in the occupational life of workers (Ritzer, 1972:362).

Rationalization

Ritzer applied Weber's notion of rationalization to the fast-food restaurant industry and the medical profession. The McDonaldization process has become Ritzer's contemporary exemplar of rationalization. His linking of rationality to various professions is in the direct tradition of Weber.

In his 1975 article "Professionalization, Bureaucratization and Rationalization: The Views of Max Weber," Ritzer explained:

> It is well known that the bulk of Weber's work examines the development of rationality in the Occident and the barriers to that development in the rest of the world. He analyzed a variety of factors that led to the rise of rationality in the West and examined a number of structures that seemed to embody that rationality. Among these structures can be included the market, bureaucracy, *and* professions. I do not mean to imply by this that the concept of the profession is as important as the others in Weber's thinking. But it is clear that a profession *is* an important example of Western rationality. Calvinism, and the asceticism it produced, played a crucial role in the development of Occidental rationality. . . . Less well known is the fact that Weber linked Calvinistic asceticism to the professions. (p. 628)

Weber had noticed that the creation of professions in social institutions had accelerated the rationality process. "Professionals contributed to the rationalization of these institutions and, conversely, the rationalizing institutions contributed to the development of the professions" (Ritzer, 1975:628). Thus, Western social institutions were becoming increasingly professionalized and rationalized, including the rise of the modern church contributing to the development of a professional priesthood. The training of legal professionals (lawyers) in specialized law schools coincided with the growing rational-legal societies of

the West. Weber believed that professional legal training was the decisive factor in the development of rational law.

Weber regarded professionalization as the integral aspect of the process rationalization, whereas Ritzer emphasized that both bureaucratization and professionalization are the keys to the rationalization of society. Ritzer (1975) argued that the intimate relationship between the processes of bureaucratization and professionalization was fast becoming an accepted sociological tenet.

In their 1988 article "Rationalization and the Deprofessionalization of Physicians," Ritzer and Walczak proposed "that increasing formal rationality is likely to lead to greater external control over physicians and to a decline in the ability of the medical profession to distinguish itself from bureaucrats and capitalists. These changes, in turn, are likely to lead to some degree of deprofessionalization of physicians" (p. 1). Ritzer and Walczak (1988:1) noted important changes and developments affecting the medical profession, including antitrust decisions, corporatization, conglomeration, bureaucratization, technological change, unionization, and the rise of McDoctors (no-appointment, walk-in medical facilities modeled after fast-food restaurants), third-party payers, health maintenance organizations (HMOs), and prospective payment systems based on preset diagnostic related groups (DRGs). The combination of increasing control over the medical profession by external organizations and internal rationalization has led to the deprofessionalization of physicians. "Such changes could have profound implications for the entire professional category since physicians have for many years been the model profession" (Ritzer and Walczak, 1988:2). Utilizing a Weberian rationalization approach, Ritzer and Walczak (1988) concluded that "the dividing line between substantively rational physicians and formally rational bureaucrats and capitalists is increasingly blurred with the result that it is harder for physicians to claim the distinctive position of profession and to have that claim accepted by the public. . . . The theory of rationalization has allowed us to see clear linkages among a series of disparate social changes and to understand how they are changing the nature of medicine and contributing to the deprofessionalization of physicians" (p. 15). Ritzer and Walczak also suggested that instead of a deprofessionalization occurrence in the medical profession, it may be that a new type of rationality is emerging, such as hyperrationalization—combining practical, theoretical, substantive, and formal rationality with the medical profession controlling it.

Changes in the medical profession are caused by the increasing level of rationalization. By definition, then, rationalization leads to the "disenchantment" of the settings in which it occurs (Ritzer, 2002a). The term *disenchantment* implies "the loss of a quality—enchantment—that was at one time very important to people. Although we undoubtedly have gained much from the rationalization of society in general, and the means of consumption in particular, we also have lost something of great, if hard to define, value" (Ritzer, 2002a:166). Efficient systems seek to eliminate anything that resembles enchantment (anything that is magical, mysterious, fantastic, dreamy, and so on) because efficient systems center on orderliness and predictability. Efficiency can be applied to the customer and the organization. Sometimes what is efficient for the customer and for management is different and sometimes overlaps. For example, a shopping mall is efficient for both the customer and the owner. The shopper has the convenience of shopping at multiple stores all in one setting, and the shop owner has numerous potential customers to draw upon. On the other hand, the practice of McDonald's limiting the sale of breakfast items to a specific hour may be efficient for the restaurant but not for the customer, who may want an Egg McMuffin in the afternoon. The fast-food industry has perfected efficiency

modes through predictability—replicated settings, scripted interactions with customers, predictable employee behavior, and predictable products.

Shopping malls and megastores (for example, Price Club) encourage mass consumption and contribute to hyperconsumption. Ritzer refers to this phenomenon as "cathedrals of consumption"—places and settings designed for consumers to spend large amounts of money. "These places do more than simply permit us to consumer things, they are structured to lead and even coerce us into consumption" (Ritzer, 2002a:162) Such settings, which came into existence after World War II, provide a new means of consumption and have dramatically transformed the very nature of consumption. "Cathedrals of consumption" are quasi-religious settings to which people make "pilgrimages" in order to practice consumer religion.

Shoppers can make these pilgrimages without money. Purchasing items that one cannot afford is no obstacle to consumption as long as one as a credit card. "The credit card, like the fast-food restaurant, is not only a part of this process of rationalization but is also a significant force in the development and spread of rationalization. Just as McDonald's rationalized the delivery of prepared food, the credit card rationalized (or "McDonaldized") the consumer loan business. Prior to credit cards, the process of obtaining loans was slow, cumbersome, and nonrationalized" (Ritzer, 2002b:178). Credit cards are based on the new ideology of rationalization. Unfortunately, they are too easy to obtain, and many users of credit cards act very irrationally in their purchasing habits and end up in debt.

Consumption and Consumerism

Ritzer's *Enchanting a Disenchanted World* (1999) is an attempt to inform consumers about the world that is created merely to sell products. He detailed how the new means of consumption are settings, or structures, that enable people to consume all sorts of products. Ritzer (1999) referred to these settings as "cathedrals of consumption." The cathedrals of consumption have an enchanted, sometimes sacred, or religious character for many of the people who visit them. The cathedral often has a magical, fantastic, enchanted setting. The enchanting market centers on consumption of the products. (Note: This practice is in violation of Ritzer's presentation of the efficient and predictable settings that corporations generally prefer.)

Technological advancements and the credit card industry have facilitated people's desire to consume. Ritzer believes that the modern capitalist system produces a climate that involves the rationalization of production with the idea of romanticizing the environment in which to consume. McDonalds, with its playlands for children and its newspapers for customers to read and feel more relaxed while consuming, provides a few examples aimed at creating a cathedral of consumption. Supermarkets (such as Wegmans, Albertsons) and department stores (such as Wal-Mart) provide delis with fresh sandwiches and dining areas to entice customers to sit and relax while consuming. Thus, the cathedrals of consumptions, although more "enchanting," are still subject to routinization and efficiency.

Ritzer (1999) indicated that this trend in consumerism will continue to expand but noted that the cathedrals will give way to the implosion of goods and services made available to order through the Internet and television shopping networks. The cathedrals will continually need to compete with one another in promotion of their enchanted environment, and many will face extinction. However, Ritzer concluded that the future will continue to be defined by consumption.

Postmodern Analysis

Since the time of the Industrial Revolution, the consumption of goods has been the driving force which sustains Western economic societies. Even though the products and means of payment have changed, the power structure remains mostly intact, with those who control the means of production demanding the same end goal: profit. Ritzer (2001a) used a modern epistemology to describe both fast-food restaurants and credit cards in terms of grand narratives: McDonaldization and Americanization. In "The 'New' Means of Consumption" (2001a), Ritzer applied key aspects of postmodern social theory not only to fast-food restaurants and credit cards, but also a broader set of phenomena that can be combined under the heading of what he called the "means of consumption." "Related innovations in the means of consumption include shopping (including mega-) malls, super-stores, cybermalls, theme parks, home shopping via television, infomercials, telemarketing, and even the somewhat older supermarkets" (Ritzer, 2001a:338).

Postmodern theory can be criticized as quasi theory, at best, that offers few new insights into social phenomena. After all, as Ritzer (2001a) questioned, "How can these phenomena (forms of consumption) be discussed under the heading of postmodernism when two of them have already been discussed as modern phenomena?" (p. 338). Ritzer answered this question by suggesting that it is "far more useful to regard modernism and postmodernism not as one epoch that follows another but as different 'modes' of analysis" (p. 338). Ritzer insisted that a postmodern perspective leads to a different set of insights into the new means of consumption than those derived from a modern viewpoint. Furthermore, Ritzer believes that the new means of consumption are social phenomena that can be usefully analyzed from both perspectives.

Critics of postmodern theory dislike, among other things, the classification of theory as "postmodern" because of its inherent bias to a certain point in history. Certainly, hundreds of years from now social theorists are going to wonder with amazement how "brilliant" social thinkers in the late twentieth century came to label a body of thought postmodern. But Ritzer (2001a) insisted that "good theory is good theory, whether it carries a modern or postmodern label. We need to spend less time worrying about how we label theory and spend more time developing and using strong, useful theoretical perspectives" (p. 357). This is clearly sound advice from Ritzer.

Social Theory

Without question, Ritzer is a master at examining, analyzing, and writing "good" theory. His social theory textbooks are classic in the field of sociology. Ritzer's theoretical contributions extend to the global society. His ideas are valuable for helping us to better understand some of the many important social-economic changes that are occurring in the contemporary world. Through his description of the McDonaldization process, Ritzer provided a warning to people that they must resist the seemingly irreversible trend of consumerism that society is currently entrenched in.

Sociology, as a science, attempts to support its theories with empirical data. Ritzer (1970) wrote, "One of the ways in which sociology advances is through the development of an hypothesis and the testing of it empirically. The result of such empirical testing may be an acceptance, a rejection, or a casting of doubt on the hypothesis. Once an hypothesis has been tested empirically, other theorists or empiricists (or both) may feel compelled to respond to the results of the empirical test" (p. 530). The highest value of sociological theory, then, is realized when it is supported by empirical data.

In his article "The Failure to Integrate Theory and Practice" Ritzer (1981a) reflected on the current state of sociology. He believes that all the great theorists were engaged in the practical implications of their theories.

Ritzer feels that Karl Marx was the most obvious example of a theorist who attempted to integrate theory with practice, while Émile Durkheim's concern about the decline of the collective conscience led him to suggest structural reforms. Ritzer is critical of modern social theorists. He challenges them to interrelate theory and practice, and to stop creating theories that are too abstract (for practice). He hopes that sociology will make a closer examination and place a higher level of concentration on the sociology of occupations and organizations.

According to Ritzer, then, social theory needs to be linked to actual practice through empirical research, and it must have a practical application. He abides by these rules not only in his own theories but when he explores others' theories as well. For example, Ritzer (1969, 1970) examined the validity of Howard Becker's "commitment theory." Becker had contended that commitment occurs through a process of placing side bets (investments). The more side bets an individual has, the greater the level of commitment. Becker theorized that a person who refuses to change jobs, even though the new job would offer a higher salary and better working conditions, must do so because of a level of commitment to the present job that offers greater rewards than a higher salary and better working conditions. With age as one variable, it was presumed that older persons would have a stronger commitment to their current job. In fact, Becker claimed that "generalized cultural expectations" would constrain the activity of job hunting by older persons. In the 1960s, when Becker developed this theory, society expected older persons to be more committed to their organizations (just as society expected organizations to be more committed to persons). Additionally, the lack of viable alternatives would further constrain older workers. Older persons are also more likely to have stronger community ties and family roots that would influence their commitment to the job. Marriage and education levels were among the other side bets that contributed to Becker's commitment theory.

After empirically testing Becker's commitment theory, Ritzer (1969) concluded:

> Although the basic process of commitment is psychological, the structural factors discussed by Becker also play a role in commitment. Once an individual has psychologically committed himself there are a series of structural constraints which, over time, serve to increase the commitment. These are the side-bets Becker has talked about. However, in our theory, they are not the major determinants for commitment, they only increase commitment once it has initially been made. (p. 478)

Ritzer demonstrated that theory can be modified and often improved. However, it is only through empirical testing that changes in theory can be justified and assertions of truth, or falsity, can claim validity.

There are many classifications of theory (for example, consensus vs. conflict; abstract vs. concrete). The macro-micro distinction is a common one in sociology. Some theorists maintain a commitment to structural analysis (macro theory) while others attempt to explain the social behavior of individuals and groups (micro theory). Randall Collins (1981) promoted a "radical microsociology." Ritzer (1985) responds by stating:

> There is nothing inherently wrong with such a theoretical (and methodological) orientation; the problem lies in the fact that Collins wishes this to become the dominant approach in sociology. The predominance of such an orientation, should it ever come to pass, would pose a number of serious problems for sociology. First, its image of the subject matter of sociology (interaction patterns) is shaped primarily by what can be studied using Collins's limited sense of empirical research. Second, Collins's single-minded focus on interaction patterns foretells, should it become the dominant focus in sociology, the loss to the field of its longstanding interest in what can be variously called consciousness, cognitive processes, the social construction of reality, or micro-subjectivity.

Concerns for such phenomena are deemed out of bounds by radical microsociology because they are not seen as amenable to empirical-scientific research. Third, radical microsociology also eschews an interest in large-scale social structures and social institutions, and for much the same reason it ignores conscious processes, they do not seem capable of being studied empirically. In sum, in pursuit of a narrow scientific ideal, Collins seems fully prepared to eliminate, or downplay, most of sociology's traditional concerns. (pp. 88–89)

Ritzer is as much a defender of traditional sociology as he is of macrosociology. The 1960s were an era dominated by macrotheories (especially functionalism and conflict), but Ritzer acknowledged the rise in popularity of microtheories in sociology during the 1980s.

In his article "The Rise of Micro-Sociological Theory," Ritzer (1985) reviewed Collins's radical microsociology and concluded that "the excessive reach and intellectual problems of radical microsociology aside, the fact remains that micro-theories and the micro-oriented paradigms with which they are associated are on the ascendancy in contemporary sociology. The 1980s are likely to belong to micro-theory in its many guises including phenomenology, ethnomethodology, existential sociology, varieties of behavioral sociology, and others (including even radical microsociology)" (p. 96).

There is clearly a place for microtheories in sociology, but it should be evident that macrostructural issues are implied domains of sociology and must never be neglected or ignored by sociologists. In fact, sociological theory has been moving in the direction of a micro-macro integration, or what is sometimes called *bridging theories*.

Metatheory

Metatheory, in sociology, involves the formal or informal study of sociological theory. In short, it is the study of theory itself. Ritzer (1988) made it clear that sociologists are not the only ones who conduct meta-analysis—reflective study of one's own discipline. There are many variants of meta-analysis, but they can all be loosely grouped under the heading of *metasociology*. Ritzer (1988b:188) defined metasociology as the reflexive study of the underlying structure of sociology in general, as well as of its various components—substantive areas, concepts, methods, data, and theories. Metatheory is concerned specifically with the study of theories, theorists, communities of theorists, and the larger intellectual and social contexts of theories and theorists.

Ritzer (1988b) distinguished four categories of metatheories:

1. **Internal-intellectual:** Derived from the work of Thomas Kuhn and others who attempted to identify major paradigms in sociology. Metasociologists working in this tradition emphasize cognitive aspects and "schools of thought" approaches.

2. **Internal-social:** Also indebted to Kuhn (as well as others), this approach emphasizes the communal aspects of various sociological theories. The tendency in this approach is to focus on relatively small groups of theorists who have direct links to one another and identifying "schools" in the history of sociology.

3. **External-intellectual:** This approach includes examining the influence of ideas in other academic fields on sociological theory and borrowing ideas, theories, concepts, and so forth from other disciplines when they can help sociological theory.

4. **External-social:** Involves shifting to the more macrolevel to look at the larger society and its impact on the creation of sociological theory.

Ritzer (1988) believe that metatheory will continue to develop and contribute to the day-to-day activities of sociologists. "One of the many important functions that metatheory can perform is to increase the 'theoretical self-consciousness' of sociologists by making the various internal and external, intellectual and social factors that lie at the base of their work more explicit and more amenable to critical analysis. While all sociologists can profit from metatheory in this sense, this is especially relevant to theorists" (p. 195). Critics (for example, Turner, 1985a, 1986b) of metatheory accuse it of being overly philosophical and creating unresolvable and unnecessary issues. Ritzer (1988b) concluded that metatheory was coming of age in the 1980s and that its future included offering a range of possibilities for the benefit of sociology, as well as an array of other disciplines.

As an example of how metatheory could benefit sociology, Ritzer (1989) published an article, "Sociology of Work: A Metatheoretical Analysis," in which he provided a metatheoretical examination of Ida Harper Simpson's overview of the history of the sociology of work. (1989) Simpson proposed that there was a relationship between changes in the sociology of work and in sociological theory. Ritzer (1989) concluded in his article that "metasociological and metatheoretical analyses of the type undertaken here and in Simpson's paper can be important aids in the advancement of sociology. Not only have we uncovered a surprising and striking parallel in the histories of two subareas within sociology, but we have shown that each has much in common with, and to gain from, the other. Now all we need is some sociologists of work to read some contemporary theory seriously and for some theorists to immerse themselves in empirical research into the workworld" (p. 600). It should be clear that Ritzer has always maintained a commitment to "good" social theory, its need to be grounded empirically, and the value of metatheoretical analysis of existing social theory in order to create better theory. In his *Metatheorizing* (1992) Ritzer made it clear that there is a need for a systematic study of sociology theory, and utilizing a metatheoretical approach is the best way to accomplish this goal.

Sociological Paradigms

An aspect of metatheorizing is the creation of paradigms in the tradition of Thomas Kuhn's work. Ritzer utilizes a paradigmatic, metatheoretical perspective as a guide of his analysis of sociological theory in his social theory textbooks. Ritzer (1981b, and 1981 with Richard Bell) examines the theoretical works of others in order to seek exemplars for specific paradigm classifications. Ritzer (2000b) believes that there are three paradigms that dominate sociology. His three paradigms are the *social-facts, social-definition,* and *social-behavior* paradigms. There are four components in each paradigm. Here is brief summary of Ritzer's three-paradigm scheme:

The Social-Facts Paradigm

1. **Exemplar:** Émile Durkheim, especially *The Rules of Sociological Method and Suicide.*
2. **Image of the subject matter:** Social factists focus on what Durkheim called *social facts,* or large-scale social structures and institutions.
3. **Methods:** Generally rely on interview questionnaire and historical-comparative methods.
4. **Theories:** Action theory, symbolic interactionism, phenomenology, ethnomethodology, and existentialism.

The Social-Definition Paradigm

1. **Exemplar:** Max Weber and his work on social action.
2. **Image of the subject matter:** How do social actors define their social situations and the effect of these definitions on ensuing action and interaction?
3. **Methods:** Social definitionists are most likely to use the interview questionnaire method but are also the most likely of sociologists to utilize the observation method.
4. **Theories:** Action theory, symbolic interactionism, phenomenology, ethnomethodology, and existentialism.

The Social-Behavior Paradigm

1. **Exemplar:** The work of B. F. Skinner.
2. **Image of the subject matter:** A focus on the "unthinking behavior" of individuals; the "response" of the stimulus-response relationship. Examination of behaviors that are "rewarding" and those that are "costly."
3. **Methods:** The distinctive method of social behaviorists is the experiment.
4. **Theories:** Behavioral sociology and, more important, social exchange theory.

Ritzer maintains a belief in the importance of metatheorizing and paradigm schemes as a means of better understanding social theory.

FINAL COMMENTS

George Ritzer's relevancy to sociological theory continues, as he remains a dominant member of the discipline. His primary contributions come from the sociology of work and occupations and social theory. Ritzer has attempted to bridge the macro-micro distinction in social theory. His doctoral dissertation, *Commitment, Professionalism, and Role Conflict Resolution,* represents a microinteractionist analysis of social behavior in the work environment. His subsequent works, especially those related to his concept of *McDonaldization,* remain his shining works of great significance.

Ritzer's McDonaldization concept has been well received by both academics and laypersons worldwide. The McDonaldization process has a profound effect on the way people conduct social behavior. More and more products (for example, television, news, fast food) are presented in an idealistic "McNugget" fashion. This is a direct result of the highly rationalized-based philosophy that guides the McDonaldization process. Ritzer indicated that this process takes place at both the macro and micro levels. The product, or cathedral of consumption, is not just one "iron cage" but many minicages that individuals choose to enter. Ritzer suggests that people change their course of action and daily habits, which ultimately pay homage to the cathedrals. For example, instead of patronizing a large corporate chain store, shop at local merchants' stores; use cash instead of credit cards; deal with "real" people instead of computer interaction (such as going inside the bank for your transaction rather than using an ATM machine); and avoid finger foods if at all possible. All of this will help reduce the controlling effects that the McDonaldization process has on today's society (Ritzer, 2001c).

Ritzer fears that the level of creativity is deeply compromised by the control element of McDonaldization; he worries that people are becoming mere consumers, lining up for the iron cage camouflaged as a glorious cathedral. I believe that the human species has survived far more dangerous threats than the creature comforts of consumption, and there will always be brilliant, innovative thinkers and practitioners who will continue to find solutions to society's social problems. George Ritzer is such a person.

With his level of production, one might suggest that Ritzer himself is a product of the McDonaldization process. The obvious difference lies in the high quality of work offered by Ritzer.

13

Jonathan H. Turner

In sociology there is little consensus on what is good theorizing, and even though Turner does have his critics, it is this author's contention that Jonathan Turner is one of the most brilliant social thinkers of contemporary times. His sociological analysis and social theorizing rank him as a true master of social theory.

A BRIEF BIOGRAPHICAL SKETCH

Jonathan H. Turner was born on September 7, 1942, in Berkeley, California. Turner is a fifth-generation Californian. He was raised in Palo Alto and Monterey. He was an athlete throughout junior high and high school, participating in a variety of sports. Turner (2002) reported that he was not very intellectual until his last two years in high school, when, suddenly, his parents' emphasis on academics (they both had master's degrees) kicked in. At that point he became an extremely compulsive worker, making up for lost time.

Turner went to college on an athletic scholarship, and after one year he left the University of California at Riverside (UCR) and trans-

Jonathan Turner, brilliant social thinker and sociological generalist.

Source: Courtesy of Jonathan Turner, University of California, Riverside

ferred to the University of California at Santa Barbara (UCSB) with the intention of playing football and tennis. However, once Turner entered UCSB he became less interested in sports and more interested in academics. He eventually received academic scholarships and abandoned sports as a means of supporting his studies.

Turner (2002) stated that his roommates called him "the machine" because he studied so hard and was so disciplined in his studying. But his dedication to scholarly pursuits paid off. By the time he went to graduate school, he was well ahead of most first-year graduate students and was able to earn his advanced degrees quickly. Although he maintains that there was no overt pressure to do well in school, his sister, who is two years older, was the first person in history to get a perfect score on the SAT examination (Turner, 2001).

As already stated, Turner began his college career at UCR and after just one year transferred to UCSB, proclaiming that he would never go back to Riverside. As we shall learn shortly, the cliché of "never say never" was applicable to Turner's proclamation.

When Turner arrived at UCSB a new program in sociology had been initiated. Several new professors came to the university, including Tamotsu Shibutani from the University of California at Berkeley, Donald R. Cressey from UCLA, and Walter Buckley from the Rand Corporation. A year later, Thomas Scheff arrived. Hence, Turner's early training was in the symbolic interactionist tradition but was also grounded in general systems theory (Buckley's specialty).

Turner began studying sociology his sophomore year, after becoming rather bored by psychology, which had been his major his freshman year. Sociology was more what Turner thought psychology would be, examining the individual from the perspective of society (Turner, 2001). He took every course the department offered and even took some graduate courses as an undergraduate. In 1965, Turner received his bachelor's degree in sociology from UCSB.

Turner was accepted at Harvard for his graduate studies, but he chose instead to attend Cornell University in order to broaden his horizons beyond symbolic interactionism. He did not consider himself a theorist in graduate school; his areas of specialization in graduate school were social psychology and organizations (Turner, 2002). But he kept attending theory classes because of his strong interest in social theory. In fact, once he started teaching theory at Hawaii in 1968, he was hooked and has not looked back since that time.

At Cornell, Turner's initial courses in sociology were taught by a disciple of Talcott Parsons, who also had had George Homans on his dissertation committee. Turner enjoyed the Parsonian scheme because everything seemed to have a place. This was especially important because Turner could now address macro issues not covered by interactionism. Turner acknowledges that the problems with functional theory are well documented, but he has always liked the "big-picture" approach of functionalism. In fact, his first book, *Patterns of Social Organization: A Survey of Social Institutions* (1972b), was very much influenced by Parsons and Neil Smelser's *Economy and Society* (1956), and throughout his career, he has always tried to think in "big pictures" (Turner, 2001). Turner (2001) stated that all of his major theory professors advocated one thing: to state arguments in testable propositions. Turner tends to think in terms of processes that flow over time and that turn back on themselves, and consequently, he is known for creating some rather complicated models when describing various social processes. Turner completed his master's degree in 1966 at Cornell and his Ph.D. in 1968.

Jonathan Turner married Susan Hainge in 1967, but they divorced in 1971 and he married Sandra Leer. Turner taught for one year at the University of Hawaii, and since 1969, he has taught at UCR. He has been department chair, has been given an award as the distinguished professor of sociology, and is a fellow of the American Association for the Advancement of Science (1997). Turner served as president of the Pacific Sociological Association (1988–1989) and president of the California Sociological Association (2000–2001).

He also has held the editorial position for *Sociological Perspectives* (1992–1996) and is the current editor for *Sociological Theory* (1999–2003). Turner has published a large number of books and articles and has lectured all over the world, serving as visiting professor in such institutions as Cambridge University, Universität Bremen in Germany, and Shandong and Nan Kai Universities in the People's Republic of China.

Within the discipline of sociology, Turner is known as a general theorist, although he has a number of more substantive specialties, including the sociology of emotions (see *On the Origins of Human Emotions*, 2000), ethnic relations, forms of conflict, social institutions, social stratification, and macrodynamics. In recent years Turner has been moving toward establishing a general theory of human organization. *Macrodynamics,* published in 1995, presents an analysis of human organization at the societal level, and his newest book, *Face-to-Face: A Sociological Theory of Interpersonal Theory of Interpersonal Behavior* (2002), has a microlevel focus.

Turner's next project is to master the mesolevel, or the domain of reality that sits between the interpersonal and societal levels. He hopes to write a book titled *The Principles of Sociology,* which will be a book of principles much like a physics text (Turner, 2001). Turner (2002) stated that his recent concern with microsocial processes represents a reemergence of the interest in social psychology that he held while attending graduate school. Combining social psychology and organizational analysis completes the circle in Turner's academic career.

In many of his publications, Turner emphasizes that sociology must evolve from the great theorists of yesterday, such as Karl Marx, Georg Simmel, Émile Durkheim, and George Herbert Mead, by taking what is relevant from their theories and applying it to new theories. Turner welcomes open criticism of his theories and ideas, in order to further knowledge within sociology, in an attempt to piece together structurally sound theories. Turner does not see the value, to sociology, of those who constantly criticize the theories and concepts of the classical giants of sociology. "We still stand in the shadows of these giants and we appear reluctant to stand on their shoulders—lest we fall down. Sociological theory is still about persons, rather than about generic processes of our universe" (Turner, 1984:38). "I can only offer the belief that it is time to pull from these and other scholars what is theoretically most useful and move on with the job of theory building" (Turner, 1993:98).

INFLUENCES

Like social thinkers, Turrner was influenced by a great number of people. Among his instructors, Turner was influenced by Tamotsu Shibutani, a symbolic interactionist; Donald R. Cressey, who was, at the time, the world's most famous criminologist; and Walter Buckley, a general systems theorist. In graduate school, it was his mentor, Robin M. Williams, a functional and conflict theorist, who had the greatest influence on Turner. Intellectually, the people most influential on Turner's thought are, at the microlevel, George Herbert Mead, Sigmund Freud, Erving Goffman, and Ralph Turner. At the macrolevel, Turner was influenced by Talcott Parsons, Peter Blau, Randall Collins, Amos Hawley, Émile Durkheim, Herbert Spencer, Karl Marx, Georg Simmel, and Max Weber. In the following pages a brief review of Marx's, Simmel's, and Weber's influence on Turner is be presented.

Karl Marx (1818–1883)

Karl Marx's commitment to social change led him to visualize social systems as plagued with elements that produce conflict. This can easily be seen in his many works pertaining to revolutionary class conflicts in industrial society (Turner, 1993). Turner organized the work of Marx (as well as that of Simmel and Weber) in such a way as to allow him to apply his own propositions to conflict theory. (Note: Turner followed the recommendations of his former professors, who taught him to state his arguments in testable propositions.) Turner (1993) stated that the more unequal the distribution of scarce resources in a system, the greater is the conflict of interest between its dominant and subordinate segments.

Marx addressed the need for the organization of the subordinates which lead to overt conflict. The need for organization is paralleled with the idea of emotional arousal. As Turner (1993) proposed, there must be a high degree of emotional arousal for the subordinates to organize, due to the substantial risks they face by opposing those who hold power. For Marx, alienation was one form of emotional arousal because it goes against people's basic needs (Turner, 1993).

In his book, *Societal Stratification: A Theoretical Analysis* (1984), Turner applied Marx's principles of stratification and described how conflict inevitably emerges with stratification. Social classes emerged through the initial concentration of control of the means of production. Production escalates in response to the elite's desire to extract more resources for further control (and profit), thereby increasing inequality (Turner, 1984). "Those who control production also have disproportionate power; in turn, they use control of production and power to extract surplus and, thereby, create and sustain inequality. In addition, they use their power to control ideological resources that legitimate inequality" (Turner, 1993:105).

Georg Simmel (1858–1918)

Concerned about the *forms* of social interaction, Georg Simmel studied the interplay between associative and dissociative processes and how they operate to create and maintain social patterns (Turner, 1993). Simmel's focus on basic forms of interaction provided Turner a microbehavioral approach to the study of conflict and a counterbalance to Marx's macro orientation. Simmel was interested in analyzing the forms of dissociation in social systems and discovering the degree of combativeness, or violence, of conflict (Turner, 1993). Simmel cited as the determinants of conflict variables such as the degree of emotional involvement of the parties to a conflict, the level of the respective solidarity among members of conflict parties, and the degree of previous harmony between members of conflict parties.

Turner learned from Simmel that not all conflicts necessarily intensify to the point of violence, and that if they do not, they can still have integrative outcomes for the social whole. Simmel's propositions also allow for inquiry into the conditions under which initially violent conflicts can become less intense and, once again, have integrative consequences for the social whole (Turner, 1993).

Max Weber (1864–1920)

Max Weber was concerned about such issues as legitimized order, authority, and domination. Weber stated that a legitimized order involves a pattern of "domination" for regulating the actions of actors. Domination involves authority, or the rights of some to control and regulate the actions of others. A social system remains integrated when patterns of domination within and between hierarchies of status groups, parties, and classes are considered appropriate, or legitimate, by the actors (Turner, 1993).

Turner viewed Weber's theory of social integration and conflict as sophisticated. "Social integration is a function of legitimacy given to elites who dominate various social arenas, most notably in material well-being (class), power (party), and honor (status groups). The very fact of domination, especially in terms of tradition, creates stratification processes that maintain a potential for their transformation, when and if charismatic leaders can emerge and successfully mobilize subordinates" (Turner, 1993:117).

CONCEPTS AND CONTRIBUTIONS

At this point it should be established that Jonathan Turner began his early training in sociology with symbolic interactionism, learned of Parsonian functionalism in graduate school—admitting his preference to always keep an eye on the big picture—and identified with the conflict theory to the point where he articulated a brilliant interpretation of it. A review of some of Turner's most significant contributions begins with his commitment to establishing "good" social theory.

Social Theory and Positivism

Jonathan Turner has attempted to integrate a variety of theoretical traditions but generally maintains a commitment to the Big Three theories found in the sociological tradition: functionalism, conflict, and symbolic interactionism. Turner also maintains a traditional stand in favor of positivism and the idea that sociology is a science. Auguste Comte, the founder of sociology, argued that sociology had reached a positivist stage and was capable of identifying "laws" of human behavior. Today, there are many sociologists who question the validity of the positivist approach. Turner (1985a) acknowledged that critics of positivism question whether human behavior

can be examined in the same manner as the natural sciences, and he asserted that such critics are interfering with the general accumulation and improvement of social theory:

> Positivism has negative connotations in sociological theory these days, being equated on the one side with raw empiricism and on the other side with naivete about the real workings of humans. My sense is that this suspicion about positivism has worked against the cumulation of knowledge about human action, interaction, and organization. . . . I would like to challenge this smug cynicism by reviewing the diverse ways that sociologists construct theory. For a discipline cumulates knowledge by building and testing theories. And so, if we find that there is little theory in a discipline, we can be sure that there is precious little knowledge about the workings of its domain of inquiry. My belief is that "theorists" in sociology rarely theorize, and as a result, we know embarrassingly little about the social universe. This lack of knowledge is not because of positivism; on the contrary, it is because we have failed to be positivists in Comte's sense of this term. (p. 24)

Turner is to be commended for his dedication to building "good" theory. He attempts to make it clear that arguing over the validity of positivism, and other such debates, only serves to interfere with good old-fashioned thinking, or social theory. Turner (1985a) summarized his commitment to positivism and social theory building by stating:

> I think that sociology has avoided the one kind of theorizing that can cumulate knowledge. We have either retreated up into the meta-theoretical stratosphere or buried ourselves under mounds of raw data. We have, in other words, avoided being positivists. We have collected myriads of facts and interpretations of them, and we have created numerous grand schemes and typologies. Robert Merton (1968) saw this some time ago in his advocacy for theories of one

middle range, but he loaded the dice to-ward more data collection. I think that we ought to go back to Comte, get comfort-able in our armchairs once again, and start theorizing. For only when theorists begin to develop abstract principles and analyti-cal models about invariant and timeless properties of the social universe can soci-ology hope to cumulate knowledge about human action, interaction, and organiza-tion. (pp. 29–30)

The diversity of opinion in sociology as to what constitutes "good" theory has been very harmful to the discipline. The lack of consensus from within has made sociology look weak to the "outside" world—both the academic and nonacademic worlds. As Stephan Fuchs and Jonathan Turner (1986) explained:

Uncertainty is high in sociology because the organizational structure of profession-al sociology is not autonomous, closely in-tegrated, and centralized. Sociology is thus "multiparadigmatic" primarily because no single, homogeneous scientific establish-ment exclusively controls the standards of epistemic legitimacy, the distribution of reputations through the publications sys-tem, and the allocation of the means of in-tellectual production. If any particular scientific establishment managed to mo-nopolize control over the production and administration of sociological knowledge, then sociology could be as "mature" a sci-ence as physics. The high level of task un-certainty in sociology thus follows from the pluralistic structure of its professional organization rather than from the pre-sumed complexity of its subject matter. . . . Moreover, sociology has thus far been un-able to achieve reputational autonomy from the lay public and competing organi-zations (religion, media, etc.). (p. 149)

Turner believes that sociology in general and social theory specifically are suffering from constant in-fighting among those found within the discipline. The debate centering on positivism and scientism has kept sociology

from reaching its full potential as a respected academic field. Turner (1990) believes that positivism is more easily applicable to sociol-ogy as a tool for research than it is for social theory:

Any reasonable assessment of sociology today would conclude that the prospects for scientific theory seem rather dim. There are, of course, many theorists who advo-cate "positivism" or the search for general laws and models that are empirically as-sessed in an effort to cumulate knowledge about how the social universe operates. But if we look at sociology as an institu-tional whole, this is certainly not the pre-vailing view, especially among those who call themselves "theorists." On the re-search side of sociology, things are not as bad, because many advocate the use of "scientific methods" and produce sugges-tive findings that have theoretical implica-tions. Yet much of the time research in sociology is theoretical, and is conducted to accommodate a patron, client, or per-sonal interest rather than a theoretical question. (Turner, 1990b:37)

Turner (1990b) promoted the idea that sociol-ogy *must* be a science:

Many sociologists want sociology to be "anything and everything for everyone," whereas I want it to be a science. . . . Science involves developing abstract propositions and models; my approach to metatheory is (1) to construct propositions and models and (2) to move back and forth between the two. (p. 51)

With his metatheorectical approach, Turner remains committed to thinking and theoriz-ing in terms of processes that flow and feed on themselves, and he parts company with defenders of metatheory like George Ritzer. Utilizing a functional analysis Turner (1988) emphasized yet again sociology's need to commit to the canons of science. "Sociology desperately needs a way to record, cata-logue, and array comparative data; notions of requisites might serve this truly 'neo' function in sociology" (p. 120).

Turner's Conflict Theory

Realizing that symbolic interactionism does not have an adequate conception of social structure and social organization, Turner (1982) concluded that it is an inadequate sociological perspective. In his view, structural functionalists fail to properly address the issue of social change, and even when they do explain social change, it is in developmental rather than revolutionary terms. In his 1975 article "A Strategy for Reformulating the Dialectical and Functional Theories of Conflict," Turner stated: "The growing disenchantment with structural-functional theory has been marked by the rise of alternative theoretical perspectives over the last two decades. One of the most conspicuous of these alternatives has been `conflict theory' which has presumably rediscovered for the discipline such phenomena as power, force, coercion, constraint, and change in social systems" (p. 433). Turner became attracted to conflict theory because it seemed to better address the macro issues than did functionalism. He turned his attention to the development of conflict theory. In his *Structure of Sociological Theory* (1982), Turner specified a number of feedback loops, or dialectical relations, that lead to his nine stages of conflict theory. Ritzer (1988a:232) outlined the nine-stage process as follows:

1. The social system is composed of a number of interdependent units.
2. There is an unequal distribution of scarce and valued resources among these units.
3. Those units not receiving a proportionate share of the resources begin to question the legitimacy of the system.
4. Deprived people become aware that it is in their interests to alter the system of resource allocation.
5. Those who are deprived become emotionally aroused.

6. There are periodic, albeit often disorganized, outbursts of frustrations.
7. Those involved in the conflict grow increasingly intense about it and more emotionally involved in it.
8. Increased efforts are made to organize the deprived groups involved in the conflict.
9. Finally, open conflict of varying degrees of violence breaks out between the deprived and the privileged. The degree of violence is affected by such things as the ability of the conflict parties to define their true interests and the degree to which the system has mechanisms for handling, regularizing, and controlling conflict.

In the first stage of Turner's conflict theory, elements of functionalism exist, as he stated that society is made up of a number of interdependent units. In *Macrodynamics* (1995), Turner described four bases of power and explained how they themselves are interrelated. The more the four mechanisms—the use of symbols, the use and manipulation of material incentives, the use of administrative structure, and the use of coercion—of power are brought together and work in unison with each other, the higher is the concentration of power. The units exist as a function of the society, serving a purpose within that society and supported by the society through other functions. There is a point where all of the functions of a society must meet, whether it is by direct or indirect means. Turner (1995) stated that it is at this conjunction that the power of a society is held.

In the second stage, Turner stated that there is an equal distribution of resources within the society. This is where actual conflict begins, because the units within the society start to realize that the spread of resources, whether material wealth, power, services, or some other resource, is disproportional, with the majority of the resources going to a minority of the population.

When frustration begins to take root within the units of the system, conflict has reached the third stage. Frustration leads to the questioning of the legitimacy of the system. The subordinates question the authority of the system. When the subordinates realize that it is in their best interest to change the system, in order to secure the proper proportionality of resources, the fourth stage has been reached. Communication among the deprived members of the system is critical in order for all to realize their situation within the system. The communication between deprived members is often controlled by those in positions of power and authority. Additionally, over a period of time, deprived groups often reach a state of hopelessness, or false consciousness, in regard to their collective plight. When word spreads among the deprived groups that mobilization has begun, further collective action is highly probable.

In the fifth stage, Turner indicated, emotions become involved in the decision-making process. Courses of action often become erratic. Subordinates initiate periodic, often disorganized, outbursts of frustration aimed at the system in the sixth stage. These outbursts bring with them the potential to become organized, thus paving the way for the beginning of direct confrontation. Those involved in the conflict grow increasingly intense about their frustrations and act increasingly emotional during the seventh stage. The escalation of emotions and the repeated commitment to the "conflict" can be attributed in part to the failure of the subordinates to gain attention from the dominant group.

The eighth stage represents the inevitable response by the power group. The power group's attempt to squash the conflict situation triggers further attempts among the subordinates to rally as many people to the cause as possible. In the ninth and final stage, Turner stated, conflict evolves into direct confrontation between the subordinates and the dominant group, or the deprived and the privileged. Turner believes that the degree of violence resulting from this conflict depends on how the parties involved in the conflict define their true interests and the extent to which the system has mechanisms for handling, regularizing, and controlling conflict.

History has shown that conflict between diverse groups is inevitable. This is especially true of ethnic groups. Social theory can be used to explain this conflict. Macrosociological theories represent the best option. In his analysis of ethnic relations theories, Turner (1986c) stated, "Most theories focus on the patterns of `antagonism' and `discrimination' between minority ethnics and the numerical majority, although exceptions are typically made for colonial systems and societies such as South Africa where a minority discriminates against the majority" (p. 403).

Macrodynamics

Turner's most noted contribution to macro theory is revealed in his *Macrodynamics: Toward a Theory on the Organization of Human Population* (1995). Turner's (1990) macrodynamic analysis was influenced, in part, by Durkheim's model:

> *The Division of Labor* (1933/1893) is, of course, the main source of Durkheim's macrostructuralism. Basically, Durkheim views the concentration of a population in ecological space—what he termed "material density"—as crucial to the division of labor, with population size and rate of growth as central "causes" of such density. But ecological conditions exert an independent effect, since the same sized population can be concentrated or dispersed as a result of varying amounts of space and geo-social configurations (natural barriers, cities, etc.). . . . Ultimately, the "division of labor," or what I term "social differentiation," is "caused" by the increased "moral density" that follows from escalated "material density." It is at this point that Durkheim's causal argument gets slippery, because he invokes a selection argument, positing natural selection as a causal mechanism that translates ecological concentration into a division of labor, or increased social differentiation. (p. 1094–1095)

Turner (1990) placed a much stronger emphasis on population size as a significant variable of macrodynamics. He drew a causal arrow directly from the population variables to competition for resources to acknowledge that "Population size, *per se,* exerts a direct influence on scarcity of resources. Competition for scarce resources thus causes conflict, under conditions of material density; and it is at this point that Durkheim invokes a selection mechanism, presumably because competition and conflict create selection pressures for specialization" (p. 1095).

Turner has consistently shown an interest in social organizations. In his *Macrodynamics* (1995), he identified seven elements that explain the organization of societies:

1. Size of population, including its rate of growth, diversity, and movements.
2. Production and amount of resource extraction and conversion.
3. Level of distribution, including amount and speed of circulation of people, materials, and information.
4. Extent of centralized power, or the degree of control and regulation.
5. Size and pattern of settlements.
6. Differentiation within and among structural units, social categories, and systems of symbols.
7. Extent of the above pressures in maintaining a society or causing its dissolution.

An increase in population causes strain on productive activities. Regulation and control of the population tighten. New ways to distribute goods and information to the masses become necessary and are accomplished through invention and innovation. Properly addressing these issues decreases the potential for societal dissolution and paves the way for further population growth.

As technology increases, so does production. Motivation for cultural items leads to material pursuit. Once a surplus exists, possession of property becomes more noticeable. Those who receive more property become more powerful. In turn, this step leads to higher levels of regulation and creates a concentration of power (Turner, 1995).

In the third element, levels of distribution, Turner was concerned with two things: moving material and information and the exchange between people. Those with power want to maintain a surplus production, although at some point, overproduction will cause the demand for products to diminish (satiation has occurred).

Turner (1995) defined *power* as "the capacity to regulate and control the actions of other members of a population and the structural units organizing these members. By regulation as control, I simply mean that one actor, or set of actors, has the capacity to affect the course of actions of other actors, or set of actors; and the greater this capacity, the more power an actor or set of actors possesses" (p. 75). Turner labeled four basic bases of power: ideological, economic, military, and political. As the population increases, a higher need for consolidated power emerges to regulate and coordinate activities.

Population affects the organization of society in two ways. If there are not enough people, the system will encourage immigration. This increase in population encourages expansion. Turner (1995) explained that densely populated areas create control problems due to emerging potential sources of counterpower from "(a) concentration of possibly readily mobile masses, (b) wealthy elite participating in exchange distribution that could challenge traditional authority, (c) the old elite threatened more and more by (a) and (b)" (p. 107). Differentiation within and among structural units may include increases in ethnic diversity and possible formations of urban masses that might mobilize to challenge the existing power group.

Turner concluded his macrodynamic analysis by stating that society must be able to handle the interaction of all these forces. If it does not, the society will disintegrate. A mechanism often employed by social systems to deal with the complexity of the integration, regulation, distribution, and coordination of units is bureaucracy.

Bureaucratization

Bureaucracies allow the performance of extensive tasks. In his "Historical Forces behind Bureaucratization" (2001), Turner credited Egypt with the initiation of bureaucracy, noting that significant projects like the building of the pyramids could not have been done without specialized labor, coordination of the roles of a large number of workers, and a hierarchical arrangement that provided an efficient chain of command. Military conquests and defense against aggressors are another reason behind the formation of bureaucracy. The extent to which the troops are organized is critical to military success. The introduction of money into the economy is another facilitating factor. Turner also proposed that the Catholic church created bureaucracies in order to expand its influence over the masses. As a social system increases in size, the need for a formal organization increases correspondingly. Some form of social control must always exist to ensure the survival of the system. In short, all four of the bases of power described by Turner utilize bureaucracy.

Inequality

Ideally, a bureaucracy is a functional device that should not only ensure the smooth operation of the various units that make up the social system but also help to prevent favoritism, or inequality, as all persons must abide by the same rules. Turner and Starnes (1976) described four components of inequality:

1. **Economic surplus:** The source of inequality and the cause of problems in distribution.
2. **Self-interest:** A source of competition among the various units.
3. **Power groups:** Those units which have won the competition for resources.

4. **Reaffirmation of power:** The proposition that those with the power will find the means to maintain their power position.

The wealthy members of society hold influence over the government, especially in economic matters. They are able to separate the middle and lower classes. The middle class unintentionally (with what Marx would call *false consciousness*) supports the wealthy and misconstrues the lower class as enemies (Turner and Starnes, 1976).

The government regulates the price of goods either to manage the ration of supply to demand or to directly influence the prices charged for goods. Quotas and taxes control the supply and demand by limiting the goods that go into and out of a country. By allowing certain companies to act as monopolies, the government can regulate the flow of goods and the profits of organizations. Also, by the limiting of imports, domestic competition is discouraged (Turner and Starnes, 1976).

Inequality is often a source of outrage, anger, frustration, revolt, and oppression in human societies. There are those who believe that certain social structures and processes have systematically regulated the social system to the extent that certain groups, especially minority groups, are relegated to conditions of poverty while living in the midst of affluence. Inequality is a result of the structure of basic social institutions and people's access to valued resources (Turner, 1977).

Social Stratification

Turner's ideas on social stratification are articulated best in his 1984 article "Some Theoretical Principles of Societal Stratification," coauthored with Robert Hanneman. Turner and Hanneman presented six theoretical principles on societal stratification and three basic social processes that lead to stratification. A review of this work begins with three generic processes that Turner and Hanneman (1984:2–4) believe cause social stratification:

1. **Distributive Processes:** Valued resources are distributed unequally among the members of a social system. At the most abstract level, these distributive processes are conceptualized in terms of the degree of concentration of three basic resources: material wealth, power, and prestige. Concentration is concerned with what proportion of persons in a social system possess what proportion of a given resource. Inequality (previously discussed) is a result of the concentration of valued resources among limited numbers of people. It is the view of Turner and Hanneman that the inequality of power and prestige can also be defined by concentration measures.

2. **"Social Class" Processes:** Social class is the realization of underlying social processes and therefore cannot be viewed as a unitary property of social systems. Turner and Hanneman focused on two discrete processes: group formation and rank. *Group formation* can be defined as the degree and extent of differentiation of homogeneous subpopulations in a system, *homogeneity* being defined as the degree to which subsets of members in a system can be distinguished by common or similar behaviors and attitudes (p. 3). *Rank* refers to the degree to which homogeneous subsets in a system can be linearly rank-ordered in terms of their imputed worthiness.

3. **Mobility Processes:** People are free to move from place to place and from position to position. In the context of stratification, the primary concern is with movement across ranked positions and/or ranked subpopulations. The degree of social mobility is defined in terms of the proportion of individuals in a society who are mobile and the distance across rank-ordered subpopulations that those who are mobile travel.

With these processes in mind, Turner and Hanneman (1984:4–19) categorized six theoretical principles, or equations, on societal stratification:

1. **Concentration of Material Wealth:** The work of Marx and Lenski had a great influence on this equation. Generic forces are related to the degree of concentration of material wealth (CMW) in a system. CMW is viewed as a positive exponential function of productivity (P) and a negative exponential function of the number of social hierarchies (NH) and the number of organization units in a system (NO). The relation between productivity and the concentration of material wealth is exponential because initial increases in P have less effect on CMW than subsequent increases. The effect of power on CMW is measured in terms of densities of organizational units (NO) and hierarchies (NH) in societies.

2. **Concentration of Power:** This equation is influenced by the ideas of Spencer and Simmel. Equation 2 states that the concentration of power (CPO) is logarithmically related to the level of perceived external threat (ET) and exponentially related to the level of (P), the degree of internal conflict or conflict potential (IC), and the volume of internal transactions (IT). These factors stand in a multiplicative relation to one another with regard to their impact on the concentration of power (COP). Increases in P create material wealth, which can be used to buy power. Once power is initially consolidated, it can then be mobilized to acquire more wealth and, consequently, even more power.

3. **Concentration of Prestige:** This equation is influenced by the Davis-Moore (1945) hypotheses and Bernard Barber's (1978) theory of occupational prestige. The degree of concentration of prestige (CPR) is a negative logarithmic function of the number of positions, as a proportion of all persons (N), that are perceived to possess power (Po), or (Po/N), and a negative exponential function of the number of positions, as a proportion of all persons (N), who are perceived to possess skill (SK), functional importance (FI), and material wealth (Mw). Prestige is a type of resource different from either material wealth or power, primarily because it is a perceptual and behavioral variable. Money and property are tangible objects, with a clear value, whereas, prestige is bestowed upon someone and represents a subjective value.

4. **Differentiation of Homogeneous Subpopulations:** This equation is concerned with the degree of differentiation among, and homogeneity in,

a society's subpopulations (*DFHO*). The degree of differentiation is a result of size (*N*); functional, spatial, and vertical differentiation; and discriminatory behavior (*D*). Spencer and Durkheim argued over a century ago that there is a direct relationship between social differentiation and population size. Basic mathematics reveals the logic of this equation, in that societies with small populations have a lower level of differentiation, whereas, larger societies always have the possibility of being highly diversified. This equation addresses not only differentiation (*DF*) but also the social forces that are related to increasing homogeneity among differentiated subpopulations. Inequality and discrimination remain the leading forces that hinder cooperation among diverse groups.

5. **Ranking of Differentiated and Homogeneous Subpopulations:** In Equation 5, conditions affecting the degree of rank ordering among subpopulations are examined. Equation 5 is influenced by Parsons's analytical model of stratification and states that "the degree of linear rank ordering among homogenous subpopulations (*RAHO*) is a logarithmic function of the degree of consensus over value standards (*CNVS*) and an exponential function of the degree of differentiation of homogeneous subpopulations (*DFHO*). Consensus over value standards is weighted more heavily than subpopulations formation" (p. 15). In brief, the focus of this equation is on how differentiated subpopulations are ranked within the social system.

6. **Mobility Processes:** Equation 6 explores the rate of mobility in society, which includes movement up and down the social ladder, as well vertical movements within the same ranking social order. Attention is also paid to whether or not individuals (or collectivities) take advantage of opportunities that present themselves. Generally speaking, the social system is designed and maintained by those in power in an attempt to maintain their advantageous position.

Turner and Hanneman did not propose that these six equations represent the only processes involved in social stratification, but it is their view that these six equations are among the most critical. They concluded that

> stratification is a social form created by the intersection of those processes involved (1) in concentrating material wealth, power, and prestige, (2) in creating subpopulations that become rank-ordered, and (3) in accelerating or lessening the movement of people and groups as they move from one ranked population to another. A "natural science of society" seeks to explain the operation of these processes; and even though Equations 1 through 6 may require refinement or be subject to empirical refutation, they represent a sincere effort to develop scientific theory in the social sciences. (Turner and Hanneman, 1984:20)

Turner's analysis of social stratification led him to believe that social forces, such as inequality and discrimination, are responsible for establishing and maintaining social inequality. Oppression is another such variable.

Oppression

Turner defined *oppression* as "successfully keeping a segment of the population from attaining access to valuable resources" (Turner, Singleton, and Musick, 1984:2–3). The most valuable resources identified by Turner are material well-being, power, and prestige. Oppression itself leads to stratification due to the unequal distribution of resources. The population is divided along these economic lines (Turner et al., 1984). According to Turner (1984), stratification is a social form consisting of three constituent processes:

1. The unequal distribution of valued resources.
2. The formation of homogeneous subpopulations.
3. The ranking of these subpopulations.

The unequal distributions of resources is a critical dimension of stratification. Some individuals and collectibles in social systems receive more of what people value in society than do others. Power groups use oppression to place groups of people in different ranks.

The caste system is an example of stratification that allows for little mobility in and out of the ranks. The lowest castes (or groupings) are the biggest victims of oppression. The greater the degree of denial of resources, the greater the level of oppression. Thus, the social structure itself is often responsible for oppression. Turner and Singleton (1978) emphasized "that most of the variance in the structure of oppression can be accounted for by structural variables" (p. 1015).

The individuals and groups of people that possess power find it advantageous to use their power to design the social system that best fits their needs. Since those with power find it beneficial to maintain their power positions, it should be understandable why those without power find it beneficial to try to improve their socioeconomic position. Turner discovered that the most down-on-their-luck people are not the most likely to revolt. Instead, revolts are caused by those who have become upwardly mobile and therefore have something to gain. In other words, the truly poor are most likely not to benefit from a successful revolt, whereas those in a better position to take advantage of the power positions in the newly emerging social system will be the most likely to participate in revolution.

Discrimination

Turner provides several features of what he called *isolated acts of discrimination*. These are acts "not sanctioned by cultural values, beliefs, or norms: they are *not* performed as matter of policy within an organization" (Turner and Aquirre, 1998:8). In other words, these are interpersonal forms of discrimination in which one person possesses a discriminatory feeling toward another and acts on it. Institutional discrimination occurs when certain practices are built into the system itself, for example, unfair housing policies and unequal treatment in the judicial system. Turner and Aquirre argued that if enough people participate in isolated acts of discrimination, the act form a pattern and become institutionalized.

Depending on the severity of the discrimination, a group may resort to one or several types of adaptation. When a group is small or relatively powerless it may have to simply learn to live with the discrimination. This state is referred to as *passive acceptance.* When a group can manage to carve a role in which it can use its creative resources and possibly prosper, it has accomplished *marginal participation. Assimilation* occurs when a group loses its distinctiveness and becomes part of the greater society. People less physically identifiable are more easily assimilated. Sometimes groups withdraw from society to support themselves. This is sometimes called *self-segregation* (for example, the Amish). A more extreme reaction to discrimination and racism is *rebellion,* which occurs when certain groups are very upset and vent their frustrations on the dominant group.

Micro Theory

As a general theorist, Turner has also made significant contributions in his micro theory. His initial training in symbolic interactionism left a permanent impression on Turner, as evidenced by his publications in the area of micro theory over three decades.

In his 1970 article "Entrepreneurial Environments and the Emergence of Achievement Motivation in Adolescent Males," Turner reviewed previous research that had traced the high need for achievement among adolescent males to certain socialization experiences in the family. Turner believes that there was something about the middle classes which affects family socialization in ways conducive to high achievement motivation. An especially important variable associated with social class is the nature of a father's occupation. Results from Turner's study indicated "that adolescents with high need-achievement come from homes where fathers engage in entrepreneurial role behavior in their occupational status. This is found to be true regardless of whether or not such an occupation is middle class or working class, or whether the community where the subject lives is highly modern or traditional. These findings are seen as specifying more exactly the social structural origins of achievement motivation" (Turner, 1970:147). Turner (1979) concluded that "fathers in entrepreneurial occupations are seen as having a set of values and psychological dispositions compatible with those socialization practices in the family which will lead to high need for achievement in their sons" (p. 163).

Turner expanded his study of motivation to the development of a sociological theory of motivation in his 1987 article, "Toward a Sociological Theory of Motivation." Turner emphasized that this theory was a work in progress, but it does represent an attempt to bring motivational dynamics back into mainstream sociological theory and research. Among the problems associated with building a sociological theory of motivation remains the lack of consensus of what exactly motivation is and how to conceptualize it for theoretical and methodological purposes. Turner (1987b) stated:

> Few would disagree with the idea that there are forces mobilizing, driving, and energizing individuals to act, interact, and organize. How to conceptualize these processes remains a controversial area in psychology, social psychology, and sociology. The seeming inability to agree on what motivation is and how to conceptualize its operation has led some to abandon the topic in favor of less problematic issues, such as specific cognitive processes in psychology and particular facets of interaction in sociology. (p. 15)

Turner developed a composite model of his motivational theory but suggested that a number of other models should also be constructed. As a result, such theories could be tested empirically. According to Turner (1987b), the point of constructing composite models is that they

> encourage the next step in building theory: the articulation of propositions. In order to test models, they need to be translated into,

or serve as inspiration for, the development of testable hypotheses. . . . Eventually, it might be possible to construct a more formal theory from these propositions, but this goal will be realized only after the relative merits of the preliminary concepts, models, and propositions are assessed in light of relevant data and alternative theories. Since motivation has not been examined either explicitly or extensively by sociologists in recent decades, it seems prudent to work in this preliminary fashion—that is, at the level of robust concepts, simple composite models, and evocative propositions. (p. 26)

Turner had promoted the use of composite models in theory building in his 1986a article "The Mechanics of Social Interaction: Toward a Composite Model of Signaling and Interpreting" as well, in which he stated:

> I am proposing a particular strategy of theory development: limit the topic to only one core process; examine diverse points of view on this process sympathetically and undogmatically; construct a simple synthetic or composite model; and then, and only then, try to (a) connect the elements of the model to what has been bracketed out and (b) elaborate upon specific causal processes. In performing (a) and (b), we should move from analytical models to propositions that state the conditions under which the elements specified in the model will vary. (p. 105)

In recent years, Turner (2003) has been working on a general theory of emotions where he seeks to integrate a variety of theoretical traditions, primarily symbolic interactionism, expectation states, and psychoanalytic theory. Turner's theory of emotion centers on people's expectations:

> The important point is that these expectations become part of individuals' definitions of the situation, especially with respect to what should transpire because of expectations aroused. Emotions are aroused when expectations are met, exceeded, or unmet. As a general rule, when people's expectations are not realized, they experience negative emotions, or various combinations of

anger, fear, and sadness. In contrast, when individuals' expectations are realized, they will experience variants of satisfaction and happiness, and if they are exceeded, people generally will feel variants of happiness. The more emotions are aroused, the more interpersonal energy evident in the behaviors of individuals. (Turner, 2003:448)

Turner is certainly consistent in his belief that sociology should be grounded in the scientific tradition, and this is true at both the macro and the micro levels of social analysis.

FINAL THOUGHTS

Throughout his career, Jonathan H. Turner has maintained a commitment to scientific inquiry and a focus on social issues that will be as important in the future as they are today. Inequality, oppression, and discrimination have existed throughout human history, and many social thinkers have attempted to discover ways to eliminate it from society. Turner has long been a champion of the rights of the oppressed, and his work is to be commended.

Turner's work on conflict theory incorporates ideas from all the major social theories: functionalism, symbolic interactionism, exchange, and, of course, conflict. He has developed a model of conflict theory that has fused the relevant ideas of the sociological giants of the past with the concerns of contemporary society. Turner's conflict theory promotes four essential elements:

1. The realization of inequality among the units found in the social system.
2. The impact of emotions on behavior.
3. The existence of organizational components for those who experience inequality.
4. The variation of conflict, some of which leads to violence and some of which does not.

Conflict theory is not Turner's only major contribution to social theory. As a generalist, he has offered a great deal of insight and analysis at the macro and micro levels, as well as attempting to bridge the gap between the two (what he calls *meso theory*).

Jonathan Turner is a brilliant contemporary social thinker and will go down in history as a sociological giant.

14

Applying Social Theory to Future Society

Among the primary purposes of *Contemporary Social Theory: Investigation and Application* (and *Classical Social Theory: Investigation and Application*) was to provide the reader an extensive, but clearly presented, review of key concepts and contributions from a select number of brilliant social thinkers over a 500-year period and to demonstrate the relevancy of this material to third-millennium society. The ability to link social thought with "real" everyday events is critical if the social sciences hope to maintain any sense of legitimacy in the academic and secular worlds. As George Homans noted, sociologists and other social scientists have made empirical discoveries and behavioral psychologists have established general propositions, but he insisted that the key *now* is to apply such propositions to all forms of human behavior, thus demonstrating their relevancy. As seen in Chapter 6, Homans outlined five distinct propositions that he felt explained all human behaviors.

George Ritzer noted that many of the great classical theorists were involved in the practical implications of their theories, especially Marx and Durkheim. Unfortunately, too many contemporary theorists are quite narrow in their theoretical approaches and often fail to fully demonstrate the practical use of their ideas.

As difficult as is the challenge of demonstrating the relevancy of social thought to everyday events, predicting the future proves to be far more complicated. The three goals of any true science are discovery, explanation, and prediction. Simply discovering a phenomenon and providing an explanation of its characteristics cannot be enough for science. As Milton Friedman (1953) argued in his *Essays in Positive Economics,* the primary test of a scientific theory is its ability to predict. Science must always concern itself with accurately predicting the consequences of discovery. Obviously, predicting the future presents a formidable challenge. Karl Marx's observations and analysis of the two-class capitalist system and its effects on the proletariat were very accurate during his lifetime. But his belief that capitalism was merely a "necessary evil" on the way to communism has been proven wrong. He failed to envision a number of changes in the socioeconomic structure (for example, labor laws, unions, profit sharing, stock options, and retirement benefits) that eventually allowed the development of a middle class, a socioeconomic class that enjoys relative wealth.

George Herbert Mead believed that it is impossible to forecast any future condition in society, for it is always the unexpected that happens and we must recognize its impact on the world (Reck, 1964). He believed that history is a progressive process that can never be completely planned and is, therefore, unpredictable. Ideas such as this are echoed by proponents of chaos theory, who insist that complex systems, including human society, are impossible to predict accurately beyond the relatively near future because of the large number of complex, uncontrollable variables. For this very reason, the social sciences face a far more difficult challenge than the natural sciences when trying to create "laws" and accurately predict future circumstances. Furthermore, it is much easier to forecast general social and technological trends than it is to predict specific political or technical events. Surely, no social scientist in the late 1990s predicted the terrorist attacks on the World Trade Center (New York City) or the Pentagon on September 11, 2001. Consequently, accurate forecasting is generally limited to social currents and trends.

I do believe, however, that this phenomenon—that the unexpected seemingly always occurs—can be factored into scientific analysis. I call this process *planned unexpectedness.* Since the unexpected always seems to occur, we must plan on its occurrence. Planned unexpectedness is similar to the behavior of individuals who "schedule" free time, or what I call *planned spontaneity.* Within a structured existence it is possible to accomplish necessary work functions and plan time that is designated for spontaneous behavior (nonobligated time frames).

Attempting to predict future behavior is important in social theory. This is especially true if for no other reason than that many decisions made by individuals involve making interpretations about present behaviors and future ramifications. Luckily, social currents and trends do exist in society. Forecasting always involves some form of historical

analysis, and history provides evidence that social patterns have maintained themselves for at least the past five centuries. Therefore, a number of social behaviors and events can be *expected* to happen. Properly identifying these consistent themes found in human society allows a limited number of high-probability predictions about the future. If these social "givens" are factored in with planned unexpectedness, predicting future society is not nearly as difficult. In this chapter, a number of central and primary social themes are explored and analyzed. Projected implications of these trends assist in the prognostication of future society.

BELIEF IN PROGRESS AND CULTURAL EVOLUTION

Nearly all social theorists grounded in the scientific tradition share in a belief that society is continuously progressing and culture is generally evolving. Progressive thinking and scientific reason are essential elements in cultural evolution. Since at least the time of the Greeks, enlightened thinkers have faced the challenges presented by those who possess an allegiance to religious faith, tradition, and/or other forms of dogmatic thinking. The Age of Enlightenment was a period in history when social thinkers were convinced that society was emerging from centuries of darkness and ignorance into an age of scientific reason and progress. These thinkers held a firm belief in the power of human reason and the ability of people to act rationally. They believed that humanity itself could be progressively altered.

Auguste Comte was a strong proponent of positivism and encouraged a society based on rationality. He argued that all societies evolved through three stages, each stage representing an improvement in thinking and political and economic development. Comte clearly viewed this evolutionary process as a sign of progress.

Charles Darwin demonstrated that evolution is a fact. He articulated a theory centered on the idea of natural selection, a process in which the more "fit" members of a particular species adapt to and survive in the environment: the members that fail to adapt simply die off. This process is viewed as progress since the genetically weaker members of a species disappear, and the more fit are allowed to live on and continue to contribute.

Herbert Spencer noted that while certain species of animals drastically alter their physical bodies in order to survive in various environments, humans remain mostly the same despite the great differences in geographic living conditions. He summarized that humans adapt not *biologically* but *culturally* to their environment. Spencer is best known for his concept of the survival of the fittest, the idea that those who keep up with the changing environment are the ones most likely to succeed and progress. He had no problem equating evolution with progress. Unfortunately, Spencer is generally viewed as a strict evolutionist, but this is a mistake, as he clearly articulated how some societies have been victims of dissolution (they fell apart because they were not strong enough to survive).

Karl Marx utilized the historic process to demonstrate that humans are not trapped in a predetermined state of being. It is humans who made history, and therefore, they can change it. Marx clearly viewed certain types of advancements as progress. He viewed capitalism as a necessary step toward his ideal progressive society: communism. Unlike Spencer, who thought government should implement a laissez-faire approach toward society because it was evolving progressively on its own, Marx felt that there are times when people must intervene in the social-economic structure for their own sake. Marx was unhappy with early capitalism and attempted to form a revolution to overthrow the existing society.

Émile Durkheim was a strong proponent of Comte's and Saint-Simon's concept of positivism. Durkheim was the first sociologist to actually use the scientific empirical method

of data collection and data analysis. He believed that social scientists could discover patterns by studying phenomena. In fact, he believed that human progress is directly tied to the successful discovery of the laws (or patterns) found in society. According to Durkheim, these laws are not different from the ones found in nature. Durkheim used the concepts *mechanical solidarity* and *organic solidarity* to demonstrate how societies evolve from primitive social structures, characterized by little division of labor, to modern ones, characterized by a great deal of differentiation. Although Durkheim was concerned that modern society might lack basic human morality, he felt that society possesses a collective conscience that serves to unite the members.

In *The Protestant Ethic and the Spirit of Capitalism* (1904–1905/1958a), Weber demonstrated that certain cultural barriers, especially those centered on religion, hamper the growth of a rational economic system. Thus, while the West was experiencing mass industrial growth and enjoying economic wealth, other societies remained primitive and economically poor. The relevance of this topic is exemplified by the growing phenomenon of globalization. The third millennium begins with a great disparity between the economically rich countries and the developing poorer nations. Without a change in cultural values and attitudes, the financially poor societies will never develop their full economic potential and will risk further polarization.

Charles Cooley lived a relatively sheltered life in Ann Arbor, Michigan, and most of his work is microsociological. He showed little interest in Darwin's view on evolution and the interrelatedness of nature. He agreed with Spencer's general conception of the progressive nature of life, but not his specific views of society. Cooley believed that human nature progresses through interactions in primary groups. In order for individuals to grow, new primary groups must be sought. Thus, a progressive society provides plenty of interaction opportunities for its members and a choice among a wide variety of primary groups.

George Herbert Mead's commitment to pragmatic thinking reveals his confidence in the unity of science and progress. He believed that scientific analysis eliminates bias and dogmatic thinking. Mead firmly believed that the use of reason and science was clearly superior to that of the Christian evangelistic ideas he had been exposed to in his youth. Science and a commitment to progress were far more important than a commitment to faith and prayer.

Contemporary theorists, as a whole, generally accept the idea and value of continued societal progress and cultural evolution. The social thinkers who do not perceive that society is progressing generally have ideas on how to reach a more desired variation of society (such as feminists who are upset by the existing social order but who have ideas on how to make society better through ideals of equality). A belief in progress is only logical; after all, any alternative belief presents a pessimistic outlook on life—not that there are not enough elements in existence that can support a negative view of the future of humankind. Sociobiologist Edward Wilson provided an example of an alarmist, pessimistic view of the future. Wilson (1975) warned that continuously accelerated evolution could bring about changes we may not like or survive. He suggested that there could be a lessening of altruistic behavior through the maladaption and loss of group-selected genes. Wilson believed that behavioral traits tend to be selected out by the principle of metabolic conservation when they are suppressed or when their original function becomes neutral in adaptive value. Such traits could largely disappear from populations in as few as ten generations, or just two or three generations in the case of humans. Valued qualities, such as cooperativenss with groupmates, may "evolve" into aggressive behaviors aimed at strangers. Possible evidence of Wilson's concern is the fact that many people today believe there is a decline in general good manners, and that more and more people act very rudely toward one another without any provocation. Beyond biological impediments to progress are the social obstacles. Among the more significant of these social obstacles to progress are tyrannical rulers. History has shown that a number of evil people have ruled their respective societies. In fact, we can *plan* on such leaders' reappearing throughout history. Repressive governments will always represent an obstacle to progress. A list of the ten worst living dictators will appear later in this chapter in the section on terrorism.

Western cultures, such as the United States, continue to place a high value on progress. New and improved forms of technology generally benefit the majority of citizens. Unfortunately, progress often comes at a cost to some, and therefore, there will be those who suffer from the negative aspects of progress. For example, expanding freeways in Los Angeles benefits those who use the freeway (the majority) but harms those who had their homes destroyed (the few, and usually politically unpowerful) to make room for the freeway. Technology creates new and improved commercial products but endangers the usefulness of the replaced products. Thus, consumers are forced to keep purchasing new material goods because the old ones have become outdated. For example, digital television implies that old television sets will become obsolete, turntables were replaced by compact disk (CD) players, and eventually a series of new technologies will render CD players obsolete.

It is reasonable to assume, however, that Western societies, especially the United States, will continue to grow and flourish throughout the third millennium. Cultures that fail to adapt to the new progressive order risk dissolution and complete elimination. The continuation of progress must be accompanied by an increased level of individual and cultural responsibility. It is the duty and obligation of social thinkers to continue serving as illustrators of the realities of society. Rational thought, education, and a clear form of communication should ensure that future society will continue to enjoy the benefits and value of progress.

TECHNOLOGICAL GROWTH

Continued progress in human society is dependent upon technological growth. Since the time of the Industrial Revolution, the human species has witnessed and enjoyed the tremendous societal improvements due to the benefits of technological growth. Examples of these benefits are nearly endless, but include such areas as a dramatic increase in life expectancy and quality of life, medical improvements, a wide variety of the material goods that make everyday tasks simple (for example, in transportation, automobiles, subways and airplanes; in food production, farm equipment, such as tractors, combines, and hay balers; in forms of communication, telephones, fax machines, and the Internet), and other everyday products of technological development that we take for granted (such as, indoor plumbing, electricity, television, and stereos). In the past 500 years human society has clearly profited from the development of technology.

Undoubtedly, technology will continue to benefit humans. It is a necessary criterion of progress and cultural evolution. A large number of technological developments are already in the works that will benefit human society in the third millennium. A few of these developments are discussed in the following pages.

Genetic Engineering

In brief, genetic engineering involves the manipulation of deoxyribonucleic acid, or DNA. An important element in the manipulation of DNA is vectors, which are pieces of DNA that can self-replicate independently of the DNA in the host cell in which they are grown. Examples of vectors are plasmids, viruses, and artificial yeast chromosomes. These vectors permit the generation of multiple copies of a particular piece of DNA, so this is a useful method of generating sufficient quantities of material with which to work. The process of engineering a DNA fragment into a vector is called *cloning* (to be discussed later in this chapter), because multiple copies of an identical molecule are produced (Singer, 1995).

In attempts to correct a genetic disorder or an acquired disease, gene therapy may be utilized. Gene therapy involves supplying a functional gene to cells lacking that function. There are two broad categories of gene therapy. The first category involves the alteration of germ cells, that is, sperm or eggs; the results is a permanent genetic change for the whole organism and subsequent generations. This *germ line gene therapy* is not considered an option in humans because of current ethical and moral considerations. The second category of gene therapy, somatic cell therapy, is analogous to an organ transplant. In this case, one or more specific tissues are targeted by direct treatment or by removal of the tissue; then the therapeutic gene or genes are added to the tissue in the laboratory, and the tissue is returned to the patient. Many clinical trials of somatic cell therapy have been started, mostly for the treatment of cancers and blood, liver, and lung disorders. In the near future, this form of genetic engineering will appear simplistic and archaic. In fact, any further discussion of the progress in genetic engineering will be outdated shortly after it is published. Suffice it to say, technological development will continue to influence this field.

Stem Cell Research and Human Cloning

The genetic makeup of humans has long puzzled scientists. As our knowledge of the genetic code increases, it becomes easier for scientific technology to benefit the human species. The beginning of the third millennium has witnessed great advancements in our knowledge of the human genome. As of this writing, we know that it takes just 30,000 to 40,000 genes to make, maintain, and repair a human. This figure represents few more than the number of genes necessary for a worm. "If you're judging the complexity of an organism by the number of genes it has, we've just taken a big hit in the pride department," (p. 1D) says the national Genome Research Institute's director, Francis Collins, who also heads the U.S. division of the international Human Genome Project (HGP) (Sternberg, 2001). This is not to suggest that the human genetic makeup is simple. The genome is a spiraling chain of chemicals running through every living being. In humans, the chain is vast, "25 times larger than any previously studied genome and eight times larger than the sum of all such genomes" (Sternberg, 2001, p.1d). Expanding knowledge of the human genome will further assist scientists who work in such areas as genetic engineering, stem cell research, and cloning. Among the first concrete benefits gained from the Human Genome Project was the creation in 2000 of a safe and speedy treatment salve to heal skin ulcers in people with poor circulation. Spokesperson David Stump of the Human Genome Sciences in Rockville, Maryland, stated that the compound, made of a protein called *keratinocyte growth factor-2* (KGF-2), is safe and accelerates healing. Nearly 4 million people in the United States face the dismal prospect of "skin breakdown" as a result of diabetes (doctors estimate that at least 10 percent of the 16 million diabetics nationwide develop chronic wounds during their lifetime) or poor circulation in their leg veins. "About half a million more people suffer venous stasis ulcers, wounds that fail to heal because damaged leg veins can't deliver sufficient blood to tissues. These wounds appear to benefit from KGF-2, which is applied to the skin" (Sternberg, 2001, p.2d).

Stem cells, or human embryonic stem (heS) cells, have the ability to self-replenish and to produce at least one descendant per cell (Holland, Lebacqz, and Zoloth, 2001). Stem cells enable the human body to regenerate tissues and other needed cells such as blood and skin (Holland et al., 2001). Only recently have scientists discovered that research on the adult stem cells is also valuable. But research conducted on embryonic stem cells is still the most valuable and has nearly unlimited uses in biotechnology research. Research on heS cells is most promising because it has been shown that as the fertilized cell divides, it can become a separate, entirely sustainable, and complete organism altogether from the original cell (Holland et al., 2001).

At the start of the third millennium, the topic of cloning is one of the most controversial subjects. In fact, the prospect of human cloning is at least partially responsible for the creation of the bioethics field (Lee and Tirandy, 2003). *Cloning* can be defined as "a group of genetically identical organisms produced without sexual reproduction; produced asexually" (McKinnell, 1985:119).

Cloning involves placing the nucleus of an adult cell in an egg from which the center has been removed and producing an embryo that is a genetic copy of the adult (Willing, 2001). Many people have an unwarranted and alarmist fear of cloning and seem to view it as the "coming of the end of humanity." An odd mix of activists, who include those on both sides of the abortion issue, is joining forces to push for a total ban on human cloning. The coalition is lobbying for a bill that would impose a ten-year prison sentence and $1-million fine on scientists who practice cloning for reproduction or research. Such alarmists need to remember that these same irrational fears were once applied to life support devices and heart transplants. The level of criticism and condemnation of cloning has not deterred scientists, as technological advancements continue in this field.

Like genetic engineering, stem cell research is an area where technological advancements will make today's breakthroughs obsolete in time.

Never-Ending Developments

As previously stated, there have been tremendous technological advancements in human society since industrialization. Developments in genetic engineering and cloning were highlighted because of their capacity to dramatically affect the future of the human species. The technological advancements in the West and especially the United States have greatly improved the lives of those who live there. At the beginning of industrialization (in the late 1700s) life expectancy for Americans was about thirty-six years. At the beginning of the third millennium the average life expectancy for all humans on the planet was sixty-three years. In the United States average life expectancy is 76.9 years for a baby born in 2000, and infant mortality has dropped to the lowest level on record. Life expectancy in underdeveloped sub-Saharan Africa is just half that in the developed world (Websdale, 2001).

Medical science and social behavioral consciousness deserve most of the credit for this dramatic difference in life expectancy. For those who can afford them (reflecting the reality of socioeconomic differences), the United States offers the best doctors and best-equipped hospitals in the world. Advancements in the medical field are startling. In 2001, a historic event occurred at a hospital in Louisville, Kentucky, when an artificial heart was transplanted into a patient. Two surgeons removed a patient's dying heart and replaced it with a mechanical heart, a yo-yo-shaped plastic-and-titanium pump weighing less than two pounds that is powered through the skin by an external battery pack. Some experts praised the new device because it is totally enclosed in the human body, sharply reducing risk of infection, a critical failure of earlier efforts.

Future society can expect further developments in the medical field. Animal clones are now giving birth, and new technologies are bringing the fate of the species within human control. Scientists are offering the opportunity to redefine, with unprecedented accuracy, what it means to be a person. The human species is nearly at a point where it can alter itself and can control genetic defects and create genes immune to known diseases. Biotech firms have positioned themselves to plunge further into such research. A biotech industry analyst asserted that the genomics revolution alone will double biotech revenues to $4 billion annually by 2005. Investors should look into newly developing technologies.

The construction industry has evolved in the area of bridge building through the use of plastics. Plastic bridges are only about one-quarter the weight of conventional bridges, so they are easier and quicker to install. Plastic bridges cost about twice as much as the usual steel-and-concrete bridges, but they won't corrode and are likely to last decades longer. Plastic bridges are made of carbon-fiber-reinforced polymers, a technology that's relatively new in work on roads and bridges. The bridge decks are paved with asphalt, so the plastic is undetectable by motorists.

Technological growth assists the human species in agriculture. At the world's largest biotech conference (San Diego, June 25, 2001) scientists revealed the so-called golden rice, engineered to produce vitamin A in the hope that developing nations can use it to stave off malnutrition. It has been successfully grown in greenhouses and will be tested outdoors soon. Mike Phillips, spokesman for the Biotechnology Industry Organization stated, "We could not have come up with a better example of what biotechnology is all about. It's a wonderful story of (how) the public and private sectors have come together" (Elias, 2001:A4). Critics view the genetically modified food as a potential health hazard and insist on further research to determine whether it is really safe for human consumption. However, in 1980, the U.S. Supreme Court authorized the patenting of a genetically modified organism (GMO), in effect, a designer life form: as a result large numbers of modified food products have flooded the marketplace (Lee and Tirandy, 2003).

Despite concerns from critics, by the start of the Third Millennium "the majority of processed foods eaten by Americans contained, to some degree or another, genetically modified ingredients. Many unprocessed foods, too, are GMO" (Lee and Tirandy, 2003:226). Genetically modified foods are becoming so commonplace that the farming of genetically modified crops is now a $600-billion-a-year industry in the United States (Lee and Tirandy, 2003). Organic farmers are concerned that their corps have become "contaminated" by neighboring genetic farms and have begun to file lawsuits. (Note: The one thing that seems most certain about future society is the continuing existence of lawyers) In France, a militant farmer, José Bove, decided to take the law into his own hands and mowed down a field of genetically modified crops owned by Cetiom, a specialist in oilseed research. The antiglobalization crusader-farmer was fined and faces possible jail time.

Developments in such areas as food production are important and will prove to be even more necessary as the third millennium proceeds. As Thomas Malthus warned human society many years ago, there is a scarce number of resources to go around. The human population is expanding at an alarming rate, and the demands placed on the planet are nearing a critical point. Technological growth must continue, not just because American prosperity depends on endless innovation and mass production of consumer products, but for the very survival of the human species.

There exist numerous examples of mundane advances in technology that affect the

everyday lives of people. Many of the automobiles that people drive are filled with luxuries unheard of just a decade ago. College students enjoy the benefits of technology in many ways. For one, meal plans are available on easy-to-use credit cards instead of the once cumbersome food stamps. It is extremely easy to log online nearly anywhere on campus, and in fact, it is now possible to do laundry online. By late 2002, over forty college campuses, all in the Midwest were featuring cyberlaundry via the eSuds system. In short, students can log onto a Web site to see if there are available machines to do their laundry, and they receive an e-mail when the load is finished. The system can automatically charge the students through their ID cards instead of their using coins. The advancements to come in the next few years and decades should be amazing.

SCARCE RESOURCES

In *An Essay on the Principles of Population* (1798) Malthus presented a pessimistic view of human society. He believed that the world's population was growing too quickly in proportion to the amount of food available. Malthus feared that the lack of natural resources would lead to such social problems as crime, poverty, and greed. Herbert Spencer felt that overpopulation and the search for scarce resources would inevitably lead to the survival of the fittest. People, and whole societies, would be in conflict with one another over the scarcity of desired resources. These conflicts would lead to political and territorial conflicts.

Demographic analysis is among the most underused determining factors for the evolution of economy and society (Cooper and Layard, 2002). By 2050, the world's population is likely to range from 8 to 12 billion, up from 3 billion in 1960. Today, anyone forty years old or older has been alive long enough to have seen the earth's population double. Rapid population growth is especially evident in the developing nations of the world. Accompanying this rapid growth is the shift of large numbers of people from rural areas to urban areas. On the positive side, the improvement in the status of women (for example, in the cash economy) in the twentieth century and especially in the last third of it is a direct result of the spread of social civil rights among the growing masses (Cohen, 2002).

Predictions regarding future population size are influenced by such factors as the spread of a global infectious disease, mass destruction due to warfare and terrorism, or such celestial events as a meteoric impact on the earth's surface. However, it is safe to forecast that in the next fifty years the human population will be bigger than it is today, that it will be more urban than it is now, and that it will be older than it was in 2000.

The ever-expanding numbers of people will put great demands on the limited natural resources. Clark Abt (2002) stated that energy demand may increase as much as sevenfold to eightfold by 2025. The world's increased need for electricity alone underscores the reality that overpopulation will undoubtedly lead to conflict over the scarcity of natural energy.

Conflict over scarce resources is not limited to the natural realm; it extends to the social world as well. Some people have more than others do—more wealth, power, prestige, and even basic rights. The distribution of significant social resources is unequal in all societies and has been so throughout all of human history. These differences determine the dimensions of stratification. Stratification exists in all societies and can be viewed as a ranking system. Ranking systems are based on the distribution of different scarce resources. Stratification also involves the arrangement of the members of a social system into levels having different or unequal evaluations. These evaluations are based on the possession of something of value (such as property, money, power, and authority).

Max Weber argued that the distribution of power and authority is the basis of social conflict. Power and authority, found in all social structures, are the central ingredients in determining one's position in the social world. However, Weber believed that people can be stratified in society by income and prestige as well. Thus, of the many scarce social resources available to the members of a society, three stand out above the rest: power, income and wealth, and prestige. *Power* is generally defined as the ability to get one's own way, despite the resistance of others. *Income* refers to the amount of money that a person or family receives over a specific period of time (usually a calendar year), while *wealth* refers to the total value of everything that a person or family owns (for example, property and other capital assists), minus any debt. *Prestige,* which is often difficult to measure, is related to the positive evaluation or social honor that one receives from others. Occupation is often a key variable in one's social prestige.

Scarce Social Resources

All people within any given society are certainly not born equal, nor do they enjoy an equal quality of life. The stratification system of a society reveals the dichotomy in the possession of scarce social resources. Those in a position of power and authority cannot be expected to voluntarily distribute their resources to others without receiving something else of value in return. Those in a position of authority make every attempt to maintain and legitimize their power. Those without power seek to exercise some control over their lives and may even challenge the existing social authority. Those in power are always smaller in number but much more organized than the masses. (The role of power in society is so important that it is discussed later under a separate heading.) As Marx so brilliantly explained, conflict between the classes is a given and has been well documented throughout history.

Income and wealth represent the most obvious evidence of stratification within a society. This is true for two primary reasons. First, differences in wealth and high income are visibly noticeable in terms of material possessions. The wealthy and rich generally live in better homes that are found in better neighborhoods, and they have easier access to society's scarce material resources. Second, income and wealth are easy to measure. A continuum of income would range from no money to the highest income. In the United States the wealthiest 2.7 million Americans have combined incomes equal to those of the bottom 100 million. The richest 1 percent of households owned nearly 40 percent of the nation's wealth in 1993, while the bottom 80 percent owned 16 percent (Walker, 1999). According to *Forbes* magazine, in 1999, for the first time ever, the 400 richest Americans had collectively amassed over $1 trillion, a figure greater than the gross domestic product of China (Galewitz, 1999).

In 1999, Microsoft chairman Bill Gates led the list of the nation's wealthiest Americans with a net worth of $85 billion. Microsoft cofounder, Paul Allen, with a net worth of $40 billion, was the second richest. The minimum net worth needed to qualify for the Forbes 400 rose to $625 million from $500 million in 1968. Nearly 40 percent of the top 400 got rich the easy way—they inherited some or all of their wealth (Galewitz, 1999).

As Weber (1946) noted, however, people of the same economic class do not necessarily interact with one another simply because of this one shared characteristic. Instead, he believed that people interact because of common lifestyles. Like-minded people respect the characteristics of those who exhibit the desired qualities of behavior. These people come to possess status within the group. This status is transformed into social prestige. There are numerous ways to gain prestige, including family name, geographic location, homes in certain neighborhoods, graduation from the "right" schools, education, income, accomplishments, titles, and public exposure.

People who have relatively equal status tend to associate with one another and to live similar lifestyles. Lifestyle is not an economic concept; it is a way of life. Does one live it with flair and enjoy every moment to the fullest, or does one complain and suffer from stress? Does one spend free time helping those less fortunate or watching television? These distinctive forms of behavior may be shown by persons of the same economic means—but they choose to live different lifestyles. However, certain lifestyle choices are economically determined. One may prefer a lifestyle that involves jet-setting to exotic locations around the globe or hope to associate with certain people who are high maintenance, but the necessity of wealth and/or high income makes it impossible for most people to accomplish these lifestyles.

Social groups are most generally formed around persons who share levels of prestige and status. Many people choose their marital partners on this concept. Deciding whom to be friends with and whom to be seen with socially is a reflection of status distinctions. People of high status and prestige usually prefer not to associate with those outside their social circle.

A critical variable in determining status and prestige is one's occupation. Occupational prestige is an indicator of one's socioeconomic status (SES). Since 1925, studies have been conducted to rate the prestige of various occupations (Goode, 1988). Respondents from over fifty countries are involved in this research. Generally, physicians, scientists, and university professors rank high in prestige, while janitors and garbage collectors rank low. On the surface this research may not seem surprising, but it is important to note that garbage collectors and other occupationally low-prestige workers may earn more money than college professors. This point further illustrates that prestige and status are not solely determined by economics.

Scarce Natural Resources

The pursuit of scarce social resources is irrelevant if one's most basic needs are not met—food, clothing, and shelter. While some people wish they had a bigger house or a home at the beach, others simply want shelter from nature's elements. Some people spend thousands of dollars on a single dress or suit, while others wear the same ragged clothing for months at a time. Concerns over such issues as self-esteem and reaching self-actualization are meaningless to people without food. The point is simple—the earth has a limited number of natural resources, many of which are irreplaceable.

The earth has a limited capacity to support life. This carrying capacity, as Catton (1980) described it, is the maximum feasible load, just short of the level that would and the environment's ability to support life. Among the many dangers facing the planet is the spread of deserts, the destruction of forests by acid rain, the stripping of large tracts of land for fuel, and the many areas where the population is exceeding the carrying capacity of local agriculture.

The demands placed on our planet are huge. Humanity is still primarily dependent on the conversion of fossil fuels (for examples heating oil, gasoline) to meet its energy needs. The consumption of fossil fuels has grown rapidly since the time of industrialization and economic development. Among the potential undesirable side effects of a dependence of fossil fuels are pollution (for example, smog and acid rain), ravaged topsoil, and changes in the global economy. Humanity has witnessed a variety of these side effects for some time now, and things will only grow worse. In 2001, the state of California was rocked by an energy crisis as rolling blackouts (lack of electrical power) startled residents. Utility bills skyrocketed and shock waves of worry consumed energy-conscious persons throughout the United States. Later in the same year Brazil faced the same energy concerns. In the throes of its worst drought in decades, the Brazilian government ordered three-quarters of its 170 million citizens to cut consumption by 20 percent or face rolling blackouts and unscheduled power interruptions. The Brazilian energy crisis threatens to cripple the economy of Latin America's most populous nation. With one of the most extensive river networks in the world, Brazil obtains more than 90 percent of its electricity from dams and has failed to invest extensively in alternatives like solar energy (Rohter, 2001).

Brazil's energy crisis is only the beginning of the discussion on the most critical natural resource of all: water. Without question, the most valuable resource on the planet is water. It is often the most taken-for-granted resource. Americans use over 5.5 million gallons of water per day, just for showers. This unusually high use of water is an example of why the United States was rated the world's most wasteful user of water by the first Water Poverty Index (Lawrence, Meigh and Sullivan 2002). The index is determined by such factors as water resources, access, capacity, use, and environmental impact.

Wasteful behavior represents a social cause of water shortage. However, nature is often responsible for water shortages as well, especially in the form of drought. The United States has access to a great deal of drinkable water, but this mighty nation is subject to periodic droughts. The most recent drought was in 2002, when the U.S. government officially stated that the drought affected more than 45 percent of the country. Effects of drought include the loss of human and animal life, destruction of crops, and, specifically in 2002, the loss of 6 million acres of mostly forest land. The weather pattern that helped to cause the drought in the United States had the opposite affect in Asia, where monsoons led to hundreds of deaths in Bangladesh and northern India

Drinkable water is a valuable global commodity. Capitalists and marketers in the

West have convinced many consumers that they must buy drinking water for "fashionable" reasons—and surprisingly many people are duped into purchasing this highly overpriced product. Many so-called natural springs water are little more than everyday tap water. Retail sales of water increase yearly. Canada and the United States pay the world's lowest and third-lowest prices for water, respectively.

The news is not so good for those who do not have such amounts of disposable income to spend on water or access to the Great Lakes, which account for one-fifth of the world's fresh water. Even in the United States, there are constant water shortage concerns in certain regions of the country. The desert southwest region (Southern California, Nevada, Arizona, and New Mexico) is in a perpetual state of concern over potential water shortages. Water executives in Nevada estimate that the existing water supply will be exhausted by 2013 (Hynes, 1994). A continuously growing population and an overdependence on the Colorado River are the primary problems. In the Pacific Northwest, a region that historically has enjoyed plentiful supplies of high-quality drinking water, a 20 percent increase in the population of Oregon and Washington since 1990 has placed a dramatic demand on drinking water. Some communities are already facing serious shortages (Larson, 2001).

Supply shortages are not the only problem associated with water. Drinkable water is continuously compromised by contamination from pesticides; runoffs from farms, factories, and urban streets; and raw sewage overflows. In 1994, the Environmental Protection Agency estimated that more than 740 million pounds of toxic chemicals pour into waterways annually in addition to tons of other pollutants ranging from used motor oil to raw sewage. (Las Vegas Review Journal, 1994)

Many other areas of the world are facing even more severe water-related problems, where the water is not drinkable, or

disappearing completely. Although 70 percent of the earth's surface is covered with water, 97.5 percent of that is sea water, leaving only 2.5 percent freshwater. Nearly 70 percent of that fresh water is frozen glacier water. More than 300 cities in China are experiencing water shortages; more than 100 are in a condition of acute water scarcity. One of the world's largest marshes, home to the Marsh Arabs of southern Iraq, has all but disappeared during the 1990s decade, according to satellite images released by the UN Environment Programme (Pearce, 2001). The images also show that 90 percent of this wildlife habitat has been lost as a result of human impacts including extensive drainage. In 1992, Saddam Hussein had the marshes drained after a rebellion by their inhabitants. To combat Saddam Hussein during the 1992 Gulf War, Turkey threatened to use its dams to stop the flow of the Euphrates altogether. Iraq threatened to bomb a Syrian dam. At the end of the second millennium Syrian fighters flew by Turkish dams. According to the United Nations, in 2003, unclean water killed more Iraqis during the U.S. invasion than bombs and bullets. In Barsa, a city of 1.5 million people, most of the residents had no access to safe water for four to five days. The inevitable conflict for water will leave many people without, and they face potential outbreaks of diarrhea and other diseases.

In Russia, much of the country's drinking water is filthy, rusty sewage pipes are bursting, and there's a lack of cash to fix the problems (Startseva, 2001). My own personal trips to Russia in 1999 and 2001 confirm the terrible water quality. The shower water at an "American" hotel in St. Petersburg (1999) was brown, and foreigners in Moscow (2001) are warned not to use the water, even for brushing their teeth.

Water problems are of concern in other parts of the world as well. The Sea of Galilee, the biblical lake where Jesus is said to have walked on water, has been pumped almost to its limit. It is now so low that salt deposits endanger the remaining amount of water (Rosenblum, 2001). Israel's other primary sources of water, aquifers within mountains along the Mediterranean coast, have been depleted by the worst drought in a century. They continue to be tapped at a much quicker rate than engineers advise.

Record droughts (2001) from the Korean peninsula through northern China and on to Afghanistan have destroyed crops and plunged tens of millions of people deeper into poverty. The United Nations reports that 5 million people face starvation in Afghanistan and neighboring Tajikistan alone. China's lack of rainfall has dried out farmland the size of Nevada and fed huge dust storms. Bad harvests in North Korea have forced the communist government to warm up to the West in exchange for food aid.

The water shortage problem cannot be emphasized enough. This critical commodity is more valuable and will serve as the catalyst for more future wars over its control and ownership than crude oil. The drying out of the vast marshes around the Euphrates and Tigris Rivers in southern Iraq is an environmental and humanitarian tragedy, caused primarily by Turkey's damming of the headwaters of the Euphrates. The spring floods had historically replenished the marshes. Turkey's plan for future dams, including the Ilisu Dam on the Tigris, will most likely seal the marshes' fate (*New Scientist*, 2001).

And so we have a future with the prospect of "water wars." The Middle East is headed in that direction at the beginning of the third millennium. The Palestinians receive a fraction of the water that goes to the Israelis. The Israelis say their developed economy needs more water. Palestinians argue that the water shortages block their development. In the Gaza Strip, Palestinians pump the last drinkable dregs of underground rivers polluted by encroaching sea water and sewage. Politicians speak of water in terms of conflict and peace: if one seeks conflict, water can

provide a plausible excuse; if one seeks peace, water is a bridge for cooperation (Rosenblum, 2001). Many countries of the world are at least partially dependent upon their primary adversaries for their drinking water. This imbalance of power sows the seeds for future conflict and war.

The third millennium will undoubtedly witness a number of tragic events related to the seriousness of a limited number of scarce resources. Water will prove to be the most precious of these scarce resources. Maintaining the rainforest, protecting ample agricultural topsoil suitable for growing food, and developing new methods to secure the energy needs of an ever-expanding population are among the critical issues related to the scarcity of natural resources. Scientists must continue to explore and develop such energy alternatives as nuclear, solar, and wind energy sources and must build more efficient homes, office buildings, automobiles, and so on.

The future is never predetermined, and therefore, a solution to the potential conflict over scarce resources does exist. The solution is a world community characterized by technological development, cooperation, understanding, and great compromise. It is a simple premise in theory but will prove to be extremely difficult in practice. This world community will be championed by the economic-political force of globalization.

THE WORLD COMMUNITY AND GLOBALIZATION

Under capitalism, wealth is concentrated in the hands of private individuals and is used to create more wealth. Governments may own property and provide services, but the private sector dominates the economy. As an ideology, capitalism implies that all individuals have the opportunity to be successful through hard work, effort, and determination. Inevitably, this system will create poorer citizens among those who do not, or cannot, flourish even when presented with nearly limitless opportunities to do so. In an effort to provide for such persons, capitalist countries in the West have developed welfare programs with varying degrees of benefits.

The continued growth of industrialization, urbanization, and capitalism set forth many trends of social change that are collectively known as *modernization.* As described by Smelser (1966) the primary characteristics of modernization are

1. **Growth in Technology:** A developing nation places more emphasis on the application of scientific knowledge and abandons reliance on irrational and traditional techniques.

2. **Advances in Agriculture:** The developing nation evolves from subsistence farming toward commercial production of agricultural goods. This process leads to the disappearance of small family-owned farms and the development of efficient corporate-run farms that specialize in growing cash crops.

3. **The Use of Machinery:** The developing society undergoes a transition from the use of human and animal power to the use a machines. These machines are operated by individuals who earn a wage and produce products for the commodities market.

4. **Ecological Arrangements:** The developing nation moves from the farm and village to urban concentrations.

Modernization affects all spheres of social life. In the political sphere, small town and village law is superseded by laws of the nation-state. Literate people are needed to operate modern machinery, so the level of education in that society increases. Increased mobility and economic demands influence the traditional extended family. Patterns of inequality in societies also change. For example, gender inequality is greatly reduced as women are in greater demand to fill positions in the new economic order. The emergence of a new class, the wage workers, increases the power of the common people, for the capitalist is now dependent upon them. However, even when unions are formed to unite the power of the wage workers, they are subjected to management backlashes, which may lead to the "busting" of the unions.

Capitalism is fueled by growth. When one marketplace becomes saturated, a new one must be developed. Western society, and especially the United States, dominates industry and the economic marketplace. Large corporations have expanded their markets throughout the world. These multinational corporations, or multinationals, are economic enterprises that have headquarters in one country and conduct business in one or more other countries (Barnet, 1980).

Development of Multinationals

Multinationals are not a new phenomenon, as commerce among nations is at least as old as the Phoenicians, whose trading ships sailed from what is now Lebanon to foreign lands more than 3,000 years ago. From then on, trading routes criss-crossed the globe, as silk, gold, spices, and tools were bartered or sold. Trading firms like the Hudson's Bay Company and the Dutch East India Company were chartered by major colonial powers and granted monopolies over the right to trade with native populations. Shipping and the development of machinery were so important to the development of industry that Thorstein Veblen based his economic theories on it. In *The Theory of Business Enterprise* (1904), Veblen described shipping as an evolutionary accomplishment and a representation of an "investment in or management of extensive mechanical appliances and processes, comparable with the facts of the modern mechanical industry" (p. 21). Shipping fed the primary motive of business, pecuniary gain. Countries that dominated shipping were able to take necessary natural materials from other, less-developed nations. The exploitation of the natural resources of one society by another society has been going on for centuries. Thus, what is now the United States was itself a victim of European multinationals.

The United States illustrates the point that nearly any nation, rich in natural resources, can become a powerful, nearly self-sufficient society. The United States developed its advanced technology through scientific and cultural achievements and became the dominator, instead of the dominated. Where other societies have failed, the United States and its capitalistic system have created some of the most powerful business operations in the world. Their growth and reach extend to all seven continents. Pepsi, Kentucky Fried Chicken, and Pizza Huts are found worldwide and are enjoyed by billions of culturally distinct groups of people. Companies such as Nike "demonstrated how in the post-1970s world of new transnational corporations, money was free to move anywhere it could find quick profit" (LaFeber, 1999:151). The Nike swoosh symbol is now recognized worldwide. The endorsement of globally known Michael Jordan greatly assisted in the name recognition of Nike.

The Universal Community and Globalization

There was a time in human history when "the community" implied a relatively small geographical area, in the immediate vicinity, where everyone knew her or his neighbors. The community has taken many structural forms over the years and may be defined as a network of social relations marked by mutuality and emotional bonds (Bender, 1991). *Community* implies shared interests, characteristics or association, as in the expression "community of interest" (Foster, 1990). Nisbet (1969) described the community as a fusion of feeling, tradition, commitment, membership, and psychological strength. The universal community involves a more extensive, macro-level network of social interactions characterized by mutuality, membership, and shared interests. The United Nations is often viewed as evidence of the universal community. In September 2002, East Timor, the world's youngest country, became the 191st member of the United Nations.

In *The Elementary Forms of Religious Life* (1912/1965), Émile Durkheim stated, "There is no people and no state which is not a part of another society, more or less unlimited, which embraces all the peoples and all the States with which the first comes in contact, either directly or indirectly; there is no national life which is not dominated by a collective life of an international nature. In proportion as we advance in history, these international groups acquire a greater importance and extent" (p. 474). Durkheim recognized nearly 100 years ago the growing phenomenon of globalization. More impressive is the fact that nearly 200 years ago Saint-Simon envisioned an international community created by technological growth and industrialization. He believed that future societies would unite and form a worldwide community based on science. The idea of a worldwide community is even more obvious today and symbolizes the new economic order.

There are a number of globalizing developments: the emergence of the global communications industry, the previously mentioned growth of the multinationals, the influence of global financial markets, global warming, and international action in support of human rights. Developments like these have brought the idea of a global society to the forefront. Of special note, the world today is more closely tied into a single economy than ever before in human history. The process of linking nations of the world together is referred to as *globalization*. "Globalization appears to be the buzzword of the 1990s, the primary attractor of books, articles, and heated debated, just as postmodernism was the most fashionable and debated topic of the 1980s. A wide and diverse range of social theorists are arguing that today's world is organized by accelerating globalization, which is strengthening the dominance of a world capitalist economic system, supplanting the primacy of the nation-state with transnational corporations and organizations, and eroding local cultures and traditions through a global culture" (Kellner,

2002:285). *Globalization* can be defined as "a social process in which the constraints of geography on social and cultural arrangements recede and in which people become increasingly aware that they are receding" (Waters, 1995:3). Globalization represents the evolution of heterogeneous cultures into a homogeneous culture that transcends all topographical boundaries placed on maps. Discussion on matters related to globalization have become commonplace since the mid-1990s.

The global economy has expanded to incorporate all or almost all areas of the world into a single, integrated economic system. This has led to greater profits for the multinationals and their stockholders but has left the less-developed nations in a state of uneasiness and even hostile resentment. According to Kellner (2002), many contemporary social theorists argue "that today's world is organized by accelerating globalization, which is strengthening the dominance of a world capitalist economic system, supplanting the primacy of the nation-state with transnational corporations and organizations, and eroding local cultures and traditions through a global culture. Marxists, world-systems theorists, functionalists, Weberian, and other contemporary theorists are converging on the position that globalization is a distinguishing trend of the present moment" (p. 265). Agreeing with Kellner's premise that globalization is eroding local systems of governance, Kought and Walker (2001) believe that "the globalization of financial markets and the concomitant restructuring decisions of firms challenge the historical legacy of national systems of governance" (p. 317). In their analysis of Germany's national economic system, Kogut and Walker (2001) argued that "these national systems are challenged by the globalization of capital and the related restructuring strategies of domestic firms" (p. 317). It should be noted that Germany is hardly a minor player in the global market. As a member of the Group of Seven (G-7)

countries (the other six are the United States, Japan, France, Britain, Italy, and Canada), it has a major say in world economics.

Capitalism represents such an effective form of production that it confers enormous power on those who control it, and this power can be used to subvert or control internal power sources. The two-class society of his era described by Marx seems to be a fair portrayal of the world system, with fully developed nations on one side of the economic system and the dependent Third World nations on the other side. The Third World nations represent areas of growth for the capitalists; however, they are dependent on the wage workers of these developing nations. In regard to the impact of globalization on future generations, questions abound: How will members of the Third World and their sympathizers react to this interdependent relationship? Will they adjust their economic and political systems, thereby changing the very fabric of their culture, so that they can benefit from these technological advancements? Or will they continue to naively fight this impending new world order of globalization? Furthermore, what will become of the growing number of American workers who are losing their jobs due to competition from cheaper wager earners outside the United States? Will the ease of world travel which globalization allows lead to the rapid spread of disease, such as the SARS virus?

The Proletariat Revolution

In the early 1990s, about one out of every four workers in the world was found in the industrial nations; by the year 2025, that ratio is projected to fall to one out of six (Bloom and Bender, 1993). The implication is that jobs are increasingly going to newly developing nations. Low labor costs are the guiding light for the capitalists. If the government of the country that hosts a multinational corporation does not demand fair wages, does not allow unions, and does not supervise the working conditions of its people, then exploitation and the early negative affects of capitalism will run rampant. Furthermore, many American and Western workers are losing their jobs. From this standpoint, globalization can be viewed as a very negative economic force.

The emergence of an increasingly global labor market has resulted in job loss and declining wages in many U.S. industries. American firms already employ an estimated 7 million more workers in other countries than just a decade ago (O'Reilly, 1992). It is very likely that human society is witnessing the emergence of a global wage, equivalent to the lowest worldwide cost of obtaining labor for a particular task, once the costs of operating at a distance are taken into account (Hecker, 1991).

The North American Free Trade Agreement (NAFTA), ratified by the United States, Mexico, and Canada near the end of the second millennium, created the world's largest trading bloc, comprising 364 million people in a $6.2-trillion economy. American opponents of NAFTA argue that millions of U.S. jobs will shift to Mexico, since Mexican workers earn considerably less than Americans. American workers and workers around the world are upset by the new economic order centered on the principles of capitalistic globalization. A large number of workers' protests have occured in the past few years and are too numerous to present here.

In brief, organizations such as the World Trade Organization (WTO), the International Monetary Fund (IMF), and the World Bank are being targeted by protesters who claim that globalization erodes human rights, causes environmental problems, threatens food and product safety standards, and further polarizes the gap between the rich and the poor, among other critical human issues and concerns.

As mentioned earlier, capitalists must continue to find new markets in order for economic growth to continue. The "sleeping giant" that is China represents the largest untapped market for capitalists. They see a nearly limitless opportunity to increase profits because of the more than 1 billion potential consumers. Unions and laborers throughout the world, including in the United States, see the potential for a decrease in tens of thousands of jobs if trade is open to China. On April 12, 2000, 15,000 union members from around the United States protested on the steps of the U.S. Capitol and marched to the halls of the U.S. Senate, then to the House of Representatives, to deliver a loud and clear message to Congress: "No Blank Check for China."

In response to critics' claims that the World Bank is insensitive to the human and environmental costs of development, it denied China a loan on July 7, 2000. The loan would have been used by China to relocate 58,000 impoverished farmers onto land that would have to be irrigated and that is now occupied by Tibetan and Mongolian herders (Moritsugu, 2000). China promised to raise its own funds and said that it would go on with the relocation project regardless of the World Bank's decision.

China's attempt to host the 2008 Summer Olympic Games was considered so important that government officials described it as a national mission. After fierce lobbying, in July 2001 the International Olympic Committee (IOC) awarded Beijing the 2008 Summer Games. As the host city, Beijing hopes to improve its international image. Industrialists predict that the games will mean greater economic development. Senior Chinese intellectuals fear that the games will only serve to strengthen the rule of the Communist Party (Pan and Pomfret, 2001). Beijing beat out Toronto (along with Paris, Istanbul, and Osaka), which had put together a strong bid and whose boosters pinned their hopes on an anti-China vote because of its poor human rights record (for example, in 2000 the Chinese government executed more people than the rest of the world combined; Sullivan,

2001) and its history of athletic substance abuse violations. California Representative Tom Lanto, of the House Foreign Relations Committee, said that the decision "truly boggles the mind" in light of China's human rights violations (*ESPN,* 2001).

Beijing's hosting the 2008 Summer Games is a sure indicator of the future—the new economic order has entered China. China could no longer be ignored. Its 1.3 billion people represent one-fifth of the world's population. As the third millennium began, the global community was nearly complete. Despite the seemingly inevitable continuation of globalization, the world's labor force continues to "fight the good fight." Protests are large in number, but small in impact. Karl Marx would surely be proud of such proletariat demonstrations. Unfortunately for the workers, these protests are likely to be as ineffective as they were in Marx's era.

Consumerism

America's consumer culture is felt throughout the world. In Beijing's Beihai Park, Chinese families line up to buy buckets of Kentucky Fried Chicken; in a Venezuelan shopping mall, Santa Claus hands out candy to holiday shoppers; and during a prison riot in Serbia, inmates negotiated with their captors by cellular telephone (Crenson, 2001). Taking a stroll through Red Square, Moscow, at the beginning of the third millennium, one could see countless Russian people talking on cell phones, using video cameras, drinking beer, and practicing their English with passing American tourists and would eventually come across a very wealthy European-style shopping mall.

On every continent, more and more people are embracing the American consumer lifestyle of convenience and abundance. Today about 1.2 billion humans—most of them in North America, Europe, Japan, and Australia—live on a par with Americans, and the numbers are growing quickly in other

parts of the world (Crenson, 2001). Automobile ownership has doubled since 1986 in Latin America and has increased by ten times in Moscow from a period beginning in 1990 and ending in 2000. U.S. policymakers, who embrace consumerism, believe that the free-market system can spread democracy and stability to all corners of the globe.

Americans, only about 5 percent of the world's population, consume one-fourth of its oil. They use more water and own more cars than anybody else, and they waste more food than most people in sub-Saharan Africa eat (Crenson, 2001). There is no doubt that many people are benefiting from, and taking advantage of, others through capitalism.

Consumerism and globalization have many negative effects. While the rich generally get richer, the poor generally remain poor. The plight of worldwide laborers has been discussed, but they are not the only ones being hurt by this imbalance of economic power. National economic systems, like those found in Germany, are being challenged by the globalization of capital and the related restructuring strategies of domestic firms. Kogut and Walker (2001) found that "without organized action in a country, the network of ownership and power loses its meaning as a national filter of global pressures" (p. 331). To illustrate the problem in Germany, the family-owned brewer Beck & Co. was up for sale after its owners concluded that the 128-year-old maker of Beck's beer is too small to compete as an independent in an increasingly global market. Most of the company's sixty-seven family shareholders voted to sell (July 2001), after an analysis by the investment firm Goldman Sachs said the brewer would struggle alone.

The global economy, with its interlinking networks and emerging markets, is vulnerable to a domino-style economic crisis. A major breakdown anywhere in the system can cause problems throughout the network. For example, a default on a loan can fuel speculation, equity market losses, and severe tightening of world credit (Thorpe, 2001). In 2001, fears that Argentina would default on some of its crushing debt load—at US$128 billion—was cause for great concern as Latin America's third largest economy struggled to pull out of nearly three years of recession. Thus, Argentina's problems were potentially felt throughout the world community.

In July 2001, a train derailment in a tunnel under Baltimore caused major disturbances in the routine lives of local residents for nearly a week. Normally, news such as this would have little impact on people outside the immediate geographic area, but in the interlinked global system this lack of interest changes. The fire caused by the derailment caused major Internet slowdowns in the Midatlantic states, and delays rippled across the country as companies diverted Web traffic to other lines. Fiber optic cable running through the tunnel was damaged by the blaze (Beimer, 2001). Keynote Systems, which tracks the performances of Web sites, said slowdowns in Atlanta, Seattle, Los Angeles, and elsewhere were related to the burned cables.

The Future

Marx's class theory can be applied to globalization. The social and economic forces of globalization leading to a single global capitalist economy appear inevitable, thus creating the potential for those countries that possess the capitalist and industrial power to dominate those who do not. But this does not have to be the case. Modernization affects all spheres of social life, and for those countries that care about the welfare of their people, the opportunities to improve the standard of living are numerous. This transition will often imply changes in cultural values, norms, and ideology. Nations can learn to evolve with the changing environment, or they can choose to be dominated by the more powerful economic force of globalization. Additionally, in the world community, although cultural values are compromised,

the traditions of individual societies remain unique, thus allowing for some sense of cultural identity. It is this very reality that helps to explain why there are such diverse regional differences in attitudes, beliefs, and values within nations.

On the downside, there is the reality of a limited number of scarce resources. It is impossible for all people of the world to enjoy the riches that the minority command, and no economic system can overcome this truth. Economically strong, the United States has one of the highest poverty rates of any developed nations. U.S. Census figures show that between 1976 and 2000, the number of poor children increased from 4.4 million in 1976 to 6.9 million in 2000 (The Annie E. Casey Foundation, 2004).

The powerful nations of the world today, especially the United States, need to be aware of their place in time. As Marx pointed out, in assessing the historical process, any nation powerful at one time must take warning of the rules of history: Things change. To protect itself, the United States must find a way to keep itself strong internally as well as protected from potential external threat. Internal strength involves keeping its own workforce employed. Corporations must be discouraged from making all of their products with foreign labor forces. If need be, the federal government must serve as watchdog and run interference. It is also necessary to keep the total population limited, by means of population control and limiting the number of immigrants allowed into the country. Primary areas of concern for securing external strength involve maintaining a strong standing army and a strong national defense, both external and domestic; keeping a watchful eye over foreign governments that have hostile intent; and protecting investments and American tourists abroad.

DEVELOPING A UNIVERSAL LANGUAGE

One of the most impressive aspects of the world community and globalization is the increased efficiency of the global communications industry. When early humans began to interact with others, finding an effective means of communication was often difficult. The human species has the capacity to think and reason and therefore possesses the ability to communicate through signs and symbols. "The ability to communicate symbolically has powerful implications for social life. This ability allows for the shifting of the very boundaries of space and time" (Ryan and Wentworth, 1999, p. 8). Through the use of signs and symbols humans are capable of expressing their hopes, dreams, desires, and values. However, as demonstrated by the game of charades, communicating simply through the use of signs and gestures is a complicated process. A word that might take a second to verbalize may require minutes to communicate through gestures.

Language

Language represents the developmental process from interpreting gestures to the capability of utilizing symbolic communication and interaction. "Language can be defined as the set of symbols by which the people who share a common culture communicate" (Farley, 1998, p. 65). Language is a quick, precise, efficient, and flexible means of communication. In fact, there is no other means of communicating complex ideas. (Note: The only exception would be the ability to read minds, which is something that I believe will be a human possibility toward the end of the third millennium.) Language not only makes communicating easier but also actually makes conceivable some ideas that would otherwise be inconceivable. Philosophy, science, and literature would not exist without language.

The value of language far exceeds the obvious benefit of making communication between individuals easier. George Herbert Mead stated that sharing a language allows one the ability to put oneself in the role of the other and makes it easier to understand why that person acts as he or she does. This reflexivity allows the development of the self. Mead felt that the structure of one's language has a great impact on one's train of thought and that it affects one's perception and definition of events. In other words, language reflects what is important to the members of a society. As new technologies develop and social change affects culture, language evolves. Words such as *dot-com, sky surfing, slamming*, and *antiglare* were among the hundreds of words appearing for the first time among 207,000 definitions found in the 1999 edition of Webster's dictionary (Pyle, 2000). By 2003, such words as *Botox* (used to eliminate wrinkles), *Viagra* (the passion-enhancing drug), *sambuca* (an aniseed liqueur served with a flaming coffee bean), *bling-bling* (elaborate jewelry and clothing and the appreciation of it; gangs often wear a lot of gold bling-bling), and *head case* (a person who exhibits irrational behavior) had been added to the *Oxford English Dictionary*. Reflecting the growing influence of computers on human communication words such as *cut-and-paste, screensavers*, and *search engines* were also added to the 187,000 definitions published by the Oxford University Press in the latest edition of its dictionary.

Comte believed that it is language that keeps the members of a society bound to one another. Language itself is a social institution because it allows people to interact with one another. From this standpoint, Comte believed that language not only promotes unity among people but also connects them with preceding generations and the culture of their ancestors. Thus, language creates an ancestral community. Comte viewed language as one of the most critical ingredients in the human community.

Herbert Spencer felt that the value of language is its integrating function. The smooth operation of society depends on individual members who all speak the same language. The future growth of society, with its accompanying increased complexity, increases the need for a common language. Furthermore, Spencer believed multiple languages spoken in the same society represent an internal threat to the state's security. There is a great deal of evidence to support Spencer's warning. Since the early 1980s, the French-speaking province of Quebec has been threatening to secede from Canada over issues of language and ethnicity (Farley, 1998). The Canadian Supreme Court allowed Quebec to require that all commercial signs in the French-speaking province carry French words at least twice as large as the words in any other language (Brown, 1999). In the United States, there are some political groups that promote the idea that this nation should have more than one "official" language (such as English and Spanish). By no means must the United States fall victim to the divisive ploy of promoting multilanguages, or it will surely face internal security problems that could threaten further growth and progress.

There are some people who have moved to the United States and fail to make learning the English language one of their top priorities. They are often shocked when they have difficulty succeeding in American society. Learning the language of the dominant culture that one resides in would seem to be a matter of logic or, at least, common sense. An American who moves to France would be expected to speak French as soon as possible. This same logic applies in the United States. The benefits of learning the language range from everyday conveniences to matters of life and death. For example, telephoning 911 for emergency help receives a quicker more efficient response in English than it does in other languages (Salonstall, 2000). Research conducted by educators has shown that students (in American elementary schools) fluent in English score significantly higher on reading exams than those students who use English as a second language. Additionally, the English-speaking children do not wait

for the less fluent students to catch up, and therefore test score differences widen (Wides, 2001).

Universal Language

Many societies battle over the issue of multiple languages. The nations of the world are becoming "Americanized," and the English language is a major aspect of this cultural intrusion. Inevitably, the nations that hope to benefit by interacting with the United States accept English as a second language. Although Mandarin, the official language of China, is the most spoken language in the world (over 900 million people), people throughout the world understand the value of learning English. English is, therefore, the primary universal language.

As U.S. capitalism spreads throughout the regions of the world, U.S. culture inevitably follows. To accept and learn U.S. culture implies learning the English language. Schoolchildren are taught English in such places as Japan and Russia. Russians eagerly look forward to speaking with American tourists, hoping to improve their English language skills. Computer programs, the Internet, and electronic mailing are dominated by the English language.

The same obvious advantages of members within a nation speaking the same language are just as obviously extended to the global community. The trend of increased globalization *is* going to continue throughout the twenty-first century. Speaking the same language will increase the level of efficiency. The ability to communicate with one another is as important as ever before. Speaking the same language ensures better understanding among the highly diverse groups of people found throughout the world.

An equally obvious response to the idea of a *universal language* is a society's reluctance or refusal to accept English as its primary language. Being forced to use a language other than one's own is something that many people are unwilling to accept. The beauty of distinct languages is that certain words are unique to the cultural experiences of people. This concept is reflected in the theory of linguistic relativity. Linguistic relativity theorists believe that language not only reflects, but also helps to shape people's perceptions of reality. The language people speak represents a cultural bias in how they categorize and interpret events. Language tells us a good deal about what is important in a culture (such as the multiple descriptions Americans use for automobiles). Language develops over a long period of time, and its diversity is a result of the various cultures that have formed as a result of human adaptation to specific natural environments. People of any given society have an attachment to their language and are reluctant to abandon it. Consequently, being forced to accept a "foreign" language is equated to losing a war (military or cultural).

I believe that advancements in technology and future communications will allow all the diverse people of the world to keep their own languages. The universal language I propose will be assisted by communication devices that will allow others to "hear" foreign languages in their own language. This technology is already in use. Telephone companies have already marketed telephones that translate language, there are computer translation programs, and the use of such advancements as holograms will become routine midway through the twenty-first century. Additionally, I believe that some day very soon, the public will have access to and the option of inserting a chip (a type of hearing aid) into their ears allowing them to understand all people. Such advancements in communication could have a huge effect on universal understanding.

THE ROLE OF RELIGION

Religion is one of the oldest social institutions in human society. Lacking technological knowledge, primitive humans were often baffled by the laws of nature. Even the simplest natural phenomena (for example, eclipses, ocean tides, and the changing seasons) were confusing. Mythical gods, complete with imagery, were created in an attempt to bring order to a seemingly chaotic world. Because of a belief in some form of a god, or a higher power, religious belief systems were created. Religion remains a major social institution because it carries out important social functions and encompasses a great variety of organizations.

Social thinkers have pondered the validity of a god or a higher power for multiple millennia. Philosophers generally debate the existence of a god, while sociologists tend to focus on the role of religion in human society. Sociologists define religion as any set of answers to the dilemmas of human existence that makes the world meaningful, a system of beliefs and rituals that serves to bind people together into a social group. Religion has played an important role in nearly all societies throughout time. The earliest forms of religion were polytheistic. Religious answers to life's mysteries were often very irrational and seldom based on fact or technological knowledge. As society evolved, a new force emerged: science. The once unexplainable natural phenomena were now being answered coherently through science. During the nineteenth century, many intellectuals believed that religion would eventually be replaced by science. Religion, they believed, was irrational and science therefore was better equipped to answer the questions that plagued humankind.

One such intellectual was Auguste Comte (1798–1857), who rejected belief in a higher power but acknowledged the value of religion in contributing to social stability. Comte recognized that it was the progress of science that had led to the French Revolution and allowed French society to move out of the obsolete theological stage of knowledge into the scientific-positivistic stage of development.

Comte hoped to develop a new religion, one based on science, with a new clergy to replace the Catholic church. He proposed a scientific-industrial social order to be lead by a new clergy of elites: the technocrats. His "positivistic church" would create the great "religion of humanity." His new nontheistic, atheistic religion came equipped with its own holy days to reaffirm positivism. Comte's primary goal was to establish a moral social order based on positivistic religion, where everyone "lived for others."

Utilizing the historic method, Karl Marx (1818–1883) agreed with Feverbach that religion is man-made; not that religion makes a man." (Tucker, 1978) Religion is simply an abstract creation that has become reified throughout time. Marx was very critical of religion, primarily because he felt that it hindered attempts to reach full human potential. Marx went so far as to state that religion is the "opiate of the masses," that it exists primarily to pacify the poor, by turning their attention away from the misery of their earthly life toward a happier one in an afterlife (Glock and Stark, 1965; McLellan, 1987). Marx argued that religion exists because it helps the ruling elite keep the masses docile, controllable, and exploitable. It does so in two ways: directly, by preaching that existing social arrangements are not only fair but sacred and therefore must be maintained, and indirectly, by focusing the believer's attention on the promise of a world beyond (Goode, 1988). Marx argued that religion serves to legitimize the social, economic, and political order and thus allows the ruling elite to continue exploiting the masses.

Marx referred to religion as a form of slavery that was explicitly evil, and hampered humans' attempt to reach their full potential (Carlebach, 1978). Marx believed that the world was a place of humans and not a place of religion. It was humans who made the world what it was and that it was up to humans to change it for the better, and no amount of church going or prayer could save the world; it was up to humans to save the world. Consequently, for Marx, religion was not necessary; it was universal only because exploitation was universal.

From Marx's perspective, religion is real only because it has become reified. Georg Simmel (1858–1918) spoke of the world of sociability as an artificial one, maintained only through voluntary interaction. Because of the often harsh reality of nineteenth-century life, Simmel found it easy to understand why persons often prefer the deceptive social world they have created and work so hard to maintain.

Max Weber (1864–1920), an intellectual of the early twentieth century, used the role of religion to help explain the growth of capitalism (see Chapter 7). In *The Protestant Ethic and the Spirit of Capitalism* (1905), Weber traced the impact of Protestantism—primarily Calvinism—on the rise of the spirit of capitalism. This spirit allowed capitalists to ruthlessly pursue economic riches; in fact, it was their ethical duty. The spirit of capitalism legitimized an unequal distribution of goods as if it were a special dispensation of Divine Providence. While Protestantism helped to explain the growth of capitalism in the West, Weber also wished to explain why capitalism had not developed in other societies. He concluded that "irrational" religious systems (Confucianism, Taoism, and Hinduism) had inhibited the growth of a rational economic system. These irrational religious systems had failed to produce the kind of people who could create a rational, capitalist economy. Obviously, many such societies still exist, as nations around the world continue in their failure to adopt the rationalistic capitalistic system.

Whereas Marx and Weber examined religion primarily from a political and economic point of view, Émile Durkheim (1858–1917), a French sociologist of the early twentieth century, described religion as a system of beliefs and practices related to sacred things that unite their adherents in a kind of moral community

(Durkheim, 1912/1965). Durkheim believed that religion binds the members of a community (society) together. In fact, religion, he argued, is the worship of society itself. In the act of worship, through religious rituals, a society's members renew their bonds with one another and with the society. Durkheim's belief that religion contributes to the stability, the cohesion, and the survival of all societies by binding a society's members together and making them loyal to it would become the foundation of functionalist thought (Goode, 1988).

Functions of Religion

Religion helps to put structure into our lives. It attempts to explain and justify our place in the world. Religion tells its adherents that the practices of a specific society are not merely a product of history but cosmic in origin—they are eternal, inevitable, God-given (Delaney, 2000a). Religion offers a version of reality that "makes sense" of a vast, ever-changing, and confusing world. Religion attempts to provide meaning in a seemingly meaningless universe. Thus, religion serves many functions for people and society, such as social solidarity (binding people together); social control (controlling behavior by telling followers what they need to do to gain salvation); ceremonies of status (rituals and rites of passage); self-esteem and identity (offering adherents a sense of belonging); social change (moral crusades); and psychological support (especially in time of need).

Dysfunctional Aspects of Religion

Although religion often promotes solidarity, it can only serve this function on the societal level if all the members of a society share the same beliefs. In the United States the vast majority of the citizens have historically identified with the Judeo-Christian tradition. Religious conflict is relatively mild in the United States, especially in comparison to other regions of the world. Some countries have competing religious groups with little in common and/or with a view one another's beliefs as "wrong" and harmful. Deep religious beliefs often create intolerant people. In turn, such intolerance of diverse religious groups has often resulted in persecution, conflict, and war.

Among the dysfunctional aspects of religion are war and conflict (religion has perhaps been the single leading cause of war and conflict throughout human history, and there are numerous examples today); religious persecution (an extreme form of intolerance toward people with different beliefs); and a number of irrationalities associated with religious beliefs. Examples of irrational religious beliefs range from the sacrificing of virgins in the past to a number of contemporary examples. In Niger, hundreds of people attacked bars and bordellos used by women accused of causing a drought. Muslim holy men claimed that the women's "indecent" dress and conduct were responsible for the lower-than-normal rainfall. A bullet-shaped hunk of granite that served as a traffic barrier in a past life has been reincarnated as a Hindu shrine in San Francisco, drawing worshippers to an out-of-the-way clearing in Golden Gate Park. Some devotees want permission to build a permanent shrine around the ex-traffic barrier. There are many examples of ultrareligious parents who refuse their children modern medicine to combat diseases, choosing prayer over treatment.

The Role of Religion in the Future

Social thinkers, and especially sociologists, have been interested in the role of religion in society for centuries. A few conclusions can be drawn. First, religion has a number of functional aspects; primarily it provides meaning and identity to billions of people. It can be a beacon of light directing people toward a path of cooperativenss and understanding.

Unfortunately, as history has demonstrated, the dysfunctional aspects of religion far outnumber the positive ones. Fanatical attachment to a belief system that lacks grounding in empirical reality continues to foster intolerance and hatred toward others, which inevitably leads to conflict and war. Attempts to foster peace in the Middle East, for example, will never be met as long as religion remains the guiding force of bigotry and hatred toward those who are different simply because of different interpretations of a god(s).

Religion is irrational. Logic dictates that the clothes women wear are not correlated to the amount of rainfall. Lunar and solar eclipses are not the result of angry gods, but merely of celestial body alignments. Religious beliefs need to be abandoned and replaced with a commitment to a global community where people help those who are different and less fortunate. This humanistic approach to the global community needs to be the catalyst for the survival of the human species. The global community must be based on rational thought guided by the process of empirical science and a commitment to technological growth.

The human species is still evolving, and therefore, society is not elevated to the point where it can fully understand the benefits of a rational-scientific structure. Consequently, the third millennium will be tarnished by the blood spilled because of religious intolerance.

POWER AND SOCIAL INJUSTICE

At this point, it has been well established that social inequality has existed throughout time. This inequality has led to many forms of power struggles, usually centered on economics and/or politics. Among the most precious scarce social resources is power. The simple reality that certain persons possess power while others do not makes social injustice an inevitable and avoidable aspect of social life. Power imbalance can exist at the individual, group, or societal level.

Exchange theorists such as George Homans and Karen Cook examined the role of power at the individual and group level, while Peter Blau investigated the effect of power on large-scale structures. Homans viewed power as the ability to provide valuable rewards (scarce resources). Those with power and authority are smaller in number and control the largest percentage of valued resources. The masses resent this social inequality, and thus, the potential for conflict exists. Conflict can be avoided if members of society believe that the distribution of rewards seems fair (distributive justice). Cook and her associates believe that social justice is related to individuals' perceptions of fairness. These perceptions are influenced by two key social factors: structural power and outcome equity. In his research on large-scale social structures, Blau found that the major determinant of legitimacy is whether subordinates feel that power is exercised fairly and generously. Legitimacy transforms power into authority because legitimacy makes it socially acceptable to obey those in the power positions.

From the exchange perspective, the underlying determinant of social equity is perceived fairness. As long as actors, groups, and societies feel that they are being treated fairly, willing cooperation and relative harmony can be expected. However, when people feel that social injustice exists, conflict becomes nearly inevitable. Conflict is found throughout the planet at the beginning of the third millennium, because many people feel they are being treated unfairly, especially as a result of new global-political-economic realities.

Weber also looked at the relationship between power and authority. He viewed power as the ability to impose one's will on another, even when the other objects. Authority, on the other hand, is legitimate power; it is power that is exercised with the consent of the ruled. He believed that authority is always associated with social positions. For example, a college professor has authority in the classroom—it is a part of the job position—but does not command the same level of compliance from a group of strangers. Authority is found in all social structures and systems, and for the most part, people willingly abide by the authority of certain social positions. People who have authority possess legitimate power.

In all social relationships—micro, group, or macro—differences exist in the possession of power. Those with power use the available resources to maintain their advantageous position. They may even resort to force (the capacity to persuade or convince, to produce with unnatural or unwilling effort) and coercion (compulsions, enforcement) as a means to influence the behavior of others. This type of abuse often leads to illegitimate forms of authority and power.

Most people realize that inequality, especially in social power, is an inevitable reality of social life. They tend to accept the existence of social inequality as long as they feel they are being treated relatively fairly and are receiving distributive justice. From a political standpoint, individuals and groups are never completely powerless. In a democratic society, people have the right to vote for their leaders. They can vote a candidate into and out of office. One can choose to run for an office and fight or attempt to rehabilitate the system from within. Contributing (time and/or money) to political campaigns is another way of exercising political power. Thus, every individual possesses some level of power. Forming power interest groups that lobby elected officials to vote a certain way is another form of political power. People can strike against, protest against, and boycott businesses and governments. In extreme cases, revolutions can overthrow existing governments, and society can be redrawn.

Social injustice and an unequal distribution of power will most certainly exist throughout the third millennium; it would be naive to think otherwise. This does not imply that social activism should be discouraged; in fact, those who feel strongly about acts of injustice should attempt to make necessary changes. Among the biggest challenges for social justice activists is the inequality found between social classes and between ethnic groups.

Social Class

Wealth and income not only lie at the core of economic stratification but are also important sources of power. After all, having wealth and high income is almost synonymous with having power. The primary issues related to social class have already been discussed in this chapter, but in regard to social inequality and the role of power, a new concern arises. Is there an obligation to assist the poor? Georg Simmel believed that the poor only emerge when society recognizes poverty as a special status and then assigns others to assist the poor. In other words, throughout most of human history little attention was given to the poor; they were on their own to either survive or perish. In a civilized society aid to the poor is often viewed as a moral obligation. Once the poor are recognized as a special group deserving of assistance, they tend to feel that society owes them. The nonpoor are not always in agreement as to whether or not they are responsible to aid others.

Globalization has caused a heightened debate over the responsibility of aid to the poor. Do the developed nations *owe* the poorer nations assistance, and if so, how much, and how will the distribution work? Officials from the International Monetary Fund and the World Bank insist they are making every effort to help the poor. Protesters disagree with this assessment (Temple-Raston and Hager, 2000).

Will the disparity between the haves and the have-nots increase or decrease during the next few centuries? The answer lies in the degree to which underdeveloped nations accept the cultural changes of the new world order ushered in by globalization. But it is safe to predict that class inequality, because of the role of power, will always exist. If class inequality is inevitable, is social justice possible among the world's diverse ethnic groups?

Race Relations

Racial and ethnic social inequality is a given in human society. People are treated unequally simply because of their race or ethnicity. Although the two terms are often used interchangeably, there is a distinct difference between one's race and one's ethnicity. A *racial group* can be defined as a category of persons who share *socially* acknowledged physical differences (for example, skin color) and are recognized by themselves and others as a distinct group. Thus, a race of people is biologically determined through cultural interterpretations. Categories of race have changed over centuries and most likely will continue to change in the future. At present, Irish-Americans might be categorized as Anglo. In the past, the Irish would have considered this label a racial insult.

In other words, labeling a person, or a group of people, as a certain race is arbitrary. Skin color, as imprecise as it is, is the current criterion. But other physical characteristics, such as height, could also be used. The Pygmies, for example, have been known to the Western world since the Greek poet Homer wrote about them in the eighth century B.C. Anthropologists define Pygmies a having full normal growth in an average male of less than fifty-nine inches in height. Pygmies speak a variety of languages, usually adapting the dialect of their neighboring tribes. Among the many other "races" of people determined by height are the Amazons of South America. In Kevin Costner's futuristic movie *Waterworld,* the evolutionary process of human adaptation to a radically changed physical environment leads to such physical mutations as developing gills and webbed

feet. These physical characteristics then become the criteria in the categorization of race. Although the movie is certainly not based on a true story, the point remains that the classification of racial groups is cultural. As will be demonstrated later in this section, this classification system is used by certain groups as a justification for treating other groups unequally.

An ethnic group is a category of persons who are recognized as a distinct group based on real or presumed cultural criteria. Shared characteristics such as religion, language, ancestry, and place of residence help to determine an ethic group. Ethnic groups are usually subsets of racial groups. Ethnic groups such as the Japanese and the Chinese are both Asian in race. For both racial and ethnic groups, membership is generally involuntary and lifelong; thus, it is an ascribed status. The fact that persons are victims due to ascribed characteristics is a true sign of social injustice. It is one thing to be labeled incompetent and to be passed over for an appointment or promotion because of personal shortcomings (achieved status), but it is truly unjust to be victimized over a characteristic that one has not chosen.

Racial and ethnic social injustice is manifested in a variety of forms. For one thing, the majority group, because of its advantage of greater numbers, often dominates minority groups in their political and cultural aspirations. Second, many people exhibit ethnocentric behavior. *Ethnocentrism* is the tendency to judge other cultures by the standards of one's own and to view one's own culture as superior. It is certainly understandable that people exhibit pride in their heritage, but concluding that other groups must therefore be inferior is problematic. Thus, ethnic celebrations such as St. Patrick's Day and Cinco de Mayo are harmless, as they represent little more than displays of cultural pride.

Racism is often a tool of oppression and is another form of social inequality. *Racism* can be defined as any attitude, belief, behavior, or social arrangement that has the intent or ultimate effect of favoring one racial or ethnic group over another (Farley, 1998). Racism involves denying certain people equal access to goods and services; it operates at both the individual and the institutional level. An example of institutional racism is redlining. Redlining involves refusing customers who live in certain neighborhoods goods and services made available to others. Recently, a record $100-million judgment was assessed against Nationwide Insurance for discrimination. The jury decision was hailed as a civil rights landmark indicating that racial redlining extends beyond the banking and mortgage industries to insurance underwriters (Fulwood, 1998). Requests for such services as taxi cabs, pizza delivery, and police are often slow or nonexistent for people who live in certain geographic areas.

Prejudice and discrimination are other forms of injustice. *Prejudice* refers to negative beliefs about a group of people, while *discrimination* is actual behavior that treats people unequally on the basis of an ascribed status. A *stereotype* is a common type of prejudice and involves an exaggerated belief concerning a group of people. Thus, prejudice is a belief, but someone who acts upon it has discriminated. For example, one might think that a certain group of people is lazy (prejudice) and then purposely not hire a member of that group for a job (discrimination).

According to the FBI, racial prejudice motivated more than half the 7,755 hate crimes committed in 1998. The news was not any better a year later, as the FBI reported that murder attributed to racial disputes and other forms of prejudice had reached a five-year high. Racial bias accounted for more than half of 7,876 incidents reported in 1999 (Johnson, 2001). In 2002, there were 7,459 single bias incidents of hate crimes. Racial bias accounted for 48.8 percent, religious bias accounted for 19.1 percent, sexual orientation bias provoked 16.7 percent and bias against

an ethnicity or national origin caused 14.8 percent of the incidents. There were 9,222 victims associated with a total of 8,832 hate crimes offenses. (National Criminal Justice Reference Service, 2004)

People can react to social injustice in a number of ways, which I call the five A's:

1. **Acceptance:** Simply taking things as they are; Marx would call this *false consciousness.*
2. **Avoidance:** Removing themselves from that society.
3. **Assimilation:** Merging and blending in with the larger society.
4. **Aggression:** Acting with hostility and violence; formenting revolution.
5. **Action:** Taking more positive steps in the form of social action in order to fight injustices.

In response to the many forms of social injustice, a number of laws have been passed to protect people from such behaviors as employment and housing discrimination. Many forms of legislation are true attempts to reach the goal of social justice. Other attempts are often empty of any significant substance and are "politically correct" in design. For example, the San Diego City Council unanimously banned the word *minority* from city documents and discussions, saying the word is disparaging. In support of the ban, Councilman George Stevens said people sometimes expect less of those who are labeled minorities. A number of Jews found the word *jewfish* inappropriate and offensive. So, for just the second time in a half century, a name change took effect. The new name is *goliath grouper*. The other name change involved the pike minnow, which was known fifty-three years ago as the *squawfish*. Joseph Nelson, committee head on Names of Fishes, doesn't expect the change to trigger a wave of "ichthyological correctness" (Lynch, 2000). Crayola announced a name change for one of its crayons for just the third time in its history. The wax stick formerly known as Indian Red, "though named for a brownish-red pigment found near India, was believed by children to represent the skin color of Native Americans." (Buffaro News, 1999:B9) The new name is *chestnut*. The other two name changes were in 1958, when *Prussian blue* became *midnight blue*, and in 1962, when *flesh* was renamed *peach* after it was pointed out that not everyone has the same color of skin.

Far beyond the concern of labels are true examples of social injustice. Around the world diverse groups of people are in constant contact with one another. History indicates that patterns of interracial and interethnic contact often have very negative outcomes. Among these patterns are

1. **Expulsion (and/or population transfer):** The forced uprooting and ejection of a minority group from the society of a dominant majority. Examples include the Gypsies, who were forced out of most European countries, and Native Americans, who were forced to live on reservations. A horrific example involves the Cherokee tribe and what has come to be known as the Trail of Tears. During this journey, thousands lost their lives.

2. **Segregation:** The separation of races, formal constraint of contact between racial or ethnic groups, with restriction to access of superior facilities and opportunities. The plight of those being forced to live on reservations is a form of segregation. In the former regime in South Africa, the white minority controlled the power and denied the colored masses equal access to the benefits of society.

3. **Slavery:** The ownership of another person. From an American perspective, the most obvious example is the slavery of blacks in the South. Slavery did not begin in the American colonies and has in fact existed throughout much of human history. Ancient Greeks, such as Aristotle, possessed slaves and felt no moral need to justify such hideous behavior. Allegations of slavery exist today in one form or another. A Nigerian-registered vessel was denied entry at two African ports because it was believed to carry 100 to 250 impoverished children intended for sale as unpaid domestic and plantation workers. The United Nations issued arrest warrants for the ship's Nigerian owner, captain, and crew (Ahissou, 2001).

4. **Annihilation and Genocide:** Mass murder of a minority group by the dominant group. As bad as slavery is, annihilation and genocide are far worse, for as the definition states, a large number of people are killed. Genocide occurs when one group feels so superior to, or so threatened by another group that they must be destroyed. It is the discussion of genocide and annihilation that leads prognosticators to conclude that future society is in real trouble. The ultimate use of power is displayed when one can physically destroy an opponent. When a group or society has justified and rationalized such behavior, issues of social justice are no longer of concern. Past examples include the following:

- Pol Pot, communist leader of the murderous Khmer Rouge, personally masterminded the extermination of one-quarter of Cambodia's people while ruling in the late 1970s.
- Adolph Hitler and Nazi Germany attempted to exterminate all Jews during World War II.
- The Turks killed 1.5 million Armenians as part of the Ottoman Empire's campaign to force them out of eastern Turkey between 1915 and 1923.
- The Taino Indians, the first people who came into contact with Christopher Columbus, were nearly annihilated by 1515.

Furthermore, the harsh reality of multiple and continuous attempts at genocide underscores the true significance of this problem. Current examples of ethnic and racial strife are numerous, for instance, ethnic slaughter in Borneo, Indonesia; race riots between English and Bangladeshi and Pakistani youths in the English midlands town of Stoke-on-Trent; multiple attempts at genocide in the Balkans between Serbs, Albanians, and Croats; and continuous battles between the Hutus and the Tutsi in Africa. In fact, many ethnic groups are involved in bloodshed throughout Africa, including Kenya, Tanzania, Rwanda, and the Sudan.

People are intolerant of one another for a number of reasons, and in some cases, the intolerance may even be justified. Nonetheless, it remains a fact that racism and prejudice, like all other behaviors, are learned behaviors. Research has shown that in Northern Ireland, Catholic and Protestant children start learning to fear and loathe each others' communities as young as age three (Pogatchnik, 2002). Since people learn hatred and racism, they can learn tolerance and acceptance. Unfortunately, this has proven to be a tough lesson to teach, as interethnic and interracial contact often results in disastrous outcomes. However, there are possible solutions to minimize this negativity. It has been popular in societies of the West to promote pluralism, or a multicultural approach, where all groups are treated equally and share equally in scarce resources. It is the idea that all groups have something to offer (to society) and therefore each culture should be maintained. This approach assumes tolerance of other groups and envisions diverse groups somehow all living harmoniously with one another. It is a wonderful idea but seldom successful in practice, as the evidence so clearly reveals it as a fallacy.

Another approach to racial harmony is amalgamation, the physical blending of two or more previously distinct groups (racial or ethnic). The children of interracial couples possess the characteristics of two previously distinct groups. The offspring eventually form their own distinct group. For example, Mexicans are an amalgamated product of Spanish explorers and Native American women. Mixed marriages, once illegal in the United States, are surging, largely because of the willingness of Asians and Hispanics to marry outside their racial and ethnic groups. There are 1.5 million mixed-race marriages in the United States, which nevertheless represent only 5 percent of all U.S. marriages. However, there is a steady and continuously growing trend (Pugh, 2001).

Racial tolerance in the United States has not been realized, but as the racial shift in population continues, perhaps citizens will begin to treat one another with more respect.

The racial profile of the United States will be quite different in the year 2050. According to U.S. Census statistics, the white population, at 70.1 percent in 2003, will dwindle to 52.8 percent in 2050. The Hispanic population will continue to accelerate and will represent 24.3 percent in 2050, a rise from 12.7 percent in 2003.

The most reasonable approach to racial social justice is a form of assimilation (the melting-pot theory). Assimilation involves the cultural blending of two or more previously distinct groups. Even the dominant group must blend in with the new. Most important, old cultural heritages, ways, and customs must be compromised. Assimilation of this sort allows for a human species convergence. This convergence process transforms the multiple races into one race—the human race. By emphasizing what we have in common with one another rather than what makes us different, diverse groups may learn to see one another as similar. After all, there are similarities among even the most hated rivals. New DNA-based research reveals a genetic link between Jews and Palestinians, suggesting the two peoples, locked in a bitter struggle for more than a century, indeed share a common ancestry dating back 4,000 years (Kraft, 2000). The study, published in the *Proceedings of the National Academy of Sciences* in Washington says the Y chromosome found in Jewish men may go back to a common pool of Middle Eastern ancestors. This study suggests that people are not very different.

That is why I propose the human species convergence theory. All the earth's people must come to realize their common roots and membership in one human race. The human species convergence is a critical step toward the world community. Without some sort of racial and ethnic convergence, the distinct groups of the world will continue to wage war with one another. Convincing diverse racial and ethnic groups of the validity of this convergence theory will be as difficult as converting the religious groups to rational-scientific thinking. Unless some unifying force unites these diverse groups, conflict and social injustice will continue.

THE FIVE HORRORISTS

Social thinkers have pondered the effects of the growing human population for centuries. Thomas Malthus was among the most extreme alarmists predicting that forces of nature would wreak havoc upon humanity and the physical environment of earth. As Malthus warned in his *An Essay on the Principles of Population* (1798), human need and greed will eventually lead to the depletion of natural resources. Utilizing mathematics, Malthus argued that the world's population was growing geometrically while humanity's ability to produce food grew only arithmetically. Nature, in an attempt to survive, will provide forces of relief from the strain created by human abuse in the form of the Four Horsemen. Malthus's Four Horsemen are war, famine, pestilence, and disease. Their purpose and function is to provide population control—they are the destroyers of human life.

Malthus's use of the Four Horsemen was, in part, an adaptation to the Bible's religious and spiritual description of the Four Horsemen of the Apocalypse. In Revelation (the last book in the bible), chapter six, the story of the Four Horsemen is unveiled. The lamb (Jesus) opened the first four seals of a scroll with seven seals. When the seals were broken four horsemen appeared. The first horsemen, riding a white horse, rode out as a conqueror intent on **conquest.** The second horsemen, riding a red horse, held a sword to be used for **war.** The third horseman, riding a black horse, was known as **famine.** The fourth horseman, riding a pale horse, was called **death.** A warning of the forthcoming Horsemen of the Apocalypse was provided in chapter four of Revelation. In brief, the Four Horsemen were under God's command and were used as a means to intimidate humanity, that God is sovereign over all, and that His enemies would some day be defeated and destroyed. Those loyal to God would be spared and enjoy eternal salvation.

The Five Horrorists, the new and more deadly "destroyers of life."
Source: Courtesy of Jarrad Lokes

The Five Horrorists represent an advanced evolutionary interpretation and development of the Four Horsemen concept. Breaking completely from the religious roots and de-emphasizing the natural component of the four horsemen, the Five Horrorists emphasize the social forces that will lead to the destruction of humanity, if left unchecked by global powers. The forces that gave way to Malthus's Four Horsemen were, in reality, both natural and social. The Five Horrorists, represent an updated version of Malthus's Four Horsemen and introduce their new, and equally deadly, partner—the *enviromare*. Enviromares are environmental–related threats, or nightmares, to humanity. Collectively, the Five Horrorists are the updated Four Horsemen (war, famine, pestilence, and disease) and the enviromares. It is my contention that the Five Horrorists represent the greatest threat to humanity, and if left unchecked, will spell the doom of human existence as we know it. The only survivors of an onslaught by the Five Horrorists will be those who are "best fit" to adapt to the new, remaining and deteriorated physical environment.

WAR

One of the most devastating forces facing humanity is *war*, so it is listed as the first horrorist. War has been waged against clans of people throughout humanity and full–fledge wars between nation–states have been waged for millenniums. As C. Wright Mills (1958a:1) stated, "To reflect upon war is to reflect upon the human condition." The very implication of the meaning of war involves lethal contact. Wars have been waged for a variety of reasons, including the seizure of territory and resources, desires for domination, revenge for past wrongs, preservation of a balance of power, love, further power, and for establishment of a legacy.

The participants of war, soldiers and non–combatant citizens alike, face death, injury, rape, and torture. Entire nations "disappear" when conquered in war and survivors of a "conquered" people have their cultures taken away from them. Even nations that "win" a war do so at great economic cost. The costs of war are very expensive (for example, it is estimated that the first year of the Iraqi War cost nearly $100 billion dollars), especially if a nation has overextended its reach of "controllable" power. In addition to having a significant political, economic, and cultural impact, wars affect the very character of society. Modern warfare, spearheaded by "advanced" technology, presents many potentially catastrophic outcomes. The use of nuclear weapons and chemical warfare could lead to a type of global devastation never before witnessed by humanity.

The relationship between war and the doctrine of the survival of the fittest reveals that the "fittest" are not always the *physically* strongest members of society. After all, soldiers generally represent the largest number of fatalities in war, and soldiers are almost always the most "fit" for war—strong able-bodied males between seventeen and thirty-two. It is estimated that a third of all English males ages seventeen to thirty-five were killed in World War I. The survivors of war must find a way to adapt to their demographically altered society in order to survive the inevitable future wars.

Clearly, war is a social creation. War is not caused by such forces of nature as wind, heat, or rain. Humans create war and that is why humanity's greatest threat is humanity itself. The masses have little say in the declaration of war. War is run by political and military leaders. The citizens are nearly powerless in decisions regarding warfare, and yet, it is all of humanity that risks extermination by this deadly horrorist.

FAMINE

Famine (from the Latin *fames*, "hunger") is the second horrorist and is the result of both social and natural forces. The word famine is used to describe conditions in which a large number of people are drastically affected by a severe scarcity of food, resulting in mass malnutrition and death. Wars and deliberate crop destruction are among the leading social forces that lead to conditions favorable for famine. Forces of nature that contribute to famine include floods, droughts, and earthquakes. History has played witness to numerous famines. The North and South American continents have been mostly immune to the affects of famine; whereas the African continent is almost continuously suffering from famine. Currently, famine in Africa is the result of drought, desertification (the spread of deserts), and a rapid population growth.

Malthus was inaccurate in his analysis of humanity's ability to produce food. He cannot be faulted for his lack of insight when considering the primitive level of technology that existed during his era. Modern technology in advanced industrialized societies has found a way to meet the expanding demand for food by an ever-growing human population. If a highly organized attempt, coupled by a true desire to feed the world's people were established, there would be enough food to feed everyone. However, people who live in "advanced" societies are often guilty of conspicuous consumption and people who live in regions known for famine often fail to engage in family planning. Both of these social issues must be addressed if there is any serious hope to eliminate this horrorist.

PESTILENCE

The third horrorist and destroyer of humanity is pestilence. Pestilence refers to plagues caused by swarms of locusts, grasshoppers, and other insects. Malthus correctly identified this horrorist as a force of nature, as locusts, grasshoppers and other insects are a part of the natural world. Locusts constantly consume vegetation. When conditions result in the lack of an adequate food supply, locusts will begin to swarm in search of food.

Swarms have been known to travel for thousands of miles and can number in the millions. A swarm numbering in the millions can consume as much in a day as ten elephants or 2,500 people (Ahuja, 2001). Although a swarm may appear to be a highly organized flying unit, it is really subject to wind currents. A strong current can dramatically alter the path of locusts.

Locusts become a threat to humanity because they destroy crops grown by humans for human consumption. When these crops are destroyed, humans die. Locusts may also spread disease and plagues (pestilence). Humans will always be subject to the potentially deadly power of insects. After all, insects greatly outnumber humans (about 80 percent of all the animals on earth have six legs, and there are more than 10 quintillion bugs in some 800,000 species), consequently, the potential for insect swarms will always exist in certain parts of the world.

In addition, their threat on humanity can be enhanced because of human negligence. Social forces such as deforestation and the draining of marshlands have led to the increasing migratory behavior of locusts and other insects. When insects cannot find food in their natural environment they will seek it elsewhere, usually resulting in crop devastation.

DISEASE

Disease, the fourth horrorist, is also the result of natural and social forces. Infectious disease has been a destroyer of human life since the dawn of humanity. The lack of even elementary forms of medical knowledge (a social factor) throughout nearly all humanity allowed for the easy spread of germs (a natural factor). Whenever any member of a community was inflicted with a disease, such as small pox, the potential for its spreading throughout the region was great.

Despite modern technology, disease is as prevalent today as in the past, although the specific diseases that kill people have changed.

Societal and environmental changes such as a worldwide, explosive population growth, expanding poverty, urban migration, and a dramatic increase in international travel and commerce, are all factors that increase the risk of exposure to infectious agents (Centers for Disease Control, 1994). Not long ago, the medical profession believed that mass death due to disease would be a thing of the past. Unfortunately, infectious disease remains a leading cause of death and disability worldwide, and this horrorist is likely to remain a destroyer of humanity in the future. The inevitability of this horrorist has led health officials to utilize the phrase "emerging infectious diseases" (EID). EIDs refer to infectious diseases that have recently (since the mid-1980s) emerged, or are likely to emerge in the near future. Among the examples of emerging infectious diseases are the human immunodeficiency virus (HIV) and acquired immunodeficiency syndrome (AIDS). Although the HIV and AIDS epidemics appear to be under control in the United States, it is predicted that by 2020, HIV will have caused more deaths than any other disease outbreak in history. Severe acute respiratory syndrome (SARS) is another EID. As an airborne virus, anyone who comes into contact with someone who has SARS, risks becoming infected.

By 2003, there were hundreds of reported deaths due to SARS. Research in 2003 indicated that in Hong Kong, nearly one of five deaths was attributed to SARS, while the Centers for Disease Control reported that 30,000 Americans died from the flu (influenza) in 2002. Furthermore, according to the National Center for Health Statistics, heart disease, cancer, and stroke, remain the three leading causes of death in the United States. Thus, while attention is given to EIDs, focus must remain on the existing diseases that confront humanity.

ENVIROMARES

As described earlier, an enviromare is an environmentally–produced nightmare which causes great harm to humanity. The enviromare is the fifth horrorist—a new destroyer of life separate from Malthus's conception of the Four Horsemen. In Malthus's era, it would appear there was little concern about protecting the environment. The environment was in fairly good condition and had been barely exposed to the harmful effects of industrialization. However, modern and advanced technology spearheaded by capitalism, was not accompanied by environmental responsibility, or basic common sense. Humans, especially industrialists, are responsible for causing great harm to the earth's physical environment—the *biosphere.* The earth's biosphere represents the life support system for every living organism on the planet, including humans. Humans have come perilously close to altering the earth's fragile ecosystem (mechanisms, such as plants, animals, and microorganisms that supply people with the essentials of life) in a potentially dangerous manner.

Although enviromares are directly associated to forces of nature (the ecosystem, the biosphere, etc.) they are also influenced by a number of social forces, such as overpopulation, a primary issue that concerned Malthus. Herbert Spencer, an admirer of Malthus, established his principle of the *survival of the fittest* due to the fight for the scarcity of goods and services when the population becomes too large. Increased population implies an increased fight for goods and services. Also, since the time of industrialization, more and more people have crowded into cities and large metropolitan areas. This large concentration of people in relatively few geographical regions on the planet places a great strain on those local environments. The increased use of burning fossil fuels furthered the deterioration of urban environments. In addition, modern industrial societies have appeared to embrace the wasteful "throwaway" mentality that is associated with conspicuous consumption and conspicuous leisure.

There exists a great variety of enviro-mares, all associated with types of pollution and they include the following:

1. **Water Pollution**

Problems related to water—especially shortages of drinkable water—have already been discussed, but water pollution presents an additional concern. Since industrialization, factories have been polluting the waters by dumping their wastes (sometimes toxic) directly into them without using any filtration process. The limited water that is drinkable on this planet has been polluted by human and animal (waste).

Some of the documented cases of abuse to our waterways are the following: In the continental United States, it is estimated that less than 100 million acres of the original 215 million acres of wetlands existing 200 years ago have survived. (U.S. Office of Technology Assessment, 1984) The greatest river basin in the United States is the 2,350-mile–long Mississippi. Thousands of industries along the Mississippi River discharge billions of pounds of toxic wastes directly into this body of water. For most of the Mississippi's length, fishing and swimming are not advised. (Turnbull, et. al., 2001) There is so much contaminated water at the river's end in the Gulf of Mexico that an area as large as the state of New Jersey, or 7,728 square miles, is biologically dead. (Grunwald, 1998; Howe, 1999)

Rivers, lakes and oceans around the globe are subject to pollution. A unique danger comes from the transportation of vast quantities of oil via ocean-going cargoships. For a variety of reasons (usually human error), problems (such as slicks) occur during transportation that often compromise the successful delivery of the oil. Worldwide ocean spills of oil involve more than 10 million gallons at a time. The *Exxon Valdez* spill ranks as only the fifty-third largest in history. (Turnbull, et al, 2001) Most major spills occur in the Persian Gulf. Oil slicks on the water cut off sunlight and absorb the oxygen in the water, destroying the ecosystem by harming plant, animal, and human life. Heated water (for example, water that comes from industries and power plants used for cooling) coming into contact with another body of water can also cause an inbalance in the ecosystem.

Today, 1 billion people lack access to clean drinking water in the developing world, and 1.7 billion do not have adequate sanitation facilities. The United Nations estimates that dirty water causes 80 percent of the disease in developing countries and kills 10 million people annually.

2. **Air Pollution**

The problems associated with air pollution are numerous. The importance of clean, breathable air should be obvious to all–it is the very essential ingredient of life. And yet, the atmosphere is bombarded by toxics, natural and manmade, on a regular basis. Discussion here will be limited and concise. Without a proper atmosphere the entire ecosystem is compromised and life forms as we know them today would cease to exist at worse, or be dramatically altered at best.

Nature plays a strong role in the compromise of clean air. Volcanic eruptions spill a variety of toxics into the air. Lightning also compromises the ecosystem by emitting nitrogen dioxide and igniting wildfires. Although humans are subject to the forces of nature, they are capable of controlling most of their own pollution-causing behaviors. The dependence on fossil burning fuels continues to contribute to conditions that cause smog and thermal inversion. In some regions of the world, living with smog (a thick haze) is a daily reality—to the point where terms such as *smog stages, smog alerts,* and *health warnings,* are a part of the daily weather forecast vocabulary. In some American cities, air is measured for levels of carbon monoxide. Carbon monoxide, which stems from the incomplete combustion of motor vehicle fuels, typically reaches unhealthful levels when vehicle exhausts are trapped by temperature inversion layers associated with cold, clear winter nights. The Pollution Standard Index, measures air in terms of health. Readings of 100 or higher are occuring far too often for the safety of human, animal and plant life.

The burning of fossils fuels is a primary culprit for the depleting ozone layer. The ozone layer is the earth's upper stratosphere which screens out a great deal of the sun's harmful ultraviolet rays. Acid rain, the greenhouse effect and global warming are among the other agents that are associated with this enviromare. Humanity must find a way to keep its atmosphere in tact or risk the obvious adverse effects.

3. **Land Pollution**

Assuming there is breathable air and clean water, one of the next essentials in the maintenance of human life is land. Land is defined as the thin layer of topsoil that is available for food crops and the grazing of domesticated animals. Among the problems caused by humans that have led to land pollution are overgrazing by domesticated animals, deforestation, agricultural mismanagement, the increased use of chemical fertilizers and pesticides, erosion, urban sprawl, and strip mining. All of these factors ultimately lead to the decay of the topsoil, resulting in land pollution.

Humans insist on constantly attempting to change the very structure of the ecosystem by utilizing damaging behaviors and this exploitation will eventually catch up with humanity. Furthermore, humans cannot continue to insist on living in areas that are not geo-friendly. Many people, for example, feel the lure of the coast and ignore warnings of impending erosion. A 2000 report by the Federal Emergency Management Agency (FEMA) predicts that unless protective measures are taken, an average of 1,500 coastal buildings—mostly houses—will be lost to erosion annually for the next sixty years at a cost of $530 million a year. (Watson, 2000) The report recommends that federal insurance rates, which are based mostly on flood risk, take erosion into consideration. Climatologists report that the nation appears to be entering a period of increased hurricane activity and the additional storms are likely to cause greater coastal erosion. (Schmid, 2000)

4. **Chemical and Nuclear Pollution**

Toxic chemicals cause a great deal of land pollution. There are over 7 million chemicals in existence and over 6,000 U.S. facilities that manufacture hazardous chemicals. The manufacturing of chemicals requires their distribution—180,000 shipments a day by truck or rail—which creates plenty of opportunity for lethal accidents. (Starr, 1985) No one, including scientists, has any clue as to what might happen when various combinations of chemicals come into contact with one another. The effects of these millions of chemicals onto our environment may be devastating and life-threatening. Often industrialists simply bury their toxic wastes underground, assuming that everything will be alright as long as these chemicals are not visible. Nuclear pollution represents another danger to the environment.

Radioactive fallout from Cold War nuclear testing around the world has caused thousands of cancer deaths. Problems at nuclear facilities should be enough to scare any sane person, let alone what fear would result if nuclear weapons are used for war, in which case, there will be only a few people remaining to worry about the resulting fallout. Clearly, chemical and nuclear pollution are the result of social forces and the old adage of "One nuclear bomb can ruin your whole day" is a drastic understatement.

5. **Solid Waste Pollution**

Almost any item can eventually become a type of solid waste. Solid waste is often a polite way of describing garbage. And, Americans produce a great deal of it—four pounds of solid waste per day, per person, for a staggering 1 trillion pounds of garbage each year. (Paul, 1986; Levine, 1988) According to the Environmental Protection Agency (EPA) Americans were producing 4.46 pounds of garbage per person, per day in 1998. Encouraging is the fact that many Americans have embraced the value of recycling—doing so at a rate of 1.26 pounds per person per day in 1998.

Nature produces wastes, but most of it is bio-degradable. If humans can extend their commitment to recycling and control wasteful behaviors, solid waste pollution can be minimized. However, certain types of waste, such as construction debris, and yard clippings will continue to plague landfills. There is so much garbage in landfills throughout the United States that scientific research is being conducted to examine the biodegradation process. Archeologist William Rathje, the nation's leading garbage researcher (garbologist as he calls himself), is the foremost authority in garbology—the careful and systematic sampling of landfill contents by empirical data analysis. The study of refuse in modern society reveals a lot about human nature. Among Rathje's findings is that biodegradation is a much slower process at landfills because people wrap their garbage so tightly. Styrofoam, fast-food containers, and disposable diapers have been demonized as the scourge of land pollution, but as Rathje indicates, when combined, they make up less than 3 percent of the volume of landfills. Before the advent of bio-degradable disposable diapers, nearly 16 billion disposable diapers (representing 2 percent of the garbage total) filled landfills yearly. The real culprits, the items that take up to half the space in landfills, are paper, construction debris, and yard cuttings.

6. **Noise Pollution**

Noise pollution is basically an intrusive noise that anyone finds to be annoying. Although some people consider noises like birds chirping as disturbing, nature is not responsible for much noise pollution. Overpopulation and a high concentration of people living in sprawling metropolitan cities are among the primary causes of noise pollution. People create noise in the form of road traffic, air traffic, rail traffic, fireworks, loud neighbors, factories, construction, lawnmowers, leaf blowers, hair dryers, and so on. All these noises surpass the acceptable decibel level for safe listening. Prolonged noise pollution may cause damage to human and animal hearing. It is nearly impossible for most people to escape the inconvenience of noise pollution for any prolonged periods. To do so, often means sacrificing the benefits of the loud society.

7. **Celestial Pollution**

Proponents for the American space industry continually point us toward reaching for the stars. The idea of space travel intrigues many people. Although some people joke about sending our trash out to space, the fact is, space is already littered with trash such as rocket fragments, used-up boosters, Soviet nuclear reactors, and so on. (Anton, 1993) Celestial pollution has little relevancy to humanity right now, but it seems probable that some day the very survival of the human species may be dependent upon space exploration, travel, and eventually colonization.

TERRORISM

Joining the Five Horrorists as a very real threat to the future of humanity is terrorism. Historically, cultures throughout the world have practiced terrorism. "The progress of mankind has been shadowed by the grisly history of torture and execution. For every shining triumph of human endeavor there has been a dark example of state-sanctioned depravity. Each illustration of courage and wisdom goes hand in hand with an unbecoming horror of human design" (Kellaway, 2000:6). Ancient Roman emperors, such as Tiberius (14–37 C.E.) and Caligula (37–41 C.E.), relied on banishment and executions as forms of terrorism to eliminate political opponents (Onwudiwe, 2002). Life during the Middle Ages was so brutal that those in power created a variety of torture devices designed to terrorize subordinates into submission. "Zealots tried to defend their religious territories by terrorizing the faithful. Politicians and priests went to greater lengths than ever to attract the attention of the people, and were frequently guided by ritual and superstition in the process, resulting in more death and human destruction through torture" (Kellaway, 2000:6). Onwudiwe (2002) explained that the "church justified cruel reprisals as a means of saving the unfortunate sinner from the devil. This zealous movement to stamp out heresy led to the Inquisition" (p. 1614). Today, the most extreme examples of terrorism are directly linked to religious zealots who show intolerance of people who believe differently from them.

Defining Terrorism

Although terrorism has existed for some time now, the modern interpretation of terrorism has its roots in the French Revolution and the Reign of Terror (1793–1794). "An important feature of his regime was his open advocacy of terror as a legitimate means to achieve revolutionary goals. Since then, both states and their opponents, and various nineteenth-and twentieth-century anarchist groups in Europe, Latin America, the Middle East, and other parts of the world have utilized acts of violence to attain political goals" (Onwudiwe, 2002:1614). Thus, a key aspect of current terrorism is its design to reach some political goal(s). Additionally, the targets tend to be noncombatants (non-soldiers), and the perpetrators are themselves generally working outside an official government. The U.S. government uses a legal definition of terrorism: "The term 'terrorism' means premeditated, politically motivated violence perpetrated against noncombatant targets by subnational groups or clandestine agents, usually intended to influence an audience. The term 'international terrorism' means terrorism involving citizens or the territory of more than one country. The term 'terrorist group' means any group practicing, or that has significant subgroups that practice, international terrorism" (Henderson, 2001:4). The FBI defines terrorism as "the unlawful use of force or violence against persons or property to intimidate or coerce a government, the civilian population, or any segment thereof, in furtherance of political or social objectives" (Whittaker, 2001:3).

Terrorists, then, use violence against innocent citizens to promote a cause that is so unpopular it cannot succeed without intimidation and violence. Just as the school bully picks on a physically weaker target, terrorists generally act in a cowardly fashion by targeting women, children, and the elderly. Although terrorists are "brave" enough to freely give up their lives for a cause that they believe in, they are cowards nonetheless because they lack the honor to face their enemies. And that is why terrorists such as those who attacked the United States on September 11, 2001, were cowards and died without honor.

Modern Terrorism and Terrorists

Most terrorists are willing to die for a cause that they strongly believe in. That in itself may be commendable, if the cause is a just

one. However, who is to say what is just and what is unjust? All religions and governments propose that they have the answers and often attempt to force their beliefs of proper behavior on others. To possess such a single-focus approach as to dedicate one's life to one cause or "calling" in life is a psychological wonderment. How do people justify dedicating their life to a single course of action? And what motivates any individual to a life of terrorist acts? Individuals must find some way to justify and rationalize their behavior. A sociological approach to explaining the motivation behind terrorism reveals that a number of conditions must exist in any given society to spark the seeds of terrorism. In other words, there must be some level of social facilitation. "This concept refers to the social habits and historical traditions that sanction the use of violence against the government, making it morally and politically justifiable and even dictating an appropriate form, such as demonstrations, coups, or terrorism. Social myths, traditions, and habits permit the development of terrorism as an established political custom. An excellent example of such a tradition is the case of Ireland, where the tradition of physical force dates from the eighteenth century" (Whittaker, 2001:15). Thus, when individuals truly believe in the cause and find themselves in an environment that promotes, or at least accepts, terrorism as a legitimate option for reaching desired political goals, terroristic behaviors are judged honorable.

Terrorism has been especially evident since the early twentieth century and the awakening of nationalist impulses. As Henderson (2001:11) explained:

> The early 20th century saw the awakening of many nationalist impulses. For example, many Jews began to embrace Zionism and its vision of a Jewish state in Palestine. Many of the Arab peoples in the Middle East developed a stronger sense of their own nationhood. Both sides began to rebel against British colonialism. Some of that rebellion

began to take the form of terrorism. Similarly, ethnic minorities that had been kept in a second-class position in their own land, such as Irish Catholics, began to develop revolutionary or terrorist organizations. Meanwhile, the Soviet Union began to organize a network of communist parties in many countries, which all sought a "proletarian revolution."

The current instability found throughout the globe will continue to breed acts of terrorism into the third millennium. There are a growing number of people who seek change, even at the cost of lost lives among innocent people. As Whittaker (2001) concluded, "Terrorism may be motivated by political, religious, or ideological objectives. In a sense, terrorist goals are always political, as extremists driven by religious or ideological beliefs usually seek political power to compel society to conform to their views. The objectives of terrorism distinguish it from other violent acts aimed at personal gain, such as criminal violence" (p. 17). Whittaker (2001) also pointed out an important irony of terrorism and terrorists, especially in regard to the reality that many terrorists die during the course of their terrorist activities: Terrorism "must be successful enough in its terrorist acts and rhetoric of legitimization to attract members and perpetuate itself, but it must not be so successful that it will succeed itself out of business" (p. 25).

There exist a large number of extremist regimes that promote terrorism as a legitimate weapon in their war to maintain power and gain dominance over others.

Veteran international journalist David Wallechinsky (2004:4-7) complied a list of the ten Worst Living Dictators (2004) after consulting independent human-rights organizations, such as Freedom House, Amnesty International, and Human Rights Watch, that are willing to expose both left and right-wing regimes. Below is a summary of these results:

1. **Kim Jong II, North Korea:** North Korea has been voted the worst nation in political rights and civil liberties for thirty-one straight years by the human-rights group Freedom House. The focus given recently to Kim's development of nuclear weapons has deflected attention from the fact that his government represses its own people more completely than any other nation in the world. Among Kim's tactics of terror are the estimated 150,000 North Koreans incarcerated in labor camps.

2. **Than Shwe, Burma:** General Than Shwe has survived a power struggle to emerge as the sole leader of Burma's military dictatorship. The use of forced labor as a form of slavery and strict adherence to the dictates of his military junta are the primary forms of terror used by General Than Shaw. Burma has more child soldiers than any other nation in the world.

3. **Hu Jintao, China:** Hu spent thirty-eight years moving up in the Communist Party hierarchy. As the president and general secretary of the party, Hu is the leader of an unusually repressive regime. More than 300,000 Chinese are serving "re-education" sentences in labor camps. China carries out in excess of 4,000 executions a year, more than all other nations combined.

4. **Robert Mugabe, Zimbabwe:** Mugabae was elected independent Zimbabwe's first prime minister, with widespread domestic and international support. In recent years, he has become increasingly dictatorial. Mugabe's government has killed or tortured more than 70,000 citizens. Mugabe has fueled racism by confiscating farms owned by whites and giving them to his supporters.

5. **Crown Prince Abdullah, Saudi:** There are no elections of any sort in Saudi Arabia. Among the terroristic behaviors used by Prince Abdullah is beheading for adultery, arbitrary arrests and torture, and a general lack of basic rights for women.

6. **Teodoro Obiang Nguema, Equatorial Guinea:** This tiny West African dictatorship nation had been ignored until major reserves of oil were discovered in 1995. U.S. oil companies have pumped billions of dollars into this country to export oil. The bulk of this money remains in the hands of Obiang, who has stated that there is no poverty in Guinea and that the people are merely used to living in a different

way. Arrest and torture of political opponents are used as a means of control over the nation's oil riches.

7. **Omar Al-Bashir, Sudan:** Sudan, the largest country in Africa, has been involved in a 20-year civil war that has claimed the lives of 2 million people and uprooted 4 million. Al-Bashir's army has routinely bombed civilians and tortured and massacred non-Muslims, particularly in the oil-producing areas of the south. Al-Bashir has a long history of providing sanctuary for terrorists.

8. **Saparmurat Niyazov, Turkmenistan:** This narcissist has his picture on all the Turkmenistan money, there are statues of him everywhere, his book *Ruklmama* (Book of the Soul) is required reading in all schools, and all government employees must memorize passages to keep their jobs. His methods of intimidation include taking rural children from their homes and forcing them to work for minimal pay. He imprisons political dissidents and subjects them to Stalin-style show trials and public confessions.

9. **Fidel Castro, Cuba:** The world's longest reigning dictator heads a government filled with corruption and zero-tolerance of criticism of the government. Human rights activists, journalists and academics are routinely harassed and/or imprisoned.

10. **King Mswati III, Swaziland:** Swaziland is the last remaining absolute monarchy in Africa. Mswati became king when he turned eighteen. Swazi courts are forbidden to issue rulings that limit the king's power. The new constitution allows for the death penalty for any criminal offense and provides for debtors' prisons.

Any list of the worst dictators risks being outdated quickly, but the point should be clear: The potential for terrorism is huge, and the future may be damned by this reality. Many of these repressive regimes serve as training grounds for terrorists who are willing to wage war on unsuspecting civilians. The Middle East in particular has become a haven for terrorist training, leaving many in that region susceptible to terrorist acts. Unfortunately, no one is immune from potential attack by terrorists. The United States has fallen victim to terrorists (some within our country, such as anti-arbortionists, KKK etc.), and throughout the world, many other countries must deal with terrorism.

Counterterrorism

There are forces in existence designed to combat terrorism. "Counterterrorism can be defined as the attempts to prevent terrorism or at least reduce its frequency and severity. Understanding the terrorist's psychology, motivations, and goals is an important part of this effort. Another part is the use of intelligence, including surveillance, eavesdropping, informers, and devices to detect bombs and weapons, such as those in airports" (Henderson, 2001:19). The modern conveniences available to all citizens (such as cell phones and other electronics) also help terrorists. The use of commercial airplanes as projectiles flown into the World Trade Center towers demonstrated just how vulnerable we all are.

Intelligence is the first line of defense against terrorism. Modern technology is an ally to counterterrorists as there are a large number of devices and tracking systems available to gather information. Accurate retrieval and interpretation of this information are still the keys to fighting terrorism. The future of humanity, or at least a good portion of it, may depend on successful counterterrorism efforts. In short, if the five enviromares do not doom humanity, acts of extreme terrorism may. Objects such as nuclear plants abound in the United States and any one of them would make a good target for terrorists. The continuing progress of humanity depends on the elite visionaries of technology and humane control over the forces of chaos.

FINAL THOUGHTS

The future is not a fixed entity, and there certainly is no such thing as destiny—for destiny implies a predetermined course of events. If destiny truly exists, then one need not worry about any course of action or the consequence of specific behaviors, because everything was meant to be—including murder, rape, injustice, and so on. Humans *do* have freewill and *are* capable of learning from their mistakes. When properly motivated and possessing key resources, humans can accomplish wonderful things.

A large number of social and natural problems confront the human species in the third millennium. Science will need to continue its battle against disease and shortages of natural resources. Nations of the world must learn to assimilate the emerging cultural expectations and demands of the new world order. Sociobiologist Edward Wilson (1975) worried that the future of humankind was in potential trouble. He suggested that continuously accelerated evolution could bring about changes we may not like. There could be a lessening of altruistic behavior through the maladaptation and loss of group-selected genes. Wilson proposed that behavioral traits are selected out by the "principle of metabolic conservation" when they are suppressed, or when their original function becomes neutral in adaptive value. Such traits may largely disappear from populations in as few as ten generations, only two or three centuries in the case of human beings. Valued qualities such as cooperativeness with groupmates may disappear completely. Wilson failed to realize the power of the socialization process. When properly motivated, humans are still capable of helping one another. Social and natural problems facing the human species can be solved, but it will take a powerful unifying force, a threat of some sort, that originates either internally (earthly) or externally (celestial).

The human species depends on continuing cultural evolution and technological growth to offset religious, racial, and ethnic intolerance. Overpopulation and the limited number of scarce resources guarantee that people in power positions will continue to thrive while others will fall victim to social injustice. The only hope for a bright third millennium is the world community, where all people learn to view one another as equals and learn to treat others fairly. Embracing the world community involves cultural adaptation and human convergence.

Many animals have shown their ability to adapt to the changing environment. Birds, for example, have learned to use telephone poles (in place of trees) as their perch. A flock of orphaned sandhill cranes, following a light plane piloted by a man in crane costume, finished a month-long 1,250-mile flight in an experiment intended to eventually help a gangly cousin: the endangered whooping crane (Leisner, 2000). If the whooping crane learns this migratory route, it may survive; if it doesn't, if it's not fit, it is likely to perish.

The human species must learn to solve the problems presented by the Five Horrorists and the emerging threat of global terrorism. If all the diverse cultures of the world refuse to accept the lifestyles of others, the "survival of the fittest" doctrine will prevail.

Bibliography

Abt, Clark. 2002. "The Future of Energy from the Perspective of the Social Sciences," 77–122 in *What the Future Holds*, edited by Richard Cooper and Richard Layard. Cambridge, MA: MIT Press.

Adams, Bert and R.A. Sydie. 2001. *Sociological Theory*. Thousand Oaks, CA: Pine Forge Press.

Adorno, Theodor. 1973. *Negative Dialectics*. New York: Seabury.

Agger, Ben. 1976. "On Happiness and the Damaged Life," pp. 12–33 in *On Critical Theory*, edited by John O'Neill. New York: Seabury.

———. 1979. *Western Marxism: An Introduction*. Santa Monica, CA: Goodyear.

———. 1992. *The Discourse of Domination: From the Frankfurt School to Postmodernism*. Evanston, IL: Northwestern University Press.

———. 1996. "Postponing the Postmodern." *Cultural Studies*. Vol. 1:37–46.

Ahissou, Virgile. 2001. "Probe Opens into Claims about Child Slave Ship." *Buffalo News*. April 18:A3.

Ahuja, Anjana. 2001. "Swarms Reach Biblical Proportions." *London Times*. June 19:11.

Alabama Academy of Honor. 2002. "Edward O. Wilson." Available: www.archives.state.al.us/famous/academy/e_wilson.

Alabama Communication Hall of Fame. 2002. "Edward O. Wilson." Available: www.communication.va.edu/dean/halloffame/wilson.

Allan, Kenneth and Jonathan H. Turner. 2000. "A Formalization of Postmodern Theory." *Sociological Perspectives*. Vol. 43, No.3:363–385.

Alexander, Jeffrey C. 1985. *Neofunctionalism and After*. Beverly Hills, CA: Sage.

Alexander, Jeffrey C. 1998. *Neofunctionalism and After*. Malden, MA: Blackwell.

America at Work. 2000a. Making the Global Economy Work for Working Families.

———. 2000b. "Impoverished Children, Working Parents." 5(5): 11.

American Sociological Association. 2002. "David Riesman." *Footnotes*. 30 (5):1.

Anderson, Margaret L. 1997. *Thinking About Women: Sociological Perspectives on Sex and Gender*. Boston: Allyn and Bacon.

Anton, Genevieve. 1993. "Researcher Warns of Junk Accumulating in Space." *Las Vegas Review Journal*. December 18:12B.

Antonio, Robert J. 1983. "The Origin, Development, and Contemporary Status of Critical Theory." *Sociological Quarterly*. 24 (Summer):325–351.

Ashcraft, Richard. 1987. *Locke's Two Treatises of Government*. London: Cambridge.

Bailey, Leon. 1994. *Critical Theory and the Sociology of Knowledge*. New York: Peter Lang.

Baber, Kristine and Colleen I. Murray. 2001. "A Post Modern Feminist Approach to Teaching Human Sexuality." *Family Relations*. 50 (1):23–31.

Baker, Stephen, Geri Smith, and Elizabeth Wiener. 1993. "Detroit South: Mexico's Auto Boom: Who Wins, Who Loses." *Business Week*. March 16:98–103.

Baldwin, John. 1986. *George Herbert Mead: A Unifying Theory for Sociology*. Beverly Hills, CA: Sage.

Barnet, R. 1980. *The Lean Years*. New York: Simon & Schuster.

Baudrillard, Jean. 1968. *Le Système des Objets*. Paris: Denoel-Gonthier.

———. 1970. *The Consumer Society*. London: Sage.

———. 1972 [1981]. *For A Critique of the Political Economy of the Sign*. St. Louis: Telos Press.

———. 1975 [1973]. *The Mirror of Production*. St. Louis: Telos Press.

———. 1976. *Symbolic Exchange and Death*. London: Sage.

———. 1981. *For a Critique of the Political Economy of the Sign*. St. Louis: Telos.

———. 1983b. *Sumulations*. New York: Semiotext(e).

———. 1986. *America*. London: Verso.

———. 1987. *Forget Foucault*. New York: Semiotext(e).

———. 1990 [1983a]. *Fatal Strategies*. New York: Semiotext(e).

———. 2003. "Jean Baudrillard Biography." Available: www.egs.edu/faculty/baudrillard.html.

Begley, Sharon. 1998. "Why Wilson's Wrong". *Newsweek.* June 22, Vol.131, (25):61–62.

Bellman, Beryl. 1975. *Village of Curers and Assassins: On the Production of Fala Kpelle Cosmological Categories.* The Hague: Mouton.

Bender, Thomas. 1991. *Community and Social Change in America.* Baltimore: John Hopkins University Press.

Berger, Peter. 1961. *The Precarious Vision.* Garden City, NY: Doubleday.

———. 1967. *The Sacred Canopy—Elements of Religion.* Garden City, NY: Doubleday

———. 1969. *A Rumor of Angels.* Garden City, NY: Doubleday.

———. 1974. *Pyramids of Sacrifice.* New York: Basic.

———. 1975. *Protocol of Damnation.* New York: Seabury Press.

———. 1977. *Facing up to Modernity.* New York: Basic.

———. 1979. *The Heretical Imperative.* Garden City, NY: Anchor.

———. 1986a. *The Capitalist Revolution.* New York: Basic.

———. 1986. "The Concept of Mediating Action," pp. 1–11 in *Confession, Conflict & Community,* edited by Richard J. Neuhaus. Grand Rapids, MI: William B. Eerdmans.

Berger, Brigitte and Peter Berger. 1983. *The War Over the Family.* Garden City, NY: Anchor.

Berger, Peter; Brigitte Berger and Hansfried Kellner. 1973. *The Homeless Mind.* New York: Random House.

Berger, Peter and Hansfried Kellner. 1964. "Marriage and the Construction of Reality." *Diogenes,* 46:1–24.

Berger, Peter and Thomas Luckmann. 1980. *The Social Construction of Reality.* New York: Irvington.

Berger, Peter and Richard J. Neuhaus. 1970. *Movement and Revolution.* New York: Anchor.

Berger, Peter and Stanley Pullberg. 1965. "Reification and the Sociological Critique of Consciousness." *History and Theory,* Vol. 4:196–211.

Bernard, Jessie. 1972. *The Future of Marriage.* New York: World Pub.

Best, Steven and Douglas Kellner. 1991. *Postmodern Theory: Critical Interrogations.* New York: Guilford.

Biemer, John. 2001. "Derailed Chemical Train Burns." *Syracuse Post-Standard.* July 20:A10.

Bienenstock, Elisa Jayne and Philip Bonacich. 1993. "Game-Theory Models for Exchange Networks: Experimental Results." *Sociological Perspectives.* 36 (2):117–135.

Blane, Howard T. and Kenneth E. Leonard, editors. 1987. *Psychological Theories of Drinking and Alcoholism.* New York: Giulford Press.

Blau, Peter. 1955. *The Dynamics of Bureaucracy.* Chicago: University of Chicago Press.

———. 1956. *Bureaucracy in Modern Society.* New York: Random House.

———. 1964. *Exchange and Power in Social Life.* New York: Wiley.

———. 1973. *The Organization of Academic Work.* New York: Wiley.

———. 1974. *On the Nature of Organizations.* New York: Wiley.

———. 1994. *Structural Contexts of Opportunities.* Chicago: University of Chicago Press.

Blau, Peter and Otis Dudley Duncan. 1967. *The American Occupational Structure.* New York: Wiley.

Blau, Peter and Robert Merton, editors. 1981. *Continuities in Structural Inquiry.* Beverly Hills, CA: Sage.

Blau, Peter and Joseph E. Schwartz. 1997. *Crosscutting Social Circles: Testing a Macrostructural Theory of Intergroup Relations.* New Brunswick, NJ: Transaction Pubs.

Blau, Peter and W. Richard Scott. 1962. *Formal Organizations.* Scranton, PA: Chandler.

Bleich, Harold. 1977. *The Philosophy of Herbert Marcuse.* Washington, DC: University Press of America.

Blewett, Stephen and Mary Embree. 1998. *What's in the Air, Natural and Manmade Air Pollution.* Ventura, CA: Seaview.

Bloom, David and Adi Bender. 1993. "Labor and the Emerging World Economy." *Population Bulletin.* Vol. 48(October):1–39.

Blumer, Herbert. 1936. "Social Attitudes and Non-Symbolic Interaction." *Journal of Educational Sociology.* Vol. 9: 515–523.

———. 1937a. "Social Disorganization and Individual Disorganization." *American Journal of Sociology.* 42 (6): 871–877.

———. 1937b. "Social Psychology," pp. 44–98 in *Man and Society,* edited by Emerson P. Schmidt. New York: Prentice Hall.

———. 1940. "The Problem of the Concept in Social Psychology." *American Journal of Sociology.* 45 (5):707–719.

———. 1948. "Public Opinion and Public Opinion Polling." *American Sociological Review.* 13 (5):542–549.

———. 1954. "What is Wrong with Social Theory?" *American Sociological Review.* 19 (1):3–10.

———. 1969. *Symbolic Interaction.* Englewood Cliffs, NJ: Prentice Hall.

———. 1973. "A Note on Symbolic Interactionism." *American Sociological Review.* 38 (6):797–798.

———. 1980. "Mead and Blumer: The Convergent Methodological Perspectives of Social Behaviorism and Symbolic Interaction." *American Sociological Review.* 45 (3):409–419.

———. 1990. *Industrialization as an Agent of Social Change,* edited with an introduction by David R. Maines and Thomas J. Morrlowe. New York: Aldine de Gruyter.

Boden, Deirdre. 1990A. "People are Talking: Conversation Analysis and Symbolic Interaction," pp. 244–273 in *Symbolic Interactionism and Cultural Studies,* edited by H.S. Becker and M. McCall. Chicago: University of Chicago Press.

———. 1990B. "The World as it Happens: Ethnomethodology and Conversation Analysis," pp. 185–213 in *Frontiers of Social Theory: The New Syntheses,* edited by George Ritzer. New York: Columbia University Press.

Bohlim, Ray. 1997. "The Little Lamb that made a Monkey of Us—Can Humans be Cloned Like Sheep?" Available: www.probe.org/lambsclon.

Borgatta, Edgar and Marie Borgatta, eds. 1992. *Encyclopedia of Sociology,* Vol. 2. New York: Macmillan.

Borstein, Seth. 2001. "Global Warming Will Raise Temperature 5 Degrees by 2100, New Study Predicts." *Buffalo News.* July 29:H6

Bottomore, Tom. 1984. *The Frankfurt School.* Chichester, England: Ellis Horwood.

Breines, Paul. "From Guru to Spectre: Marcuse and the Implosion of the Movement," pp. 1–21 in *Critical Interruptions,* edited by Paul Breines. New York: Herder and Herder.

Bronner, Stephen Eric, and Douglas Kellner. 1983. *Passion and Rebellion*. New York: Universe Books.

Bronner, Stephen Eric, and Douglas Kellner, editors. 1989. *Critical Theory and Society*. New York: Routledge.

Brown, Barry. 1999. "Quebec Sign Ruling Calls off the 'Language Police.'" *Buffalo News*. October 24:A5.

Brumberg, Joan Jacobs. 1988. *Fasting Girls: The Emergence of Anorexia Nervosa as a Modern Disease*. Cambridge, MA: Harvard University Press.

———. 1997a. *The Body Project: An Intimate History of American Girls*. New York: Random House.

———. 1997b. "Silicone Valley." *The Nation*. December 29.

———. 2001. "Toronto Beaten by the Numbers: China's Billion." *Buffalo News*. July 14:A3.

Buffalo News. 1999. "Raw Umbers and Burnt Siennas of the World: Unite!" March 15:B9.

———. 2000a. "The Index." March 30:C1.

———. 2000b. "May Day Protestors Clash with Police in U.S. Cities." May 2:A2.

———. 2000c. "Tensions Force Scrapping of Genocide Resolution." October 20: A3.

———. 2000d. "What Lewis Wishes He Had Said." February 19:C7.

Cairus, Dorion. 1976. *Conversations with Husserl and Fink*. The Hague: Martinus Nijhoff.

Calhoun, Craig. 1993. "Habitus, Field, and Capital: The Question of Historical Specificity," pp.61–88 in *Bourdieu: Critical Perspectives*, edited by Craig Calhoun, E. LiPuma and M. Postone. Chicago: University of Chicago Press.

Camic, Charles. 1991. *Talcott Parsons: The Early Essays*. Chicago: University of Chicago Press.

Caputo, John. 1999. "Commentary on Ken Schmitz; Postmodernism and the Catholic Tradition." *American Catholic Philosophical Quarterly*. 73 (2):253–259.

———. 2000. "Philosophy and Prophetic Postmodernism: Toward a Catholic Postmodernism." *American Catholic Philosophical Quarterly*. 74 (4):249–267.

Carlebach, Julius. 1978. *Karl Marx and the Radical Critique of Judaism*. Boston: Routledge & Kegan Paul.

Catton, W.R. 1980. *Overshoot: The Ecological Basis of Revolutionary Change*. Urbana: University of Illinois Press.

Centers for Disease Control. 1994. "Addressing Emerging Infectious Disease Threats: A Prevention Strategy for the United States Executive Summary." 43 (RR-5):1–18.

Charon, Joel M. 1989. *Symbolic Interactionism*, 3rd ed. Englewood, Cliffs, NJ: Prentice Hall.

Cicourel, Aaron V. 1964. *Method and Measurement in Sociology*. New York: Free Press.

Clayman, Steven E. 1993. "Booing: The Anatomy of a Disaffiliative Response." *American Sociological Review*. 58:110–130.

Clecak, Peter. 1973. *Radical Paradoxes*. New York: Harper & Row.

Clements, Richard. 1999. "Prevalence of Alcohol-Use Disorders and Alcohol-Related Problems in a College Student Sample." *Journal of American College Health*. 48 (3):111–118.

Coakley, Jay. 2001. *Sport in Society*. Boston: McGraw-Hill.

Cockerham, William. 1995. *The Global Society*. New York: McGraw Hill.

Cohen, Joel. 2002. "The Future of Population," pp. 29–75 in *What the Future Holds*, edited by Richard Cooper and Richard Layard. Cambridge, MA: MIT Press.

Collins, Patricia Hill. 1986. "Learning From the Outsider Within: The Sociological Significance of Black Feminist Thought." *Social Problems*. 33 (6):514–532.

———. 1989a. "A Comparison of Two Works on Black Life." *Signs*. 14 (4):875–884.

———. 1989b "The Social Construction of Black Feminist Thought." *Signs*. 14 (4):745–773.

———. 1990. *Black Feminist Thought*. Cambridge, MA: Unwin Hyman.

———. 1992. "Transforming the Inner Circle: Dorothy Smith's Challenge to Sociological Thought." *Sociological Theory*. 10:73–80.

———. 1996. "What's in a Name? Womanism, Black Feminism, and Beyond." *Black Scholar*. 26 (1):9–17.

———. 1997. "Comment on Hekman's 'Truth and Method: Feminist Standpoint Theory Revisited: Where's the Power?'" *Signs*. 22 (2):375–381.

Collins, Randall. 1971A. "A Conflict Theory of Sexual Stratification." *Social Problems*. 19:3–12.

———. 1971b. "Functional and Conflict Theories of Educational Stratification." *American Sociological Review*. 36:1002–1019.

———. 1974. *Conflict Sociology: Toward an Explanatory Science*. New York: Academic Press.

———. 1975a. "The Basics of Conflict Sociology," pp. 56–61 in *Conflict Sociology*. New York: Academic Press.

———. 1975b. *Conflict Sociology*. New York: Academic Press.

———. 1979. *The Credential Society*. New York: Academic Press.

———. 1981. "On the Micro Foundations of Macro Sociology." *American Journal of Sociology*. 86:984–1014.

———. 1985. *Sociology of Marriage and Family: Gender, Love and Property*. Chicago: Nelson-Hall.

———. 1986a. "Is 1980's Sociology in the Doldrums?" *American Journal of Sociology*. 91:1326–1335.

———. 1986b. "The Passing of Intellectual Generations: Reflections on the Death of Erving Goffman." *Sociological Theory*. 4:106–113.

———. 1986c. *Weberian Sociological Theory*. Cambridge: University Press.

———. 1988. "Women and Men in the Class Structure." *Journal of Family Issues*. 9 (1): 27–50.

———. 1989. "Sociology: Proscience or Antiscience?" *American Sociological Review*. 54(February):124–139.

———. 1990a. "Market Dynamics as the Engine of Historical Change." *Sociological Theory*. 8 (2): 111–135.

———. 1990b. "Reply: Cumulation and Anticumulation in Sociology." *American Sociological Review*. 55 (3):462–463.

———. 1993a. "Liberals and Conservatives, Religious and Political: A Conjecture of Modern History." *Sociology of Religion*. 54(2):127–146.

———. 1993b. "Maturation of the State-Centered Theory of Revolution and Ideology." *Sociological Theory*. 11 (1):117–128.

———. 1994. "Why the Social Sciences Won't Become High-Consensus, Rapid-Discovery Science." *Sociological Forum*. 9 (2):155–177.

———. 1997. "An Asian Route to Capitalism: Religious Economy and the Origins of Self-transforming Growth in Japan." *American Sociological Review*. 62 (6):843–865.

———. 1998a. "The Sociological Eye and its Blinders." *Contemporary Sociology*. 27 (1):2–7.

———. 1998b. *The Sociology of Philosophies*. Cambridge, MA: Norton & Company.

———. 1999. *Macro-History: Essays in Sociology of the Long Run*. Stanford, CA: University Press.

———. 2000. "The Sociology of Philosophies: A Precis." *Philosophy of the Social Sciences*. 30(2):157–201.

Comte, Auguste. 1851. *System of Positive Polity*, Vol. 1. New York: Burt Franklin.

———. 1852. *System of Positive Polity*, Vol. 2. New York: Burt Franklin.

———. 1854. *System of Positive Polity*, Vol. 4. New York: Burt Franklin.

———. 1891. *The Catechism of Positive Religion*. Clifton, NJ: Kelley.

———. 1896. *Positive Philosophy*, translated by Harriet Martineau. London: Bell.

Conant, James and John Haugeland (editors). 2000. *The Road Since Structure*. Chicago: The University of Chicago Press.

Cook, Karen. 1987. "Emerson's Contribution to Social Exchange Theory," pp. 209–222 in *Social Exchange Theory*, edited by Karen Cook. Beverly Hills, CA: Sage.

———. 1998. *Curriculum vitae*.

Cook, Karen and Richard Emerson. 1978. "Power, Equity and Commitment in Exchange Networks." *American Sociological Review*. 43 (October): 721–739.

Cook, Karen, Richard Emerson, Mary Gilmore, Toshio Yamagishi. 1983. "The Distribution of Power in Exchange Networks: Theory and Experimental Results." *American Journal of Sociology*. 89:275–305.

Cook, Karen and Karen Hegtvedt. 1983. "Distributive Justice, Equity and Equality." *Annual Review of Sociology*. 9:217–241.

Cook, Karen and Mary Gillmore. 1984. "Power, Dependence, and Coalitions." *Advances in Group Processes*. 1:27–58.

Cook, Karen and J.M. Whitmeyer. 1992. "Two Approaches to Social Structure: Exchange theory and Network Analysis." *Annual Review of Sociology*. 18:109–127.

Cook, Karen and Judith Howard. 1992. "Recent Theoretical Advances in Social Psychology: Progress and Promises." *Social Psychology Quarterly*. 55(2):87–93.

Cooley, Charles. 1902. *Human nature and the Social Order*. New York: Scribners.

———. 1909. *Social Organization*. New York: Scribners.

———. 1964. *Human Nature and the Social Order*, introduction by Philip Rieff, Foreword by Herbert Mead. New York: Schocken.

Cooper, Derrick. 1991. "On the Concept of Alienation." *International Journal of Contemporary Sociology*. 28:7–26.

Cooper, Richard and Richard Layard, editors. 2002. *What the Future Holds*. Cambridge, MA: MIT Press.

Cope, Kevin Lee. 1999. *John Locke Revisited*. New York: Twayne.

Coser, Lewis. 1956. *The Functions of Social Conflict*. New York: Free Press.

———. 1964. "The Political Functions of Eunuchism." *American Sociological Review*. 29 (6):880–885.

———. 1965a. *Georg Simmel*. Englewood Cliffs, NJ: Prentice Hall.

———. 1965b. *Men of Ideas: A Sociologist's View*. New York: Free Press.

———. 1967. *Continuities in the Study of Social Conflict*. New York: Free Press.

———. 1972a. "The Alien as a Servant of Power: Court Jews and Christian Renegades." *American Sociological Review*. 37 (5):574–581.

———. 1972b. "Marxist Thought in the First Quarter of the 20th Century." *American Journal of Sociology*. 78 (1): 173–201.

———. 1974. *Greedy Institutions: Patterns of Undivided Commitment*. New York: Free Press.

———. 1975. "Presidential Address: Two Methods in Search of a Substance." *American Sociological Review*. 40 (6): 691–700.

———. 1976. "Sociological Theory From the Chicago Dominance to 1965." *Annual Review of Sociology*. (2):145–160.

———. 1977. *Masters of Sociological Thought*, 2nd ed. New York: Harcourt, Brace & Jovanovich.

———. 1982. "Remembering Gouldner: Battler, Conquistador, and Free Intelligence." *Theory and Society*. 11 (6): 885–888.

———. 1988. "Primitive Classification Revisited." *Sociological Theory*. 6, (1):85–90.

———. 1993. "A Sociologist's Atypical Life." *Annual Review of Sociology*. Vol. 19:1–15.

Coser, Lewis and Irving Howe, editors 1973. *The New Conservatives: A Critique from the Left*. New York: Quadrangle/New York Times Books.

———. 1954. "Images of Socialism," pp. 29–47 in *Legacy of Dissent*, edited by Nicolaus Mills. New York: Simon & Schuster.

Coser, Rose Laub and Lewis Coser. 1979. "Jonestown as a Perverse Utopia: A Greedy Institution in the Jungle." *Dissent*. Spring:159–165.

Craig, Steve. 2002. *Sports and Games of the Ancients*. Westport, CT: Greenwood Press.

Crenson, Matt. 2001. "As the World Adopts America's Consumer Culture, Shortages Loom." *Buffalo News*. January 21:F1.

Curra, John. 2003. *The Human Experience*. Boston: Allyn and Bacon.

Cuzzort, R.P. and Edith W. King. 1995, 5th ed. *Twentieth-Century Social Thought*. Fort Worth: Harcourt Brace.

Dahrendorf, Ralf. 1959. *Class and Class Conflict in Industrial Society*. Stanford: Stanford University Press.

———. 1968. *Essays in the Theory of Society*. Stanford: Stanford University Press.

Darwin, Charles. 1955. *The Expression of the Emotions in Man and Animals*. New York: Philosophical Library.

Davidson, Arnold I. 1997. *Foucault and His Interlocutors*. Chicago: The University of Chicago Press.

Davis, Kingsley. 1959. "The Myth of Functional Analysis as a Special Method in Sociology and Anthropology." *American Sociological Review*. 24:757–772.

Deegan, Mary Jo. 1989. *American Ritual Dramas*. New York: Greenwood Press.

Deely, John. 1994. *New Beginnings; Early Modern Philosophy and Postmodern Thought*. Buffalo: University of Toronto Press.

Delaney, Tim. 2000a. "The Building Blocks of Religion." *New Zealand Rationalist & Humanist Journal*. (Winter):2–8.

———. 2000b. "Humanistic Issues in Genetic Engineering, Fertility, and Cloning," pp.214–219 in *Science and Society*, edited by Harry Birx. St. Petersburg, Russia: Russian Academy of Sciences.

———. 2001. *Community, Sport and Leisure*, 2nd edition. Auburn, NY: Legend Books.

———. 2002a. "Collective Violence," pp. 246–251 in *Encyclopedia of Crime and Punishment*, Vol. 3. Thousand Oaks, CA: Sage.

———. 2002b. "Karl Marx and Social Change: From Early Capitalism to Emerging Capitalism," pp. 41–70 in *Values, Society & Evolution*, edited by Harry Birx and Tim Delaney. Auburn, NY: Legend Books.

———. 2002c. "The Spy Next Door." Book review in *Library Journal*. (February) 15:162.

———. 2004. *Classical Social Theory: Investigation and Application*. Upper Saddle River, NJ: Prentice Hall.

Delaney, Tim and Allene Wilcox. 2002. "Sports and the Role of the Media," pp. 199–215 in *Values, Society and Evolution*, edited by Harry Birx and Tim Delaney. Auburn, NY: Legend Books.

DeLindt, Jan and Wolfgang Schmidt. 1971. "Alcohol Use and Alcoholism." *Addictions*, 18 (Summer):1–14.

Denzin, Norman K. 1969. "Symbolic Interaction and Ethnomethodology: A Proposed Synthesis." *American Sociological Review*. 34 (6):922–934.

———. 1987. *Alcoholic Self*. Thousand Oaks, CA: Sage.

———. 1991. *Images of Postmodernism: Social Theory and Contemporary Cinema*. London: Sage.

Derrida, Jacques. 1976. *Of Grammatology*. Baltimore, MD: Johns Hopkins University Press.

———. 1978. *Writing and Difference*. Chicago: University of Chicago Press.

———. 1997. "To Do Justice to Freud: The History of Madness in the Age of Psychoanalysis," pp. 57–104 in *Foucault and His Interlocutors*, edited by Arnold I. Davidson. Chicago: The University of Chicago Press.

De Villiers, Marq. 2001. *Water, the Drop of Life*. Minneapolis, MN: North World Press.

Diamond, Jared. 1999. *Guns, Germs, and Steel*. New York: Norton.

Dominguez, Alex. 2001. "'Greenhouse Effect' is Confirmed by Satellite Data." *Buffalo News*. March 15:A7.

Dorgan, William J. 2002. "Alcoholism: Disease or Vice?" *Modern Machine Shop*. 74 (12):112.

Douglas, Jack. 1980. *Introduction to the Sociologies of Everyday Life*. Boston: Allyn and Bacon.

Drew, Paul and Anthony Wootton, editors. 1988. *Erving Goffman: Exploring the Interaction Order*. Boston: Northeastern University Press.

Dreyfus, Hubert L. and Paul Rabinow. 1982. *Michel Foucault*. Chicago: University Press.

Dronberger, Ilse. 1971. *The Political Thought of Max Weber: In Quest of Statesmanship*. New York: Meredith Corporation.

Durkheim, Émile 1965 [1912]. *The Elementary Forms of Religious Life*. New York: Free Press.

———. 1973 [1914]. "The Dualism of Human Nature and its Social Condition," pp. 149–163 in *Émile Durkheim: On Morality and Society*, edited by K. Bellah. Chicago: University of Chicago Press.

Eddy, J.A. and H. Oescher, editors. 1993. *Global Changes in the Perspective of the Past*. New York: Wiley.

Edelson, Edward. 1992. *Clean Air*. New York: Chelsea House Publishers.

Edwards, Harry. 1973. *Sociology of Sport*. Homewood, IL: Dorsey Press.

Elias, Paul. 2001. "Fortified Rice a Sticky Topic at Biotech Conference." *Buffalo News*. June 26:A4.

Emerson, Richard. 1972a. "Exchange Theory, Part I: A Psychological Basis for Social Basis for Social Exchange," pp. 38–57 in *Sociological Theories in Progress*, Vol. 2, edited by J. Berger, M. Zelditch, and B. Anderson. Boston: Houghton Mifflin.

———. 1972b. "Exchange Theory, Part II: Exchange Relations and Networks," pp. 58–87 in *Sociological Theories in Progress*, edited by J. Berger, M. Zelditch, and B. Anderson. Boston: Houghton Mifflin.

Enoch, Mary Anne and David Goldman. 2002. "Problem Drinking and Alcoholism: Diagnosis and Treatment." *American Family Physician*. 65(3):441–448.

ESPN. 2001. "SportsCenter: Beijing Wins 2008 Summer Olympics." Aired July 14.

Faberman, Harvey A. 1991. "Symbolic Interaction and Postmodernism: Close Encounter of a Dubious Kind." *Symbolic Interaction*. 14:471–488.

Farber, Marvin. 1943. *The Foundation of Phenomenology*. Cambridge, MA: Harvard University Press.

Farganis, James. 2000. *Readings in Social Theory*, 3rd ed. Boston: McGraw Hill.

Farley, John. 1998. *Sociology*, 4th edition. Upper Saddle River, NJ: Prentice-Hall.

Fay, Brian. 1975. *Social Theory and Political Practice*. Boston: Unwin Hyman.

———. 1987. *Critical Social Science: Liberation & Its Limits*. Ithaca, NY: Cornell University Press.

Feldman, Stephen M. 2000. *American Legal Thought From Premodern to Postmodern: An Intellectual Voyage*. New York: Oxford Press.

Fine, Gary Alan. 1993. "The Sad Demise, Mysterious Disappearances, and Glorious Triumph of Symbolic Interactionism." *Annual Review of Sociology*. 19:61–87.

Flavin, Christopher. 1987, "Reassessing Nuclear Power," pp. 57–80 in *State of the World*, edited by Lester Brown. New York: Norton.

Flew, Anthony. 1994. "E.O. Wilson after Twenty Years, is Human Sociobiology Possible?" *Philosophy of the Social Sciences*. 24 (3):320–335.

Fletcher, Michael and Greg Sandoval. 2003. "Panel Rejects Title IX Overhaul Yet Urges Latitude in Enforcement." *Buffalo News*. January 31:A1.

Fontana, Andrea and Frederick Preston. 1990. "Postmodern Neon Architecture: From Signs to Icons." *Studies in Symbolic Interaction*. 11:3–24.

Forrest, Gary. 1975. *The Diagnosis and Treatment of Alcoholism*. Springfield, IL: Thomas Books.

———. 1995. *Chemical Dependency and Antisocial Personality Disorder*. New York: The Haworth Press.

Foster, Janet. 1990. *Crime and Community in the City*. New York: Routledge.

Foucault, Michel. 1965. *Madness and Civilization: A History of Insanity in the Age of Reason*. New York: Vintage.

———. 1966a. *The Order of Things: An Archaeology of the Human Sciences*. New York: Vintage.

———. 1966b. "The Prose of the World." *Diogenes*. 53:17–37.

———. 1969. *The Archaeology of Knowledge and the Discourse on Language*. New York: Harper Collophon.

———. 1975. *The Birth of the Clinic: An Archaeology of Medical Perception*. New York: Vintage.

———. 1978. *The History of Sexuality*. New York: Pantheon Books.

———. 1980. *The History of Sexuality: An Introduction*. Vol. 1. New York: Vintage.

———. 1983. "Afterword: The Subject and Power," pp. 208–226 in *Michel Foucault: Beyond Structuralism and Hermeneutics*, edited by H.L. Dreyfus and P. Rabinow. Chicago: The University of Chicago Press.

———. 1985. *The Use of Pleasure: The History of Sexuality*. Vol. 2. New York: Pantheon.

———. 1995. "Madness, The Absence of Work." *Critical Inquiry*. 21(Winter):290–298.

Francoise, Michel. 2001. "McDonald's the Testing Ground for Russia's New Unionists." *AFP Moscow, Russia*. March 8:1–3.

Frey, James H. and Tim Delaney. 1996. "The Role of Leisure Participation in Prison: A Report From Consumers." *Journal of Offender Rehabilitation*. 23(1/2):79–89.

Friedman, Michael. 1993. "Remarks on the History of Science and the History of Philosophy," pp. 37–54 in *World Changes*, edited by Paul Horwich. Cambridge, MA: The MIT Press.

Friedman, Milton. 1953. *Essays in Positive Economics*. Chicago: University of Chicago Press.

Fuchs, Stephan. 2001. "Networks and Systems," pp. 129–139 in *Talcott Parsons Today*, edited by A. Javier Trevino, foreword by Neil J. Smelser. New York: Rowman & Littlefield.

Fuchs, Stephan and Jonathan H. Turner. 1986. "What Makes a Science 'Mature'?: Patterns of Organizational Control in Scientific Production." *Sociological Theory*. (2):143–150.

Fulwood III, Sam. 1998. "Nationwide Ordered to Pay $100 million in Federal Suit over Racial Redlining." *Los Angeles Times*. October 28:A8.

Galewitz, Phil. 1999. "Wealth of Richest 400 Americans tops $1 Trillion for First Time." *Buffalo News*. September 24:A1.

Garfinkel, Harold. 1956. "Conditions of Successful Degradation Ceremonies." *American Journal of Sociology*. 61 (March):420–424.

———. 1963. "A Conception of, and Experiments with, 'Trust' as a Condition of Stable and Concerted Actions," pp. 187–238 in *Motivation in Social Interaction*, edited by O.J. Harvey. New York: Ronald.

———. 1967. *Studies in Ethnomethodology*. Englewood Cliffs, NJ: Prentice Hall.

———. 1988. "Evidence for Locally Produced, Naturally Accountable Phenomena of Order, Logic, Reason, Meaning, etc. In and as of the Essential Quiddity of Immortal Ordinary Society (I of IV): an Announcement of Studies." *Sociological Theory*. (1):103–109.

———. 1996. "Ethnomethodology's Program." *Social Psychology Quarterly*. 59 (1):5–21.

———. 2002. *Ethnomethodology's Program: Working out Durkheim's Aphorism*, edited and introduced by Anne Warfield Rawls. New York: Rowman & Littlefield.

Garner, Roberta, editor. 2000. *Social Theory*. Orchard Park, NY: Broadview.

Gay, Peter. 1969. *The Enlightenment: An Interpretation*. New York: Norton & Company.

Gerth, Hans and C. Wright Mills. 1953. *Character and Social Structure*. New York: Harcourt, Brace and World.

Giddens, Anthony. 1971. *Capitalism and Modern Social Theory*. Cambridge: University Press.

———. 1976. *New Rules of Sociological Method*. London: Hutchinson

———. 1977. *Studies in Social and Political Theory*. London: Hutchinson.

———. 1979. *Central Problems in Social Theory: Action, Structure and Contradiction in Social Analysis*. Berkeley: University of California Press.

———. 1984. *The Constitution of Society: Outline of the Theory of Structuration*. Cambridge: University Press.

———. 1987. *Sociology: A Brief But Critical Introduction*, 2nd edition. New York: Harcourt, Brace & Jovanovich.

———. 1990. *The Consequence of Modernity*. Stanford, CA: Stanford University Press.

———. 1991. *Modernity and Self-identity: Self and Society in the Late Modern Age*. Cambridge: Polity Press.

———. 1992. *The Transformation of Intimacy*. Stanford, CA: Stanford University Press.

———. 1994. *Beyond Left and Right*. Cambridge: Polity Press.

———. 2000a. *Runaway World*. New York: Routledge.

———. 2000b. *The Third Way and its Critics*. Malden, MA: Polity Press.

Gilligan, Carol. 1982. *In a Different Voice*. Cambridge, MA: Harvard University Press

———. 1998. "Remembering Larry." *Journal of Moral Education*. (2)125–140.

Gilligan, Carol, Janie Victoria Ward and Jill McLean Taylor. 1988. *Mapping the Moral Domain: A Contribution of Women's Thinking to Psychological Theory and Education*. Cambridge, MA: Harvard University Press.

Glaser, Barney G. and Anselm L. Strauss. 1965. *Awareness of Dying*. Chicago: Aldine

Glock, Charles and Rodney Stark, 1965. *Religion and Society In Tension*. Chicago: Rand McNally.

Goffman, Erving. 1956. "Embarrassment and Social Organization." *American Journal of Sociology*. 62 (3): 264–271.

———. 1959. *Presentation of Self in Everyday Life*. Garden City, NY: Anchor.

———. 1961a. *Asylums*. Garden City, NY: Doubleday Anchor Books.

———. 1961b. *Encounters; Two Studies in the Sociology of Interaction*. Indianapolis: Bobbs-Merrill.

———. 1963a. *Behavior in Public Places: Notes on the Social Organization of Gatherings*. Glencoe, IL: Free Press.

———. 1963b. *Stigma*. Englewood Cliffs, NJ: Prentice Hall.

———. 1967. *Interaction Ritual*. Garden City, NY: Anchor.

———. 1971. *Relations in Public*. New York: Basic Books.

———. 1972. *Strategic Interaction*. New York: Ballantine.

———. 1974. *Frame Analysis*. New York: Harper Colophon.

———. 1979. *Gender Advertisements*. New York: Harper and Row.

———. 1981. *Forms of Talk*. Philadelphia: University of Pennsylvania Press

———. 1983a. "Felicity's Condition." *American Journal of Sociology*. 89 (1):1–53.

———. 1983b. "The Interaction Order: American Sociological Association, 1982 Presidential Address." *American Sociological Review*. 48 (1):1–17.

Goode, Erich. 1988. *Sociology*, 2nd edition. Englewood Cliffs, NJ: Prentice-Hall.

———. 1997. *Deviant Behavior*, 5th edition. Upper Saddle River, NJ: Prentice Hall.

———. 2001. *Deviant Behavior*, 6th edition. Upper Saddle River, NJ: Prentice Hall.

Goodwin, Charles. 1984. "Notes on Story Structure and The Organization of Participation," pp. 225–246 in *Structures of Social Action*, edited by J.M. Atkinson and J. Heritage. Cambridge: Cambridge University Press.

Gottlieb, Michael. 2001. "The Next 20 Years." *Moscow Times*. June 7:8.

Grafholf, Richard, editor. 1978. *The Theory of Social Action*. Bloomington; Indiana University Press.

———. 1989. *Philosophers in Exile*. Bloomington, IN: Indiana University Press.

Greisman, Harvey C. 1986. "The Paradigm that Failed," pp.273–291 in *Structures of Knowing*, edited by R.C. Monk. Lanhan, MD: University Press of America.

Griffin, Em. 1991. "A Different Voice of Carol Gilligan." *A First Look at Communication Theory*. Boston: McGraw Hill.

Groves, W. Byron and Robert J. Sampson. 1986. "Critical Theory and Criminology." *Social Problems*. 33(61): 538–575.

Grunwald, Michael. 1998. "Shell Pays $1.5 Million for Polluting River; U.S. Effects Crackdown on Mississippi." *Washington Post*. September 10:A3.

Guardian Weekly. 2000. "Rich Live Longer, Poor Die Younger in Divided World." July 6–12:3.

Gurko, Miriam. 1974. *The Ladies of Seneca Falls*. New York: Schocken Books.

Gutting, Gary. 1994. *The Cambridge Companion to Foucault*. Cambridge: University Press.

Habermas, Jurgen. 1970. *Toward A Rational Society: Student Protests, Science, and Politics*. Boston: Beacon.

———. 1973. "What Does a Crisis Mean Today: Legitimation Problems in Late Capitalism." *Social Research*. 40 (4): 39–64.

———. 1984. *The Theory of Communicative Action*, Volume One. Boston: Beacon.

———. 1987a. *The Philosophical Discourse of Modernity*, translated by Frederick Lawrence. Cambridge, MA: The MIT Press.

———. 1987b. *The Theory of Communicative Action*, Volume Two. Boston: Beacon.

———. 1989. "The Tasks of a Critical Theory of Society," pp. 292–312 in *Critical Theory and Society*, edited by Stephen Eric Bronner and Douglas Kellner. New York: Routledge.

———. 1991. "A Reply," pp.214–264 in *Communicative Action*, edited by Alex Honneth and Hans Joas. Cambridge, MA: The MIT Press.

———. 1997. "Modernity: An Unfinished Project," pp. 38–55 in *Habermas and the Unfinished Project of Modernity*, edited by Maurizio Passerin d'Entreves and Seyla Benhabib. Cambridge, MA: The MIT Press.

———. 1998. "Remarks on Legitimation Through Human Rights." *The Modern Schoolman*. 75:87–100.

Haddock, Patricia. 2000. *Environmental Time Bomb*. Berkeley Heights, NJ: Enslow.

Hardt, Hanno. 1986. "Critical Theory in Historic Perspective." *Journal of Communication*. 36:144–154.

Harding, Sandra. 1986. "The Instability of the Analytical Categories of Feminist Theory." *Signs*. 11 (4):645–664.

———. 1989a. "How the Women's Movement Benefits Science: Two Views." *Women's Studies International Forum*. 12 (3): 271–283.

———. 1989b. "Women as Creators of Knowledge." *American Behavioral Scientist*. 32 (6): 700–707.

———. 1992. "After the Neutrality Ideal; Science, Politics, and Strong Objectivity." *Social Research*. 59 (Fall): 567–87.

———. 2000. "After the Common Era." *Signs*. 25 (4): 1041–1044.

Harding, Sandra and Merrill B. Hintikka, editors. 1983. *Discovering Reality*. Boston: D. Reidel.

Hartmann, Susan. 1998. "Feminism and Women's Movements," pp.41–45 in *Reading Women's Lives*, edited by Mary Margaret Fonow. Needhan Heights, MA: Simon & Schuster.

Harvey, David. 1989. *The Condition of Postmodernity*. Cambridge, MA: Blackwell.

Hawley, Amos H. 1986. *Human Ecology: A Theoretical Essay*. Chicago: University of Chicago Press.

———. 1992. "The Logic of Macrosociology." *Annual Review of Sociology*. 18:1–14.

Hecker, Steven. 1991. *Labor in a Global Economy: Perspectives From the United States and Canada*. Eugene, OR: Labor Education and Research Center, University of Oregon.

Heckert, Druann Maria. 2000. "Positive Deviance," pp. 29–41 in *Constructions of Deviance: Social Power, Context, and Interaction*, 3rd edition, edited by Peter Adler and Patricia Adler. Belmont, CA: Wadsworth.

Hefner, Philip. 2001. "Understanding Religion: The Challenge of E.O. Wilson." *Zygon*. 36 (2):241–248.

Hegel, Georg Wilhelm Friedrich. 1931. *The Phenomenology of Mind*. New York: Macmillan.

Hegtvedt, Karen, Elaine Thompson and Karen S. Cook. 1993. "Power and Equity: What Counts in Attributions for Exchange Outcome?" *Social Psychology Quarterly*. 56:100–119.

Heidegger, Martin. 1996. *Being and Time*. Albany, NY: State University of New York Press.

Hekman, Susan. 1997. "Truth and Method: Feminist Standpoint Theory Revisited." *Signs*. 22 (2):341–363.

Held, David. 1980. *Introduction to Critical Theory*. Berkeley: University of California Press.

Henderson, Harry. 2001. *Terrorism*. New York: Facts on File.

Henslin, James. 1993. *Sociology*. Boston: Allyn & Bacon.

———. 1994. *Social Problems*. Englewood Cliffs, NJ: Prentice-Hall.

Herbert, Josef. 2000. "Life in the Late 21st Century Will Change as Weather Heats up, Report Says." *Buffalo News*. June 9:A2.

Heritage, John. 1984. *Garfinkel and Ethnomethodology*. Cambridge, MA: Polity Press.

Heritage, John and David Greatbatch. 1986. "Generating Applause: A Study of Rhetoric and Response in Party Political Conference." *American Journal of Sociology*, 92:110–157.

Hewitt, John P. 1998. *The Myth of Self-Esteem*. New York: St. Martin's Press.

Hilgart, Art. 1997. "Sanctioned Sociopathy." *Humanist*. 57(1):3.

Hobbes, Thomas. 1971. *Leviathan*, edited by Michael Oakeshoti. New York: Collier-Macmillan.

Hochschild, Arlie Russell. 1973. *The Unexpected Community*. Berkeley: University of California Press.

———. 1979. "Emotion Work, Feeling Rules, and Social Structure." *American Journal of Sociology*. 85:551–573.

———. 1983. *The Managed Heart: Commercialization of Human Feeling*. Berkeley: University of California Press.

————. 1994. "Inside the Clock Work of Male Careers," pp. 125–139, in *Gender and the Academic Experience*, edited by Kathryn P. Meadow Orlans and Ruth A. Wallace. Lincoln: University of Nebraska Press.

————. 1997. *The Time Bind*. New York: Henry Holt.

Holland, Suzanne, Karen Lebacqz, and Laurie Zoloth, eds. 2001. *The Human Embryonic Stem Cell Debate: Science, Ethics, and Public Policy*. Cambridge, MA: MIT Press.

Homans, George. 1941. *English Villagers of the Thirteenth Century*. Cambridge, MA: Harvard University Press.

————. 1950. *The Human Group*. New York: Harcourt & Brace.

————. 1951. "The Western Electric Researches," pp. 201–241 in *Human Factors in Management*, edited by S.D. Hoslett. New York: Harper.

————. 1958. "Social Behavior as Exchange." *American Journal of Sociology*. 63:597–606.

————. 1961. *Social Behavior: Its Elementary Forms*. New York: Harcourt, Brace and World.

————. 1962. *Sentiments and Activities*. New York: Free Press.

————. 1967. *The Nature of Social Science*. New York: Harcourt, Brace and World.

————. 1969. "The Sociological Relevance of Behaviorism," pp. 1–24 in *Behavioral Sociology*, edited by R. Burgess and D. Bushell. New York: Columbia University Press.

————. 1984. *Coming to My Senses: The Autobiography of a Sociologist*. New Brunswick, NJ: Transaction Books.

Homans, George C. and Charles P. Curtis, Jr. 1970. *An Introduction to Pareto: His Sociology*. New York: Howard Fertig.

Horkheimer, Max. 1947. *The Eclipse of Reason*. New York: Oxford University Press.

————. 1974. *Critique of Industrial Reason*. New York: Seabury Press.

————. 1982. *Critical Theory; Selected Essays*. New York: Continuum. .

Horkheimer, Max and Theodor W. Adorno. 1944. *Dialectic of Enlightenment*. New York: Continuum.

Horowitz, Irving L. 1983. *C. Wright Mills: An American Utopian*. New York: Free Press.

Horwich, Paul, editor. 1993. *World Changes: Thomas Kuhn and the Nature of Science*. Cambridge, MA: MIT Press.

Howe, Linda. 1999. "Short Updates about Environmental Problems." *Earth Files*. Available: www.earthfiles.com/earth083.

Hoy, David Couzens and Thomas McCarthy. 1995. *Critical Theory*. Oxford: Blackwell.

Hunt, Morton. 1990. *The Compassionate Beast: What Science is Discovering About the Humane Side of Human Kind*. New York: William Morrow.

Husserl, Edmund. 1931. *Ideas.* New York: Macmillan.

————. 1950. *Ideem I*. The Hague: Martinus Nijhoff.

————. 1964. *The Idea of Phenomenology*, translated by William P. Alston and George Nakhnikian, and introduction by George Nakhnikian. The Hague: Martinus Nijhoff.

————. 1965. *Phenomenology and the Crisis of Philosophy*, translated with an introduction by Quentin Lauer. New York: Harper & Row.

————. 1966. *The Phenomenology of Internal Time-Consciousness*, edited by Martin Heidegger, introduction by Calvin O. Schrag. Bloomington, IN: Indiana University Press.

————. 1972. "A Reply to a Critic of My Refutation on Logical Psychologism." *Personalist*, 53:5–13.

————. 1977. "Psychological Studies in the Elements of Logic." *Personalist*, 58:297–320.

————. 1998. "The Phenomenology of Monadic Individuality and the Phenomenology of the General Possibilities and Compossibilities of Lived-Experiences: Static and Genetic Phenomenology." *Continental Philosophy Review*, 31:143–152.

Hynes, Mary. 1994. "Nevada's Water Plan." *Las Vegas Review Journal*. February 2:1B.

Jagtenberg, Tom and David McKie. 1997. *Eco-Impacts and the Greening of Postmodernity*. Thousand Oaks, CA: Sage.

James, William. 1948 [1890]. *Principles of Psychology*. Cleveland: Word Publishing.

Jameson, Fredric. 1971. *Marxism and Form*. Princeton: Princeton University Press.

————. 1981a. *The Political Unconscious*. Ithaca, NY: Cornell University Press.

————. 1981b. "Reification and Utopia in Mass Culture." *Social Text*. 1:139.

————. 1984. "Postmodernism on the Cultural Logic of Late Capitalism." *New Left Review*. 146:53–92.

————. 1989. "Afterward—Marxism and Postmodernism," pp. 369–387 in *Postmodernism, Jameson, Critique*, edited by Douglas Kellner. Washington, DC: Maisonneuve Press.

————. 1990. "Modernism and Imperialism," pp. 43–66 in *Nationalism, Colonialism, and Literature*, edited by Terry Eagleton, Fredric Jameson and Edward W. Said. Minneapolis: University of Minnesota Press.

————. 2000. "Postmodernism on the Cultural Logic of Late Capitalism," pp.539–557 in *Social Theory*, edited by Roberta Garner. Orchard Park, New York: Broadview.

Jay, Martin. 1973. *The Dialectical Imagination: A History of the Frankfurt School and the Institute of Social Research 1923–1950*. Boston: Little & Brown.

Jefferson, Gail. 1979. "A Technique for Inviting Laughter and Its Subsequent Acceptance Declination," pp. 79–96 in *Everyday Language; Studies in Ethnomethodology*, edited by G. Psathas. New York: Irvington.

————. 1984. "On the Organization of Laughter in Talk About Troubles," pp. 346–369 in *Structures of Social Action*. Cambridge: Cambridge University Press.

Jencks, Christopher and David Riesman. 1968. *The Academic Revolution*. Garden City, NY: Doubleday.

Joas, Hans. 1985. *George Herbert Mead: A Contemporary Re-examination of His Thought*. Cambridge: MIT Press.

Johnson, Benton. 1975. *Functionalism in Modern Sociology: Understanding Talcott Parsons*. Morristown, NJ: General Learning Press.

Johnson, C.C. 1974. "The Aerial Migration of Insects," pp. 117–130 in *Ecology, Evolution, and Population Biology*, introduction by Edward O. Wilson. San Francisco, CA: W.H. Freeman and Company.

Johnson, Kevin. 2001. "Hate-Related Murders hit 5-Year High." *USA Today*. February 14:8A.

Kallen, Horace. 1956. *The Social Dynamics of George H. Mead*. Washington, DC: Public Affairs Press.

Kaufman, Michael. 2002. "Robert K. Merton, Versatile Sociologist and Father of the Focus Group, Dies at 92." *New York Times*. February 24.

Kellaway, Jean. 2000. *The History of Torture of Execution.* New York: Lyons Press.

Kellert, Stephen R. and Edward O. Wilson, editors. 1993. *The Biophilia Hypothesis.* Washington, DC.: Shearwater Books.

Kellner, Douglas. 1977. *Karl Korsch: Revolutionary Theory.* Austin: University of Texas Press.

———. 1983. "Expressionism and Rebellion," pp. 3–39 in *Passion and Rebellion,* edited by Stephen Eric Bronner and Douglas Kellner. New York: Universe Books.

———. 1984. *Herbert Marcuse and the Crisis of Marxism.* Berkeley: University of California Press.

———. 1989a. *Critical Theory, Marxism, and Modernity.* Baltimore: John Hopkins University Press.

———. 1989b. *Jean Baudrillard: From Marxism to Post Modernism and Beyond.* Stanford, CA: Stanford University Press.

———. 1990. *Television and the Crisis of Democracy.* Boulder, CO: Westview.

———. 2002. "Theorizing Globalization." *Sociological Theory.* 20 (3):285–305.

———. 2003. "Herbert Marcuse." Available: www.uta.edu/-huma/illuminations/kellner.

Kemper, Theodore D. and Randall Collins. 1990. "Dimensions of Microreintation." *American Journal of Sociology.* 96 (1):32–68.

Kivisto, Peter. 1998. *Key Ideas in Sociology.* Thousand Oaks, CA: Pine Forge Press.

Knoke, David. 1990. *Political Networks.* Cambridge: University Press.

Kougat, Bruce and Gordon Walker. 2001. "The Small World of Germany and the Durability of National Networks." *American Sociological Review.* 66(June): 317–335.

Kohlberg, Lawrence and Carol Gilligan. 1971. "The Adolescent as a Philosopher: The Discovery of the Self in a Post Conventional World." *Daedalus.* 100:1051–1086.

Kornblum, William. 1991. *Sociology,* 2nd edition. Austin, TX: Holt, Rinehart & Winston.

———. 1993. *Sociology,* 3rd edition. Austin TX: Holt, Rinehart & Winston.

———. 1994. *Sociology,* 3rd edition. Fort Worth, TX: Harcourt Brace.

Korsch, Karl. 1971. *Marxism and Philosophy.* New York: Monthly Review Press.

Kovach, Bill. 1997. "E.O. Wilson's Last Class." *Nieman Reports.* 51 (1):96.

Kraft, Dina. 2000. "DNA Study Genetically Links Jews and Arabs." *Buffalo News.* May 10:A10.

Kritzman, Lawrence, editor. 1998. *Michel Foucault: Politics, Philosophy, Culture.* New York: Routledge.

Kuhn, Thomas. 1962, *The Structure of Scientific Revolutions.* Chicago: University of Chicago Press.

LaFeber, Walter. 1999. *Michael Jordan and the New Global Capitalism.* New York: Norton.

Lane, Ruth. 1994. "Structural-Functionalism Reconstructed." *Comparative Politics.* July:461–474.

Larson, Douglas. 2001. "Technological Promises, Scientific Disputes." *Phi Kappa Phi Journal.* Spring:6.

Las Vegas Review Journal. 1994. "Clean Water Act Proposed by Administration." February 2:5A.

Lauer, Quentin. 1965. *Phenomenology and the Crisis of Philosophy.* New York: Harper & Row.

Lawrence, Peter, Jeremy Meigh and Caroline Sullivan. 2002. "The Water Poverty Index: An International Compromise." *Keele Economic Research Papers.* Available: www.keele.ac.uk/depts/ec/web/papers.

Lederer, Edith. 2001. "World Leaders will Craft Plan to Fight Aids." *Buffalo News.* June 24:A10.

Lee, Henry C. and Frank Tirandy. 2003. *Blood Evidence.* Cambridge, MA: Perseus.

Lee, Jean. 2001. "Africa, Asia to Lead Population Boom despite Aids' Toll." *Buffalo News.* February 28:A3.

Leisner, Pat. 2000. "Orphaned Crane Flock Migrates, Led by Pilot." *Buffalo News.* November 12:A14.

Lemert, Charles. 1997. *Postmodernism is Not What You Think.* Malden, MA: Blackwell

Lemert, Charles C. and Garth Gillan. 1982. *Michel Foucault: Social Theory and Transgression.* New York: Columbia University Press.

Lenski, Gerhard. 1966. *Power and Privilege: A Theory of Social Stratification.* New York: McGraw-Hill.

———. 1970. *Human Societies: An Introduction to Macrosociology.* New York: McGraw-Hill.

———. 1994. "Societal Taxonomies: Mapping the Social Universe," *Annual Review of Sociology.* 20:23.

Lenski, Gerhard, Patrick Nolan, and Jean Lenski. 1995. *Human Societies: An Introduction to Macrosociology,* 7th edition. New York: McGraw-Hill.

Levin, William C. 1991. *Sociological Ideas,* 3rd ed. Belmont, CA: Wadsworth.

Levi-Strauss, Claude. 1967. *Structural Anthropology,* translated by Clarie Jacobsen and Brooke Grundfest Schoepf. Garden City, NY: Anchor Books.

Lewontin, R.C. 1977. "Biological Determinism as a Social Weapon." In Ann Arbor Science for the People Editorial Collective, *Biology as a Weapon.* Minneapolis, MN: Burgess.

———. R.C. 1982. *Human Diversity.* New York: Scientific American Library.

Levine, Donald. 1971. *Georg Simmel.* Chicago: University of Chicago Press.

Levine, Michael. 1988. "The Trash Mess Won't be Easily Disposed of." *Wall Street Journal.* December 15:14.

Lindersmith, Alfred R., Anselm L. Strauss, and Norman K. Denzin. 1991. *Social Psychology,* 7th edition. Englewood Cliffs, NJ: Prentice Hall.

Lindsey, Linda L. and Stephen Beach. 2003. *Essentials of Sociology.* Upper Saddle River, NJ: Prentice Hall.

———. 2004. *Sociology.* Upper Saddle River, NJ: Prentice Hall.

Lipshires, Sidney. 1974. *Herbert Marcuse: From Marx to Freud and Beyond.* Cambridge, MA: Schenkman.

Livingston, Eric. 1986. *The Ethnomethodological Foundations of Mathematics.* London: Routledge and Kegan Paul.

Locke, John. 1967. *Two Treatises of Government: A Critical Edition,* introduction by Peter Laslett.

Loeb, Michel. 1986. *Noise and Human Efficiency.* New York: Wiley & Sons.

Long, Robert Emmett. 1989. *The Promise of Water Disposal.* New York: H.W. Wilson.

Lopreato, Joseph. 1967. "Class Conflict and Images of Society." *The Journal of Conflict Resolution.* 11 (3):281–293.

Los Angeles Times. 1998. "A Wife's Role is 'To Submit,' Baptists Declare." June 10:A1.

Luft, Sebastian. 1998. "Husserl's Phenomenological Discovery of the Natural Attitude." *Continental Philosophy Review*, 31: 153–170.

Luhmann, Niklas. 1983. "Insistence on Systems Theory: Perspectives From Germany—An Essay." *Social Forces*. 61 (June):987–996.

———. 1984. "The Self-Description of Society: Crisis Fashion and Sociological Theory." *International Journal of Comparative Sociology*. 25 (Jan/Apr):59–72.

Lukacs, Georg. 1923. *History and Class Consciousness*. Berlin: Malik Verlag.

Lumsden, Charles J. and Edward O. Wilson. 1981. *Genes, Mind and Culture*. Cambridge, MA: Harvard University Press.

Lynch, Marika. 2000. "Jewfish now Extinct—The Name, not the Grouper." *Syracuse Post Standard*.

Lynch, Michael. 1985. *Art and Artifact in Laboratory Science: A Study of Shop Work and Shop Talk in a Laboratory*. London: Routledge and Kegan Paul.

Lyotard, Jean-Francois. 1979. *The Postmodern Condition: A Report on Knowledge*. Minneapolis:University of Minnesota Press.

———. 1992. "Mainmise." *Philosophy Today*. (Winter):419–427.

———. 1993. *The Postmodern Explained*. Minneapolis: University of Minnesota Press.

———. 1999 [1984]. *The Postmodern Condition: A Report on Knowledge*. Minneapolis: University of Minnesota Press.

Lyotard, Jean-Francois and Gilbert Larochelle. 1992. "That Which Resists, After All." *Philosophy Today*. (Winter): 402–414.

Machalek, Richard. 1992. "Why are Large Societies Rare?" *Advances in Human Ecology*. 1:33–64.

MacIntyre, Alasdair. 1970a. *Herbert Marcuse*. New York: Viking.

———. 1970b. *Marcuse*. Bungay, Suffolk, Great Britain: Fontana.

Mackinnon, Catherine A. 1982. "Feminism, Marxism, Method and the State: An Agenda for Theory." *Signs*. 7:515–544.

———. 1983. "Feminism, Marxism, Method and the State: Toward Feminist Jurisprudence." *Signs*. 8:635–58.

Madison, Gary and Marty Fairbairn, editors. 1999. *The Ethics of Postmodernity*. Evanston, IL: Northwestern University Press.

Malinowski, Bronislaw. 1926. *Crime and Custom in Savage Society*. London: Routledge and Kegan Paul.

Malnic, Eric and Tom Gorman. 2000. "Agency to Buy Desert Dumps for L.A. Trash." *Los Angeles Times*. August 10:B5.

Malthus, Thomas. 1798. *An Essay on the Principle of Population*. London.

Mannheim, Karl. 1936. *Ideology and Utopia*. New York: Harcourt, Brace and Company.

Manning, Philip. 1992. *Erving Goffman and Modern Sociology*. Sanford, CA: Stanford University Press.

Marcuse, Herbert. 1960. "Activity of Dialectic." *Diogenes*. 31:80–88.

———. 1964. *One-Dimensional Man*. Boston: Beacon Press.

———. 1966. *Eros and Civilization*. Boston: Beacon Press.

———. 1968a. *Negations*. Boston: Beacon Press.

———. 1968b. "Re-examination of the Concept of Revolution." *Diogenes*. 64:17–26.

———. 1969. *Essay of Liberation*. Boston: Beacon Press.

———. 1972. *Studies in Critical Philosophy*. Boston: Beacon Press.

———. 1989. "Philosophy and Critical Theory," pp. 58–74 in *Critical Theory and Society*, edited with an Introduction by Stephen Eric Bronner and Douglas Kellner. New York: Routledge.

———. 1998. *Technology, War and Fascism*. New York: Routledge.

Markula, Pirkko. 2003. "The Technologies of the Self: Sport, Feminism, and Foucault." *Sociology of Sport Journal*. 20 (2):87–107.

Martin, Bill. 1992. *Matrix and Line*. Albany: State University of New York Press.

Martindale, Don. 1988. *The Nature and Types of Sociological Theory*. Prospect Heights, IL: Waveland Press.

Martinich, Aloysius. 1999. *Hobbes a Biography*. New York: Cambridge University Press.

Marx, Karl. 1964. *The Economic & Philosophic Manuscripts of 1844*, edited by Dirk Strunk. New York: International Publishers.

———. 1932 [1848]. *The Communist Manifesto*. New York: International Publishers.

———. 1906 [1867]. *Das Kapital*. New York: Modern Library.

Marx, Karl and Friedrich Engels. 1970 [1845–46]. *The German Ideology, Part 1*, edited by Robert Tucker. New York: Norton & Company.

———. 1978. "Manifesto of the Communist Party," pp. 469–500 in *The Marx-Engels Reader*, edited by Robert Tucker. New York: Norton & Company.

Maryanski, Alexandra and Jonathan H. Turner. 1991. "The Offspring of Functionalism: French and British Structuralism." *Sociological Theory*. 9 (1):106–115.

Maslow, A.H. 1936. "The Role of Dominance in the Social and Sexual Behavior of Infra-human Primates: IV, the Determination of Hierarchy in Pairs and in A Group." *Journal of Genetic Psychology*, 49(1):161–198.

McCarthy, Thomas. 1979. *The Critical Theory of Jurgen Habermas*. Cambridge, MA: MIT Press.

McConnaughey, Janet. 1998. "Initially Biased." *Los Angeles Times*. March 28:A10.

McCormick, Peter and Frederick A. Elliston, editors. 1981. *Husserl: Shorter Works*. Notre Dame, IN: Notre Dame University Press.

McKinnell, Robert G. 1985. *Cloning of Frogs, Mice and Other Animals*. Minneapolis, MN: University of Minnesota Press.

McLellan, David. 1969. *The Young Hegelians and Karl Marx*. New York: Macmillan.

———. 1987. *Marxism and Religion*. New York: Harper and Row.

———. 1990. *Karl Marx: Selected Writings*. Oxford: Oxford Press.

McPhail, Clark and Cynthia Rexroat. 1979. "Mead vs. Blumer: The Divergent Methodological Perspectives of Social Behaviorism and Symbolic Interaction." *American Sociological Review*. 44 (3):449–467.

Mead, George Herbert. 1934. *Mind, Self, & Society*, edited and with an introduction by Charles W. Morris. Chicago: University of Chicago Press.

———. 1936. *Movements of Thought in the Nineteenth Century*. Chicago: University of Chicago Press.

———. 1938. *The Philosophy of the Act.* Chicago: University of Chicago Press.

———. 1959. *The Philosophy of the Present.* LaSalle, IL: Open Court.

———. 1964. *Selected Writings,* edited by Andrew Reck. Indianapolis, IN: Bobbs-Merrill.

———. 1982. *The Individual and the Social Self: Unpublished Work of George Herbert Mead.* Chicago: University of Chicago Press.

Mendelson, Jack H. and Nancy Mello. 1985. *Alcohol Use and Abuse in America.* Boston: Little Brown.

Merton, Robert K. 1938. "Social Structure and Anomie." *American Sociological Review.* 3:672–682.

———. 1968 [1949]. *Social Theory and Social Structure.* New York: Free Press.

———. 1957a. "Priorities in Scientific Discovery: A Chapter in the Sociology of Science." *American Sociological Review.* 22 (6):635–659.

———. 1957b. "The Role Set: Problems in Sociological Theory." *British Journal of Sociology.* 2:106–120.

———. 1957c. "Social Structure and Anomie." *American Sociological Review.* 22 (6):672–682.

———. 1959. "Social Conformity Deviation and Opportunity—Structure." *American Sociological Review.* 24: 177–189.

———. 1987. "The Focused Interview and Focus Groups: Continuities and Discontinuities." *Public Opinion Quarterly.* 51 (4):550–565.

———. 1996 [1994]. "A Life of Learning," pp. 339–359 in *Robert K. Merton: On Social Structure and Science,* edited by Piotr Sztompka. Chicago: University Press.

———. 1995. "The Thomas Theorem and the Matthew Effect." *Social Forces* 74 (2):379–424.

———. 1997. "On the Evolving Synthesis of Differential Association and Anomie Theory: A Perspective from the Sociology of Science." *Criminology.* 35 (3):517–523.

Merton, Robert K., Alisa P. Gray, Barbara Hockey, and Hanan C. Selvin, editors. 1952. *Reader in Bureaucracy.* New York: Free Press.

Meyer, Lois. 1985. *Making a Scene: Probing the Structure of Language in Sibling Interaction.* Unpublished manuscript. University of California, Berkeley.

———. 1988. "It was No Trouble: Achieving Communicative Competence in a Second Language," pp. 195–221 in *Developing Communicative Competence in a Second Language,* edited by Robin Scarcella, Elain Anderson and Stephen Krashin. New York: Newbury House.

Michelmore, Bill. 2000. "Cataracts Big Suicide Lure." *Buffalo News.* May 1:A1.

Michener, H. Andrew, John D. DeLamater, and Sharon H. Schwartz. 1986. *Social Psychology.* San Diego: Harcourt Brace Jovanovich.

Miller, David. 1973. *George Herbert Mead; Self, Language, and the World.* Austin: University of Texas Press.

Miller, James. 1993. *The Passion of Michel Foucault.* New York: Anchor.

Mills, C. Wright. 1940. "Situated Actions and Vocabularies of Motive." *American Sociological Review.* 5 (6):904–913.

———. 1943. "The Professional Ideology of Social Pathologists." *American Journal of Sociology.* 49 (2):165–180.

———. 1946. "The Middle Classes in Middle-Sized Cities: The Stratification and Political Position of Small Business and White Collar Strata." *American Sociological Review.* 11 (5):520–529.

———. 1948. *The New Men of Power.* New York: Harcourt, Brace and Jovanovich.

———. 1951. *White Collar.* New York: Oxford University Press.

———. 1956. *The Power Elite.* New York: Oxford University Press.

———. 1958. *The Causes of World War Three.* New York: Simon & Schuster.

———. 1958. "The Structure of Power in American Society." *British Journal of Sociology.* 9(1):29–41.

———. 1959. *The Sociological Imagination.* New York: Oxford University Press.

———. 1962. *The Marxists.* New York: Dell.

———. 2002. "The Promise," pp. 1–7 in *Mapping the Social Landscape,* edited by Susan J. Ferguson. Boston: McGraw Hill.

Mitcheil, J. Clyde. 1974. "Social Networks." *Annual Review of Anthropology.* 3:279–99.

Mokhiber, Russell and Leonard Shen. 1981. "Love Canal," pp. 268–310 in *Who's Poisoning America: Corporate Polluters and Their Victims in the Chemical Age,* edited by Ralph Nader, Ronald Brownstein, and John Richards. San Francisco: Sierra Club.

Molm, Linda and Karen Cook. 1995. "Social Exchange and Exchange Networks," pp. 209–235 in *Sociological Perspectives in Social Psychology,* edited by K.S. Cook, G.A. Fine, and J. House. Boston: Allyn and Bacon.

Mommsen, Wolgang and Jurge Osterhammel, editors. 1987. *Max Weber and His Contemporaries.* Boston: Allen & Unwin.

Moritsugu, Ken. 2000. "China Denied Loan by the World Bank." *Philadelphia Inquirer.* July 8:A4.

Morrow, Raymond A. with David D. Brown. 1994. *Critical Theory and Methodology.* Thousand Oaks, CA: Sage.

Moya, Paula M.L. 2001. "Chicana Feminism and Post Modernist Theory." *Signs.* 26 (2):441–483.

Mueller-Vollmer, Kurt, editor. 2000. *The Hermeneutics Reader.* New York: Continuum.

National Criminal Justice Reference Service. 2004. "Hate Crime Resources – Facts and Figures." Available: www.ncjrs.org/hate_crimes/facts.

National Institute on Alcohol and Alcoholism. 1992. "Alcohol Alert; The Genetics of Alcoholism." July 18:357.

Natural Connections. 2002. "Edward O. Wilson Profile." Available: dnr.metroke.gov/swd/naturalconnetions/edward_wilson_bio

Neuhas, Richard J., editor. 1986. *Confession, Conflict and Community.* Grand Rapids, MI: William B. Eerdmans.

New Scientist. 2001. "Water Wars." May 19:3.

Nicholson, Carol. 1989. "Postmodernism, Feminism, and Education: The Need for Solidarity." *Educational Theory.* 39 (3):197–205.

Nicolaus, Martin. 1973. *Grundrisse: Foundations of the Critique of Political Economy,* translated by Martin Nicolaus. New York: Vintage.

Nisbet, Robert. 1965. *Emile Durkheim.* Englewood Cliffs, NJ: Prentice-Hall.

———. 1969. *Social Change and History.* New York: Oxford University Press.

Norris, Christopher. 1990. *What's Wrong with Postmodernism.* Baltimore: Johns Hopkins University Press.

———. 1993. *The Truth About Postmodernism*. Cambridge, MA: Blackwell.

Ober, John David. 1970. "On Sexuality and Politics in the Work of Herbert Marcuse," pp. 101–135 in *Critical Interruptions*, edited by Paul Breines. New York: Herder and Herder.

Off-line Productions. 1997. "Interview transcripts of George Ritzer." Available: www.spanner.org/mclibel/interviews/ritzer_George.html.

Onwudiwe, Ihekwoaba D. 2002. "Terrorism," pp.1614–1624, in *Encyclopedia of Crime & Punishment*, Vol. 3. Thousand Oaks, CA:Sage.

O'Reilly, Brian. 1992. "Looking Ahead: Jobs are Fast Moving Abroad." *Fortune*. December 19:52–66.

Palmer, Richard E. 1969. *Hermeneutics*. Evanston, IL: Northwestern University Press.

Pampel, Fred. 2000. *Sociological Lines and Ideas*. New York: Worth.

Pan, Philip and John Pomfret. 2001. "Beijing's Joy is Olympic." *Washington Post*. July 14:A1.

Pangman, Julie K. 1995. *Guide to Environmental Issues*.

Parsons, Talcott. 1942. "Some Sociological Aspects of the fascist Movements." *Social Forces*, 21:138–147.

———. 1949 [1937]. *The Structure of Social Action*. Glencoe, IL: Dorsey Press.

———. 1951. *The Social System*. Glencoe, IL: Free Press.

———. 1954. *Essays in Sociological Thought*. Glencoe, IL: Free Press.

———. 1956a. "A Sociological Approach to the Theory of Organizations I." *Administrative Science Quarterly*. June: 63–85.

———. 1956b. "A Sociological Approach to the Theory of Organizations II." *Administrative Science Quarterly*. Sept: 225–239.

———. 1965 [1960]. *Structure and Process in Modern Societies*. New York: Free Press.

———. 1964. *Social Structure and Personality*. New York: Free Press.

———. 1966. *Societies*. Englewood Cliffs, NJ: Prentice Hall.

———. 1969. *Politics and Social Structure*. New York: Free Press.

———. 1971. *The System of Modern Sociology*. Englewood Cliffs, NJ: Prentice Hall.

Parsons, Talcott and Robert Bales. 1955. *Family, Socialization and Interaction*. Glencoe, IL: Free Press.

Parsons, Talcott, Robert F. Bales and Edward A. Shils. 1953. *Working Papers in the Theory of Action*. Glencoe, IL: The Free Press.

Parsons, Talcott and Gerald Platt. 1973. *The American University*. Cambridge, Mass: Harvard University Press.

Parsons, Talcott and Neil Smelser. 1956. *Economy and Society*. New York: Free Press.

Patterson, Orlando. 2002. "The Last Sociologist." *New York Times*. May 19:15.

Paul, Bill. 1986. "Congregation is Rapidly Coming of Age." *Wall Street Journal*. March 2:6.

Pearce, Fred. 2001. "Iraqi Wetlands Face Total Destruction." *New Scientist*. May 19:4.

Pettas, William and Steven L. Gilliland. 1992. "Conflict in the Large Academic Library: Friend or Foe?" *Journal of Academic Librarianship*. 18 (1):24–29.

Pfuetze, Paul. 1961. *Self, Society and Existence: Human Nature and Dialogue in the Thoughts of George Herbert Mead and Martin Buber*. New York: Harper Torch Books.

Philips, John. 2000. *Contested Knowledge: A Guide to Critical Theory*. New York: Zed Books.

Pogatchnik, Shawn. 2002. "Northern Ireland's Children Taught to Hate at an Early Age, Study Finds." *Buffalo News*. June 25.

Pope, Stephen. 2001. "Engaging E.O. Wilson: Twenty-Five Years of Sociobiology," *Zygon*. 36 (2):233–240.

Popkewitz, Thomas and Lynn Fendler, editors. 1999. *Critical Theories in Education*. New York: Routledge.

Pressler, Charles and Fabio Dasilua. 1996. *Sociology and Interpretation: From Weber to Habermas*. Albany: State University of New York Press.

Pugh, Tony. 2001. "Mixed Marriages increase in U.S., Indicating Crumbling of Racial Walls." *Buffalo News*. March 25:A5.

Pyle, Richard. 2000. "Webster's Stays 'Edgy' with New Additions." *Buffalo News*. June 26:A7.

Rainey, James. 1996. "A Change in Behavior Sought." *Los Angeles Times*. July 17:B1.

Randall, Vicky. 1991. "Feminism and Political Analysis." *Political Studies*. 39:513–532.

Rasmussen, David M. 1990. *Reading Habermas*. Cambridge, MA: Blackwell.

Reck, Andrew. 1964. *Selective Writings; George Herbert Mead*. Chicago: University of Chicago Press.

Reynolds, Larry. 1990. *Interactionism; Exposition and Critique*, 2nd ed. Dix Hills, NY: General Hall.

Reynolds, Larry. 1993. *Interactionism: Exposition and Critique*, 3rd ed. Dix Hills, NY: General Hall.

Rich, Adrienne. 1976. *Of Women Born: Motherhood as Experience and Institution*. Cambridge, MA: Harvard University Press.

Riesman, David. 2001 [1950]. *The Lonely Crowd*. New Haven, CT: Yale University Press.

———. 1951. "Some Observation of Social Science Research." *Antioch Review*. S51(11):259–278.

———. 1955. *Individualism Reconsidered*. New York: Doubleday.

———. 1956. *Constraint and Variety in American Education*. Lincoln: University of Nebraska Press.

———. 1980. *On Higher Education*. San Francisco: Jossey-Bass.

Riesman, David, with Nathan Glazer. 1952. *Faces in the Crowd*. New Haven, CT: Yale University Press.

Riesman, David and Verne A. Stadtman, editors. 1973. *Academic Transformation*. New York; McGraw Hill.

Riley, Alexander Tristan. 2002. "Durkheim Contra Bergson? The Hidden Roots of Postmodern Theory and the Postmodern Return of the Sacred." *Sociological Perspectives*. 45(3):243–265.

Risman, Barbara. 1986. "Can Men 'Mother'?: Life as a Single Father." *Family Relations*. 35:95–102.

———. 1988. "Just the Two of Us: Parent-Child Relationships in Single-Parent Homes." *Journal of Marriage and the Family*. 50:1049–1062.

———. 1998. *Gender Vertigo: American Families in Transition*. New Haven, CT: Yale University Press.

Ritzer, George. 1968. *Commitment, Professionalism, and Role Conflict Resolution*. Ann Arbor, MI: University Microfilms.

———. 1969. "An Empirical Study of Howard Becker's Side-Bet Theory." *Social Forces*. 47 (4):475–478.

———. 1970. "On the Problem of Classifying Commitment Theory." *Social Forces*. 48 (4):530–533.

———. 1972. *Man and His Work: Conflict and Change.* New York: Appleton-Century-Crofts.

———. 1975. "Professionalization, Bureaucratization and Rationalization; The Views of Max Weber." *Social Forces.* 53 (4): 627–634.

———. 1981a. "The Failure to Integrate Theory and Practice: The Case of the Sociological Work." *Journal of Applied Behavioral Science.* July/August/September:376–380.

———. 1981b. "Paradigm Analysis in Sociology: Clarifying the Issues." *American Sociological Review.* 46 (2): 245–248.

———. 1983. "The McDonaldization of Society. " *Journal of American Culture.* 6:100–107.

———. 1985. "The Rise of Micro-Sociological Theory." *Sociological Theory.* 3 (11):88–98.

———. 1988a. *Contemporary Sociological Theory*, 2nd edition. New York: Knopf.

———. 1988b. "Sociological Metatheory: A Defense of a Subfield by a Delineation of its Parameters." *Sociological Theory.* 6 (2):187–200.

———. 1989. "Sociology of Work: A Metatheorectical Analysis." *Social Forces.* 67 (3):593–604.

———. (editor) 1992. *Metatheorizing.* Newbury Park, CA: Sage.

———. 1993. *The McDonaldization of Society.* Newbury Park, CA: Pine Forge Press.

———. 1994. *Sociological Beginnings: On the Origins of Key Ideas in Sociology.* New York: McGraw-Hill.

———. 1996. *The McDonaldization of Society*, 2nd edition. Thousand Oaks, CA: Pine Forge Press.

———. 1999. *Enchanting a Disenchanted World: Revolutionizing the Means of Consumption.* Thousand Oaks, CA: Pine Forge Press.

———. 2000a. *Classical Sociological Theory*, 3rd edition. Boston: McGraw Hill.

———. 2000b. *The McDonaldization of Society.* Thousand Oaks, CA: Pine Forge Press.

———. 2000c. *Modern Sociological Theory*, 5th edition. Boston: McGraw Hill.

———. 2000d. *Sociological Theory*, 5th edition. Boston: McGraw Hill.

———. 2001a. "The 'New' Means of Consumption.," pp. 337–359, in *Illuminating Social Life*, edited by Peter Kivisto. Thousand Oaks, CA: Pine Forge Press.

———. 2001b. "The Weberian Theory of Rationalization and the McDonaldization of Contemporary Society, "pp. 47–71 in *Illuminating Social Life 2nd ed*, edited by Peter Kivisto. Thousand Oaks, CA: Pine Forge.

———. 2001c. "Ways to Cope with McDonaldization." Available: www.umd.edu.

———. 2002a. "Cathedrals of Consumption," pp. 162–170 in *McDonaldization: The Reader*, edited by George Ritzer. Thousand Oaks, CA: Pine Forge Press.

———. 2002b. "Credit Cards, Fast-Food Restaurants, and Rationalization," pp. 178–184 in *McDonaldizaion: The Reader*, edited by George Ritzer. Thousand Oaks, CA: Pine Forge Press.

———. 2002c. "McJobs: McDonaldization and its Relationship to the Labor Process," pp. 141–147 in *McDonaldizaion: The Reader*, edited by George Ritzer. Thousand Oaks, CA: Pine Forge Press.

———. 2003. *Contemporary Sociological Theory and Its Classical Roots.* Boston: McGraw Hill.

Ritzer, George and Richard Bell. 1981. "Emile Durkheim: Exemplar for an Integrated Sociological Paradigm?" *Social Forces.* 59 (4):966–995.

Ritzer, George and David Walczak. 1988. "Rationalization and the Deprofessionalization of Physicians." *Social Forces.* 67 (1):1–22.

Roan, Sharon L. 1989. *Ozone Crisis.* New York: Wiley.

Robillard, Albert B. and Christopher Pack. 1976–1982. Research and didactic videotapes, occasional papers, in-house memoranda, tape and video recorded rounds and medical and clinic conferences, and lectures. Department of Human Development, Michigan State University.

Robinson, Paul A. 1969. *The Freudian Left.* New York: Harper & Row.

Rockmore, Tom. 1989. *Habermas on Historical Materialism.* Bloomington: Indiana University Press.

Rogers, Keith. 1994. "U.S. Ignored Warning on Nuke Testing." *Las Vegas Review Journal.* February 6:1A.

Rogers, Mary F. 1983. *Sociology, Ethnomethodology, and Experience.* New York: Cambridge University Press.

Rohter, Larry. 2001. "Brazilians Stunned by Energy Rationing." *Moscow Times.* June 7:11.

Rosemond, John. 2000. "Self-Esteem Overrated." *Buffalo News.* June 26:A10.

Rosenblum, Mort. 2001. "Mideast Drought Adds to Political Pressures." *Buffalo News.* July 8:A4.

Ross, Emma. 2002. "Husbands, Too, May Be Suffering, Study Suggests." *Buffalo News.* October 5:A2.

Rousseau, Jean-Jacques. 1973. *The Social Contract and Discourses*, edited by G.D.H. Cole. New York: Dutton.

Ruane, Joseph and Jennifer Todd. 1988. "The Application of Critical Theory." *Political Studies.* 36:533–538.

Ryan, John and William Wentworth. 1999. *Media and Society.* Boston: Allyn and Bacon.

Saint-Simon, Claude-Henri. 1807. *Introduction to the Scientific Studies of the 19th Century.* Paris.

———. 1813. *Essays on the Science of Man.* Paris.

Saltonstall, Dave. 2000. "Lacking Spanish-Speaking Operators, New York Contracts Out 911 Calls." *New York Daily News.* July 3:12.

Scheffler, Israel. 1974. *Four Pragmatists: A Critical Introduction to Pierce, James, Mead, and Dewey.* New York: Humanities Press.

Schegloff, Emmanuel. 1979. "Identification and Recognition in Telephone Conversation Openings, pp. 23–78 in *Language: Studies in Ethnomethodology*, edited by G. Psathas. New York: Irvington.

Schmid, Randolph. 2000. "Federal Agency Warns of Erosion Threat." *Indianapolis Star.* June 28:A3.

Schrag, Calvin O. 1997. *The Self After Postmodernity.* New Haven CT: Yale University Press.

Schuckit, Marc. 1984. *Drug and Alcohol Abuse; A Clinical Guide to Diagnosis and Treatment*, 2nd ed. New York: Plenum Press.

Schutz, Alfred. 1962. *Collected Papers.* The Hague: Marinus Nijhoff.

———. 1967. *The Phenomenology of the Social World*, introduction by George Walsh. Evanston, IL: Northwestern University Press.

Schutz, Alfred and Thomas Luckmann. 1973. *The Structures of the Life-World*, translated by Richard M. Zaner and H. Tristram Engelhardt, Jr. Evanston, IL: Northwestern University Press.

Scientific American. 1974. *Ecology, Evolution, and Population Biology,* introduction by Edward O. Wilson. San Francisco, CA: Freeman.

Scimecca, Joseph. A. 1997. *The Sociological Theory of C. Wright Mills.* Port Washington, NY: Kennikat.

Seidman, Steven 1991. "The End of Sociological Theory: The Postmodern Hope." *Sociological Theory.* 9(2):132–146.

———. 1991 [1983]. *Liberalism and the Origins of European Social Theory.* Los Angeles: Norton.

Seligman, Linda. 2001. *Systems, Strategies, and Skills of Counseling and Psychology Therapy.* Upper Saddle River: Prentice Hall.

Shalin, Dmitri. 1986. "Pragmatism and Social Interactionism." *American Sociological Review.* 51:9–29.

———. 1991. "The Pragmatic Origins of Symbolic Interactionism and the Crisis of Classical Science." *Studies in Symbolic Interaction.* 12:223–251.

———. 1993. "Modernity, Postmodernity, and Pragmatist Inquiry: An Introduction." *Symbolic Interaction.* 16 (4):-303–332.

Sheehan, Thomas. 1981. "Husserl's Critique of Psychologism," pp.143–145 in *Husserl: Shorter Works,* edited by Peter McCormick and Fredrick A. Elliston. South Bend, IN: University of Notre Dame Press.

Shribman, David. 1989. "Even After 10 Years, Victims of Love Canal Can't Quite Escape it." *Wall Street Journal.* March: A1.

Shumway, David. 1989. *Michel Foucault.* Boston: Twayne.

Sichuan, Lucy A. 1985. *Plans and Situated Actions: The Problem of Human-Machine Communication.* Palo Alto, CA: Xerox Palo Alto Research Center.

Simmel, Georg. 1897–1899. "The Persistence of the Social Group." *American Journal of Sociology,* 3(5):662–698.

———. 1900. *Philosophie des Geldes.* Leipzig: Duncker und Humblot.

———. 1950. *The Sociology of Georg Simmel: Early Essays,* translated by Kurt H. Wolff. Glencoe, IL.: Free Press.

———. 1956 [1908]. "Conflict" in *Conflict and the Web of Group Affiliation* translated by Kurt H. Wolff, New York: Free Press.

———. 1971 [1908]. "The Poor," pp. 150–178 in *Georg Simmel,* edited by D. Levine. Chicago: Chicago Press.

Simpson, Ida Harper. 1989. "Sociology of Work: Where Have the Workers Gone?" *Social Forces.* 67:563–81.

Singer, Sam. 1995. *Human Genetic.* Freeman.

Singleman, Peter. 1992. "Exchange as Symbolic Interaction: Convergence Between two Theoretical Perspectives." *American Sociological Review.* 37:414–424.

Skvoretz, John David Willer and Thomas J. Fararo. 1993. "Toward Models of Power Development in Exchange Networks." *Sociological Perspectives.* 36 (2):95–115.

Smelser, Neil J. 1966. *Social Structure and Mobility in Economic Development.* Chicago: Aldine.

———. 1998. "The Rational and the Ambivalent in Social Sciences." *American Sociological Review.* 63 (1):6.

Smith, Dorothy. 1974. "Women's Perspective as a Radical Critique of Sociology." *Sociological Inquiry.* 44:7–13.

———. 1975. "An Analysis of Ideological Structures and How Women are Excluded: Consideration for Academic Women." *Canadian Review of Sociology and Anthropology.* 12:353–369.

———. 1979. "A Sociology for Women," in *The Prism of Sex: Essays in the Sociology of Knowledge,* edited by J.A.

Sherman and E.T. Beck. Madison: University of Wisconsin Press.

———. 1987. *The Everyday World as Problematic: A Feminist Sociology.* Boston: Northeastern University Press.

———. 1990. *The Conceptual Practices of Power: A Feminist Sociology of Knowledge.* Boston, Northeastern University Press.

———. 1993. "The Standard North American Family." *Journal of Family Issue.* 14 (5):50–65.

———. 1997. "Comment of Hekman's Truth and Method: Feminist Standpoint Theory Revisited." *Signs.* 22(2): 393–398.

———. 2000. "Schooling for Inequality." *Signs.* 25 (4): 1147–1151.

Smith, Steven B. 1987. "Hegel's Idea of a Critical theory." *Political Theory.* 15 (1):99–126.

Spencer, Herbert. 1851. *Social Statics.* London: Chapman.

———. 1860. *The Social Organism.* London: Greenwood.

———. 1864. *The Principles of Biology.* New York: Appleton.

———. 1896. *The Study of Sociology.* New York: Appleton.

———. 1898. *Principles of Sociology.* New York: Appleton.

Spotts, Peter N. 2002. "Stem Cell Advances Stoke Debate on Cloning." *Christian Science Monitor.* June 2 USA Section:02.

Spykman, Nicholas. 1965. *The Social Theory of Georg Simmel.* New York: Atherton.

Starr, Mark. 1985. "American's Toxic Tremors." *Newsweek.* August 26:100–106.

Startseva, Alla. 2001. "Gosstroi Looks to France for Water." *Moscow Times.* June 7:3.

Stein, Jill Marie. 1997. "Re: Harold Garfinkel." Email correspondence available: http://csf.colorado.edu./mail/-socgrad/May97/0077.

Sternberg, Steve. 2001. "Human Genome Makes Mind-boggling Reading." *USA Today.* February 12:1D, 2D.

Stone, Gregory P. 1962. "Appearance and the Self," pp.86–118 in *Human Behavior and Social Processes,* edited by Arnold Rose. Boston: Houghton Mifflin.

Stone, Gregory P. and Harvey A. Farberman. 1970. *Social Psychology Through Symbolic Interaction.* Waltham, MA: Ginn-Blaisdell.

Strauss, Anslem. 1956. *The Social Psychology of George Herbert Mead.* Chicago: University Press.

———. 1964. *George Herbert Mead on Social Psychology: Selected Papers.* Chicago: University of Chicago Press.

Strydom, Piet. 2001. "The Problem of Triple Contingency in Habermas." *Sociological Theory.* 19 (2):165–186.

Stryker, Sheldon. 1987. "The Vitalization of Symbolic Interactionism." *Social Psychology Quarterly.* 50 (1):83–94.

Sullivan, Jerry. 2001. "Chinese People Describe the Games." *Buffalo News.* July 15:B1.

Sundow, David. 1978. *Ways of the Hand.* Cambridge, MA: Harvard University Press.

Takahashi, Nobuyuki. 2000. "The Emergence of Generalized Exchange." *American Journal of Sociology.* 105: 1105–1134.

Taylor, Jill McLean, Carol Gilligan and Amy M. Sullivan. 1995. *Between Voice and Silence.* Cambridge, MA: Harvard University Press.

Temple-Raston, Dina and George Hager. 2000. "Global Leaders Acknowledge Need for Change." *USA Today.* April 17:4A.

Thayer, H.S. 1968. *Meaning and Action: A Critical History of Pragmatism.* New York: Bobbs-Merrill.

The Annie E. Casey Foundation. 2004. "Percent of Children in Poverty." Available: www.aecf.org/kidscount.

Thibaut, John and Harold Kelley. 1959. *The Social Psychology of Groups.* New York: Wiley.

Thompson, Kenneth. 1979. *Ethics, Functionalism and Power in International Politics.* Baton Rouge, LA: Louisiana University Press.

Thomson, Garret. 1993. *Descartes to Kant.* Prospect Heights, IL: Waveland Press.

Thorpe, Jacqueline. 2001. "Argentine Crisis Spreads." *Financial Post.* July 12:C1.

Tilman, Rick. 1984. *C. Wright Mills: A Native Radical and His American Intellectual Roots.* University Park: Pennsylvania State University Press.

Tong, Rosemarie. 1989. *Feminist Thought.* Boulder, CO: Westview Press.

Trevino, A. Javier. 2001. *Talcott Parsons Today.* New York: Bowman & Littlefield.

Trivers, R.L. 1971. "The Evolution of Reciprocal Altruism." *Quarterly Review of Biology.* 46(4):35–57.

Tuaolo, Esera. 2002. "Free and Clear." *ESPN The Magazine.* November 11:72–77.

Tucker, Robert C., editor. 1978. *The Marx-Engels Reader*, 2nd edition. New York: W.W. Norton & Company.

Turnbull, Linda, Elaine Hendrix and Borden Dent. 2001. *Atlas of Crime.* Phoenix: Oryx Press.

Turner, Jonathan H. 1970. "Entrepreneurial Environments and the Emergence of Achievement Motivation in Adolescent Males." *Sociometry.* 33 (2):147–165.

———. 1972a. *American Society: Problems of Structure*, 2nd edition. New York: Harper & Row.

———. 1972b. *Patterns of Social Organization: A Survey of Social Institutions.* New York: McGraw-Hill.

———. 1973. "From Utopia to Where?: A Strategy for Reformulating the Dahrendorf Conflict Model." *Social Forces.* 52 (2) :236–244.

———. 1974. *The Structure of Sociological Theory.* Homewood, IL: Dorsey Press.

———. 1975. "A Strategy for Reformulating the Dialectical and Functional Theories of Conflict." *Social Forces.* 53 (3):433–444.

———. 1976. "Marx and Simmel Revisited: Reassessing the Foundations of Conflict Theory." *Social Forces.* 53 (4): 618–627.

———. 1977. *Social Problems in America.* New York: Harper & Row.

———. 1982 [1978]. *The Structure of Sociological Theory*, 2nd edition. Homewood, IL: Dorsey Press.

———. 1984 *Societal Stratification; A Theoretical Analysis.* New York: Columbia University Press.

———. 1985a. "In Defense of Positivism." *Sociological Theory.* 3:24–30.

———. 1985b. *Herbert Spencer: A Renewed Appreciation.* Beverly Hills, CA: Sage.

———. 1986a. "The Mechanics of Social Interaction: Toward a Composite Model of Signaling and Interpreting." *Sociological Theory.* 4 (1):95–105.

———. 1986b. *The Structure of Sociological Theory*, 4th ed. Chicago: Dorsey Press.

———. 1986c. "Toward a Unified Theory of Ethnic Antagonism: A Preliminary Synthesis of Three Macro Models." *Sociological Forum.* 1 (3):403–427.

———. 1987a. *Social Theory Today.* Stanford, CA: Stanford University Press.

———. 1987b. "Toward a Sociological Theory of Motivation." *American Sociological Review.* 52 (February): 15–27.

———. 1988. *A Theory of Social Interaction.* Stanford, CA: Stanford University Press.

———. 1990a. "Emile Durkheim's Theory of Social Organization." *Social Forces.* 68 (4):1089–1103.

———. 1990b. "The Misuse and Use of Metatheory." *Sociological Forum.* 5 (1):37–53.

———. 1993. *Classical Sociological Theory: A Positivists' Perspective.* Chicago: Nelson-Hall.

———. 1995. *Macrodynamics: Toward a Theory on the Organization of Human Populations.* New Brunswick, NJ: Rutgers University Press.

———. 2000. *On the Origins of Human Emotions.* Stanford, CA: Stanford University Press.

———. 2001. "Historical Forces Behind Bureaucratization." *Sociology*, 2nd ed. New York: Harper & Row

———. 2002. Biography information provided by an email reply from Turner, and information provided by the University of California Riverside website. Available: www.JOHNATHANTURNER.@UCR.EDU.

———. 2002. *Face to Face: Toward a Sociological Theory of Interpersonal Behavior.* Stanford, CA: Stanford University Press.

———. 2003. *The Structure of Sociological Theory.* Belmont, CA: Wadsworth.

Turner, Jonathan H. and Adalberto Aguirre. 1998. *American Ethnicity: The Dynamics and Consequences of Discrimination*, 2nd edition. Boston: McGraw-Hill.

Turner, Jonathan H. and Robert Hanneman. 1984. "Some Theoretical Principles of Societal Stratification." *Sociological Theory.* 2:1–22.

Turner, Jonathan H. and Alexandra Maryanski. 1988. "Is Neofunctionalism Really Functional?" *Sociological Theory.* 6 (1):110–121.

Turner, Jonathan H., Royce Singleton and David Musier. 1984. *Oppression: A Socio-History of Black-White Relations in America.* Chicago: Nelson-Hall.

Turner, Jonathan H. and Royce Singleton. 1978. "A Theory of Ethnic Oppression: Toward a Reintegration of Cultural and Structural Concepts in Ethnic Relations Theory." *Social Forces.* 56 (4):1001–1018.

Turner, Jonathan H. and Charles Starnes. 1976. *Inequality; Privilege and Poverty in America.* Pacific Palisades, CA: Goodyear.

Turner, Stephen P. 1993. "The End of Functionalism." *Philosophy of the Social Science.* 23:228–242.

Udry, J. Richard. 1994. "The Nature of Gender," *Demography.* 31:561–573.

———. 1995. "Sociology and Biology: What Biology Do Sociologists Need to Know?" *Social Forces.* 73:1267–1278.

U.S. Office of Technology Assessment. 1984. *Wetlands: Their Use and Regulation.*

van den Berb, Axel. 1980. "Critical Theory; Is There Still Hope?" *American Journal of Sociology.* 86 (3):449–478.

van den Berghe, Pierre L. 1973. *Age and Sex in Human Societies: A Biosocial Perspective.* Belmont, CA: Wadsworth.

———. 1975. *Man in Society: A Biosocial View.* New York: Elsevier.

———. 1977. "Sociobiology, Dogma, and Ethics," *Wilson Quarterly.* Summer:121.

———. 1977–1978. "Bridging the Paradigms." *Society.* 15:42–49.

Veblen, Thorstein. 1904. *The Theory of Business Enterprise.* New York: Scribner's.

Walker, Lewis. 1999. "Why Some People are Poor." *On Wall Street.* November:127.

Wallace, Ruth and Alison Wolf. 1999. *Contemporary Sociological Theory,* 5th ed. Upper Saddle River, NJ: Prentice Hall.

Wallechinsky, David. 2003. "The 10 Worst Living Dictators." *Parade Magazine.* February 16:4–6.8

Waters, Malcolm. 1995. *Globalization.* London: Routledge.

Watson, Traci. 2000. "Lure of the Coast Tends to Drown out Erosion Alerts." *USA Today.* June 28:10A.

Weber, Marianne. 1907. *Ehefrau und Mutter in der Rechtsentwicklung.* Tubingen: J.C.B. Mohr.

Weber, Max. 1946. *From Max Weber: Essays in Sociology,* translated and edited by H. Gerth and C. Wright Mills. New York: Oxford University Press.

———. 1947. *The Theory of Social and Economic Organization,* translated by A.M. Parsons and T. Parsons. New York: Free Press.

———. 1949 [1903–1917]. *The Methodology of the Social Sciencesed* edited by Edward Shils and Henry Rinch. New York: Free Press.

———. 1958a [1904–1905]. *The Protestant Ethic and the Spirit of Capitalism.* New York: Scribners

———. 1958b [1915]. "Religious Rejections of the World and Their Directions," pp.323–359 in *From Max Weber: Essays in Sociology,* edited by H. Gerth and C.W. Mills. New York: Oxford University Press.

———. 1978. *Economy and Society,* edited by Guenter Roth and Claus Witch. Berkeley: University of California Press.

Websdale, Neil. 2001. *Policing the Poor.* Boston: Northeastern University Press.

West, Candance and Sarah Fenstermaker. 1995. "Doing Gender." *Gender and Society.* 9:8–37.

Whitmeyer, Joseph M. 2001. "Measuring Power in Exchange Networks." *Sociological Perspectives.* 44 (2):141–162.

Whittaker, David, editor 2001. *The Terrorism Reader.* New York: Routledge.

Whitteil, Giles and Oliver August. 2001. "Locust Army Marches on its Stomach." *London Times.* June 19:1.

Wides, Laura. 2001. "English Fluency Widens Test Score Gaps." *Daily Breeze.* August 17:A1.

Wieder, D. Lawrence. 1974. *Language and Social Reality.* The Hague: Mouton.

Williams, Frank P. and Marilyn D. McShane. 1994. *Criminological Theory.* Englewood Cliffs, NJ: Prentice Hall.

Willits, F. K. and D. M. Cridger. 1998. "Religion and Well-Being: Men and Women in the Middle Years." *Review of Religious Research.* 26:332–342.

Wilson, Edward O. 1971. *The Insect Societies.* Cambridge, MA: Harvard University Press.

———. 1974. *Ecology, Evolution and Population Biology.* San Francisco: W.H. Freeman.

———. 1975. *Sociobiology: The New Synthesis.* Cambridge, MA: Harvard Press.

———. 1978. "Introduction: What is Sociobiology?" pp. 1–12 in *Sociobiology and Human Nature: An Interdisciplinary Critique and Defense,* edited by Michael S. Gregory, Anita Silven, and Diane Sutch. San Francisco: Jossey-Bass.

———. 1980. *Sociobiology: The Abridged Edition.* Cambridge, MA: Harvard University Press.

———. 1984. *Biophilia.* Cambridge, MA: Harvard University Press.

———. 1990a. *The Ants.* Cambridge, MA: Harvard University Press.

———. 1990b. "Insects," in *Omni.* Sept, Vol. 12, Issue 12:6.

———. 1992. *Diversity of Life.* Cambridge, MA: Harvard University Press.

———. 1994. *Naturalist.* Covelo, CA: Shearwater Books.

———. 1998. *Consilience.* New York: Knopf.

———. 2002a. *The Future of Life.* New York: Knopf.

———. 2002b. "Hotspots," in *National Geographic.* January, Vol. 201, Issue 1:86–89.

———. 2002c. "Speciation and Biodiversity," an interview with Edward O. Wilson. Available: www.actionbio-science.org/biodiversity/wilson.

Wilson, Jeff, 2000. "Ashes to Ashes, Dust to Moon Dust." *Buffalo News.* May 10:A3.

Wolf, Naomi. 1991. *The Beauty Myth; How Images are Used Against Women.* New York: William Morrow.

The Women's Right National Historical Park Service (1848) in Sencca Falls, NY.

Yamagishi, Toshio and Karen Cook. 1993. "Generalized Exchange and Social Dilemma." *Social Psychology Quarterly.* 56(4):235–248.

Yamagishi, Toshio, Mary Gilmore, and Karen Cook. 1988. "Network Connections and the Distribution of Power in Exchange Networks." *American Journal of Sociology.* 93:833–851.

Younts, Wesley and Charles Mueller. 2001. "Justice Processes; Specifying the Mediating Role of Perceptions of Distributive Justice." *American Sociological Review.* 66 (February):125–145.

Zeitlin, Irving. 1981. *Ideology and Development of Sociological Theory,* 2nd ed. New York: Harcourt, Brace & Jovanovich.

Zimmerman, Don and Melvin Pollner. 1970. "The Everyday Life," pp. 80–103 in *Understanding Everyday Life,* edited by Jack Douglas. Chicago: Aldine.

Zimmerman, Don and Jack Whalen. 1987. "Multi-party Management of Single Telephone Calls: The Verbal and Gestural Organization of Work in an Emergency Dispatch Center." Presented at the Surrey Conference on Video, University of Surrey, Guildford, England.

Zimmerman, Don and D. Lawrence Wieder. 1970. "Ethnomethodology and the Problem of Order: Comment on Denzin," pp. 285–298 in *Understanding Everyday Life,* edited by Jack Douglas. Chicago: Aldine.

Index

of social world, 188–90
time, 186–87
See also Berger, Peter; Husserl, Edmund;
Schutz, Alfred
philosophes, 8–9
physical strength, 33, 97, 101
Piaget, Jean, 37, 219
play, 36–37, 114
political correctness, 347
politics
Berger, 197–98
critical theory, 238, 241, 247–50
Mills, 84, 87
and social justice, 345
third way (Giddens), 64
Weber, 72–73
Pollner, Melvin, 174–75
pollution, 353–56
Pope, Stephen, 32, 33
population
forced relocation, 348
size, 312, 316, 327, 338
Wilson, 22, 24, 25, 29, 31
See also demographics
positivism
Comte, 321, 341–42
critical theory, 249, 255
defined, 14
postmodernism, 272, 285
Turner, 309–10
postmodernism
in art, 254
and consumption, 299–300
critics, 286, 289, 299
deconstruction, 263, 277
feminism, 208–9
language, 263, 274
and Marxism, 256
and media, 252, 278, 289
method, 253, 260, 263, 270, 274, 282, 283, 285
origins, 260–61
premises, 261–63
and scientific method, 95
significance, 285–86, 289
on signs, 276
terminology, 262
See also Baudrillard, Jean; Derrida, Jacques; Foucault,
Michel; Giddens, A.; Jameson, Fredric; Lyotard,
Jean-François; Riesman, David
poverty, 204, 312, 345
power
Berger, 197–98
(R.) Collins, 96, 97
in conflict theory, 70–71
Coser, 77
Dahrendorf, 89–90
differentials, 149
Emerson, 154
exchange theory, 137, 144, 147, 149, 154, 344
and gender, 154, 229
Giddens, 62–64
Hobbes, 5
Industrial Revolution, 12

and inequality, 333, 345
least interest principle, 147
Machiavelli, 3–4
Mills, 84–86, 302
Parsons, 66
postmodernism, 284–85
in primitive society, 101
Rousseau, 8
Turner, 311, 313, 314, 315, 317
van den Berghe, 33–34
Weber, 72, 328, 344
See also authority
power-dependence, 152, 154
power elite, 85, 87, 100, 102
pragmatism, 107–10
prediction, 104, 294, 321–23
prestige, 315, 328–29
primitive societies
differentiation, 60
kinship, 42
modernization, 333
power, 101
reciprocity, 134–35
sports, 36–37
prisons, 283–84
problem-solving, 191
production
Marx, 71
means of, 101, 308
postmodernism, 279, 286
surplus, 313
professions, 37, 103, 297–98
progress, 9, 321–24
property, 5–6, 90, 313
for Marx, 71–72, 91
propositional approach, 15
Protestant ethic, 43, 54
proximity, 78
psychoanalysis, 318–19
psychological egoism, 4, 6
psychologism, 183

Q
qualitative approach, 16
quality, 293, 294
quantification, 16, 293

R
Rabinow, Paul, 283, 284
race, 346–50
and cognition, 37
cultural goals, 55
and degradation, 172
feminism, 204, 206, 209, 215–19
radicalism, 241–42, 252
rank, 315, 316, 328
Rathje, William, 355–56
rationalism, 6, 8–9
rationality
Comte, 329, 341
critical theory, 239, 240, 247–49
ethnomethodology, 175